Lecture Notes in Computer Science 10428

Commenced Publication in 1973
Founding and Former Series Editors:
Gerhard Goos, Juris Hartmanis, and Jan van Leeuwen

Editorial Board

David Hutchison
Lancaster University, Lancaster, UK
Takeo Kanade
Carnegie Mellon University, Pittsburgh, PA, USA
Josef Kittler
University of Surrey, Guildford, UK
Jon M. Kleinberg
Cornell University, Ithaca, NY, USA
Friedemann Mattern
ETH Zurich, Zurich, Switzerland
John C. Mitchell
Stanford University, Stanford, CA, USA
Moni Naor
Weizmann Institute of Science, Rehovot, Israel
C. Pandu Rangan
Indian Institute of Technology, Madras, India
Bernhard Steffen
TU Dortmund University, Dortmund, Germany
Demetri Terzopoulos
University of California, Los Angeles, CA, USA
Doug Tygar
University of California, Berkeley, CA, USA
Gerhard Weikum
Max Planck Institute for Informatics, Saarbrücken, Germany

More information about this series at http://www.springer.com/series/7409

Marijn Janssen · Karin Axelsson
Olivier Glassey · Bram Klievink
Robert Krimmer · Ida Lindgren
Peter Parycek · Hans J. Scholl
Dmitrii Trutnev (Eds.)

Electronic Government

16th IFIP WG 8.5 International Conference, EGOV 2017
St. Petersburg, Russia, September 4–7, 2017
Proceedings

Springer

Editors
Marijn Janssen
Delft University of Technology
Delft
The Netherlands

Karin Axelsson
Linköping University
Linköping
Sweden

Olivier Glassey
University of Lausanne
Lausanne
Switzerland

Bram Klievink
Delft University of Technology
Delft
The Netherlands

Robert Krimmer
Tallinn University of Technology
Tallinn
Estonia

Ida Lindgren
Linköping University
Linköping
Sweden

Peter Parycek
Donau-Universität Krems
Krems
Austria

Hans J. Scholl
University of Washington
Seattle, WA
USA

Dmitrii Trutnev
ITMO University
St. Petersburg
Russia

ISSN 0302-9743 ISSN 1611-3349 (electronic)
Lecture Notes in Computer Science
ISBN 978-3-319-64676-3 ISBN 978-3-319-64677-0 (eBook)
DOI 10.1007/978-3-319-64677-0

Library of Congress Control Number: 2017947762

LNCS Sublibrary: SL3 – Information Systems and Applications, incl. Internet/Web, and HCI

Printed on acid-free paper

This Springer imprint is published by Springer Nature
The registered company is Springer International Publishing AG
The registered company address is: Gewerbestrasse 11, 6330 Cham, Switzerland

Preface

The IFIP EGOV-EPART2017 conference was a high-caliber multitrack conference including a doctoral colloquium dedicated to the broader area of electronic government and electronic participation. Scholars from around the world have attended this premier academic forum for over 15 years, which has given it a worldwide reputation as one of the top two conferences in the research domains of electronic, open, and smart government, and electronic participation. This year there were submission from 34 countries.

The call for papers attracted completed research papers, work-in-progress papers on ongoing research (including doctoral papers), project and case descriptions, as well as workshop and panel proposals. The acceptance rate was 46%. This conference of five partially intersecting tracks presents advances in the socio-technological domain of the public sphere demonstrating cutting-edge concepts, methods, and styles of investigation by multiple disciplines. The papers were distributed over the following tracks

- The General E-Government Track
- The General eParticipation Track
- The Open Government, and Open and Big Data Track
- The Policy Modeling and Policy Informatics Track
- The Smart Governance, Smart Government, and Smart Cities Track

Among the full research paper submissions, 34 papers (empirical and conceptual) from the General EGOV Track, the Open Government and Open/Big Data Track, and the Smart Governance/ Government/Cities Track were accepted for Springer's LNCS EGOV proceedings (vol. 10428), whereas another 14 papers of completed research papers from the General ePart Track and the Policy Modeling and Policy Informatics Track went into the LNCS ePart proceedings (vol. 10429).

The papers in the General EGOV/Open Big Data/Smart Gov Tracks have been clustered under the following headings:

- Smart Governance, Government and Cities
- Services
- Organizational Aspects
- Government Infrastructures
- Big and Open Linked Data (BOLD)
- Open Government
- Evaluation

As in the previous years and per the recommendation of the Paper Awards Committee under the leadership of Olivier Glassey of the University of Lausanne,

Switzerland, the IFIP EGOV-EPART2017 Conference Organizing Committee again granted outstanding paper awards in three distinct categories:

- The most interdisciplinary and innovative research contribution
- The most compelling critical research reflection
- The most promising practical concept

The winners in each category were announced in the award ceremony at the conference dinner, which has always been a highlight of the IFIP EGOV-EPART conference series.

Many people make large events like this conference happen. We thank the over 100 members of the IFIP EGOV-EPART 2016 Program Committee and dozens of additional reviewers for their great efforts in reviewing the submitted papers. We would like to express our gratitude to Dmitrii Trutnev and Andrei V. Chugunov and their team from the ITMO University for the organization and the management of all the details locally.

Information Technologies, Mechanics and Optics (ITMO) is one of the leading higher education institutions in Russia, providing training and research in advanced science, humanities, engineering, and technology. Founded in 1900, the ITMO University has grown to an organization of over 13,000 students and earned its name "National Research University," blending the culture of innovation and discovery with world-class education (http://en.ifmo.ru/). The E-Governance Center (eGov Centre) was launched in May 2009 as a department at the ITMO University. The eGov Center purpose is to concentrate intellectual and organizational resources in order to support the development and dissemination of eGovernment/Open Government solutions in Russia and Eurasia (http://egov.ifmo.ru/en/about).

September 2017

Marijn Janssen
Olivier Glassey
H. Jochen Scholl

Organization

The IFIP EGOV-EPART 2017 Organizers

Marijn Janssen	Delft University of Technology, The Netherlands (2017 Lead Organizer)
Karin Axelsson	Linköping University, Sweden
Yannis Charalabidis	University of the Aegean, Greece
Andrei V. Chugunov	ITMO University, Russia
Olivier Glassey	University of Lausanne, Switzerland
Bram Klievink	Delft University of Technology, The Netherlands
Robert Krimmer	Tallinn University of Technology, Estonia
Ida Lindgren	Linköping University, Sweden
Panos Panagiotopoulos	Queen Mary University of London, UK
Theresa A. Pardo	Center for Technology in Government, University at Albany, SUNY, USA
Peter Parycek	Danube University Krems, Austria
Efthimios Tambouris	University of Macedonia, Greece
Hans Jochen Scholl	University of Washington, USA
Øystein Sæbø	Agder University, Norway
Dmitrii Trutnev	ITMO University, Russia
Anneke Zuiderwijk-van Eijk	Delft University of Technology, The Netherlands

IFIP Working Group 8.5 Elected Officers

Chair

Hans Jochen Scholl	University of Washington, USA

Vice Chair

Marijn Janssen	Delft University of Technology, The Netherlands

Secretary

Olivier Glassey	University of Lausanne, Switzerland

Conference Chairs

Marijn Janssen	Delft University of Technology, The Netherlands
Hans Jochen Scholl	University of Washington, USA
Efthimios Tambouri	University of Macedonia, Greece
Ida Lindgren	Linköping University, Sweden

Theresa A. Pardo	Center for Technology in Government, University at Albany, SUNY, USA
Peter Parycek	Danube University Krems, Austria
Anneke Zuiderwijk-van Eijk	Delft University of Technology, the Netherlands
Olivier Glassey	University of Lausanne, Switzerland
Dmitrii Trutnev	ITMO University, Russia
Andrei V. Chugunov	ITMO University, Russia

General E-Government Track

Hans Jochen Scholl	University of Washington, USA
Marijn Janssen	Delft University of Technology, The Netherlands

General eParticipation Track

Efthimios Tambouris	University of Macedonia, Greece
Øystein Sæbø	Agder University, Norway
Panos Panagiotopoulos	Queen Mary University of London, UK

Open Government and Open and Big Data Track

Ida Lindgren	Linköping University, Sweden
Bram Klievink	Delft university of Technology, The Netherlands
Robert Krimmer	Tallinn University of Technology, Estonia

Policy Modeling and Policy Informatics Track

Theresa A. Pardo	Center for Technology in Government, University at Albany, SUNY, USA
Yannis Charalabidis	University of Aegean, Greece

Smart Governance, Smart Government, Smart Cities, and Smart Regions Track

Peter Parycek	Danube University Krems, Austria
Olivier Glassey	University of Lausanne, Switzerland
Karin Axelsson	Linköping University, Sweden

PhD Colloquium

Ida Lindgren	Linköping University, Sweden
J. Ramon Gil-Garcia	Center for Technology in Government, University at Albany, SUNY, USA
Anneke Zuiderwijk-van Eijk	Delft University of Technology, The Netherlands

Program Committee

Suha Al Awadhi	Kuwait University, Kuwait
Renata Araujo	UNIRIO, Brazil
Jansen Arild	University of Oslo, Norway
Karin Axelsson	Linköping University, Sweden
Frank Bannister	Trinity College Dublin, Ireland
Jesper B. Berger	Roskilde University, Denmark
Lasse Berntzen	Buskerud and Vestfold University College, Norway
Paul Brous	Delft University of Technology, The Netherlands
Wojciech Cellary	Poznan University of Economics, Poland
Bojan Cestnik	Temida d.o.o., Jožef Stefan Institute, Slovenia
Yannis Charalabidis	University of the Aegean, Greece
Soon Ae Chun	City University of New York, USA
Wichian Chutimaskul	King Mongkut's University of Technology Thonburi, Thailand
Peter Cruickshank	Edinburgh Napier University, UK
Todd Davies	Stanford University, USA
Sharon Dawes	Center for Technology in Government, University at Albany/SUNY, USA
Fiorella de Cindio	Università di Milano, Italy
Robin Effing	University of Twente, The Netherlands
Annelie Ekelin	Linneaus University, Sweden
Elsa Estevez	National University of the South, Argentina
Sabrina Franceschini	Regione Emilia-Romagna, Italy
Ivan Futo	Multilogic Ltd., Hungary
Andreas Gabor	Corvinno Technology Transfer Center Nonprofit Public Ltd., Hungary
Mila Gasco	University at Albany SUNY, USA
Katarina Gidlund	Midsweden University, Sweden
J. Ramon Gil-Garcia	Centro de Investigación y Docencia Económicas, Mexico
Olivier Glassey	Université de Lausanne, Switzerland
Göran Goldkuhl	Linköping University, Sweden
Dimitris Gouscos	University of Athens, Greece
Joris Hulstijn	Tilburg University, The Netherlands
Johann Höchtl	Danube University Krems, Austria
M. Sirajul Islam	Örebro University, Sweden
Tomasz Janowski	Gdańsk University of Technology, Poland
Arild Jansen	University of Oslo, Norway
Marijn Janssen	Delft University of Technology, The Netherlands
Haziq Jeelani	Galgotias University, India
Carlos Jiménez	IEEE e-Government, Spain
Luiz Antonio Joia	FGV/EBAPE, Escola Brasileira de Administração Pública e de Empresas, Brazil
Nikos Karacapilidis	University of Patras, Greece

Bram Klievink	Delft University of Technology, The Netherlands
Roman Klinger	University of Stuttgart, Germany
Ralf Klischewski	German University in Cairo, Egypt
Helmut Krcmar	Technische Universität München, Germany
Robert Krimmer	Tallinn University of Technology, Estonia
Juha Lemmetti	Tampere University of Technology, Finland
Azi Lev-On	Ariel University Center, Israel
Ida Lindgren	Linköping University, Sweden
Miriam Lips	Victoria University of Wellington, New Zealand
Helen Liu	The University of Hong Kong, SAR China
Euripidis Loukis	University of the Aegean, Greece
Luis Luna-Reyes	University at Albany, SUNY, USA
Cristiano Maciel	Universidade Federal de Mato Grosso, Brazil
Gregoris Mentzas	National Technical University of Athens, Greece
Michela Milano	DISI Università di Bologna, Italy
Yuri Misnikov	Institute of Communications Studies, University of Leeds, UK
Gianluca Misuraca	European Commission, JRC-IPTS, Italy
Catherine Mkude	University of Koblenz, Germany
Carl Moe	Agder University, Norway
José María Moreno-Jiménez	Universidad de Zaragoza, Spain
Morten Nielsen	Tallinn University of Technology, Estonia
Vanessa Nunes	UnB/CIC, Brazil
Adegboyega Ojo	National University of Ireland, Ireland
Christian Østergaardmadsen	IT-University of Copenhagen
Panos Panagiotopoulos	Queen Mary University of London, UK
Eleni Panopoulou	University of Macedonia, Greece
Theresa Pardo	University at Albany, SUNY, USA
Peter Parycek	Danube University Krems, Austria
Marco Prandini	Università di Bologna, Italy
Barbara Re	University of Camerino, Italy
Nicolau Reinhard	University of São Paulo, Brazil
Andrea Resca	Cersi-Luiss Guido Carli University, Italy
Michael Räckers	European Research Center for Information Systems (ERCIS), Germany
Mihoko Sakurai	University of Agder, Norway
Gustavo Salati	Unicamp, Brazil
Rodrigo Sandoval Almazan	Universidad Autonoma del Estado de Mexico, Mexico
Rui Pedro Santos Lourenço	Universidade de Coimbra, Portugal
Sabrina Scherer	University of Koblenz-Landau, Germany
Marc Schmalz	University of Washington, USA
Hans J. Scholl	University of Washington, USA
Gerhard Schwabe	Universität Zürich, Switzerland
Johanna Sefyrin	Linköping university, Sweden
Toramatsu Shintani	Nagoya Institute of Technology, Japan
Luizpaulo Silva	UNIRIO, Brazil

Uthayasankar Sivarajah	Brunel Business School, Brunel University, UK
Maria Sokhn	University of Applied Sciences of Switzerland, Switzerland
Henk Sol	University of Groningen, The Netherlands
Mauricio Solar	Universidad Tecnica Federico Santa Maria, Chile
Maddalena Sorrentino	University of Milan, Italy
Witold Staniszkis	Rodan Systems, Poland
Leif Sundberg	Mid Sweden University, Sweden
Delfina Sá Soares	University of Minho, Portugal
Øystein Sæbø	University of Agder, Norway
Efthimios Tambouris	University of Macedonia, Greece
Yao-Hua Tan	Delft University of Technology, The Netherlands
Peter Teufl	IAIK/Graz University of Technology
Dmitrii Trutnev	e-Government Technologies Center of ITMO University, Russian Federation
Jolien Ubacht	Delft University of Technology, The Netherlands
Jörn von Lucke	Zeppelin Universität Friedrichshafen, Germany
Andrew Wilson	University of Brighton, UK
Adam Wyner	University of Aberdeen, UK
Mete Yildiz	Hacettepe Üniversitesi, Turkey
Chien-Chih Yu	National ChengChi University, Taiwan
Deniz Zeytinoğlu	TÜBİTAK, Turkey
Anneke Zuiderwijk	Delft University of Technology, The Netherlands

Contents

Infrastructures

Big and Open Linked Data

Open Government

Evaluation

Smart Governance, Government and Cities

Designing Information Marketplaces for Disaster Management

Ralf Klischewski(✉) and Yomn Elmistikawy

German University in Cairo, 11432 Cairo, Egypt
ralf.klischewski@guc.edu.eg

Abstract. Disaster management always needs to strike a balance between preparedness and flexibility. The challenges of industrial crisis information management are manifold, out of which we address the question: How to create the best possible information sharing solution for a given environment and crisis situation? This ongoing design science research has identified essential components to be assembled in an 'information sharing kit', including description of informational needs, data model, categorization of ICT components, and guidelines for kit usage. All of these can and should be further developed towards a localized crisis information sharing kit, on the basis of which specific information sharing solutions can be set up in order to create information marketplaces for response and recovery whenever crises occur. Insights from this research are expected to inform disaster preparation in practice, especially in ICT empowered community settings such as smart cities, and to identify more clearly the (research) needs for standardization in disaster-related information management and integration.

Keywords: Disaster management · Information sharing · Information marketplace · Localized information sharing kit · Design science research

1 Introduction

Industrial disasters often cause loss of human life and damage to the environment. The disastrous impacts even increase when information sharing during crisis management does not succeed to orient and empower the stakeholders involved towards appropriate action. While the advancements in information and communication technology (ICT) entail new opportunities for information sharing, disaster management is challenged by the growing availability of potential relevant information sources as well as by the complexity of managing the collection, processing and sharing of data through multiple channels with those who have urgent, but mostly specific informational needs.

For adequate reaction, disaster management always needs to strike a balance between preparedness and flexibility. But how to reach this balance on the level of computer-supported information sharing is still unclear. Therefore our research question is: How can the stakeholders in charge create a suitable ICT infrastructure for information sharing during specific crisis response and recovery? We propose using an information

M. Janssen et al. (Eds.): EGOV 2017, LNCS 10428, pp. 3–12, 2017.
DOI: 10.1007/978-3-319-64677-0_1

marketplace as guidance for implementation information sharing solutions for disaster management. Essential components can be assembled into a localized ‘information sharing kit’ during disaster preparation, and based on such readiness a specific information marketplace can be set up ad hoc whenever a crisis occurs.

The next section briefly characterizes the unique attributes of industrial disasters, crises management and related challenges of information sharing. Section 3 conceptualizes the idea of information marketplaces for disaster management as an open ensemble of accessible structured data supplies and explicit use-case based informational demands to be matched through dedicated algorithms. Section 4 reports about the ongoing design science research to provide a proof-of-concept for this approach. The conclusion signifies the contribution to the field and points to future research.

2 Informational Challenges in Industrial Disaster Management

A crisis is an unfamiliar event that has a low probability of occurring while causing high-risk consequences if not managed properly. Industrial crises are classified as accidental crises, when caused by technical errors that are equipment related, or as intentional crises, when the cause is human error from poor performance. These accidents are stem from factories such as nuclear power stations, energy factories, toxic material using factories or normal factories that could catch fire. Situated mostly in urban areas, industrial crises are especially difficult to manage because of the number and diversity of actors involved, the variety (and often volatility) of needed data and information to be processed and communicated, and the complexity and vulnerability of the ICT infrastructure in place.

An industrial crisis involves internal stakeholders (e.g. employees and managers) and external stakeholders (e.g. media, civilians) [24] as well as disaster management organizations (DMOs), including public safety personnel, healthcare, transportation, the government, and sometimes even the army [4]. These stakeholders are expected to make sense of the situation while there is shortage of information as well as short-time for response [13].

The negative impact of industrial crises often increases due to information management problems among these stakeholders during the management of the crisis. The process of managing an industrial crisis is divided into different phases, each with different information management challenges. Most authors agree to the basic classification into pre-crisis, crisis and post-crisis phases, albeit with variations regarding pre-crisis activities. Here we adopt the approach of Hilliard et al. [9] to differentiate only two pre-crisis phases, preparedness and mitigation, followed by the remaining phases response (during the crisis) and recovery (post-crisis).

During pre-crisis phases data is collected to evaluate the organization’s performance, i.e. to assess the preparedness for a crisis, including role awareness, prerequisites for crisis response, and actions for crisis prevention [25]. Another stream of data sourcing regarding previous crisis triggers, abnormal factory performance measurements and environmental data is used to detect anomalies [2], predict crises [18], generate vulnerability maps, identify crisis management requirements [1], and assess risks and vulnerabilities [3, 8].

All the stakeholders involved in the crisis should be kept up-to-date with each other's performance evaluation and early warning signals in order to ensure preparation alignment and to avoid role duplication, missing requirements or preparing plans that do not match the crisis requirements [25]. However, a lack of common ground in terms of terminology and means of communication [19] as well as each entity focusing on its own needs may hinder this information sharing and coordination [4].

During crisis response the events are monitored and immediate response is offered accordingly including rescue, evacuation, issuing warnings, and updating the public with ongoing events [1, 7]. As poor response might lead to an even more severe disaster than the crisis itself, the right information must reach the right person at the right time to carry out timely response. However, the information sharing in this phase is challenged by the low cohesiveness of the crisis management teams; e.g. due to role duplication across different organizations [25], the shortage of time available for the teams that often had not worked together before to nurture ties and build trust in each other, and/or the lack of common ground between these teams where each team has its own processes to handle a crisis, its own terminologies used during communication, and its own ICT support. Accordingly, it is difficult to access and filter the right information to be shared and to identify appropriate channels for information sharing. Furthermore, crisis information overload, along with the limited availability of communication channels, often lead to bottlenecks in information flow, causing communication failure and delays in data collection and processing; possible implications include inefficient filtering of information and the information getting outdated due to the continuous change in circumstances [7, 16].

Any delay in data collection would lead to going blind into the interpretation phase [24], resulting into either incomplete or conflicting interpretation of the crisis events. For interpretation, the inconsistent/irrelevant data is removed and the remaining data is analyzed to reach an understanding about the crisis [7, 25]. The information sharing itself then is often impaired by reduction of available communication channels, emergence of new uncontrolled communication channels (e.g. social media), poor communication filters to prioritize information and to distinguish between crucial and safe-to-ignore information [7, 16, 19], and low vertical and horizontal interaction inside and across DMOs [11].

Day et al. [6] summarized the challenges in data collection as inadequate stream of information, data inaccessibility, data inconsistency, low information priority, source identification difficulty, storage media alignment, and unreliability. These challenges include inadequate data collection methods, time pressure and limited resources for decision-making, as well as conflicting crisis interpretation and data processing [13]. Scholl et al. [24] found that hazard-related planning is not sufficient to support systematic information collection and sharing and that standardized information sharing procedures and information integration practices are lacking; from the technical perspective they call for more research on common information architecture and information system platforms. Challenges are also faced in designing audience-specific messages [7], and often no attention given to sharing crisis information with citizens affected by the crisis [16].

In principle, an abundance of ICT is available to handle the information management and communication during an industrial crisis. For example, DMOs often use Disaster Management Decision Support Systems to collect and analyze data for supporting crisis response [1]. However, a crisis experiment implemented by Bharosa et al. [4] showed that even though 72% of participants see ICT as valuable, 74.7% are not satisfied with existing ICT solutions.

With the advancements in public infrastructure, especially in smart cities, and an ever increasing range of data from IoT-related sensors and smart cards [12] new options for improving data sourcing and processing in various phases of disaster management need to be explored. Opportunities for information sharing according to the users' needs nowadays include more dedicated channels and platforms such as smart phones, internet, social networks, online-mapping and cloud computing [20], and the public infrastructure should be linked with applications, social learning and governance to build knowledge bases for citizens and enable collaboration [10, 15].

Thus, the public infrastructure offers an opportunity to overcome the information management challenges in crisis management by utilizing its technological solutions during response and recovery: sharing the crisis details, and the response and precautions to be taken to the affected citizens; sharing up-to-date information between the DMOs needed for crisis management; ICT solutions offering a balance between flexibility and preparedness in the communication during crisis. Scholl and Patin [22] emphasize that actionable information requires "resilient information infrastructures" that should be "redundant and resourceful", i.e. combining ICT with social, organizational, and knowledge assets.

3 Information Marketplaces for Disaster Management

Given the array of potentially valuable data sources and the challenge to manage comprehensive information sharing in very short time, new option for automating the information sharing have to be explored. Numerous research papers have pointed out the challenges, but solutions have been rarely proposed. Accordingly, our research question is: How to design a suitable ICT infrastructure for information sharing during crisis response and recovery? The vision is that stakeholders in charge may implement a situated information marketplace based on a kit of publicly available and/or prefabricated components.

Information marketplaces have been mainly studied from the economic perspective and also have been used to conceptualize the 'smart city' [5]. The core idea is that 'raw data' is transformed and/or perceived as a valuable information product to be consumed by those in need for this information (and who are willing to pay a premium for it). In disaster management, multiple stakeholders are in need of comprehensive and diverse information, most of which is predictable in principle, but not specifically. The types of stakeholders and their communications channels also can be largely foreseen (depending on the type of crisis) but again not the specific persons or groups. However, the preparation of disaster management includes multiple scenarios of crisis analysis and response through which informational needs and available data and its accessibility can be identified in advance, at least in principle, allowing for preparing the information sharing based on a standardization presenting potentially relevant data as an informational product to be consumed. If we aim also for automating the match between informational demands and supplies, then also the informational needs have to be described in a standardized way, i.e. through generally known attributes, to enable a matching algorithm to present relevant data to the right informational users through the available channels. To some extent Saleem et al. [21] had prototyped this idea in terms of a "Business Continuity Information Network"; for this purpose they had identified (a) the necessary informational components as disaster management dataspace, disaster recovery resources identification, situation awareness, dynamic contact management, and intelligent decision support, as well as (b) algorithms for retrieving and presenting relevant information to users.

In our approach, we take the idea of an information marketplace to the next level of abstraction so that the elements of the information flow realization become visible and each of these elements can be supported by selected kit components. Hence, the information marketplace is conceptualized as an open ensemble of accessible structured data supplies and explicit use-case based informational demands, both matched through algorithms that may follow different types of market regulations (see Fig. 1).

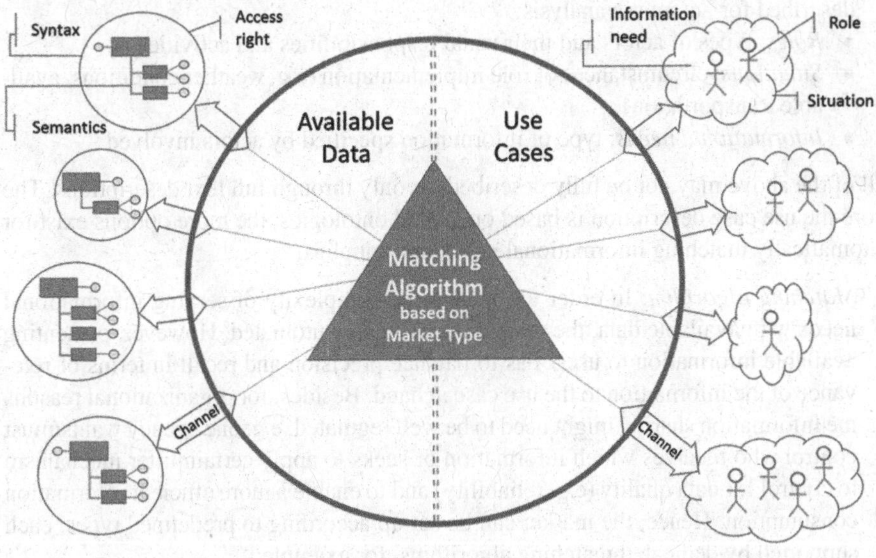

Fig. 1. Conceptualizing an information marketplace for disaster management

While every community may prepare for such market in its own fashion, the mechanism of any electronic marketplace requires similar components and preparations:

1. *Available data*: Turning data into useful information can only happen when

- information users know about its existence (presentation to users is to be organized by the matching)
- users have the right to access the data
- users are able to manage the communication channel for accessing the data
- the data can be processed based on the known syntax (e.g. XML, streaming data, VoIP)
- the meaning of the data (semantics) is known and can be related to the users' needs

How to define the semantics can follow different paths. Existing ontologies should be reused as much as possible, and given communities can identify their own categories of meaning. For example, Pan et al. [16] have identified and described four types of crisis response information: personnel status, infrastructure, crisis management and notification, area access. Standardized descriptions in each of these areas could be used to describe informational needs in various use cases and to define and annotate metadata for the available datasets (see [14] for review of available ontologies). In any case, it needs a standardized description and architecture of what Scholl et al. [23] call "essential elements of information."

2. *Use cases*: Turning data into useful information happens only when users can meaningfully interpret the data for improving their action. For matching the available data with the information demand, the different cases of information use have to be described for automatic analysis:
   - *Roles*: types of actors and their usual responsibilities and activities
   - *Situations*: circumstances of role implementation (e.g. weather conditions, available transportation)
   - *Informational needs*: type of information specified by actors involved

All of the above may not be fully described, or only through full text descriptions. The more the use case description is based on shared ontologies, the more options exist for automatically matching informational needs and supplies.

3. *Matching algorithm*: In order to manage the complexity of serving informational needs with available data, the matching should be automated. However, presenting available information to users has to balance precision and recall in terms of relevance of the information to the use case at hand. Besides, for organizational reasons the information sharing might need to be well regulated, e.g. one agency wants/must control who receives which information or seeks to apply certain filter mechanism to control for data quality (e.g. reliability) and to enable a more efficient information consumption. Hence, the market can be set up according to predefined types, each supported by dedicated matching algorithms, for example:
   - *Free market*: all participants can see, access and consume all available data
   - *Central Agency*: the visibility of data, all matchmaking, and all information consumption is controlled by one central agency in charge
   - *Demand pull*: a given description of a use case is automatically analyzed and available data is constantly provided based on predefined rules

- *Supply push*: whenever new data is available potential users are notified; users may define certain subscriptions (feeding filters)

The DMOs and the community at large should agree on the type(s) of market to prepare for. However, during crisis the applicable type might even change due to situated analysis of the information demand and supply.

4 Designing an Information Sharing Kit for Crisis Management

This ongoing research has adopted a design science approach, which is the process of creating new and innovative artifacts to address a certain problems. It explores the opportunity of using existing ICT components to prepare a "crisis management information sharing kit" (i.e. not a ready-made solution) that can be flexibly used to set up an information market for specific crisis incidents in a given environment (e.g. a smart city). In this section we discuss the approach to and the results of the design science phases as structured by Peffers et al. [17].

Beyond literature review *problem understanding and identification* was achieved through interviews with personnel from DMOs, followed by assessing different crisis scenarios. Semi-structured interviews were conducted with the sheriff's deputy of a police station and a lieutenant-colonel in fire department located in a very large city. The interview questions asked for crisis notification (how? when?), exchange of crisis incident information in real-time with other DMOs (what information is shared and how?), information to be shared with citizens (what information and how?), problems of information sharing, informational needs related to types of industrial accident (what information from which source?). Interview results revealed marginal use of ICT for data sourcing and information sharing processes as well as a lack of clear instructions on information to be shared between DMOs and between police officers/fire fighters and affected citizens during industrial crisis. Furthermore, available crisis documentation was used for problem confirmation and objectives identifications. Governmental and news reports have been analyzed regarding crises that occurred during the last ten years in industrial facilities facing a fire, a leak, an explosion and/or building collapse (Fukushima 2011; Kaohsiung 2014; Savar/Rana Plaza 2013; Ludwigshafen/BASF 2016; Waco/West Fertilizer 2013; Port Wentworth/Georgia Sugar Refinery 2008). In line with previous literature it was found that, even though some information sharing happened, multiple challenges still hindered timely information sharing especially among DMOs and between DMOs and citizens and that appropriate ICT solutions have usually not been in place.

The basic *design objective* is to enable key stakeholders to set up and/or adapt ICT solutions for providing the needed information during response and recovery of the industrial crisis in focus. The core objective is to design artifacts for supporting a strategic approach that identifies and creates components as far as possible during crisis preparation in order to swiftly and flexibly realize a situated ICT-powered information market when needed during crisis response and recovery.

The *artifact design* includes so far:

- Informational demands are categorized into person/organization account, situation assessment, rescue alert, relief claim, volunteer request, supply request, evacuation/routes, medical care, specific roles (e.g. fire fighters, police officers) and DMO monitoring, exemplified by 70 user stories (i.e. intended/planned activities that require specific information)
- Entity relationship diagram with several hundred entities, relationships and attributes as a possible blueprint for stakeholders to identify and model relevant data
- Categorization of typical ICT infrastructure components for channel management, including hardware, software (in particular the market place mechanics), operating system, data management and storage, telecommunication, internet platform, standards (e.g. ontologies), and even consultants or other IT services
- Guidelines to assist kit users in (a) preparing their localized information sharing kit (including analysis of past/expected local crises, identifying users and their informational needs, preparing access to available data, developing information sharing mechanisms and test solutions) as well as (b) transforming the localized kit (including crisis analysis, specifying users' information needs and communication channels, choosing and combining existing components, making adjustments) into an actual information sharing solutions for crisis management (e.g. mobile apps, information portals, multi-layered maps, news feeds, billboards; see Fig. 2)

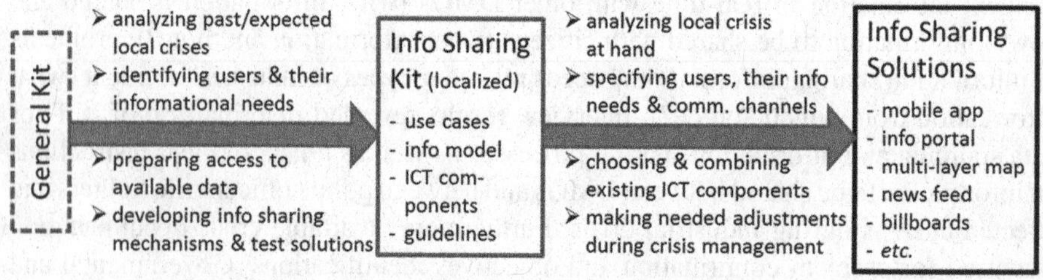

Fig. 2. Transformation of the information sharing kit into ready-to-use solutions

The *artifact demonstration* aims to involve numerous and diverse members of DMOs trying to use the kit components during a simulation of crisis preparation and management. The *artifact evaluation* then focuses on the usability of the kit and its effectiveness in terms of creating suitable localized 'markets' for crisis-related information sharing. Data collection for evaluation includes observation during simulation as well interviews of participants after simulation.

5 Conclusion

Previous research has found that information sharing during disaster management is not adequately supported by ICT solutions. As standardized data management and information integration procedures and practices are still in its infancy, disaster management has difficulties in striking a balance between preparedness and flexibility. In order to support responsible stakeholders we propose using an information marketplace as guidance for the implementation of specific information sharing solutions for disaster management. The ongoing design science research has identified essential components to be assembled in an 'information sharing kit', including description and categorization of informational needs, data model, categorization of ICT components, and guidelines for kit usage. These can and should be specified and further developed towards a localized crisis information sharing kit. On the basis of the localized kit specific information sharing solutions can be set up in order to create information marketplaces for response and recovery whenever crises occur.

This research is expected to contribute to our understanding how to design situated information sharing solutions for industrial crisis management. However, it tackles only one facet of the complexity inherent in industrial crisis management which is the *approach* towards creating the best possible solution for a given environment and crisis situation. Other aspects such as data accessibility, system interoperability, cloud-based components, information integration, semantic standardization are essential for implementing solutions, but the development and/or improvement of these is outside the scope of this research. Rather we seek to test to what extent stakeholders in charge (who are not ICT experts) find the vision of an information marketplace and the components of the 'information sharing kit' (including guidelines) helpful to create information sharing solutions that serve their needs. Insights from this research are expected to inform disaster preparation in practice, especially in ICT empowered community settings such as smart cities, and to identify more clearly the (research) needs for standardization in disaster-related information management and integration.

References

1. Ashgar, S., Alahkoon, D., Chuilov, L.: Categorization of disaster decision support needs for the development of an integrated model for DMSS. Int. J. Inf. Technol. Decis. Mak. **7**, 115–145 (2008)
2. Beinat, E., Bannink, I., Oldani, G., Sagl, G., Steenbruggen, J.G.M.: A Review of Emerging Technologies for Crisis Management—Social Media, Internet of Things and Big Data. Sensible Future Foundation, University of Salzburg; Dutch Ministry of Infrastructure and Environment (2012)
3. Berke, P., Smith, G., Lyles, W.: Planning for resiliency: evaluation of state hazard mitigation plans under the disaster mitigation act. Nat. Hazards Rev. **13**, 139–149 (2012)
4. Bharosa, N., Lee, J., Janssen, M.: Challenges and obstacles in sharing and coordinating information during multi-agency disaster response: propositions from field exercises. Inf. Syst. Front. **12**, 49–65 (2010)
5. Cosgrave, E., Arbuthnot, K., Tryfonas, T.: Living labs, innovation districts and information marketplaces: a systems approach for smart cities. In: Conference on Systems Engineering Research, Procedia Computer Science, vol. 16, pp. 668–677 (2013)
6. Day, J.M., Junglas, I., Silva, L.: Information flow impediments in disaster relief supply chains. J. Assoc. Inf. Syst. **10**, 637–660 (2009)
7. Hale, J.E., Dulek, R.E., Hale, D.P.: Crisis response communication challenges building theory from qualitative data. J. Bus. Commun. **42**, 112–134 (2005)

8. Highfield, W.E., Peacock, W.G., Van Zandt, S.: Mitigation planning. Why hazard exposure, structural vulnerability, and social vulnerability matter. J. Plan. Educ. Res. **34**, 287–300 (2014)
9. Hilliard, T., Scott-Halsell, S., Palakurthi, R.: Elements that influence the implementation of crisis preparedness measures by meeting planners. J. Conting. Crisis Manag. **19**, 198–206 (2011)
10. Hollands, R.G.: Will the real smart city please stand up? Intelligent, progressive or entrepreneurial? City **12**, 303–320 (2008)
11. Kapucu, N., Arslan, T., Demiroz, F.: Collaborative emergency management and national emergency management network. Disaster Prev. Manag. Int. J. **19**, 452–468 (2010)
12. Kyriazis, D., Varvarigou, T., Rossi, A., White, D., Cooper, J.: Sustainable smart city IoT applications: heat and electricity management & eco-conscious cruise control for public transportation. In: 14th IEEE International Symposium and Workshops on a World of Wireless, Mobile and Multimedia Networks, pp. 1–5 (2013)
13. Ley, B., Ludwig, T., Pipek, V., Randall, D., Reuter, C., Wiedenhoefer, T.: Information and expertise sharing in inter-organizational crisis management. Comput. Support. Coop. Work (CSCW) **23**, 347–387 (2014)
14. Liu, S., Brewster, C., Shaw, D.: Ontologies for crisis management: a review of state of the art in ontology design and usability. In: Proceedings of the 10th International ISCRAM Conference, pp. 349–359 (2013)
15. Nam, T., Pardo, T.A.: Conceptualizing smart city with dimensions of technology, people, and institutions. In: Proceedings of the 12th ACM Annual International Digital Government Research Conference, pp. 282–291 (2011)
16. Pan, S.L., Pan, G., Leinder, D.: Crisis response information networks. J. Assoc. Inf. Syst. **13**, 31–56 (2012)
17. Peffers, K., Tuunanen, T., Rothenberger, M., Chatterjee, S.: A design science research methodology for information systems research. J. Manag. Inf. Syst. **24**, 45–77 (2008)
18. Peng, Y., Zhang, Y., Tang, Z., Li, S.: An incident information management framework based on data integration, data mining, and multi-criteria decision making. Decis. Support Syst. **51**, 316–327 (2011)
19. Reddy, M., Paul, S., Abraham, J., McNeese, M., DeFiltch, C., Yen, J.: Challenges to effective crisis management: using information and communication technologies to coordinate emergency medical services and emergency department teams. Int. J. Med. Inf. **78**, 259–269 (2009)
20. Roche, S., Propeck-Zimmermann, E., Mericskay, B.: GeoWeb and crisis management: issues and perspectives of volunteered geographic information. GeoJournal **78**, 21–40 (2013)
21. Saleem, K., Luis, S., Deng, Y., Chen, S., Hristidis, V., Li, T.: Towards a business continuity information network for rapid disaster recovery. In: Proceedings of the International Conference on Digital Government Research, pp. 107–116 (2008)
22. Scholl, H.J., Patin, B.J.: Resilient information infrastructures: criticality and role in responding to catastrophic incidents. Transform. Gov. People Process Policy **8**, 28–48 (2014)
23. Scholl, H.J., Ballard, S., Carnes, S., Herman, A., Parker, N.: Informational challenges in early disaster response: the massive Oso/SR530 landslide 2014 as case in point. In: Proceedings of the 50th IEEE Hawaii International Conference on System Sciences (2017)
24. Seeger, M.W., Sellnow, T.L., Ulmer, R.R.: Communication, organization, and crisis. Commun. Yearb. **21**, 231–277 (2012)
25. Van de Walle, B., Turoff, M.: Decision support for emergency situations. Inf. Syst. E-Bus. Manag. **6**, 295–316 (2008)

A Unified Definition of a Smart City

Arkalgud Ramaprasad[1], Aurora Sánchez-Ortiz[2(✉)], and Thant Syn[3]

[1] University of Illinois at Chicago, Chicago, IL 60607, USA
prasad@uic.edu
[2] Universidad Católica del Norte, Antofagasta, Chile
asanchez@ucn.cl
[3] Texas A&M International University, Laredo, TX 78041, USA
thant.syn@tamiu.edu

Abstract. There is some consensus among researchers that the first urban civilization labeled a 'city' was Sumer in the period 3,500–3,000 BC. The meaning of the word, however, has evolved with the advancement of technology. Adjectives such as digital, intelligent, and smart have been prefixed to 'city', to reflect the evolution. In this study, we pose the question: What makes a 'Smart City', as opposed to a traditional one? We review and synthesize multiple scientific studies and definitions, and present a unified definition of Smart City—a complex concept. We present the definition as an ontology which encapsulates the combinatorial complexity of the concept. It systematically and systemically synthesizes, and looks beyond, the various paths by which theory and practice contribute to the development and understanding of a smart city. The definition can be used to articulate the components of a Smart City using structured natural English. It serves as a multi-disciplinary lens to study the topic drawing upon concepts from Urban Design, Information Technology, Public Policy, and the Social Sciences. It can be used to systematically map the state-of-the-research and the state-of-the-practice on Smart Cities, discover the gaps in each and between the two, and formulate a strategy to bridge the gaps.

Keywords: Smart cities · eGovernment · Ontology · Framework

1 Introduction

Cities around the world play a key role in the global economy as centers of both production and consumption, generating a large portion of the world's GDP [1]. The growth of cities since the industrial revolution has reached unprecedented levels. The population division of the United Nations has estimated that in 2016 54.5 per cent of the world's population lived in urban settlements and by 2050 this number will rise to 67% [2]. This considerable growth in cities' population will require major urban infrastructure developments in order to cope with the demand of its inhabitants. IEC [3] estimates that the infrastructure development for the next 35 years will surpass the one built over the last 4,000 years. Unquestionably, cities are complex systems and the rapid urban growth that brings traffic congestion, pollution, and increasing social inequality may turn the

M. Janssen et al. (Eds.): EGOV 2017, LNCS 10428, pp. 13–24, 2017.
DOI: 10.1007/978-3-319-64677-0_2

city into a point of convergence of many risks (economic, demographic, social, and environmental). That could seriously surpass their ability to provide adequate services for their citizens [4]. However, well managed cities can provide multiple benefits to the people living there since they produce economies of scale by sharing amenities such as transport, sport and entertainment facilities, business services, broadband, etc. [5]. The World Economic Forum also suggested that cities provide proximity and diversity of people that can be an incentive for innovation, and create employment as exchanging ideas breeds new ideas [6].

Governments and researchers since the 1990s have been using the term 'Smart Cities' as a fashion label, or because it could help certain cities to distinguish and promote themselves as innovative. Being a Smart City is an aspiration for some cities who have been developing long term plans to achieve this purpose. But, this is still a challenge for other that are facing this process sightlessly basically because concept is still ambiguous [7]. Giddens [8] suggested that the modernization process in the cities are linked to risks and many of them are "manmade risks", that have arisen because of the development of new technologies and the advances in scientific knowledge which are associated to the smartness of the city. In this context, Liotine et al. [9] considers the term Smart City as an anthropomorphism (attribution of human characteristics to the city) because it is based on the ability of the city to sense and respond to its challenges smartly—using natural and artificial intelligence embedded in the city's information systems.

There have been numerous studies attempting to define the Smart City concept, but it is still a difficult challenge to tackle. It is a multidisciplinary concept and to define 'Smart' is difficult. The first attempts to define the concept were focused on the smartness provided by information technology for managing various city functions [10–19]. Lately the studies have widened their scope to include the outcome of the Smart City such as sustainability, quality of life, and services to the citizens [20–30]. Murgante and Borruso [31] warned that cities, in the rush of being considered part of the "Smart umbrella", can be susceptible to ignore the importance of becoming sustainable and if they focus solely on improving technological systems they can easily become obsolete.

The assessment of the level of smartness of cities have also become important for researchers and government officials. They have developed rankings that considers variables like economy, infrastructure, innovation, quality of life, resilience, transportation, urban development, etc. [32–34].

Despite the vast literature on smart cities, or because of it, there are more than thirty-six definitions of the term. They address different, but relevant, aspects of the construct. However, the literature does not provide a unified a definition of the construct that is (a) inclusive of the present definitions, and (b) extensible to accommodate the evolution of the construct. We logically deconstruct the construct to define it using an ontology. The proposed definition unifies the present definitions. It can be extended, scaled, and refined/coarsened as necessary [35, 36].

2 Conceptualizing Smart Cities

The term city has been used since ancient times to describe certain urban communities by some legal or conventional definitions. The definitions can vary between regions or nations. The use of the term smart city is more recent and its early use can be traced to the initial use of information technology in urban environments. Many studies have reviewed the literature's definitions and dimensions of a smart city, characterizing and identifying variables and elements to groups them. The authors of these studies include Giffinger et al. [33], Albino et al. [37], Chourabi et al. [38].

Caragliu et al. [7] found some elements that could characterize a smart city. They include (a) utilization of networked infrastructure to improve economic and political efficiency and enable social, cultural, and urban development; an underlying emphasis on business-led urban development; (b) a strong focus on the aim of achieving the social inclusion of various urban residents in public services; (c) profound attention to the role of social and relational capital in urban development; and (d) social and environmental sustainability as a major strategic component. Albino et al. [37] also identified some common characteristics of a smart city that include: (a) a city's networked infrastructure that enables political efficiency and social and cultural development; (b) an emphasis on business-led urban development and creative activities for the promotion of urban growth; (c) social inclusion of various urban residents and social capital in urban development; and (d) the natural environment as a strategic component for the future.

How we can include all the elements and dimensions that could encapsulate the smart city concept in a unified definition is then the challenge of this study. It is based on an extensive literature analysis and using more than thirty-six different definitions of this concept from disciplines as diverse as urban studies, computers and information technology, sociology, and public health [10, 37–40].

There is no doubt that a Smart City is a multidisciplinary concept that embodies not only its information technology infrastructure but also its capacity to manage the information and resources to improve the quality of lives of its people. The use of information technology has been considered as a key factor in the smartness of a city since it can sense, monitor, control and communicate most of the city services like transport, electricity, environment control, crime control, social, emergencies, etc. [31, 41, 42]. While the information technology can make a city smart (or smarter), the city itself is an entity with multiple stakeholders seeking diverse outcomes. The proposed unified definition integrates the two aspects.

3 Frameworks and Rankings of Smart Cities

Many frameworks have been proposed to encapsulate the critical elements in smart cities, and the underlying relationships between the elements. Some frameworks stress technology and infrastructure as the main components, while others emphasize looking people´s wellbeing. Brandt et al. [43] developed a framework for smart cities based on (a) the information systems research literature within the smart city context, and (b) the insights from interviews with municipal stakeholders from European cities. Their framework combines the resource-based and the ecosystem views to provide a comprehensive representation of the smart city. In this context, they discuss the types of resources a smart city can rely on such as built capital, human capital, natural capital, and information technology infrastructure. In their view the ecosystem includes the stakeholders within the city (city administration, businesses, and resident commuters, etc.).

Chourabi et al. [38] propose a framework that attempts to incorporate sustainability and livability issues, as well as internal and external factors affecting smart cities. They identify eight factors that, based on the literature at that time, were considered fundamental to the comprehension of smart city initiatives and projects. They include: management and organization, technology, governance, policy, people and communities, the economy, built infrastructure, and the natural environment. The same spirit of providing a more integrated perspective of smart cities prevails in Neirotti et al. [4] who present a taxonomy of domains. They divide the research articles into 'Hard' and 'Soft' domains. They grouped the key elements into six categories: natural resources and energy; transport and mobility; buildings; living; government; economy and people.

Giffinger et al. [33] also conceive a framework, based on the literature, for ranking smart medium-sized cities in Europe. They conceive a smart city as one that would excel, in a forward-looking way, in six characteristics: smart economy, smart people, smart governance, smart mobility, smart environment, and smart living. Similarly, Lombardi et al. [16] proposed a framework based on the concept of the Triple Helix [44] that relates university, industry, and government. They identify five clusters of elements in their analysis: smart governance, smart human capital, smart environment, smart living, and smart economy. The indicators for the dimensions in the framework were designed using a focus group and experts in different disciplines to allows a future classification of smart city performance and the relations between components, actors, and strategies.

Most of the analyzed frameworks agree on one or more factors but there is not a complete convergence among them and their relationships. Thus, to synthesize the smart city concept systematically and systemically we propose a unified definition of Smart City as a high-level ontology.

4 A Unified Definition of a Smart City

Our definition of a Smart City is shown in Fig. 1 and described below. It is presented as a high level ontology as described by Ramaprasad and Syn [36] and Cameron et al. [35], in the context of public health informatics and mHealth respectively. It is similar to the approach used by Ramaprasad et al. [45] and Ramaprasad et al. [46] to study eGovernment. (Note: Words referring to those in the framework are capitalized in the text.)

Smart								City		
Structure		**Functions**		**Focus**		**Semiotics**		**Stakeholders**		**Outcomes**
Architecture	[to]	Sense	[+]	Cultural	[+]	Data	[by/from/to]	Citizens	[for]	Sustainability
Infrastructure		Monitor		Economic		Information		Professionals		QoL
Systems		Process		Demographic		Knowledge		Communities		Equity
Services		Translate		Environmental				Institutions		Livability
Policies		Communicate		Political				Businesses		Resilience
Processes				Social				Governments		
Personnel				Technological						
				Infrastructural						

Illustrative Components (total components = 7*5*8*3*6*5 = 25,200):
Architecture to sense economic information by/from citizens for QoL.
Systems to process environmental data by governments for livability.
Policies to communicate technological knowledge by professionals for resilience.
Processes to translate political information to citizens for sustainability.

Glossary:
Smart: Capable of intelligent sense and response through semiotics.
Structure: The structure required to manage the semiotics.
Architecture: The overall architecture to manage the semiotics.
Infrastructure: The physical and virtual infrastructure to manage the semiotics.
Systems: The computer, social, and paper based systems to manage the semiotics.
Services: The computer, social, and paper based services to manage the semiotics.
Policies: The policies on managing the semiotics.
Processes: The processes to manage the semiotics.
People: The people responsible for managing the semiotics.
Function: The functions required to manage the semiotics.
Sense: To sense the semiotic elements.
Monitor: To monitor the semiotic elements over time.
Process: To process the semiotic elements.
Translate: To translate the semiotics into action/control.
Communicate: To communicate the semiotic elements.
Focus: The focus of intelligent sense and response -- smartness.
Cultural: Cultural dynamics of the city.
Economic: Economic dynamics of the city.
Demographic: Demographic dynamics of the city.
Environmental: Environmental dynamics of the city.
Political: Political dynamics of the city.
Social: Social dynamics of the city.
Technological: Technological dynamics of the city.
Infrastructural: Infrastructural dynamics of the city.
Semiotics: The iterative process of generating and applying intelligence.
Data: The symbolic representation of sensations and measurements.
Information: The relationship among the data elements.
Knowledge: The meaning of the the relationships among the data elements.
City: A city capable of intelligent sense and response
Stakeholders: Those affecting and affected by the city.
Citizens: The citizens of the city.
Professionals: The professionals of the city.
Communities: The communities of the city.
Institutions: The institutions of the city.
Businesses: The businesses of the city.
Governments: Federal, State, and Local governments.
Outcomes: The desired outcomes of a smart city.
Sustainability: Sustainability of the city.
QoL: Quality of life of the stakeholders.
Equity: Equity among the citizens of the city.
Livability: The livability of the city.
Resilience: The ability of the city to resile.

Fig. 1. A unified definition of a smart city

A Smart City is a compound construct with two parts, each of which is a complex construct. It can be represented as:

$$Smart\ City = f(Smart + City)$$

The City is defined (for this paper) by its Stakeholders and the Outcomes. Thus:

$$City = f(Stakeholders + Outcome)$$

The desirable outcomes of a Smart City include its Sustainability, Quality of Life (QoL), Equity, Livability, and Resilience. Thus:

$$Outcomes \subset \left[Sustainability,\ Quality\ of\ Life,\ Equity,\ Livability, Resilience\right]$$

The Stakeholders in a city include its Citizens, Professionals, Communities, Institutions, Businesses, and Governments. Thus:

$$Stakeholders \subset \left[Citizens, Professionals, Communities, Institutions, Businesses, Governments\right]$$

Thus, the effects on 'citizens' QoL', 'communities' equity', 'businesses' resilience', and 27 ($6 \times 5 - 3$) other possible combinations of Stakeholder and Outcome, defines the smartness of a city.

Semiotics—the iterative process of generating and applying intelligence—forms the core of smartness. The focus of smartness may be many aspects of interest to the stakeholders to obtain the desired outcomes. It depends on the structure and functions of the systems for semiotics. Thus:

$$Smart = f(Structure + Function + Focus + Semiotics)$$

In the iterative Semiotics process, Data are converted into Information, Information to Knowledge, and the Knowledge is then translated into smart actions. Thus:

$$Semiotics \subset \left[Data, Information, Knowledge\right]$$

The focus of Semiotics may be Cultural, Economic, Demographic, Environmental, Political, Social, Technological, and Infrastructural. The semiotics of each focus will affect the corresponding smartness of the city, its stakeholders, and the corresponding outcomes. Thus:

$$Focus \subset [Cultural, Economic, Demographic, Environmental, Political, Social, Technological, Infrastructural]$$

The Structure and Functions of its Semiotics (Data, Information, Knowledge) management system will determine the smartness of a city. The Functions include Sensing, Monitoring, Processing, Translating, and Communicating [41]. Thus:

$$Functions \subset [Sense,\ Monitor, Process, Translate, Communicate]$$

The Structure includes the Architecture, Infrastructure, Systems, Services, Policies, Processes, and Personnel. Thus:

$$Structure \subset [Architecture, Infrastructure, Systems, Services, Policies, Processes, Personnel]$$

Concatenating the four left dimensions, the smartness of city will be a function of its 'architecture to sense cultural data', 'policies to communicate environmental knowledge', and 838 ($7 \times 5 \times 8 \times 3 - 2$) other combinations in 'Smart' encapsulated in the definition.

Taken together, there are $7 \times 5 \times 8 \times 3 \times 6 \times 5 = 25{,}200$ potential components of a smart city encapsulated in the definition. A truly smart city is one that has realized a significant proportion of them. Thus, cities may be smart in different ways and to different degrees. Four illustrative components are listed below the ontology in Fig. 1. They are illustrated below:

- Architecture to sense economic information by/from citizens for QoL. The architecture to periodically sense the QoL of the citizens of the city, and to make the data available to the citizens.
- Systems to process environmental data by governments for livability. Systems to determine air and water pollution levels, and warn the citizens when they exceed acceptable thresholds.
- Policies to communicate technological knowledge by professionals for resilience. Policies to share knowledge about the technological vulnerabilities of a city, for example its data networks, to assure quick response and recovery in the event of a natural disaster.
- Processes to translate political information to citizens for sustainability. Processes (town-hall meetings, online forums, etc.) to translate the political manifestos into policies and practices that may affect the sustainability of the city.

A component of a Smart City may be instantiated in many ways, not just one. Thus, the 25,200 components encapsulated in the definition may be reflected in innumerable ways in research and practice. Similarly, the innumerable instantiations may be mapped onto the 25,200 components to obtain a comprehensive view of the 'bright', 'light', 'blind/blank' spots/themes in Smart Cities research and practice. The 'bright' spots/themes are those that are heavily emphasized because they are important or are easy. The 'light' spots/themes are those that are lightly emphasized because they are unimportant or are difficult. The 'blind/blank' spots/themes are those that have been overlooked or are logically infeasible.

The ontology defines Smart City simply and visually, without compromising its underlying combinatorial complexity. It is systemic and systematic. Its dimensions (columns) are based on research and practice in the domain. Further, the definition encapsulates all possible components of a Smart City, however many there are. We can describe any research or practice in the domain using the definition.

In summary, the unified definition presented as an ontology represents our conceptualization of Smart Cities [47]. It is an "explicit specification of [our] conceptualization," [48] and can be used to systematize the description of the complexity of domain knowledge [49]. The ontology organizes the terminologies and taxonomies of the domain. "Our acceptance of [the] ontology is... similar in principle to our acceptance of a scientific theory, say a system of physics; we adopt, at least insofar as we are reasonable, the simplest conceptual scheme into which the disordered fragments of raw experience can be fitted and arranged." [50] The many definitions of a Smart City can also be mapped onto the unified definition. It is a domain ontology that "helps identify the semantic categories that are involved in understanding discourse in that domain." [51, p. 23] Ontologies are used in computer science, medicine, and philosophy. Our ontology of a Smart City is less formal than computer scientists', more parsimonious than medical terminologists', and more pragmatic than philosophers'. It is designed to be actionable and practical, and not abstract and meta-physical. Its granularity matches that of the discourse in research and facilitates the mapping and translation of the domain-text to the framework and the framework to the domain-text.

5 Discussion

The Smart City ontology presented in this article provides a path to conceptualize systemically and systematically this novel domain including, refining, and extending previous definitions and conceptualizations of smart cities in a simple but powerful way. The ontology deconstructs the smart city concept into its basic dimensions and elements allowing the visual representation as a graphic-table and the articulation of its components using structured natural English revealing the combinatorial complexity of smart cities. This ontology is logically constructed but it is grounded in the literature and practice of smart cities. The multidisciplinary nature of the topic required to draw upon concepts from Urban Design, Information Technology, Public Policy, and the Social Sciences. The analysis of previous research included more than thirty definitions of the concept, articles about smart cities and rankings currently in use. This ontological framework for smart cities can be a tool for researchers and practitioners to visualize the appropriate elements and components of a smart city.

The logical construction of the ontology minimizes the errors of omission and commission. Smart city is a compound construct of two parts, Smart and City, and every one of it is at the same time composed of other dimensions and elements. For example, the City part of the smart city construct in the ontology encompasses the effect of stakeholders on the desirable outcomes. Most researchers in the information technology field focus their definitions of smart cities on the electronified functions provided to the citizens without consideration of the outcome (Sustainability, Quality of Life, Equity, Livability, Resilience). However, for the urban related disciplines the sustainability and quality of life has been the critical issues associated to most smart city definitions but electronic means have not been always part of those definitions (error of omission). The Smart part of the ontology compels the researcher to structure this part from the logical perspective of the term, the disciplines that converge in it and what is defined by other researchers as smartness (for example Debnath, Chin, Haque and Yuen [41] and Akhras [42] considered sensing, processing and decision making, acting (control), communicating, predictability, healing and preventability fundamental in the smartness of a city). Smart then was deconstructed into four dimensions (Structure, Function, Focus, and Semiotics) where structure, functions, and focus provide the means for semiotics which represents in detail the iterative process of generating and applying intelligence. Thus, the ontology can help specify the four dimensions and its elements for enabling a combination of them, instead of specifying it just generally (error of commission).

Finally, the ontology function as a multi-disciplinary lens. The Structure, Functions, and Semiotics are drawn from the information systems literature and refined for Smart City; the Focus, Stakeholders and Outcomes dimensions are drawn from the Public Administration, Urban Design, Public Policy, and the Social Sciences. The ontology compels the user to analyze different aspects of smart cities and synthesize solutions by drawing upon these disciplines.

6 Conclusion

In this paper, we have proposed an ontology that characterizes the logic of the Smart City domain and can be used to study this domain from many perspectives, at different levels of complexity, and at the desired level of detail. The main contribution of this study is the Smart City Ontology which was based on the logic behind the concept and the mapping of the numerous definitions of the term in the literature. The initial review revealed a clear separation among definitions coming from the information technology field, where the focus was on infrastructure, from those from the urban design and the social sciences where the emphasis was on the outcome (mainly sustainability and quality of life).

The Smart City Ontology will be an essential tool that can be used by planners and government officials to: (a) assess the level of smartness of their cities from many perspectives at different levels of complexity (b) provide a roadmap for new smart city designs (c) guide cooperative thinking among government agencies and other stakeholders (d) map the state-of-the-practice and unveil the bright, light and blind/blank spots of cities. Finally, this Smart City Ontology is fundamental for researchers because it allows them to map the state-of-the-research of the domain and it will permit them to systematically identify the 'bright', 'light', and 'blind/blank' spots in the literature. This mapping could reveal the gaps in the literature and practice, and the opportunities for research in various disciplines encompassed in this ontology.

Last, the unified definition of a Smart City as an ontology is in structured natural English, as opposed to linear natural English of the other traditional definitions reviewed in the paper. Thus, it retains its semantic interpretability while at the same time encapsulating the complexity of the construct. Further, the definition can be adapted as the construct evolves and to different contexts, because of its modular structure. It can be plastic. The definition can be expanded by adding an additional dimension (column), and reduced by eliminating a dimension. For example, Temporality of Outcomes (Short term, Medium term, and Long term) can be an additional dimension; or the elements of Outcomes can be aggregated under the broad term of a Smart City, and the dimension could be eliminated. The definition can be refined by adding subcategories of an element, and coarsened by combining several elements. For example, Governments (Stakeholder), can be subcategorized as Federal, State, and Local Governments; and Institutions and Businesses can be combined as Organizations. The unified definition should serve as a seed for the evolution of the research and practice in the Smart Cities domain.

References

1. Cohen, B.: Urbanization in developing countries: current trends, future projections, and key challenges for sustainability. Technol. Soc. **28**, 63–80 (2006)
2. United Nations, P.D.: The World's Cities in 2016. United Nations (2016)
3. IEC: Orchestrating Infrastructure for Sustainable SmartCities. International Electrotechnical Commission (2014)
4. Neirotti, P., De Marco, A., Cagliano, A.C., Mangano, G., Scorrano, F.: Current trends in Smart City initiatives: some stylised facts. Cities **38**, 25–36 (2014)
5. Swinney, P.: Why are Cities Important? (2014)
6. WEF: Global Risks 2015 Report. World Economic Forum (2015)
7. Caragliu, A., Del Bo, C., Nijkamp, P.: Smart Cities in Europe. J. Urban Technol. **18**, 65–82 (2011)
8. Giddens, A.: Runaway World: 1999 Reith Lecture. Website: news.bbc.cu.uk/hi/english/static/events/reith 99 (1999)
9. Liotine, M., Ramaprasad, A., Syn, T.: Managing a Smart City's resilience to Ebola: an ontological framework. In: 2016 49th Hawaii International Conference on System Sciences (HICSS), pp. 2935–2943. IEEE (2016)
10. Nam, T., Pardo, T.A.: Conceptualizing smart city with dimensions of technology, people, and institutions. In: Proceedings of the 12th Annual International Digital Government Research Conference: Digital Government Innovation in Challenging Times, pp. 282–291. ACM
11. Harrison, C., Eckman, B., Hamilton, R., Hartswick, P., Kalagnanam, J., Paraszczak, J., Williams, P.: Foundations for Smarter Cities. IBM J. Res. Dev. **54** (2010)
12. Washburn, D., Sindhu, U., Balaouras, S., Dines, R.A., Hayes, N., Nelson, L.E.: Helping CIOs understand "smart city" initiatives: Defining the Smart City, Its Drivers, and the Role of the CIO. Forrester Research, Cambridge (2010)
13. Bakıcı, T., Almirall, E., Wareham, J.: A smart city initiative: the case of Barcelona. J. Knowl. Econ. **4**, 135–148 (2013)
14. Eger, J.M.: Smart growth, smart cities, and the crisis at the pump a worldwide phenomenon. I-WAYS J. E-Gov. Policy Regul. **32**, 47–53 (2009)
15. Lazaroiu, G.C., Roscia, M.: Definition methodology for the smart cities model. Energy **47**, 326–332 (2012)
16. Lombardi, P., Giordano, S., Farouh, H., Yousef, W.: Modelling the smart city performance. Innov. Eur. J. Soc. Sci. Res. **25**, 137–149 (2012)
17. Mulligan, C.E., Olsson, M.: Architectural implications of smart city business models: an evolutionary perspective. IEEE Commun. Mag. **51**, 80–85 (2013)
18. Coe, A., Paquet, G., Roy, J.: E-governance and smart communities: a social learning challenge. Soc. Sci. Comput. Rev. **19**, 80–93 (2001)
19. Townsend, A.M.: Smart Cities: Big Data, Civic Hackers, and the Quest for a New Utopia. WW Norton & Company (2013)

20. Anthopoulos, L.: Defining smart city architecture for sustainability. In: Proceedings of the 14th IFIP Electronic Government (EGOV) and 7th Electronic Participation (ePart) Conference 2015. Presented at the14th IFIP Electronic Government and 7th Electronic Participation Conference 2015, pp. 140–147. IOS Press (2015)
21. Bifulco, F., Tregua, M., Amitrano, C.C., D'Auria, A.: ICT and sustainability in smart cities management. Int. J. Public Sector Manag. **29**, 132–147 (2016)
22. Herrschel, T.: Competitiveness and sustainability: Can 'Smart City Regionalism' square the circle? Urban Stud. **50**, 2332–2348 (2013)
23. Lee, J., Kim, D., Ryoo, H.Y., Shin, B.S.: Sustainable wearables: wearable technology for enhancing the quality of human life. Sustainability **8** (2016)
24. Huston, S., Rahimzad, R., Parsa, A.: 'Smart' sustainable urban regeneration: Institutions, quality and financial innovation. Cities **48**, 66–75 (2015)
25. Shapiro, J.M.: Smart cities: quality of life, productivity, and the growth effects of human capital. Rev. Econ. Stat. **88**, 324–335 (2006)
26. Ahvenniemi, H., Huovila, A., Pinto-Seppä, I., Airaksinen, M.: What are the differences between sustainable and smart cities? Cities **60**, 234–245 (2017)
27. Aloi, G., Bedogni, L., Di Felice, M., Loscri, V., Molinaro, A., Natalizio, E., Pace, P., Ruggeri, G., Trotta, A., Zema, N.R.: STEM-Net: an evolutionary network architecture for smart and sustainable cities. Trans. Emerg. Telecommun. Technol. **25**, 21–40 (2014)
28. Hara, M., Nagao, T., Hannoe, S., Nakamura, J.: New key performance indicators for a smart sustainable city. Sustainability **8** (2016)
29. Marsal-Llacuna, M.L.: City indicators on social sustainability as standardization technologies for smarter (citizen-centered) governance of cities. Soc. Indic. Res. **128**, 1193–1216 (2016)
30. Lee, J., Lee, H.: Developing and validating a citizen-centric typology for smart city services. Gov. Inf. Q. **31**, S93–S105 (2014)
31. Murgante, B., Borruso, G.: Cities and smartness: the true challenge. Int. J. Agric. Environ. Inf. Syst. **6**, 5 (2015)
32. IESE: Ranking The World's 'Smartest' Cities. Forbes. Forbes (2016)
33. Giffinger, R., Fertner, C., Kramar, H., Kalasek, R., Pichler-Milanovic, N., Meijers, E.: Smart Cities. Ranking of European Medium-Sized Cities, Final Report, Centre of Regional Science, Vienna, UT (2007)
34. Giffinger, R., Gudrun, H.: Smart cities ranking: an effective instrument for the positioning of the cities? ACE: architecture. City Environ. **4**, 7–26 (2010)
35. Cameron, J.D., Ramaprasad, A., Syn, T.: An ontology of mHealth. Int. J. Med. Inform. 16–25 (2017)
36. Ramaprasad, A., Syn, T.: Ontological meta-analysis and synthesis. Commun. Assoc. Inf. Syst. **37**, 138–153 (2015)
37. Albino, V., Berardi, U., Dangelico, R.M.: Smart cities: definitions, dimensions, performance, and initiatives. J. Urban Technol. **22**, 3–21 (2015)
38. Chourabi, H., Nam, T., Walker, S., Gil-Garcia, J.R., Mellouli, S., Nahon, K., Pardo, T.A., Scholl, H.J.: Understanding smart cities: an integrative framework. In: 2012 45th Hawaii International Conference on System Science (HICSS), pp. 2289–2297. IEEE (2012)
39. Zubizarreta, I., Seravalli, A., Arrizabalaga, S.: Smart city concept: what it is and what it should be. J. Urban Plan. Dev. **142**, 04015005 (2015)
40. Marsal-Llacuna, M.L., Colomer-Llinas, J., Melendez-Frigola, J.: Lessons in urban monitoring taken from sustainable and livable cities to better address the Smart Cities initiative. Technol. Forecast. Soc. Chang. **90**, 611–622 (2015)
41. Debnath, A.K., Chin, H.C., Haque, M.M., Yuen, B.: A methodological framework for benchmarking smart transport cities. Cities **37**, 47–56 (2014)

42. Akhras, G.: Smart materials and smart systems for the future. Can. Mil. J. **1**, 25–31 (2000)
43. Brandt, T., Donnellan, B., Ketter, W., Watson, R.T.: Information systems and smarter cities: towards an integrative framework and a research agenda for the discipline. AIS Pre-ICIS Workshop—ISCA 2016 (2016)
44. Leydesdorff, L., Deakin, M.: The triple-helix model of smart cities: a neo-evolutionary perspective. J. Urban Technol. **18**, 53–63 (2011)
45. Ramaprasad, A., Sánchez-Ortiz, A., Syn, T.: An ontology of eGovernment. In: Tambouris, E., et al. (eds.) EGOV 2015. LNCS, vol. 9248, pp. 258–269. Springer, Cham (2015). doi: 10.1007/978-3-319-22479-4_20
46. Ramaprasad, A., Sánchez-Ortiz, A., Syn, T.: Gaps in local eGovernment research: an ontological analysis. In: Proceedings of the 21st Americas Conference on Information Systems (AMCIS 2015), Puerto Rico, USA (2015)
47. Gruber, T.R.: Ontology. In: Liu, L., Özsu, M.T. (eds.) Encyclopedia of Database Systems. Springer, New York (2008)
48. Gruber, T.R.: Toward principles for the design of ontologies used for knowledge sharing. Int. J. Hum. Comput. Stud. **43**, 907–928 (1995)
49. Cimino, J.J.: In defense of the desiderata. J. Biomed. Inform. **39**, 299–306 (2006)
50. Quine, W.V.O.: From a Logical Point of View. Harvard University Press, Boston (1961)
51. Chandrasekaran, B., Josephson, J.R., Benjamins, V.R.: What are ontologies, and why do we need them? IEEE Intell. Syst. **14**, 20–26 (1999)

Towards a Capabilities Approach to Smart City Management

Anushri Gupta(✉), Panos Panagiotopoulos(✉), and Frances Bowen(✉)

School of Business and Management, Queen Mary University of London, London, UK
{anushri.gupta,p.panagiotopoulos,f.bowen}@qmul.ac.uk

Abstract. Smart cites are rapidly gaining momentum but our understanding of their underlying management framework has to a large extent been unexplored. Under the different initiatives within the label of smart cities, there is no systematic understanding of how city decision makers manage the configuration of resources and processes within the dynamic urban environment. This research in progress paper develops a research agenda on the capabilities of smart city management by synthesising the findings of 72 papers. Further to consolidating the enabling aspects of technology and data as key resources is smart city development, the review leads to the identification of dynamic, operational, cultural and management capabilities. The paper concludes by discussing the value of this approach for future work in the area of smart cities.

Keywords: Smart city management · Capabilities · Systematic review

1 Introduction

Rapid urbanisation, in the early 21st century, has resulted in complex challenges in the social, environmental, economic aspects of a city. Smart cities have been an important theme of research within the scholarly community, with the use of the term being evident mainly since 1998. An undeniable and important part of developing smarter cities has been about the role digital infrastructure to deliver smart services [1, 2]. Nevertheless, there are many more issue to consider as smart cities lie at the intersection of environment, technology and innovation – altogether creating a complex environment for stakeholders to collaborate and co-create value.

Key themes in the smart city literature include innovation, citizens, infrastructure and standards; with focus on the characteristics [3]; dimensions [4, 5]; social aspects, participatory (smart) governance [6–8] and smart city viability determinants [9]. At large, there is considerable research focusing on integrated digital infrastructure for smart city solutions and citizen-centric governance. As the implementation of smart city initiatives progresses, we need to conceptualise how complicated stakeholder interactions can be managed and sustained within a dynamic urban environment. With few exceptions [10, 11], such research on the strategic, governance and management elements of smart cities remains mostly at an early stage.

M. Janssen et al. (Eds.): EGOV 2017, LNCS 10428, pp. 25–35, 2017.
DOI: 10.1007/978-3-319-64677-0_3

This paper addresses the question of: *"Which capabilities can facilitate the effective management of smart city services?"* The aim is to present an emerging research agenda on the capabilities of smart city development. This is achieved with the help of a systematic review of 72 relevant papers that provide evidence on how resources are deployed and configured to develop capabilities for smart city management. First we develop the conceptual foundations and then outline the methodology and findings of the review.

2 Capabilities and the Management of Smart Cities

Dynamic capabilities are a theoretical concept that originates from the resource-based view of the firm with wide applications in the management literature e.g. [12, 13]. In the business world, dynamic capabilities refer to processes by which managers develop and configure organisational competencies within dynamically-evolving markets. In the public sector, dynamic capabilities have been introduced in the context of performance improvement, optimal resource management and knowledge sharing where strategic approaches remain prevalent despite the lack of competition [14, 15].

In digital government research, capabilities have been used to capture the complex alignment between new technologies and organizational characteristics of government agencies; such examples include business process management [16], interoperability [17] or big data readiness capabilities [18]. In particular, Klievink and Janssen [19] integrate dynamic capabilities with maturity models to describe the stages involved in the implementation of joined-up government. In the context of these applications, capabilities are conceptualised both as an analytical framework to describe how processes of resource configuration occur and a summary concept to outline the different capabilities involved to enable a technological transition (e.g. joined-up government).

A key point from the above studies is that capabilities allow to modify and align resources and process with varying (internal and external) environments. This provides a useful springboard to conceptualise the different complexities involved in the management of smart city initiatives. Smart city managers need to make decisions related to the use of a large pool of resources (e.g. data, people, technology) within a large number of interrelated processes (e.g. new initiatives, existing workflows, local governance frameworks). For instance, Meijer et al. [8] suggest that cities need to be responsive to the rapidly changing external environment and improve the efficiency and sustainability of such initiatives by developing internal capabilities accordingly. Rezende and Kohls [20] also clearly outline how 'smartness' refers to contextual conditions like the social, economic and political systems along with technology diffusion. Dameri and Benevolo [10] posit that smart city is not only a technical - economic system but also a social system of complicated stakeholder interactions such as local communities, businesses and public-private organisations. At a theoretical level, studies have looked at public value creation and management issues in the context of smart governance [11, 21].

In brief, a capabilities perspective can make a twofold contribution: (1) help consolidate the stream of academic work related to the management of smart cities and (2) point to the specific capabilities that can enable smart city objectives such as shared value creation and asset management, drawing on previous experiences from the current evidence base. In the next section, we outline this approach via a systematic review.

3 Methodology

A literature review was conducted to collect and assess current evidence regarding the management of smart cities in a systematic and transparent way [22, 23]. We sought to identify the relevant academic sources and overview the evidence from the perspective of capabilities. Based on previous work, a total of 18 relevant search terms used in the smart city domain were identified [24–26]. The search terms were used to query the Web of Science database and extract the relevant literature using the search parameters shown in Table 1. The 967 results retrieved from Web of Science were further scrutinised to obtain 72 relevant papers to conduct a systematic literature review. This was done in several stages of iteration after screening the abstracts of the papers for relevance. Relevance was defined in terms of information related to the management of smart cities, e.g. purely technical papers in the field of GIS (geographical information systems), telematics and informatics, decision support systems or articles in the categories of urban planning and development, architecture, psychology were excluded. Also, a few articles in conference proceedings had to be excluded at this stage due to lack of access.

Table 1. Literature search terms (Timespan: 1997–2017; Citation Index: SSCI, CPCI-SSH, ESCI)

Set	Search terms	Hits
1	("smart city" OR "digital city" OR "intelligent city" OR "virtual city" OR "information city" OR "knowledge city" OR "cyber city" OR "eco city" OR "ubiquitous city")	791
2	("smart cities" OR "digital cities" OR "intelligent cities" OR "virtual cities" OR "information cities" OR "knowledge cities" OR "cyber cities" OR "eco cities" OR "ubiquitous cities")	578
3	#1 OR #2	1091
4	Result #3 filtered using; English, Article & Proceedings	967

The literature assessment was based on Inan et al. [27] and Teece et al. [12] where organisational capability is composed of operational and dynamic capabilities, both of which are influenced by contextual factors such as organisational culture and learning. Using this as a foundation, several sub-capabilities are identified with respect to dynamic, operational, learning and cultural capabilities. As capabilities are configuration of people, resource, technology and organisations; the capabilities are assessed by identifying the key enablers hinted at in the literature and the way in which the scholars discuss its deployment for value creation. It is the latter that has an implication towards the organisational process (also referred to as routine) being implemented and assists to evaluate the impact of configurations of enablers on smart city performance. The routines listed in Sect. 4 are specific to the capability cluster being discussed.

4 Findings

The 72 papers studied were mainly published between 2006–2016, with an approximate 60% coverage together in the years 2015 and 2016. Also, out of the 72 papers, 21 were conference proceedings while the rest were journal articles. The most widely covered proceedings were "19th International Scientific Conference on Economics and Management (2 papers)" and "15th IFIP Electronic Government EGOV 8th Electronic Participation EPART Conference (3 papers)"; The journal articles largely covered were "Social Science Computer Review (9)", "Technological Forecasting and Social Change (5)", "Government Information Quarterly (6)", "Innovation and the Public Sector (4)" and "Electronic Government and Electronic Participation (4)". Using Web of Science 'analyse results' feature, it turned out that the major contribution, came from categories like "Information Science Library Science (40.27%)", followed by "Management (27.77%)", "Social Sciences Interdisciplinary (23.61%)" and "Business (20.83%)".

4.1 Dynamic Capabilities

As stated in [12], dynamic capabilities are highly relevant in context of rapid technologically changing markets; thus a technical perspective on capabilities by focusing on the 'digital infrastructure' theme of smart cities. The key enablers identified are technology (sensors, connectivity, digital platforms, smartphones, applications) and data (data science: storage – processing - visualisation). In alignment with Teece et al. [12], the implied routines identified from the literature are: (1) 'sensing' - surveillance of technological externalities on public services, (2) 'seizing'- referring to the context of privacy enhancing technologies and secure transactions, (3) 'transforming' - towards new techniques for optimisation of public services, designed to obtain feedback and (4) 'reconfiguration'- implying at decision-making tools for sustainable realignment of assets with the technological evolving contexts (Table 2).

Table 2. Overview of dynamic capabilities identified

Enablers	Routines	Capabilities	Description	References
Technological/digital infrastructure-enabled by technology and data	Reconfiguration	Technological asset management	The ability to design tools and techniques for digital infrastructure maintenance, scaling, data modelling and visualization; to eventually drive capital	[28]
	Sensing and seizing	Digital governance capability	The ability of policy makers to judge influence of technological externalities on citizen security and design privacy considerate policies accordingly.	[29, 30]
	Transforming	Digital enterprise capability	Design of tools and platforms that allow for the ability to develop cross reference services and transform with evolving technological trends	[31]

Technological Asset Management. Considering sensory and unstructured (big) data as an enabler for smart city services, Hashem et al. [28] provide a multi-layered framework for integrated data asset management. The authors highlight how this model aids in reconfiguring the policy implications by making the case of Stockholm. Stockholm incorporated data management of waste collecting vehicles to address traffic and environmental issues which resulted in reconfiguration of policy to a shared waste management vehicle fleet.

Digital Governance Capability. Belanche-Gracia et al. [29] conducted an empirical study of smartcard payment in Zaragoza Spain. Besides illustrating user generated data as an enabler for optimising public services; the study highlights the need for public authorities to sense privacy and security threats of citizens and act accordingly. In the same context, with examples from Rotterdam, Van Zoonen [30] proposes a 2 × 2 privacy framework to aid public authorities to seize security breaches. The privacy framework assesses which technology-data applications are likely to raise privacy concerns.

Digital Enterprise Capability. By conducting a case study of Trafpoint mobile application, Johannessen et al. [31] illustrate how the deployment of gamification techniques by city authorities, aids in transforming city services. The study depicts that Trafpoint drives implicit participation allowing public authorities to cross reference crowd sourced data.

4.2 Operational Capabilities

Operational capabilities are the ability to continuously and efficiently perform daily activities while simultaneously designing techniques to improve performance. While the former implies the 'continuous improvement' routine; the latter hints at 'strategy planning' routine. Capabilities identified here take into consideration the social, economic and political contextual conditions and thus have a key impact on sustainable performance. Here, with respect to the 'innovation' theme in the smart city literature the key enablers identified are mainly (1) data for data-driven innovation, (2) public-private partnership for open innovation and (3) citizens for social innovation. In terms of 'leadership management' theme, the key enabler identified is open data (Table 3).

Government Interoperability Capability. By assessing the public services offered by the City Hall in Chicago, Rezende and Kohls [20] states that e-Gov provides the opportunity for departments within public organisation to redefine the data interoperability systems; consequently fostering data driven innovation. A similar study of eCityGov alliance in the Pacific Northwest of the USA, by Scholl et al. [32], introduces the concept of ICT resource pooling to improve e-services. In this context, ICT are the enablers for governments to continuously improve e-services on the basis of data driven innovation.

Social Monitoring Capability. Conducting a sentiment analysis on Twitter data, [33] consolidate the manner in which implementation of social media platforms by public

Table 3. Overview of operational capabilities identified

Enablers	Routine	Capabilities	Description	References
Innovation-enabled by data, public-private stakeholders and citizens.	Continuous improvement	Government interoperability capability	The information sharing ability amongst municipal levels to be viable	[20, 32]
		Social monitoring capability	The ability to foster social innovation via social media and applications	[33]
		Performance management capability	Design of tools that foster data driven decision making besides civic participation	[34]
		Cross-sector collaboration capability	The ability to design techniques that empower public-private-people partnerships to foster entrepreneurial spirit and strengthen economy	[6, 21]
Leadership Management – Enabled by open data	Strategy	Systems integration and co-ordination capability	The design of systems infrastructure that allows for capturing holistic view during decision making	[35]
		Open government data (OGD) capability	Ability to make data about government operations and decision making to public thereby increasing accountability and transparency in public services	[36]

bodies enables social innovation - fostering civic participation and feedback. This in turn proves beneficial for city authorities to improve welfare services and raise in terms of accountability.

Performance Management Capability. Abella et al. [34] provide another illustration of data driven innovation in smart cities. In doing so the authors emphasise the need for tools for timely release of information and geo-location of data, to improve city service performance.

Cross-Sector Collaboration Capability. Considering 4P (public-private-people) partnership as a key enabler for smart city services, Nam and Pardo [6] study the case of the Philly 311 non-emergency programme in Philadelphia for effectiveness, efficiency and transparency in service delivery. In this study the author's highlight the importance of both internal and external collaboration (open innovation) to continuously improve services. On similar lines, Chatfield and Reddick [21] study Japan's Kitakyushu smart community project to identify antecedent conditions required for smart city implementation. In doing so authors posit that smart city implementations require bottom-up approach; implying collaboration of stakeholders from various sectors in the city to create shared value.

Systems Integration and Co-ordination Capability. Taking into account the conflict for policy makers in integrating traditional decision making models with citizen feedback (enabled by open and crowdsourced data); Boukhris et al. [35] propose the multi-criteria decision-making (MCDM) model. This model assists decision makers in strategic planning and provides them with the best alternative(s); as MCDM models allows for ranking and weighing citizen input.

Open Government Data Capability. Based on the empirical study conducted in Spain, Carrasco and Sobrepere [36] address five dimensions of OGD out of which 'Strategy' dimension has been emphasised as the most important. This dimension assesses the overall vision, governance, institutional and legal framework of open government data initiative.

4.3 Learning and Cultural Capabilities

These capabilities are the foundations on which other capabilities are realized. With respect to learning capabilities the key enablers identified are the city stakeholders who regularly hone their skills; while with respect to cultural capabilities the key enablers identified are the city structure and history (Table 4).

Table 4. Overview of learning and cultural capabilities

Enablers	Routine	Capabilities	Description	References
City stakeholders–firms, government, university and citizens	Skills training - (creativity, intelligence, soft skills, hard skills, technological skills)	Learning capability	Considering city as a social system, it is the ability to develop skills for knowledge based urban development; where intelligence is the key to effectively utilise internal and external knowledge	[37, 38]
City structure and history	Support mechanisms/behaviour that supports innovation	Cultural capability	Ability to build and improve facilities that encourage tourist attractions, creative talent and attract inward investment	[39]

Learning Capability The importance of knowledge transfer amongst city actors during the design phase of smart city environments is emphasised by [37]. The authors state that the exchange of domain knowledge is highly tacit in nature; which, at times leads to loss of valuable information. The study suggests that this can be overcome by studying knowledge transfer in human-computer interactions. In a similar context, by assigning knowledge as a central factor to foster productivity of welfare services, Donolo [38] stresses the importance of soft skills as an essential capability in the knowledge society.

Cultural Capability Looking at cities as centres of production and growth - to drive inward investment, Markatou and Alexandrou [39] stress the importance of factors like city branding, urban environment, presence of prestigious universities.

5 Conclusion and Research Agenda

This research in progress attempts to expand the growing area of smart city management by establishing an initial theoretical connection to the capabilities approach. The review of 72 related papers led to the new types of capabilities that included dynamic, operational, learning and cultural capabilities, which altogether reflect the diversity of approaches in relation to smart city management. Dynamic capabilities assist in decision-making with respect to technological evolution, whereas operational capabilities assist in evaluating changes in terms of socio-economic-political contexts. Cultural and learning capabilities are an antecedent to dynamic and operational capabilities as they relate to the contextual factors of smart cities. The capabilities listed provide a snapshot of the smart city literature in the social sciences.

By consolidating the different aspects of smart city management, several new links also emerge as: (1) dynamic capabilities mainly impact information and policy development of city services, (2) operational capabilities predominantly impact the execution and (3) learning and cultural capabilities influence the procedure of smart city services. Furthermore, the capabilities point to the use of specific resources to achieve smart city outcomes especially, when it comes to new forms of data and information sharing (e.g. social monitoring, interoperability and open data capabilities). This has been better understood by linking the capabilities to illustrative examples from the literature.

Future work can consider both the theoretical and practical levels of smart city capabilities. At the conceptual level, there is scope to link capability development to stage models of smart city evolution and value creation activities. Such an approach seems possible at the stage where both the implementation of smart cities is progressing rapidly and there is a body of related academic work (most relevant papers in the review were published recently). At the practical level, although the integration of the resources within city infrastructure and citizen adoption is quite established, realising capabilities and underlying processes can allow to explore the configuration of hard and soft infrastructure in cities. Thus, cities with more limited resources can develop smarter and resilient services, catering specifically to the city characteristics.

In terms of empirical studies, capabilities can be a useful lens both for case study explorations of smart city management and as a framework to design survey-based instruments. Particularly related to the latter, there is a lot to learn about city managers' perceptions of the enablers of smart city management. There is good scope to identify new capabilities that have yet to be reported within the academic literature but are related to the challenging implementation of new initiatives such as different types of data- open data [36], crowdsourced data [31] and big data [28]. A practical example of a complex data driven decision making platform is London Datastore. It aims to create a city data market by 'opening' the data collected at the expense of the public, to all. However, such platforms face issues like data sharing, interoperability. Thus, a future research agenda which assesses capabilities like data sharing, data interoperability and even data infrastructures; as part of complex smart city infrastructure seems promising.

References

1. Harrison, C., Donnelly, I.A.: A theory of smart cities. In: Proceedings of the 55th Annual Meeting ISSS—2011, Hull, p. 55 (2011)
2. Anthopoulos, L.: Defining smart city architecture for sustainability. In: Electronic Government Electronic Participation, pp. 140–147 (2015)
3. Sinkiene, J., Grumadaite, K., Liugailaite-Radzvickiene, L.: Diversity of theoretical approaches to the concept of smart city. In: 8th International Scientific Conference "Business and Management", pp. 933–940 (2014)
4. Juceviþius, R., Patašienơ, I., Patašius, M.: Digital dimension of smart city: critical analysis. Proc. Soc. Behav. Sci. **156**, 146–150 (2014)
5. Gil-Garcia, J.R., Zhang, J., Puron-Cid, G.: Conceptualizing smartness in government: an integrative and multi-dimensional view. Gov. Inf. Q. **33**, 524–534 (2016)
6. Nam, T., Pardo, T.A.: The changing face of a city government: a case study of Philly311. Gov. Inf. Q. **31**, S1–S9 (2014)
7. Rodríguez Bolívar, M.P., Meijer, A.J.: Smart governance: using a literature review and empirical analysis to build a research model. Soc. Sci. Comput. Rev. **34**(6), 673–692 (2016)
8. Meijer, A.J., Gil-Garcia, J.R., Rodríguez Bolívar, M.P.: Smart city research: contextual conditions, governance models, and public value assessment. Soc. Sci. Comput. Rev. **34**, 647–656 (2016)
9. Anthopoulos, L., Fitsilis, P.: Evolution roadmaps for smart cities: determining viable paths. In: 13th European Conference eGovernment (ECEG 2013), pp. 27–35 (2013)
10. Dameri, R.P., Benevolo, C.: Governing smart cities: an empirical analysis. Soc. Sci. Comput. Rev. **34**, 693–707 (2016)
11. Castelnovo, W., Misuraca, G., Savoldelli, A.: Smart cities governance: the need for a holistic approach to assessing urban participatory policy making. Soc. Sci. Comput. Rev. **34**, 724–739 (2016)
12. Teece, D.J., Pisano, G., Shuen, A., David Teece, M.J.: Dynamic capabilities and strategic management. Strateg. Manag. J. **187**, 509–533 (1997)
13. Eisenhardt, K.M., Martin, J.A.: Dynamic capabilities: what are they? Strateg. Manag. J. **21**, 1105–1121 (2000)
14. Pablo, A.L., Reay, T., Dewald, J.R., Casebeer, A.L.: Identifying, enabling and managing dynamic capabilities in the public sector. J. Manag. Stud. **44**, 687–708 (2007)

15. Kim, S., Lee, H.: The impact of organizational context and information technology on employee knowledge-sharing capabilities. Public Adm. Rev. **66**, 370–385 (2006)
16. Niehaves, B., Plattfaut, R., Becker, J.: Business process management capabilities in local governments: a multi-method study. Gov. Inf. Q. **30**, 217–225 (2013)
17. Pardo, T.A., Burke, G.B.: Improving Government Interoperability: A Capability Framework for Government Managers. Center for Technology in Government, pp. 1–24 (2008)
18. Klievink, B., Romijn, B.-J., Cunningham, S., de Bruijn, H.: Big data in the public sector: uncertainties and readiness. Inf. Syst. Front. **19**, 1–17 (2016)
19. Klievink, B., Janssen, M.: Realizing joined-up government—dynamic capabilities and stage models for transformation. Gov. Inf. Q. **26**, 275–284 (2009)
20. Rezende, D.A., Kohls, J.B.: Public services and electronic government Chicago's digital city. In: International Conference on Social Science and Management—ICSSM, pp. 1–9 (2014)
21. Chatfield, A.T., Reddick, C.G.: Smart city implementation through shared vision of social innovation for environmental sustainability: a case study of Kitakyushu, Japan. Soc. Sci. Comput. Rev. **34**, 757–773 (2016)
22. Tranfield, D., Denyer, D., Smart, P.: Towards a methodology for developing evidence-informed management knowledge by means of systematic review. Br. J. Manag. **14**, 207–222 (2003)
23. Briner, R.B., Denyer, D.: Systematic review and evidence synthesis as a practice and scholarship tool. In: Rousseau, D.M. (ed.) The Oxford Handbook of Evidence-Based Management, pp. 112–129. Oxford University Press, New York (2012)
24. Schaffers, H., Komninos, N., Pallot, M., Trousse, B., Nilsson, M., Oliveira, A.: Smart cities and the future internet: towards cooperation frameworks for open innovation. In: Domingue, J., Galis, A., Gavras, A., Zahariadis, T., Lambert, D., Cleary, F., Daras, P., Krco, S., Müller, H., Li, M.-S., Schaffers, H., Lotz, V., Alvarez, F., Stiller, B., Karnouskos, S., Avessta, S., Nilsson, M. (eds.) FIA 2011. LNCS, vol. 6656, pp. 431–446. Springer, Heidelberg (2011). doi:10.1007/978-3-642-20898-0_31
25. Komninos, N.: Intelligent cities: variable geometries of spatial intelligence. Intell. Build. Int. **3**, 172–188 (2011)
26. Anthopoulos, L., Fitsilis, P.: Using classification and roadmapping techniques for smart city viability's realization. Electron. J. e-Gov. **11**, 326–336 (2013)
27. Gurkan Inan, G., Bititci, U.S.: Understanding organizational capabilities and dynamic capabilities in the context of micro enterprises: a research agenda. Proc. Soc. Behav. Sci. **210**, 310–319 (2015)
28. Hashem, I.A.T., Chang, V., Anuar, N.B., Adewole, K., Yaqoob, I., Gani, A., Ahmed, E., Chiroma, H.: The role of big data in smart city. Int. J. Inf. Manag. **36**, 748–758 (2016)
29. Belanche-Gracia, D., Casaló-Ariño, L.V., Pérez-Rueda, A.: Determinants of multi-service smartcard success for smart cities development: a study based on citizens' privacy and security perceptions. Gov. Inf. Q. **32**, 154–163 (2015)
30. Van Zoonen, L.: Privacy concerns in smart cities. Gov. Inf. Q. **33**, 472–480 (2016)
31. Johannessen, M.R., Berntzen, L.: Smart cities through implicit participation: using gamification to generate citizen input for public transport planning. In: Electronic Government and Electronic Participation (2016)
32. Scholl, H.J., Alawadhi, S.: Smart governance as key to multi-jurisdictional smart city initiatives: the case of the eCityGov Alliance. Soc. Sci. Inf. **55**, 255–277 (2016)
33. Estévez-Ortiz, F.-J., García-Jiménez, A., Glösekötter, P., Rey, U., Carlos, J.: An application of people's sentiment from social media to smart cities. Prof. LA Inf. **25**, 1699–2407 (2016)
34. Abella, A., Ortiz-De-Urbina-Criado, M., De-Pablos-Heredero, C.: Information reuse in smart cities' ecosystems. Prof. La Inf. **24**, 1699–2407 (2015)

35. Boukhris, I., Ayachi, R., Elouedi, Z., Mellouli, S., Amor, N.: Ben: decision model for policy makers in the context of citizens engagement: application on participatory budgeting. Soc. Sci. Comput. Rev. **34**, 740–756 (2016)
36. Carrasco, C., Sobrepere, X.: Open government data: an assessment of the Spanish municipal situation. Soc. Sci. Comput. Rev. **33**, 631–644 (2015)
37. Pourzolfaghar, Z., Helfert, M.: Investigating HCI Challenges for Designing Smart Environments. In: HCI in Business, Government, and Organisations: Information Systems, HCIBGO 2016, PT II (2016)
38. Donolo, M.: The knowledge society and the capability approach in the perspective of sustainable development in Europe. In: Vision 2020: Innovation, Development Sustainability, and Economic Growth, pp. 1–5 (2013)
39. Markatou, M., Alexandrou, E.: Urban system of innovation: main agents and main factors of success. Proc. Soc. Behav. Sci. **195**, 240–250 (2015)

Towards "Smart Governance" Through a Multidisciplinary Approach to E-government Integration, Interoperability and Information Sharing: A Case of the LMIP Project in South Africa

More Ickson Manda(✉)

University of the Witwatersrand, Johannesburg, South Africa
moreikson@gmail.com

Abstract. The integration and interoperability of e-government systems, and information sharing is essential in transforming governments to "smart governments" that deliver services to enhance the socio- economic inclusion and the quality of life of its citizens. The aim of this doctoral study is to understand institutional barriers to e-government integration, interoperability and information sharing preventing governments from transforming to smart governments. The study is an interpretive case study, using South Africa as a unique case of a developing country which has adopted the "smart" agenda. Findings will contribute to theory through advancing knowledge in the new research area of smart government as well as contributing to practice through generating applicable knowledge on digital transformation in the public sector.

Keywords: Smart government · Smart governance · Integration · Interoperability · Institutional theory · E-government

1 Introduction

E-government integration, interoperability and effective information sharing is one of the key priorities governments worldwide are implementing to increase efficiency in service delivery and to improve synergies across government agencies [15]. This is increasingly becoming important as governments are pressured to respond to the needs of the so called "smart society" though "smart governance" [11]. Smart societies leverage the power of technology for socio-economic development and other purposes [4, 9]. 'Smart governments' thus leverage the power of technology, knowledge and innovation in governing and service delivery. Information sharing, interoperability and integration of e-government are key in transforming governments to "smart governments" [9]. South Africa is one of the few countries in Africa that have adopted the 'smart' agenda in its bid to improve the lives of its citizens [11]. The lack of interoperability and integration has been identified by the South African government as one of the barriers in transforming the public service [23]. The absence of 'integrated information systems' for skills supply and demand across government for example, has

M. Janssen et al. (Eds.): EGOV 2017, LNCS 10428, pp. 36–44, 2017.
DOI: 10.1007/978-3-319-64677-0_4

compromised the ability of government agencies to effectively collaborate in addressing developmental issues such as skills for inclusive growth [21].

South Africa has come up with measures aimed at improving integration, interoperability and information sharing. A significant example is the Labour Market Intelligence Partnership (LMIP) project launched in 2012 to build integrated systems for reliable collection, collation, analysis and sharing of reliable labour market intelligence to support evidence based decision making. The LMIP project thus presented an opportunity to conduct a study to understand the barriers governments face in integrating and interoperating their systems in their bid to transform to smart governments that are innovative, efficient, accountable, transparent and inclusive.

This study contributes to theory and knowledge in the discipline of e-government by using an institutional based view and multidisciplinary approach in understanding e-government integration and interoperability. Various disciplinary perspectives (information systems, information science, political science and public administration) are used to understand the complex social, political, economic, technical and regulative issues surrounding e-government. The use of multidisciplinary studies in e-government is supported by [18] who cited the fragmentation of literature in e-government as part of the problem in understanding complex issues such as integration and interoperability. The practical contribution would be to generate applicable knowledge on e-government integration and interoperability to promote digital transformation of the public sector.

2 Problem Statement and Purpose

The interoperability and integration of e-government systems, and information sharing has captured the attention of governments due to increased pressure to improve governance, service delivery and quality of life of citizens through offering 'smart' services. Integration and interoperability enable faster, efficient, effective and more comprehensive service delivery to citizens, business and collaboration among government agencies [18]. Governments are however still experiencing blockages in transforming to "smart governments" due to challenges with the integration and interoperability of e-government systems [4, 5, 15, 18, 19].

The purpose of the study is to understand e-government integration and interoperability institutional barriers so as to improve systems integration and interoperability for promoting collaboration and a seamless flow of information, knowledge and innovation across government for improving governance. In understanding the barriers, I use an institutional perspective and multidisciplinary approach.

2.1 Research Question

To address the problem highlighted above, **the main question** posed in this study is:

How can e-government integration and interoperability given its complexity be improved using a multidisciplinary approach and institutional perspective to help transform governments into "smart governments"?

The following research **sub-questions** are posed:

1. *What is the extent of e-government integration, interoperability and cross boundary information sharing in South Africa?*
2. *What institutional barriers is the South African government facing in its bid to improve information sharing, integration and interoperability of its systems for strengthening smart governance?*
3. *How has the South African government responded to institutional barriers to e-government information sharing, integration and interoperability?*

3 Related Work

Interoperation and integration of e-government systems, information, processes, institutions, and physical infrastructure to provide better services and create an enabling environment is an enabler of smart governance [4]. Governments, both developed and developing, are thus embarking on initiatives to transform to smart governments that deliver better services and quality of life to their citizens. According to [15], integration and interoperability is however "not an end in itself but an enabler for helping government use technology to improve government services and operations. Citizens do not demand interoperability; rather, systems must be interoperable to effectively meet citizens' demands". Interoperability also plays a major role in improving government efficiency through enhancing government communication, administrative efficiency and streamlining processes which improves the quality of public service delivery [26]. Information sharing, interoperability and integration of e-government systems increase Government to Government (G2G) efficiency. G2G efficiency has an impact on the performance of other e-government services, such as Government to Citizen (G2C) and Government to Business (G2B) [26].

Previous studies (mostly from developed countries) in e-government integration, interoperability and information sharing such as [3, 4, 15, 18, 19] identified constraints such as policy, legislation, resourcing, leadership, structures and technology etc. Few such studies from developing countries exist and this presented an opportunity to contribute to literature by attempting to understand some of these barriers using a multidisciplinary approach and institutional perspective. The socio-historic, socio-economic and political contexts, which are important in understanding developmental issues such as e-government, are some of the key focal areas in this study.

3.1 Key Definitions

Smart government and related concepts are still fairly new and scholars have not agreed on what it entails [5, 17]. It has been characterized as the use of technologies in the provision of services, [5] for example, argues that a smart government "integrates information sources of multiple departments and multiple business system functions on a large scale, and then provides the on-demand dynamic portfolio smart services". It has also been defined as a government that "uses sophisticated information technologies to interconnect and integrate information, processes, institutions, and physical infrastructure to better serve citizens and communities" [4]. Scholl and AlAwadhi [17] adopted a technological neutral definition. They define smart government as "the intelligent and adaptive office, authority, or function of governing" and smart governance as "the capacity of employing intelligent and adaptive acts and activities of looking after and making decisions about something". Keeping in line with a technological neutral definition emphasising Holland's [7] call for social inclusion in smart agendas, I define smart government as:

An accountable and transparent government that is digitally transformed, innovative, uses knowledge, social, economic and political systems, and other tools for effective internal functioning, governance and service provision, in the pursuit of inclusive growth.

Integration, interoperability and information sharing are also interrelated terms which have been confused by some scholars [19]. I adopt the following definitions:

E-government Integration is "the forming of a larger unit of government entities, temporary or permanent, for the purpose of merging processes and/or sharing information" [18].

Interoperability "represents a set of multidimensional, complementary, and dynamic capabilities needed among these networks of organizations in order to achieve successful information sharing" [15].

Inter-agency information sharing is the exchanging of information between government agencies or giving agencies in the same network access to information [3].

Scholl et al. [19] concluded that integration, interoperability and information sharing are "intertwined and inextricably interrelated". They proposed the use of the compound acronym of INT-IS-IOP as a term for integration (INT), information sharing (IS), and interoperation/interoperability (IOP). This approach is adopted in this study.

4 Theoretical Framing

Institutional theory, a multidisciplinary theory with roots in sociology, political science and economics underpins this study. It is "one of these more integrative approaches that recognize the importance of the context in which ICT are embedded and help to understand the influences of various factors on their selection, design, implementation, and use" [12]. The "IS field's practical interest in the development, use, and management of information systems may have diverted analysts to lower levels of analysis and hence, away from studying how regulative processes, normative systems, and cultural frameworks shape the development of e-government systems…" [14]. However, developments in technology have led to an emphasis on information systems research that seeks to understand its impact on institutions and their immediate environments [10, 14]. In this study I explore how the three pillars of institutions (regulative, normative and cultural-cognitive) identified by [20] influence digital transformation. Institutional theory is based on the belief that organizations, and the individuals who populate them, are shaped by rules, norms, values, beliefs, and taken-for-granted assumptions that are partly of their own design become established as authoritative guidelines for social behavior [20].

Institutional isomorphism is also used to understand institutional barriers to integration and interoperability and how pressure to achieve legitimacy influences institutional transformation. Legitimacy is defined as, "a generalized perception or assumption that the actions of an entity are desirable, proper, or appropriate within some socially constructed system of norms, values, beliefs, and definitions" [24].

5 Methodology

In social sciences, the choice of methodology is influenced by the nature of the phenomena or problem [13]. The methodological choices made in this study were as a result of their appropriateness in addressing the research problem through the **research question** and **sub-questions** highlighted in Sect. 2 and Subsect. 2.1.

5.1 Research Philosophy

This study assumes an interpretevist qualitative paradigm as it seeks to generate an understanding of the social, political, technological, and economic context inherent in e-government. This is key in gaining insights into the complex issues surrounding e-government integration and interoperability. The role of the researcher in interpretevist research is to interpret his or her own understanding of phenomena hence the principle of objectivity common in positivist research will not be applied in this study.

5.2 Research Design

An interpretive case study research design is adopted in this study. The case study method has gained popularity due to a shift of information systems research from a technical perspective towards an organizational and social perspective where the emphasis is the study of social and organizational issues such as culture, behaviour and structure in relation to technology [1]. The complexity of the e-government information sharing, integration and interoperability problem being investigated in this study justifies the use of this approach. One of the primary outcomes of this study is to contribute towards building theory in e-government which is still in its developmental stages. This also justifies the use of a case study method which is appropriate in theory building where theory is absent or is still in formative stages [1]. Theory building in e-government has largely been influenced by research originating from developed countries. An opportunity is being missed for researchers from developing countries to share their knowledge and experiences in contributing to the body of knowledge especially in social sciences where the social context influences how we view the world.

5.3 Data Collection

For the purposes of collecting data, documents, semi-structured interviews and a review of literature are used in this study. Purposive sampling was used to select the participants (a minimum of 10 senior officials) responsible for policy and ICT from across six national departments. Additional participants will be selected through snowball sampling. More than one approach in collecting data (triangulation) was used so as to minimise the exclusion of any relevant evidence taking into account the complexity of the problem. Moreover, no single source of data could adequately provide required data to answer the questions posed in this study, hence prompting the use of multi-sources of data. The data collection methods used each have their own strengths and play a complementary role in addressing the weaknesses in each.

5.4 Data Analysis

Qualitative analysis, whose role is to understand and make sense of phenomena and to uncover emerging themes, patterns, and insight rather than predicting or explaining, was done simultaneously with data collection so as to identify gaps in the data as recommended by Bhattacherjee [2]. The role of qualitative data analysis is to understand and make sense of phenomena and to uncover emerging themes, patterns, and insight rather than predicting or explaining [2].

Thematic analysis was used in analysing data. Coding was conducted in interview and documentary data so that evidence could be put into a limited number of categories appropriate to the research problem for easy analysis. A combination of open (inductive) and closed (deductive) coding was used. Closed coding was used to select themes identified from literature and theory while open coding was used to identify new themes that emerged during the data collection and analysis process.

6 Discussion of Preliminary Results

In this section, I discuss the preliminary results from evidence gathered from documents and interviews conducted so far. Although it's still too early to draw conclusions, some of the findings so far point to institutional leadership, collaboration and coordination, information and communication infrastructure, policy and legislation as some of the contentious issues in South Africa's digital transformation efforts.

Institutional leadership: In the transformation to smart government, leadership plays an important role in providing strategic direction, putting in place coercive mechanisms such as regulations, structures and norms that help shape desired behavior in institutions. Leadership also influences the transformation of cultural-cognitive elements such as practices, beliefs and shared values. Despite some of the notable achievements such as the development of supportive policies, leadership remains one of the most significant challenges in digital transformation in South Africa. This ranges from lack of clarity of roles between the various key departments driving the smart agenda resulting in lack of accountability, government department 'turf wars' and dysfunctional structures. The institutional leadership challenge in the smart government agenda in South Africa has compromised transformation due to poor coordination of resources and institutional activities.

Collaboration, coordination and integration of services: The government of South Africa has recognised the role of collaboration in realising its vision of a digitally transformed and smart government. Inter-organizational collaboration defined by [16] as involving "sets of negotiations that are demanded by the lack of predefined institutional roles that accompany market and authority based relationships", is a key enabler of integrated government. The clustering of government departments is one strategy that has been used to foster collaboration, coordination and integration. Preliminary findings show that inter-governmental collaboration and integration are more pronounced within departments in the same cluster e.g. security cluster. Collaboration and integration is likely to happen when institutions share a common mandate. Trusting relations are thus more likely to be reinforced and reproduced when there are strong institutional forces promoting common obligations on both parties [12].

Social and political cohesion was also found to influence collaboration and integration as it cements trust in inter-organizational relations [8]. The lack of social and political cohesion is one of the significant barriers in policy development and implementation. Government sometimes finds itself at odds with citizens, private business, civil society and other social partners due to lack of cohesion. This suggests that full institutionalization or sedimentation of 'smart governance' which is characterized by social cohesion, trust, established structures, norms and practices is far from being reached.

An analysis of the interview data conducted so far further revealed that power and politics in institutions play a significant role in the success of integration initiatives in government. An understanding of the interplay between power, politics, collaboration, trust and institutionalization of new structures, systems, norms and value systems has the potential to contribute to institutional theory and will be investigated further.

Information and communication infrastructure: Preliminary findings pointed to the poor state of communication and information infrastructure such as broadband in South Africa as a cause for concern. Broadband connectivity is a key technology for digital connectivity, without which interoperability and integration of systems is compromised. This has also been a threat to "inclusive government", a key dimension of smart government identified by Gil-Garcia et al. [6]. The poor state of ICT infrastructure including electricity in rural areas where 40% of South Africa's population lives, is a threat to government vision of being a smart government that governs a smart, connected and digitally inclusive society by 2030 [22]. Smart government is about inclusivity and creation of a smart and connected citizenry [11]. The current state of affairs is likely to exclude the already marginalized citizenry and increase the connectivity divide. A smart, connected and engaged citizenry promotes participative government, a key outcome of smart government identified by [6]. Citizen participation and engagement is also important in legitimising governments and their institutions whose existence is primarily to serve the interests of its citizens.

Innovative policy and legislative framework: Legislative reforms and innovative policies are important regulative institutional mechanisms for supporting the smart agenda. Legislation and policies allow governments to put in place resources and governance mechanism (smart governance) in response to challenges brought by the smart society. The journey to smart governance in South Africa began in 1998 after the Presidential Review Commission on the performance of the public sector identified the governance of information resources and ICT in the public sector as key in its transformation [25]. South Africa has developed a comprehensive e-government policy and legislative framework which addresses crucial issues such as the integration of services and systems, interoperability, cyber-security, personal privacy and infrastructure development. What remains a significant challenge is the implementation of policy and legislation as witnessed by delays in implementation of key policies and legislation such as the Protection of Personal Information Act (2013), Integrated ICT Policy initiated in 2013 and Cybercrimes bill promulgated in 2015. Issues of trust, privacy and security thus remain an 'Achilles heel' in the current framework due to delays in implementation. This is worsened by poor policy and legislation harmonization as new policies and legislation are developed. This ultimately compromises the effectiveness of policy and legislation as mechanisms for effecting transformation.

Mimetic pressures in the setting of development agenda, including ICT policy direction have been evidenced. South Africa's adoption of the Digital Migration Policy and Strategy (a key strategy for broadband penetration) derives from the 2006 International Telecommunications Union resolution where member states were given a June 2015 deadline to migrate. South Africa's failure to meet the deadline points to poor policy implementation, especially where policy direction is influenced by external forces without sufficient resourcing. Governments especially in developing countries, often have to choose between international standards and best practices, and domestic priorities such as poverty reduction and reducing inequalities etc. This conflict is likely going to lead to governments failing to effectively implement policies as they often aim to please both. Domestic priorities are essential as governments use social obligation as a basis for legitimacy. Externally, governments are coerced to comply with international regulations for legitimising themselves in the global context.

References

1. Benbasat, I., Goldstein, D.K., Mead, M.: The case research strategy in studies of information systems. MIS Q. **11**(3), 369–386 (1987)
2. Bhattacherjee, A.: Social Science Research: Principles, Methods, and Practices. USF Tampa Bay Open Access Textbooks Collection, Book 3 (2012)
3. Dawes, S.S.: Interagency information sharing: expected benefits, manageable risks. J. Policy Anal. Manage. **15**(3), 377–394 (1996)
4. Gil-Garcia, J.R.: Towards a smart State? Inter-agency collaboration, information integration, and beyond. Inf. Polity **17**(3, 4), 269–280 (2012)
5. Gil-Garcia, J.R., Helbig, N., Ojo, A.: Being smart: emerging technologies and innovation in the public sector. Gov. Inf. Q. **31**(1), 11–18 (2014)
6. Gil-Garcia, J.R., Zhang, J., Puron-Cid, G.: Conceptualizing smartness in government: an integrative and multi-dimensional view. Gov. Inf. Q. **33**(3), 524–534 (2016)
7. Hollands, R.G.: Will the real smart city please stand up? Intelligent, progressive or entrepreneurial? City **12**(3), 303–320 (2008)

8. Huddy, L., Sears, D., Levy, J. (eds.): Group identity and political cohesion in Oxford Handbook of political psychology. Oxford University Press, New York (2013)
9. Jimenez, C.E., Solanas, A., Falcone, F.: E-government interoperability: linking open and smart government. Computer **47**, 22–24 (2014)
10. Luna-Reyes, L.F., Gil-García, J.R.: Using institutional theory and dynamic simulation to understand complex e-government phenomena. Gov. Inf. Q. **28**(3), 329–345 (2011)
11. Manda, M.I., Backhouse, J.: Towards a "Smart Society" through a connected and smart citizenry in south africa: a review of the national broadband strategy and policy. In: Scholl, H.J., et al. (eds.) EGOVIS 2016. LNCS, vol. 9820, pp. 228–240. Springer, Cham (2016). doi:10.1007/978-3-319-44421-5_18
12. Marchington, M., Vincent, S.: Analysing the influence of institutional, organizational and interpersonal forces in shaping inter-organizational relations. J. Manage. Stud. **41**(6), 1029–1056 (2004)
13. Noor, K.B.M.: Case study: a strategic research methodology. Am. J. Appl. Sci. **5**(11), 1602–1604 (2008)
14. Orlikowski, W.J., Baroudi, J.J.: Studying information technology in organizations: research approaches and assumptions. Inf. Syst. Res. **2**(1), 1–28 (1991)
15. Pardo, T.A., Nam, T., Burke, G.B.: E-government interoperability interaction of policy, management, and technology dimensions. Soc. Sci. Comput. Rev. **30**(1), 7–23 (2012)
16. Phillips, N., Lawrence, T.B., Hardy, C.: Inter-organizational collaboration and the dynamics of institutional fields. J. Manage. Stud. **37**(1), 23–43 (2000)
17. Scholl, H.J., AlAwadhi, S.: Creating smart governance: the key to radical ICT overhaul at the city of Munich. Inf. Polity **21**(1), 21–42 (2016)
18. Scholl, H.J., Klischewski, R.: Government integration and interoperability: framing the research agenda. Int. J. Public Adm. **30**(8), 889–920 (2007)
19. Scholl, H.J., Kubicek, H., Cimander, R., Klischewski, R.: Process integration, information sharing, and system interoperation in government: a comparative case analysis. Gov. Inf. Q. **29**, 313–323 (2012)
20. Scott, W.R.: Institutions and Organizations. Sage, Thousand Oaks (2014)
21. South Africa: LMIP launch Minister's speech (2012). http://www.hsrc.ac.za/uploads/
22. South Africa: National development plan. www.gov.za/issues/key-issues
23. South Africa: National Integrated ICT policy discussion paper (2015). http://www.gov.za/documents/national-integrated-ict-policy-discussion-paper-comments-invited
24. Suchman, M.: Managing legitimacy: strategic and institutional approaches. Acad. Manage. Rev. **20**(3), 571–610 (1995)
25. The Presidency: Report of the Presidential Review Commission on the Reform and Transformation of the Public Service in South Africa, Pretoria (1998)
26. Zheng, D., Chen, J., Huang, L., Zhang, C.: E-government adoption in public administration organizations: integrating institutional theory perspective and resource-based view. Eur. J. Inf. Syst. **22**, 221–234 (2013)

Service Delivery

New Channels, New Possibilities: A Typology and Classification of Social Robots and Their Role in Multi-channel Public Service Delivery

Willem Pieterson[1(✉)], Wolfgang Ebbers[1], and Christian Østergaard Madsen[2]

[1] University of Twente, Enschede, The Netherlands
{w.pieterson,w.e.ebbers}@utwente.nl

[2] IT University of Copenhagen, Copenhagen, Denmark
chrm@itu.dk

Abstract. In this contribution we discuss the characteristics of what we call the fourth generation of public sector service channels: social robots. Based on a review of relevant literature we discuss their characteristics and place into multi-channel models of service delivery. We argue that social robots is not one homogenous type of channels, but rather breaks down in different (sub)types of channels, each with different characteristics and possibilities to supplement and/or replace existing channels. Given the variety of channels, we foresee challenges in incorporating these new channels in multi-channel models of service delivery. This is especially relevant given the current lack of evaluations of such models, the broad range of channels available, and their different stages of deployment at governments around the world. Nevertheless, social robots offer an potentially very relevant addition to the service level landscape.

Keywords: Multi-channel management · Social robots · Service channels · eGovernment · Service delivery

1 Introduction

The public sector service channel landscape has been in continuous movement since the 1990s. Currently a new generation of service channels is arriving: social robots fueled by artificial intelligence [1–4]. Not only do new channels arrive (such as conversational bots), we could also see a large degree of robotization of existing types of service channels, such as the telephone being replaced by conversational robots. The impact of this change could be large. Estimates suggests that sophisticated algorithms could substitute for approximately 140 million full-time knowledge workers worldwide and computers increasingly challenge human labor in a wide range of cognitive tasks [5]. The message seems clear; a new generation of service channels is arriving and could impact the current way channels are utilized by governments. But how exactly? What is the nature of these social robots and how will they fit into the multi-channel service delivery mix? These are important questions for several reasons. The first is cost. An increasing number of channels also leads to an increase in costs. Every single channel requires a specific

M. Janssen et al. (Eds.): EGOV 2017, LNCS 10428, pp. 47–59, 2017.
DOI: 10.1007/978-3-319-64677-0_5

technical infrastructure and resources [6]. Examples of these resources are staff, staff training and the branding of the channel to match the identity of the organisation. The second is quality of services and making sure the right services are delivered to the right citizens using the right channel. Scholars [7] argue that certain channels are suited for certain types of services, but this suitability may vary for different types of citizens. Lastly, although scholars and practitioners argue that electronic channels supplement, rather than replace traditional channels, the interplay between traditional and e-government channels remains to be explained [8]. We also need to determine how newer generations of service channels interact with existing channels and how these interactions impact the evaluations and success of public service delivery. This exploratory paper aims to find an answer to three interrelated questions:

1. What exactly is this new generation of social robot channels?
2. What are the characteristics of these channels regarding service delivery?
3. What is the position of these channels in the (multi-)channel mix?

The answers to these questions can help practitioners who wish to start incorporating new types of channels. Furthermore, this paper aims to set the agenda for future studies on the role and position of newer generations of service channels. This paper starts with a discussion of the various generations of service channels up until now. We briefly discuss the rise of previous generations of service channels and the properties of the various types of channels, as well as their position within existing frameworks for multichannel service delivery. Lastly, we discuss some (research) challenges regarding social robots as new channels.

2 Generations of Service Channels

The landscape of service channels has undergone significant changes in the past three decades. Traditionally (before the 1990s), most public services were dealt with in person, using the mail, via the phone [9]. The three channels of phone, mail and in-person (a.k.a. front desk or face-to-face) have been labeled as the 'traditional' service channels to separate them from the new 'electronic' service channels [7] that started to appear in the 1990s. We would argue that the utilization of the internet and advances in technology have led to several (partially overlapping) phases of electronic channel evolution. Table 1 summarizes these phases.

Phase 1 started in the 1990s with the widespread adoption of internet technologies. Even though the internet has been around since the 1960s [10], the widespread adoption of the technology did not happen until the 1990s. The first set of channels based on internet technology (websites and email) were hailed by many as bringing significant opportunities for governments to improve both the quality of service delivery, as well as reduce its cost [11]. This led to the first generation of electronic channels becoming leading in many government service strategies.

Table 1. Overview of generations of channels.

G	Period	Label	Alternative(s)	Example channels
0	<1990s	Traditional	–	In-person, telephone, mail
1	1990s	Electronic	Digital	Website, email
2	2000s	Social	Social media, Web 2.0, Government 2.0	Social media (e.g. social networking sites, (micro-)blogging, wikis)
3	2010s	Mobile	M-Government	Smartphones, responsive sites, mobile apps
4	2020s	Robot	(Social) Robots, Robotization	Social & conversational robots, artificial intelligence, virtual intelligence

As the internet matured, the capabilities of the infrastructure increased and new channels were developed. This gave rise to a second phase of electronic channels, which we label as social channels or alternatively Web2.0 [12]. This Web 2.0 consists of new platforms for interactions characterized by extensive input from citizens, for example in the integration of knowledge and co-production of web services. Once again, we witnessed hopeful views on how a Government2.0, based on Web2.0 would be beneficial [e.g. 14]. As a result, many governments started using social media or other Web2.0 technologies to communicate with their citizens. A study in the Netherlands [15], for example, found that all municipalities were active on Twitter, about 90% on Facebook and about 60% on YouTube in 2015.

Even though many governments are not active on every kind of social channel, yet another generation of channels appeared. Since the arrival of mobile phone technologies in the 1990s governments have been working on "M-government" initiatives [c.f. 16], for example via SMS messages. Fueled by the increased capabilities of wireless infrastructures and the invention of smartphones in the late 2000s, even more service channel opportunities were developed, such as special mobile websites, adaptive websites and dedicated mobile apps.

So far, we have seen that we can distinguish between different phases in the development of different (government) service channels. At the time of their arrival, they were all hailed as offering great new possibilities to improve service delivery. Lastly, in all cases governments, as well as their citizens started adopting these channels, albeit at different paces. Regarding the first generations of electronic channels it seems that saturation in the adoption by governments in most (Western) countries has been achieved [17], although the degree to which services are fully interactive and integrated [11] varies. The second and third phases are still in progress in most countries, with the adoption of mobile apps by governments being still relatively in its infancy. However, we believe a new –fourth– generation of electronic channels, one driven largely by artificial intelligence and robotization is now arriving. In the next section, we will discuss the characteristics of this fourth generation in detail.

3 The Fourth Generation of Electronic Channels

While the first generation of electronic channels was fueled by internet technologies themselves, the second generation was fueled by broadband internet and the increased technological capabilities of the internet technologies; the third generation was fueled by advances in wireless technologies and wireless broadband. The fourth is driven by advances in artificial intelligence that allow in part for the automation or robotization of existing channels and in part the creation of a new set of channels.

Artificial intelligence (AI) in its broadest sense is a field attempting to understand intelligent entities [18]. Therefore, one of the main goals of AI is to create technologies that are smart enough to think and act like humans. In practice, AI is used to create smarter technologies that can make decisions or support decision making.

The term artificial intelligence itself is by no means a new concept. The phrase "artificial intelligence" was coined in 1956 at a conference in Dartmouth [19]. However, it was not until recently that artificial intelligence matured. Real world examples of AI are smart assistants (such as Apple's Siri) and self-driving vehicles. What all these technologies have in common is that artificial intelligence is the 'engine' that enables intelligent robots to supplement or replace humans in a wide range of activities.

The development of robots to replace human labor is in itself nothing new. The emergence of real robots dates from 1954 when George Devol and Joe Engleberger created the first industrial robots. By 2008, the world robot population was estimated at 8.6 million, the same as the state of New Jersey. This number includes 7.3 million service robots compared and 1.3 million industrial robots [20].

Most of these existing robots are being used for relatively simple, boring, dangerous or dirty tasks [21]. There are obvious reasons for this. Many routines tasks (such as welding components in a car factory) are easiest to robotize and since robots know no emotions, it was obvious that they were deployed first for tasks that humans perceive as being dangerous or dirty (such as defusing bombs). However, as robots' capabilities evolve, it becomes possible that they are able to execute more and more complicated tasks [2]. Several experts expect that that within the next two decades robots will be as commonplace as computers are right now [22].

Various types of classifications for robots exist. For example, we can distinguish between certain types of "assistive social robots" [23]. "Service-type" robots serve such purposes as helping elderly persons dress, bathe, eat, move around, etc. "Companion-type" robots play a more therapeutic role by interacting with seniors in order to stimulate their emotional and physical health. Bainbridge et al. make another important distinction for communication purposes, namely the difference between physical and virtual robots [24]. This distinction can have important consequences for the quality of the communication interaction. For purposes of this paper, we focus on a special class of robots, namely social robots. There are two types of definitions of social robots. In one type the social interactions among robots themselves are emphasized [e.g. 4]. The second type, and our focal point, is on the social interactions between humans and robots. This type of social robot can be defined as *"an autonomous or semi-autonomous robot that interacts and communicates with humans by following the behavioral norms expected by the people with whom the robot is intended to interact"* [25].

Within this definition, it is possible to distinguish between different types of social robots. For example, following our discussion above, we can distinguish between social robots that are physically present versus those that are completely virtual. For the context of service delivery, we distinguish between three types or classes of social robots; (1) Software agents, (2) Virtual and virtuality enhancing robots, and (3) Physical social robots. The difference between the three stems from their nature and the degree to which they represent a physical reality. Software agents live completely in the background and feed into existing channels. For example, a human agent having chat/IM conversations with citizens could be replaced by a software agent. The service experience changes very little and the impact of the robot is mostly in the back-office. Virtual and virtuality enhancing robots change reality or create new realities, without being tangible. The two channels here are virtual and augmented reality. In contrast to software agents they do affect the front-office design and experience more elaborately. Lastly, physical social robots have a physical presence. They are physical entities that interact with humans either taking a human (humanoid or android) shape or a non-human shape. This physical presence creates, as we will see below, possibilities to move around as well as exploit the physical features to enhance or enrich the service encounter. Below we will discuss each type and sub-type briefly.

3.1 Software Agents

The first type consists of so-called software agents. These agents can be defined as "a self-contained, autonomous software module that performs assigned tasks from the human user and interacts/communicates with other applications and other software agents in different platforms to complete the tasks" [26]. The key characteristic, from our point of view, of these software agents lies in the notion that they (a) exist in software form only, (b) they support users with certain tasks and/or (c) complete tasks assigned by the user. For example, chat software can respond to user inquiries and intelligent agents (such as Apple's Siri) can complete tasks assigned by users such as making appoints). For the purpose of service delivery and in line with the literature on characteristics of service channels [27], we can sub-divide the broader class of software agents into three possible service channels:

Chat bots are software agents that focus on written/text language. This is very similar to existing chat or email channels, but with the human agent in the back office replaced or supported by software modules that respond to inquiries.

Conversational bots focus on spoken language and as such offer an alternative to telephone interactions. Conversational bots are more complicated to realize than chat-bots based on the more complicated nature of emulating speech. These conversational bots could be used in customer contact centers to respond to questions or help citizens solve ambiguous or complex problems.

Intelligent agents. The last type of software agents integrates chat and conversational bots into one system that can respond to inquiries or execute tasks. Several of these intelligent agents are currently on the market and the most well-known examples are Apple's Siri, Microsoft's Cortana and Google's Assistant. These intelligent agents react to spoken or typed commands and integrate tightly with existing systems.

Intelligent government agents could, for example, support citizens with any transactions they need to complete (e.g. pay parking tickets, file taxes) or find relevant information on government websites about certain topics.

3.2 Virtual and Virtuality Enhancing Robots

Virtual and virtuality enhancing robots are the second type of social robots. A key characteristic of virtual and virtuality enhancing robots is that they create a visual output based on imagery. This can take one of two forms: (1) it can be an augmentation of reality or (2) it can be a new version or virtualization of an existing reality. While these two types of augmented and virtual reality have this 'graphic' nature in common. They differ in key areas. Augmented reality differs from virtual reality in that "in a virtual environment the entire physical world is replaced by computer graphics, AR enhances rather replaces reality" [28]. We will discuss both briefly.

Augmented reality (AR) was first coined as a concept in the year 1992 [29] and is said to have three key goals: (a) create virtual references between reality and virtuality, (b) augment or enhance this virtual experience in real time and (c) create (real-time) interactivity between the virtual world and the real world. While the concept has been around since the 1990s and has seen some practical use (e.g. in cockpits), it was not until recently that many started talking about the broader societal adoption of augmented reality, fueled by tech demonstrations of (for example) Microsoft's HoloLens and previously Google Glass. Augmented reality could enhance public service encounters. For example, citizens could experience how new constructions would change their current streetscape (and better thus participate in the decision making process). During in person interactions, augmented reality could hypothetically be used to display key components of the spoken conversation creating additional communication cues that could enrich the communication.

Virtual reality (VR) can be defined as an immersive interactive multimedia and computer-simulated reality that can digitally replicate an environment [based on 30]. As such, one of the key goals of virtual technology development is to realize and improve the experience of telepresence [31]. This creates possibilities for public services in several ways. For example, in the design and participation processes of public (construction) processes, virtual reality can be used to show new construction where nothing currently exists and thus get input from citizens. In personal service encounters, virtual reality could be used to emulate a service environment for people who are unable to travel to service desks for personal contact. This could lead to better quality services for several segments of the civil population.

3.3 Physical Social Robots

The third and final class of social robots consists of those robots with a physical appearance. These types of robots have been around for a number of decades. Especially, as receptionists and office companions physical social robots are becoming increasingly popular [32]. We can also break physical social robots down into several sub-types: Non-Humanoid Robots and Humanoids. Main difference in the context of service delivery between the two is that the human resemblance of humanoids could potentially create a "richer" communication experience.

Non-humanoids are robots that take the shape of any object or animal, as long as it does not resemble a human being. Sony's Aibo "robodog" launched in 1999 is a well-known example of a non-humanoid. These non-humanoids could be used in public service settings where little to no communication is involved and where the ambiguity [7] of the communication process is low. For example, non-humanoids could guide visitors to their proper location in governmental buildings and serve as mobile versions of interactive booths or kiosks where citizens can complete self-service tasks.

Humanoids or also called Androids are robots that take a human like physical form. As such, they can emulate human-esque conversation styles and include aspects of human behavior such as body language. This addition potentially provides a very rich communication experience, especially since it comes to more emotional, personal topics or issues with high levels of ambiguity. Research choice that people tend to choose channels that offer many (communication) cues when services are more personal, more emotional and more ambiguous [27]. At the same time do research findings show that humans treat computers—and consequently robots—as social entities [33] or people [34], supporting the argument that humanoids could play an important role in emotional, personal and ambiguous social service encounters akin to the aforementioned "Companion-type" robots used in care settings. From that perspective, humanoids could even fulfill an important role in lessening emotional burdens on service agents that deal with emotional citizens struggling with complex problems.

4 Characteristics of Intelligent Channels

One of the obvious key questions regarding these new channels is what their characteristics are and how they can be used in service delivery processes. This can help us understand how they can be used in service delivery processes and to what extent these channels could replace existing service channels. Currently no complete overview exists comparing intelligent channels with each other and/or to other channels. In general terms Norman [35] compares the differences between robots and people and focuses mostly on the degree to which people and robots differ in terms of creativity, logical thinking, level of organization, etc. This comparison does not, however, include a diverse set of intelligent channels. More complete comparisons of channels do exist. Wirtz and Langer [6], for example, compare some 15 channels (comprising all channels from generations 0–3) on their cost benefit ratio, communication capability and service provision capacity. However, this model does not include any of the fourth generation channels and it is not granular enough for our purposes because it assumes that 'service provision capacity' is a one dimensional property. We follow the line of communication scholars [36] and previous multi-channel studies [7] that argue that services have multiple properties (for example in terms of the levels of ambiguity and complexity of the service) and different types of services require different types of channels. More comprehensively, van Dijk [37] reviews numerous theories that deal with characteristics of media or channels, and presents his model of "communication capacities" based on these theories. However, this model also does not include any of the new intelligent channels.

Since no complete overviews comparing the characteristics of intelligent channels exist, we propose such an overview ourselves, based on existing publications. We include in our overview several key characteristics of channels, such as the speed of the interaction, the ease of use and their stimulus richness (or communication capacity). This stimulus richness has been linked to the ambiguity of services [7] as well as emotional and personal aspects of public service delivery [27]. Furthermore, and building on this, in terms of channel/service fit, we include the ability to reduce complexity and ambiguity [7]. Lastly, we include how these channels could supplement existing channels in the short term and potentially replace channels in the long term. At present we do not believe any of the channels are ready to replace any channels in full, let alone replacing humans with robots that are (deservedly or not) perceived as autonomous, responsive, artificial beings that are able to perform complex tasks. This might change in the long term where intelligent channels could replace (human fueled, yet similar) channels (but where there might still be some kind of human back up or fall back option).

One of the defining characteristics of the intelligent channels is the higher level of stimuli richness, compared to most other electronic channels from the first, second and third generation. For example, an intelligent assistant who has access to personal information could allow for a highly personalized conversation with high levels of language variety using both written and oral cues. As such, many of these channels potentially offer greater capabilities to reduce ambiguity in many service delivery processes. We see this as one of the greatest general opportunities of social robots in terms of improving service delivery processes as currently the more expensive telephone and in-person channels are being used to reduce ambiguity [7].

We do need to stress though that, while it may come across as such, we do not intend to present this table as a fixed and rigid overview of characteristics of channels. For example, the media richness perspective, on which we draw in our assessment of the stimuli richness, has been criticized for being too rigid in assigning characteristics to media, while in reality the richness of a certain channel is fluid and depends such factors as the experiences of the communicators and the specific context in which the communication takes place [see e.g. 27, 38].

5 Integration in Multi-channel Models

The last relevant question is what the place of the new fourth generation should be in the channel mix offered by government organizations. In this section, we discuss the extent to which new channels fit existing models (Table 2).

Table 2. Characteristics of social robots.

Property	Software agents			Virtual and virtuality enhancing robots		Physical social robots	
	Chat bots	conversatio nal bots	Intelligent assistants	AR	VR	Non-humanoid Robots	Humanoids
Speed/ interactivity	Medium	High	High	Medium	Medium	Medium	High
Ease of use	High	Med/High	Med/High	Low/Med.	Low/Med.	Low/Med.	
Stimuli richness	Low	Medium	Medium	High	Med/High	Medium	High
Ability to reduce complexity	Med/High	Med/High	High	Medium	Medium	Medium	Medium
Ability to reduce ambiguity	Medium	High	High	High	High	Medium	High
Short term channel supplement/ long term replacement	Chat, Email	Telephone	Chat, Email, Telephone, Social Media, Apps, Website	Front Desk, Telephone	Front Desk, Telephone,	Front Desk	Front Desk

Note: This overview and assessment is based on the current and near future capabilities of these channels. Obviously, their capabilities and capacity for service delivery will evolve in the future.

Several models combine properties of service channels and how these channels can be positioned to deliver certain services to certain citizens (or businesses) [see e.g. 6, 7, 39, 40]. These models differ in their focus on different aspects of multi-channeling. In that sense, the three models have complementary value. However, the models share a number of drawbacks in relation to social robots. The first is that none of the models includes robots as channels. Secondly, no model includes mechanisms or facilities on how to assess or implement the replacement or compliment of new to existing channels. Thirdly, all different models see the existing channels as discrete entities with a (fixed) set of properties. This could create problems for social robot channels that very often combine properties of different existing channels, which may evolve over time as the underlying artificial intelligence improves. For example, does the capability of a humanoid social robot to reduce ambiguity change as the humanoid becomes more human and is able to increase its 'richness' [36] by evoking more natural language? Related to this change, is the response and the responsiveness of humanoids perceived as more or as less sincere and as more or as less autonomous than that of human beings? And more importantly, how do these perceptions relate to the perceived problem solving and perceived ambiguity decreasing capacity, thus influencing the replacement capacity of a robot related channel?

As such, the role of social robots within multi-channel service delivery seems promising given their characteristics, but their fit in the current channel strategies seems unclear. None of the existing multi-channel models seem well equipped to incorporate the fourth generation of electronic channels, let alone any future new channels. This is even more problematic given the realization that even now we lack insights on the effectiveness of existing channel strategies. Dawes [41] argues that in the literature there is a low emphasis on the "the substantial impacts of a multitude of service channels on the organization". Gagnon et al. posit that "multi-channel public delivery services has not been covered in the literature […] in such depth" [40]. So, if the literature gives us little guidance on the current state of the art, how are we to deal with upcoming developments?

6 Conclusions and Discussion

In this paper we focused on the arrival of a new 'generation' of service channels; social robots. These social robots are different from previous generations of service channels in that they are fueled by artificial intelligence. Compared to older generations of channels this allows for richer service experiences which, in certain cases, could offer experiences similar to human interactions. This leads to the possibility that intelligent channels could replace traditional human channels. One of the features of these intelligent channels is that they create the possibility to reduce ambiguity, which until now has been a dominant feature of telephone and in-person channels.

In this, it is important to realize that robots do not form one homogenous channel but break down in several types of service channels with different characteristics. Based on these characteristics we argue that these social robots (a) offer the possibility to supplement several of the existing channels thereby (potentially) improving service delivery and lessening the burden on the organization and its (human) agents, (b) in the future may replace some of the existing channels as (amongst others) the artificial intelligence behind these channels improves sufficiently and (c) could create new service channel opportunities that currently do not exist.

The position of social robots in the multi-channel mix is rather unclear. As we argued above, social robots is a collection of channels that all have different opportunities that could potentially supplement or replace existing channels. They are better suited to reduce ambiguity than most other channels. However, currently no multi-channel models exist that integrate social robots and no studies exist comparing social robots to other generations of channels in terms of their effectiveness and efficiency in public service delivery settings. As such, both more theoretical and empirical work is needed in this area.

Furthermore, while several governmental agencies may already be using robots and looking to implement them, most governments are still working on the successful implementation of channels from the third, second, and perhaps even the first generation of electronic channels. As such, organizations may be working on channel strategies based on many different channels, all with different characteristics and –technical and organizational– requirements. It is not hard to imagine that this turns the management of this multitude of channels into a complicated affair. This leads to a word of caution to organizations wanting to start using social robots to make sure the organization is 'ready' to start working with these channels.

Lastly, every single generation of channels is being heralded as offering great opportunities to improve service delivery and reduce costs. With the field evolving so rapidly it is doubtful whether the potential of each single generation of channels has been realized. While we have no studies available testing the hypothesized benefits of each generation of channels, we do have some information about the digitalization of government in the past 20 years in general, which so far has not been very successful [42]. Thus, while we are hopeful about the possibilities of social robots for service delivery, we also urge the field to temper any optimism and first explore the theoretical and practical aspects of social robots in terms of achieving organizational goals.

References

1. van Eeuwen, M.: Mobile Conversational Commerce: Messenger Chatbots as the Next Interface Between Businesses and Consumers. University of Twente, Enschede (2017)
2. De Graaf, M.M.A, Ben Allouch, S.: What are people's associations of domestic robots? Comparing implicit and explicit measures. In: 25th IEEE International Symposium on Robot and Human Interactive Communication (RO-MAN), pp. 1077–1083 (2016)
3. Dautenhahn, K.: Getting to know each other—artificial social intelligence for autonomous robots. Robot. Auton. Syst. **16**(2–4), 333–356 (1995)
4. Dautenhahn, K., Billard, A.: Bringing up robots or—the psychology of socially intelligent robots: from theory to implementation. In: Proceedings of Autonomous Agents (1999)
5. MGI: Disruptive technologies: Advances that will transform life, business, and the global economy. Technology Republic. McKinsey Global Institute (2013)
6. Wirtz, B.W., Langer, P.F.: Public multichannel management–an integrated framework of off- and online multichannel government services. Public Organ. Rev. 1–18 (2016)
7. Ebbers, W.E., Pieterson, W.J., Noordman, H.N.: Electronic government: Rethinking channel management strategies. Government Information Quarterly **25**(2), 181–201 (2008)
8. Madsen, C.Ø., Kræmmergaard, P.: How to succeed with multichannel management? Int. J. Public Adm. Digit. Age (IJPADA) **3**(4), 94–110 (2016)
9. Reddick, C., Anthopoulos, L.: Interactions with e-government, new digital media and traditional channel choices: citizen-initiated factors. Transform. Gov. People Process Policy **8**(3), 398–419 (2014)
10. Hafner, K., Lyon, M.: Where Wizards Stay Up Late: The Origins of the Internet. Simon and Schuster, New York (1998)
11. Layne, K., Lee, J.: Developing fully functional e-government: a four stage model. Gov. Inf. Q. **18**(2), 122–136 (2001)
12. Chadwick, A., May, C.: Interaction between states and citizens in the age of the internet: "eGovernment" in the United States, Britain, and the European Union. Governance **16**(2), 271–300 (2003)
13. Osimo, D.: Web2. 0 in Government: Why and How? Seville. European Commission Joint Research Centre Institute for Prospective Technological Studies (2008)
14. Tapscott, D., Williams, A.D., Herman, D.: Government 2.0: transforming government and governance for the twenty-first century. New Paradig. **1** (2008)
15. Kok, DeVoogd: Open gemeenten. De sociale media almanak voor gemeenten (2015)
16. Lawrence, P., Littman, L.: Preparing wireless and mobile technologies in government. (2002). http://www.businessofgovernment.org
17. Eurostat: Key figures on the digital economy and society. (2017). http://ec.europa.eu/eurostat/web/digital-economy-and-society/data/database. Accessed 14 Feb 2017

18. Russell, S., Norvig, P., Intelligence, A.: A Modern Approach. Artificial Intelligence, pp. 25–27. Prentice-Hall, Englewood Cliffs (1995)
19. Kernaghan, K.: The rights and wrongs of robotics: ethics and robots in public organizations. Can. Public Adm. **57**(4), 485–506 (2014)
20. Guizzo, E.: World robot population reaches 8.6 million. IEEE Spectr. (2010). http://spectrum.ieee.org/automaton/robotics/industrial-robots/041410-world-robot-population. Accessed 20 Jan 2017
21. Takayama, L., Ju, W., Nass, C.: Beyond Dirty, Dangerous, and Dull: What Everyday People Think Robots Should Do. HRI 2008, Amsterdam, The Netherlands (2008)
22. Siciliano, B., Khatib, O. (eds.): Springer Handbook of Robotics. Springer, Cham (2016). doi: 10.1007/978-3-319-32552-1
23. Broekens, J., Heerink, M., Rosendal, H.: Assistive social robots in elderly care: a review. Gerontechnology **8**(2), 94–103 (2009)
24. Bainbridge, W.A., Hart, J., Kim, E.S., Scassellati, B.: The effect of presence on human-robot interaction. In: The 17th IEEE International Symposium on Robot and Human Interactive Communication. RO-MAN 2008, pp. 701–706. IEEE, August 2008
25. Bartneck, C., Forlizzi, J.: A design-centred framework for social human-robot interaction. In: 13th IEEE International Workshop on Robot and Human Interactive Communication. ROMAN 2004, pp. 591–594. IEEE, September 2004
26. Popirlan, C.I.: Knowledge processing in contact centers using a multi-agent architecture. WSEAS Trans. Comput. **9**(11), 1318–1327 (2010)
27. Pieterson, W., Teerling, M., Ebbers, W.: Channel perceptions and usage: beyond media richness factors. In: Wimmer, Maria A., Scholl, Hans J., Ferro, Enrico (eds.) EGOV 2008. LNCS, vol. 5184, pp. 219–230. Springer, Heidelberg (2008). doi: 10.1007/978-3-540-85204-9_19
28. Milgram, P., Zhai, S., Drascic, D., Grodski, J.: Applications of augmented reality for human-robot communication. In: IROS 1993. Proceedings of the 1993 IEEE/RSJ International Conference on Intelligent Robots and Systems' 93, vol. 3, pp. 1467–1472. IEEE, July 1993
29. Caudell, T.P., Mizell, D.W.: Augmented reality: an application of heads-up display technology to manual manufacturing processes. In: Proceedings of the Twenty-Fifth Hawaii International Conference on System Sciences, 1992, vol. 2, pp. 659–669. IEEE, January 1992
30. David, R., Stahre, J., Wuest, T., Noran, O., Bernus, P., Fast-Berglund, Å., Gorecky, D: Towards an operator 4.0 typology: a human-centric perspective on the fourth industrial revolution technologies. In: CIE46 Proceedings, 29–31 Oct 2016, Tianjin, China (2016)
31. Lau, H.F., Lau, K.W., Kan, C.W.: The future of virtual environments: the development of virtual technology. Comput. Sci. Inf. Technol. **1**(1), 41–50 (2013)
32. Niculescu, A., van Dijk, B., Nijholt, A., Li, H., See, S.L.: Making social robots more attractive: the effects of voice pitch, humor and empathy. Int. J. Soc. Robot. **5**(2), 171–191 (2013)
33. Nass, C., Steuer, J., Tauber, E.R.: Computers are social actors. In: Proceedings of the SIGCHI Conference on Human Factors in Computing Systems, pp. 72–78. ACM, April 1994
34. Reeves, B., Nass, C.: The Media Equation. How People Treat Computers, Television, and New Media like Real People and Places. CSLI Publications and Cambridge (1996)
35. Norman, D.A.: Things that make us smart: defending human attributes in the age of the machine. Addison-Wesley Pub. Co., Bosto (1993)
36. Daft, R.L., Lengel, R.H.: Organizational information requirements, media richness and structural design. Manag. Sci. **32**(5), 554–571 (1986)
37. Van Dijk, J.: The Network Society. Sage Publications, London (2012)
38. Ngwenyama, O.K., Lee, A.S.: Communication richness in electronic mail: critical social theory and the contextuality of meaning. MIS Q. **21**, 145–167 (1997)

39. Madsen, C.Ø., Kræmmergaard, P.: Channel choice: a literature review. In: Tambouris, E., Janssen, M., Scholl, H.J., Wimmer, M.A., Tarabanis, K., Gascó, M., Klievink, B., Lindgren, I., Parycek, P. (eds.) EGOV 2015. LNCS, vol. 9248, pp. 3–18. Springer, Cham (2015). doi: 10.1007/978-3-319-22479-4_1
40. Gagnon, Y.C., Posada, E., Bourgault, M., Naud, A.: Multichannel delivery of public services: a new and complex management challenge. Int. J. Public Adm. **33**(5), 213–222 (2010)
41. Dawes, S.S.: An exploratory framework for future e-government research investments. In: Proceedings of the 41st Annual Hawaii International Conference on System Sciences, pp. 201–201. IEEE, January 2008
42. Waller, P., Weerakkody, V.: Digital Government: overcoming the systemic failure of transformation. Working Paper 2. Brunel University, London (2016)

External User Inclusion in Public e-Service Development: Exploring the Current Practice in Sweden

Jesper Holgersson[1,2(✉)], Karin Axelsson[2], and Ulf Melin[2]

[1] School of Informatics, University of Skövde, 541 28 Skövde, Sweden
jesper.holgersson@his.se

[2] Division of Information Systems, Department of Management and Engineering, Linköping University, 581 83 Linköping, Sweden
{jesper.holgersson,karin.axelsson,ulf.melin}@liu.se

Abstract. For the last decade e-government research has underlined the importance of an external user perspective in public e-service development and there have been numerous attempts to provide guidance and directions for government agencies in this matter. Individual research studies show little progress in this matter, but a more generalisable picture of the current state of external user inclusion is missing. The aim of this paper is to provide a better and more generalisable understanding of Swedish government agencies' current practice of external user inclusion in public e-service development. In order to do so, we have interviewed Swedish government agencies regarding their perceptions on external user inclusion. Our findings show mixed results regarding attitudes towards and current practice of external user inclusion. It is clear that organisational size and previous experience of public e-service development matter. At the same time challenges such as a general lack of resurces and a lack of time are seen as general barriers, regardless of agency level and size.

Keywords: e-Government · Public e-service development · External user inclusion · Government agencies · County councils · Municipalities

1 Introduction

Public e-service, i.e. government's provision of electronic service to inhabitants of the society, such as citizens and business organisations, is a central and vital component in e-government programs, digital agendas, and policies worldwide. When introducing public e-services, governments' main priorities have been to enhance internal efficiency in terms of automating internal, manual processes and any user considerations have been left out [1, 2]. As a consequence, most public e-service development projects have been characterised by an inside out perspective in where external user considerations have been given little attention [3]. At best, external user considerations have been guessed or assumed by public e-service developers instead of thoroughly analysed [4]. As a direct consequence, several public e-service initiatives have failed since the external users, e.g. the citizens, have preferred other existing and more traditional service channels, such

M. Janssen et al. (Eds.): EGOV 2017, LNCS 10428, pp. 60–70, 2017.
DOI: 10.1007/978-3-319-64677-0_6

as phone, mail or physical visits, simply because they do not see the point in using the electronic variants. However, in e-government research [e.g. 4, 5] as well as in government steering documents and digitalisation plans and agendas [e.g. 6, 7], the importance of an increased attention towards external users in public e-service development is emphasised. The common belief is that such an increased attention towards e.g. citizens enhance the probability for successful public e-service development and deployment [8]. However, despite these efforts little seems to happen in practice: public e-services are still being developed mainly from an internal perspective favouring inter-organisational values and goals over user oriented goals [e.g. 9–11]. Though, being valuable contributions, it is clear that most reports on external user inclusion in public e-service development are based in individual case studies which hardly ever lead to any generalisable findings [12]. At the same time, as concluded by Bannister and Connolly [13], the amount of valid case studies within the e-government research field are significant. What is missing is a more general and generalisable understanding of external user inclusion in public e-service development. As a first step, we have chosen to address a Swedish development context. Hence, the aim of this paper is to provide a better and more general understanding of Swedish government agencies' current practice of external user inclusion in public e-service development. In doing so we add new findings to the e-government research field when highlighting to what extent external users are included in public e-service development in Sweden, agencies' future directions within this matter, and underlying motives for their choice of direction.

The paper is structured as follows. In the following section we present related research whereas we in the third section outline our research design. Section four presents our analysis for each government agency level respectively. The paper is ended by results and conclusions in where research implications and suggestions for future research are discussed.

2 Related Research

The need for external user influences in public e-service development is a valuable and much needed component that enhance the probability for successful public e-service development and deployment [8], or as Jones et al. [14, p. 150] put it: "*key to the success of any e-government deployment is the citizen*". External user inclusion in public e-service development is discussed in different terms in e-government research. Lindblad-Gidlund [15] discusses it in terms of citizen driven development whereas Olphert and Damodaran [16] use the concept of citizen participation. Another commonly used term in e-government research is user participation [e.g. 17, 18] where the users, most often referred to as the citizens, should be playing an active role in the public e-service development process in terms of highlighting needs and experienced problems that can be eased or solved via public e-services. Worth highlighting is that external user inclusion should not be mistaken for e-participation. E-participation is related, but different concept where citizens take part in democratic processes regarding e.g. political decisions and policy making [19] whereas user participation focuses on representing external user interests in public e-service development [5].

As highlighted in the introduction it seems that despite numerous research efforts where the importance of external user inclusion are highlighted, little progress is to be found in practice. Illustrating examples are found mainly in Scandinavian research studies of user participation where the possibility to take an independent position has been seen as natural elements in research since the 1970s [20, 21].

Scandurra et al. [9] report findings from a case study on the development process of online electronic health records. They found that external user inclusion during the development process was limited to a few poorly documented focus group meetings with patient organisations with no real impact on the development process. Axelsson et al. [10] have analysed the development process of anonymous exams at a Swedish university. The findings presented conclude that external user inclusion can be characterised as a mix between informal and formal user representation in where different user groups were included to different degrees in the development process. In another case study of the development process of electronic driving license applications, Axelsson and Melin [11] conclude that no real external user considerations were made during the development process which in turn also implied that user impact in the development of public e-service was more or less absent.

One notable exception is provided by Lindblad-Gidlund [22] who presents a practitioners' perspective of external user centredness in public e-service development within one Swedish government. In the study, several practitioners are interviewed regarding their experiences of and attitudes towards external user inclusion in public e-service development which provides a general picture within one government. However, the results provided by Lindblad-Gidlund [22] are hard to generalise. What is missing is a more general overview of government agencies' attitudes towards and

3 Research Design

This study is based on semi structured interviews [23] with Swedish government agencies in their role as public e-service providers. In Sweden, government agencies are classified into three levels: (1) national, (2) regional, and (3) local [24]. In order to identify general patterns highlighting potential similarities and differences, all government agency levels were included in the interview study. In total, 24 interviews were conducted, distributed over 6 municipalities representing local government agencies, 6 county councils representing regional government agencies, and 7 government authorities representing national government agencies.

The size of the agencies varied. As an example, the number of residents for the municipalities interviewed were between 5.000 and 140.000 whereas the county councils were of similar size. For government authorities, there were major differences in size in terms of the number of employees, ranging from less than 5.00 to more than 10.000. The respondents at each agency were selected based on their current involvement and overall insights into public e-service development projects and had work titles such as project manager, CIO, and business developer. In some agencies, more than one suitable respondent were identified, but in most cases one respondent per government agency was interviewed. As stated, the interviews were semi structured, i.e. a fixed interview guide was used as a template for all interviews but with the option to ask clarifying questions whenever needed.

The interview guide contained a basic set of questions covering the topics: (1) the government agency´s viewpoint and current provision of public e-services, (2) the government agency´s general view of external user inclusion in public e-service development, (3) how external user inclusion currently is practiced within the government agency, and (4) challenges and potential problems based on experiences of external user inclusion in public e-service development projects. The interviews were carried out either face-to-face or via telephone and lasted about 30 to 45 min each and were thereafter transcribed. The analysis was conducted row by row from the transcribed interviews in order to identify answers to the basic set of topics on which the interviews were based. The main goal with the interviews was to obtain rich and qualitative data on public e-service providers' attitudes towards and experiences of external user inclusion in public e-service development projects. The study is based on a qualitative and interpretive research approach [23, 25, 26], since the main interest lies in understanding and explaining government agencies' attitudes towards and experiences of external user inclusion in their role as public e-service providers. This means that the main focus of this study is to explore Swedish government agencies' current situation in order to understand the current practice in public e-service development with respect to if and how external users are included in public e-service development projects.

4 Analysis

The analysis of the empirical data reveals major differences both between and within different government agency levels. In the following sections we will present our findings for each government agency level respectively. It should be noted that all citations from the empirical data (interviews) have been translated from Swedish.

4.1 Government Authorities

When analysing the empirical data from government authorities, is becomes clear that external user inclusion in public e-service development is seen as an important component in order to provide good public e-services: "*It is the core of the development process, to meet the needs of the users. It is the linchpin to deliver something good which generate value. In order to meet our customers' needs and processes we need to have user participation*". It seems clear that government authorities have realised the importance of including needs and perspectives from the main user group of public e-services, which is illustrated by the following quote: "*The main target group for us are genealogists and our goal is to serve them properly. We know quite a lot about this target user group and many of our employees are researchers themselves*".

When it comes to how external user inclusion is present in public e-service development, the level of maturity varies. Some government authorities have fixed routines for how external user interest should be included in public e-service development whereas others have no such formal process. The most common approach is to collect opinions, comments and complaints via customer services. One illustrating example of such a routine is shown in the following quote: "*We get quite a lot of information through something called the official mailbox. There are very many comments. There were many comments when we started in 2002 regarding the possibility to declare taxes electronically online. In the declaration period, we received about 150 comments per day. It was ordinary people on the street who submitted their views on how to think*". Other government authorities have more or less fixed networks of external users, mostly in terms of business organisations, who can be contacted on short notice in order for fast responses in different matters related to public e-service development, or as the following quote illustrate: "*We collect our focus groups from different regional channels and meet them close to their home field*". As it seems, government authorities where the main user group are business organisations, seem to have a better and more efficient dialogue if compared to government authorities where citizens are the main target user group.

When it comes to limiting conditions and potential challenges hindering external user inclusion, government authorities have similar experiences. One often mentioned drawback of external user inclusion is a fear of disappointed users where high user expectations cannot be met: "*That's what is usually discussed, when you sit and prototype and try to design something, when there is a disappointment among the users when the result is not in line with the expectations*". Another commonly discussed challenge is time in terms of impatient users who want quick results which cannot be delivered simply because the reality is far too complex, as the following quote illustrate: "*It's problematic when I meet young entrepreneurs who want everything to go so fast and be so easy. It can be a problem since the tax legislation is not that easy, especially VAT is complicated and cannot be simplified. It is difficult to get these people to realise that sometimes you cannot just answer yes or no without requiring a little more than that*". Time is also discussed in relation to competence, i.e. the ability to put needs and ideas into practice and present design suggestions quickly in order to keep the external users interested in being included: "*A prerequisite is that you can quickly create prototypes that can be discussed and then quickly begin a realisation of it to design and deliver something a few months after that. It must go fast, it cannot be as it is today where it takes a year to do a teeny thing, we would not make it, they [the users] would be mad at us. You are completely useless, they would think*".

4.2 County Councils

During the analysis of the empirical data from county councils the general attitude towards external user inclusion is positive. County councils agree upon that there is a need for a more nuanced picture of needs and expectations from external users in public e-service development, but at the same time clarity and consistency regarding how such work should be carried out is perceived to be missing, or as the following quotes highlight: "*I would like to include representatives of various user groups in the development process, such as through focus groups. Today there is often very little focus on the person who will finally use the service*", and "*I have not seen a nationwide methodology that should be applied in e-service development. There is too little support to get to the different end users in a good well thought through manner*".

On a general level, external user inclusion in public e-service development within county councils is present in various forms, often in terms of involving different patient groups in the development process. Often, such efforts have been focusing on appearance and user interaction whereas needs and functionality have been given less attention, as highlighted in the following quote: "*The patient organisations involved include rheumatism, visually impaired, etc. We have also tested the system on citizens who have not used the service before and gathered comments we tried to consider*". In larger public e-service initiatives, it is in most cases politicians who decide what to initiate without taking into account if there is any expressed need from the expected users, i.e. the citizens. The following two quotes provide illustrative examples of this situation: "*I have a good example, we have developed a price comparison service in dentistry and the service was very complicated. When asking questions to people it becomes clear that they really do not want it, they are not interested. They say they would rather compare the quality and other criteria than those we [the politicians] have set. No one wanted to be involved, either residents or dentists, but it was still politically decided that it [the e-service] would be developed*", and "*In most cases it is not needs from patients but other sources which initiates development. For example, the app we talked about, it was the politicians who decided that it would be developed. This was no good solution and I think that the citizens got no value out of it*".

When analysing challenges and limiting conditions for external user inclusion it becomes clear that time and a general lack of resources are the main delimiters for increased inclusion of e.g. patients. As the following quotes highlight, lack of time is a problem since development work often is carried out as projects and time to delivery of individual project goals is often limited, which in turn implies that basic identification of external users' needs cannot be prioritised: "*I think we would have been working in another way if we had more time. Since the project is an EU project which is limited to three years we have to keep up the pace. We have decided that we will start with a basic version of the system that we launch and then we can always go back and improve it when we get new input*". Also, resources in general is highlighted as a barrier towards increased external user inclusion: "*We would like to have a larger panel that could have tested but we have not, we have not had the time or resources to work with larger groups*". Also, ability and willingness to participate is seen as a challenge that hinders external user inclusion, i.e. limited knowledge of the healthcare domain and little engagement in health care services per se may hinder external user inclusion initiatives, as exemplified in the following quote: "*The knowledge is limited to know what to ask for…It is generally really hard to get people who want to participate*".

4.3 Municipalities

When analysing the empirical data from municipalities, it is clear that size of the organisations and number of inhabitans matters. In general, larger municipalities exhibit a larger number of deployed public e-services which at the same time can be considered as more mature. When plotted on the four stage maturity model provided by Layne and Lee [27], it is clear that e-services provided by smaller municipalities often end up as catalogue services whereas e-services provided by larger municipalities to a larger extent end up as transaction and in some cases as vertically integrated e-services. When analysing the empirical data, it becomes apparent that smaller municipalities with very limited resources exhibit a somewhat negative attitude towards public e-services per se. Such municipalities experience no pressure from citizens to offer service electronically and the usage frequency of existing e-services is in many cases sparse. The following quotes serve as illustrating examples: "*We see ourselves no winnings at all to provide e-services, simply because there are no demands. We know this since we talk with representatives at different administrations and they say that there are no citizens who are requesting e-services. There are no savings with e-services, just cost increases alone*" and "*If you for example consider the application for alcohol permits, we maybe have four errands per year. To develop an e-service for this is simply not worth-while*". Instead, the main driver for public e-service development is considered to be based mainly on political agendas, as highlighted in the following quote: "*There is no explicit agenda for developing public e-services. The decisions taken politically are probably based on a desire to be a part of a trend. 10–15 years ago, all municipalities should have IT-strategies which have never been read or followed, it is simple a part of the trend*". This situation is also reflected in how external user inclusion is viewed by small municipalities, or as one respondent puts it: "*I don't believe in the idea*". However, other small municipalities are at a general level positive towards external user inclusion, but when it comes to actually implementing it they are sceptic, as the following quotes illustrate: "*To have users as a part of the development process would have been terrific, but how do you do it?*", and "*We have not yet had the opportunity to have the users in the development process but I think it would be a great idea to test it…although it seems hard to actually realise it, but it has been discussed*".

When analysing the empirical data from larger municipalities another picture emerges. There is a higher general interest towards transforming manual services into e-services since there is a belief that such transformations will reduce the administrative burden that most administrative units perceive, or as one respondent puts it: "*The reason to why they want to digitise more is that you simply want to do things more effectively and easier to access centrally*". However, the degree of which external users are included in e-service development is still very limited, as exemplified by the following quotes: "*That [external user inclusion] is something that we work too little with. It feels a bit awkward to ask users what they want. We have been a bit cowardly there and instead passed it on the administrations that have better knowledge of the citizens and also receive a lot of feedback from citizens*", "*We don't ask, instead we test what works and what doesn't. If it works it works*", and "*We have not yet had the opportunity to include the users in the development….as it is today, it is the administrations' needs that steer and what they think the citizens need*". However, there is one exception. One of the larger municipalities states that they are developing a process description for how external users should be included in public e-service development projects. However, this is not yet in operation but the basic idea is that development initiatives should be based on citizen inputs. Thereafter, the remaining part of the development process will be managed internally. Potential external user inclusion in the actual development process is not yet investigated, or as the respondent state: "*We have not thought much about whether users should be involved in the development process. We have no plan at present but we are not completely uninterested*".

When analysing limiting conditions and potential challenges hindering external user inclusion, the municipalities' arguments are rather similar. A general theme is a lack of resources which in most cases refers to economy and time available. For smaller municipalities this comes as no surprise; at the moment they seem to be struggling with just put any services online. However, also large municipalities experience the same basic problems, i.e. including external users is too expensive, or as the following quotes state: *"Time and money obviously limit how you can work towards citizens"*, and *"Actually it is a question of resources, to cope with doing it [external user inclusion] alongside everything else. We are not enough people to be able to cope with it"*. Other challenges highlighted are how included external users would be representative for other ones as well as a fear of disappointing included external users, as one respondent puts it: *"It must of course be done properly, it must be fair [external user representation]. If you bring in citizens to participate and then an e-service is developed that doesn't meet the initial expectations…I don't think that is very good*".

5 Results and Conclusions

The aim of this paper was to provide a better and more generalisable understanding of Swedish government agencies' current practice of external user inclusion in public e-service development. As shown in the analysis, organizational size matters when it comes to perspectives and real life experiences of external user inclusion in public e-service development.

Government authorities in general exhibit a more open attitude towards external user inclusion if compared to county councils and municipalities. This is not surprising as public authorities per se are more experienced in developing e-services as well as having larger resources, which in turn means that they have more experience of both successes as well as failures. When it comes to municipalities and county councils with less experiences of public e-service development, a more negative attitude is found. Public e-service development in general and external user inclusion in particular is instead seen as yet another directive that is laid upon already burdened systems developers who are trying their best to just get something online in order to appease politicians and decision makers. As highlighted by Holgersson, Alenljung and Söderström [28], most municipalities, especially the smaller ones, experience a different reality if compared to larger, more experienced government agencies in terms of available resources (e.g. financial, competence) as well as the number of e-services that must be developed. As pointed out by Bernhard [29], municipalities is the agency level that has the closest relation to the citizens on the street-level in where a wide range of services are provided, if compared to government authorities that can focus on just a few nationwide services with a larger volume of users and a different scale in many dimensions. The somewhat sceptic attitude towards external user inclusion within foremost municipalities, but also in county councils, may also depend on a possibly multi-dimensional, gap between administrations and public e-service developers. In municipalities, it is usually the internal IT department that is responsible for public e-service development projects, but at the same time it is the administrations that will use e-services as a means to provide service to e.g. citizens. Obviously, the interest to make better adjustments to an invisible user is limited for IT departments already burdened with other work duties (e.g. making the daily IT environment) where public e-services are just another task laid upon everything else.

We have identified that the current practice of external user inclusion follows more or less the same pattern as attitudes towards external user inclusion. As revealed in the analysis, government authorities are more experienced in developing public e-services and also possess a larger amount of resources in terms of e.g. financial resources, competence and time. Moreover, in most cases, government authorities already have existing work procedures for how to include an external user perspective in public e-service development, and so do county councils to some extent. The level of formality for how external users are included in public e-service development by municipalities is significantly lower, not at least when it comes to smaller municipalities. However, it is important to address what external user inclusion really means in practice. As discussed in the related works section, user participation has been put through in e-government research as a means to assure that external needs are included in public e-service development [18]. In user participation, users, e.g. citizens in this case, should be actively involved during the development process [30]. As found in the empirical data, none of the interviewed government agencies at any level exhibits such an approach towards external users. Instead, external users are often included very early and in some cases also late in the development process, but not as active agents during the development process.

Challenges and limiting conditions are more or less the same for all levels of government agencies independent of size. A lack of time as well as a lack of resources is seen as a hinder for external user inclusion. An important aspect highlighted is a lack of knowledge for how to include external users. It seems like each agency at any level is more or less isolated from other agencies' experiences. It is also clear that previous attempts to provide guidance and more concrete advice for how to include external users [e.g. 31, 32] seem to be too context independent and homogenous. As shown in the analysis, the reality is much more complex and the conditions for developing public e-services vary greatly. Based on the analysis made, it comes as no surprise that such general directives seem to have little impact since the underlying preconditions are so different.

One interesting observation found is a contradiction between the common belief that public e-service initiatives in most cases are initiated as means to enhance internal efficiency by e.g. reducing the number of service errands handled manually by civil servants [see e.g. 1, 2, 33]. As it appears, far from every government agency has internal efficiency and reduced manual handling of service errands at the top of the agenda when initiating public e-service development projects. Instead, political agendas as well as a genuine strive for better service provisioning without any internal winnings per se seem, to be important drivers in many agencies. As pointed out by Rose et al. [34], the public sector has deep-rooted value traditions which are very hard to change. However, it seems like there may be a new public e-service ethos evolving within government agencies and we believe there is an ample opportunity for more research to explore these findings further.

The findings presented in this paper add new insights to the e-government research field by providing a more general and generalisable understanding of external user inclusion in public e-service development. However, the research presented addresses a Swedish development context and the conclusions are therefore difficult to generalise outside Sweden. Hence, we call for further research within this area also in other development contexts in order to obtain more generalisable results.

References

1. Asgarkhani, M.: The effectiveness of e-service in local government: a case study. Electr. J. E-Gov. **3**, 157–166 (2005)
2. Anthopoulos, L.G., Siozos, P.S., Tsoukas, I.A.: Applying participatory design and collaboration in digital public services for discovering and re-designing e-Government services. Gov. Inf. Q. **24**, 353–376 (2007)
3. Millard, J.: Government 1.5—is the bottle half full or half empty? Eur. J. ePract. **9**, 1–16 (2010)
4. Axelsson, K., Melin, U., Lindgren, I.: Exploring the importance of citizen participation and involvement in e-government projects—practice, incentives and organization. Transform. Gov. People Process Policy **4**, 299–321 (2010)
5. Karlsson, F., Holgersson, J., Söderström, E., Hedström, K.: Exploring user participation approaches in public e-service development. Gov. Inf. Q. **29**, 158–168 (2012)
6. OECD: Focus on Citizens-Public Engagement for Better Policy and Services (2009)
7. European eGovernment Action Plan: The European eGovernment Action Plan 2011–2015 Harnessing ICT to promote smart, sustainable & innovative Government. Brussels (2011–2015)
8. Holgersson, J., Karlsson, F.: Public e-service development: understanding citizens' conditions for participation. Gov. Inf. Q. **31**, 396–410 (2014)
9. Scandurra, I., Holgersson, J., Lind, T., Myreteg, G.: Development of novel eHealth services for citizen use—current system engineering vs. best practice in HCI. In: Kotzé, P., Marsden, G., Lindgaard, G., Wesson, J., Winckler, M. (eds.) INTERACT 2013. LNCS, vol. 8118, pp. 372–379. Springer, Heidelberg (2013). doi:10.1007/978-3-642-40480-1_24
10. Axelsson, K., Melin, U., Lindgren, I.: Public e-services for agency efficiency and citizen benefit—findings from a stakeholder centered analysis. Gov. Inf. Q. **30**, 10–22 (2013)
11. Axelsson, K., Melin, U.: Six key lessons for e-government projects. In: Scholl, H.J., Janssen, M., Traunmüller, R., Wimmer, M.A. (eds.) EGOV 2009, pp. 93–103. Linz, Austria (2009)
12. Larsson, H., Grönlund, Å.: Future-oriented eGovernance: the sustainability concept in eGov research, and ways forward. Gov. Inf. Q. **31**, 137–149 (2014)
13. Bannister, F., Connolly, R.: The great theory hunt: does e-government really have a problem? Gov. Inf. Q. **32**, 1–11 (2015)
14. Jones, S., Hackney, R., Irani, Z.: Towards e-government transformation: conceptualising "citizen engagement". Transform. Gov. People Process Policy **1**, 145–152 (2007)
15. Gidlund, K.L.: One for all, all for one—performing citizen driven development of public e-services. In: Tambouris, E., Macintosh, A., Bruijn, H. (eds.) ePart 2011. LNCS, vol. 6847, pp. 240–251. Springer, Heidelberg (2011). doi:10.1007/978-3-642-23333-3_21

16. Olphert, W., Damodaran, L.: Citizen participation and engagement in the design of e-government services: the missing link in effective ICT design and delivery. J. Assoc. Inf. Syst. **8**, 491–507 (2007)
17. Folkerd, C., Spinelli, G.: User exclusion and fragmented requirements capture in publicly-funded IS projects. Transform. Gov. People Process Policy **3**, 32–49 (2009)
18. Verne, G., Braaten, I.: Participation for the unengaged. In: Proceedings of the 13th Participatory Design Conference: Short Papers, Industry Cases, Workshop Descriptions, Doctoral Consortium Papers, and Keynote Abstracts—vol. 2, pp. 1–4. ACM, Windhoek, Namibia (2014)
19. Sæbø, Ø., Flak, L.S., Sein, M.K.: Understanding the dynamics in e-Participation initiatives: looking through the genre and stakeholder lenses. Gov. Inf. Q. **28**, 416–425 (2011)
20. Marti, P., Bannon, L.J.: Exploring user-centred design in practice: some caveats. Knowl. Technol. Policy **22**, 7–15 (2009)
21. Bjerknes, G., Bratteteig, T.: User participation and democracy. a discussion of scandinavian research on systems development. Scand. J. Inf. Syst. **7**, 73–98 (1995)
22. Lindblad-Gidlund, K.: Designing for all and no one—practitioners understandings of citizen driven development of public e-services. In: Proceedings of the 12th Participatory Design Conference: Research Papers, vol. 1, pp. 11–19. ACM, Roskilde, Denmark (2012)
23. Patton, M.Q.: Qualitative Research & Evaluation Methods. Sage, London (2002)
24. Government Offices: How Sweden is governed. In: Government Offices (ed.) Stockholm (2014)
25. Braa, K., Vidgen, R.T.: Interpretation, intervention, and reduction in the organizational laboratory: a framework for in-context information system research. Account. Manag. Inf. Technol. **9**, 25–47 (1999)
26. Walsham, G.: Interpretive case studies in IS research: nature and method. Eur. J. Inf. Syst. **4**, 74–81 (1995)
27. Layne, K., Lee, J.: Developing fully functional E-government: a four stage model. Gov. Inf. Q. **18**, 122–136 (2001)
28. Holgersson, J., Alenljung, B., Söderström, E.: User participation at a discount—exploring the use and reuse of personas in public e-service development. ECIS 2015. AIS, Münster (2015)
29. Bernhard, I.: Local e-Government in Sweden—municipal contact center implementation with focus on citizens and public administrators. J. Community Inform. **10**, 1–15 (2014)
30. Cavaye, A.L.M.: User participation is systems development revisited. Inf. Manag. **28**, 311–323 (1995)
31. The Swedish delegation for eGovernment: Vägledning för behovsdriven utveckling. In: e-delegationen, S. (ed.) (2012)
32. Holgersson, J.: User participation in public e-service development—guidelines for including external users. School of informatics. Ph.D. University of Skövde, Skövde (2014)
33. Ilshammar, L., Bjurström, A., Grönlund, Å.: Public e-services in Sweden: old wine in new bottles. Scand. J. Inf. Syst. **17**, 11–40 (2005)
34. Rose, J., Persson, J.S., Heeager, L.T., Irani, Z.: Managing e-Government: value positions and relationships. Inf. Syst. J. **25**, 531–571 (2015)

Georgia on My Mind: A Study of the Role of Governance and Cooperation in Online Service Delivery in the Caucasus

Morten Meyerhoff Nielsen(✉) and Nato Goderdzishvili

United Nations University, Operating Unit on Policy-Driven Electronic Governance (UNU-EGOV), Rua de Vila Flor 166, 4810-445 Guimarães, Portugal
meyerhoff@unu.edu, ngoderdzishvili@dea.gov.ge

Abstract. Georgia's achievements in public sector modernisation have been lauded, since 2004, for their ability to increase transparency, fight corruption, ease the way of doing business and improve public service delivery to citizens. Information Communication Technology (ICT) played an important role as an enabler of public sector reform. Despite this, research into the Georgian model of governance and inter-governmental cooperation is extremely limited. Similarly, literature reviews have, in recent years, pointed out limitations in the understanding of technology use in public service delivery and, particularly, the role governance, cross-governmental decision making, and cooperation play when introducing ICT solutions and online services to citizens. As part of a larger qualitative, multi-country comparison, this article analyses the Georgian approach to electronic governance (eGovernance). The analysis highlights the influence of politically motivated and driven public sector reforms underpinned by ICT use for better service delivery, transparency and a fight against corruption in the period 2004–2012. Despite early success in relation to ICT infrastructure, standards and roll-out to key enablers, the article finds that the electronic government (eGovernment) eco-system is fragmented and that the use of public and private online service (eService) is limited, despite high internet penetration and usage. The key barrier found is the lack of an effective governance and inter-governmental cooperation model to improve cooperation between government actors (e.g. data collection, quality and reuse, shared infrastructure, systems and service), build on existing infrastructure and enablers to optimize the value-added of earlier investments – particularly in relation to electronic identity management (eID), digital signatures (eSignature) and eServices. Georgia would benefit from a more formalized approach to ICT related programmes and projects by considering an IT-implementation model to effectively manage risk, improve benefit realization and link individual key performance measurements (KPI) to those of the eGovernment strategy and action plan.

Keywords: eGovernance · eGovernment · eService · Use · Inter-governmental corporation · Analysis · Georgia

M. Janssen et al. (Eds.): EGOV 2017, LNCS 10428, pp. 71–91, 2017.
DOI: 10.1007/978-3-319-64677-0_7

1 Introduction

Googling Georgia two things are guaranteed: first, confusion between the European Republic of Georgia or the southern US state of Georgia, and second, the post-Rose Revolution wave of successful public sector improving transparency, fighting corruption and providing a more effective service delivery. The question remains: what has allowed a small, low income country in the Caucasus region to seemingly succeed where others have not and is the answer to the apparent success found in the governance model and level of inter-governmental corporation?

Multiple research disciplines have analysed the public sectors IT and technology use. Academics in public administration (PA) [1–6], information systems (IS) management [2, 3, 7–10], or electronic government and governance (eGovernment and eGovernance) [11–16], have all highlight the failures of the public sector to apply Information Communication Technology (ICT) with real success. Often cited mistakes include blindly digitising current processes [13, 16, 17] and focusing on technology and supply [18–20] rather than value-adding outcome and impact of IT and technology [4, 21, 22] – not only in relation to ICT use in public administration but in particular when it comes to the provision of online services (eService) for citizens [20, 23].

To address multiple models for assessment have been proposed. The so-called stage and maturity models have been a key tool of academics, consultants and international organisations in assessing the relatively success of eGovernment across countries since the 1990s. A major flaw of the models is non-the-less their focus on supply, technology and organisational issues but with a rather limited understanding of public service delivery, especially if enabled by ICT [8, 20, 23, 24]. In addition, multiple authors – including the 2016 review of maturity models, public sector reform, IT governance, eGovernment literature by Meyerhoff Nielsen [23] – finds that current research does not adequately addresses the role of governance and cooperation in ensuring the successful supply and use of online eService's. In fact, front-office service provision and back-office integration are mixed-up in the majority of maturity models. For example, one-stop shop portals do not constitute a form of transaction, but are rather an indicator of the degree with which authorities cooperate and integration in the production and provision of services via a joint portal [20, 23]. While Heeks tries to address this by proposing a two-dimensional matrix model distinguishing between the front- and the back-office [25], the proposed model does not account for eGovernance or take-up [26].

Similarly, none of the analysed maturity models addresses governance directly [23, 26]. Davison [27], Iribarren et al. [8], Janowski [28], Kalambokis et al. [29], Shareef et al. [30] and Waseda [31] models highlight management and coordination issues, such as the existence of chief information officers (CIO). Cooperation, on the other hand, is indirectly addressed in most models. This is expressed in terms of vertical and horizontal integration, the sharing of information and data between public authorities (even the private and third sector), and the existence of one-stop shops [26, 32, 33], but again there is limited focus on the role of governance in proposing a national vision and strategy, let alone in ensuring the required cooperation between actors or ensuring the realization of the envisioned effects.

To investigate the role of governance and inter-governmental cooperation in the successful supply and citizen use of eService's, this article analyses the Georgian use of ICT in public administration and eGovernment. The aim is two-fold: *to identify the Georgian features and lessons learned in relation to the role of eGovernance and inter-governmental cooperation and to add the Georgian lessons to a future cross-country comparison.*

To address the stated aim, this article starts by outlining the methodology used (Sect. 2). The Georgian experience is presented using the conceptual framework, including background indictors and preconditions (Sect. 3), before the national approach to governance, cooperation model and eGovernment is outlined (Sect. 4). Key enablers and services supplied and their use (Sect. 5) is presented before observations and conclusions are presented (Sect. 6).

2 Methods

As part of a larger study address the research gaps in relation to eGovernment governance and cross-governmental cooperation identified by Meyerhoff Nielsen [23], a classical exploratory, qualitative, case study methodology framework [34–36] is applied to enable a with-in case analysis.

An adapted version of Krimmer's context, content, process model (CCP model) [28] as used by Meyerhoff Nielsen for the Estonian [37], Faroese [38] and Danish cases [39], a Danish-Japanese [40] plus a Estonian-Georgian comparison [41] is chosen to allow for future cross-country comparison. The conceptual model consists of four macro-dimensions: Background indictors; national governance and cooperation model; national approach to eGovernment; and effect measurements and preconditions. Each dimension explains a key area that influences processes, choices and outcomes in relation to eService supply and take-up. Using the framework for the with-in case analysis to identify the governance mechanisms in play will allow the author to make a cross-case comparison to determine the correlation (i.e., the more of Y, the more X) between a strong cooperative governance model (cause) and the introduction of online services (effect 1) and subsequent citizen use of the online service delivery channel (effect 2).

Using the framework, this article identifies Georgia's respective strengths and weaknesses in relation to the country's respective governance models and eGovernment experiences since 1991, but with a particular focus on the period since 2010. Georgia has been chosen for two main reasons: it is a rarely studied but potentially interesting case representing a small, low income, centralised country [34, 36, 42]. This allows the author to later compare Georgia to a high-income centralised micro-state like the Faroe Islands, a medium-income and centralized country of similar size like Estonia, a more populated, high-income, decentralised country like Denmark and a large, highly decentralized, high-income country such as Japan. Georgia, similarly, offers a chance to look at the role of governance and intergovernmental cooperation in a different socio-economic context and helps the author isolate the role they play in the supply and take-up of citizen online services.

Primary sources used include relevant academic literature, relevant policy documents, national and international statistical sources e.g. International Telecommunications Union (ITU) [43] and UNDESA's eGovernment Readiness Index [44–46]. The written sources are complimented with a small number of interviews carried out in May 2015 and February 2017.

3 Results

As a result of history and culture, countries operate in different contexts and offer different perspectives and experience when it comes to eGovernment and online service provision for citizens. Similarly, population size, income levels, administrative systems, and complexity vary. It is therefore important to put things in context.

3.1 Socio-economic Background

Georgia is, in socio-economic terms, a small but relatively populated country. Georgia is a small economy with a large trade deficit, but good GDP growth following a period of stagnation from 2008 until about 2014. The country is considered a nation state but with strong regional identities. The country, despite immigration, experiences population growth due to increased birth-rates [47, 48]. For details see key statistics in Table 1.

Table 1. Key socio-economic statistics 2016 [47, 48]

Population (January 2016)	3,720,400
Territorial size	69.700 km^2
Population density	57.3 per km^2
Official languages	Georgian, Abkhazian (in Abkhazia)
Ethnic groups	Georgian 86.8%, Azeri 6.3%, Armenian 4.5%, other 2.3% (incl. Russian, Ossetian, Yazidis, Ukrainian, Kist, Greek)
Median age and life expectancy	38 and 74.4 years
Population growth	−0.05%
Urbanization	53.6%
GDP 2016 (est.)	€13.67 billion
GDP per capita 2016 (est.)	€5,025
GDP growth rate 2016 (est.)	3.4%
Unemployment 2016 (est.)	12.1%
Imports 2016 (est.)	€6.43 billion
Exports 2016 (est.)	€2.69 billion

4 Internet Access and Use

For online service delivery to succeed, internet access and a minimum level of digital literacy and competences are essential pre-conditions. As an indicator of digital literacy levels individuals actual use of the internet, online banking and shopping sites are used (eBanking and eCommerce respectively). To put Georgia in context, Table 2 includes the average for the EUs 28 member states.

Table 2. Individual and household access to, and use of the internet, 2010–2016, selected years (EU28 country average in brackets) [49]

	2010	2013	2016 [50]
Household internet access [51]	27% (70%)	82% (79%)	95% (86%)
Individual with mobile internet [52]	18.80%# (21%*)	42.74%# (24%)	63% (27%)
Individual using the internet (at least once a week)	– (65%)	45.5%** (72%)	90% (79%)

Authors estimation based on 0.70 million and 1.59 million transactions in 2010 and 2013 respectively.
* 2011 data. ** 2012 data

While data is available from the International Telecommunications Union (ITU), other and more recent and seemingly reliable (see discussion by Meyerhoff Nielsen [53]) data is available from other sources. Generally, the ITU data shows a more bleak picture of internet access and use in Georgia compared to e.g. the US Aid financed survey of 1,500 Georgians in 2016. While both sources show growth in household internet access, it is particularly impressive the fact that 90% of households in a low-income country like Georgia choose to pay for internet access. Combined with the high level of actual internet use, this confirms that the pre-conditions for introduction online government services and citizens actual use of them exist in Georgia.

5 eGovernment and Governance

Georgia has, since the November 2003 Rose Revolution, actively pursued public sector reform. In particular, the period of 2004 to 2014 saw a massive change. Political initiative and a willingness to transform the public sector had wide spread public support and has created a solid ICT and legal foundation. The strategic focus was on transparency, accountability, efficient and effective public service delivery [54–56]. The role of ICT in underpinning the strategic objectives is therefore helpful for understanding the Georgian context and eGovernment outcomes.

5.1 Strategic Focus Since 1991

The Georgian eGovernment focus can be divided in two main periods: fragmented and uncoordinated use of ICT in the period 2004–2014, followed by attempts to introduce a more formalized approach and coordinated approach from 2014, as outlined in Table 3.

Table 3. eGovernment in Georgia, 2004–2018 [54–57]

2004–2014 ICT use in the public section	While no national eGovernment strategy or action plan in the period was active, individual initiatives in line ministries were implemented. As part of a general drive for public sector reform, increased access to public services, transparency and an anti-corruption drive, ICT use was initially focused on the creation of basic information systems, digitalizing internal information resources, automating information flows, creating data centres, and connecting national authorities with their regional offices
2014–2018 Digital Georgia – eGovernment strategy and action plan	The first formal eGovernment strategy and action plan was approved in 2014 with the aim of making Georgia's public sector more efficient and effective, offering integrated, secure, and high quality eServices, improve usage and participation, and enabling ICT-driven sustainable economic growth
	Strategy focuses on 11 thematic directions (i.e. eService's, eParticipation and Open Government, eHealth, Public Finance Management System, eBusiness, making Georgia a regional ICT-Hub Georgia, infrastructure, cyber security; skills development and e Inclusion) grouped into service areas, future excellence, ICT enablers as well as horizontal measures such as enabling frameworks, governance and awareness. The strategy has success criteria and is underpinned by an action plan with associated KPIs
	The eGeorgia strategy is part of the Public Administration Reform Roadmap 2020 [58], which is an "umbrella" framework also including the Open Government Partnership, Anti-corruption, Public Finance Management System Reform, Regional Development, Civil Service Reform and eGovernment directions and action plans

While the first decade of eGovernment and ICT use was uncoordinated and without a comprehensive "whole-of-government" vision, the use of ICT in the political drive for the transformation of the public administration have reflected similar patterns seen in Europe, the former Soviet Union and beyond (albeit at different pace), that is: infrastructure roll-out, backend systems, launch of key enablers like eID and core registers, increased access to public sector services, digital literacy and, subsequently on governance structures, standards, eService supply and use [40, 44–46, 53, 57, 59–62].

The introduction of the first actual eGovernment strategy and action plan has to date born little fruit. Despite extensive consultation of government stakeholders in 2012–2013, political approval and subsequent incorporation into the Public Administration Reform Roadmap 2020, funding has been limited and delayed [54–56, 63, 64]. A mid-term review consisting of three-days of stakeholder workshops facilitated by a team of international experts aimed to re-ignite the strategy and action plan. The result is a prioritisation of a number of building blocks in 2017–2018, in particular the reinforcement of effective enabling frameworks, such as the governance structure, enforcing eID management, increase back-office digitisation and the provision of more user-friendly eServices and ensure their actual use [54, 57, 64–66].

5.2 Governance Model and Institutional Framework

Georgia is in many ways a small and highly centralized country. The central government institutions are few and provide most public services for citizens. Nine regions exist but have limited public service responsibility. Of the 74 municipalities, only the four main urban centres Batumi, Kutaisi, Telavi and the capital, Tbilisi, have the financial and human resources to provide citizen orientated services in larger numbers. The government and public authorities are actively trying to change this through the Public Service Hall and Community Center concepts – providing back-end systems, access to relevant registers and skills development [54, 57, 64, 67, 68]. Table 4 summarizes the general approach to public service delivery in Georgia.

Table 4. General governance and institutional framework [69–71]

National institutional framework and governance	Mostly centralized, decisions are made and executed on high horizontal level. Multi-level management approach is not implemented yet. eGovernment and ICT related initiatives are concentrated within key public agencies. Local governance with low capacity to deliver eService's and use ICT with interactions with citizens and businesses. The development of local eGovernment infrastructure and provision of eServices to local population is centrally implemented by the Public Service Development Agency within the MoJ
Decentralisation of government authority	Limited, due to limited or lack of capacity in local governance level

Like governance in general, Georgia's approach to ICT reflects the country's context, experience and public sector capacities, including decision making processes, the degree of cooperation between authorities and different levels of government, the private sector, civil society, and the research community.

Politically, Georgia has seen three distinct political periods since gaining independence in the wake of the Soviet Union collapse. From 1991 to 2003 the newly independent Georgia was dominated by the former elite, economic contraction and social upheaval, the Rose-Revolution 2003 against rampant corruption and inefficiency lead to a center-right reformist government lead by United National Movement (UNM), economic growth and a professionalization of the public administration. In the aftermath of the 2008 war, economic stagnation and increased dissatisfaction with the UNM government led the newly formed Georgian Dream party to win the 2012 Parliament elections and the 2013 Presidential elections. Since 2012, the economy has been slow to recover and at time showed a fragmented political focus. The post-2012 result has been a relatively small and professional public sector, but also resulted in deterioration of Georgia's positions government and eParticipation international rankings [44–46, 60, 72].

Historically, policies, strategies, action plans and institutionalized processes have often been fragmented or lacking. Focus has been on implementation of overall policy objectives rather than on formal processes, coherence of the overall ICT framework for the public sector or system documentations [54, 63, 73]. Georgian successes has initially been based on the political vision and willingness to reform the public sector, scrap old processes and legislation in favour of ICT systems, a more professional civil service – even firing 60,000 police officers to achieve the political vision of more efficient, effective, transparent and accountable government and service delivery [58, 74].

In relation to the eGovernance model, Georgia initially did not have a formalised structure focusing on ICT use in the public sector. The first attempt to formalise the institutional framework for eGovernment and ICT related intergovernmental cooperation emerged in 2007. The CIO Council was established and chaired by Prime Minister, the deputy chair was the MoJ and secretarial support by DEA – the mandated and regulatory authority for eGovernment. All relevant line-ministries and ICT related agencies were members of the CIO Council, as were key national ICT experts (incl. from the private sector and NGOs – and interestingly also from of US Aid). The CIO Council was responsible for the strategic direction and horizontal coordination, initiation and approving the eGovernment strategy, budgetary support, allocation of inter-agency support if required. The aim was to ensured cooperation and collaboration among key stakeholders. The MoJ constituted the mandated authority for eGovernment issues, with the actual implementation delegated to DEA. Authorities were generally responsible for ICT initiatives for their respective areas and service portfolios [54, 55, 57].

To increase the efficiency of inter-governmental cooperation in relation to ICT, CIO Council was replaced in 2014 with an eGovernment Unit based in the cabinet office [75]. In practice the change was never effectuated as the Unit had either limited or no staff. The subsequent vacuum has in effect allowed authorities to peruse their own agendas, set their own priorities and hampered the effective coordination of ICT in Georgia. This lack of inter-governmental coordination is a real barrier for enforcement of national standards for e.g. interoperability (IOP), reuse of data, usability requirements in eService's etc. It has also lead to lack of transparency of ICT project plans, objectives, budgets and activities. Ineffective, overlapping and redundant ICT investments is the result of the weakened governance model, as is unclear mandates, responsibilities and general lack of knowledge sharing and low exploitation of available skills [54, 65].

As a result, the 2016 mid-term of the 2014–2018 eGovernment strategy have recommended a new governance structure which is summarised in Table 5.

Table 5. eGovernment governance and cooperation actors and responsibilities [54, 65, 75, 76]

Responsible authority for eGovernment strategy	The eGovernment Development Unit (eGDU) within the Department of Political Analysis (DPA) of the Administration of Government (i.e. the cabinet office) is responsible for strategic planning, planning, horizontal and vertical coordination eGovernment When drafting strategies, stakeholders are consulted through both informal meetings, public hearings and debates. Georgia tends to use international experts or international organizations (e.g. EU, OECD, UN) for expert opinions on the draft strategy documents On both strategic and operational levels, the Legal Entity of Public Law in the MoJs DEA is a key supporting authority for the cabinet office and leads and organizes the strategy drafting and consultative process. In practice, the DEA is the liaison body for public and private organization, collects input, organizes stakeholder meetings, workshops with external partners (including international organizations and foreign experts), draft position papers and preparing briefs
Responsible authority for action plan	On the strategic and operational levels, the DEA is responsible for the oversight, coordination and monitoring of all eGovernment initiatives in the national action plan. The DEA provides the status updates and associated recommendations to the eGDU and the cabinet office, while the cabinet office has the final say in any decisions, including in cases of diverting opinions, disagreements or a lack of compliance with the eGovernment strategy and action plan objectives The DEA is supported by thematic work groups of line ministries and stakeholder forums. The thematic work groups are formed to coordinate individual action plan initiatives and meet almost monthly
Responsible authority for initiating and coordinating new eGovernment strategies and action plans	The DEA is responsible and mandated to initiate and coordinate eGovernment strategies and action plans with active involvement of all stakeholders. The DEA is guided by the cabinet office and eGDU vision and input from relevant authorities

(*continued*)

Table 5. (*continued*)

Chairperson organization	The Prime Minister chairs both the cabinet and the eGDU
Hosting organization and secretariat	eGDU is part of the cabinet office but supported by the mandated MoJ and the specialized agency DEA
Member organizations	Members of the eGDU are the DPA (housing the eGDU), DEA, ministry and agency CIOs, different eGovernment Legal Entities of Public Law, the National Regulatory Authority, the Georgian IT Innovation Center, NGOs and other civil society watchdogs like Transparency International and sometimes donor organizations (US AID, UNDP, EU, etc.)
National governance and cooperation model	The national coordination and collaboration mechanism is not fully implemented and therefore not reinforced. Many aspects of eGDU and DEA are currently duplicated
Process of eGovernment strategy and action plan development and approval (from idea to approval by government)	Centralized, initiated and coordinated by the DEA, but hybrid as MoJ/DEA is responsible to the cabinet office and DPA which provides the vision and strategic direction, and to which issues can also be escalated eGovernment strategies are initiated and drafted by the DEA, based on the direction given by the DPA, and in consultation with relevant stakeholders. Prior to finalization, the DPA ensures that strategy, action plan and their success criteria and KPIs reflects a "whole-of-government" approach, that all relevant stakeholders were consulted and is aligned with the general national strategic development framework, vision and strategic objectives The DPA may solicit additional external experts or organizations (domestic and international) for input and adjust the DEA provided draft. The aim is to ensure ownership domestically, limit resistance to the strategic direction and initiatives as well as align the eGovernment strategy with international best practice and development in EU member states. The DPA is responsible for submitting the final strategy and action plan to the cabinet office for government

(*continued*)

Table 5. (*continued*)

	approval and executing the strategy through decree
eGovernment strategy legality	Yes, the eGovernment strategy is an integral part of Public Administration Strategy and Roadmap of Georgia which is approved by Prime Minister decree and is thus legally enforceable
Action plan (i.e. is the strategy underpinned by an action plan)	The process and responsibilities are the same as for the eGovernment strategy
Action plan legally binding	Yes, as part of the eGovenrnment strategy, the action plan is legally enforceable

As outlined in Table 5, the Georgian eGovernment model has a high level of complexity. It can nonetheless be boiled down to three layers: the strategic level, the operational level, and the daily implementation level.

At the strategic level, the eGDU ensures that all governance processes, strategic visions and long-term decisions are in line with the political agenda of the country and, at the same time, that high political will is properly translated into executive action plans. All horizontal eGovernment and ICT projects, new initiatives and new authorities are discussed, evaluated and approved by strategic level. The eGDU carries out its work based on input from the MoJs specialised agency DEA, which is the mandated body for ICT and eGovernment.

At the operational level, the execution and management of the eGovernment decisions made at strategic level is carried out by the mandated body DEA. The DEA provides support to the strategic level in the planning and implementation of the strategic priorities, monitors eGovernment activities and implements a number of key initiatives as well – in short, the DEA ensures the strategic alignment and coordination of eGovernment activities in the short, medium and long term.

Daily implementation has always been decentralized to responsible line-ministries and authorities, but from 2016 onwards a co-ordination mechanism in the form of thematic work groups has been introduced. Each thematic work group is responsible for the implementation of their respective action plan initiatives and report to DEA on progress, risks and for potential conflict resolution. The DEA, in turn, presents regular management overviews to the eGDU and the cabinet office, including the escalation of issues to be solved at cabinet level. The model is illustrated in Fig. 1 and further summarised in Table 6 below – where the strategic and tactical level is merged to allow for easier comparison with other case studies.

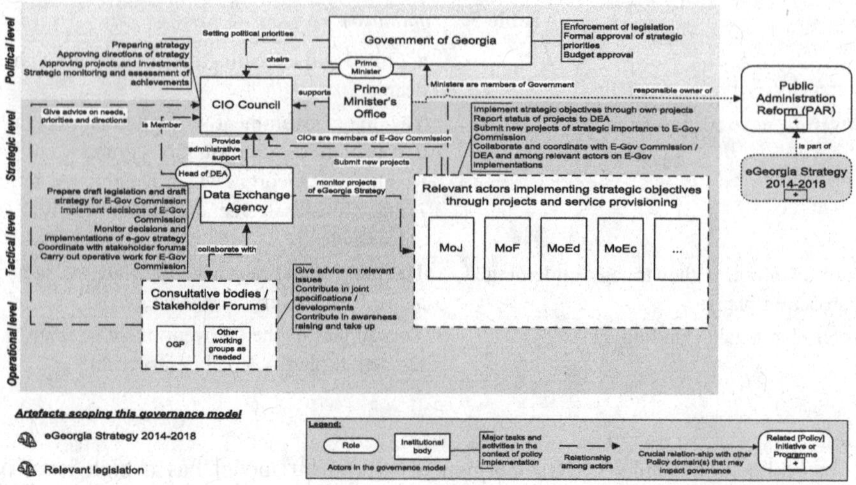

Fig. 1. eGovernance and coordination model [65]

Table 6. eGovernance and coordination model implemented in 2016–2017 [54, 65, 75, 76]

	Co-ordination of the implementation of strategy	Wider co-ordination of the development of information society
Vision		Administration of the Government of Georgia Civil society organizations
Strategy	Administration of the Government of Georgia DEA	
Implementation of action plans	DEA	DEA, Communication Regulatory Body
Daily implementation and everyday work	Individual Ministries and responsible field agencies	
	Thematic work groups/networks	

6 Key Enablers, Citizen eServices, Their Use and Impact

Having confirmed that the required infrastructure and digital literacy exist (Sect. 3), outlined the strategic eGovernment focus over time and described the governance and cooperation model (Sect. 4), what has Georgia achieved in terms of the roll-out (supply) of key enablers and citizen eservices and impact (i.e. demand and use)?

Due to the fragmented eco-system for ICT and public sector services online, it is not easy to get a full picture. Key enablers, such as electronic identities (eIDs), digital signatures (eSignatures), core government registries (e.g. cadastral, property, population, business, vehicle registries), most national authorities have websites with information, a national Government Gateway is in place for data distribution and re-use, as is the www.opendata.ge portal, the statistical services www.geostat.ge and a national one-stop-portal www.my.gov.ge [56, 63, 77].

That said, the impact and value-added of the individual initiatives are hard to assess. The Government Gateway has seen a steady increase in the number of public and private authorities integrate to the centralized service bus – almost 70% from 23 organizations in 2014, 26 in 2015, to 39 in 2016 – but the value of annual transactions have fallen 20% from approximately 55 million in 2015 to circa 44 million in 2016 [78]. The number of datasets available on the open data portal have increased 82.5% from 263 datasets in 2015 and 480 in 2016 [78]. By comparison, www.my.gov.ge only has 56 eServices available and the number of users is low, as highlighted in Table 7, and most users looked for information rather than transactional eServices. For instance, in 2016, 35% looked for information related to legal acts and public hearings, 18% looked for tax relation information, 17% visited the property registry, 16% looked for information related to border crossings, and 14% searched the vehicle registry for data [78].

Table 7. my.gov.ge use 2012–2016, selected years [78]

	2012	2013	2014	2015	2016
Registered users			7,740	4,650	40,026
Number of services	1,319	21,082	52,343	46,652	69,665
Repeat use per user*	–	–	6,76	10,03	1,74
% of population*	–	–	0,21	0,12	1,08

* Author's estimation.

The existence of eID/eSignature, digital post box solutions and a few select number of citizen service areas are confirmed in Table 8. What is harder to assess is the actual volume of public service delivery online – or degree of digitization (i.e. % of service delivery volume online). Where available the degree of digitization is included in Table 8.

Available data shows a mixed picture. A relatively large number of Georgians have an eID/eSignature enabled ID card and almost all tax returns are submitted online. There is only limited use of FixMyStreet type solutions. By contrast to the successful introduction online tax forms and the enabling eID and eSignature most high-volume/high-frequency service areas such as social benefits, registering a new address, daycare, schools, universities are not available as eServices despite the existence of the required registries, good quality data and the document and data exchange infrastructure. Similarly, both citizens and authorities seem unaware of the potential efficiency of integrating services on the national portal or sending messages digitally via the joint-governmental digital post infrastructure provided by www.my.gov.ge.

Table 8. Individual use of the internet 2014–2016, selected years

	eService availability	Degree of digitization (i.e. % of service delivery volume online)		
		2010	2013	2016
eID/eSignature [50]	Yes		48.3% (2015)*	62,7%
Digital post [78]	Yes		584 (2015)	1,869
Tax declaration [50, 79]**	Yes	c. 35%	96%	96%
Register for school	No			
Register for university	No			
Apply for student grant	No			
Change of address	No			
Housing subsidy	No			
Apply for pension	No			
Report vermin (FixMyStreet) [80]	Yes		400 reports	51 reports
Report theft	No			

* Author's estimation based on 2015 volume of 1,800,000.
** Author's estimation based on volume in 2010 of 678,770 electronic declarations, in 2013 of 2,526,004, in 2015 of 2,784,186 and in 2016 of 2,627,850.

Considering the limited data availability for eService use, statistics for the proportion of citizens use of online banking (eBanking), shop online (eCommerce) and their level of online interaction with public authorities is a useful substitute. Unfortunately, data is only available for 2016 and presented in Table 9.

Table 9. Citizens use of eBanking, eCommerce and interaction with public authorities online (at least once per year) 2010–2016, selected years (EU28 country average in brackets) [49, 50]

	2010	2013	2016*
Online banking	– (36%)	– (42%)	21% (49%)
Online commerce	– (40%)	– (47%)	14.6% (55%)
Interacted with government online	– (41%)	– (41%)	– (48%)
Obtained info. from a gov. website	– (37%)	– (37%)	28.7% (42%)
Downloaded a form (for submission)	– (26%)	– (25%)	9% (29%)
Submitted a complete form (eService)	– (21%)	– (21%)	9.3% (28%)

* Georgian data is comparable to EuroStat data as it follows the same data collection methodology, although collected by US Aid funded national survey "Georgia Good Governance Initiative: E-Readiness Study in Georgia".

Despite the fragmented online service offers (depending on the service areas), the data in Table 9 highlights that the Georgians do use both private and public sector eServices, albeit at a far lower level than their general use of the internet – and most likely consisting of social media and online entertainment. While general internet access and use is higher than the EU28 average (see Table 2), Georgian use of eBanking, eCommerce and eGovernment services are all substantially lower (see Table 9). An interesting "Georgian dilemma" as actual use and households propensity to purchase internet for home use is on par with the most wired countries in the world, including other successful eGovernment service providers like Denmark, the Netherlands, and Estonia [39, 40, 49, 53].

7 Observations and Conclusions

Backoffice ICT use in Georgia has been a success, as has the introduction of key enablers, relevant registers and standards. Similarly, a number of high-volume, high-frequency online services are available. The areas of open data, data reuse in government and eParticipation can be improved, but show some initial promise - particularly in relation to the open data portal. Georgia faces a number of recurrent challenges, including: limited budget availability; a shortage or underutilization of qualified staff; expensive infrastructure; a lack of some key national standards; data compatibility; and security issues [64]. These challenges are amplified by the vacuum left by an inefficient or missing governance structures to ensure cross-governmental cooperation and joint-development, and has led to a fragmented ICT framework [55, 63, 65, 66, 72].

While Georgians household propensity to purchase internet access and citizens general use of the internet is higher than the EU28 average (see Table 2), the use of banking, commerce and government online service offers is by comparison all substantially lower (see Tables 2, 7–9). Despite the success in rolling-out the required internet infrastructure, the limited use of government eServices points to the influence of two inter-connected factors:

- While key enablers like eID and eSignatures are already rolled-out and available through the national ID card, actual use is limited. Online services need to be used to add value to the user and provide the envisaged return on investment, but this requires a coordinated and joint-governmental approach to usability and channel strategies, which are still lacking. Georgian authorities therefore need to increase their corporation to ensure that the national my.gov.ge portal contains all government eServices, no matter the responsible authority, that single-sign-on is implemented and that there is a common look-and-feel across different service delivery areas.
- The lack of eID/eSignature use, limited public awareness of online service offers and the value of using them, a lack for channel strategies and promotion of public sector eService – maybe even a lack of trust in online transactions involving payment and personal data. The limited public awareness and lack of channel strategies seem to be influenced by issues related to governance and inter-governmental cooperation.

While distributed responsibility is a common feature in most countries, Georgia currently does not have a fully functioning mechanise to ensure cooperation and compliance with the national eGovernment vision, established mandates and standards.

Similarly, there is currently no actual mechanism to ensure adequate funding of ICT projects, bind to together fragmented initiatives or to ensure compliance with established mandates, standards etc. This points to the importance of cooperation between authorities and the level of integration between entities in the provision and production of services, as proposed by authors such as Heeks [5, 25], Lee and Kwak [32] Chen and Mingins [33]. The Georgian case therefore provides additional evidence in support of the positive role inter-governmental cooperation plays in the introduction and take-up of eService. In the Georgian context, the vacuum left by an un- or understaffed eGDU, and an unclear mandate for the DEA to take on this responsibility, is partly to blame for the current stagnation in relation to eGovernment and online service use.

The eGovernance model currently being implemented may be complicated on paper but could in theory be a solution – although it is worth simplifying it. In fact, many aspects of the eGDU and the DEA seem to be duplicated, which results in misunderstanding amongst stakeholders, resistance to comply with mandatory requirements specified in the joint-governmental policies and strategies – not least the eGovernment strategy and action plan. While strategic initiatives are in the process of improving local government capacities and their user of ICT, municipalities are remarkably absence in past, present and future eGovernment governance and inter-governmental cooperation models which are still largely planned vertically with national line ministries and agencies.

Similarly, the less than optimal use of joint infrastructures like the www.mygov.ge portal and eID/eSignature are examples of how benefit realization and value creation of ICT investments is not maximized due to authorities incompliance or limited support for key strategic objectives. Thus, the Georgian case highlights the importance of good management and coordination of government eGovernment activities in support of authors such as Davison [27], Iribarren et al. [8], Janowski [28], Kalambokis et al. [29], Shareef et al. [30], Waseda [31] and organizations such as the OECD [81].

In conclusion, *the Georgian case adds support to the initial question asked i.e. that there is a positive relationship between a strong cooperative eGovernance model (cause) and the introduction of online services (effect 1) and subsequent citizen use of the online service delivery channel (effect 2).* The Georgian experience highlights the importance of a formal governance model for ICT use. A governance model with clear and recognized mandates to ensure that decisions are made, conflicts are resolved, and the strategic visions, objectives and outcomes are achieved. While the existence of a national CIO (like the eGDU) or specialized government entity for eGovernment (like the DEA) does not guarantee success, the current vacuum in Georgia is a clear example of what often happens when a mechanism to ensure compliance with a strategic vision, decision making and conflict resolution is missing. The positive impact of informal and personal networks and the role of individuals in driving a vision, ensuring coordination and inter-governmental cooperation can play also emerge in the Georgia case, but with limited results. While having at least a partial mandate, the DEA staff has not been able to fully convince line ministries of the need for cooperation rather than launching overlapping or conflicting initiatives. While initially successful, the Georgian approach to eGovernance and inter-governmental cooperation would benefit from a streamlining of potentially overlapping mandates and the formalisation of informal networks.

This will help minimize the risk of failure if consensus cannot be reached and if personal and institutional capacities or contacts do not exist (or fail).

Acknowledgements. This paper is a result of the project "SmartEGOV: Harnessing EGOV for Smart Governance (Foundations, methods, Tools)/NORTE-01-0145-FEDER-000037", supported by Norte Portugal Regional Operational Programme (NORTE 2020), under the PORTUGAL 2020 Partnership Agreement, through the European Regional Development Fund (EFDR). It was also supported in part by funding from Tallinn University of Technology, Project B42; OGI - Open Government Intelligence project in the EU Horizon 2020 framework program, grant agreement 693849.

References

1. Bannister, F., Connolly, R.: Transformation and Public Sector Values, in tGov 11. Brunel University, London (2011)
2. Brown, C.V., Magill, S.L.: Alignment of the IS functions with the enterprise: toward a model of antecedents. MIS Q. **18**(4), 371–403 (1994)
3. Brown, A.E., Grant, G.G.: Framing the frameworks: a review of IT governance research. Commun. Assoc. Inf. Syst. **15**(1), 38 (2005)
4. Cordella, A., Bonina, C.M.: A public value perspective for ICT enabled public sector reforms: a theoretical reflection. Gov. Inf. Q. **29**(4), 512–520 (2012)
5. Heeks, R.: Implementing and Managing eGovernment: An International Text. Sage, New York (2005)
6. Pollitt, C., Bouckaert, G.: Public Management Reform: A Comparative Analysis-New Public Management, Governance, and the Neo-Weberian State. Oxford University Press, Oxford (2011)
7. Klischewski, R., Scholl, H.J.: Information quality as capstone in negotiating e-government integration, interoperation and information sharing. Electron. Gov. Int. J. **5**(2), 203–225 (2008)
8. Iribarren, M., Concha, G., Valdes, G., Solar, M., Villarroel, M.T., Gutiérrez, P., Vásquez, Á.: Capability maturity framework for eGovernment: a multi-dimensional model and assessing tool. In: Wimmer, M.A., Scholl, H.J., Ferro, E. (eds.) EGOV 2008. LNCS, vol. 5184, pp. 136–147. Springer, Heidelberg (2008). doi:10.1007/978-3-540-85204-9_12
9. Ross, J.W., Weill, P., Robertson, D.: Enterprise Architecture as Strategy: Creating a Foundation for Business Execution. Harvard Business Press, Harvard (2006)
10. Poeppelbuss, J., et al.: Maturity models in information systems research: literature search and analysis. Commun. Assoc. Inf. Syst. **29**(27), 505–532 (2011)
11. Heeks, R., Bailur, S.: Analyzing e-government research: perspectives, philosophies, theories, methods, and practice. Gov. Inf. Q. **24**(2), 243–265 (2007)
12. Huijboom, N., et al.: Public Services 2.0: the impact of social computing on public services. In: Institute for Prospective Technological Studies, Joint Research Centre, European Commission. Luxembourg: Office for Official Publications of the European Communities, Luxembourg (2009)
13. Traunmüller, R., Wimmer, M.A.: e-government at a decisive moment: sketching a roadmap to excellence. In: Traunmüller, R. (ed.) EGOV 2003. LNCS, vol. 2739, pp. 1–14. Springer, Heidelberg (2003). doi:10.1007/10929179_1

14. Millard, J., Luca, C., Galasso, G., Riedl, R., Neuroni, A.C., Walser, K., Hamida, S., Huijboom, N., Meyerhoff Nielsen, M., Leitner, C., Fehlmann, A., Scherrer, R.: European eGovernment 2005–2007: Taking Stock of Good Practice and Progress Towards Implementation of the i2010 eGovernment Action Plan, p. 80 (2007)
15. Christine Leitner, J.-M.E., Heinderyckx, F., Lenk, K., Nielsen, M.M., Traunmüller, R.: eGovernment in Europe: The State of Affairs, p. 66 (2003)
16. Bannister, F.: Dismantling the silos: extracting new value from IT investments in public administration. Inf. Syst. J. **11**(1), 65–84 (2001)
17. de Bri, F., Bannister, F.: Whole-of-government: the continuing problem of eliminating silos. In: Proceedings of the 10th European Conference on eGovernment, pp. 122–133. National Centre for Taxation Studies and University of Limerick, Ireland (2010)
18. Janssen, M., Charalabidis, Y., Zuiderwijk, A.: Benefits, adoption barriers and myths of open data and open government. Inf. Syst. Manag. **29**(4), 258–268 (2012)
19. Lips, M.: E-government is dead: long live public administration 2.0. Inf. Polity **17**(3), 239–250 (2012)
20. Meyerhoff Nielsen, M.: Supply and use of citizen eServices: an analysis of selected national experiences in relation to existing governance and cooperation models. NISPAcee J. Public Admin. Policy **23** (2015)
21. Bannister, F.: The curse of the benchmark: an assessment of the validity and value of e-government comparisons. Int. Rev. Admin. Sci. **73**(2), 171–188 (2007)
22. Andersen, K.V., Henriksen, H.Z.: E-government maturity models: extension of the Layne and Lee model. Gov. Inf. Q. **23**(2), 236–248 (2006)
23. Meyerhoff Nielsen, M.: The Role of Governance, Cooperation, and eService Use in Current eGovernment Stage Models. Hawaii (2016)
24. Pöppelbuß, J., Röglinger, M.: What makes a useful maturity model? A framework of general design principles for maturity models and its demonstration in business process management. In: ECIS, vol. 11(3) (2011)
25. Heeks, R.: A Better eGovernment Maturity Model, in iGovernment Briefing. University of Manchester, Manchester (2015)
26. Meyerhoff Nielsen, M.: Governance failure in light of Government 3.0: foundations for building next generation eGovernment maturity models. In: Ojo Jeremy, A.M. (ed.) Government 3.0—Next Generation Government Technology Infrastructure and Services—Opportunities, Enabling Technologies, Challenges and Roadmaps. FORTHCOMING 2017, PAIT—Public Administration and Information Technology
27. Davison, R.M., Wagner, C., Ma, L.C.: From government to e-government: a transition model. Inf. Technol. People **18**(3), 280–299 (2005)
28. Janowski, T.: Digital government evolution: from transformation to contextualization. Gov. Inf. Q. **32**(3), 221–236 (2015)
29. Kalampokis, E., Tambouris, E., Tarabanis, K.: Open Government Data: A Stage Model. In: Janssen, M., Scholl, H.J., Wimmer, M.A., Tan, Y. (eds.) EGOV 2011. LNCS, vol. 6846, pp. 235–246. Springer, Heidelberg (2011). doi:10.1007/978-3-642-22878-0_20
30. Shareef, M.A., et al.: e-Government Adoption Model (GAM): differing service maturity levels. Gov. Inf. Q. **28**(1), 17–35 (2011)
31. Obi, T.: WASEDA—IAC Internationl e-Government Index. Waseda University and IAC International Agency of CIO Tokiyo (2015)
32. Lee, G., Kwak, Y.H.: An open government maturity model for social media-based public engagement. Gov. Inf. Q. **29**(4), 492–503 (2012)

33. Chen, J.Y.Y., Mingins, C. A three-dimensional model for E-government development with cases in China's regional E-government practice and experience. In: ICMeCG, 2011 Fifth International Conference on Management of e-Commerce and e-Government. The Institute of Electrical and Electronics Engineers Inc, Wuhan, pp. 113–120 (2011)
34. Benbasat, I., Goldstein, D.K., Mead, M.: The case research strategy in studies of information systems. MIS Q. 369–386 (1987)
35. Rohlfing, I.: Case Studies and Causal Inference: An Integrative Framework. Palgrave Macmillan, New York (2012)
36. Yin, R.K.: Case Study Research: Design and Methods. Sage, New York (2013)
37. Meyerhoff Nielsen, M.: eGovernance and online service delivery in Estonia. In: 18th International Digital Government Research Conference on Digital Government Research, DG.O 2017. New York (2017); (forthcoming)
38. Meyerhoff Nielsen, M.: Digitising a small island state: a lesson in Faroese. In: Proceedings of the 9th International Conference on Theory and Practice of Electronic Governance. 2016. ACM
39. Meyerhoff Nielsen, M.: Governance and online service delivery: the danish case. In: 15th IFIP Electronic Government (EGOV) and 8th Electronic Participation (ePart) Conference 2016. IOS Press, Guimarães (2016)
40. Meyerhoff Nielsen, M.: eGovernment and governance: the Danish–Japanese timelines and models compared. CeDEM Asia **2016**, 53–66 (2012)
41. Meyerhoff Nielsen, M.: Citizen Use of Government eServices: Comparing Use, Governance and Cooperation Models in Estonia and Georgia, in 25th NISPAcee Annual Conference—Innovation Governance in the Public Sector. NISPA, Kazan (2017)
42. Collier, D., Mahoney, J.: Insights and pitfalls: selection bias in qualitative research. World Polit. **49**(01), 56–91 (1996)
43. ITU—Internet Telecommunications Union. Worlds Telecommunication/ICT Indicators Database (2014). http://www.itu.int/en/ITU-D/Statistics/Pages/publications/wtid.aspx
44. UNDESA—United Nations Department of Economic and Social Affairs, E-Government Survey 2010: Leveraging e-government at a Time of Financial and Economic Crisis. United Nations, New York (2010)
45. UNDESA—United Nations Department of Economic and Social Affairs, E-Government Survey 2012: E-Government for the People. United Nations, New York (2012)
46. UNDESA—United Nations Department of Economic and Social Affairs, E-Government Survey 2014: E-Government for the Future We Want. United Nations, New York (2014)
47. CIA—Central Intelligence Agency. The World Factbook (2015). 1 July, 2014 [cited 2015 1 October]. https://www.cia.gov/library/publications/the-world-factbook/rankorder/2119rank.html
48. GeoStat—National Statistics Office of Georgia. Key indicators. 2016 [cited 2017 13 February 2017]. http://www.geostat.ge/index.php?action=0&lang=eng
49. Eurostat. Information society household survey. 2016 [cited 2016 29 June 2016]. http://ec.europa.eu/eurostat/web/information-society/data/database
50. US Aid, Georgia Good Governance Initiative: E-Readiness Study in Georgia (Nationwide Survey). US Aid, Burlington (2017)
51. Caucasus Research Resource Center. Webhome. 2016 [cited 2017 13 February 2017]. http://caucasusbarometer.org/ge/cb2013ge/WEBHOME/
52. Georgian National Communications Commission. 2015 წლის საქმიანობის ანგარიში 2016 [cited 2017 13 February 2017]. https://www.gncc.ge/uploads/other/1/1976.pdf
53. Nielsen, M.M.: E-governance and stage models: analysis of identified models and selected Eurasian experiences in digitising citizen service delivery. IJEG Int. J. Electron. Gov. **12**(2), 107–141 (2016)

54. Interview 1—Key staff at DEA—Data Exchange Agency, Governance and online service delivery and use in Georgia, M. Meyerhoff Nielsen, Editor (2017)
55. Interview 2015—Key staff at DEA—Data Exchange Agency, Group interview with key staff at DEA—Data Exchange Agency, M. Meyerhoff Nielsen, Editor (2015)
56. Goderdzishvili, N., Gvenetadze, T.: Georgia's successful journey to e-government. In: Proceedings of the 8th International Conference on Theory and Practice of Electronic Governance. ACM (2014)
57. Krabina, B.L., Liu, P.-W., Meyerhoff Nielsen, M., Millard, J., Reichstädter, P., Wimmer, M.: A Digital Georgia: e-Georgia strategy and action plan 2014–2018, DEA—Data Exchange Agency, Editor. Government of Georgia, Tblisi (2014)
58. Government Planning and Innovation Unit, Public Administration Reform Roadmap 2020, Government Planning and Innovation Unit, Editor. Government of Georgia, Tblisi (2015)
59. JoinUP, eGovernment in Estonia, February 2016, Edition 18.0. EC—European Commission, Brussels (2016)
60. UNDESA—United Nations Department of Economic and Social Affairs, E-Government Survey 2008: From e-Government to Connected Government. United Nations, New York (2008)
61. Heeks, R.: Understanding and Measuring eGovernment: International Benchmarking Studies. UNDESA workshop, "E-Participation and E-Government: Understanding the Present and Creating the Future", pp. 27–28. Budapest, Hungary (2006)
62. Meyerhoff Nielsen, M., Bagarukayo, K.: The role of governance in the supply and take-up of government eServices: the case of Kenya, Uganda, Rwanda and South Africa. In: Kaur, H.L., Ewa, Adam, M. (eds.) Catalyzing Development Through ICT Adaption: The Developing World Experience. Springer, New York City (forthcoming)
63. Gvenetadze, I.: Georgian e-Government Model in the Reform of Public Administration, D.-D.E. Agency, Editor. DEA—Data Exchange Agency, Tblisi (2017)
64. Gvenetadze, I.: Georgia's Successful Journey to E-Government, D.-D.E. Agency, Editor. CU4EU (2016)
65. Millard, J., Maria, W., Reichstädters, P.: Update on e-Georgia Strategy 2014–2018: Implementation and Prioritization Roadmap 2017–2018 (INTERNAL DOCUMENT), DEA —Data Exchange Agency, Editor. Government of Georgia, Tblisi (2017)
66. Turashvili, T.: Georgia in UN E-Government Survey—Results and Recommendations. 2016 [cited 2017 11 February 2017]. https://idfi.ge/en/georgia-in-the-un-e-governance-research-review-of-findings-and-recommendations
67. Public Service Development Agency. Community Centre. 2017 [cited 2017 13 February 2017]. http://www.centri.gov.ge/en/about-us/history
68. საქართველოს მთავრობის დეცენტრალიზაციისა და თვითმმართველობის განვითარების სტრატეგიის ძირითადი პრინციპები 2013–2014 წლებისთვის, in 223. Legislative Herald of Georgia, Georgia (2013)
69. საქართველოს კონსტიტუცია, in 768. Legislative Harald of Georgia, Georgia (1995)
70. Resolution 188 (2004) on Local and Regional Democracy in Georgia, in 188. Council of Europe, Georgia (2004)
71. Public Relations Service. Introducing e-Governance in Local Self Governments. 2017 [cited 2017 15 February 2017]. http://sda.gov.ge/?page_id=7492&lang=en
72. IDIF—Institute for Development of Freedom of Information, E-Governance and E-Transparency—International Tendencies and Georgia. IDIF—Institute for Development of Freedom of Information, Tblisi (2016)
73. Administration of Government, მთავრობის დოკუმენტის სისტემის რეფორმის სტრატეგია, A.o. Government, Editor. Government of Georgia, Tblisi (2015)

74. Administration of Government, Social-economic Development Strategy of Georgia: GEORGIA 2020, Administration of Government, Editor. Government of Georgia, Tblisi (2014)
75. Administration of Government, Organigram of Georgian Government, Administration of Government, Editor. Government of Georgia, Tblisi (2014)
76. On the Creation of the Legal Entity of Public Law (LEPL)—Data Exchange Agency, in 1536-RS. Legislative Herald of Georgia, Georgia (2009)
77. Obi, T.: WASEDA—IAC International e-Government Index, G.S.o.A.-P.S. Toshio Obi Laboratory, Editor. Waseda University, Tokyo (2016)
78. DEA—Data Exchange Agency, Various use statistics for key infrastructure, M. Meyerhoff Nielsen, Editor. DEA–Data Exchange Agency, Tbilsi (2017)
79. Revenue Service, Annual report of Revenue Service of Georgia, 2010, R. Service, Editor. Ministry of Finance, Tblisi (2016)
80. Transparency International. Fix my street, Georgia. 2017 [cited 2017 15 February 2017]. https://www.chemikucha.ge/en/
81. OECD, Recommendation of the Council on Digital Government Strategies 15 July 2014—C (2014)88. OECD, Paris (2014)

Time to Refuel the Conceptual Discussion on Public e-Services – Revisiting How e-Services Are Manifested in Practice

Ida Lindgren(✉) and Ulf Melin

Information Systems, Department of Management and Engineering, Linköping University, Linköping, Sweden
{ida.lindgren,ulf.melin}@liu.se

Abstract. There are various models and frameworks describing the nature of e-services in the public sector. Many of these models are based on previous conceptualizations and have evolved over time, but are first and foremost conceptual creations with weak empirical grounding. In the meantime, practitioners in the field have continued to further develop e-services, and new advancements in technology have enabled new solutions for e-services. In the light of advancements in practice, and the limitations seen in current conceptual work concerning public e-services, we identify a need to refuel the conceptual discussion on e-services in the public sector by empirically investigating how e-services can be manifested in practice. The aim of this paper is to illustrate the possible variations of e-services in practice, and to discuss this variation in relation to the conceptual representation of the phenomenon. Based on qualitative interviews with employees involved with e-service development and provision at a large governmental agency, we illustrate that an 'e-service' can take on many different forms within an organization; ranging from downloadable forms, to complicated self-service systems that require expertise knowledge and IT-systems with specific processing capacity. The notion that all services mediated through a website can be understood under one general umbrella term, without further categorization, needs to be challenged.

Keywords: e-Services · Public sector · e-Government · Conceptual models · Empirical grounding

1 Introduction

Providing public services online, e-services, has long been promoted as a way to innovate public sector operations and to open up for a more transparent and democratic society. Governmental agencies and other public organizations have spent considerable efforts on developing e-services as a substitute or complement to traditional, manual or face-to-face, services [2]. As a result, e-services have become a routinely used channel of communication and interaction between citizens and public administrations [4]. Still, both practitioners and researchers in the field claim that there is a very large variation

M. Janssen et al. (Eds.): EGOV 2017, LNCS 10428, pp. 92–101, 2017.
DOI: 10.1007/978-3-319-64677-0_8

in the extent to which e-services are implemented in the public sector, and in the quality of these services [8]. Developing e-services, and ensuring their uptake, has proven difficult and the underlying reasons for why e-service development is challenging are of course many. Lack of sufficient resources and know-how is highlighted, as well as insufficient understanding and involvement of important stakeholders in the development process [3].

Some scholars have pointed to the conceptual vagueness of the e-service concept in itself, and claimed that the conceptual confusion around this phenomenon is one reason for slow advancements in this field [10]. Lindgren and Jansson [18] illustrate how the concept of public e-services has suffered from "conceptual stretching" [23], i.e. vague conceptualization; it can be everything or nothing. The conceptual vagueness of the phenomenon has gained attention in the research literature; today, there are various models and frameworks describing the nature of e-services [10, 11]. These models are typically conceptual constructions and we identify a lack of grounding of these models in practice. In the meantime, practitioners in the field have continued to further develop e-services and new advancements in technology have enabled new solutions for e-services, e.g. improved performance concerning processing and storage, as well as increased use of mobile devices [4]. In the light of recent advancements in practice, and the limitations identified in current conceptual work concerning public e-services, we argue for a need to refuel the conceptual discussion on e-services by empirically investigating how e-services can be manifested in practice.

The aim of this paper is to illustrate possible variations of e-services in practice, and discuss this variation in relation to the conceptual representation of the phenomenon. This work is built on the assumption that there are different types of e-services, and that there is a gap between how we discuss public e-services in the research literature, and the nature of the e-services provided by public organizations. In order to investigate this assumed gap between how e-services are perceived in literature and practice, our work departs from three different conceptual models and one particular public organization.

2 Method

The empirical part of this paper is based on a single qualitative and interpretative case study (cf. [19, 27]) focusing on how a Swedish governmental agency (The Swedish Transport Administration) works with e-services. This paper is written in the context of a research project investigating the development and use of e-services in that particular agency. The aim of the project is to better understand how public sector organizations can work with e-service development in order to ensure that these services add value for both internal and external stakeholders. Focus include investigating how e-service development is governed and on conceptual refinement of "e-service" as a general concept. The initiatives described in this paper can be categorized as an act of engaged scholarship [26], meaning that we have tried to combine theoretical and conceptual development with efforts to contribute to the government agency's problem solving activities.

Qualitative data generation and analysis was conducted in an iterative manner and include three different sources;

- **Document studies** were performed to get an overview of the governmental agency's work with e-services. We have focused especially on three strategy (policy) documents that steer the development and provision of e-services in the organization; (a) the IT Strategy, (2) the Digitalization Strategy, and (3) the Service Strategy.
- **25 semi-structured interviews** [20] where conducted over a period of 21 months (March 2015–Dec 2016) with representatives from several business areas and hierarchical levels at the headquarters and different divisions of the organization (e.g. strategic planning, communications, IT-department, controlling, customer service, business development). 17 of the interviews were conducted face-to-face, and eight were conducted using telephone. The interviews were guided by open ended questions and focused on e.g. how the respondents define e-services; how they interpret the strategies mentioned above; management issues linked to e-services; and present challenges and possibilities associated with e-services.
- A hermeneutic **literature review** [5] was used to increase our understanding of concepts and the managerial challenges of e-service development, provision, and use. We have explored themes that surfaced continuously during the emerging analysis of the empirical data from interviews and documents from the government agency. The results of this review are presented in the next section.

The analysis was performed during the research period when interviews were transcribed (partially, when deeper knowledge were needed) and the responses were categorized inductively, as a part of a content analysis approach [15]. Working with the analysis in this way is an example of a reflexive research process [1], generating categories based on the empirical data while using theory as a guide (e.g. previous research on conceptualizations of public e-services) [27].

3 Public e-Services in the e-Government Research Literature

The literature on e-services in the public sector is growing and includes a large number of various concepts used more or less synonymously, such as *public e-service* [13], *e-service* [14], *digital service* [22], *e-Public-Service* [17], *e-government service* [9], and *Web site channel* [6]. As a response to this variation in terminology, Lindgren and Jansson [18] presented a generic framework for understanding public e-services as having three dimensions. First, a public e-service must be understood as a service process, that should create some value for both user and supplier. Second, this service process is mediated through some internet-based and interactive IT artifact, that is integrated with other IT-systems in the supplying organization. Third, e-services provided by public organizations must be understood as *public* services mediated online, and thereby as access to governments and public organizations per se [12]. For example, this last dimension entails a set of public values, as well as specific regulatory frameworks and relationships between government and citizen, to be considered.

Other scholars have identified the need for more detailed classifications or characterizations of e-services in the public context. The result is considerable literature on how to distinguish one type of e-service from another, first and foremost with regards to their so-called *maturity*. The idea of assessing maturity stems from the seminal paper by Layne and Lee [16], and has later been manifested in a number of different frameworks. Although the wording is slightly different in these models (e.g. [25, 28]), four typical stages can be identified;

1. a website providing *information* about the agency and its services,
2. a website providing *interactive information* about the agency and its services, or providing the possibility to contact people and get further information through *communication,*
3. a website providing functions allowing the visitors to *hand in and retrieve* personal information, and
4. a website with network functions for *proactive and joined-up services* involving several agencies and institutions, for handling *complete service transactions*.

According to critics of these models (e.g. [4, 7, 10]), stage models represent a naïve and techno-centric view on technology in which the maturity characteristics of an e-service are assessed without investigating the actual demand for and use of the service. The evolutionary aspect also implies that the higher stages are inherently better than the lower. The result of this kind of model is that policy makers may be deceived into using the stage models in a normative manner and thereby strive for higher stages on weak, or even false, grounds [7].

More recently, Jansen and Ølnes [10, 11] conducted a rigorous review of current literature on public e-services, and presented a framework for categorizing digital interaction between government and citizens/businesses. In contrast to other similar frameworks, Jansen and Ølnes [10] focus not only on the mode of interaction, but also on the purpose, content, and outcome of the interaction for both provider and receiver. The main categories in their framework are the following;

1. *Simple, one-way information provision* – provide documents to users for downloading.
2. *Two-way communication and information provision* – provide specific information services on user request.
3. *Dynamic, secure interaction between user and system* – initiate a well-defined data handling process, complete an electronic form.
4. *Secure transaction and contraction* – carry out a specific task, regulated by law, which may be part of public service provision.
5. *Complete transaction process* – initiate and execute a complete set of tasks, e.g. case handling.
6. *Support functions* – execute a process that is necessary/required for executing a task, e.g. log in, eSignature.

These three frameworks presented above focuses on different aspects of public e-services. The dimensions presented by Lindgren and Jansson [18] tries to capture the common denominator of the different processes/systems included in the public e-service concept. The maturity stage models, e.g. Wimmer [28], captures different degrees of interactivity seen in different public e-services. And finally, the work by Jansen and Ølnes [10, 11] describes different modes of interaction, and the purpose, content, and outcome of this interaction for both provider and receiver. We now turn to our empirical example, to illustrate and analyze how public e-services can be manifested in practice.

4 e-Services at the Swedish Transport Administration

The Swedish Transport Administration is a government agency responsible for long-term planning of the transport system for all types of traffic, as well as for building, operating, and maintaining public roads and railways. The organization has approximately 6.500 employees and is organized in different divisions and geographic regions in Sweden. The organization was formed in 2010, as a consequence of a merger between two agencies; where one agency was previously responsible for roads, and the other for railways. Today, the agency is also responsible for administering the theoretical and practical tests needed to receive a driving license and a taxi driver badge, as well as the theoretical test for the professional know-how needed for a transport license and certificate of professional competence [24].

The organization is divided into a number of departments and is characterized by the participants as a classic 'silo' organization, in which the various departments govern much of their own work. Each department is responsible for the development and provision of its own e-services, but these e-services are then accessed from a shared website (the official website of the organization). Looking at the website, the organization provides a very large number of e-services. Some respondents claim that they provide around 80 different e-services, but since the responsibility for the e-services is spread across various actors in the organization, it is difficult to get a comprehensive overview of the exact number of e-services provided by the organization. In addition, several participants report that there is an ongoing discussion in the organization as to what the 'e-service' concept means; despite the fact that there is a definition of 'e-service' adopted in the organization that can be found on their intranet: "*E-service. A service that is provided through an electronic interface, and that is completely or partially delivered electronically. An e-service can for example provide information directly on the website, be a part of a case handling process, and sometimes demand log in. Downloadable forms, or other documents that are printed and saved in the computer to be sent separately as a letter or email, are not considered to be e-services. Hyperlinks to e-mail available on the website are also not considered as e-services.*" (our translation from Swedish).

When interviewing employees in the organization, we asked all participants to describe how e-services are manifested in their organization. In the organization, all e-services are accessible from a single webpage, with an underlying hierarchical tree structure of webpages. Looking at the site where all e-services are presented, alongside the interview material, we see that the e-services provided by the Swedish Transport Administration can be divided into five different types. We have extracted these types inductively from the empirical material and labelled them as follows:

1. **Information e-service** – a link that gives access to forms and documents.
2. **Automated (self-service) e-service** – an interactive interface that enables self-service for the user, with no human involvement in the back-office.
3. **Mediating e-service** – an interactive interface that mediate/is part of a service process, in which the user indirectly interacts with a case handler.
4. **e-Service portal** – an interactive interface that presents several related e-services together.
5. **Open data** – API's provided online that other organizations can download and use.

The first type, *information e-service*, refer to forms and documents made available on the website. Most participants add that these documents are not 'proper' e-services according to the organization's definition, but that these documents are still made accessible on the same website (context) as the other e-services. The second type, *automated (self-service) e-service*, refers to e-services with no human involvement in the back-office parts of the system. In this organization, there are only a limited amount of automated e-services provided and these are typically directed towards a set of well-known professional users that are frequent users of these particular services. One example is an e-service for administrating special transport permits for heavy goods on the road, which transport companies can use in a self-service way. The third type of e-service above, *mediating e-service*, refers to an e-service that is part of a larger service process, in which the user indirectly interacts with a case handler. This is perhaps the archetype of e-service. In this organization, the complexity of these services ranges from uncomplicated forms in which citizens can fill in information to be handled by case handlers at the administration, to very complex systems in which railway operators can plan and apply for capacity on the railway infrastructure. The last example requires both expert users and very specific IT-systems on both the user and supplier side, concerning both software and processing capacity. The forth type, *e-service portal*, refers to a one-stop-shop made up by several related e-services. The e-service portals are typically directed to the administration's contract customers. The services provided within the portal can be of all of the different types above. An example of such an e-service portal is a portal directed towards railway operators, in which the service for planning and applying for railway capacity mentioned above is included. The last type, *open data*, refers to the open data offered by the organization. In this particular organization, a recent decision has been made to perceive Open Data as a service, and hence also as an e-service. The open data provided through API's include data sets covering maps, traffic data (e.g. for public roads, railways, and ferries), and basic facts of the organization. In a sense, Open Data could be understood as the first type of e-service, information e-service, but both technical solution and content is different from the typical documents provided in the first type of e-service.

5 Discussion

As can be seen in the categorization above, a 'public e-service' at the Swedish Transport Administration can refer to many different kinds of services and technical solutions. The inductive categories are similar to the generic e-service models provided in the literature. We soon identified that there were conceptual challenges related to e-services in the organization too; just as in the literature. The general e-service definition adopted by the organization includes all inductively generated types, except for the first; information e-service. But when you look closer at the definition, it seems to refer to any kind of interface on their website, except those that link to a downloadable document or email. Interestingly, in their work practice, *everything* online that has some interactive feature is treated in terms of being an e-service on the organizational website. In this particular organization, the 'e-service' concept hence becomes the kind of stretched term that Lindgren and Jansson [18] are describing; it means just about anything that is provided online. For the participants that are working with the actual development and provision of these e-services, this definition is not informative and even creates problems. It *does* matter what kind of e-service you have at hand; e.g. it matters a great deal when it comes to e-service policy, development, provision and use if the e-service is used (1) to perform and deliver a fully automated decision; (2) as part of a service process involving a case handler; (3) to be part of a set of interrelated e-services, presented together in a portal; or (4) to present a packaged data set as open data. It also matters if the user is known, such as professional contract customers, or if the e-service is directed towards the more vaguely understood citizen or an unknown entrepreneur using open data. This in turn brings different consequences for how to understand what capabilities for e-service development and delivery are needed in the organization concerning service architectures, processes, policies, and reference models able to consider specificities of the local context [4].

The inductively generated categories above show many similarities with the maturity stage models; with the important difference that there are no normative connotations regarding the value of the respective kind of e-service. When comparing the framework presented by Jansen and Ølnes [10] with the inductively generated categories, we see that the first category in our inductive categorization, 'information e-service', matches with the first one in Jansen and Ølnes' framework, 'simple one-way information provision'. But thereafter, it is clear that our inductively derived categories are differentiating e-services in a different way. Applying Jansen and Ølnes' framework on e-services in our case organization would help describe the mode of interaction for each e-service under study. However, their framework does not include any aspects concerning type of users involved, nor the notion of Open Data as an e-service. According to the framework presented by Jansen and Ølnes, open data access could indeed be classified as 'simple one-way provision of information'; but open data provision requires a lot of work behind the scenes, in comparison to uploading a form online. Considering how much work the Swedish Transport Administration puts into the packaging of their data in API's, it seems reasonable to add this type to our understanding of public e-services. In sum, each model and categorization discussed in this paper, including the inductive categories, captures certain – and slightly different – aspects of public e-services. But they also leave other aspects out of the description; none of these models/categorizations seem to be exhaustive or useful if used in isolation.

6 Concluding Remarks and Future Research

Our analysis is based on a limited amount of literature and one single case. Still, several interesting points can be made when investigating similarities and differences between the theoretically driven conceptualizations of public e-services in the research literature, and how e-services can be manifested in practice. Above, we illustrate that an 'e-service' can take on many different forms within an organization; ranging from simple downloadable forms, to complicated self-service systems that require expertise knowledge and IT-systems with specific processing capacity from both user and supplier. The notion that all services mediated through a website can be understood under one general umbrella term, without further categorization, must therefore be challenged. There seems to exist a need for a general definition that can be used to understand the core of the public e-service concept; but in order to understand how public e-services can play out in practice, we need more detailed characterizations of the concept. The existing models presented for this purpose capture various aspects, but are still limited. We argue for a more comprehensive and scalable typology that can be used to categorize public e-service for multiple purposes. For example, the models/typologies present today lack information on (1) type of technical solution, (2) type of public service, as well as (3) type of user. We also identify a need to separate the types of public e-service from the normative notion that one type is inherently better than the other. For this purpose, we would like to call for further empirical investigations of how e-services are manifested in practice. By refueling the conceptual discussion on public e-services with further inductively induced categorizations of the phenomenon – as both process and technology – better conceptualizations can be made that, in turn, can be used to address the prevailing challenges with public e-service development.

Acknowledgements. This work was supported by the Swedish Transport Administration.

References

1. Alvesson, M., Sköldberg, K.: Reflexive Methodology: New Vistas for Qualitative Research, 2nd edn. SAGE, London (2009)
2. Ancarani, A.: Towards quality e-services in the public sector: the evolution of web sites in the local public service sector. Manag. Serv. Qual. **15**(1), 6–23 (2005)
3. Axelsson, K., Melin, U., Lindgren, I.: Public e-services for agency efficiency and citizen benefit—findings from a stakeholder centred analysis. Gov. Inf. Q. **30**(1), 10–23 (2013)

4. Bertot, J., Estevez, E., Janowski, T.: Universal and contextualized public services: digital public service innovation framework. Gov. Inf. Q. **33**(2), 211–222 (2016)
5. Boell, S., Cecez-Kecmanovic, D.: A hermeneutic approach for conducting literature reviews and literature searches. Commun. Assoc. Inf. Syst. **34**(1), 257–286 (2014)
6. Ebbers, W.E., Pieterson, W.J., Noordman, H.N.: Electronic government: rethinking channel management strategies. Gov. Inf. Q. **25**(2), 181–201 (2008)
7. Goldkuhl, G., Persson, A.: From e-ladder to e-diamond—re-conceptualising models for public e-services. In: Proceedings of the 14th European Conference on Information Systems (ECIS2006), Göteborg, Sweden (2006)
8. Jacobson, D.I.: Adopting and refining e-services—the role of organization size. Public Organ. Rev. 1–13 (2016)
9. Jansen, J., de Vries, S., van Schaik, P.: The contextual benchmark method: benchmarking e-government services. Gov. Inf. Q. **27**(3), 213–219 (2010)
10. Jansen, A., Ølnes, S.: The muddy waters of public e-services—the use and misuse of the concept and how to get out of the maze. Syst. Signs Actions **8**, 76–94 (2014)
11. Jansen, A., Ølnes, S.: The nature of public e-services and their quality dimensions. Gov. Inf. Q. **33**(4), 647–657 (2016)
12. Jansson, G., Lindgren, I.: Putting "public" back into public e-services: a conceptual discussion. In: Scholl, H.J., et al. (eds.) Electronic Government and Electronic Participation. Joint Proceedings of Ongoing Research and Projects of IFIP EGOV and IFIP ePart 2012. Trauner Verlag, Linz (2012)
13. Karlsson, F., Holgersson, J., Söderström, E., Hedström, K.: Exploring user participation approaches in public e-service development. Gov. Inf. Q. **29**(2), 158–168 (2012)
14. Kaisara, G., Pather, S.: The e-Government evaluation challenge: a South African Batho Pele-aligned service quality approach. Gov. Inf. Q. **28**(2), 211–221 (2011)
15. Krippendorff, K.: Content Analysis: An Introduction to Its Methodology, 2nd edn. SAGE Publications, Thousand Oaks (2004)
16. Layne, K., Lee, J.: Developing fully functional e-Government: a four stage model. Gov. Inf. Q. **18**(2), 122–136 (2001)
17. Lenk, K.: Electronic Service Delivery—a driver of public sector modernization. Inf. Polity **7**, 87–96 (2002)
18. Lindgren, I., Jansson, G.: Electronic services in the public sector: a conceptual framework. Gov. Inf. Q. **30**(2), 163–172 (2013)
19. Myers, M.D.: Qualitative Research in Business & Management. Sage Publications, Thousand Oaks (2009)
20. Myers, M.D., Newman, M.: The qualitative interview in IS research: examining the craft. Inf. Organ. **17**(1), 2–26 (2007)
21. Pollitt, C.: Mainstreaming technological change in the study of public management. Public Policy Adm. **26**(4), 377–397 (2011)
22. Re, B.: Quality of (Digital) Services in e-Government. Ph.D. thesis, School of Advanced Studies—Doctorate course in Information science and complex systems (cycle XXII). University of Camerino, Italy (2010)
23. Sartori, G.: Concept misformation in comparative politics. Am. Polit. Sci. Rev. **64**(4), 1033–1053 (1970)
24. The Swedish Transport Administration. http://www.trafikverket.se/en/. Accessed 12 Jan 2017
25. Statskontoret: The 24/7 Agency. Criteria for 24/7 Agencies in the Networked Public Administration. Report no. 2000:41 (2000)

26. Van de Ven, A.H.: Engaged Scholarship—A Guide for Organizational and Social Research. Oxford University Press, Oxford (2007)
27. Walsham, G.: Interpretive case studies in IS research: nature and method. Eur. J. Inf. Syst. **4**(2), 74–81 (1995)
28. Wimmer, M.: Integrated service modelling for online one-stop government. Electron. Mark. **12**(3), 149–156 (2002)

Organizational Aspects

e-Government and the Shadow Economy: Evidence from Across the Globe

Linda Veiga[1,2] and Ibrahim Kholilul Rohman[2(✉)]

[1] Universidade do Minho and NIPE, Campus de Gualtar, 4710-057 Braga, Portugal
[2] United Nations University-Operating Unit on Policy Driven Electronic Governance (UNU-EGOV), R. de Vila Flor 166, 4810-225 Guimarães, Portugal

linda@eeg.uminho.pt, rohman@unu.edu
http://www1.eeg.uminho.pt/economia/linda/
https://egov.unu.edu/

Abstract. The shadow economy can be defined as economic activities that escape detection in the official estimates of the Gross Domestic Product (GDP). A larger size of the informal sector poses a significant challenge for policymaking as it reduces the reliability of official estimators and increases the likelihood of adopting ineffective policies. Furthermore, the shadow economy may also influence the allocation of resources. The phenomenon is particularly important in the developing world. This paper aims to investigate a possible contribution of e-Government (eGov) to mitigate the problem of the shadow economy. We argue that the implementation of eGov will allow the government to reduce the administrative burden costs, reduce tax evasion, and allow citizens to act as whistle-blowers, all of which may eventually lower the size of the shadow activities. Since the implementation of eGov corresponds to the stage of infrastructure development in the Information and Communications Technologies (ICTs), the diffusion of eGov also requires particular threshold points by which the impact can only be seen. We investigate the data of 147 countries during the period 2003–2013, where the data on estimated shadow economy (based on [1]) and eGov index (based on [2]) are both available. We found that increasing the eGov index significantly reduces the size of the shadow economy. Moreover, the marginal impact is greater in the developed and higher income countries. This sheds a light on the importance to achieve a sufficient level of critical mass in eGov infrastructure before countries are able to reap the benefits of the initiatives.

Keywords: e-Government · Shadow economy · Growth · Developing countries · Public administration

1 Introduction

The shadow economy (SE) -unrecorded and unreported economic activities- has been a problem hampering economic progress in many countries for a long time [1]. Among others, [3] highlight its impact on tax revenue, [4] on regional public debts, and [5, 6] on the unemployment rate. On the financial sector, SE associates with a higher inflation rate [7], higher interest rates, a greater probability of sovereign default [8], and an

M. Janssen et al. (Eds.): EGOV 2017, LNCS 10428, pp. 105–116, 2017.
DOI: 10.1007/978-3-319-64677-0_9

adverse effect on credit ratings [9]. At the industry level, [10] concluded that firms choosing to enter the SE tend to produce negative spillover effects denoted by lower productivity and the propensity to innovate.

The study by [11] found that the SE is negatively correlated with the wealth of nations. [12] corroborated this result with a finding that a 1% increase in the SE lowers the growth rate of the "official" GDP by 0.6% in developing countries. [13] warned that once SE is established, it is hard to remove. The size of the SE is quite huge, especially in the developing regions. Table 1 shows the distribution between regions and the World Bank's income level.

Table 1. The size of shadow economy (% to GDP) between region and income, average 2003–2013 and the *standard deviation*

Regions	The World Bank income classifications			
	High income	Higher middle income	Lower middle income	Low income
East Asia & Pacific	17.63 (*7.22*)	38.25 (*13.19*)	31.11 (*14.87*)	
Europe & Central Asia	21.65 (*7.83*)	41.02 (*8.84*)	50.64 (*9.55*)	
Latin America & Caribbean	33.59 (*14.20*)	38.70 (*10.51*)	62.96 (*10.98*)	51.11 (*3.53*)
Middle East & North Africa	17.46 (*6.22*)	24.46 (*7.91*)	36.44 (*5.20*)	
North America	21.97 (*13.84*)			
South Asia		21.32 (*2.65*)	35.09 (*11.54*)	42.98 (*5.99*)
Sub-Saharan Africa		29.36 (*11.20*)	36.39 (*11.56*)	45.14 (*14.82*)

Table 1 shows that the average ratios of the SE on GDP ranges between 43 to 51% in low income countries, and that those in Latin America and the Caribbean are more prone to these activities than those in South Asia and Sub-Saharan Africa. We also see an indication of spatial effect in Latin America and South Asia based on the values of the standard deviation. Thus, adding to its enormous size, the lower standard deviation indicates a contagion of the SE phenomenon across countries in these regions. In the Sub-Saharan Africa, on the opposite, there is a more clustered outcome due to the disparities of economic progress between countries. Furthermore, the range of the SE in the lower middle-income countries is wider (between 30 to 63%) than the low-income group, again showing a higher incidence in Latin America and Caribbean than in any other regions. In East Asia and the Pacific, we see a greater deviation in the Pacific region. The proportion of the SE in the higher middle-income countries is somewhat lower (between 20–40%) compared with previous two groups, where countries in (Eastern) Europe and Central Asia have the greatest proportion of SE. The performance of countries is relatively uniform when looking into its standard deviation, especially in South Asia where the standard deviation is very low. Moving towards higher income countries the proportion is much smaller (between 17–34%), but the largest incidence is still found in Latin America and the Caribbean, also with a greater variation between countries.

Three preliminary conclusions can be drawn from this table. First, that SE is relatively clustered in specific countries (in this case Latin American and Caribbean countries); second, the incidence is significantly larger in low income countries; and third, the phenomenon is contagious across countries in specific regions inferred from the lower standard deviations like those in South Asia and Latin America and the Caribbean.

A study by [14] defined e-Government as the use of ICTs in the public sector involving several actors and encompassing various interaction patterns in a continuously changing environment. [15] emphasized a need to conduct more studies on the effects of eGov on economic and business activities and, as such, our paper aims to contribute to this niche in the literature.

Conceptually, the link between the potential roles of eGov on economic sustainability, and specifically the SE, can be inferred from [13]. The study mentioned that the primary cause of a shadow activity is an attempt to avoid predatory and obstructive regulations. Thus, if institutional and regulatory problems are addressed, the government might expect a reduction of the shadow activities. The size of the administrative burden can be astounding. [16] estimated that the total administrative burden on businesses within the European Union was around 600 billion euros per year, ranging from 1.5% of GDP in the UK and Sweden to 6.8% of GDP in Hungary, Greece, and the Baltic States. Thus, the implementation of eGov aimed at reducing the administrative burden on businesses is believed to gauge better policies, better implementation, better compliance and, ultimately, better government. Since 2007, Europe has targeted to reduce administrative by 25% in 2012 leading to an increase of 1.4% of EU GDP [17].

The purpose of the study is to investigate a possible role of digital government in reducing the SE through administrative burden reduction. This paper answers two research questions. First, does the implementation of eGov contribute to a reduction in the size of the SE? Second, is there a threshold point by which eGov development is more effective to reducing the size of the SE? The analysis is carried out at different levels of income and regions in order to see the heterogeneity between groups of countries (mainly contrasting the phenomenon in the developed versus developing countries).

2 On the Determinants of the Shadow Economy

Previous studies (e.g. [18]) defined the SE as activities operating outside the principal legal and social structures of the economic system. In Eastern Europe, the SE primarily concerns with the market sector but operates outside the system of economic planning, and involves the private mobilization of means of production. Contrary, in the Western Europe, the SE is associated with the 'black economy' dealing with the tax evasion, fraudulent claims for unemployment benefit and all non-marketed productive activities not included in the national accounts.

There are several determinants affecting the size of the SE. In a phenomenon called hysteresis, [13] found a negative but asymmetric association between GDP and SE. To illustrate, a US$1 decrease of GDP is associated with a 31-cent increase in the size of the SE, whereas a US$1 increase of GDP results in only a 25-cent decrease SE. The study also showed that firms in a more specialized economy have a lower incentive to enter the shadow activities.

Other main determinants concern with the taxation regime and institutional setting. The studies by [19–21] found that the burden of taxation is among the main determinants in the EU countries and particularly in Spain [22]. [23] pointed out that bureaucratic complexity also contributes to the SE. [24] stressed the role of institutional factors by which [4] exemplified with the degree of the corruption level. [25] backed this argument by analyzing 126 countries over 1996–2012, and found that corruption and the SE are related complementarily.

There are other factors worth addressing. [5] stressed the role of inequality, [26] on literacy rates and [27] on ICT usage (e.g. the Internet). Moreover, while most studies found negative sides of SE, [28, 29] found a positive relationship between formal economic activities and SE in Greece and Mexico, respectively.

3 The Role of Technology and e-Government

The eGov policy is a complex interaction. [30, 31] showed that implementing workable e-Government systems requires bringing together different perspectives of stakeholders during implementation. [32] found that transforming Business-to-Government information exchange might result in more efficiency and reduction of redundant controls. [33] summed that implementing eGov in the U.S. Government's General Services Administration (GSA) helps federal agencies to better serve the public by offering superior workplaces, expert solutions, and management policies.

Moreover, as the main vein in eGov implementation is ICT devices, we argue that the nature of network externality as it exhibits in ICT also applies to eGov. The value of ICT services depends on its network: if there are enough adopters, the good becomes valuable. The point of critical mass is mentioned in many ICT studies (e.g. [34, 35]). Details of the study by [35, 36] ascertained the need to achieve a critical mass in order to obtain increased economic growth. Based on these studies, we also assume that a critical mass is also required in the eGov implementation.

4 Methodology and Data

4.1 On Collection of the Data on the Shadow Economy

There are two possible avenues which can be employed to estimate SE: the direct and indirect approaches [37]. The direct approach is operationalized by assigning a well-designed surveys or samples based on voluntary replies, or tax auditing and other compliance methods. The main disadvantages of this method are the flaws inherent in all surveys hence the results depend greatly on the respondent's willingness to cooperate.

The second avenue is to use indirect approaches or indicator approach. Among these, six main strategies can be implemented. *First*, by measuring the discrepancy between national expenditure and income statistics; *second*, between the official and actual labor force; *third*, between the volume of transaction and GNP (see [38] for detail); *fourth*, by assuming that the SE increases the demand for currency; *fifth*, by estimating the physical inputs (for instance electricity (see [39] for details); and *sixth* by using econometric modeling. The main weakness of indirect approaches concerns with the double accounting issue. Thus, comparing the direct and indirect approaches, [38] suggested that the later should be used as the upper-bound.

In this study, the data on the size of the SE was obtained from [1] which uses the multiple indicators multiple causes (MIMIC) approach to estimate the SE. The concept of the MIMIC model is to examine the relationships between a latent variable "sizes of SE" with a number of observable variables by using their information of covariance. The detail of MIMIC model is thoroughly explained in [37].

The estimated SE used in this study covers all market-based legal production of goods and services that are hidden from public authorities for one or combinations of the following reasons: to avoid payment of taxes, to avoid payment of social security contributions, to avoid certain legal labor market standards and to avoid complying with certain administrative procedures, such as completing statistical questionnaires [1].

4.2 On the e-Government Index

Taking into account the analysis implemented by [39], we decided to use the UNDESA index [2] in this study. The study [39] compared the following three indices published internationally based on the reproducibility, coverage of observation, qualitative assessments, and national scope:

- The index constructed by Accenture, which assesses, on a yearly basis, e-Government efforts in 20 + countries since 2000;
- The Brown University's (Prof. West and his research team) index which is released annually since 2001;
- And [1], which assesses the e-Government readiness among UN's members, since 2002.

The UNDESA eGov development index (EGDI) is reported based on a comprehensive survey of the online presence of all 193 United Nations Member States, which assesses national websites and how e-Government policies and strategies are applied in general and in specific sectors for the delivery of essential services. The EGDI is not designed to capture e-Government development in an absolute sense; but to give a performance rating of national governments relative to one another. Although the basic model has remained consistent, the precise meaning of these values varies from time to time. Moreover, the index is a simple average of the normalized scores of the three most important dimensions of e-Government, namely: (1) scope and quality of online services (Online Service Index, OSI), (2) development status of telecommunication infrastructure (Telecommunication Infrastructure Index, TII), and (3) inherent human capital (Human Capital Index, HCI).

4.3 Other Data and Econometric Model

Our main variable of interest to explain the level of the SE is the eGov index. However, to avoid the omitted variable bias problem, other control variables commonly used in the literature are also considered. These include the GDP per capita at purchasing power parity in thousands of 2011 US dollars (*GDPpc*), the general government final consumption expenditure as a percentage of GDP (*Gov%GDP*), the degree of openness of the economy measured by the sum of exports and imports over GDP (*Openness*), and the inflation rate (*Inflation*). All variables were obtained from the World Bank dataset. These variables were also chosen because they exist for 145 of the 147 countries for which data on the SE and the EGDI is available.[1]

The estimated baseline model was the following:

$$SE_{it} = \propto + \beta EGDI_{it-1} + \gamma \sum_{j=1}^{n} Control_{jit-1} + \theta \sum_{k=1}^{6} \text{Region}_{kit} + e_{it} \quad (1)$$

Where *i* stands for country, *t* for year, *SE* for shadow economy, *EGDI* for the e-Government development index, *Control* for a vector of control variables, *Region* for a vector of dummies for the World Bank's regions, and *e* for the error term. α and β represent coefficients, and γ and θ vectors of coefficients to be estimated. The EGDI and all control variables were lagged one year because it takes time for them to have an impact on the SE and to mitigate endogeneity problems.

Since the EGDI is only available for specific years (2003, 2004, 2005, 2008, and every two years thereafter), the index was not built to capture e-Government development in an absolute sense but rather to assess the diffusion of e-Government through a comparison of national governments relative to one another. Moreover, as the index's methodology changed over time [2], we decided to work with cross-sections of countries for each year that the index is available. The model was first estimated by OLS, using heterokedasticity-consistant error terms. Since the estimated SE never yields values below zero or above 100, the data is censored, which implies that performing a Tobit estimation is a more appropriate estimation method.

In addition, as a robustness test, and taking into account that the size of the informal sector is always between zero and one (or one hundred), the model was also estimated with the Fractional Probit model [40].

---

1 Several other variables, for which less data is available, were also used in preliminary analysis but results remained essentially the same. Among others, we used the share of taxes on GDP, the share of part-time/long-term employment on total employment, and the real interest rate from the World Bank dataset; a dummy for democracies from POLITY IV; the human capital index from the World Economic Forum; the economic freedom of the world index and the black-market exchange rates index from the Fraser Institute; and finally, the index of socio-economic conditions from the International Country Risk Guide.

5 Results

The econometric results for the three methods mentioned above are presented in Table 2. Columns 1 to 3 are for a cross-section of countries in 2013, and column 4 for 2004. These two years are, respectively, the most recent and the first year for which we were able to run the cross-section. As can be seen from the table, results are very similar regardless of the estimation procedure used, or the year analyzed.[2] The estimated coefficient for the EGDI is negative and statistically significant in all specifications, indicating that countries with a better performance in the EGDI tend to have a lower SE. As expected, countries with a higher GDP per capita have a smaller informal sector. This result is consistent with previous studies, even though [8] found a non linear relationship between the two variables. The dummies for the World Bank's regions reveal that the share of the SE in GDP is significantly larger in Latin American and Caribbean countries (Region 3). For OLS and fractional probit estimations, in 2013, there is evidence that it is lower in the Middle East & North Africa (Region 4) and South Asia (Region 6). Finally, the control variables *Gov*, *Open* and *Inflation* did not turn out as statistically significant in any regression. Given that the results are similar across the three methods, and the nature of our dependent variable, results for subsequent estimations are reported only for the Tobit estimation.

In order to test which component of the EGDI is most influential on the size of the SE, we included each of them in the same regression. Results reported in column 1 of Table 3,[3] suggest that only the telecommunication infrastructure index (TII) is a significant determinant of the SE.[4] The estimated coefficient is negatively signed and highly statistically significant. However, since the three components of the EGDI are strongly correlated, we decided to include each of them separately in the estimations. Results indicate that they are all statistically significant and negatively signed. Therefore, there is also evidence that progress in the Online Service Index (OSI) and Human Capital index (HC) reduce the size of the informal sector though TII shows the biggest magnitude among three sub-indices.

[2] Estimations were also performed for each year for which the EGDI is available. Results are available from the authors upon request.

[3] To economize space, in Table 3 we only report the estimated coefficients associated with the e-indices but the estimated regressions included the same controls as those of Table 3 (Eq. 1).

[4] TII currently takes into account the number of: internet users, fixed-broad band subscriptions, wireless broadband subscriptions, fixed-telephone subscriptions and mobile-cellular subscriptions.

Table 2. Results using different econometric methods and years

VARIABLES	OLS 2013	Tobit 2013	Frac. Probit 2013	Tobit 2004
EGDI	−0.263***	−0.263***	−0.21**	−0.237***
	(−2.967)	(−3.432)	(−2.35)	(−3.965)
GDPpc	−0.246***	−0.246***	−0.0035***	−0.175**
	(−3.073)	(−2.855)	(−3.67)	(−2.606)
Gov	0.170	0.170	0.18	0.072
	(0.680)	(0.636)	(0.76)	(0.348)
Open	−0.032	−0.032	−0.017	−0.089
	(−0.506)	(−0.514)	(−0.27)	(−1.246)
Inflation	−0.015	−0.015	−0.026	−0.084
	(−0.0882)	(−0.0807)	(−0.17)	(−0.582)
Region3	9.934***	9.934***	0.093***	7.747***
	(3.144)	(3.331)	(3.37)	(2.911)
Region4	−5.239**	−5.239	−0.051**	−3.819
	(−2.098)	(−1.482)	(−1.99)	(−1.198)
Region6	−8.231*	−8.231	−0.077*	−3.323
	(−1.832)	(−1.508)	(−1.82)	(−0.765)
Constant	50.02***	50.02***	−0.21**	43.84***
	(9.709)	(11.33)	(−2.35)	(11.75)
N. observations	145	145	145	145
R-squared	0.433			
Log-likelihood		−571.0	−90.2	−543.5

Notes: The estimation method used in each regression and the year is indicated in the title of the respective column. Marginal effects (in percentage points) are reported for the Fractional Probit method. Robust t-statistics in parentheses. ***p < 0.001, **p < 0.05, *p < 0.1.

Table 3. EGDI and its components

Variables	(1)	(2)	(3)	(4)
TII	−0.277***	−0.296***		
	(−2.715)	(−4.120)		
OSI	0.0402		−0.141**	
	(0.505)		(−2.218)	
HCI	−0.0705			−0.203***
	(−0.840)			(−3.054)
N. observations	145	145	145	145
Log-likelihood	−568.2	−568.6	−574.3	−572.2

Notes: Results for a cross-section of countries for the year 2013 using the Tobit estimation method. Estimations include the same controls as those of Table 3. Robust t-statistics in parentheses. ***p < 0.001, **p < 0.05, *p < 0.1.

The following step of the analysis was to split the sample according to the World Bank's income groups and regions. Results are presented in Table 4. In order to economize space, we only show the estimated coefficients for the EGDI, but all estimations include the same controls as those of Eq. 1, except for the regions' dummies. Table 4 reveals that EGDI seems to exert a bigger influence on the size of the SE in high income countries, suggesting that the ability of e-Government to reduce the SE can only be expected after countries reach certain levels of economic and e-Government development. The mean value of the EGDI in the high-income countries is 0.68, much higher than for the other income groups.

Table 4. Results by income class

Variables	High income	Low income	Lower middle income	Upper middle income
EGDI	−0.306** (−2.359)	−0.325 (−1.102)	0.357 (1.144)	0.240 (1.352)
N. observations	47	23	35	40
Log-likelihood	−162.3	−85.1	−143.4	−149.8

Notes: Results for a cross-section of countries for the year 2013 using the Tobit estimation method. Robust t-statistics in parentheses. ***$p < 0.001$, **$p < 0.05$, *$p < 0.1$.

We also estimated the same analysis by region and found that the largest coefficient (in absolute terms) was obtained for the East Asian and Pacific countries, and the smallest for the Middle East, North African and Sub-Saharan countries. Only for the countries in the Latin America and Caribbean region did the EGDI turn out not to be statistically significant.

6 Discussion

As the Digital Government landscape is continuously and dynamically evolving, it is important that policymakers and government executives evaluate the Digital Government decisions and foresee its impact on society. The purpose of this study is to investigate a possible role of digital government in reducing the SE activities - a long problem which has hampered many countries, especially the developing ones. We investigate whether the implementation of eGov has contributed to a reduction in the size of the SE and if a minimum level of eGov development is required for it to effectively decrease the size of the informal sector.

The contribution of this study is twofold: (1) we provide empirical evidence, based on a large sample of countries, on the potential impact of eGov (proxied by EGDI-UNDESA) to mitigate the problem of the SE; (2) we show that the impact differs across income and geographic groups of countries, which suggests that it is necessary to achieve a minimum level of economic and eGov infrastructure before a country can reap the benefits from the initiative. Decomposing the sample by income groups, we found the impact of the EGDI on the reduction of the SE is statistically significant in the high-income group. The result is consistent when the analysis is performed at the region level showing the greater impact at the regions entailing a greater economic progress. Our findings are consistent with previous studies on the need to achieve critical mass of ICT (telecommunications and broadband) before expecting a wider spill of the impacts on the economy and society. By disentangling the sub-indices, we can interpret these results as follows: unless a country has achieved at least 26% fixed broadband subscribers and 70% internet users, they might not be able to expect the spillover effect of the eGov development. These figures are obtained from the mean values of both variables in the high-income countries.

The paper also stresses the need to implement a more concrete and thorough eGov road map, especially in developing countries, to reduce the administrative burden and the size of the SE. We acknowledge there is room for improvement on methodological aspects and econometric modeling. We are also aware that, given the complexity of the problems associated with these phenomena, our recommendation should not be seen as a sole panacea. However, we believe that improvements in e-Government may represent a more efficient and socially acceptable strategy to control SE activities than the adoption of punitive measures.

Acknowledgements. The authors are very grateful to Friedrich Schneider for providing the data on the estimates for the SE. This research was supported by the Programa Operacional da Região Norte, NORTE2020, in the context of project NORTE-01-0145-FEDER-000037 (SmartEGOV). This work was also carried out within the funding of COMPETE reference number POCI-01-0145-FEDER-006683 (UID/ECO/03182/2013), with the FCT/MECs (Fundação para a Ciência e a Tecnologia, I.P.) financial support through national funding and by the ERDF through the Operational Program on Competitiveness and Internationalization - COMPETE 2020 under the PT2020 Partnership Agreement.

References

1. Hassan, M., Schneider, F.: Size and development of the shadow economies of 157 countries worldwide: updated and new measures from 1999 to 2013. IZA Discussion Paper 10281, Institute for the Study of Labor (IZA) (2016)
2. United Nations Department of Economic and Social Affairs (UNDESA): E-government surveys (various years of datasets) (2006). https://publicadministration.un.org/egovkb/en-us/Reports/UN-E-Government-Survey-2016
3. Mazhar, U., Méon, P.-G.: Taxing the unobservable: the impact of the shadow economy on inflation and taxation. World Dev. **90**, 89–103 (2017)
4. González-Fernández, M., González-Velasco, C.: Analysis of the shadow economy in the Spanish regions. J. Policy Model. **37**, 1049–1064 (2015)
5. Dell'Anno, R.: Analyzing the determinants of the shadow economy with a "separate approach". An application of the relationship between inequality and the shadow economy. World Dev. **84**, 342–356 (2016)
6. Giles, D.E.A., Tedds, L.M.: Taxes and the Canadian underground economy. Canadian Tax Foundation = L'Association canadienne d'études fiscales, Toronto (2002)
7. Prinz, A., Beck, H.: In the shadow of public debt: are there relations between public debt and the shadow economy? Econ. Anal. Policy **42**, 221–236 (2012)
8. Elgin, C., Uras, B.: Homeownership, informality and the transmission of monetary policy. European Banking Center Discussion Paper Series No. 2014-005; CentER Discussion Paper Series No. 2014-045. http://dx.doi.org/10.2139/ssrn.2488419

9. Markellos, R.N., Psychoyios, D., Schneider, F.G.: Sovereign debt markets in light of the shadow economy (February 29, 2012). http://dx.doi.org/10.2139/ssrn.1773343
10. Amendolagine, V., Capolupo, R., Ferri, G.: Innovativeness, offshoring and black economy decisions. Evidence from Italian manufacturing firms. Int. Bus. Rev. **23**, 1153–1166 (2014)
11. Chong, A., Gradstein, M.: Inequality, institutions, and informality. IDB Working Paper No. 427 (2004). http://dx.doi.org/10.2139/ssrn.1818716
12. Schneider, F.: Shadow economies around the world: what do we really know? Eur. J. Polit. Econ. **21**, 598–642 (2005)
13. Eilat, Y., Zinnes, C.: The shadow economy in transition countries: friend or foe? A policy perspective. World Dev. **30**, 1233–1254 (2002)
14. Larsson, H., Grönlund, Å.: Future-oriented eGovernance: the sustainability concept in eGov research, and ways forward. Gov. Inf. Q. **31**, 137–149 (2014)
15. van den Boer, Y.: What's your favorite blend? Analyzing source and channel choices in business-to-government service interactions Enschede: Universiteit Twente. doi: 10.3990/1.9789036536639
16. Kox, H.: Intra-EU Differences in Regulation-Caused Administrative Burden for Companies, p. 136. CPB Memorandum, The Hague (2005)
17. European Commission: Measuring administrative costs and reducing administrative burdens in the EU (2007). http://europa.eu/rapid/press-release_MEMO-06-425_en.htm?locale=en
18. Smith, J.D.: Market motives in the informal economy. In: Gaertner, W., Wenig, A. (eds.) The Economics of the Shadow Economy, pp. 161–177. Springer, Heidelberg (1985)
19. Blackburn, K., Bose, N., Capasso, S.: Tax evasion, the underground economy and financial development. J. Econ. Behav. Organ. **83**, 243–253 (2012)
20. Quintano, C., Mazzocchi, P.: The shadow economy beyond European public governance. Econ. Syst. **37**, 650–670 (2013)
21. Stankevičius, E., Vasiliauskaitė, A.: Tax burden level leverage on size of the shadow economy, cases of EU countries 2003–2013. Procedia Soc. Behav. Sci. **156**, 548–552 (2014)
22. Markandya, A., González-Eguino, M., Escapa, M.: From shadow to green: linking environmental fiscal reforms and the informal economy. Energy Econ. **40**, S108–S118 (2013)
23. Goel, R.K., Nelson, M.A.: Shining a light on the shadows: identifying robust determinants of the shadow economy. Econ. Model. **58**, 351–364 (2016)
24. Torgler, B., Schneider, F.: The impact of tax morale and institutional quality on the shadow economy. J. Econ. Psychol. **30**, 228–245 (2009)
25. Cooray, A., Dzhumashev, R., Schneider, F.: How does corruption affect public debt? An empirical analysis. World Dev. **90**, 115–127 (2017)
26. Chaudhuri, K., Schneider, F., Chattopadhyay, S.: The size and development of the shadow economy: an empirical investigation from states of India. J. Dev. Econ. **80**, 428–443 (2006)
27. Elgin, C.: Internet usage and the shadow economy: evidence from panel data. Econ. Syst. **37**, 111–121 (2013)
28. Aristidis, B., Ioannis, M.: The absorption of a shadow economy in the Greek GDP. Procedia Econo. Finance **9**, 32–41 (2014)
29. Macias, J.C.A.B., Cazzavillan, G.: Modeling the informal economy in Mexico. A structural equation approach. J. Dev. Areas **44**, 345–365 (2010)
30. Azad, B., Faraj, S.: e-Government institutionalizing practices of a land registration mapping system. Gov. Inf. Q. **26**, 5–14 (2009)
31. Rowley, J.: e-Government stakeholders—who are they and what do they want? Int. J. Inf. Manag. **31**, 53–62 (2011)

32. Bharosa, N., Janssen, M., Wijk, R.V., Winne, N.D., Voort, H.V.D., Hulstijn, J., Tan, Y.-H.: Tapping into existing information flows: the transformation to compliance by design in business-to-government information exchange. Gov. Inf. Q. **30**, S9–S18 (2013)
33. Guttman, M., Parodi, J.: Real-Life MDA: Solving Business Problems with Model Driven Architecture. Elsevier/Morgan Kaufmann Publishers, Amsterdam (2007)
34. Meade, N., Islam, T.: Modelling and forecasting the diffusion of innovation—a 25-year review. Int. J. Forecast. **22**, 519–545 (2006)
35. Röller, L.-H., Waverman, L.: Telecommunications infrastructure and economic development: a simultaneous approach. Am. Econ. Rev. **91**, 909–923 (2001)
36. Torero, M., Chowdhury, S.K., Bedi, A.S.: Introduction and overview. In: von Braun, J., Torero, M. (eds.) Information and communication technologies for development and poverty reduction: The potential for development and poverty reduction, pp. 21–63. John Hopkins University Press, Baltimore (2006)
37. Schneider, F., Bühn, A.: Estimating the Size of the Shadow Economy Methods, Problems and Open Questions. CESifo, Munich (2013)
38. Feige, E.L.: Defining and estimating underground and informal economies: the new institutional economics approach. World Dev. **18**, 989–1002 (1990)
39. Berntzen, L., Olsen, M.G.: Benchmarking e-Government—A Comparative Review of Three International Benchmarking Studies. In: 2009 Third International Conference on Digital Society (2009)
40. Papke, L.E., Wooldridge, J.M.: Econometric methods for fractional response variables with an application to 401 (K) plan participation rates. J. Appl. Econ. **11**, 619–632 (1996)

Networks of Universities as a Tool for GCIO Education

Luís S. Barbosa[1,2] and Luís Paulo Santos[3,4(✉)]

[1] UNU-EGOV - United Nations University, Guimarães, Portugal
barbosa@unu.edu
[2] INESC TEC, Braga, Portugal
[3] CSIG - INESC TEC, Vila Real, Portugal
[4] University of Minho, Braga, Portugal
psantos@di.uminho.pt

Abstract. Networking and collaboration, at different levels and through differentiated mechanisms, have become increasingly relevant and popular as an effective means for delivering public policy over the past two decades. The variety of forms of collaboration that emerge in educational scenarios makes it hard to reach general conclusions about the effectiveness of collaboration in general and of inter-institutional networks in particular. The university environment is particularly challenging in this respect as typically different agendas for collaboration and competition co-exist and are often promoted by very same entities. Although no 'one-fits-all' model exists for the establishment of a network of universities, the prime result of the research reported in this paper is that the concept of such a network is a most promising instrument for delivering specific services within the high education universe. In this context, the paper discusses the potential of these networks for the design of educational programmes for the GCIO (Government Chief Information Officer) function and proposes a set of guidelines to successfully establish such networks.

Keywords: GCIO · Networks of universities · Educational programmes

1 Introduction: Networks for GCIO Education

Government Chief Information Officer (GCIO) refers to a leadership position on Information Technology (IT) within a government organization. In general, a GCIO [3,5] is responsible for developing and managing IT capabilities within an agency, for strategically aligning such capabilities with existing organizational objectives, and for leading the organization towards adopting new strategic objectives made possible by the dynamics of digitization. Although the concrete characterization of this function may depend on the national context (namely, on the maturity level of digital governance mechanisms), its relevance is widely acknowledged.

M. Janssen et al. (Eds.): EGOV 2017, LNCS 10428, pp. 117–127, 2017.
DOI: 10.1007/978-3-319-64677-0_10

If the function is emerging, the design of specific educational programmes for GCIO training is still an open issue in most countries. Some Governments in the developing world (e.g., Mozambique and Colombia) are pursuing an integrative strategy, building on their university systems' resources, to foster synergies and establishing institutional partnerships to jointly deliver GCIO training programmes. In such a context, the present paper discusses the establishment of network of universities (NoU) to deliver GCIO related education, as a cost-effective alternative.

Networking and collaboration have become increasingly popular as an effective means for delivering public policy over the past two decades. Governments became commissioners of services and partners in delivery networks rather than direct services providers [8]. Indeed, there is a current global trend of governments to empower different stakeholders, from individuals and communities to institutions and networks, as an opportunity to achieve better governance, and to harness the power of technology to deliver new and better services. Networks as frameworks for public policy are supported by digital technology, which allows for ever greater volumes of information to be collected and stored, and facilitates information sharing among agencies and organisations, through electronic communication and shared or jointly accessible databases and repositories.

This paper's context is provided by the prospect of structuring a GCIO-related education NoU in a developing country. The relevance of this study is further compounded by the perceived growth of the importance of networking and cooperation structures in education. Inter-institutional cooperation, despite its tremendous potential, is by no means straightforward. Collaborating actors need to possess sufficient cognitive distance for new insights to emerge, but at the same time need to be similar enough for dialogue to be possible and constructive, thus imposing upper bounds on cognitive distance. The educational context, moreover, is complex [7]. The autonomy of universities implies the existence of diverse missions, goals and agendas, leading, over the last decades, to a greater emphasis on competition rather than collaboration. The consolidation of a bidding culture where an increased part of funding is obtained through competitive processes, the public availability of institutional performance data and related ranks, the need to compete for students, seem incompatible with promoting a culture of sharing and collaboration. However, NoUs stimulate deeper organisational learning and have potential for redesigning local systems and structures by promoting different forms of collaboration, linkages, and multi-functional partnerships.

Methodology and paper's structure. The paper studies the concept of a network of universities in order to identify a set of guidelines for establishing such a network devoted to GCIO-related education. This is done through a literature review, surveyed in Sect. 2, followed by a detailed analysis of six interviews to leading actors in different kinds of networks of universities. Each interview, conducted either face-to-face or through videoconference, followed a specific protocol which covers the following six areas of inquiry: (i) context and structure; (ii) governance; (iii) membership and interaction; (iv) activities; (v) challenges; and (vi) success factors.

The networks analized here are quite heterogeneous, ranging from typical bottom-up networks, promoted by groups of academics, to top-down ones, created by inter-governmental initiatives, and others exhibiting mixed profiles. They are also distinguished by scope, mission, object, activities, governance and forms of interaction. This analysis is documented in Sect. 3.

Finally, Sect. 4 concludes the paper by enumerating a number of guidelines for the design and maintenance GCIO-related educational programmes.

2 A Brief Review of Literature

According to [2], the concept of a network of universities covers two dimensions: (1) the collaboration through partnerships intended to strengthen the individual institutions in the fulfilment of their missions, and (2) purpose-driven platforms to address specific issues, typically societal challenges (e.g. global health, food security, etc.). In both cases, the success of inter-institutional collaboration projects depends on the clear perception, by all partners, that the collaboration in the process configures a win-win situation for all involved agents [4].

In a number of illustrative case-studies that can be found in the literature, the political context emerges as a key-issue for the network, particularly for the development and sustainability of partnerships. One reason for failure is the lack of suitable legal regulation [1]; another is insufficient funding. A clear political framework and full autonomy to educational institutions seem essential for maintaining any collaboration process. Thus, the success of this collaboration depends on the commitment and interaction amongst all stakeholders.

The case-study described by Chapman et al. [2] shows the importance of networks of universities as a way to ensure social and educational development. Consequently, the focus is put on the definition of the network's structure and its operational model. The sustainability of the network depends on the ability to keep the partners informed, engaged and involved in the decision-making process as well as in the activities developed. This implies a set of indicators that are essential for networks success, namely the organisational issues in the operation of university networks (e.g. value of university networks; *loci* of leadership matters; transparency versus bureaucracy); and the academic staff issues in the operation of university networks (e.g. staff incentives, bureaucratic complexity).

External success factors for networks include: suitable motivation for collaboration between partners; incentives that connect appropriate rewards with organisational goals; and an accountability system that encourages collaboration (see e.g., [7,10]). On the other hand, typical difficulties [1] include:

- Imperfect information: the network objectives and the partners' role need to be clear from the beginning.
- Uncertainty and immeasurability: the partners may not be able to accurately evaluate the quality of each other's potential contribution.
- Irreversibility: The partners may be reluctant to make contributions to the relationship that cannot be reversed if the relationship ends (for example, the sharing of intellectual property).

- Absence of focal points: Without them agreements become less likely and may have impact on partners' commitment and engagement.
- Disincentives to share gains.
- Sustainability: partnerships will need to be 'renewed' if they are to be sustained, perhaps through the renegotiation of points of focus.

The literature also identifies a number of risks associated to the establishment of networks in educational contexts that include:

- Poor performance by any of the partners may lead the network as a whole to underperform or even fail in the delivery of essential services [6].
- The level of resources required to set up collaboration and the additional workload that can result for staff in partner organisations [9].
- Delays in the decision-making process due to the negotiation processes.
- Power imbalances between different network partners and goal incongruence, which may lead to major misunderstandings.
- Poor network culture and, in particular, the fact that network management is not usually part of the training or career path of civil servants.

3 State of the Practice: Expert Interviews

This section introduces six examples of successful networks of universities. The choice considered their heterogeneity in terms of scope, mission, structure and forms or governance, membership and interaction, The six cases are based on detailed expert interviews to leading actors in each of the networks, according to a specially designed protocol.

AUN – *ASEAN University Network of the Association of Southeast Asian Nations*, Thailand (www.aunsec.org). AUN is a multi-country, broad scope network of universities established by the Governments of ASEAN Member Countries in 1995. It has a clear institutional strategic focus aimed at facilitating regional inter-university cooperation.

RedUNCI – *Red de Universidades Nacionales con Carreras de Informática*, Argentina (redunci.info.unlp.edu.ar). Joins together a number of Argentinian universities offering degrees in Informatics. It was created in 1996 to extend to Informatics, as a new academic discipline, an internationally funded core programme for scientific development in Argentina.

UASnet – *Universities of Applied Sciences Network*, EU (www.uasnet.eu). Created in 2011, to build a representative instance for Applied Sciences Universities within the EU and strengthen the integration and contribution of the UAS sector within the research and innovation strategy of Europe.

MAP-i – *MAP Doctoral Programme in Comp. Sci.*, Portugal (mapi.map.edu.pt). Launched in 2007 to establish an inter-university doctoral programme in Computer Science, open to the international, highly-competitive PhD market. It joins together the three top public universities in the North of Portugal, involving eight research centres.

CIO University – United States of America. Active from 1998 until 2014, this virtual university was established as a consortium of seven North American universities, to other graduate level programs addressing the essential knowledge, skills and abilities of federal CIOs.

REDCUPS – *Red Colombiana de Instituciones de Educación Superior Promotoras de Salud,* Colombia (www.aunsec.org). It was founded in 2010 as a network of universities, under their own leadership, in order to articulate efforts to strengthen the contribution of universities to the promotion of Health, and optimise resources in what concerns training, qualification of processes and institutional capacity building.

The main findings of this exercise, classified with respect to the categories mentioned in Sect. 1, are presented in the sequel.

Context, purpose and structure. The first conclusion than can be drawn from the expert interviews concerns the suitability of the concept of a network of universities as an instrument for delivering specific services related to the high education universe. Moreover, these forms of association can: (1) expand the scope and reach of activities that a single university can perform; (2) enrich a university's mission; and (3) address endogenous and exogenous challenges through new tools.

MAP-I, RedUNCI and REDCUPS are examples of networks created to address specific challenges in the core mission of a university: the design of a top quality doctoral programme in the first case (MAP-i), the consolidation of Informatics as a new curricular area and collection of professional careers in the second (RedUNCI), and the involvement of higher education institutions in promotion of public health at a national level (REDCUPS). In all cases, the network brought together extra resources and critical mass.

The CIO University network had a different nature that emerged as a collective project in response to a mandate from a governmental agency designed to address a very specific need: Federal agency CIO training. It was perceived from the outset that the desired goals could be more easily achieved through a network of complementary institutions than by a single university implementing a new stand-alone programme.

Both AUN and UASnet respond to more global needs: the overall development and strengthening of the higher education system in Southeast Asia, in the former case, and the establishment of a representative instance and an institutional voice for universities with a more applied focus within the European Union, in the latter.

The existence of a clear, shared mission seems to be a decisive factor across the cases. The six networks studied were created to address a specific and well-identified problem – not a 'small', operational one, such as getting access to extra core funding. The association scheme, although implemented in different ways, was clearly understood as the most effective, if not the only, way to achieve the set of objectives defined.

The expert interviews also revealed the diversity of forms that the creation of a network of universities may take. Some of the networks studied, such as AUN and CIO University, were built by external initiative, where the governmental or even international, inter-governmental level acted as a driving force. In the cases of RedUNCI and MAP-i, the idea of a network emerged within the academic community and later made its way to the highest levels of the university management structure. Finally, the case of UASnet is an example of a network also promoted from inside the academic system, but at the level of an inter-university cooperation structure, the UAS Rector's Conference in Europe.

Networks can also emerge along a bottom-up or a top-down process. RedUNCI, REDCUPS, MAP-I and UASnet are examples of the first modality, the CIO University and AUN, of the latter. In all cases, however, a strong institutional commitment, involving the right level of responsibility (i.e. the administration of the member universities, the inter-university structure or the governmental agency) was given. Commitment beyond constituting a success factor, seems to be a necessary condition for the NoU very existence.

Governance. Network governance assumes different formats depending on where the main locus of institutional responsibility resides. The 'external stakeholder', as in the cases of AUN or the CIO University, plays an important role in the decision-making process. The networks established internally to a set of universities, such as MAP-i, RedUNCI, REDCUPS, and, to a certain extent, ASUnet, exhibit open, peer-based, essentially democratic and representative governance bodies at the relevant level of representation. In all cases, however, it seems that successful networks favour:

- a simple, often minimalistic governance structure;
- a decision-making process based on consensus, which is actively sought;
- and an effective, dedicated administrative support.

Interaction and membership. In all the cases effective interaction among the relevant actors, both at the institutional and personal levels, is clearly present, explicitly desired and sought through dedicated communication strategies and clear management rules. Creating trust among all the players seems essential for the network to achieve its aims and become smoothly integrated in the university ecosystem. Several communication strategies were mentioned in the interviews, essentially supported by digital technology and collaborative platforms. This seems, however, to be the easy part: promoting interaction supposes more active policies. Two of them were mentioned, with different flavours, in all interviews:

- The importance of acting in a transparent way, with clear operation rules and open decision processes. In the case of MAP-i, in which the network activities imply/promote some form of competition among the involved universities and academics, the open-call principle established for all resource-concerned decisions plays a fundamental role in ensuring the smooth operation of the network and increasing collaboration between academics.
- The effort to create a collective identity and a sense of membership to the network among not only institutional stakeholders, but also individual actors, from academics and students to managers and secretarial support. In some cases this even lifts to explicit branding activities.

The decision to admit new members is always made by consensus. Structural stability is implicitly regarded as a network asset.

Activities. The activities developed by the six networks analysed are rather specific to each domain of intervention and, as expected, driven by each network mission. Curricular development and management, course delivering, organisation of conferences and workshops, branding management, promotion of mobility and internationalization, are typical examples. Key aspects to emphasize include:

- Having a clear action focus and activity plan, shared by the whole network, is perceived as a relevant element in building the network identity, known and recognised among the partners and externally.
- Regard the role of the network as subsidiary to the normal activity of each member institution. In some cases, MAP-i being the typical example, the network is actually offering an activity which has replicas at the local level, and some competition seems inevitable. The crucial point to overcome this sort of possibly disruptive effect, is to build the awareness that the network, even in a somehow competing situation, brings real added-value to each partner, in the form of tangible or intangible assets.

Challenges. Most of the challenges that the five networks face are concerned with improving administrative support (UASnet and MAP-i) and keeping or increasing the funding level (AUN, UASnet, CIO University). Improving the coordination structure was additionally identified through the RedUNCI case. A second category of challenges concerns the operation of the network itself: accomplishing the mission is always understood as a challenge, which is probably an interesting indicator of the vitality of the five networks studied. This category includes:

- Enduring (as UASnet puts it, 'continue to do well what as been done well from the outset', or, for CIO University after its official closing, to keep the market value of its brand certificate);
- Scaling;
- The ability to cope with its own success and avoid denying internal and external expectations (AUN);
- Pursuing difficult objectives and being more and more ambitious with respect to attainable objectives; and
- The broad scope of the network mission (RedUNCI mentions, for example, the heterogeneity and extension of the Argentinian high education systems) and some institutional resistances to change.
- Finally, the need to seek and maintain a high level of personal and institutional motivation, and the ability to generate institutional processes able to internally appropriate the network experience and incorporate it in the mainstream dynamics of the university (REDCUPS).

Success factors. The following issues were identified as main success factors in the six expert interviews:

- clear mission and objectives from the outset;
- ability to focus in its mission over time;
- shared values leading to a collective sense of identity;
- clear institutional support at the suitable level of responsibility;
- effective support structure at the operational level;
- wide involvement of the community;
- past achievements and quality of the work done;
- collaborative culture (enforced at the management level and promoted along the whole network); and, in several cases, participative governance models;
- the inclusion within international dynamics of already established associations of universities;
- effective interaction between stakeholders; and
- establishment of trust and even of personal links and friendship among the main actors, over time.

The special roles played by some partners with high levels of institutional commitment to the network, are mentioned, namely by RedUNCI, as a success factor for the whole network. Equally important, however, seems to be the ability of the latter to integrate and manage smoothly such proactive behaviour.

These findings are consistent with what is reported in the literature, as reported above. The following aspects, however, were not mentioned so emphatically in our own expert interviews, although they can be found implicitly there:

- The relevance of the political and cultural context; and
- A rigorous balance of local autonomy and ability to compromise.

4 Concluding: Guidelines for a NoU for GCIO Education

From the research reported, the following guidelines emerged to frame the establishment of networks of universities to jointly deliver GCIO-related education.

Guideline 1: Definition of a clear mission statement. The question of which are the network's goals should be the starting point for its establishment and development. Goals need to be clearly formulated and linked to specific actions. There need to be clear benefits to all organisations within the network, or lead to an overarching outcome that is of importance and relevance to all network actors. Preferably, main goals should be made measurable, so that they can be clearly monitored for achievement. A network is always a means to an end, and not an end in itself. This awareness is essential to build a set of shared goals and mission.

Guideline 2: Identification of stakeholders and clear articulation of a uniform or differentiated membership scheme. The identification of stakeholders and articulation of a membership scheme entails the need for a detailed analysis of existing competences GCIO-related education within each national higher education system. This should be undertaken in three complementary movements:

- The identification of main training and capacity building needs within the public and the private sector, that this network may address;
- The design of a matrix of core competencies for the identified curricular needs; and
- The identification of existent degrees, courses or even just curricular areas, within each national high education system.

Guideline 3: Definition of the loci of initiative and responsibility in the network and its fundamental structure. The *loci* of the initiative, responsibility for the network, and its structure do not need to coincide, or even overlap, but can be distributed among the stakeholders to a greater or lesser extent. The expert interviews analysed in this paper illustrate different configurations that should be assessed in face of concrete context.

Guideline 4: Definition and planning of the network activity. The definition and planning of a network should be directly related to the mission statement and specify the extent of involvement and collaboration of each partner. Some categories of activities for the envisaged network can already be anticipated:

- Identification of core competencies and curricular design through collaborative research involving the network stakeholders;
- Delivering specific courses in collaboration and/or certifying existing courses and their combination; and
- Organisation of global activities (e.g. thematic conferences; joint workshops with communities practice, typically at sectorial levels; common graduation ceremonies; publications of dissertations, case studies or lecture notes, etc.).

Guideline 5: Development of policies for promoting membership and interaction. Active policies for promoting membership and interaction among the network need to be planned beforehand. A main challenge in setting up a network of universities is the creation of trust. Trust is based above all on shared values and personal relations between staff active in the network. While it is desirable at the outset, where that is not the case trust may emerge over the course of collaborating through interaction between the partners. A step-by-step approach to building trust through small-scale collaborations before going on to deeper relationships may be effective in this regard.

Guideline 6: Definition of a realistic model. The definition of a realistic operational model for the administration of the network, with a clear provision for shared resources, administrative support and funding. Those aspects, namely the suitable definition of sustainable funding models, were mentioned across the different expert interviews as a potential source of risks.

Guideline 7: Definition of a suitable policy for branding management. An aspect identified in all expert interviews was the relevance of a suitable policy for branding management. This should begin at an early stage of the network establishment, coming directly from the definition of the mission statement and the corresponding activity planning.

Guideline 8: Establishment of clear communication channels. Finally, it is necessary to establish clear communication channels within the network. This aspect also requires proper attention in the network design phase. In view of the difficulties involved in collaboration and networking, and the room for misunderstanding, communication among all partners is absolutely crucial. Communication flows are hard enough to effectively organise within an organisation, let alone within a collaborative network, and this is therefore a key task.

The proposed guidelines emerged from a qualitative, case-based research. We believe they offer a useful working framework, which needs to be instantiated and suitably adapted to each particular implementation context.

Acknowlegdments. This paper is a result of the project *SmartEGOV: Harnessing EGOV for Smart Governance (Foundations, Methods, Tools)* NORTE-01-0145-FEDER-000037, supported by Norte Portugal Regional Operational Programme (NORTE 2020), under the PORTUGAL 2020 Partnership Agreement, through the European Regional Development Fund (EFDR).

References

1. Boggs, A., Trick, D.: Making college-university collaboration work: Ontario in a national and international context. Technical report, Toronto: Higher Education Quality Council of Ontario (2009)
2. Chapman, D.W., Pekol, A., Wilson, E.: Cross-border university networks as a development strategy: lessons from three university networks focused on emerging pandemic threats. Int. Rev. Educ. **60**, 619–637 (2014)
3. Cohen, J.F., Dennis, C.M.: Chief information officers: an empirical study of competence, organisational, positioning and implications for performance. S. Afr. J. Econ. Manag. Sci. **13**(2), 203–221 (2010)
4. Dorner, N., Morhart, F., Gassmann, O., Tomczak, T.: Collaboration and partnership for equitable improvement: Towards a networked learning system? On the Horizon **19**(3), 217–225 (2007)
5. Estevez, E., Janowski, T.: A comprehensive methodology for establishing and sustaining government chief information officer function. In: Proceedings of the 8th International Conference on Theory and Practice of Electronic Governance, ICEGOV 2014, pp. 235–243. ACM, Guimaraes, October 2014
6. Goldsmith, S., Eggers, W.D.: Government by Network: The New Shape of the Public Sector. Brookings Institution Press, Washington, DC (2004)
7. Havlicek, J., Pelikan, M.: The globalization of higher education - be responsible and survive the changes. Int. Educ. Stud. **6**(4), 217–224 (2013)

8. Mickelthwait, J., Wooldridge, A.: The Fourth Revolutions: The Global Race to Reinvent the State. The Penguin Press, New York (2014)
9. Nooteboom, B.: Inter-firm Collaboration, Networks and Strategy: An Integrated Approach. Routledge, New York (2004)
10. Obst, D., Kuder, M., Banks, C.: Joint and double degree programs in the global context: Report on an international survey. Technical report. Institute of International Education, New York (2011)

From a Literature Review to a Conceptual Framework for Health Sector Websites' Assessment

Demetrios Sarantis[1(✉)] and Delfina Sá Soares[1,2]

[1] United Nations University Operating Unit on Policy-Driven Electronic Governance, Campus de Couros, Rua Vila Flor 166, 4810-445 Guimarães, Portugal
{sarantis, soares}@unu.edu

[2] Department of Information Systems, ALGORITMI Center, University of Minho, Campus de Azurém, Azurém, 4800-058 Guimarães, Portugal

Abstract. Health sector institutions' websites need to act as effective web resources of information and interactive communication mediums to address the versatile demands of their multiple stakeholders. Academic and practitioner interest in health sector website assessment has considerably risen in recent years. This can be seen by the number of papers published in journals. The purpose of this paper is twofold to further establish the field. First, it offers a literature re-view on hospitals' websites assessment. Second, it offers a conceptual framework to address the website assessment issue in health sector. The proposed assessment framework focuses on four main criteria: content, technology, services, and participation being evaluated by the use of several indicators. Academics, hospital practitioners, public officials and users will find the review and the framework useful, as they outline major lines of research in the field and a method to assess health institution websites.

Keywords: eGovernment · eHealth · Assessment framework

1 Introduction

The traditional face-to-face patient interaction with a health services provider is be-coming less common, replaced gradually by frequent interactions with the respective health-sector web portals. It is thus increasingly important for these organizations to have an effective web presence. Furthermore, patients demand an effortlessly usable, gateway to initiate interaction, making an aptly organised portal crucial feature of the modern health care organization [1].

With patients taking over more responsibility for their own health care decision, web is an appropriate media to facilitate information exchange between patients and health-services providers. Increasingly, hospital websites are beginning to operate as extension of hospital services, offering access to a range of information and applications [2]. Therefore, in an effort to facilitate the public's access to reliable information

M. Janssen et al. (Eds.): EGOV 2017, LNCS 10428, pp. 128–141, 2017.
DOI: 10.1007/978-3-319-64677-0_11

and to useful services from hospital websites, we consider that it is crucial to be able to assess health-sector organisations' portals.

Health sector institutions' websites evaluation contribute to maximize the exploitation of invested resources by organizations in the development of user-perceived quality websites. Evaluation on websites related to medical health has recently become a hot topic in the studies of health informatics and information management. Reviewing relative literature, it can be found that there are several studies related to evaluation on health-sector websites, each one assessing a variety of elements. But there is not yet an unequivocal definition of the concept of health sector website quality and the discourse about health sector institutions websites' quality evaluation remains open [3].

The overarching aim of the present study is to review and analyse existing literature research efforts in the area of hospital website assessment and based on the extracted results, to propose an assessment framework that can integrate the identified aspects.

This paper is organized in six sections. Next section presents relative background information. The third section introduces the methodology applied, while section four reviews and analyses existing website quality assessment efforts in health sector. Section five analyses the proposed health sector website assessment instrument. Finally, section six presents the conclusions and possible future research steps.

2 Background Information

Compared to other areas of eGovernment, where assessment has been conducted more systematically for longer period (i.e. municipality services), the assessment of eHealth systems deployment is lagging behind. Hospital portals and web based systems provide patients more information, and more involvement in their healthcare, they improve access to health advice and treatment and can make healthcare systems more efficient if the patient-centred care aim is to be achieved [4].

Eighty percent of Internet users, or about 93 million Americans, report using the Internet as a resource for researching and making health care decisions [5]. A 2010 survey [6] of public, private and university hospitals in Europe showed that 81% have one or more electronic patient records systems in place, but only 4% grant patients online access to their health information. 71% use online eBooking systems for patients' appointments with medical staff but only 8% offer patients the opportunity to book their own hospital appointment online. Only 30% use ePrescription for medicines, 8% telemonitor patients at home, 5% have some form of electronic exchange of clinical care information with healthcare providers in other EU countries.

Research in the area of health sector website assessment appears essential in order to identify the gaps and improve their overall performance. Most research on this field is focused on information context, software quality and usability issues. Nevertheless, hospital web sites should fulfil objectives beyond the delivery of accurate information and state of the art software solutions.

3 Methodology

In our literature review, we selected to conduct an exploratory study approach since it helps to acquire insight into the available literature by identifying the conceptual content of the field and by contributing to theory development towards formulating our conceptual framework [4]. The research methodology encompasses three phases.

3.1 Material Collection

In the present study, six well-known academic online databases, Science Direct, EB-SCOHost, Google Scholar, Web of Science, Scopus and Wiley Online Library were selected to search for relevant studies. The literature search was carried out in article titles from 2000 to February 2017 (time of the final search). The search for related publications was mainly conducted as a structured keyword search. The resulting search equation was defined using the Boolean operators "AND" and "OR". The searching process was based on following keywords (hospital OR health sector) AND (web site OR website) AND (quality OR evaluation OR assessment). At the end of the database search, 45 published articles were found. Final selection of articles was carried out according to compliance with inclusion and exclusion criteria. Inclusion criteria were: the documents should be original articles published in peer reviewed journals or conferences. Only articles where the complete text was available for retrieval were included. Exclusion criteria comprised: studies which did not contain at least one health sector website evaluation aspect were excluded. Also, excluded were those which did not make specific references to website characteristics. Among these papers, 16 were determined as the suitable ones and were selected. In addition, a secondary search was carried out in article abstracts to locate possible relative resources which do not include some of the keywords in their titles. Four relative articles have been found.

3.2 Content Analysis

Content analysis was based on exploratory study of the selected articles carried out using systematic check techniques, on existing health sector web presence assessment studies. This type of research was chosen because it can provide significant insight into a given situation, facilitating the identification and structuring of new problems. The different assessment approaches have been analysed, extracting the significant elements of which they consist.

3.3 Conceptual Framework Synthesis

In designing the assessment framework, the following steps have been followed:

I. Gleaning the main assessment elements from the selected literature.
II. Propose framework's main assessment criteria.
III. Allocate the identified elements of content analysis to the proposed criteria.
IV. Propose indicators to assess each criterion.

4 Related Works

Apart from research concerning general approaches of website evaluation and evaluation on websites subjected to commerce, government and education, there are several studies focusing on quality assessment of health-sector organisations' websites. In this section, we review the existing literature on latter ones.

Llinás et al. [5] evaluate and compare the user-orientation of Spanish, American and British hospital websites. In their descriptive study, they evaluate websites according to readability, accessibility and the quality of information provided. Lewiecki et al. [6] develop and evaluate measurement tools to determine the quality of osteoporosis websites for patients. They use indicators in the categories of content, credibility, navigability, currency, and readability. Moreno et al. [3] present a qualitative and user-oriented methodology for assessing quality of health-related websites based on a 2-tuple fuzzy linguistic approach. To identify the quality criteria set, a qualitative research has been carried out using the focus groups technique. According to the qualitative research results they define five quality dimensions, credibility, content, usability, external links and interactivity services. Huerta et al. [1] and Huerta et al. [7] assess the web presence of hospitals and their health systems based on five dimensions, accessibility, content, marketing, technology, and usability. Tsai and Chai [8] developed an evaluation questionnaire for nursing websites covering overall impression, download and switch speed, accessibility and convenience, web page content, and compatibility with common browsers. Randeree and Rao [9] consider the following factors for evaluating health sector websites: access/usability, audience, accuracy, timeliness, content, authority, and security. Guardiola-Wanden-Berghe et al. [10] conducted an observational, descriptive and cross-sectional study carried out using systematic check techniques, on assessment of documentary and content quality assessment of eating disorder websites. Rezniczek et al. [11] evaluate the quality of websites of Obstetrics and Gynecology departments in German-speaking countries using Google search rank, technical aspects, navigation and content as objective criteria. Maifredi et al. [12] explored the characteristics of the contents and the user-orientation of Italian hospital websites. The analysis considered Italian hospitals with a working website assessing technical characteristics, hospital information and facilities, medical services, interactive on-line services and external activities.

Bilsel et al. [13] present a quality evaluation model which consists of seven major e-service quality dimensions, including tangibles, reliability, responsiveness, confidence, empathy, quality of information, and integration of communication issues of websites. Moslehifar et al. [14] study focus in four different categories such as general information, accessibility of websites, functionality of websites, and facilities information provided in websites. Patsioura et al. [15] proposed framework focuses on three main criteria, information, communication and electronic services. Norum [16] evaluates the quality of Norwegian cancer hospitals' Websites according to general information, hospital details and technical aspects. Calvo [17] assesses the quality and describe characteristics of websites of large Spanish hospitals evaluating the global quality, accessibility, usability, interactivity, updating, quality model and information. Liu et al. [18], focus on the evaluation of quality of hospital websites in China using a pre-defined objective criterion based on content, function, design, and management & usage. Garcıa-Lacalle et al. [19] determine which factors have an influence on website adoption and level of development over time. The used checklist includes elements such as general information, contacting information, web linkage, quality of care, information for patients, information about resources and performance, site navigation and usability, health information, services provided to professionals and facilitating transactions. Gruca and Wakefield [20] evaluate the status of US hospital websites examining the following features: electronic documents, providing decision aids, linkages to partners, building trust via external verification, facilitating transactions, multiparty targeting, self-service information and discussion forums. The study conducted by Mira et al. [21] on the readability and accessibility of Spanish hospital websites concludes that they need to be more patient oriented because the websites visited did not fulfil even half of the readability and accessibility attributes required by widely used standards. Mancini et al. [22] found that the enforcement of accessibility regulations has helped to significantly improve hospital website accessibility in Italy.

5 Assessment Framework

Based on the analysis of the above evaluation studies, we propose four fundamental health sector website assessment criteria – Content, Technology, Services and Participation – which cover the whole spectrum of the identified assessment elements of our literature review.

Table 1 classifies the identified assessment elements found in literature into each of the four proposed assessment criteria.

Health sector website evaluators must be able to clearly identify whether specific goals or targets have been met and where adaptations to institution's website strategy appear to be necessary. Progress toward achieving health institutions web presence goals can be tracked by selecting specific indicators that correspond and evaluate each of these criteria (Table 2). The performance indicators enable measurement of progress towards the achievement of the key objectives for each criterion, which in turn permits the ongoing evaluation of success in implementing the hospital's website aimed strategy.

Table 1. Significant identified elements assigned to the proposed criteria

Study	Content	Technology	Services	Participation
[1]	Content	Technology, accessibility, usability	–	Marketing
[3]	Content, credibility	Usability, external links	–	Interactivity services
[5]	Address/contact, general information, services, patient information, research and teaching	Page features, page layout, page update, technical features	–	Patient interaction, media
[6]	Content, credibility, timeliness	Navigability, readability,	–	–
[7]	Content	Technology, accessibility, usability	–	Marketing
[8]	Overall Impression, Content	Download and switch speed, accessibility and convenience, browser compatibility	–	Interactivity services
[9]	Accuracy, authority, content, timeliness	Accessibility and usability, audience, security and privacy	–	–
[10]	Content, document features	–	–	–
[11]	Content	Navigation, technical aspects	–	Google search rank
[12]	Hospital information and facilities, hospitalization and medical services, external activities	Technical aspects	Appointments	Forum
[13]	Reliability, empathy, quality of information	Tangibles, responsiveness, assurance	Integration of communication	–
[14]	General information characteristics, functionality characteristics, facilities characteristics	Accessibility characteristics	–	–
[15]	Information gathering	–	Communication & transaction	–
[16]	General information, hospital information	Technical aspects	–	–
[17]	Presented information, updating the contents, quality references, information for the professionals, supplier information	Accessibility, usability	Interactivity and relationship with users	–
[18]	Function, content, design	Management & usage	–	–
[19]	General information, contacting information, web linkage, quality of care, information for patients, information about resources and performance	Site navigation and usability	–	Health information, services provided to professionals, facilitating transactions
[20]	Electronic documents, providing decision aids, linkages to partners, building trust via external verification	–	Facilitating transactions	Multiparty targeting, self-service information, discussion forums
[21]	–	Readability, accessibility	–	–
[22]	–	Accessibility	–	–

Table 2. Criteria and indicators allocated to each of them

Content	Technology	Services	Participation
• Hospital information • Quality metrics • Organisational structure • Medical information • Patient information • Research and teaching	• Navigability • Accessibility • Usability/readability • Credibility • Privacy/security	• Administration procedures • Appointments • Patient Care • Inter-hospital communication • Communication with Others	• Community interaction • Media • Advertising/marketing

5.1 Content

Content criterion evaluates the presence of information relevant to the user. It evaluates the quality, availability, relevancy, completeness and concise representation of specific information that it is expected to be provided in a health's sector institution website. Thereinafter the proposed indicators are analysed.

Hospital Information
Most of the hospitals provide general health information [10, 18]. The simplest health sector websites consist of electronic versions of their printed materials. Using these capabilities, a hospital website can provide up-to-date information in a cost-effective and involving manner. Hospital designation and logo on the home page are usually included in the home page [11, 14, 18, 20]. Almost all sites include information such as a general phone number for the hospital, fax number, postal address, e-mail address, VAT number, a map or directions to the hospital, parking information, transportation information and a history of the institution [5, 12, 13, 15, 16, 19, 20]. Additional elements are illustration of complementary services (press, cafeteria, Wi-Fi, telephone etc.), phone directory of the institution and emergency information [16]. Few take advantage of the available technology to provide a virtual tour of their facilities [5].

Quality Metrics
Public reporting of hospital quality data, empowers patients, referring physicians, and purchasers of health care with the information needed to make informed decisions regarding their care [20]. It also encourages hospitals and physicians to participate in continuous performance improvement by creating a healthy and competitive environment for better patient outcomes. Consequently, more and more hospitals are considering reporting their organizational quality metrics on their websites. Quality elements include the waiting list, the number of available beds, the admissions number report, the nosocomial infection rate, the inpatient mortality rate and the surgical mortality rate [14, 16, 17, 19].

Organisational Structure
The organisation chart depicts institution's structure, it defines the hierarchy and the different roles that are involved [5]. Emphasizing on openness and accountability and attempting to make the provided services more patient-centred, lead hospitals to publish their services charter. Essential information is the list of clinical services avail-able at the hospital, the list of outpatient hospital services available (consultation,

diagnostic services), the list of departments or units providing patient services, their relative working hours, their locations and their contact details [5, 9, 11, 12, 13, 14, 15, 16, 18, 19].

Medical Information

Hospital physicians should have their own place on a hospital's website given their importance to the success of a hospital. Clearly, there is an incentive for hospitals to link website visitors with doctors having an existing relationship with the hospital. For potential patients, an electronic version of doctors printed directory is essential [18]. Apart from the list of employed doctors, sites should include doctor's phone number, email address, picture, education/certification and relative practice information [6, 12, 18–20].

In this section health-disease specific information and relative treatment information is included [19]. It should also be provided the possibility to read online or to download health-care booklets and a medical glossary [12].

Patient Information

A clear description of patient's rights and obligations is essential. Information that should be adequately addressed is the related indications for hospital admission and discharge. The website contains different types of admission, information and rules to be followed on admission, during hospitalisation and discharge as well as information to obtain a copy of the medical documents [5, 12, 19]. It also provides information for visitors [5]. Details of how to pay prescription charges, about private consultations/services and fees and information for foreigners is provided in this section [14].

Research and Teaching

Many hospitals have a teaching mission. Those institutions include in their website, information about graduate medical education in general and information for medical students, undergraduate or postgraduate courses that are held at the hospital, schedule of activities that take place at the hospital (courses, workshops and conferences), scientific studies that the hospital promotes or is involved in and publications of the hospital itself [5, 20].

Hospital libraries represent the most accessible source for medical information and services. Doctors, nurses, and other health professionals request information from hospital libraries related to a current case or clinical situation. The ability of hospital's website to provide relative information about the library presence, address, working hours, publications catalogue and available services (reading, loans, copies) is important [5, 9].

5.2 Technology

This criterion appears to be a mixture of, mainly technical, items that relates to easy navigation, website quality, visual appeal, functionality and reliability. The technology criterion is related to how the content and services are assembled and made available on a website. Technology criterion is analysed in the following indicators.

Navigability

Navigability indicator examines the easiness that the user finds the required piece of information by moving through the website. Elements that are evaluated include effective use of hyperlinks and the degree to which the interface helps the user orient himself within the website [3, 5–7, 9, 12, 14].

Accessibility

Accessibility indicator refers to the practice of removing barriers that prevent inter-action with, or access to website, by people with disabilities or people with restricted computer literacy [1, 5, 7, 14, 17]. Elements that should be addressed include semantically meaningful HTML tags, textual equivalents provided for images, links named meaningfully, text and images that are large or enlargeable, flashing effects which are avoided or made optional, content that is written in plain language, compliance with WCAG W3C guidelines, compatibility with different browsers and access from various devices [1, 3, 5, 8, 11].

Usability/Readability

Usability indicator evaluates the ease of use of the website. Information should be presented concisely, without ambiguity and each item should be placed in the appropriate area [6, 8, 13]. Some of the common aspects of usability are simplicity, consistency, familiarity, clarity and relevancy [3, 8, 13, 19]. For prospective and current patients to effectively use the information available at a hospital's website, they must have a search tool [5, 8, 12, 14, 16]. A search engine allows a patient to locate information without knowing how the hospital has organized website's content. Other essential features include website map, content in foreign languages, quick load time, graphics that open conveniently, website pages that can be printed, individual sub-pages that have specific and meaningful titles [1, 5–9, 12, 14, 17].

Credibility

Because of the critical role of hospital websites in human's health, credibility indicator is critical. Elements that should be evaluated include author and date of the provided information and the text quality which should be grammatically and spelling correct [1, 3, 7, 9]. Interest conflict declaration, date of last website update, HON (Health on the Net) foundation code certification, webmaster characteristics and sources and references should be clearly listed [3, 5, 6, 8, 9, 10, 13, 15].

Privacy/Security

Health sector website privacy holds profound implications since service delivery impacts human life, legality and social policy. Related information presentation and dissemination has raised privacy concerns among both consumers and providers. A privacy policy describing the website's information practices should be easily accessible on the site [13]. Issues regarding patient confidentiality, copyright notice and terms of use, must be specifically addressed to become widely available [9, 18].

Inclusion of trust symbols (e.g. Verisign) allow a hospital website to stand out from the increasingly crowded internet marketplace. Security management tools and usage is an important part of the website. Other elements included in this indicator are general disclaimers, ownership of the site and provision of a secure website using encryption techniques (e.g. HTTPS) [3].

5.3 Services

The growth of consumerism and the proliferation of internet accessible sources of health-related information have modified the traditional roles of provider and patient. The trend towards creating individual patient profiles personalising the provided electronic services can bring many benefits to both hospital and patient. Personalised content can be provided during interactions with all users and this might improve loyalty to a particular hospital.

This criterion includes electronic healthcare scheduling, prescription renewal or drug acquisition, automation of hospital's back-office procedures, forms availability on website, electronic completion of administrative transactions and on-line appointments.

Administration Procedures

Health institutions can use online forms or provide standardised documents for downloading and uploading, to their users [5, 19]. In this way, they simplify and optimise the administrative interaction with their customers. Taking this notion one step further, they can establish the use of digitally signed documents enabling the full electronic administration cycle.

Experiences in other e-commerce areas create high expectations to hospital customers for what is possible. Hospital websites are expected to facilitate interaction between visitors and the hospital staff [15, 17]. In order to achieve cost savings and streamline the treatment, hospitals allow visitors to submit e-mail requests for general health information [3, 5, 17, 19, 20]. Some of them provide the capability for referring doctors to use e-mail referral forms or furthermore enable interactive communication applications [17].

Appointments

Translating visitor's interest in a hospital into action is one of the most important purposes of a hospital website. Online appointments and user membership registration are functions that should be included [14, 18]. Some hospitals enable their customers to interactively schedule appointments via web forms or via e-mail [12, 20]. These forms include the patient's phone numbers, address, reason for appointment, best time to reach and preferred location for appointment. Some websites include a printable checklist of items to bring to the hospital in the appointment [20].

Patient Care

Features evaluated in this indicator provide an important link between patients and hospitals. Supporting professional practice, asynchronous communication between the patient and the physician is implemented through email or through web-based message exchange systems [8, 13]. Some hospitals offer real-time chat sessions between doctors and patients, providing in this way the opportunity to the patient to pose follow-up questions [18]. Through their websites, hospitals provide access to patient's medical records system that creates and maintains all patient data electronically [9]. The system captures patient data, such as patient personal data, requests, lab orders, medications, diagnoses and procedures, at its source at the time of entry.

Inter-hospital Communication
Ubiquitous, secure electronic exchange of patient's clinical data and patient's record among hospitals/laboratories, through appropriate web interfaces, helps lessen the disruption from parallel electronic and paper-based medical record systems, thereby decreasing physician time costs and optimising service provision to the patient [23, 24].

Communication with Others
Electronic exchange of data and documents with other organisations, especially with public administration authorities, exploit the existing possibilities to automate bureaucratic procedures completion [3, 15].

5.4 Participation

Participation criterion is used to describe the interaction between hospital, patients and online communities on the web. Online communities often involve members to provide content to the website and contribute in some way. Examples of such include forums, complaints forms, interaction with the media and hospital's marketing activities. Hospital sites can host patient support groups, interact with community organisations and become a portal for physician organisations and private medical offices.

Community Interaction
Hospital websites are aim principally to communicate with existing or prospective patients. While many visitors to a hospital's website may have similar generic health questions or medical service needs, there is a significant heterogeneity across the entire visitor spectrum. Each patient has unique needs based on his health conditions. At the same time, the hospital must find ways to treat these widely-varied conditions efficiently. If hospitals can effectively meet patients' widely varying information needs by using internet technology rather than more personnel, they further their twin goals of better health for patients and higher efficiency [14]. One such technology is a threaded discussion forum (e.g. diseases, allergies, treatments etc.) where visitors can post questions, and receive answers that other visitors may also access easily [3, 8, 12, 19, 20]. They often use these tools to build a community of users to strengthen the relationship with their potential and current patients [13, 18]. In order to be effective, hospitals must make a commitment to moderate the forums and provide timely as well as accurate feedback to participants.

Media
Many hospitals exploit the immediacy of the web to report current news about the institution, press releases and internal announcements [5, 14, 17]. In addition to general health information, many hospitals also inform the community about health events [14, 20]. Using internet is more cost effective than printing and distributing calendars through postal mail. It is expected hospitals to allow visitors to sign-up for newsletter or e-mail notices of community health events of interest.

Marketing/Advertising
A hospital's website is one of its public faces [25]. Some hospitals use their websites to promote their work, and keep in touch with the different types of stakeholders [10, 14,

17, 19]. Hospitals can use their website to expand the reach of their medical practices to anyone with Internet access and advertise the international availability of their services [1, 7, 11].

Website sponsors and investors should be also clearly disclosed and possible advertising material should be differentiated form other content [6]. Social media applications can be included in this category (Facebook, Twitter, LinkedIn etc.) [14].

Financial information, including insurance details, can be included in their websites [14]. Hospital websites can be a convenient way for health care providers to analytically inform patients of their liability regarding insurance issues.

6 Conclusions and Future Work

Our review of related research has shown that hospital website assessment process can be based in four criteria, content, technical, services and participation. We identified 18 evaluation indicators which can be used to assess the above criteria.

Our framework has been designed to focus on how a specific health sector institution website applies its goals and objectives. The framework could help hospital management, health sector officials and website managers to understand causal links that show "how" and "where" a website is consistent with its strategy. This study should also be of interest to technology practitioners and researchers, as the findings shed light on the further development of performance measurements for hospital websites. To fulfil a strategic evaluation, we recommend that domain experts have a better understanding of the website's aims and evaluate the site according to those.

Next step of our research will be to determine specific metrics and relative weights for each indicator in order to implement a concrete assessment instrument for health sector institutions web presence. Hospital websites assessment instrument, apart for health institutions' managers, will allow patients to search for hospitals and compare them based on their performance on various quality measures.

In terms of practical application, we plan to use it in Portuguese hospital's website assessment and discuss the results with hospitals' management and health sector authorities. This will complement views expressed in individual discussions and group workshops, to assess practical acceptability in a better way.

Health-sector websites are the public face of most hospitals, integrating the hospital, the citizen, the physician, and the patient [9]. Website visitors will expect to complete their transactions with the hospital via the web. If they do not take advantage of the available technology to serve and interact effectively with their patients, then hospitals will have a greatly reduced role in many future health care decisions [20].

Acknowledgements. This paper is a result of the project "SmartEGOV: Harnessing EGOV for Smart Governance (Foundations, methods, Tools)/NORTE-01-0145-FEDER-000037", supported by Norte Portugal Regional Operational Programme (NORTE 2020), under the PORTUGAL 2020 Partnership Agreement, through the European Regional Development Fund (EFDR).

References

1. Huerta, T.R., Hefner, J.L., Ford, E.W., McAlearney, A.S., Menachemi, N.: Hospital website rankings in the United States: expanding benchmarks and standards for effective consumer engagement. J. Med. Internet Res. **16**(2) (2014)
2. Leonardi, M.J., McGory, M.L., Ko, C.Y.: Publicly available hospital comparison web sites: determination of useful, valid, and appropriate information for comparing surgical quality. Arch. Surg. **142**(9), 863–869 (2007)
3. Moreno, J.M., Del Castillo, J.M., Porcel, C., Herrera-Viedma, E.: A quality evaluation methodology for health-related websites based on a 2-tuple fuzzy linguistic approach. Soft Comput. **14**(8), 887–897 (2010)
4. Berwick, D.M., Nolan, T.W., Whittington, J.: The triple aim: care, health, and cost. Health Affairs (Millwood) **27**(3), 759–769 (2008)
5. Reid, P., Borycki, E.M.: Emergence of a new consumer health informatics framework: introducing the healthcare organization. Stud. Health Technol. Inform. **164**, 353–357 (2011)
6. European Commission, eHealth Action Plan 2012–2020 - innovative healthcare for the 21st century (2012)
7. Shields, P.M., Tajalli, H.: Intermediate theory: the missing link in successful student scholarship. J. Public Affairs Educ. **12**(3), 313–334 (2006)
8. Llinás, G., Rodríguez-Iñesta, D., Mira, J.J., Lorenzo, S., Aibar, C.: A comparison of websites from Spanish, American and British Hospitals. Methods Inf. Med. **47**, 124–130 (2008)
9. Lewiecki, E.M., Rudolph, L.A., Kiebzak, G.M., Chavez, J.R., Thorpe, B.M.: Assessment of osteoporosis-website quality. Osteoporos. Int. **17**(5), 741–752 (2006)
10. Huerta, T.R., Walker, D.M., Ford, E.W.: An evaluation and ranking of children's hospital websites in the United States. J. Med. Internet Res. **18**(8) (2016)
11. Tsai, S.L., Chai, S.K.: Developing and validating a nursing website evaluation questionnaire. J. Adv. Nurs. **49**(4), 406–413 (2005)
12. Randeree, E., Rao, H.R.: E-health and assurance: curing hospital websites. Int. J. Electron. Healthc. **1**(1), 33–46 (2004)
13. Guardiola-Wanden-Berghe, R., Sanz-Valero, J., Wanden-Berghe, C.: Quality assessment of the website for eating disorders: a systematic review of a pending challenge. Ciencia & Saude Coletiva **17**(9), 2489–2497 (2012)
14. Rezniczek, G.A., Küppers, L., Heuer, H., Hefler, L.A., Buerkle, B., Tempfer, C.B.: Quality of websites of obstetrics and gynecology departments: a cross-sectional study. BMC Pregnancy Childbirth **15**(1), 103 (2015)
15. Maifredi, G., Orizio, G., Bressanelli, M., Domenighini, S., Gasparotti, C., Perini, E., Caimi, L., Schulz, P.J., Gelatti, U.: Italian hospitals on the web: a cross-sectional analysis of official websites. BMC Med. Inform. Decis. Mak. **10**(1), 17 (2010)
16. Bilsel, R.U., Büyüközkan, G., Ruan, D.: A fuzzy preference? Ranking model for a quality evaluation of hospital web sites. Int. J. Intell. Syst. **21**(11), 1181–1197 (2006)
17. Moslehifar, M.A., Noor, A.I., Sandaran, S.C.: Assessing the quality of trust features on website content of top hospitals for medical tourism consumers. Malays. J. Commun. **2**(1), 469–489 (2016)
18. Patsioura, F., Kitsiou, S., Markos, A.: Evaluation of Greek public hospital websites. In: ICE-B - International Conference on e-Business, Proceedings, pp. 223–229 (2009)
19. Norum, J.: Evaluation of Norwegian cancer hospitals' web sites and explorative survey among cancer patients on their use of the internet. J. Med. Internet Res. **3**(4) (2001)
20. Calvo-Calvo, M.A.: Quality and characteristics of websites of large Spanish hospitals. Rev. Esp. Doc. Cient. **37**(1) (2014)

21. Liu, X., Bao, Z., Liu, H., Wang, Z.: The quality and characteristics of leading general hospitals' Websites in China. J. Med. Syst. **35**(6), 1553–1562 (2011)
22. García-Lacalle, J., Pina, V., Royo, S.: The unpromising quality and evolution of Spanish public hospital web sites. Online Inf. Rev. **35**(1), 86–112 (2011)
23. Gruca, T.S., Wakefield, D.S.: Hospital web sites: promise and progress. J. Bus. Res. **57**(9), 1021–1025 (2004)
24. Mira, J.J., Llinás, G., Tomás, O., Pérez-Jover, V.: Quality of websites in Spanish public hospitals. Med. Inform. Internet Med. **31**(1), 23–44 (2006)
25. Mancini, C., Zedda, M., Barbaro, A.: Health information in Italian public health websites: moving from inaccessibility to accessibility. Health Inform. Libr. J. **22**(4), 276–285 (2005)

Organizational Learning to Leverage Benefits Realization Management; Evidence from a Municipal eHealth Effort

Kirsti Askedal[1(✉)], Leif Skiftenes Flak[1], Hans Solli-Sæther[2], and Detmar W. Straub[3]

[1] University of Agder, Gimlemoen 25, 4604 Kristiansand, Norway
kirsti.askedal@uia.no
[2] Norwegian University of Science and Technology, Larsgårdsvegen 2, 6009 Ålesund, Norway
[3] Georgia State University, Atlanta, GA 30302-4015, USA

Abstract. While work with benefits realization requires organizational learning to be effective, emphasis on organizational learning is hard to find in benefits realization studies. To remedy this research gap, we study how organizational learning theory can contribute to improve benefits realization processes. A qualitative approach was used to gain in depth understanding of benefits realization in an ICT healthcare services project. We found that individual learning is present, but organizational learning has not been given explicit attention neither in the project nor in the literature of benefits realization management. We argue that the individual learning in the project forms an excellent basis for organizational learning, i.e., in the form of organizational structures, routines, and methods for benefits realization.

Keywords: Benefits management · Organizational learning theory · Complex organizations · Public sector · eHealth

1 Introduction

To prepare for the rapid demographic changes and the increased number of citizens suffering from non-communicable and compounded diseases [1, 2], the healthcare sector is dependent on innovation to manage future service-provision. This, among other topics, is emphasized by the European Commission when they included *Health, Demographic Change and Wellbeing* in their framework for research and innovation, *Horizon 2020* [3].

Where will this innovation occur? Information and communication technologies (ICTs), a wide range of which are being implemented into the healthcare sector [4, 5], are interventions supporting people in living safe and independent in their own homes; they can also improve quality of life and provide efficient and effective services. Even though there is enthusiasm to use information and communication technology (ICT) in healthcare services [6], adoption often occurs without a true understanding of the added value of ICT to healthcare service or a comprehensive evaluation of the health impact [4, 6, 7].

M. Janssen et al. (Eds.): EGOV 2017, LNCS 10428, pp. 142–153, 2017.
DOI: 10.1007/978-3-319-64677-0_12

In the field of eHealth, it seems difficult to realize expected benefits [5, 8, 9] and varying levels of effects are reported by patients and healthcare professionals [6, 10]. Hofmann [11] argues it should be seen as a moral problem, i.e., not having knowledge of the effects of technology, as ICT is rapidly being adopted into many countries' healthcare services. Authorities have been hesitant in making benefit realization approaches a requirement, but are eager to better understand the potential benefits and how to produce them [12].

Several benefits realization tools for public sector have been developed and these are increasingly being adopted by praxis [12, 13]. There is, however, little empirical evidence of the benefits realization process as it occurs in practice [14]. As technology is seen as a helping tool for managing the future challenges in the healthcare services and are progressively being integrated into the healthcare services, there is a need for research to document whether ICT contributes and how the public sector should work to secure such gains.

Learning to use benefits management tools and methods is generally related to a common understanding of those representatives involved in the effort. They are typically healthcare professionals with little or no experience with benefits realization management. However, to increase benefits realization, means identifying potential benefits and manage the process. Thus, knowledgeable representatives are key. For health care professionals to become knowledgeable they must learn and experience from the process. Our approach to learning and knowledge is based on how individual knowledge is central in the organizational learning [15].

The research question for our study is: How can organizational learning affect complex benefits realization?

2 Theory

This section introduces benefits management [16] and organizational learning theory [17] as appropriate analytic lenses for our study. Benefits management emphasizes organizational development and innovation, includes a wide range of potential benefits, and looks at what is appropriate for addressing the complexity in public sector relevant to explicit stakeholder foci. Organization learning theory states that, in order to be competitive in a changing environment, organizations must change their goals and actions to reach these goals. In the public sector, individual learning transforms into organizational learning when information is shared and stored in the organization memory in such a way that it influences rules, values, attitudes and actions.

2.1 Benefits Management Model

In the middle of 1990s, a process model of benefits management was developed through a research project in benefits management at the Cranefield School of Management Information System Research Centre (ISRS) [18]. With experiences from many organizations, this model has been extended and refined, and presented in detail in the book to Ward and Daniel [16]; Benefits Management: *Delivering Value from IS & IT Investments.*

Working with benefits realization, trough the model to Ward and Daniel [16] is like an iterative process. The model emphasizes organization development and innovation and consists of five stages, with different activities related to each stage, illustrated in Fig. 1.

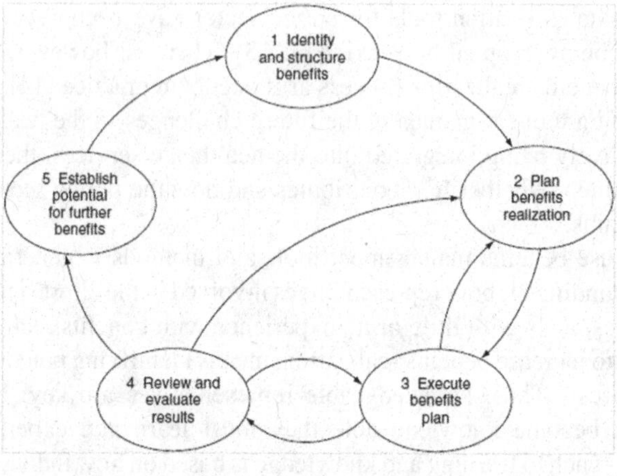

Fig. 1. Benefits management model [16, p. 105].

Ward and Daniel [16] point out that there is an inherent interdependency of benefits realization and change management in their approach and that is the reason why they call it Benefits Management. This state that it is not only about the implementation of technology, but also changes in the organizational processes, the roles and working practices individually or in team inside the organizations and in some cases outside the organizations. The term Benefits Management is defined by [16, p. 36] as: *"The process of organizing and managing such that the potential benefits arising from the use of IS/IT are actually realized*".

Even though there are different models of the benefits management process, the main principles are often similar to the Ward and Daniels model [16] and their model has also been an inspiration for the Norwegian work in that field [12, 13].

It is important to understand the strategic context in which IT investments are being made [16], and for this reason, we state that the context for our research is municipal health organizations. A characterizing feature of public organizations is the diversity of different stakeholders and competing interests [19]. Unlike the private sector, the public sector must strive to develop services which can be used by everyone in the community [16].

A critical issue in enabling organizations to realize benefits from IT investments, is the ability of the organization to embed individual learning into organizational structures and routines [16]. During the benefits realization process, learning occurs on the individual level among the people that carry out the various analyses comprising the benefits realization method. However, translating these insights into organizational learning does not happen automatically but require specific attention from the organization.

2.2 Organizational Learning Theory

Organizational learning occurs when individuals within an organization experience a problematic situation and inquire into it on behalf of the organization. In order to transcend to the organizational level, learning that results from organizational inquiries must become embedded in the images of organization held in its members' minds and/or in the epistemological artefacts (e.g., the cognitive maps, memories or programs) embedded in the organizational environment [17]. Single loop learning adjusts the action, but not the objectives behind the activity. Double loop learning alters or rejects the established governing objectives and produces a major and fundamental change in the organization's mission. Double loop learning is thus closely linked to an organization's ability to develop and increase their performance, e.g. by realizing benefits from IS & IT investments.

Senge [20] points out that learning organizations engaged in systematic organizational development depend on five conditions for success. These five conditions are: (1) to facilitate personal mastery; (2) to create mental models; (3) to build a shared vision; (4) to develop group learning through good leadership; and (5) to engage in systems thinking. The idea is that the whole will be greater than the sum of the parts. This can be done e.g. by including employees in benefits realization and change management. Ownership to the process will facilitate individual learning, which can build group learning (project) and ultimately organizational learning.

Nonaka and Takeuchi [21] introduced the SECI-model which has become the cornerstone of knowledge creation and transfer theory, illustrated in Fig. 2.

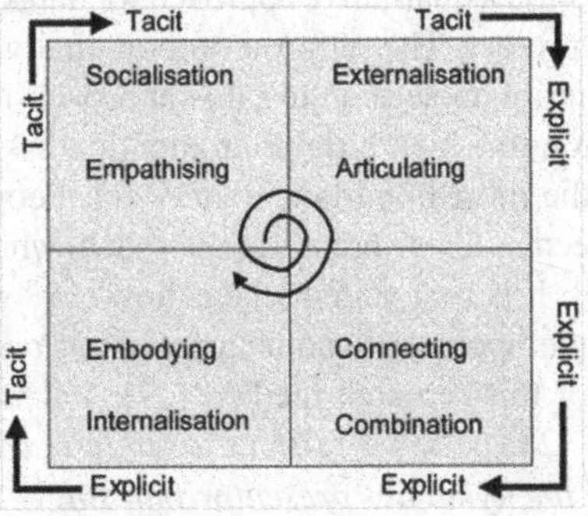

Fig. 2. The SECI-process [22, p. 12].

The four dimensions of the model – socialization, externalization, combination, and internalization – explain how tacit and explicit knowledge are converted into organizational learning. The first dimension, socialization, is explained to be the process of converting tacit knowledge through shared experiences like spending time together. When tacit knowledge is articulated into explicit knowledge it is called externalization, who is the second dimension in the SECI-process. Explicit knowledge can be shared with others, e.g. in processes and routines, and become basis of new knowledge. The third dimension is called combination, and occurs when explicit knowledge is converted into more systematic and complex sets of explicit knowledges, and distributed to the members of the organization. Internalization is the fourth dimension, and happens when explicit knowledge created and shared in the organization is converted into individual tacit knowledge. When individual tacit knowledge is shared with others, it can start a new spiral of knowledge creation [22].

Organizations that share knowledge and experience contribute to innovation and learning across organizational boundaries and thus create benefits for one or more partners. Knowledge sharing is focused both on creating new knowledge, sharing knowledge, and applying knowledge. Sometimes knowledge sharing is perceived to be difficult to carry out. There can be structural, political, personal or cultural obstacles or barriers that must be overcome. Legislation can be such an obstacle for ICT in healthcare services.

To synthesize our brief review of the benefits management and organizational learning literature, we suggest that a benefits management model for improving benefits realization in an organization can be combined with organization learning. The first challenge is to properly understand the strategic context and conduct the activities of identification, planning, execution, reviewing, and establishing potential for further benefits. The second challenge is to move from individual learning to organizational learning. This challenge involves probing how organizations can take interpreted knowledge held by individuals and use it to change organizational actions/goals.

3 Method

Based on the research question a qualitative approach for data collection was considered most appropriate for this project. The purpose of a qualitative approach is to obtain a richer description of the problem setting and this approach is especially useful when investigating a phenomenon to which little prior attention has been paid [23].

Case study is one of the most important sources for theory development in social science [24], and can be seen as a non-proactive approach, who "study the phenomenon after the fact" [25, p. 326]. It is best suited when "how" or "why" questions are being sat and when focus is a contemporary phenomenon within a real-life context [26]. There are different definitions for this research method [27], and we apply the definition of case study by Eisenhardt [28, p. 534]: "*The case study is a research strategy which focuses on understanding the dynamics present within single settings*".

Based on the need for knowledge about benefits realization process, this project is designed as a single-case study, with an interpretive approach. We have followed the five components of case study research design proposed by Yin [26, p. 29] where the unit of analysis is the knowledge creation process in complex benefits realization setting, within a municipal healthcare context. Data is collected through participant-observation (see Sect. 3.1. for details about the role of the researcher), and field notes are analyzed as an interactive process among the researchers with use of different interrelated elements illustrated in Creswell [29, p. 185].

3.1 Case Description

In 2015, one municipality in Norway, on behalf of two counties (made up of 30 municipalities), was asked by the central government to establish a Response Central for managing safety alarms and other sensors for recipients of municipal healthcare services.

After the business plan for the Response Central was developed and parallel to other important clarifications (i.e., how to cooperate with other municipalities in the region, and preparation for procurement), it was decided by the steering committee to focus on benefits realization. One of the researchers was given the task of managing the benefits realization process, hence referred to as the benefits realization process manager. As it was considered to be extensive and time-consuming to agree on a common benefits realization plan across the potential cooperation partners (municipalities), the initial aim was to develop a general benefits realization plan for one of the municipalities, with an intention to share the document with the cooperation partners as a starting point for them to manage benefits realization process in their own organizations.

Different methodologies for benefits realization were reviewed. The KommIT methodology [30] was considered by the benefits realization process manager to be the most transparent and useful for this project. This methodology is inspired by the work of Ward and Daniel [16]. Table 1 illustrate the different stages from the two stated methodologies and how they relate. The project is still running with only results from stage 1 and part of stage 2 of the methodology being completed.

Table 1. Overview of the stages for benefits management model [16] and KommIT methodology [30]

Benefit management model	KommIT methodology
1. Identify and structure benefits	1. Concept; identify and assess benefits
2. Plan benefits realization	2. Plan; plan benefits realization
3. Execute benefits plan	3. Execute; manage benefits realization during project
4. Review and evaluate results	4. Hand over; hand over benefits realization from project to operation
5. Establish potential for further benefits	5. Realize; benefits realization in operation

4 Results

During a three-month period, a number of activities were conducted following the KommIT methodology. This resulted in important and necessary discussions among key stakeholders. Several inputs were fruitful for benefits realization in this specific case, but the core discussion was related to the benefits realization process in general. It was the first time this specific methodology was used in this sector and the benefits realization process manager had no practical experiences with it in advance. Thus, the project was dependent on and tried to strictly follow the methodology. Based on experiences to a given point in time, some minor changes were made to secure progress and maintain the schedule.

In the following, the purpose and challenges of the two stages will be outlined. Then, an overview of individual learning related to the stages from the perspective of the benefits realization process manager will be presented (Table 1).

4.1 Stage 1 - Concept; Identify and Assess Benefits

According to the KommIT methodology, the purpose of this partial stage is to analyze potential benefits linked to the specific ICT-project. What kind of positive effects can the municipality expect? Will there be changes in work-processes? Who are the stakeholders? Are the changes sufficient to justify the project?

One of the main challenges in managing this stage was related to stakeholders' insecurity about the purpose for the benefits realization process. The decision to establish the Response Central was taken before the project were started and was the driver for this process. Some of the stakeholders expressed skepticism based on experiences from similar processes, where identified benefits and assumptions for savings have had a directly negative impact on their budgets without taking the necessary prerequisites into account. Questions like: "Is the process just a cover for justifying the investment" arose.

Given the skepticism in the organization towards change and the fact that the project affected several departments, all the units were invited to process for identifying benefits during this stage. Some of the stakeholders were concerned that this would be just another shadow process. However, it seems that all of the stakeholders were satisfied with the thorough review of the concept and the possibility of asking clarifying questions. This involvement led to project ownership and important stakeholders were identified. However, it seemed difficult to achieve the desired openness, due to a major stakeholder focus on prerequisites and emphasizing that the defined benefits merely showed a potential. Because of this suspicion, some vital information may have been held back.

4.2 Stage 2 - Plan; Plan Benefits Realization

The KommIT methodology next suggests that the planning stage purpose is to link identified benefits to specific targets, define measurement indicators, actions, and assign responsibility for benefits realization to stakeholders in the organization. This phase starts after the project is accepted based on the benefits analysis in the previous phase.

The principles underpinning the development of the benefits realization plan appear simple and easy to implement. Developing a benefits realization plan across different units within one organization was, however, challenging in praxis because the plan needed to be broadly accepted in the organization to ensure benefits realization. The stakeholders had different perspectives to the identified benefits. Some were only willing to pay attention to qualitative effects, like safety and service quality, but others were willing to discuss direct or indirect economic benefits as well. This may be related to organizational roles or professional background. Most of the identified benefits proved to be qualitative as the organizational changes and ICT investment will affect the budget in a negative way the next years. In short term, this project will cost a lot of money, but in long term, the investment can help to prepare for the future challenges the healthcare services are facing. When it was experienced to be challenging in one organization with different units, developing the same plan for a consortium of organizations, thought to be the overall goal at the start, is obviously even more challenging.

Since this was the first time a benefits realization process was conducted systematically in the healthcare services in the municipality, there were no established structures for where to discuss and ask for advice throughout the process. The benefits realization process manager had to rely on the method and justify for stakeholders both "why focus on benefits realization in general" and facilitating the benefits realization process in the specific circumstance. General organizational guidance for managing processes like this would have been very useful in a project which involves several departments in one organization/across different organizations.

Table 2 summarizes the individual learning in the project based on experiences from stages 1 and 2 from the perspective of the benefits realization process manager.

Table 2. Individual learning from the KommIT methodology stages in Praxis

Stage	Individual learning from stage
1. Concept: identify and consider benefits	1. An agreement of purpose for the benefits realization process and the investment is critical. To communicate a clear problem understanding at the grass root level is needed 2. A combination of competence (e.g. healthcare, technical and innovation) is necessary for modeling current and future work-processes 3. Analyzing changes in work-processes and identifying benefits are important activities for stakeholder involvement and ownership of the benefits realization process and the project in general 4. The identified benefits at this point outlines potential, and it is important to identify and be aware of the prerequisites 5. Due to a constantly evolving project, stakeholder analysis must be seen as an iterative process 6. A thorough stakeholder analysis is critical to ensure an adequate change management process and high degree of realization of the identified benefits 7. If an action (here the Response Central) to a challenge is determined in advance, an analysis of benefits is a demanding activity due to the stakeholders' uncertainty about the motive for the benefits realization process
2. Plan: plan benefits realization	1. Organizational support is needed to manage a benefits realization process in complex projects and organizations 2. A distinct unit for managing processes like this had been very useful in a project who involves several departments in one organization/across different organizations 3. A benefits realization plan has limited value unless accepted broadly in the organization. This requires substantial effort

5 Discussion

Organizational learning capability is related to both organizational and managerial characteristics and factors that enable the organizational learning process [31]. Dimensions of a learning organization consist of: continuous learning, dialogue and inquiry, collaboration and team learning, systems to capture learning, empowered employees, connected organizations, and strategic leadership [32].

The issue of organizational learning has not been given explicit attention in the benefits realization literature. We argue that this is a major shortcoming and that organizational learning is instrumental in enabling organizations to realize benefits from their ICT investments. We consider organizational learning theory to be a valuable contribution to the benefits realization literature and propose that the practical benefits realization methods should incorporate mechanisms for organizational learning.

The individual learning outlined in Table 2 provides a good basis and can give input to necessary organizational learning. E.g. the need for a broad competence base when modelling processes in Stage 1 indicate that the organization should facilitate exactly this in future endeavors. Further, the expressed need for a distinct coordination unit in Stage 2 suggest that the organization needs to establish such a unit to support similar future efforts. Gladly, the organization in the present case are these days planning to establish a portfolio office, who will be responsible for coordinate and manage projects and help department managers to run processes like this. More examples of how individual learning can be transferred into organizational learning can be found in Table 3.

Results presented from this case can be seen in relation with three of the dimensions presented in the SECI-process [22]. The trigger for the knowledge creating process was the steering committee's focus on benefits realization, and the available methodologies (e.g. KommIT methodology) for running such processes in public sector provided by other organizations (internalization). The benefits realization process manager had some tacit knowledge and this were converted through shared experiences when stakeholders in the project spending time together through this process (socialization). The individual tacit knowledge gained from the process has in this paper being articulated into explicit knowledge (externalization). One part of this dimension is illustrated in Table 2, and another can be viewed in Table 3, where suggestions of how to transfer individual learning (tacit knowledge) into organizational learning (explicit knowledge) is presented. The suggestions to organizational learning from this case can be used for input to the portfolio office, and maybe be implemented in future projects and revised methodologies for benefits realization in public sector (combination).

In summary, we propose the following two additions to existing benefits realization methods: (1) Individual learning should be specified and (2) Individual learning should be translated into organizational learning.

Table 2 summarized the individual learning from the case. Table 3 illustrates how individual learning can be transformed into organizational learning.

Table 3. Examples of transferring individual learning into organizational learning

Stage	Individual learning from stage	Suggestions to organizational learning
1. Concept: identify and consider benefits	1. An agreement of purpose for the benefits realization process and the investment is critical. To communicate a clear problem understanding at the grass root level is needed 2. A combination of competence (e.g. healthcare, technical and innovation) is necessary for modeling current and future work-processes 3. Analyzing changes in work-processes and identifying benefits are important activities for stakeholder involvement and ownership of the benefits realization process and the project in general 4. The identified benefits at this point outlines potential, and it is important to identify and be aware of the prerequisites 5. Due to a constantly evolving project, stakeholder analysis must be seen as an iterative process 6. A thorough stakeholder analysis is critical to ensure an adequate change management process and high degree of realization of the identified benefits 7. If an action (here the Response Central) to a challenge is determined in advance, an analysis of benefits is a demanding activity due to the stakeholders' uncertainty about the motive for the benefits realization process	• Stimulate the organization to be adaptable to change • Communicate accurate and clear information at different levels in the organization • Use standardized methodology for project- and benefits realization • Ensure that persons involved in the project (in different stages and activities) have the right skills and competence for the tasks • Allocate sufficient resources, both human and economical
2. Plan: plan benefits realization	1. Organizational support is needed to manage a benefits realization process in complex projects and organizations 2. A distinct unit for managing processes like this had been very useful in a project who involves several departments in one organization/across different organizations 3. A benefits realization plan has limited value unless accepted broadly in the organization. This requires substantial effort	• Clarify roles and descriptions of who is responsible for change management, benefits realization management. This needs to be communicated and well known in the organization • Establish a unit for support and advise in such processes (e.g. a portfolio office)

6 Conclusion

This study explored the research question "How can organizational learning affect complex benefits realization?". Based on a qualitative case study of a complex benefits realization effort in a health care context, we derived several individual learning points based on the benefits realization process manager´s experiences. The nature of the learning points suggests that the organization would benefit from embedding these insights into revised practice in future benefits realization efforts or put another way; ignoring the individual learning would be likely to cause frustration and low organizational performance in future efforts. On this basis, we suggest two contributions to the benefits realization methods: (1) Individual learning should be specified and (2) Individual learning should be translated into organizational learning. We used the case to illustrate how individual learning can be transformed into organizational learning.

7 Implications

Although it is developed several benefits realization tools for public sector, there is little evidence on the benefits realization process in practice [14]. This study highlights the process, focusing on municipal health- and care services. It also sees a benefits realization method in the perspective of organizational learning theory. The result can be used as a guide for enabling organizations to realize benefits from IT investments and how they can embed individual learning into organizational structures and routines. This project will hopefully lead to better benefits realization processes when implementing technology in practice, and to develop already existing benefits realization tools.

References

1. Barnett, K., et al.: Epidemiology of multimorbidity and implications for health care, research, and medical education: a cross-sectional study. Lancet **380**(9836), 37–43 (2012)
2. World Health Organization: 10 facts of ageing and the life course. http://www.who.int/features/factfiles/ageing/en/ (2014)
3. European Commission: Health, Demographic Change and Wellbeing. http://ec.europa.eu/programmes/horizon2020/en/h2020-section/health-demographic-change-and-wellbeing (2014)
4. Martin, S., Kelly, G., Kernohan, W.G., McCreight, B., Nugent, C.: Smart home technologies for health and social care support. Cochrane Database Syst. Rev. (4), CD006412 (2008). doi:10.1002/14651858.CD006412.pub2
5. Henderson, C., et al.: Cost-effectiveness of telecare for people with social care needs: the Whole Systems Demonstrator cluster randomised trial. Age Ageing **43**(6), 794–800 (2014)
6. Wootton, R.: Twenty years of telemedicine in chronic disease management—an evidence synthesis. J. Telemed. Telecare **18**(4), 211–220 (2012)
7. World Health Organization: Connecting for health: Global Vision, Local Insight. http://www.who.int/ehealth/resources/wsis_report/en/ (2005)
8. Essén, A., Conrick, M.: New e-service development in the homecare sector: beyond implementing a radical technology. Int. J.Med. Inform. **77**(10), 679–688 (2008)
9. Henderson, C., et al.: Cost effectiveness of telehealth for patients with long term conditions (Whole Systems Demonstrator telehealth questionnaire study): nested economic evaluation in a pragmatic, cluster randomised controlled trial. BMJ **346**, f1035 (2013)
10. Steventon, A., et al.: Effect of telehealth on use of secondary care and mortality: findings from the Whole System Demonstrator cluster randomised trial. BMJ **344**, e3874 (2012)
11. Hofmann, B.: Ethical challenges with welfare technology: a review of the literature. Sci. Eng. Ethics **19**(2), 389–406 (2013)
12. Flak, L.: Gevinstrealisering og offentlige IKT-investeringer. Universitetsforlaget AS, Oslo (2012)

13. Hellang, Ø., Flak, L.S., Päivärinta, T.: Diverging approaches to benefits realization from public ICT investments: a study of benefits realization methods in Norway. Transform. Gov. People Process Policy **7**(1), 93–108 (2013)
14. Ashurst, C., Doherty, N.F., Peppard, J.: Improving the impact of IT development projects: the benefits realization capability model. Eur. J. Inf. Syst. **17**(4), 352–370 (2008)
15. Chiva, R., Alegre, J.: Organizational learning and organizational knowledge: towards the integration of two approaches. Manag. Learn. **36**(1), 49–68 (2005)
16. Ward, J., Daniel, E.: Benefits Management: Delivering Value from IS & IT Investments. Wiley Series in Information Systems. Wiley, Chichester (2006)
17. Argyris, C.S., Schön, D.: Organizational Learning II: Theory, Method and Practice. Addison-Wesley, Reading, PA (1996)
18. Ward, J., Taylor, P., Bond, P.: Evaluation and realisation of IS/IT benefits: an empirical study of current practice. Eur. J. Inform. Syst. **4**(4), 214–225 (1996)
19. Pang, M.-S., Lee, G., DeLone, W.H.: IT resources, organizational capabilities, and value creation in public-sector organizations: a public-value management perspective. J. Inform. Technol. **29**(3), 187–205 (2014)
20. Senge, P.: The Fifth Discipline: The Art and Practice of the Learning Organization. Crownb Pub., Fort Collins (2006)
21. Nonaka, I., Takeuchi, H.: The Knowledge Creating Company: How Japanese Companies Create the Dynamics of Innovation. Oxford University Press, New York, NY (1995)
22. Nonaka, I., Toyama, R., Konno, N.: SECI, BA and leadership: a unified model of dynamic knowledge creation. Long Range Plan. **33**(1), 5–34 (2000)
23. Johannessen, A., Tufte, P.A., Kristoffersen, L.: Introduksjon til samfunnsvitenskapelig metode. Abstrakt forlag as, Oslo (2005)
24. Andersen, S.S.: Casestudier: forskningsstrategi, generalisering og forklaring. Fagbokforlaget, Oslo (2013)
25. Cole, R., Purao, S., Rossi, M., Sein, M.: Being proactive: where action research meets design research. In: ICIS Proceedings, 27 (2005)
26. Yin, R.K.: Case Study Research: Design and Methods. Sage, London (2013)
27. Gerring, J.: What is a case study and what is it good for? Am. Polit. Sci. Rev. **98**(02), 341–354 (2004)
28. Eisenhardt, K.M.: Building theories from case study research. Acad. Manag. Rev. **14**(4), 532–550 (1989)
29. Creswell, J.W.: Research Design: Qualitative, Quantitative, and Mixed Methods Approaches, 3rd edn. Sage, London (2009)
30. The Norvegian Association of Local and Regional Authorities: Gevinstkokebok for IKT-prosjekter i norske kommuner. http://www.ks.no/contentassets/af1d839033564d188081b64e8eec02a8/13224-ks-kommit-gevinstkokebok.pdf (2013)
31. Chiva, R., Alegre, J., Lapiedra, R.: Measuring organisational learning capability among the workforce. Int. J. Manpower **28**(3/4), 224–242 (2007)
32. Marsick, V.J.: The dimensions of a learning organization questionnaire: introduction to the special issue examining DLOQ use over a decade. Adv. Dev. Hum. **15**(2), 127–132 (2013)

Towards a Repository of e-Government Capabilities

Soumaya I. Ben Dhaou(✉)

United Nations University, Operating Unit on Policy-Driven Electronic Governance (UNU-EGOV), Guimarães, Portugal
bendhaou@unu.edu

Abstract. The paper aims to contribute to the development of an e-Government capabilities repository. The purpose of this repository is to increase the level of success of the e-Government projects and initiatives. The results are based on an examination of a multidisciplinary body of knowledge, an iterative structured methodology and a comparative in-depth case study performed in two Canadian public administrations. We analyzed the data to identify the presence or absence of the capabilities, the evolution of these capabilities and their interrelationship. We proposed a preliminary knowledge repository of e-Government capabilities composed of 4 interdependent categories: the strategic capabilities, the project capabilities, the business capabilities and the technological capabilities.

Keywords: e-Government · Organizational capabilities · Dynamic capabilities · Repository · Case study

1 Introduction

The goal of this paper is to present a work-in-progress towards the development of an e-Government capabilities repository. The aim of this repository is to support Government and public administration (PA) in the development, deployment and/or renewal of their e-Government transformation strategy.

This repository can be presented as a reference guide to the required capabilities for the successful deployment of an e-Government initiative or project. It can help governments, particularly from developing countries, to increase the level of success and avoid risk in undertaking any types of e-Government initiatives and organizational change. In other words, this repository may be utilized as a tool for PA, ministries and public agencies, firstly for identifying the needed capabilities prior to starting any e-Government initiatives related to electronic service delivery; when they develop their e-Government project/strategy or when they face challenges and difficulties during the e-Government development process. Secondly, it will also serve as a diagnostic tool for defining what are the existing capabilities that can be leveraged for the e-Government deployment and evaluating the strength and weaknesses of these capabilities. Thirdly, this repository will help clearly define the gap between the required capabilities and the existing one in the PA and facilitate the organizational change.

M. Janssen et al. (Eds.): EGOV 2017, LNCS 10428, pp. 154–165, 2017.
DOI: 10.1007/978-3-319-64677-0_13

This preliminary version of the repository is developed based on in-depth case studies realized in two different Canadian PA. The e-Government transformation is studied here using a strategic management and capabilities perspective. This perspective provided a rich and in-depth observation of the phenomenon studied.

This paper starts by introducing a brief description of the theoretical framework. Then, the methodology is described, followed by the comparison between the studied cases. Finally, in the results section, the first version of the e-Government capabilities repository is presented.

2 Theoretical Background

The goal of this section is to introduce the theoretical framework of organizational capabilities proposed in the literature that serve as starting point for our research.

The organizational capability concept was intensively studied in the strategic Management field. Several researches were dedicated to define and simplify the understanding of the organizational capabilities concept (Amit and Schoemaker 1993; Collis 1994; Grant 1991; Zollo and Winter 2002). Based on the synthesis of these definitions, an e-Government capability is defined for this research as the leveraging, the combination and the coordination of resources, competencies and knowledge through different processes to set up e-Government project (or initiative).

The presence of organizational capability is firstly based on the identification or the existence in the organization or availability outside of the organization of resources, competencies and knowledge. Secondly, it is through specific processes and at a certain point in time that the organizational capabilities are effectively materialized.

This definition implies that any strategic initiatives or project is based on the existence in the organization of capabilities (Renard and Soparnot 2010). When an organization is planning to set up and/or deploy its strategy, it should previously identify and assess its available organizational capabilities. Depending on the situation and the strategic objectives the organization wants to achieve, they will determine which organizational capabilities are required to be mobilized at which level and which capabilities will need to be created, acquired or developed. Referring to an organizational capabilities knowledge repository can facilitate this activity. This repository will play the role of diagnostic tool for the organization where we can retrieve a classification of needed organizational capabilities for a specific strategy.

St-Amant and Renard (2004) proposed a first body of knowledge (BoK) for e-Government service delivery. This BoK is composed of two broad groups of capabilities, the capabilities of progression (1) and the capabilities of context (2). These two groups of capabilities are composed of different categories and management domain.

The capabilities of progression (1) refer to the capabilities that support the realization of the e-Government project. This group of capabilities contributes directly to the creation and/or development of the other type of capabilities. The capabilities of progression are divided in two categories. Firstly, the change management capabilities are adopting an organizational behaviour approach that emphasizes more the human and organizational aspects of the progression. These capabilities are facilitating issues such as human resource management, personal and organizational development. Secondly, the management by project is more techno-economic oriented analysis of the progression. This category focuses on the management of deliverables: how to plan, organize, coordinate and assess deliverables. It is targeting one specific e-Government initiative and cannot be generalized to the whole e-Government project. The project approach of e-Government is adopting a production perspective that require to fully understand and assess the needs to determine among others a precise budget and scheduling to realize deliverables that answer to clear and known functional specifications.

The capabilities of context (2) are the existing capabilities in the organization. They exist through the service delivery processes already available to the citizens. This group of capabilities is divided in three classes: Information and Business Governance capabilities, Business capabilities and Information resources management capabilities.

The Information and Business Governance capabilities are composed firstly of the organizational capabilities required for the coordination between the top management and stakeholders of different business, specific to each PA on one side and its related information on the other side. Secondly, the business capabilities are composed of the set of capabilities that allows organizing, planning, directing and assessing of all the business resources allocated to e-Government projects. Thirdly, the information management capabilities define the capabilities the organizing, planning, directing and assessment of all the information resources allocated to e-Government projects. This set of capabilities may be under the responsibility of internal or/and external experts and specialists.

3 Methodology

The research project is to present the preliminary stages in the development of a repository of e-Government capabilities based on St-Amant and Renard (2004) body of knowledge for e-Government service delivery as theoretical framework to realize our empirical study and propose a more accurate and updated repository of e-Government capabilities.

This research is using an exploratory design combining different qualitative methods to reach the objective. Firstly, a document analysis synthesizing scientific and practical knowledge in the field strategic management, information system management and e-Government was realized. We reviewed and codified explicit knowledge available such as books, academic papers, research reports, white papers, body of knowledge and repositories in various disciplines. Secondly, a comparative in-depth case studies methodology for gathering evidence was used. The case studies methodology had the purpose to operationalize the e-Government capabilities and to test the framework. This first test remains exploratory in nature and needs to be examined within a broader context. This study required a detailed description of the environment, which allows the exploration of unforeseen elements and relationships to offer better insights into the organizational dimensions.

The case studies were conducted in two Canadian administrations named GOP and MINR[1]. The research design was developed based on Carrol and Swatman's (2000) "structured case study" model based on a pre-defined research cycle and Yin's (2002) "embedded case study sampling strategy". The data collection methods include the analyses of multiple documents and archival records, participation in meetings and workshops and individual semi-structured interviews. It provided richness, depth and validity of information. Such triangulation reduces bias and it is recommended in case research (Yin 2002). Atlas/ti content analysis software was used to codify the qualitative data. Given the exploratory nature of the research, different analysis techniques were used including narrative strategy, explanation building, temporal bracketing, and pattern matching. With respect to the various sources of information, the researchers were able to develop a qualitative in-depth compilation of data within study's environment, as well as a storytelling of events and activities focused specifically on developmental issues.

St-Amant and Renard (2004) BoK for e-Government service delivery served as a starting point for collecting, coding and analysing the data. This framework was progressively reviewed throughout the different analysis iterations as described by Fig. 1.

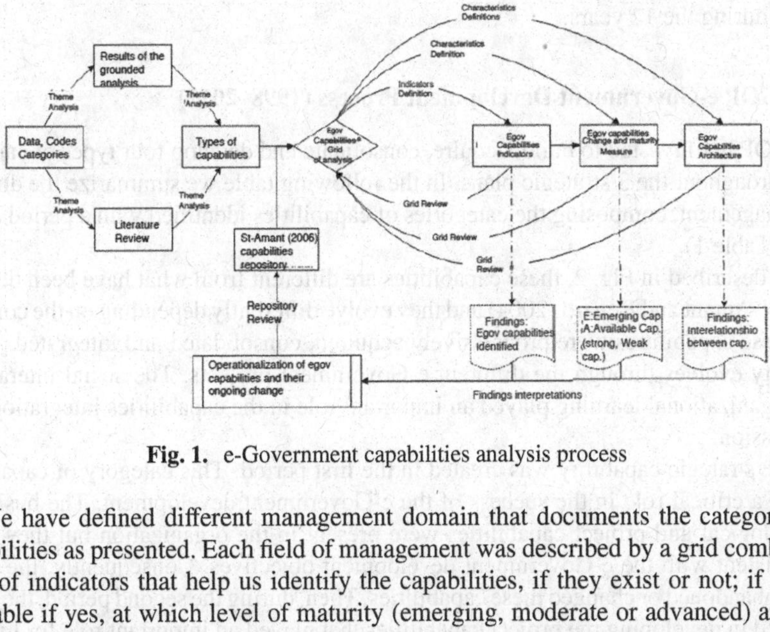

Fig. 1. e-Government capabilities analysis process

We have defined different management domain that documents the categories of capabilities as presented. Each field of management was described by a grid combining a set of indicators that help us identify the capabilities, if they exist or not; if it was available if yes, at which level of maturity (emerging, moderate or advanced) and the level of strength. Finally, we noticed that the interrelationship between these capabilities is also an important factor to study that leads us to define the integration of the capabilities.

[1] The two institutions requested from the researcher to use the acronymes for any publications related to the cases.

4 Analysis and Findings

The GOP and MINR are the pioneers in the implementation of e-Government in Canada. The GOP is an autonomous PA created in 1965 to manage pension plan annuities. It is directed by a board that votes, allocates budgets, takes decisions and authorizes major initiatives. A cabinet shuffle in early 2000 marked a turning point in the type of management and led to the adoption of a new e-Government vision. The GOP's e-Government development is presented as a broad transformation called "Service delivery renewal" to meet the challenges of a growing demands (given the reversed pyramid of age) and the pressures of efficiency.

The MINR is the largest, the most strategic ministry, as well as the most complex one. It is creating 85% of the revenue for the government. Since its creation in 1961, the MINR knew several important organizational transformations with a solid history of in successful project management and Information system development.

In both PA, the e-Government development process started at the beginning of the 2000's. We have examined this development process through 3 strategic plans of 4 years. In the following paragraphs we will describe the capabilities identified in both organization during the 12 years.

4.1 GOP e-Government Development Process (1998–2012)

The GOP has invested to build, acquire, consolidate and develop four types of capabilities throughout the 3 strategic plans. In the following table we summarize the domain of management, composing the categories of capabilities identified with a period at the GOP (Table 1).

As described in Fig. 2, these capabilities are different from what have been defined in by St-Amant and Renard (2004) and they evolve differently depending on the context.

These capabilities were progressively acquired, consolidated and integrated. Their maturity evolves through the different e-Government projects. The social interaction and organizational learning played an important role in the capabilities integration and progression.

The strategic capability was created in the first period. This category of capability played a critical role in the success of the e-Government development. The business, technological and project capabilities were present in the organization but they were inconsistent with the e-Government development objectives. Consequently, the GOP either abandoned or changed these capabilities. Then, during the second period, the GOP invested in developing the project capabilities that played an important role for linking and integrating all the capabilities. Also, they consolidated the technological and business capabilities. Efforts were invested for jointly developing the business and the technological elements of the e-Government. This collaboration was a source of innovation at different level. These innovations became new projects adopted and enhanced all capabilities (Fig. 3).

Table 1. Identified e-Government capabilities at the GOP

e-Government phases	e-Government capabilities
1998–2004: "Service Renewal strategy project": infrastructure implementation and the development of the first e-services (online presence, interactive pdfs forms)	Creation of a strategic capabilities: strategic thinking, management of the deployment of e-Government project, resources allocation, Business and IT Governance Management, creation of internal and external value, Partnership management Enhancement of Project capabilities: communication management, quality management, risk management, project management, change management, support management Business capabilities leveraging: service delivery management, management of the relationship with partners, management of IT impact, information management, results management and human resource management IT capabilities leveraging and consolidation: Management of IT strategy, strategic planing and support management, enterprise architecture, IS development management, IS human resource management, IS service management
2004–2008: "Internal digitalization and shared infrastructure": technological development, online service adoption, collaboration for shared infrastructure and integrated e-services	Consolidation of strategic capabilities: better adaptation to the environment and flexibility, resource allocation and internal value creation, customer value creation, partnership multiplication and management of the IS/Business Governance Development and consolidation of the Project capabilities: Exploitation of the existing skills in project management, adoption of new competencies. learning new techniques and tools in project management, learning change management Technological capabilities consolidation: Learning and adapting new technologies, knowledge acquisition and creation in web-based technology Leveraging business capabilities: secure the success of change management, skills development in customer needs analysis and data collection
2008–2012: "Multichannel strategy and Organizational transformation": transfer to online services, workflow and organizational change to increase the efficiency, value-added services and increase cooperation and partnership	Leveraging of the strategic capabilities: Continuous strategic brainstorming, strategy deployment management, resource allocation and value creation, Business and IT Governance, external value creation and partnership management Redefinition of Project capabilities: communication management, quality management, risk management, project management, change management, support management, creation of new performance unit, management and organization by project Enhancement of the Business capabilities: Learning the management of a new channel, management of new roles and new jobs in the PA and create customer relationship management Leveraging the acquired technology capabilities: exploitation of the newly acquired capabilities into new project, new partnership between IS/Business

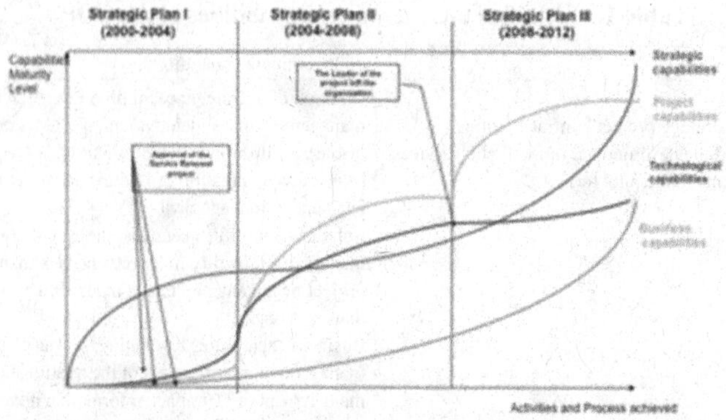

Fig. 2. e-Government capabilities development at the GOP

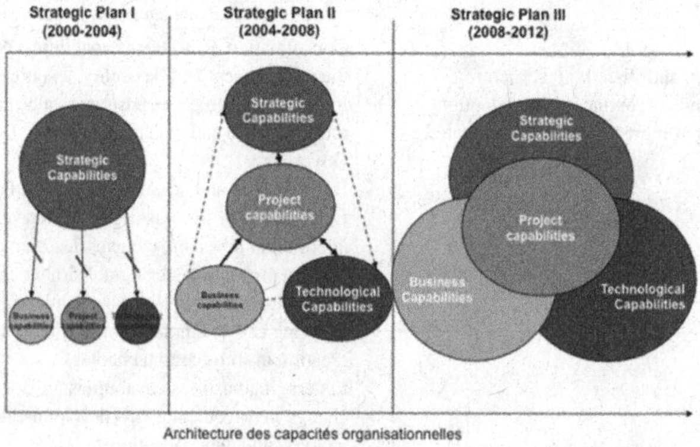

Fig. 3. GOP's architecture of e-Government capabilities

4.2 MINR e-Government Development Process (1998–2012)

The MINR's e-Government development followed a different journey. They focus mainly on the internal strength during the two first strategic plans: The technology and the project management. In the middle of the third strategic plan, the e-Government development process was aborted for a lack of performance, low level of registration and use of the system, overbudget and implementation delays. Even if it is publicly described as a technological success. It was considered as an important organizational and project failure. In 2008, they officially admit the failure of the project and progressively retracted (Table 2).

The MINR leveraged the existing knowledge, skills and resources in term of project and technological capabilities. These two types of capabilities were developed and consolidated prior to the e-Government project. It was considered as reference in terms of know-how, methods, project and change management in the government. The MINR had a long history of success in IS and IT projects. The MINR was able to easily adapt to the Internet platform technologies and infrastructure. It was the first one to develop complex technologies, such as online authentication and identification. They strengthened the technological capability by developing their knowledge through training and seminars, they increased the resources by partnering with external firms and hire IT experts and consultant.

Table 2. Identified e-Government capabilities at the MINR

e-Government phases	e-Government capabilities
1998–2004: Consultation and e-Government appropriation	Leveraging of Project capabilities: Project management, methodology and change management IT capabilities leveraging and consolidation: Existing capabilities used previously in the development of internal information system and Intranet implementation
2004–2008: Development and implementation of the public service delivery	Development and consolidation of the technological capabilities: Enterprise architecture, web technology skills and knowledge acquisition, application management, infrastructure management Consolidation of the project capabilities: The IT department took the leadership from the project management resources. it was totally absorbed and more and more isolated from the organizational to an independent office dedicated with a strong IT expertise
2008–2012: Record of a failure, Progressive divestment and exit from the project Postmortem analysis and inspection Timid and slow relaunch of the e-Government development	Development of the technology capabilities: Security knowledge and skills acquisition, Internet and Web technology consolidation, Identification and authentication, software development

We observed the development and maturity of the technological capabilities through 3 strategic plans. During the first period, the MINR decided not to leverage neither develop the business capabilities and develop the e-Government separately from the organization. The project capabilities were leveraged but the organization did not invest until they were progressively absorbed and strengthened the technological instead of developing a dynamic project capability (Fig. 5). The technological capabilities, with the number of online service developed and the technological project undertaken, was consolidated and strengthened very fast. The MINR became a reference for all the PA (Figs. 4 and 5).

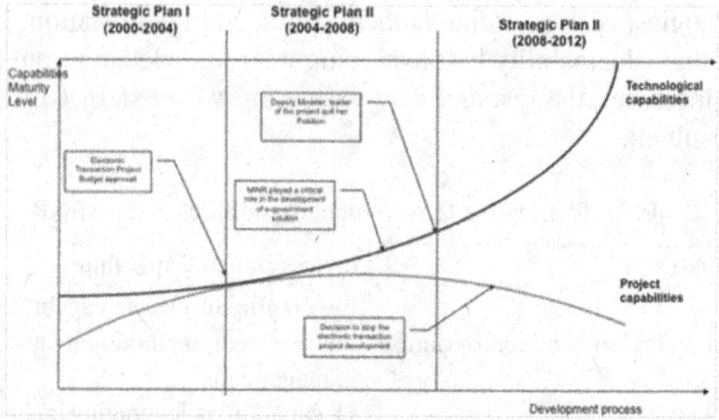

Fig. 4. e-Government capabilities development at MINR

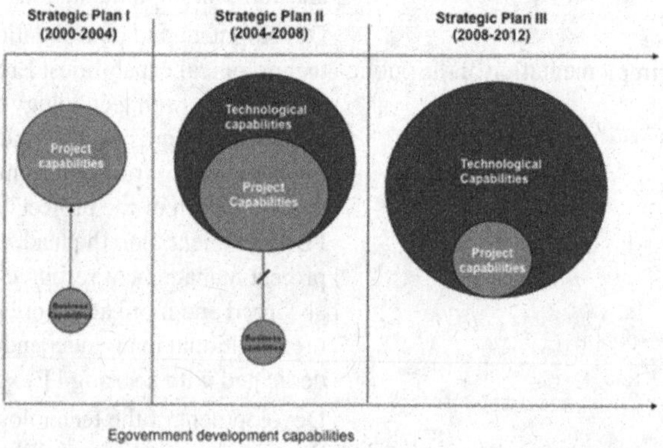

Fig. 5. MINR's e-Government capabilities architecture

However the project was led by an IT team that concentrates all the efforts on the IT aspects and loose track of all the project management dimensions such as budget management, schedule and planing management and performance management. Also, the lack of communication and collaboration with the business resources and the lack of knowledge and consultation of the business during the first period led to serious difficulties in the e-Government development process and impacted in the quality of online service developed. It also explain the very low registration and adoption of the online service. The investment was made mainly on the technological resources, competencies and knowledge. It became the predominant e-Government capability. They have failed to develop or acquire any other type of capabilities.

5 Discussion and Conclusion

The GOP and MINR cases confirmed the need of a combination of interrelated capabilities to develop the e-Government. To identify this capabilities we use as starting point St-Amant and Renard (2004) theoretical framework that we progressively reviewed and enriched using a triangulation between the data collection, the analysis techniques, and the literature review.

Firstly, one of the main difficulty we faced using St-Amant and Renard's Framework is that the strategy formulation is supposed to be predetermined confirming that the strategy is already defined. Our results show that it is not the case, at least in the Canadian PA. The strategy is not always defined, neither is clear. Both organizations did not have any strategic capabilities when they started the e-Government project. The development of this type of capabilities played a major role in the success of the GOP throughout the strategic plans, while the absence of the strategic capabilities was one of the most important causes behind the failure of the e-Government project for the MINR after more than 7 years of e-Government development.

Secondly, the project capabilities were added and redefined as dynamic capabilities that have a transformative potential for PA and impacted on the capabilities of context that are already available in the organization. Thirdly, what emerges from the data is that e-Government is not predetermined but evolves throughout projects. Each new initiative launched created change and required constant adaptation. In other words, the e-Government is not a goal or finality, but rather a continuous change that requires constantly revision of the stock of available capabilities. Finally, we have proposed a revisited framework of capabilities based on 4 interrelated and integrated categories. We have operationalized the capabilities based on the iteration strategy reviewing constantly the data and the literature. We have identify the need of a combination of four types of capabilities to the development to support the continuous change: Strategic, project, business and technological. Acquiring these capabilities is important, but it is not enough. It is as important to adapt, develop and renew these capabilities in order to avoid rigidities.

In conclusion we propose a revisited repository of e-Government capabilities (Fig. 6). The repository is based on a set of premises. The first premise states that government and PA requires the presence of capabilities (dynamic and/or organizational) that they will have or that they will need in order to realize successfully the e-Government transformation and overcome the challenges of e-Government service delivery adoption and implementation (they are facing today or in the future). The second premise is that the repository is composed of different ideal-type of capabilities needed that means it can differ or require adaptation depending on the context. Last premise specifies that the absence of one of these capabilities could be critical for the success of an e-Government service delivery implementation.

The identification of the e-Government capabilities is challenging. Firstly, the capabilities can be determined through the produced outcomes. According to Croom and Batchelor (1997), capabilities are revealed through time. They are observed in actions (Renard and Soparnot 2010). Data were here coded and analysed by examining the activities of the e-Government development process and highlighting the capabilities that were leveraged if existing or developed within the process. Secondly, the organizational capabilities show the organizational know-how. And given the tacit nature of some capabilities, the interpretation, the perceptions and the understanding of the interviewed constitute the foundation to explore the nature and maturity of the identified capabilities.

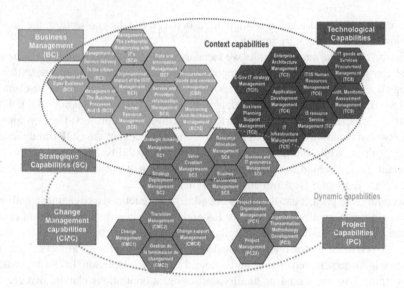

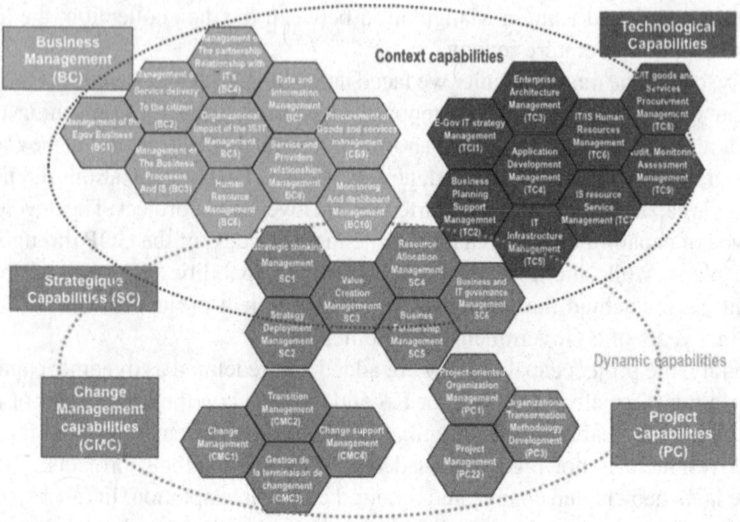

Fig. 6. e-Government capabilities repository

Finally, the e-Government capabilities are described specifically to their context. It is important to explore and develop control criteria for social interactions (Nonaka et al. 1996). These processes helped identifying the capabilities, their absence or presence, and helped interpreting as well.

This repository is a first stage that requires to be consolidated and constantly updated based and adapted based on new case studies.

Acknowledgment. This paper is a result of the project "SmartEGOV: Harnessing EGOV for Smart Governance (Foundations, methods, Tools)/NORTE-01-0145-FEDER-000037", supported by Norte Portugal Regional Operational Programme (NORTE 2020), under the PORTUGAL 2020 Partnership Agreement, through the European Regional Development Fund (EFDR).

References

Amit, R., Schoemaker, P.J.: Strategic assets and organisational rent. Strateg. Manag. J. **14**(1), 33–46 (1993)

Carrol, J.M., Swatman, P.A.: Structured-case: a methodological framework for building theory in information systems research. Eur. J. Inform. Syst. **9**(4), 235–242 (2000)

Collis, D.J.: Research note: how valuable are organizational capabilities. Strateg. Manag. J. **15**(1), 143–152 (1994)

Grant, P.M.: The resource based theory of competitive advantage: implications for strategy formulation. Calif. Manag. Rev. **33**(3), 114–135 (1991)

Croom, S., Batchelor, J.: The development of strategic capabilities: an interaction view. Integr. Manuf. Syst. J. **8**(5), 29–312 (1997)

Nonaka, L., Takeuchi, H., Umemoto, K.: A theory of organizational knowledge creation. Int. J. Technol. Manag. **11**(7–8), 833–845 (1996)

Renard, L., Soparnot, R.: Proposition d'un modèle de management stratégique de l'entreprise par les capacités organisationnelles. Gestion **27**(6), 23–38 (2010)

St-Amant, G.E.: Carte conceptuelle des capacités de transformation organisationnelles pour réaliser les défis d'Aé. Cahier de recherche ESG-UQÀM (2006)

St-Amant, G.E., Renard, L.: Premier référentiel de connaissances associées aux capacités organisationnelles de l'administration électronique. Manag. Int. **9**(1), 49–68 (2004)

Strauss, A., Corbin, J.: Basics of Qualitative Research: Grounded Theory, Procedures and Techniques. Sage, Newberry-Park (1998)

Yin, R.K.: Case Study Research Design and Methods, vol. 2. Sage, Thousand Oaks (2002)

Zollo, M., Winter, S.: Deliberate learning and the evolution of dynamic capabilities. Organ. Sci. **13**(3), 339–351 (2002)

A Social Cyber Contract Theory Model for Understanding National Cyber Strategies

Raymond Bierens(✉), Bram Klievink, and Jan van den Berg

Faculty of Technology Policy and Management, Delft University of Technology, Jaffalaan 5, 2628 BX Delft, Netherlands
r.h.bierens@tudelft.nl

Abstract. Today's increasing connectivity creates cyber risks at personal, organizational up to societal level. Societal cyber risks require mitigation by all kinds of actors where government should take the lead due to its responsibility to protect its citizens. Since no formal global governance exists, the governmental responsibility should start at the national level of every country. To achieve successful management of global cyber risks, appropriate alignment between these sovereignly developed strategies is required, which concerns a complex challenge. To create alignment, getting insight into differences between national cyber strategies, is the first step. This, in turn, requires an appropriate analysis approach that helps to identify the key differences. In this article, we introduce such an analysis approach based on social contract theory. The resulting analysis model consists of both a direct and an indirect type of social cyber contract between governments, citizens and corporations, within and between sovereign nations. To show its effectiveness, the proposed social cyber contract model is validated through an illustrated case examining various constitutional rights to privacy, their embedding in the national cyber strategies and how their differences could cause potential barriers for alignment across sovereignties.

Keywords: National cyber strategy · Social contract · Privacy · Cyber security · National security · Cyber risk

1 Introduction

More and more cyberspace is becoming an unsafe global environment to operate in. Today's increasing connectivity creates cyber risks at personal, organizational up to societal level. Societal risks require mitigation by government that has the responsibility to protect its citizens. Since no formal global governance exists, man-aging cyber risks should start by accepting the sovereignty of every country in cyberspace.

Studies into national cyber security strategies between 2005 and present by CCDCOE [1], OECD [2] and UNIDIR [3] plus scientific organizations Istituto Affari Internazionali [4] and TNO [5] show that for many governments sovereignty is the basis of their national cyber security strategy as part of its constitutionally agreed responsibilities. Australia [6], Austria [7], Estonia [8], Finland [9], Germany [10, 11], Hungary

M. Janssen et al. (Eds.): EGOV 2017, LNCS 10428, pp. 166–176, 2017.
DOI: 10.1007/978-3-319-64677-0_14

[12], Japan [13], Netherlands [12, 14], Spain [15], United Kingdom [16] and United States [17, 18] all explicitly mention sovereignty in their national cyber strategy.

To achieve successful management of global cyber risks requires increased alignment is necessary between these sovereignly developed national cyber strategies. Studies by Instituto Affari Internazationali [4] and TNO [5] already confirmed the potential barriers arising by the lack of agreed definitions around cyberspace, and above all of their harmonization between national cyber strategies. Priorities for national cybersecurity strategies will vary by country. In some countries, the focus may be on protecting intellectual property, and still others may focus on improving the cybersecurity awareness of newly connected citizens [19]. Some nations fear (potential) cyber-attacks by terrorists on their Critical National Infrastructure, others consider information published in cyber space by terrorists, the ability for terrorists to communicate using ICT, and the gathering of intelligence on terrorists or foreign nations as topics that belong to their national cyber security strategy [5].

Insight is the first step into identifying the actual barriers that create differences between national cyber strategies and therefore can limit the alignment between them. Using social contract theory, this article introduces a direct and indirect type of social contract between governments, citizens and corporations, within and between sovereign nations. This results in a proposed social cyber contract model that is validated through an illustrated case examining various constitutional rights to privacy and their embedding in the national cyber strategies and potential barriers across sovereignties that rise from that.

The fluid nature of security threats and global cooperation suggest the need for flexibility in governance and policy structures. However, in a democratic society, such flexibilities must also be accompanied by a commensurate level of trust and accountability to citizens [20]. The balance between the needs for privacy versus national security is a typical example of that. In 2011, Casman [21] used social contract theory to demonstrate the government's obligation to provide security in lieu of privacy in the post-09/11 United States. Transparency and privacy are considered as important societal and democratic values to create an open and transparent government. Only by conceptualizing these values in this way, the nature and impact of open government can be understood, and their levels be balanced with security, safety, openness and other socially-desirable values [21]. On the topic of privacy, national cyber strategies show that privacy is less common as research by Luijff [22] comparing 19 national cyber strategies shows the

Table 1. Luijff, Besseling and De Graaf.

Country	Privacy protection actions
Germany	Specifically defined[a]
United Kingdom	None defined
Netherlands	Specifically defined
United States	None defined

[a] Research [22] did not include 2016 German Strategy that specifically defines privacy actions.

differences for the researched national cyber strategies of Germany, Netherlands, United Kingdom and United States (Table 1).

Using social contract theory, this article introduces a direct and indirect type of social contract between governments, citizens and corporations, within and between sovereign nations. This results in a proposed social cyber contract model that is validated through an illustrated case examining various constitutional rights to privacy and their embedding in the national cyber strategies and potential barriers across sovereignties that rise from that.

The first part of this article researches direct social contract between government and its citizens in Germany, Netherlands, United Kingdom and United States. For each of these countries, the relationships between their constitution and their national cyber strategy is made on the topic of privacy. The second part of this article focusses on the indirect social cyber contract which consists of two agreements: between government and corporations and between citizens and corporations. Together, these two agreements form are subsidiary to the direct social contract as written down in the Constitution. After the introduction of the direct and indirect social contract, a single integrated social cyber contract model is introduced and used to examine if this leads to insights into potential barriers between two spheres of sovereignties.

In its last paragraph, the article defines two preliminary conclusions regarding the added value of using the social contract theory for understanding national cyber security strategies, including the introduction of a direct and indirect social contract as part of a single social cyber contract model.

2 Why the Social Contract Perspective?

In 1987 the National Regulatory Research Institute published their perspective on social contract and telecommunications regulations [24]. After 09/11 the social contract Casman [21] used social contract theory to redefine the balance between privacy and national security. As of 2008, the Internet Security Alliance brought social contract theory into cyberspace [25, 26]. Central in all of these publications is the role and behavior of government towards its citizens as written down in the Constitution and is executed between governments, citizens and corporations. In a democratic market-driven society citizens have option of choice between different parties as well as corporations and can take visible and researchable actions if they feel rebalancing of the social contract is needed. For that reason, social contract as part of the field of political science is used in this research.

As an alternative, the field economical sciences was considered. National cyber security from an economic perspective, usually related to GDP, focusses on the economic aspects such as efficiency of national cyber strategies [24], Also the dependency on global economy leaves little individual influence for Governments and therefore providing insights into potential causes for differences and similarities of national cyber strategies.

The second alternative field of science considered is technical. Cyberspace can be defined as a network of (in)direct connected devices. Cyberspace largely operates through commercial technology and communication corporations that operate globally. Because of this, governments cannot autonomously change the technical workings of cyberspace. This disfavors the technical field as a potential cause for differences and similarities.

3 The Direct Social Cyber Contract Between Government and Citizens

The purpose of national security is to protect the safety of a country's secrets and its citizens [25]. This includes kinetic (real) threats and digital (virtual) cyber threats. Within each sovereignty, this responsibility is written down in the constitution. Within a sovereign democratic country, the Constitution of a country is the most important legal document, and has been described as the great law before which all other laws of a society must bow. It describes the core values, roles and responsibilities that apply to all citizens and government alike. A constitution becomes effective through people's consent and willingness to abide by it. This is done through social contract, and as such, a constitution is considered to be a contract [26]. A nation's constitution is therefore considered to be the most common written representation of a social contract [23]. In return for receiving security, citizens fulfill their own described responsibilities to obey the law. This social contract applies to both the kinetic and the digital domain.

A good example of the applicability of the constitution are the articles on privacy. Below are the articles found in the German Constitution ("Basic Law") and the Dutch Constitution ("Grondwet").

Germany – Article 10 (Privacy of correspondence, posts and telecommunications)

(1) The privacy of correspondence, posts and telecommunications shall be inviolable.
(2) Restrictions may be ordered only pursuant to a law. If the restriction serves to protect the free democratic basic order or the existence or security of the Federation or of a Land, the law may provide that the person affected shall not be informed of the restriction and that recourse to the courts shall be replaced by a review of the case by agencies and auxiliary agencies appointed by the legislature.

Netherlands – Article 13 (Privacy)

(1) The privacy of correspondence shall not be violated except in the cases laid down by Act of Parliament, by order of the courts.
(2) The privacy of the telephone and telegraph[1] shall not be violated except, in the cases laid down by Act of Parliament, by or with the authorisation of those designated for the purpose by Act of Parliament.

The United Kingdom does not have a written constitution that enshrines a right to privacy for individuals and there is no common law that provides for a general right to privacy. The UK has, however, incorporated the European Convention on Human Rights

[1] On April 18th, the Dutch House of Representatives ("Tweede Kamer") accepted the proposal to add digital communications to this article of its constitution.

[27] into its national law, which provides for a limited right of respect towards an individual's privacy and family life. This right is embedded in the UK Government's 1998 Data Protection Act [28] which aims to "to strike a balance between the rights of individuals and the sometimes competing interests of those with legitimate reasons for using personal information."

In comparison, the United States Constitution does not explicitly include the right to privacy. However, the Supreme Court has found that the fourth amendment to the US Constitution implicitly grants a right to privacy against governmental intrusion:

(1) The right of the people to be secure in their persons, houses, papers, and effects, [a] against unreasonable searches and seizures, shall not be violated, and no Warrants shall issue, but upon probable cause, supported by oath or affirmation, and particularly describing the place to be searched, and the persons or things to be seized

The German and Dutch Constitution are the basis for the national cyber security strategy. The 2016 German Cyber Security Strategy [10] explicitly reflects its constitution in the following paragraph:

Secure, confidential, non-manipulative electronic communications is fundamental to the exercise of the right to a private environment, the right to privacy of the citizens.

The Dutch Cyber Security Strategy [14] also refers to its constitutional paragraph on privacy in the following paragraph:

The government in an international context will also enter into a dialogue with relevant private parties and will act in a framework-developing and standards-developing fashion to protect the privacy and security of users.

By Executive Order of President Obama, a Commission on Enhancing National Cybersecurity published the following recommendations in December 2016 [33]:

The next Administration should launch a national public–private initiative to achieve major security and privacy improvements by increasing the use of strong authentication to improve identity management. … An effective identity management system is foundational to managing privacy interests and relates directly to security.

Germany and Netherlands explicitly refer to privacy on an individual level resulting in a strong recommendation for encryption for their communication. However, in Germany, this encryption is unconditional and without access for anyone including its own Government. In The Netherlands, uncontrolled access by its intelligence agencies is considered but has yet to be mapped against its Constitution and is therefore not yet approved. The United States does not recommend encryption outside reach of its own intelligence agencies but in-stead recommends strong authentication but with access to both corporations and citizens by law enforcement if national security requires. However, this recommendation follows their Fourth Amendment which protects its citizens against unreasonable searches and seizures.

The Constitution can be seen as a direct social contract between two parties. Comparing four constitutions shows a relationship between the Constitutions and the national cyber strategies from each nation. The constitution, and therefore the social contract, does also apply to the digital domain. This article defines the Constitution, if applicable on the digital domain, as the direct social cyber contract. Since Constitutions differ between countries, subsequently so do their national cyber strategies and (for example) their right to (digital) privacy derived from these strategies.

4 The Indirect Social Cyber Contract Between Government, Corporations and Citizens

With the emergence of private companies in general, and privatized companies that are part of critical national infrastructure in particular, a third party entered social contract theory at the beginning of the 20th century: corporations. Corporations are formed by citizens who create a new legal entity together that has its own roles and responsibilities within a country with the most common purpose to maximize profits. Within a sovereign state, the Constitution also applies to the activities executed by corporation that have their legal entity within that same sovereign state. Since their purpose of profit maximization can cause conflicts with the social contract between citizens and government, the role of sovereign states expands to ensure corporations acted within the already agreed social contract.

To provide this assurance, laws and regulations are applied specifically for corporations while taking into account other drivers such as competitive market forces between corporations and citizens. These competitive market forces are assumed to have a positive effect on the behavior of corporations. In case these drivers are limited, such as within a monopoly, the government will increase its control and strengthen its laws and regulations.

Each government has to decide how to regulate their corporations, both critical infrastructure and non-critical infrastructure. Their options are to enforce and/or to incentivize. There are two key elements to ISA's Cyber Security Social Contract. Firstly, cyber security is seen an enterprise-wide risk management problem which must be understood as much for its economic perspectives as for its technical issues. Secondly is that government's primary role ought to be to incentivize the investment required to implement the standards, practices, and technologies that have already been shown to be effective in improving cyber security. This became the basis for the regulation of US Corporations through the NIST Cybersecurity Framework [32] that was initiated and supported by ISA's cyber security social contract.

The German National Cyber Strategy takes the opposite approach and has decided for enforcement. Their strategy (Bundesamt fur Sicherheit in der Informationstechnik 2011) states:

The public and the private sector must create an enhanced strategic and organizational basis for closer coordination based on intensified information sharing. To this end, cooperation established by the CIP implementation plan is systematically extended, and legal commitments to enhance the binding nature of the CIP implementation plan are examined.

The Dutch Government takes a risk-based approach, to increase the resilience of vital services and processes and work to an effective joint public-private and civil-military response, and with the help of our international partners [12].

The agreement between Government and Corporations are ultimately intended for execution of the agreement between Government and Citizens in the Constitution. Therefore, the Terms and Conditions (T&C's) agreed between Corporations and Citizens must be taken into consideration as well. This social contract is between a corporation and its customer, the citizen. Similar to democratic government, a citizen has the freedom of choice. In Government, this choice is made during the elections, with corporations, that choice is made through market forces. If one does not like the Terms & Conditions (T&C's), and unless there is a monopoly, the freedom to select another is there. The T&C's of the corporation must, off course, comply with the Constitution of the sovereign nation its legal entity operates.

In each cyber security strategy there are specific agreements between Government and corporations to ensure execution of the social contract between government and citizens. Each sovereign state selects its own method cooperation within this agreement to mitigate cyber security risks, ranging from enforcement to incentivizing its corporations. Between Corporations and Citizens there are also specific social contract agreements through the acceptance of T&C's. The two agreements (Government – Corporation, Corporation – Citizen) together fall under the Constitution within the sovereignty and are in this research defined as an indirect social cyber contract.

5 Integrating into a Single Model

The previous two paragraphs have introduced the following two social cyber contracts:

1. A *direct social cyber contract* between Government and citizens that is based upon the Constitution and all cyberspace related policies that are derived from it.
2. An *indirect social cyber contract* that to ensure execution of the first by legal entities other than people that consist of two agreements:
   a. An agreement between Government and Corporations formalized through regulation;
   b. An agreement between Citizens and Corporations formalized through market forces regulating the agreed T&C's;

The social cyber contract model in Fig. 1 shows the graphical representation of these two models and how they interact within a single sovereignty.

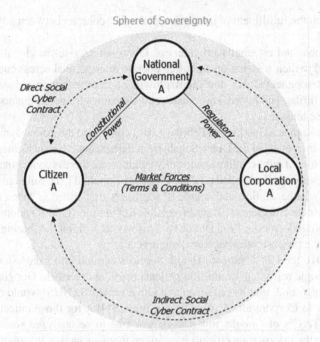

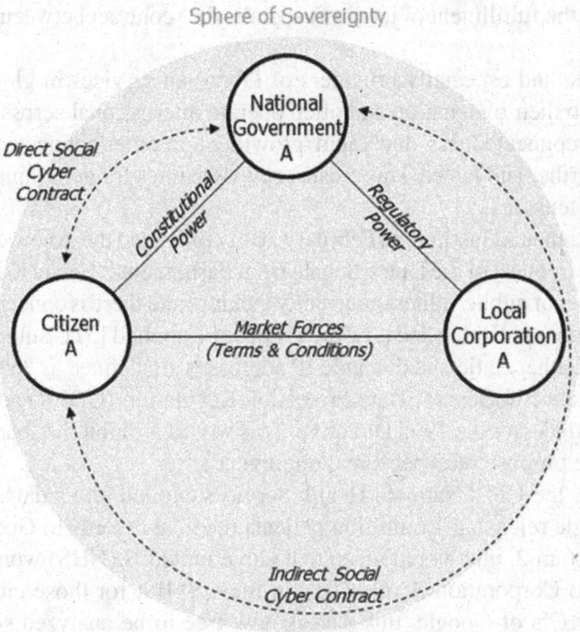

Fig. 1. The social cyber contract model.

6 Conflicting Social Cyber Contracts Between Spheres of Sovereignty

This research focusses on the possible causes why alignment of national cyber security strategies can cause barriers to data sharing within and between sovereignties.

In order to assess if social cyber contract theory contributes to this research into possible causes, a case study on privacy has been used. Due to the lack of alignment, one would expect to see conflicts between countries where the direct social cyber contract, and subsequently also the indirect social cyber contract, are different.

Let's take two countries, A and B, where in both countries the direct and indirect social cyber contract are successfully fulfilled between citizens, government and corporations, but they are different in content. If citizen B than decides to use the service of corporation A, this citizen will have to accept the Terms & Conditions from corporation A for that specific service. However, these T&C's have been developed and executed as part of the social cyber contract fulfillment in country A.

Should country B has a different social contract, this is no longer applicable. Citizen B has now, often unknowingly, become part of the indirect social cyber contract in country A. And this is only the best case. Worst case is that citizen B within country A, since he is not part of the sovereignty A, is without any legal protection at all.

In both situations, government B can no longer deliver upon its direct social contract since corporation A and government A are outside of its regulatory power. Therefore, government B can no longer fulfill his indirect social cyber contract which can have implications on the fulfillment of its direct social cyber contract between government B and citizens B.

Corporations, and especially providers of IT-driven services in global cyberspace are not limited to their own nation and often operate international across countries. The increasing interconnectedness and rapid growth of internet-connected devices only enhances this further and faster. This creates new dynamics for governments that potentially can cause tensions.

The Dutch Rathenau Institute in February 2017 confirmed these new dynamics when their analysis, by request of the Dutch Senate from Parliament ("Eerste Kamer"), showed that the protection of public values is currently lacking, and there is conceptual confusion over what rules are applicable and how they should be applied [31]. Sullivan and Burger [32] examine whether static and dynamic IP addresses are defined as "personal data" as defined in the new EU General Data Protection Regulation (GDPR) adopted in April 2016 and its predecessor the 1995 Directive. This would prohibit the sharing of it across countries for the purpose of cyber threat intelligence.

In May 2016 the UK's National Health Services entered into a data-sharing agreement with Google releasing 1.6 million patients medical records to Google. Applying this case to diagram 2, that would mean that Government B (NHS) would release data about citizens to Corporation A (Google), in the US. But for those citizens that also accepted the T&C's of Google, this data is now free to be analyzed since Google is allowed to use the information citizens have given them, as well as information Google gets from using their services. Even though people felt this as a clear violation of their civil rights and therefore of their social contract, legally that is more complicated since (Fig. 2):

1. Each citizen willingly accepted the T&C's of Google before using the services;
2. The T&C's and associated data storage policies are compliant with the Constitution of the United States, being the ultimate legal entity of Google.

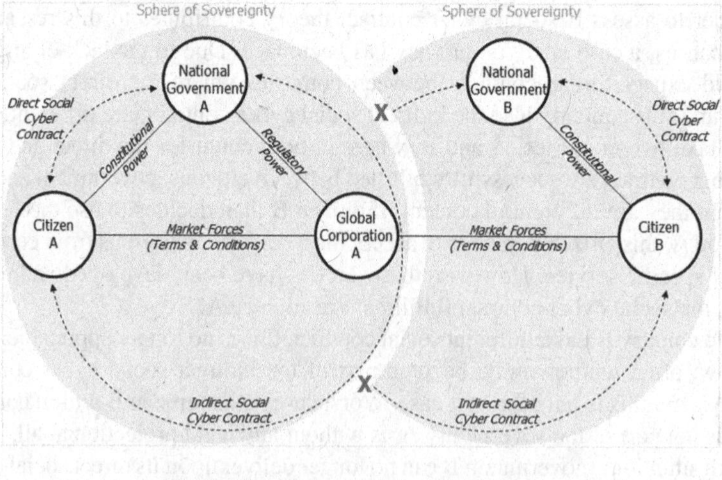

Fig. 2. Conflicting social cyber contracts.

The NHS example also shows that when data is shared, it does not immediately violate any social contract. But when combined with other sources, it can quickly become an invasion of privacy.

7 Preliminary Conclusions

The first preliminary conclusion of this ongoing research is that because since cyber risk can have societal impact, the government has an important role in executing its social contract responsibilities as defined in the constitution. Since every constitution is built upon the sovereignty of a nation, so is every national cyber security strategy. Constitutional differences, such as illustrated in this article for the topic privacy, can create differences between these cyber strategies.

The important role of private companies to maintain the internet's infrastructure, as well as providing new technology-driven IT services around the world, makes it necessary for explicitly defining their role within the social contract. The second preliminary conclusion is that the introduction of the direct and indirect social contract provides insight on the relationship between government, citizens and corporation. Using the topic of privacy, this article shows that a single integrated social contract model also can identify differences between multiple sovereignties if citizens from one country start using IT services from a global country that falls under a different sovereignty.

References

1. CCDCOE: National Cyber Security Framework Manual. NATO CCD COE Publications (2012)
2. OECD: Cybersecurity Policy Making at a Turning Point - Analysing a New Generation of National Cybersecurity Strategies, Brussels (2012)
3. UNIDIR: Cybersecurity and Cyberwarfare (2011)
4. Istituto Affari Internazionali: Ambigious Definitions in the Cyber Domain, Rome (2011)
5. Luiijf, K., Besseling M., Spoelstra, M., de Graff, P.: Ten National Cyber Security Strategies - A Comparison, The Hague (2013)
6. Ministry of Interior: Strong and Secure - A Strategy for Australia's National Security, Canberra (2013)
7. BundeskanzlerAmt Osterreich: National Cyber Security Strategy, Vienna (2013)
8. Ministry of Defence: National Defence Strategy, Talinn (2013)
9. Ministry of Interior: Finland's National Cyber Security Strategy, Helsinki (2013)
10. Bundesamt fur Sicherheit in der Informationstechnik: Germany_BSI_2011_Cyber Security Strategy for Germany, Berlin (2011)
11. Bundes Ministerium des Innern: Cyber Security Strategy for Germany, Berlin (2016)
12. National Cyber Security Center: National Cyber Security Strategy, Prague (2013)
13. Information Security Policy Council: Cyber Security Strategy, Tokyo (2013)
14. National Cyber Security Center: National Cyber Security Strategy 2, The Hague (2013)
15. Gobierno De Espana: National Cyber Security Strategy, Madrid (2013)
16. HM Government: Securing Britain in an Age of Uncertainty, London (2010)
17. White House: Cyberspace Policy Review, Washington (2010)
18. White House: National Security Strategy, Washington (2015)

19. Microsoft: Developing a National Strategy for Cybersecurity, Redmont (2013)
20. Bertot, J.C., Seifert, J., Jaeger, P.: Securing the homeland in the digital age: issues and implications for policy and governance. Gov. Inf. Q. **32**, 105–107 (2015)
21. Casman, B.: Security vs. Privacy: The Use of Social Contract Theory to Support the Government's Obligation to Provide Security in Lieu of Privacy. University of Nevada, Las Vegas (2011)
22. Jansen, M., van den Hoven, J.: Big and Open Linked Data (BOLD) in government: a challenge to transparancy and privacy. Gov. Inf. Q. **32**, 363–368 (2015)
23. Luiijf, E., Besseling, K., de Graff, P.: Nineteen national cyber security strategies. Int. J. Crit. Infrastruct. **9**, 3–31 (2013)
24. The National Regulatory Research Center: A Perspective on Social Contract and Telecommunications Regulation. The National Regulatory Research Center, Columbus (1987)
25. Internet Security Alliance: The Cyber Security Social Contract, Arlington (2008)
26. Internet Security Alliance: Social Contract 2.0, Arlington (2010)
27. Brangetto, P., Aubyn, M.K.S.: (2015) Economic aspects of national cyber security strategies, Tallinn
28. Macmillan Dictionary: National Security Definition. In: Macmillan Dictionary. http://www.macmillandictionary.com/dictionary/british/national-security. Accessed 16 Jan 2017
29. Nyamaka, D.M.: Social contract theory of John Locke in the contemporary world. In: Selected Works of Daudi Mwita Nyamaka Mr. Saint Augustine University of Tanzania (2011)
30. The United States Constitution as Social Compact: American Philosophical Society. Proc. Am. Philos. Soc. **131**, 261–269 (1987)
31. European Union: European Convention for the Protection of Human Rights and Fundamental Freedoms, Brussels (1998)
32. UK Government: Data Protection Act 1998, London (1998)
33. Commission on Enhancing National Cybersecurity Report: Report on Securing and Growing the Digital Economy, Washington (2016)
34. National Institute of Standards & Technology: NIST Cybersecurity Framework. In: National Institute of Standards & Technology. http://www.nist.gov/cyberframework/. Accessed 12 Feb 2014
35. Rathenau Instituut: Opwaarderen - Borgen van publieke waarden in de digitale samenleving, The Hague (2017)
36. Sullivan, C., Burger, E.: "In the public interest": the privacy implications of international business-to-business sharing of cyber-threat intelligence. Comput. Law Secur. Rev **33**, 14–29 (2016)

The E-governance Development in Educational Sector of Republic of Moldova

Lucia Casap[1] and John Sören Pettersson[2(✉)]

[1] Academy of Economic Studies, Banulescu-Bodoni 61, Chişinău, Republic of Moldova
lucia.casap@gmail.com
[2] Karlstad Business School, Karlstad University, Universitetsgatan 2, 651 88 Karlstad, Sweden
john_soren.pettersson@kau.se

Abstract. During the last years e-governance is being implemented in many countries. Within the same country, the level of achieved results can vary significantly between sectors. The implementation of e-governance in Republic of Moldova has had a good start, but some stagnation in the implementation of the e-governance agenda is registered. In the educational sector, the implementation is still at the low level. This practical paper surveys the e-tools in the educational sector of the Republic of Moldova, thus revealing the e-governance level of the sector. By comparing with the usage of IT tools in the Swedish educational system, and identifying the benefits and issues met during their development, it proposes a way for future implementation of the e-governance agenda in the educational sector in Moldova. While Moldova as a country has extensive Internet coverage, Sweden was choose for the comparison because of its Internet coverage plus its focus on furthering the skills of its workforce and also the considerable efforts of e-governance agenda implementation.

Keywords: E-governance · Educational sector · EMIS

1 Introduction

Realizing the possibilities of building trust between governments and citizens by using internet-based strategies to involve citizens in the policy process, and thus demonstrating government transparency and accountability [1, p. 752], the Government of Republic of Moldova defined an e-governance agenda in 2005. The implementations were initialized in 2010 with a major project financed by the World Bank and administrated by the government. The Electronic Government Center (EGC) is responsible for developing and implementing the government technologic modernization agenda: 429 public services are described on the EGC platform www.servicii.gov.md; 102 of these services are available on-line. A large share of the developed services is implemented for the citizens and business sector (issuance and verification of registration documents, fiscal services etc.) [2, pp. 5–10]. Although there are good examples of e-services in Moldova, the educational system remains underserved.

M. Janssen et al. (Eds.): EGOV 2017, LNCS 10428, pp. 177–186, 2017.
DOI: 10.1007/978-3-319-64677-0_15

The share of Internet users in the Republic of Moldova passed 66% in 2014 [3]. Many of them, including public employees, teachers, students, pupils and their parents are potential beneficiaries of e-governance in the educational sector. The aim of e-governance in education sectors would be to improve information and service delivery, encourage student participation in the decision making process, making administration transparent and effective, and give institutions a new channel of educational deployment [4]. With the start of big reforms in various levels of the educational sector to increase quality, equity and efficiency of the system, the implementation of the e-governance in this sector is mandatory according to a Governmental decision 2014 [5].

This paper has the aim to identify the available e-tools in the educational sector of Republic of Moldova. The results are compared with Sweden to propose the way for implementation of Moldova's e-governance agenda the in educational sector. The decision to use Sweden as a inspirational source was based on Sweden's focus on education and training skills of its workforce, and indeed being the country leading the top of the most competitive economies in Europe when this decision was made (2012) [6]. Later it has also held the top position in the E-Government UNDP Survey [7, p. 111].

The following section frames the present study in the discussion of e-government and e-governance. Section 3 describes the methods applied for data collection and data analysis. Section 4 presents the e-governance context of the educational sector in the Republic of Moldova, while Sect. 5 presents the results of a comparative analysis of e-governance in educational sector of Moldova and Sweden. Finally, Sects. 6 and 7 discuss conclusions and recommendations for future development of e-governance in educational sector of the Republic of Moldova.

The paper is a result of the UNESCO Obuchi Fellowship 2015 and a part of the first author's PhD studies. The future aspects to be analysed are teachers, pupils and parents' perspective in Moldova. The final results of this research are envisaged to support the current development of the sector e-governance in the Republic of Moldova and to constitute a valuable case study for countries with similar profile.

2 E-governance and E-Government in Education

The literature is dealing with two distinct definitions: e-governance and e-government. Although some sources do not distinguish these two definitions, there are an increasing tendency to separate them [7, p. 75]. E-government provides better services to citizens by effective use of ICTs improving the system of government [8], while the e-governance deals with the whole spectrum of the relationship and networks within government regarding the usage and application of. E-government is a narrower scope focusing the development of online services to the citizen, more the "E" on any particular government service – such as e-Tax, e-Transportation or e-Health [9, p. 3].

E-governance induces cost savings in the medium to the long term. In the short term, however, staffing and costs tend to increase, as government must offer multiple delivery platforms (both the traditional and e-government) during the initial transition [10]. According to Bhatnagar, a key trend in developing countries is to build for service delivery around tax collection, customs and procurement. This have been popular among governments and quickly embraced because it creates more efficient means to collect revenue; this being critical for governments that are cash constrained. Departments with regulatory functions have been quick to embrace e-government, while developmental departments such as education and health have been slow [11, p. 34].

The fields of implementation of e-governance are [10]:

- e-administration – refers to improving of government processes and of the internal workings of the public sector with new ICT (Information and communication technology) executed information processes;
- e-services – refers to improved delivery of public services to citizens. Some examples of interactive services are: requests for public documents, requests for legal documents and certificates, issuing permits and licenses;
- e-democracy – implies greater and more active citizen participation and involvement enabled by ICTs in the decision-making process.

The present study is connected to all three fields with its focus on the educational sector's IT infrastructure (however, in this paper we leave the field types implicit).

According to Bhatnagar, there are two ways to implement e-Governance in a country: bottom-up or top-down. Usually, big countries are more willing to have a bottom-up approach, leaving various institutions to develop their own projects. In this case, the biggest problem is of interconnection of these solutions. For small countries it is more common to have a top-down approach. A solution in both situations is the creation of a national agency, which assures the coordination of the solutions [11, pp. 74–75].

Governments establish national agencies responsible for implementing the e-government agenda nationwide. Agencies also measure the results of e-government principles application and use of ICTs to the fullest potential, to verify progress and planned performance improvement. This allows agencies to better manage their information resources including their investments in information technology [12, p. 7].

For a better management of the educational sector, it is not primarily e-services that should be developed but a platform with basic information about the sector: number of institutions, teachers, pupils etc. Good infrastructure is needed, as is obvious from countries where a system exists at the ministry without digital connection to all the places where input data is gathered or used [13].

An Education Management Information System (EMIS) is a Management Information System designed to manage information about an educational sector. An EMIS is a repository for data collection, processing, analysing and reporting of educational information including schools, students, teachers and staff. The EMIS information is used by the Ministries of Education, NGOs, researchers, donors and other education stakeholders for research; policy and planning; monitoring and evaluation; and decision making. EMIS information is specifically used to create indicators that monitor the performance of an education system and to manage the distribution and allocation of educational resources and services. The EMIS is expected to collect, process, utilize, and disseminate education data [13].

In the world there are many types of EMIS, some resources are open and can be adapted to the needs of the country, others are paid. Here should be mentioned the UNESCO initiative from 2010 to create an open solution database for the EMIS that provides all the necessary toolkits for data collection and analysis, and trainings for the responsible of data input and their analysis [14]. However, the authorities may opt to create their own system, depending on the specific country and indicators that wants to collect. Organization of the data collection varies from country to country. Some countries collect data via the Internet, other have had to rely on manually and physical means, a fact which may severely hamper the efficience of the EMIS [13].

3 Research Methods

For the analysis of the current situation regarding e-governance in the educational sector in Sweden and Moldova a secondary data analysis and a survey by interviews were done. Beside the secondary data analysis, a total number of 40 in-depth interviews were conducted. In Sweden, 25 interviews were performed in Karlstad Municipality with representatives from all educational levels. Previous experience of the Information Systems Department at Karlstad University in matter of the Education Management Information Systems research helped with choice of location in Sweden but interviews at the university level were conducted with educationalists and administrative staff outside the IS department. In Moldova, 15 interviews were conducted with representatives from all educational levels in the capital area. The technique of in-depth interviews rather than a massive employment of questionnaires was chosen as the longer discussions make it possible to better uncover presumptions among interviewees that the researcher did not imagined beforehand. To ensure the data accuracy, the interviews were conducted in both countries with the respondents representing central/local authorities and institutions from educational sector. The aim of the in-depth interview was to map available e-tools used by the educational sectors, their deployment, usage and benefits.

The comparative analysis of existing e-governance tools in the educational sectors of Moldova and Sweden was applied at the second step for data analysis. The aim of this method was to reveal:

- The countries way of applying e-governance at various tiers of the educational sector; and
- The future way of e-governance development in educational sector of Republic of Moldova, based on identified practices, issues and benefits.

4 E-governance Context of the Moldovan Educational Sector

Realizing the necessity to improve the quality of governance and to make the public service expenditure more efficient, the Moldovan government started the e-governance implementation in 2010. Some public e-services were already available, for example fiscal taxation, population documentation services, services of the Ministry of Internal Affairs. Other services, for example, open data, mobile digital signature etc. were introduced on-line by the EGC mentioned before.

Working in conditions of limited budgets, usually authorities must decide in which sectors to invest in e-governance as noted in Sect. 2. The situation is characteristic also for the Republic of Moldova, where the largest number of e-services was introduced in revenue-producing ministries.

The rate of citizens that require on-line public services increased from 9% in 2012, to 16% in 2014, according to EGC [15]. A barrier for increasing the share of on-line public services access is the lack of publication of information about their availability on various sites. It is thus difficult to find them, and there is a lack of skills of people to use on-line services.

According to the Strategic Program for Governance Technological Modernization, all the public services will be available also electronically till 2020 [16]. Arguably, the started reforms in the educational sector to increase quality, equity and efficiency, provide the right ground to start implementation of the e-governance agenda in the sector. Along with implementation of e-governance it is necessary to consider a promotional strategy of e-services and a strategy for increasing user's skills of e-services [17, p. 6].

According to the Moldova Education Strategy 2020 [5, pp. 12–18], from *government's perspective*, the biggest problems in the educational sector of Republic of Moldova are:

- Demographic decline leads to continued decline in part of the population included in education;
- Investment in education does not ensure national economic competitiveness;
- The lack of connection between education and labour market.

The strategy identifies three main actors: Government (central and local public authorities), institutions and parents/pupil. These actors have different demands. A single solution cannot solve all actors' issues; a reform at each educational level is necessary. At various levels of educational sector of Moldova has started major reforms to increase the quality, equity and efficiency in education. E-governance implementation in the field is necessary to monitor the reform results. Moldova has an undeniable advantage of territorial and financial accessibility of the Internet [18, p. 24]. Although there are good examples of e-governance tools in the Moldovan educational sector, still the e-governance in this sector remain underdeveloped for the moment.

5 Comparative Analysis of E-Tools in Moldovan and Swedish Educational Sector

A detailed analysis of available e-governance tools in educational sectors reveal a relative low level of e-governance implemented in Moldova. The situation varies depending on the educational level. For example, in general school, high school and university level, the number of available e-governance tools are higher than in pre-school level and Vocational Education and Training (VET) level. The number of e-governance tools in educational sector of Sweden does not vary so much from one level to other. In Sweden, several e-tools are developed for each actor of educational sector.

1. **At preschool level** of Republic of Moldova websites are seldom available. These are most common in private kindergartens. Institutions or public authorities do not have any system for digital recording of pupils or employees from kindergartens. In Sweden, at the municipal level are available platforms that offer to the interested persons information about each kindergarten and group, provide forms for admission and information about kids menu and activities. Municipal administrators have access to the information regarding pupils and kindergarten employees. At the municipal level is available an analytical tool which provides reports and possibilities for various data analysis. Institutions have access to the information regarding their pupils and their presence, employees and their presence, finances and teachers schedules. Teachers can access information regarding their schedule.
2. **At compulsory school level**, Moldova has some institutions websites and EMIS system based on which it was possible to create an open data platform. The implementation of the EMIS started in Moldova in 2007 with the Government Decision no. 270 of 13.04.2007 on approval of the "Concept of educational information system" [18]. The first pilot rounds of data collection took place in 2011–2012 [19]. Subsequently, in 2013 EMIS was adapted and implemented in all institutions of 1–12 grades. Currently, the EMIS system includes a spectrum of indicators on institutions, staff, and pupils [20]. The public authorities can manage the available information; the responsible from institutions have access to the system twice a year for updateing the data. The representatives of schools need to introduce data on the platform, the main data being in paper based registers, which is the main source of information for schools decisions. Parents have access to some information on a website created by a NGO with the support of the World Bank. In Sweden, similar to preschools, the same type of e-governance tools are available to the actors in the compulsory schools, whether private or public.
3. **At lyceum level**, Moldova has similar e-governance tools as compulsory school. Additional, at the national level there is a diplomas issuing platform. The central authorities manage the information. Institutions introduce information once a year. When the system opens for a second time each year, teachers/officers have a tool for data verification and correction. Parents and pupils can verify on the website the authenticity of the documents. For Sweden, see VET below.
4. **At VET level,** some institutions from Moldova have websites. No other e-governance tools are available. In Sweden for institutions of this level (Gymnasium) there is available a municipal platform with information regarding all institutions, with services for admissions guiding and admission platform. The extension of institutions websites offers information regarding course schedules for each student, food menu, information regarding students free time activities. For institutions, information is available regarding pupils and employees, financial information and teacher schedule. At the municipal level, administrative employees have access to the information regarding students and employees and a tool which generates reports and helps to analyse data. The parents are provided with information regarding students' presence at school and in case of absence, the system sends a message to the parents. Students have access to the library information and course learning platform.

5. **At Higher Education**, Moldovan institutions have websites; some have internal systems for employees' and students' information providing students information regarding course schedule and marks. Several institutions use learning platforms. Integrated information is not available at national level. For interested persons are available information regarding diploma authenticity and there is a diploma issuing platform. In 2016 started a wide national project for library systems integration. Swedish institutions have also their own websites providing information regarding available faculties. For students there is a national platform for admission which also provides the institutions with information regarding students. The institutions' administration has access to a platform for diploma issues that is connected to the platform for admission. Students have web access to the libraries and to learning platforms with detailed information and with possibility to distance study. Teachers have a system for scheduling and publishing course activities (Table 1).

Table 1. The available e-governance tools in educational sector of Republic of Moldova and Sweden

Levels of education	Moldova	Sweden
Preschool level	- Some institutions websites	- Municipality platform - Groups websites - Platform with information about pupils - Platform for pupils presence - Admission forms for pupils - Analytic tool for reports - System for teachers – schedule - Platform with financial information
Compulsory school	- EMIS - Open data platform - Some institutions websites	- Municipality platform - Classes websites - Platform with information about pupils - Platform for pupils presence - Admission platform for pupils - Analytic tool for reports - System for teachers – schedule - Platform with financial information
Lyceum	- EMIS - Open data platform - Some institutions websites - Diplomas issues platform - Diplomas verification platform	- Municipality platform - Institutions websites - Platform with information about pupils - System for aggregate data about pupils - Platform for pupils presence
VET level	- Some institutions websites	- Admission platform for pupils - Analytic tool for reports - System for teachers – schedule - Courses, Learning platform - Library platform - Platform with financial information
Higher education	- Institutions websites - Courses schedule - Information regarding grades - Diplomas issues platform - Diplomas verification platform - Library system - Learning platform	- Institutions websites - Platform with information about students - Admission platform for students - Information regarding grades - Diplomas issues platform - Teachers system (schedule) - Library platform - Courses, learning platform

6 Discussion and Conclusion

Analysing the implementation of e-governance in educational sector in Moldova, it can be observed that the major achievement of the e-governance is implementation of EMIS system, thanks to which was possible the development of the open data platform. At VET level, similar to preschool level and higher education even this possibilities are not available. The university level has some e-governance tools as, diploma issue and verification, courses and learning platform, library system, but only the library system started to be integrated between institutions at the moment (spring 2016). Other systems are sporadic and there is no integrated system regarding the students at this education level. In Sweden the EMIS system is not available except for the admission and study results system, which are national, but at the level of institutions are available all necessary e-governance tools for obtain information about the education sector. For Sweden it is more a necessity to integrate available services than to develop new ones.

The EMIS system in Republic of Moldova brings definitive benefits. However, its existence only at the level of general education significantly reduce the availability of information necessary for decision making in the entire educational system. Thus, there are many cases where officials are in need of some information have to use the phone. This method is demanding for both the central authorities and institutions, making inevitable the duplication of effort and information.

The lack of e-services such as admission, absence information, marks information, or sometimes basic information regarding institutions, in on-line format for parents and their children limit the educational sector transparency, increase the service access time and the staff time to spend on service to parents, pupils and employers.

The aim of this paper was to to identify the available e-services, e-administration and e-democracy solutions in the educational sector of Republic of Moldova. The results of the conducted study reveal that in Moldovan educational sector the number of available e-governance tools varies from one educational level to another. Considering the fact that there are not many integrated e-service, the Government succeeded in implementation of EMIS that is mandatory to monitor the reforms results. A key factor of a successful EMIS is access and use by the institutions of the data that they have entered. The actual system offers a limited access for the school representatives. In this situations representatives of institutions are likely to abandon data entry or to input data in an erroneous form because of tools absence for data verification and a perception of existent IS unusefulness. The actual EMIS is more oriented to solve the needs of public authorities instead of institution management or citizens. The lack of availability of the EMIS in preschools, VET and Higher Education, reduces significantly the advantages offered by the system.

Moldova e-governance implementation has a top-down approach. The central public authorities remain the main actors responsible for the e-governance agenda implementation. The situation is explained by the absence of sufficient budgets for local authorities to develop their own e-tools. In comparison, e-governance in Sweden have a bottom-up approach. The institutions have their own e-governance tools. The local public authorities have several platforms that allow them to process data and to offer e-services to the population. The extent of the electronic support at various educational levels does not vary very much. Here should be mentioned that the availability of some of the tools can vary from one municipality to another, as the country has a decentralized administration.

7 Recommendations

Considering the results, the future e-governance agenda in Moldova educational sector may have a combination of top-down approach and where is possible a bottom-up approach. The implementation of EMIS at all education levels will allow performing a comprehensive monitoring and evaluation of the implemented reforms impact. Each level should be approached individually, having the specific issues and needs. A wider access to the input data for institutions administers will allow development of an institutions proactive marketing approach. The parents, students and pupils can benefit from published open data.

Simultaneously, central public authorities can select a sample of institutions where to develop, introduce, test and adjust new e-tools in educational sector. This way can help to improve the developed e-tools until they are ready to meet necessaries requirement for implementation at the national level. The experience from Sweden show that developed e-tools should be developed near users for later integration. The responsibility of the Electronic Government Center in this case is to monitor and ensure the compatibility of developed new e-governance tools.

References

1. Pundhir, S., Sharma, D.: Benefits of E-governance in India. Int. J. Sci. Technol. Manag. **6**(2), 751–755 (2017)
2. E-Government Center: E-Transformation of Government in Moldova, Achievements and Results in 2013–2015. E-Government Center, Chisinau (2016)
3. E-Government Center, "www.egov.md," Sondaj național anual 2014, 12-06-2015. http://www.egov.md/ro/resources/polls/sondajul-2014capitolul-inivelul-de-dotare-cu-calcultare-si-acces-la-internet
4. Sami, A., Mudasir, S.M.: E-governance in education: areas of impact and proposing a framework to measure the impact. Turk. Online J. Distance Educ. (TOJDE) **14**(2), 305–313 (2013)
5. Ministry of Education.: "EDUCAŢIA-2020," Strategia sectorială de dezvoltare pentru anii 2014–2020, p. 47
6. Media Team.: "Ranking: the top most competitive economies in Europe (2012)
7. United Nations: E-Government Survey 2016. United Nations, New York (2016)
8. Heeks, R.: Success and Failure in e-Government Projects. The University of Manchester's Institute for Development Policy and Management (2008)
9. NITC Nepal Government.: Introduction to e-Government and its Scenario in Nepal. National Information Technology Center (2014)
10. "www.wikibooks.org," E-government/The Goals of E-Government. Accessed 17 March 2016
11. Bhatnagar, S.C.: E-government: From Vision to Implementation: A Practical Guide with Case Studies, p. 203 (2004)
12. Perillo, V.T.: E-government: Innovation, Collaboration and Access, p. 205. Nova Science Publishers, Inc., New York (2009)

13. Wicander, G.: Mobile Supported e-Government Systems, Analysis of the Education Management Information System (EMIS) in Tanzania. Karlstad University, Karlstad (2011)
14. "www.educationinnovations.org," http://www.educationinnovations.org/program/openemis. Accessed 15 May 2017
15. E-Government Center, "www.egov.md," National Annual Survey "Citizens' perception, uptake and support for the e-Transformation of Governance in the Republic of Moldova", 2015. http://www.egov.md/en/resources/infographics/infographicthe-rate-citizens-who-required-public-services. Accessed 15 June 2015
16. "www.egov.md," When will electronic services become available? http://www.egov.md/en/about/faq. Accessed 2015 June 2015
17. OECD.: Efficient e-Government for Smarter Public Service Delivery. OECD e-Government Studies, p. 29 (2010)
18. Budeanschi, Dumitru: Availability of Open Data in Education. Exper Grup, Chisinau (2014)
19. Hotărâre Nr. 270 din 13.04.2007 cu privire la aprobarea Concepţiei sistemului informaţional educaţional. "www.lex.justice.md," http://lex.justice.md/index.php?action=view&view=doc&lang=1&id=322761. Accessed 29 March 2015
20. Declaraţia Ministrului Educaţiei. "www.noi.md," http://www.noi.md/md/print/news_id/35176. Accessed 29 March 2015

A Review of the Norwegian Plain Language Policy

Marius Rohde Johannessen(✉), Lasse Berntzen, and Ansgar Ødegård

University College of Southeast Norway, Notodden, Norway
{marius.johannessen,lasse.berntzen,ansgar.odegard}@usn.no

Abstract. In this paper, we examine the policy documents that define the Norwegian policies on language use in the public sector, with an emphasis on how ICT is mentioned as a tool for creating a public sector language citizens find easy to understand. Norway and other countries have had a series of projects aimed at making the public sector use plain language in their communication with citizens. We present two example cases of successful plain language use and one less successful case, and discuss these cases using the lens of new institutional theory. We argue that the institutional context of change and user-centricity have had a major impact on the success of our example cases.

Keywords: eGovernment · Public sector renewal · Plain language · Institutional theory · Policy

1 Introduction

Language use and language policies are matters of great public interest, as language can be an instrument of inclusion or exclusion, discriminate or include certain groups and act to reinforce or break up existing power structures [1]. The ways in which we use language can be seen as a constant ideological battle about discourse, social control and social structure [2].

Public sector, or bureaucratic, language, has emerged in its current form because of the bureaucratic logic of impersonality, rationality and objective, rule-based decision-making [3], and the result has often been a language system that is difficult for users of public services to interpret. Partly because of the need for precise formulations dictated by bureaucratic logic, but also because of professionals using the terminology specific to their professions.

From a democratic perspective, the use of complex language is a problem, as it denies citizens the opportunity to participate in policymaking and to influence decision-making. The representative democratic ideal is that every citizen has both the right and the opportunity to be heard by elected officials. The use of language may be a major barrier to democratic participation and citizen access to the public sector, and plain language is thus an important prerequisite for eGovernment and eDemocracy [4]. This has been discussed since the 1980's when several scholars began arguing for the use of "plain English" in the public sector [3], as bureaucratic language had become difficult to understand for ordinary citizens.

M. Janssen et al. (Eds.): EGOV 2017, LNCS 10428, pp. 187–198, 2017.
DOI: 10.1007/978-3-319-64677-0_16

Plain language has emerged in recent years as an international topic[1], and in Norway, the plain language project emerged in 2008 as part of the government's initiative to modernize the public sector [5]. The project is grounded in several policy documents, and ICT plays a central role in this effort [6], with a clear user-centric perspective on how digital communication channels should function.

Our objective with this paper is to examine the relationship between policy, technology and institutional culture in the plain language project. We do this by analyzing policy documents addressing plain language, looking for explicit mentions of ICT in these documents, and by examining two example cases of successful plain language work: The Norwegian tax administration and the Norwegian Public Roads administration. We contrast these successful cases with the case of the welfare agency NAV, which has not been as successful [7]. We apply institutional theory as our lens in order to explain these different results. This approach addresses Axelsson et al.'s call for research on policy documents in a wider range of contexts [8].

The rest of the paper is structured as follows: Sect. 2 presents related research on language use and institutional theory. Section 3 outlines our research approach. In Sect. 4 we present our findings from the analysis of policy documents and example cases, and we discuss these findings in light of institutional theory in Sect. 5. Section 6 presents our conclusion and suggestions for further research.

2 Related Research

In this section, we discuss previous research on plain language, provide a brief overview of the Norwegian efforts in this area, and situate plain language in the wider context of digitizing the public sector in order to make it more effective and efficient. Further, we provide a brief overview of institutional theory as our analytical lens.

2.1 Plain Language from a User-Centric Perspective

Plain language is defined as "correct, clear and user-centered language in texts from government" [9] (authors' translation), and should involve organizing information so that the most important points come first, breaking complex information into understandable chunks, using simple language and defining technical terms and using the active voice [10]

Researchers have discussed plain language at least since the 1980's [3]. OECD countries have emphasized the use of plain language in government for long time, and 23 countries had implemented plain language strategies in the year 2000, with varying degrees of success. The OECD considers plain language as important for facilitating transparency and accountability in government [11]. In the Nordic countries, Sweden has been the driving force of plain language, and the Swedish efforts to simplify government communication has been an inspiration for Norwegian policy-makers [12].

[1] See f.ex the plain language network: http://plainlanguagenetwork.org.

Plain language did not receive much attention in Norway until the government initiated the project "klarspråk" (plain language) in 2008. The objective of the project was to improve communication between citizens and government, and the project involved more than 60 government agencies at the national level [5]. Evaluators [5] considered the initial project successful, and it was renewed in 2013 as the project "Plain language in public administration". This recent project is a collaborative effort between the Norwegian Agency for Public Management and eGovernment (DIFI) and the Norwegian Language Council. DIFI has created an online course for plain language use, and DIFI in collaboration with the language council has set up the web site "klarsrpåk", which provides guidelines, case studies, examples of good communication, language games and quizzes, as well as a project guide for planning and executing plain language projects in government agencies [12].

In order to involve municipalities as well as national government, the municipal organization KS has become involved, and is currently offering plain language courses to municipalities and working on guidelines for plain language, which will be presented as an e-learning application when completed. They have also set up a plain language award that goes to the municipality that has been most active in promoting and using plain language in the past year [13].

There are several approaches to evaluating plain language. Readability indexes are algorithms that attempt to calculate the readability of a text [14]. The two main index types are readability instruments aimed at assessing print and web-based information and word recognition and comprehension tests [15]. These indexes measure for example character, word and sentence length to determine the complexity of a text [15]. By paying attention to the number of words and syllables we use when writing, we can make our texts easier to understand [16]. However, a recent study indicated that readability indexes are not necessarily the most reliable tool for plain language work [17]. Nonetheless, readability indexes remain one important part of the plain language toolbox, and there is ongoing research on the automation of text simplification, where readability indexes are applied along with synonym dictionaries to replace difficult words in sentences [18]. The second approach is to apply writing techniques aimed at clarity. These techniques involve guidelines for the structuring of texts, choice of words, layout and more. There are several published guidelines, focusing on different areas of the writing process [19]. The third approach differs from the other two, in that the focus is on evaluating the result of a text; How well is it understood? Are readers able to act on the content? Visual representation and communication is seen as important in this approach, and usability testing is the preferred way of evaluating texts [19].

The Norwegian plain language project recommends that writers should emphasize the latter approach, but does recommend some use of guidelines and readability indexes as supplements to user evaluations [9]. However, both DIFI's online course and the "klarspråk" web site's writing tips rely heavily on checklists and examples of structure and writing styles. The project guide presents guidelines and examples of usability testing, recommending this for agencies who are working consistently on plain language.

Plain language is, in both national and municipal policies, placed in the context of modernization and digitization of the public sector, and mentioned as an essential aspect of a user-centric government. In the white paper "Digital Agenda for Norway" [6], the government outlines its policy for a cost-efficient, digitized public sector. One of the two key objectives of the white paper is to create a citizen-centric mindset in government. Public services should be presented as coordinated and complete, even if a service involves several agencies and levels of government. Information sharing is another key element of the policy. Services that are not designed form a user-centered perspective tend to have a much lower rate of adoption [20]. Usability testing is essential in user-centric government [21], hence the strong focus on testing in the Norwegian policy. In public sector projects, the user groups are many and diverse, and there can be very large differences in the objectives of citizens using the system and the government officials at the other end. This presents an additional challenge for user-centric government [22], and could also be seen as one of the reasons why the Norwegian plain language project downplays the importance of "simple" language. Certain user groups are both able to and require, communication to be precise and sometimes complex [9]. Usability testing with selected target groups is thus the only approach that can facilitate these many and varied user groups.

Despite this strong policy focus on user-centricity, eGovernment projects have had a tendency to be focused around the service being delivered, and citizen needs have not been taken into account [23]. In the next section, we present institutional theory as a possible explanation for this.

2.2 Neo-Institutional Theory and Organization Identity Theory

From a Neo-Institutional perspective, the concept of plain language might be considered one of many recipes for modernizing the organizational field of public sector organizations within the ideas of New Public Management, which might be characterized a global mega trend in modernizing the public sector organizations since the introduction in the 1980's [24].

Organizations adapt to what they believe society expect from them [25] and organizational changes thus emerge as a result of isomorphic processes [26] not necessarily founded in instrumental and rational reasons alone. This leads to institutional isomorphism and similarity between organizations [26]. However, when the institutional environments are ambiguous and pluralistic, there is a tendency of decoupling action from formal structure in order to maintain organizational efficiency [25].

As Meyer and Rowan [27] suggest, organizations embrace the wider culture and values institutionalized and legitimated in the society. Hence, the introduction of plain language may be explained within the frames of modern values and organizational phenomena like citizen-centrism, consumer dialogue, impression management and organization image.

Despite the focus on legitimacy through ceremonial changes and the tendency of decoupling action from formal structure, the adoption and implementation of the concept of plain language might be characterized as organization identity work [28]. Within a dynamic perspective on organization identity [29], an ongoing and ever moving relation between culture and image is affecting organization identity – "where we come from" and "who we are becoming" as an organization. This tension between the roots, history and traditions of the organization and the future represented by the image is to a great extent occupied with aligning the organization to expectations from the environments and the society.

Focusing only on "who we are becoming" might lead to adoption of plain language as neither accepted by the employees nor implemented and used in accordance with the ideas of the concept. On the other hand, focusing only on culture, traditions and the past might cause organizations to become immune to impulses, demands and changes initiated in the external environments. This might explain resistance to change, and should be taken in consideration when adopting concepts like plain language.

Seemingly contradictory theoretical perspectives like neo-institutional theory and organization identity theory might be of crucial importance when explaining adoption and implementation of new concepts. Formation of identity and construction of legitimacy through isomorphic processes are two sides of the same coin [30]. Thus, adopting and implementing plain language without involving and connecting with the culture, roots and traditions of the organization presumably will lead to ceremonial changes with no or little influence on the quality of dialogue with the citizens. In accordance with [31], we suggest a multidimensional time perspective when adopting new concepts. In order to succeed we recommend paying attention to both the past traditions and at the same time focus on the future, including changing expectations in society.

3 Research Approach

The purpose of this paper is to examine the relationship between policy, technology and institutional culture in the plain language project. Policy documents can carry ideas from high-level to concrete policy [8]. This paper addresses the call for research on policy documents in a wider range of contexts [8], by examining policy documents in the Norwegian Plain language project. The study was conducted using a qualitative, interpretive approach.

We have collected the policy documents that the Norwegian Language council report are central to the plain language projects: Two white papers outlining the government strategy on language and digitization[2], the government communication policy[3], the egovernment policy[4] and the strategy for accessibility[5]. We also have e-mail interviews with representatives from DIFI and KS, where we asked about status and future plans for the plain language project. Data for the two example cases are from DIFI's evaluation of government organizations working with plain language.

A policy analysis process can focus on policy problems, performance, expected and observed outcomes, as well as the actions that a policy leads to [32]. We focus our analysis on problems (understood as target audience, value propositions and social aspects of the policy) and expected outcomes and actions, especially involving communication and ICT. Actors, the acts performed by actors and their engagement with artefacts are typical characteristics of an interpretive approach to policy analysis in concrete

[2] st.meld 27 (http://ow.ly/8kLj308wr5q) & 35 (http://ow.ly/jvut308wraz).
[3] http://ow.ly/h9Ku308wrlE.
[4] http://ow.ly/C7HB308wt16.
[5] http://ow.ly/LbOb308wrt6.

cases [33]. Analysis of the documents have been conducted using discourse analysis [34] We have chosen two example cases, the Norwegian tax administration and the Norwegian Public Roads administration to examine how policy flows from high-level objectives to practical implementation. We apply institutional theory as our lens in order to explain why these two projects were successful in translating policy into action.

4 Findings

4.1 Policy Analysis

We have analyzed five policy documents, explicitly mentioning plain language: The «digital agenda» and «language policy» are white papers from government presented for discussion in parliament. The government communication policy presents the high-level policy for communication at all levels of government, and is a framework that can be used for further planning. The government accessibility strategy outlines the strategy for including people with accessibility challenges in society, and the language and digitization policy outlines the plan for modernizing and renewing the public sector. Table 1 summarizes the problem areas, plain language and related ICT aspects of these policy documents.

The five policy documents deal with plain language from different perspectives. The *language policy's* purpose is to outline a policy for the continued use of Norwegian language in all levels of society. Here, plain language is addressed as important for citizens, but the policy also discusses the need for complexity and emphasizes language education. The policy only mentions ICT as a contextual factor: As a driver for the requirement of higher literacy skills and as a threat to small languages such as Norwegian.

The *communication policy* builds somewhat on the language policy, but the purpose is to facilitate communication between citizens and government. Information and inclusion in public matters is the focal point of the policy. Plain language is mentioned as being important in order to reach the objectives of openness, participation and inclusion. ICT receives little attention. The only mention if ICT is that the public sector needs to use the possibilities offered by new communication technologies.

The *eGovernment policy* is more explicit on the role of ICT, and is the first document where digitization and plain language is set in the context of a more efficient public sector. Digitization is seen as essential for service delivery and the inclusion of all citizens, and the policy is more explicit on which tools (digital mailbox, user-centric design, common core components and digital communication as standard) to implement.

The *Accessibility strategy* addresses the needs of disabled people. In 2014 regulua-tion was introduced to facilitate accessibility in digital communication, and this strategy outlines the process for an accessible public sector. The document states that plain language is essential for accessibility, especially for people with certain kinds of cognitive disabilities. ICT plays a large role in this, and the document outlines 14 detailed points for accessible ICT. The points discuss what to do, but the responsibility for how is delegated to DIFI.

Table 1. Overview of policies

	Problem area (target audience, social aspects, values)	Communication & plain language	ICT/outcome aspects
Language policy (2008)	Create a common language policy across government to ensure consistency. Preserve the Norwegian language in a globalized world. Reveal hidden, language-based power structures. Points to socio-demographic differences in language skills	Acknowledges role of tradition in language use as barrier to plain language. Simplify bureaucratic language where possible, but some texts require precision and complexity. Improve language education	Information society increases necessity of mastering language. IT (Internet) a challenge for continued use of Norwegian language
Communications policy (2009)	Inform and include citizens in policy-making and service creation	Openness, participation, reaching everyone, coherence in communication across gov' agencies. Plain language important to reach everyone	Exploit new technologies
eGovernment policy (2012)	Digitize the public sector to a) create a more effective and efficient public sector, and b) to improve service delivery and communication with citizens.	1/3 find it difficult to understand public communication. Objective: All communication from government should follow plain language guidelines	Government communication to be digital (digital first choice) Digital mailbox User-centricity Create common set of core components
Accessibility strategy (2015)	Create a society where everyone is able to participate, also disabled people	Plain language important for accessibility	14 detailed policies on ICT/accessibility. Addresses "what", but not "how"
Digital agenda (2016)	ICT is rapidly changing society on all levels. We must use ICT to create a) a user-centric, effective and efficient public sector and b) Innovation, value and equal possibilities for participation	Plain language increases use of digital services, and ensures more people can take part. Young adults no not understand how to use current services	User-centricity Coordination across government departments Digital first choice Digital skills in schools Continue to build digital infrastructure (mobile, fibre)

The *Digital agenda* is the most recent policy, released in 2016. The ambitions of the digital agenda pull together a lot of the content from the previous policies, and present a vision of a user-centric government that talks in a way people can understand. This document is much more emphatic in stressing the point that government agencies can no longer act as silos, but need to work together to solve complex social problems.

Together, the five policy documents present a clear vision for a user-centric government, where plain language is essential for inclusive and efficient communication.

4.2 Example Cases: Successful Digitization and Plain Language

The Norwegian tax administration and the Norwegian Public Roads administration have both worked extensively with plain language in the past years, and both agencies report that plain language has led to measurable improvements.

The tax administration has been leading the way in digitizing the public sector, and the main driver is the change from defining themselves as a control and surveillance agency into a service agency whose purpose is to help citizens, organizations and businesses. At the same time, they are focused on becoming more effective and efficient, and are working to improve digital self-service solutions on their web site, which is constantly updated. Plain language is part of this change into a user-centric service organization. When changing something, they start by inviting user feedback via their "beta" blog. For example, their tax return simplification project received feedback from 11.000 users and was tested over several iterations. They combined workshops with employees, aimed at understanding the internal processes and regulation, with user testing and user feedback. This thorough understanding of the regulations and processes involved in tax deductions allowed the design team to create a front-end where users did not have to know the details in order to get the reporting right. The results have been positive. The commuter part of the project led to a 40% decline in complaints on tax returns, a 200% increase in site visits and a significant reduction in calls and e-mails about commuter tax deductions as users were able to use and understand the information on the web site.

The public roads administration ran a plain language project from 2011 to 2012. The project was run by their communication department, and included users from several of the other departments in the agency. After the project was completed, they implemented plain language as part of the everyday work processes in the organization. As with the tax administration, the public roads administration also has a holistic approach, seeing plain language as part of their overall drive to become a user-centric organization. They have redesign their web site emphasizing self-service in order to save resources and be more efficient. Frequently used services such as change of ownership forms for cars are now digitized and automated, making the process of buying and selling used cars much easier. They have also worked on changing the wording of standard letters, in order to make them easier to understand. Each of these letters are sent to a million users every year, so even a marginal increase in the public's ability to understand and act on a letter provides significant savings. The new letters were user-tested over two iterations. In the final test, users reported they spent significantly less time understanding the message and the actions they were required to take. Internally, the new letters led to a 40% reduction in calls from frustrated citizens who did not understand the content.

In contrast to these successful cases, we have the NAV reform, where three agencies (unemployment, social services, welfare) merged into the welfare agency NAV. Despite a user-centric focus, NAV is criticized for being removed from the users and for extensive use of bureaucratic language [35]. A major reason for this is said to be the merger itself, with massive challenges stemming from the merger of three different organizational cultures [7]. While the plain language policy development reads as a linear progression, the policies behind the NAV reform have suffered from several changes in direction both before and after the merger was initiated [7]. While NAV has been slowly improving, they still lag far behind colleagues in other agencies and users, in usability tests conducted by the first author, report that navigating the self-service web site can be both frustrating and difficult.

5 Discussion

Both the tax and public roads administrations report that organizational change was essential for their plain language success. While plain language initially was a separate project, it was later implemented as an integrated part of everyday work tasks and practices within the wider context of user-centricity and modernization through citizen self-service. Employees are positive, as they see that this approach has benefits in the form of fewer phone calls and complaints and more time for other and more interesting work.

While these two examples show how plain language and digitization can be implemented, the e-mail interviews with DIFI and KS confirms that despite a decade of plain language work, a lot remains to be done. Municipalities have only recently begun working with plain language, and large agencies such as NAV still have a long way to go.

Organizational theory can help explain these differences. Organizations adapt to the wider societal context, but in pluralistic organizational environments decoupling can occur [25, 26]. The tax and public roads administrations have internalized the digitization and plain language policies, and are working towards becoming service-organizations with the "client" (citizen) in focus. They have done this by seeing plain language, modernization and digitization as parts of an overall strategy, and made sure that this strategy is made part of the organizational culture. They have embraced the values legitimated in society [27], as communicated by the policy documents related to plain language. NAV on the other hand, has struggled with a huge reform, having to merge cultures with at times very different understandings. Evaluations of the reform [7] points to the problems stemming from this as well as the changes in the policies related to the reform as important for the current situation in the agency.

The organization identity tension between where we come from and who we are becoming [28, 29] is also handled differently. The tax and public roads administrations have managed to handle this tension. While they are focusing heavily on the future and implementing strategies that ca be seen as a clear break with the past, they remain anchored in the existing organizational culture, as exemplified in the workshops held with case handlers, aimed at understanding and building services around existing processes, but which also manages to appear as user-friendly and understandable to citizens. NAV's problem with merging different cultures appears to create a stronger tension, as employees struggle to find their place in a new organization. This makes it more difficult to cope with the expectations from policies on user-centricity and plain language. Management and policy has a strong focus on "who we are becoming", while employees seem more concerned with culture, change fatigue and finding their place.

6 Conclusion and Future Research

In this paper, we have examined the policy documents relevant for plain language work in Norway. The five policy documents we have analyzed reveal a gradually evolving policy, which begins with a pure language focus and evolves into a holistic and ambitious plan that sees plain language as an important part of creating a more efficient and user-centric public sector. Further, we have examined example cases to analyze how agencies translate the policy to action. Finally, we have applied organization theory to discuss the differences in results in our example cases, showing that policy implementation require organizations that are able to successfully handle the tension between past traditions and existing organizational culture, and future expectations and direction.

The main limitation with our study is that we have used secondary data, DIFI evaluations, in discussing the cases. While this is sufficient to provide an overall picture, future research should focus on in-depth observation of government agencies in order to verify our conclusions.

Further, we argue that there is a need for research into other aspects of plain language. We have discussed the organizational aspect of translating the plain language policy to action. Another issue is how the policies are interpreted and implemented. Plain language is easily seen as a text-only issue, involving readability of information. The policy documents discuss why and what should be done, but leave the how to the agencies implementing policy. The egovernment and digital agenda policies do mention briefly that language can also involve visualization of information, and we argue that while simplifying language is important, other possibilities to increase understanding of public sector information, mainly by using techniques of visualization, are equally important. Techniques such as flowcharts, timelines, map-based information, video and animation can play an important role in helping citizens understand information from government. There is evidence of this in the cases, as both agencies have redesigned their web sites to be visually oriented. The public roads agency have created a map-based solution for traffic monitoring and flow. The tax agency has redesigned several of their services as step-by-step guides relying heavily on visual and typographic elements. There are other examples as well, found in municipalities and other government agencies. The digital planning dialog[6], implemented in several municipalities, is a map-based solution for municipal planning where visualization has replaced long written documents. Several municipalities have implemented video streaming of meetings, survey results are presented using visualization[7] and open data policies are being implemented. However, these remain scattered examples. We are still sorely lacking an updated policy where the concept of plain language also includes these aspects, and future research should examine how different forms of communication can complement each other in order to continue working towards user-centricity and plain language as tools for modernizing government.

---

[6] http://ow.ly/eIeY308EeSC.

[7] www.bedrekommune.no.

References

1. Sonntag, S.K., Cardinal, L.: State traditions and language regimes: conceptualizing language policy choices. In: Sonntag, S.K., Cardinal, L. (eds.) State State Traditions and Language Regimes. McGill-Queen's University Press, Montreal & Kingston (2015)
2. Woolard, K.A., Schieffelin, B.B.: Language ideology. Annu. Rev. Anthropol. **23**, 55–82 (1994)
3. Sarangi, S., Slembrouck, S.: Language, Bureaucracy and Social Control. Routledge, London (2013)
4. Lutz, B.: Plain language: an important basis of e-democracy and open government. In: Parycek, P., Edelmann, N. (eds.) CEDEM 16—Conference for E-Democracy and Open Government. Danube University, Krems (2016)
5. Dahle, M., Ryssevik, J.: Klart vi kan! En evaluering av effektene av prosjektet "klart språk i staten". In: Rapport 2013:11. Bergen (2013)
6. Digital agenda for Norge: IKT for en enklere hverdag og økt produktivitet, k.-o. moderniseringsdepartement (ed.). Oslo (2016)
7. Andreassen, T.A., Aars, J.: Den store reformen: Da NAV ble til. Universitetsforlaget, Oslo (2015)
8. Axelsson, K., Melin, U., Granath, M.: In search of ICT in smart cities – policy documents as idea carriers in urban development. In: Scholl, H.J., Glassey, O., Janssen, M., Klievink, B., Lindgren, I., Parycek, P., Tambouris, E., Wimmer, M.A., Janowski, T., Sá Soares, D. (eds.) EGOVIS 2016. LNCS, vol. 9820, pp. 215–227. Springer, Cham (2016). doi: 10.1007/978-3-319-44421-5_17
9. Kvarenes, M., et al.: Klar, men aldri ferdig. En praktisk veileder i klarspråksarbeid. Språkrådet (2011)
10. Kandula, N.R., et al.: The relationship between health literacy and knowledge improvement after a multimedia type 2 diabetes education program. Patient Educ. Couns. **75**(3), 321–327 (2009)
11. Deighton-Smith, R.: Regulatory transparency in OECD countries: overview, trends and challenges. Aust. J. Public Administration **63**(1), 66–73 (2004)
12. Klarspråksarbeid i andre land. [cited 27 02 2017]. http://www.sprakradet.no/Klarsprak/om-klarsprak/hva-er-klarsprak/Klarspraksarbeid-i-andre-land/ (2016)
13. KS. Klart språk. [cited 27 02 2017]. http://www.ks.no/fagomrader/utvikling/digitalisering/klart-sprak/ (2016)
14. McCallum, D.R., Peterson, J.L.: Computer-based readability indexes. In: Proceedings of the ACM'82 Conference. ACM (1982)
15. Friedman, D.B., Hoffman-Goetz, L.: A systematic review of readability and comprehension instruments used for print and web-based cancer information. Health Educ. Behav. **33**(3), 352–373 (2006)
16. Flesch, R.F.: How to Write Plain English—A Guide for Lawyers and Consumers. Harper & Row, New York (1979)
17. Dahlia, J., Wray, D.: Reassessing the accuracy and use of readability formulae. Malay. J. Learn. Instr. **11**, 127–145 (2014)
18. Shardlow, M.: A survey of automated text simplification. Int. J. Adv. Comput. Sci. Appl. (2014)
19. Professionalising plain language options paper. In: Plain—7th Biannual Conference. Plain English Foundation, Sydney (2009)
20. Bertot, J.C., Jaeger, P.T.: The E-Government paradox: Better customer service doesn't necessarily cost less. Gov. Inf. Q. **25**(2), 149–154 (2008)

21. Bertot, J.C., Jaeger, P.T., Grimes, J.M.: Using ICTs to create a culture of transparency: E-government and social media as openness and anti-corruption tools for societies. Gov. Inf. Q. **27**(3), 264–271 (2010)
22. Axelsson, K., Melin, U., Lindgren, I.: Exploring the importance of citizen participation and involvement in e-government projects: Practice, incentives, and organization. Transform. Gov. People Process Policy **4**(4), 299–321 (2010)
23. Anthopoulos, L.G., Siozos, P., Tsoukalas, I.A.: Applying participatory design and collaboration in digital public services for discovering and re-designing e-Government services. Gov. Inf. Q. **24**(2), 353–376 (2007)
24. Røvik, K.A.: Trender og translasjoner: ideer som former det 21. Århundrets organisasjon. Universitetsforlaget, Oslo (2007)
25. Boxenbaum, E., Jonsson, S.: Isomorphism, diffusion and decoupling. In: The Sage Handbook of Organizational Institutionalism, pp. 78–98 (2008)
26. DiMaggio, P.J., Powell, W.W.: The New Institutionalism in Organizational Analysis. University of Chicago Press, Chicago (1991)
27. Meyer, J.W., Rowan, B.: Institutionalized organizations: formal structure as myth and ceremony. Am. J. Sociol. **83**(2), 340–363 (1977)
28. Røvik, K.A.: Identitetsutvikling i moderne organisasjoner. Magma **1**(1), 41–51 (1998)
29. Hatch, M.J., Schultz, M.: The dynamics of organizational identity. Hum. Relat. **55**(8), 989 (2002)
30. Pedersen, J.S., Dobbin, F.: In search of identity and legitimation: bridging organizational culture and neoinstitutionalism. Am. Behav. Sci. **49**(7), 897–907 (2006)
31. Ødegård, A.: Organisasjonrs tilpasning til radikale reformer—mellom tradisjon og fornyelse. Magma. **2017**(2) (2017)
32. Dunn, W.L.: Public Policy Analysis, 5th edn. Routledge, London (2016)
33. Yanow, D.: Accessing local knowledge. In: Hajer, M.A., Wagenaar, H. (eds.) Theories of Institutional Design: Deliberative Policy Analysis: Understanding Governance in the Network Society. Cambridge University Press, Cambridge (2003)
34. Granath, M.: The smart city—how smart can 'IT' be?: discourses on digitalisation in policy and planning of urban development. In: Linköping Studies in Arts and Science, p. 226. Linköping University Electronic Press, Linköping (2016)
35. Lundberg, K.G.: Uforutsigbare relasjoner: Brukererfaringer, NAV-reformen og levd liv (Ph.D. thesis). University of Oslo, Oslo (2012)

ICT and Financial Inclusion in the Brazilian Amazon

Luiz Antonio Joia(✉) and Ricardo Paschoeto dos Santos

Getulio Vargas Foundation, Rua Jornalista Orlando Dantas 30, Room 205, Rio de Janeiro 22231-010, Brazil
luiz.joia@fgv.br, ricardopas@bol.com.br

Abstract. The challenge of providing the infrastructure of public services in the less developed regions of Brazil has mobilized the Brazilian government in the quest for new and creative approaches that can reduce the major inter-regional disparities in the country. One of the initiatives implemented include access to the financial system, since, by way of example, such access is almost non-existent on Marajó Island in the state of Pará in the Brazilian Amazon. To change this reality, an innovative e-government project is the itinerant bank branch installed in a boat, named *Agência Barco*, to serve the riverine populations of regions with low population density, transportation difficulties and limitations in access to information and communication technology (ICT). Thus, the main objective of this research is to identify how the financial inclusion indicators have been influenced by the work of Agência Barco on Marajó Island from the ICT standpoint. The results obtained led to the conclusion that Agência Barco has been able to attend the needs of access to financial products and services demanded by the population of Marajó Island, as well as identify opportunities for broadening financial education and inclusion through this e-government venture.

Keywords: Financial inclusion · Development · ICT for development · *Agência Barco* · Marajó island

1 Introduction

Studies of the World Bank [1] and the Brazilian Institute of Geography and Statistics [2], among others, point to a continuous improvement of social and economic development indicators in Brazil in the last two decades, with a reduction of inequalities between income classes. However, when analyzing the Brazilian Municipal Human Development Index, regional inequalities are perceived, and it is possible to identify a broad variance in the opportunities available to Brazilians [3].

These inequalities also prevail in access to financial services, which can be seen in the indicators of the Financial Inclusion Reports of 2010 and 2015, which reveal a wide dispersion between the Units of the Federation [4, 5], as in March 2015 when 240 municipalities were without banking services of any kind (branches, service outlets or ATMs). Furthermore, in March 2015 a total of 1922 Brazilian municipalities did not have bank branches, i.e. 34.5% of Brazilian municipalities [5]. Therefore, there is still vast asymmetry in Brazil in access to and use of banking services [6].

M. Janssen et al. (Eds.): EGOV 2017, LNCS 10428, pp. 199–211, 2017.
DOI: 10.1007/978-3-319-64677-0_17

Thus, this article seeks to investigate an ICT-equipped itinerant bank in vessels—an e-government project developed by Caixa Econômica Federal (CAIXA[1]) and named Agência Barco[2]—which seeks to attend the populations of riverine regions with access to banking services, in cities where there is not a single local bank branch. In specific terms, the universe of this work includes the Agência Barco that serves Marajó Island[3] in the state of Pará—a region with a low human development index (HDI), including the city of Melgaço, which has the lowest HDI in Brazil [3]—aiming to identify how the Agência Barco, by means of ICT, influences the financial inclusion of the Marajó Island region.

2 Theoretical Background

2.1 ICT and Financial Inclusion

For the Brazilian Central Bank, financial inclusion is the process of effective access and use by the population of financial services suited to their needs, thereby contributing to their quality of life. However, not all individuals and companies have access to the financial system, either due to the lack of availability of services and products for given sectors of society or the lack of a financial culture among the people.

Despite progress in the relationship between citizens and the financial system and the increased presence of financial institutions in almost all Brazilian municipalities due to the success of the Banking Correspondent (BC) model [7, 8], the country still has less than half of the number of bank branches per capita existing in developed countries [9].

Moreover, by adopting a holistic approach, studies on ICT4D—Information and Communication Technology for Development—seek to analyze how ICT can promote development while respecting the complexity of local, national and international conditions [10]. Thus, ICT is the latest enabler of financial inclusion, since its mass diffusion is the most significant technological change in low-income communities in recent years, leading to the emergence of inclusive financial services, especially those related to mobile communication technology [10].

2.2 The Dynamic Info-Inclusion Model (2iD)

In an attempt to overcome the lack of research in the ICT4D field in Brazil, Joia [11, 12] proposed the dynamic info-inclusion model (2iD), which evaluates digital inclusion encompassing both political, technical, educational and social aspects, as well as the dynamics of a virtuous cycle of participation and empowerment, as shown in Fig. 1.

---

1 CAIXA is a Brazilian federal bank in charge of implementing social programs in the country.

2 Agência Barco means Riverboat Branch in English.

3 More information about Marajó Island is available at https://en.wikipedia.org/wiki/Maraj%C3%B3, retrieved on January 19, 2017.

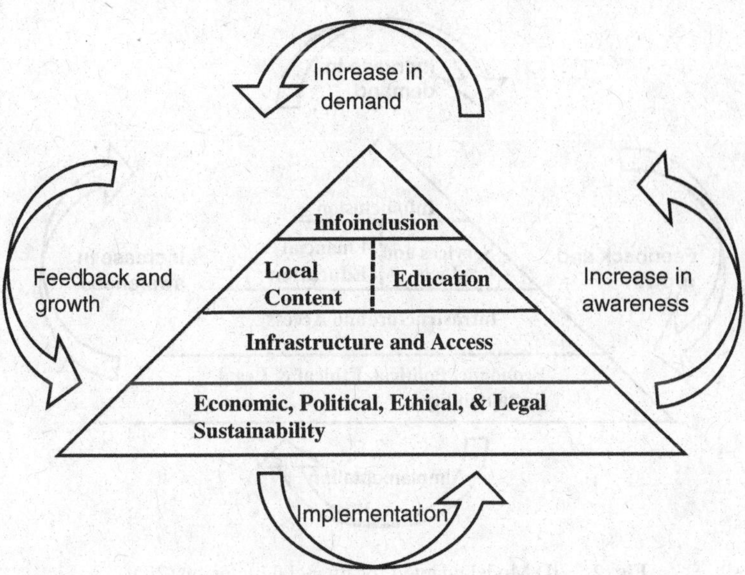

Fig. 1. Dynamic Info-inclusion Model (2iD). *Source*: Adapted from Joia [11, p. 308]

In this context, Joia [11, 12] suggests that the sustainability of digital inclusion should include not only financial and economic factors, but also factors that reflect the government's concern for the continuity of public policies for digital inclusion. Furthermore, according to the author, the "education" component in the model should go beyond the mere training of individuals, incorporating awareness of the opportunities generated by ICTs for socio-economic change. Moreover, the author stresses the need to consider the environment and the context, in order to create specific content that meets the expectations and needs of the location of the individuals in which it develops the info-inclusion project.

On the other hand, in the dynamic process of implementation of actions, there occurs increased awareness of individuals, particularly the awakening of interest in issues relating to the use of ICT. From that moment onwards, these individuals begin to demand content, education, services and access to ICT. The feedback, coupled with the broadening of the empowerment cycle arising from this dynamic, generates the implementation of new initiatives for digital inclusion, as seen in Fig. 1.

2.3 The 2iD Model Adapted to Financial Inclusion (2iDf)

For the development of this research, the 2iD dynamic info-inclusion model created by Joia [11, 12] was adapted to evaluate financial inclusion, as shown in Fig. 2. For this purpose, the theoretical framework that supports the components of the 2iD model adapted to financial inclusion, called 2iDf, is presented in Fig. 3.

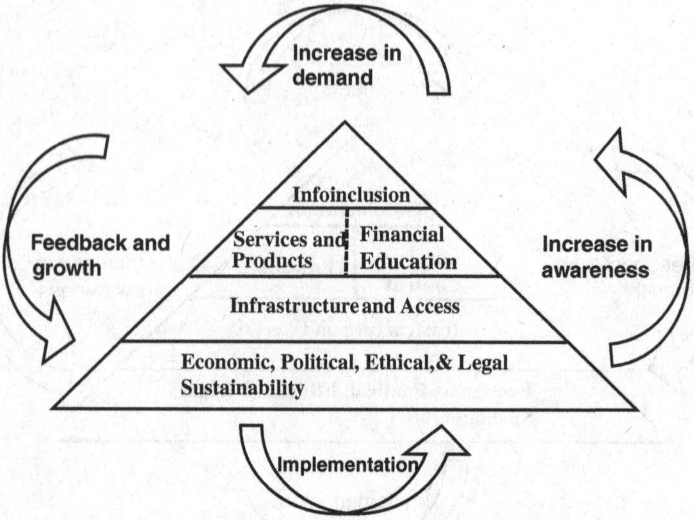

Fig. 2. 2iD Model adapted for financial inclusion (2iDf)

Component of The Model	Sources
Infrastructure and Access	[4,13-14]
Banking Installations and ICT	[4,14]
Services and Products	[4,14]
Costs	[9,15,16]
Financial Education	[13,16]
Enhancement of the Financial Resources	[8,17]
Generation of Income	[18]
Promote the Use of Electronic Transactions	[8,19,20,21]
Services and Products	[20,22]
Sustainability	[15,16,23,24]
Implementation	[11,12,16,24]
Increase in Demand	[4,11,14,26]
Feedback and Growth	[11,14,22]

Fig. 3. Theoretical framework for the 2iD model adapted for financial inclusion (2iDf)

Thus, in the adapted model of Fig. 2, the following aspects of financial inclusion are addressed:

- Infrastructure and access—This deals with the creation of individual and collective conditions for the population of the locations to access financial services involving:
  - The presence of banking facilities and technological resources;
  - Availability of services and products;
  - Accessible cost for access to the Agência Barco and the products offered.

- Financial Education—This deals with the training of people to use the products offered in all its possibilities, comprising:
  - Presentation of the characteristics of products and services that enhance the financial resources of the citizen;
  - Presentation of the characteristics of products and services to support entrepreneurial activities that can generate more income in the locations;
  - Promotion of the use of electronic transactions, thereby replacing cash.
- Services and Products—This involves offering of a portfolio of financial products and services that takes into consideration the reality of the financial inclusion in each location served.
- Sustainability—This involves the maintenance and updating of financial products and services offered in the locations, including economic aspects—logistic costs, personnel and ICT—as well as aspects related to public policies and legal and ethical issues.

Just as with the 2iD model of Joia [11], the dynamic process of the 2iDf model perceives the government as being responsible for implementing the financial inclusion initiatives. In this dynamic process, through the implementation of financial inclusion actions, there is an increase in the awareness of individuals, particularly the awakening of interest in questions relating to the use of financial products and services. Thereafter, these individuals begin to demand more financial services and products, more educational activities and, consequently, more access to technologies that enable the use of financial services. The feedback coupled with the broadening of the empowerment cycle resulting from this dynamic leads to the implementation of new financial inclusion initiatives.

3 Methodological Procedures

This article used the case study method [27], with data collection by means of interviews and direct observation. For the processing and analysis of data, the content analysis technique [28] and the application of the dynamic info-inclusion model adapted to financial inclusion (2iDf) were used.

Thus, a single case study is investigated with one unit of analysis [27] represented by a service outlet of the Marajó Island Agência Barco of CAIXA, with data obtained from document research, a questionnaire and interviews. A directed sample is used, in which individuals are selected on the basis of certain characteristics regarded as relevant by the researchers and participants [29], and employing techniques of content analysis for data analysis [30].

3.1 Data Collection

To achieve the objectives proposed in this case study a literature review was initially conducted on the subject in question. Documents were also gathered from the financial institution under analysis, IBGE, UNDP and the Central Bank.

Open interviews were conducted [31] with employees of the financial institution to assist in providing an in-depth description of the case in order to identify relevant information not available in documentary sources. However, in order to grasp the perception of the Agência Barco users regarding the services and aspects of financial inclusion, semi-structured interviews were staged [32]. The interviews were conducted during the visit of one of the researchers to the Agência Barco in Marajó. A total of 23 clients and five employees from CAIXA and five servants of organizations involved participated in these interviews, which were recorded and later transcribed verbatim for analysis. Moreover, asystematic non-participant direct observation was also conducted [31].

All the above data were obtained over the course of five days in July 2015 during a trip made by one of the researchers in the Agência Barco in the Marajó Island in Brazilian Amazon.

3.2 Data Analysis

Interviews conducted with Agência Barco clients and employees were handled with content analysis techniques, with a priori categorization based on constructs of the 2iDf model, with alphanumeric coding and grouping by frequency of occurrence, i.e. by repeating of contents common to the majority of respondents [28]. The categorization followed the mixed model [33], that is, it made it possible to add new categories as registration units were regrouped.

To assist in the analysis of content, lexical analysis (which applies statistical methods to the description of the vocabulary) was applied before the analysis of content. This was done to ensure that the data analysis therefrom was fully implemented, encompassing several possibilities that might arise or emerge [34].

Registration units for clipping of excerpts were defined by words and expressions that alluded to the static and dynamic components of the 2iDf model. Lexical analysis led to the initial identification of 864 words and phrases which, in turn, were grouped into 235 initial categories. The recurring process of lexical analysis and analysis of content led to a new categorization phase, totaling 97 categories with 821 occurrences (see Fig. 4). From this phase of the review process onwards, the intermediary categories were also coded according to their influence—positive or negative—in relation to the components of the 2iDf model. The data were interpreted by means of comparison with the constructs highlighted in the theoretical framework, which supported the components of the 2iDf model, seeking to identify the impact of the Agência Barco on financial inclusion of locations served, and to identify which of the components of the 2iDf model generated opportunities for actions that could contribute to regional development.

Components of the 2iD Model adapted for Financial incluison	Categories	Frequency of remarks per category	Frequency of remarks per component of the model
Infrastructure and access	ICT	45	430
	Co sts	85	
	Physical Structure	14	
	Promotion	129	
	Complementary services (Lottery and BC)	121	
	Team	19	
	Availability	17	
Financial e ducation	Guidance	85	179
	Ease of use	60	
	Innovation	34	
Products	Supply	112	112
Sustentainability	Politics	46	51
	Economics	5	
	Legal	0	
	Ethics	0	
Awareness	Insertion	9	17
	Community	8	
Increase in demand	New services	18	18
Growth	Initiatives	15	15

Fig. 4. Categories of the content analysis

4 The "Agência Barco" Case

CAIXA is a Brazilian public bank having experience in the operation of social programs of the Federal Government and of banking inclusion to expand attendance to populations still without access to banking services, especially through Banking Correspondents. However, in many areas with difficult access by land, or very far from municipalities with dynamic economic activity, there are difficulties for the business model of the Banking Correspondents to attend the needs of the populations. This situation is especially relevant in the riverine locations of the states of the Amazon region, where river trips between towns and larger cities can take more than one day.

In this scenario in which barriers to the physical presence of banking institutions are well-nigh insuperable, the 'Itinerant Riverine CAIXA Service Units' project, which became known as Agência Barco, was conceived.

The Agência Barco consists of boats designed and built exclusively for operation of a bank agency where bank staff perform their activities like any other bank branch of the institution. In addition, the boats are equipped with infrastructure for support to partnerships with other agencies of the Federal and State Government. These include, among others, the Ministry of Health, Ministry of Culture, Ministry of Labor, Ministry of Education, Secretariat on Policies for Women, as well as Courts of Justice to carry out public and institutional policies in the locations.

The Marajó Island Agência Barco was inaugurated in January 2014 to serve ten cities: Soure, Salvaterra, Ponta de Pedras, Muana, São Sebastião da Boa Vista, Curralinho, Bagre, Breves, Melgaço and Portel. It is a vessel with three decks, with a total area of one thousand and seventy-seven square meters, with capacity for seventy-six people seated in the service area of one hundred and forty square meters, plus a further twenty passengers who remain on the boat throughout the trip, namely five employees of CAIXA, five employees of the organizations involved, four security guards and six crew members.

One of the prerequisites for opening the Agência Barco imposed by the regulatory bodies was that no cash would be stored or transacted on the boat for security reasons. Thus, the business strategy has the support of a lottery office in each city served by the boat, such that the amounts in cash can be handled by these service outlets, also operated locally by CAIXA.

The Agência Barco makes a monthly trip, referred to as a cycle, remaining two days on average in each location, working during normal banking hours and offering all the services of a normal branch, except for cash transactions. The displacement between cities is usually at the end of the day in the early evening and night, depending on the sailing conditions and the weather (wind, rain, etc.). The main services offered are: opening accounts, microcredit operations, financing of building materials, security bonds, life insurance, direct consumer credit, registration and resetting passwords on federal government citizen cards, registration and regularization of the social integration program, release of length of service pension funds, release of unemployment benefits, registration and regularization of social security cards, family allowance benefits, among others.

The technological solution for the Agência Barco includes satellite communication to connect to the CAIXA Datacenter located in Brasilia, which is structured to support real time data and voice applications with autopointing and autotracking mechanisms. These functions enable execution and transmission of back-end processes of the Agência Barco, even with the vessel in transit, and reduce the occurrence of communication failures due to movement of the boat on its moorings. The satellite connection is concentrated in the teleport of the telecommunications services operator and forwarded by terrestrial circuits to the CAIXA Datacenter located in Brasilia. In addition to this, the vessel is equipped with direct access to the Internet via cell phone networks.

5 Results

Of the ten municipalities served by the Agência Barco on Marajó Island, eight are classified as having low or very low human development and only two are classified as having medium human development, which is well below the Brazilian global HDI [3]. Moreover, only four of the ten municipalities served by the Agência Barco have bank branches, and only the municipality of Breves has a CAIXA branch, which is the financial institution responsible for putting the public policies of the federal government into operation.

The Financial Inclusion Index of the State of Pará was analyzed in the second Financial Inclusion Report of the Brazilian Central Bank [4], with Marajó Island featuring the lowest indicators of the state, which confirms the lack of the availability of banking services in the Agência Barco operating region.

It was revealed that the majority of the customers interviewed (47.8%) had little schooling (incomplete primary education) and a little over half of the sample received social benefits from the federal government—with only one respondent stating that this is the main source of family income.

Of the twenty-three customers interviewed, approximately 50% knew of the existence of the Agência Barco through third parties, i.e. a neighbor or relative saw the boat in the harbor and passed on the information, and six customers interviewed came to the branch by boat, coming from tributaries or creeks in the regions surrounding the cities.

In addition to this, there has been a marked increase in cell phone penetration, with all of the customers confirming that they owned cell phones, although around half of them did not have any form of Internet access.

Of the twenty-three respondents, 40.9% reported having no formal relationship with financial institutions through checking or savings accounts, though only three said they had never had a bank account. In addition, more than half of the respondents reported their preference for full withdrawal of money deposited in a bank account.

With respect to financial education, there was little experience or awareness regarding other products such as, for example, loans and investments among those interviewed.

The content analysis conducted resulted in tables that summarize the opinions of respondents regarding the presence of each of the components of the 2iDf model. They identified the intermediate categories and their frequency of occurrence, as well as the influence of each intermediate category in the final category, namely a positive influence or presence of aspects related to a given component of the model or a negative influence or no aspects related to a given component of the model.

The perception of the existence of the static elements of the 2iDf model proves to be more accentuated than the dynamic components, as evidenced by a higher frequency of comments—attaining more than 93% of all remarks made by respondents. Thus, the low frequency of remarks related to the dynamic aspects of the model suggests that the financial education process failed to generate awareness of the potential opportunities offered by financial inclusion in the daily lives of individuals [12].

To assess the relative impact of the presence of each static component of the 2iDf model, a scale was created with three levels to represent the perception of the presence of a given component of the model and its positive aspects—Fig. 5 and Table 1.

Perception of presence of the component	Caption
High> 75%	
25% <= Average <= 75%	
Low < 25%	

Fig. 5. Classification of the components of the 2iDf model

Table 1. Scale of the presence of the static components of the 2iDf model

Static component of the model	Total Frequency	Positive Frequency	Positive Frequency (%)
Infrastructure/access	430	212	49.30%
Education	179	179	46.93%
Services/Products	112	97	86.61%
Sustainability	51	41	80.39%

Based on the above scale, a graphical representation of the results analyzed is shown in Fig. 6, associated with the perceptions of the presence of positive aspects of the static components of the 2iDf model.

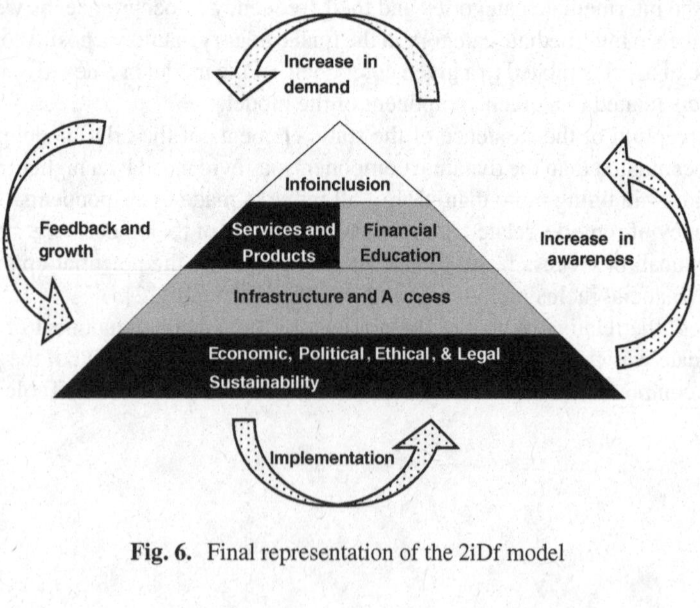

Fig. 6. Final representation of the 2iDf model

6 Conclusions

This research identified the need for investment in ICT infrastructure to meet the commercial agreements in order to provide a wider range of services, as well as enable partnerships with other state and federal agencies for services related to issuance of documents and processing retirement benefits, for example. In addition, the need to create incentives for dissemination of ICT infrastructure in regions with lower population density was identified, such as for example, the creation of basic cell phone packages with access to transaction services (cell phone banking, credit and debit transactions, cell phone payment).

It is also clear that without minimum financial education of the customers, it will be difficult for Agência Barco to offer more than the most basic and simple financial services to the population served.

Lastly, it was perceived that the riverine population in Marajó Island is still not even aware of the potential benefits accrued from being financially included as the dynamic components of the 2iDf model were not considered important by the local population.

In sum, financial inclusion is still a challenge in Brazil and tackling this situation depends on technological innovations, business models and public policies that can provide faster inclusion of the population currently excluded from financial system in the country.

References

1. World Bank: World development indicators (2015). http://data.worldbank.org/country/brazil#cp_wdi. Accessed 10 May 2015
2. IBGE: Informações Sociais, Demográficas e Econômicas (2015). http://www.ibge.gov.br/home/disseminacao/eventos/missao/informacoessociais.shtm. Accessed 5 Mar 2015
3. UNDP: Índice de desenvolvimento humano municipal brasileiro (2013). http://www.br.undp.org/content/brazil/pt/home/library/idh/o-idhm-do-brasil.html. Accessed 19 Jan 2017
4. BCB: Relatório de Inclusão Financeira N. 2. Brasília (2011). www.bcb.gov.br/?INCFINANC. Accessed 2 May 2016
5. BCB: Atendimento bancário no país—Distribuição do quantitativo de municípios por Região e UF. Brasília (2015). http://www.bcb.gov.br/htms/deorf/d201503/Quadro04-Atendimento banc?rionoPa?s-Distribui??odoQuantitativodeMunic?piosporRegi?oeUF.pdf. Accessed 2 May 2016
6. Crocco, M.A., Santos, F., Figueiredo, A.: Exclusão financeira no Brasil: uma análise regional exploratória. Revista de Economia Política **33**, 505–526 (2013)
7. Jayo, M., Diniz, E.: Um mapeamento descritivo dos modelos de gestão de redes de correspondentes bancários no Brasil. Revista de Administração da USP **48**, 621–634 (2013)
8. Leonardi, P.M., Bailey, D.E., Diniz, E.H., Sholler, D., Nardi, B.: Multiplex appropriation in complex systems implementation: the case of Brazil's correspondent banking system. MIS Q. **40**, 461–473 (2016)
9. Bader, M., Savoia, J.R.F.: Logística da distribuição bancária: tendências, oportunidades e fatores para inclusão financeira. Revista de Administração de Empresas **53**, 208–215 (2013)

10. Heeks, R.: Do Information and comunication technologies (ICTs) contribute to development? J. Int. Dev. **22**, 625–640 (2010)
11. Joia, L.A.: Bridging the digital divide: some initiatives in Brazil. Electr. Gov. Int. J. **1**, 300–315 (2004)
12. Joia, L.A.: Inclusão digital no Brasil: um modelo heurístico de natureza dinâmica. In: Martins, P.E.M., Pieranti, O.P. (eds.) Estado e gestão pública: visões do Brasil contemporâneo, 1st edn, p. 340. FGV Editora, Rio de Janeiro (2006)
13. Beck, T., De La Torre, A.: The basic analytics of access to financial services. Financ. Markets Inst. Instr. **16**, 79–117 (2007)
14. Heeks. R., Molla, A.: Impact assessment of ICT-for-development projects: a compendium of approaches. In: Working Paper on Development Informatics, Manchester (2009)
15. Kleine, D., Unwin, T.: Technological revolution, evolution and new dependencies: what's new about ICT4D? Third World Q. **30**, 1045–1067 (2009)
16. Gloukoviezoff, G.: The link between financial exclusion and over-indebtedness (2006). https://gloukoviezoff.files.wordpress.com/2009/01/wp-link-fe-oi.pdf. Accessed 10 Jan 2015
17. Diniz, E.H.: Correspondentes Bancários e Microcrédito no Brasil: Tecnologia Bancária e Ampliação dos Serviços Financeiros para a População de Baixa Renda. FGV/EAESP/GVPesquisa, pp. 1–102 (2007)
18. Dymski, G.A.: Financial globalization, social exclusion and financial crisis. Int. Rev. Appl. Econ. **19**, 439–457 (2005)
19. Brandão, J.L.: Perspectivas para os celulares dos pobres servirem a políticas de inclusão financeira e de governo eletrônico: a proposição do Ministério do Desenvolvimento Social no Governo Lula. In: Proceedings of the XXXV Encontro Nacional dos Programas de Pós-Graduação em Administração (EnANPAD, Rio de Janeiro) (2011)
20. Heeks, R., Amalia, M., Kintu, R., Shah, N.: Inclusive Innovation: Definition, Conceptualisation and Future Research Priorities. Working Paper on Development Informatics. Manchester (2013)
21. Diniz, E.H., Bailey, D.E., Sholler, D.: Achieving ICT4D project success by altering context, not technology. Inf. Technol. Int. Dev. **10**, 15–29 (2014)
22. Heeks, R.: The IC T4D 2.0 Manifesto: Where Next for ICTs and International Development? Working Paper on Development Informatics. Manchester (2009)
23. Kempson, E., Atkinson, A., Pilley, O.: Policy level response to financial exclusion in developed economies: lessons for developing countries. Bristol (2004)
24. Sarma, M.: Index of Financial Inclusion. Discussion Papers in Economics. Nova Delhi (2008)
25. Unwin, T.: The technologies: identifying appropriate solutions for development needs. In: Unwin, T. (ed.) ICT4D: Information and Communication Technology for Development. Cambridge University Press, Cambridge (2009)
26. Sanford, C., Cojocaru, L.: Do Correspondents Improve Financial Inclusion? Evidence from a National Survey in Brazil. Bankable Frontier Associates, Somerville (2013)
27. Yin, R.K.: Estudo de Caso: Planejamento e Métodos, 4th edn. Bookman, Porto Alegre (2010)
28. Bardin, L.: Análise de Conteúdo, 7th edn. Almedina, São Paulo (2011)
29. Gil, A.C.: Como Elaborar Projetos de Pesquisa, 4th edn. Atlas, São Paulo (2002)
30. Silva, A.H., Fossá, M.I.T.: Análise de Conteúdo: Exemplo de Aplicação da Técnica para Análise de Dados Qualitativos. In: Proceedings of IV Encontro de Ensino e Pesquisa em Administração e Contabilidade, Brasília (2013)
31. Marconi, M., Lakatos, E.: Fundamentos de metodologia científica, 5th edn. Atlas, São Paulo (2003)
32. Trivinos, A.N.S.: Introdução à pesquisa em ciências sociais: a pesquisa qualitativa em educação. Atlas, São Paulo (1987)

33. Laville, C., Dionne, J.: A construção do saber: Manual de metodologia da pesquisa em ciências humanas. Artmed, Porto alegre (1999)
34. Freitas, H., Janissek, R.: Análise Léxica e Análise de Conteúdo: Técnicas complementares, sequenciais e recorrentes para exploração de dados qualitativos. Sphinx-Sagra, Porto Alegre (2000)

Infrastructures

Blockchain Technology as s Support Infrastructure in e-Government

Svein Ølnes[1(✉)] and Arild Jansen[2]

[1] Western Norway Research Institute, Sogndal, Norway
sol@vestforsk.no
[2] University of Oslo, Oslo, Norway
arildj@jus.uio.no

Abstract. The blockchain technology, including Bitcoin and other crypto currencies, has been adopted in many application areas during recent years. However, the main attention has been on the currency and not so much on the underlying blockchain technology, including peer-to-peer networking, security and consensus mechanisms. This paper argues that we need to look beyond the currency applications and investigate the potential use of the blockchain technology in governmental tasks such as digital ID management and secure document handling. The paper discusses the use of blockchain technology as a platform for various applications in e-Government and furthermore as an emerging support infrastructure by showing that blockchain technology demonstrates a potential for authenticating many types of persistent documents.

Keywords: e-Government · Bitcoin · Blockchain · ICT platform · Information infrastructure

1 Introduction

Bitcoin and the underlying blockchain technology have met with significant acceptance in recent years. Since its inception less than ten years ago, primarily as a crypto currency, the technology has been developed as a platform for various applications in different areas, not only in the banking and financial sector. We find applications in other areas where secure transactions have to be carried out in an otherwise unsecure, unreliable environment like the Internet, even without the need for a trusted third-party [1, 4]. Bitcoin, including peer-to-peer networking, blockchain and consensus mechanisms provide secure identification and authentication in various types of distributed computing environments.

Some of the most important features of the open blockchain technology are its global nature and reach, its built-in transparency and its independence of third party trust. These features are not of equal importance for all governments but will be more important in countries vulnerable to corruption and lack of trust in general than in countries that enjoy a high degree of trust from its citizens and businesses. However, also these countries

M. Janssen et al. (Eds.): EGOV 2017, LNCS 10428, pp. 215–227, 2017.
DOI: 10.1007/978-3-319-64677-0_18

can benefit from the global reach and transparency that the open blockchain technology offers.

Although blockchain technology has grown remarkably as a support for many innovations, it is still a somewhat immature technology. The blockchain technology at the present time seems primarily suitable for digital ID management and secure record-keeping and document-handling, which of course are core governmental activities. A blockchain contains a secure, verifiable record of every single transaction ever made [2], whether it is a financial transaction or a transaction involving a governmental procedure (e.g. recording and timestamping a public document). This gives the technology a potential for beneficially changing secure document management in the public sector.

Secure document-handling functions, including digital signatures, certificates etc., are still an area having many different systems and practical arrangements and often creating a lot of confusion for non-specialist users.

The blockchain technology offers a high level of security; the administration of a blockchain based document management may become simpler, and not least, it will be open and more transparent.

The specific aim of this paper is to discuss in what ways and the extent to which the Bitcoin blockchain technology can be regarded as a general platform and possible service infrastructure. Thus the research objectives of our paper are:

To understand the Bitcoin/blockchain technology as

(1) *an emerging platform*
(2) *potentially as a support infrastructure.*

for improving the digitalization in public sector

A brief clarification of our terminology is needed. We use "Bitcoin/blockchain technology" throughout the paper to mean the blockchain network and database that are underlying Bitcoin, including the peer-to-peer networking, consensus rules and security mechanisms (even though this term has been criticized by e.g. van Valkenburgh [3]. Otherwise, we will explicitly name the specific platform or application in question. In addition, Bitcoin with a capital 'B' is used to denote the system while bitcoin with a small 'b' is used to denote the currency. Furthermore, our paper mainly discusses open blockchains [networks], because closed systems are never able to build an infrastructure.

1.1 Method Description

Our research approach is exploratory, analyzing the diffusion of blockchain technology in an information-infrastructure perspective. The conceptual style of the paper is most appropriate since the use of blockchain technology is almost non-existent in e-Government, as recent publications show [4]. The regulatory side of crypto currencies is important for governments, but it falls outside the scope of this article.

Our selection of literature is based on the snow-ball method [5], starting with seminal research papers on the subject, then including their referenced papers. We have also searched the extensive e-Government Research Library (EGRL) v. 12.0. However, although the EGRL 12.0 contains a huge collection of peer-reviewed papers within the e-Government field, almost no references can be found to Bitcoin and/or blockchain technology. This was also confirmed in a literature study from 2016 [4]. In the added publications in EGRL since v. 11.5 from 2016 a paper on virtual currency regulation can be found [6] searching for "bitcoin" or "blockchain". The latter paper, however, is not relevant to our discussion.

1.2 Structure of the Paper

The rest of the paper is organized as follows. Section 2 provides a description of the technological foundation, focusing on the Bitcoin and the blockchain technology and some current applications. Section 3 analyzes this technology in an information infrastructure perspective. In Sect. 4, we discuss some potentially interesting applications of the technology within the application area of digital ID management, including authentication, and the last chapter concludes our findings by addressing future research.

2 Bitcoin and Blockchain Technology

The virtual currency bitcoin is associated with a distributed ledger technology called the blockchain. It was first presented to a cryptography mailing list [7] by the posting of a white paper titled "Bitcoin – A Peer-to-Peer Electronic Cash System" in late 2008 by an author named Satoshi Nakamoto [8], presumably a pseudonym. The Bitcoin system enables users to transact directly in an open and unsecure network, like the Internet, without the use of an intermediary. This peer-to-peer system was released as open source software and launched in 2009 [7]. It has been running continuously since then and has grown to facilitate several hundred thousand transactions per day.

Bitcoin builds on research in cryptography including earlier attempts to create virtual currencies [10–13]. The core principles of Bitcoin are (1) the peer-to-peer architecture, (2) the novel use of blockchain as storage, including time stamping and validation of transactions, and (3) the consensus mechanisms framing the rules and the security model [3]. The blockchain itself is a distributed database that maintains a continuously growing list of ordered records called *blocks*, containing *transactions*. A transaction can hold different types of data. Each block contains a timestamp and a cryptographic link to the previous block [9]. In Bitcoin, the individual bitcoins are also linked together through the transactions (ibid.).

Currently the Bitcoin blockchain is limited to handling a theoretical maximum of seven transactions per second [8] and is therefore not ideal for high volume transactions. However, for efficient storing of more persistent objects and assets (e.g. certificates, licenses etc.) it is ideal. These types of objects do not change ownership so frequently that the relatively slow transaction speed of Bitcoin is challenged. The relatively low cost of transactions, combined with a high degree of security, promises cost-efficient and secure storage of various types of assets, in addition to interoperability due to its open, distributed, and global architecture. This can also consolidate assets like certificates, diplomas, licenses etc. The public sector can benefit from a readily available platform and possibly avoid costly investments.

Bitcoin solved the former problem of avoiding double-spending (spending a single digital token twice) by using a proof-of-work (PoW) method inspired by HashCash [11] and Reusable Proof of Work (RPOW) [14] combined with a consensus-based system among the Bitcoin peers [8]. The PoW-based security model relies on the presumption that the cost of compromising the system must outweigh the profit from doing so. The PoW in Bitcoin is primarily to find a hash value based on the combination of the hash value of the previous block, a "nonce" and the hash of the new block [9]. Hash functions are used for authentication of documents and are also crucial in verifying and validating digital signatures [15].

Although this paper focuses on the blockchain technology per se, it is important to understand how the bitcoin currency and the underlying blockchain technology is tightly interwoven [9]. An open, permissionless blockchain cannot exist without incentives or recompensing mechanisms like Bitcoin (ibid.). Even if the blockchain can contain information other than the bitcoin currency transactions, the currency is a crucial incentive to secure the transfer of ownership of information and assets. The possibility to earn new bitcoins is what keeps miners spending resources (mainly hardware and electricity) on finding the specific hash value and thereby securing the transactions (ibid.). The massive amounts of resources spent on computing hash values make Bitcoin by far the most secure blockchain system in operation today [16].

There is a common misconception that blockchain technology itself comes with a built-in security [3]. Instead, the opposite is true; the security mechanism needs to be specified. There is a fundamental difference between an open blockchain and a closed (private) blockchain [3]. *Open* blockchains, like e.g. Bitcoin and Ethereum, are permissionless systems in which everyone can join and even develop additional solutions, and therefore they need a security model to secure the transactions and, furthermore, to integrate a consensus mechanism. The only model operating at scale today is the PoW model. *Closed* blockchains, on the other hand, must rely on traditional security mechanisms in order to prevent unwanted access and modification to the blockchain.

At a technical level, Bitcoin relies on two fundamental cryptographical functions: public key cryptography for making digital signatures [17] and hash functions for validation of signatures and transactions [1]. A Bitcoin transaction is a digital signature which signs a transaction containing the payer's address, the recipient's address, and the amount of bitcoins transferred [9]. The transaction is propagated to the Bitcoin network, e.g. the nodes comprising all users of the Bitcoin core program and eventually bundled with other transactions to be included in a block (ibid.). The new block is attached to the blockchain through a *mining* process where computer power is used to solve a mathematical puzzle, the proof of work (PoW) part [9]. The miner who first finds the right answer to the puzzle gets a reward in newly minted bitcoins. Miners' contribution in the Bitcoin system together with the control mechanisms of full node clients render it possible to eliminate the use of a third-party for approval [8].

Bitcoin was the first implementation of a virtual currency system. During subsequent years, numerous copies have been made, resulting in new virtual currencies called *altcoins*; at present there are hundreds of them (see coinmarketcap.com). These altcoins can also be seen as alternative platforms for digital currency solutions and real-life and real-time testbeds for new features. Among these are Ethereum, focusing on smart contracts [18], Monero, Dash and Zcash, all of which provide more privacy than Bitcoin [19].

An important part of blockchain development is its governance. In Bitcoin, no group of stakeholders (e.g. miners, full node clients, core developers) is in charge, and consensus between the different groups has to be reached. Changes to the protocol are proposed through BIPs (Bitcoin Improvement Proposals) and are then voted on by miners. Full node clients "vote" by downloading upgraded versions of the reference client, or choosing not to download [20]. However, the recent scaling debate concerning whether to raise the size of blocks to achieve better throughput and ease the pressure of unconfirmed transactions piling up has raised concerns and caused many people to describe the debate as a governance crisis [20]. Bitcoin does not have any way of managing conflicts and that can lead to paralyzing deadlocks, which seems to be the situation now (ibid.). The governance of blockchain technologies is important if the technology also is to be used as a platform for public digital services.

Almost all altcoins derive from Bitcoin and share the fundamental design principles. They distinguish themselves from Bitcoin in different ways, e.g. monetary policy, capacity, hashing methods etc. Altcoins are incompatible with Bitcoin, and when a crypto currency performs a hard fork (a change in protocol that is not backward compatible), there is a risk that a new altcoin will be the result, if the participants do not agree unanimously on the change. An example of this is the Ethereum platform that split in two (Ethereum and Ethereum Classic) after a controversial hard fork in 2016.

3 Blockchain in an Infrastructure Perspective

An ICT infrastructure is usually regarded as the collection of hardware and software components, including networks that are required to enable communication and interoperations between ICT systems. Thus, they form a different "unit" of design when compared with traditional classes of IT solutions. Hanseth and Lyytinen [21] define these design classes in their order of increasing complexity as: (1) IT capabilities, (2) applications, (3) platforms, and (4) information infrastructures (IIs).

We see that Bitcoin (and other virtual currencies based on blockchain technology) clearly fulfills the characteristics of an application, understood as a suite of IT capabilities, being developed to meet a set of specified user needs within a select set of communities. Furthermore, we will argue that the growth of blockchains (including the consensus and security mechanisms) are becoming platforms for many applications, such as securing document handling and other types of digital assets, gradually building a heterogeneous and growing user base. However, one challenge is how to maintain backward compatibility as well as horizontal equivalence across different combinations of capabilities.

3.1 Blockchain Technology and Information Infrastructure

ICT infrastructures, as defined above, are primarily understood as technical facilities. However, the advent of the Internet, and more precisely the worldwide web, illustrated a need for a holistic, socio-technical and evolutionary approach when studying such networks of distributed, and thereby interlinked information systems, usually denoted as information infrastructure. Following Hanseth and Lyytinen [21], we understand *Information Infrastructure (II)* as *"a shared, open and unbounded, heterogeneous and evolving socio-technical system consisting of a set of IT capabilities and their user, operations, and design communities."* Because of its dispersed and distributed ownership, the lack of centralized control is a fundamental attribute of information infrastructure. Consequently, different actors shape, maintain, and extend information infrastructure "in modular increments, not all at once or globally" [22].

From the outset, Bitcoin was designed as a cryptocurrency and was not intended to comprise a general-purpose platform for public sector use. However, as we have noted above, a number of new applications have been built on the permissionless Bitcoin/blockchain platform (see e.g. Fig. 1), clearly indicating the potential of this technology to be *shared* across multiple communities in various ways. Furthermore, its developments also demonstrate its *openness and evolving* nature, including a growing number of new applications, as we have illustrated in Sect. 2.

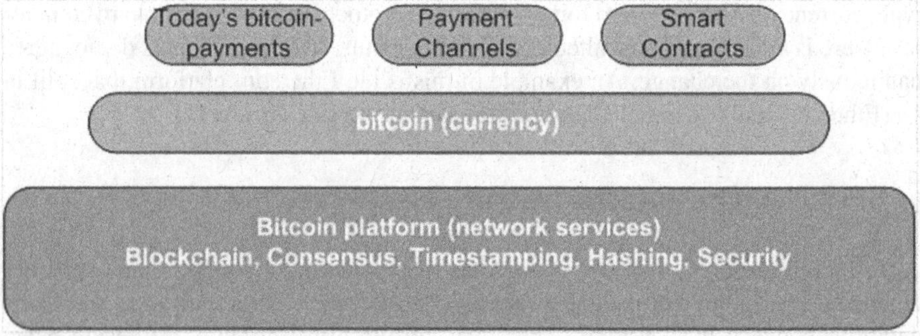

Fig. 1. Bitcoin's layered architecture

The *control* of an information infrastructure is typically distributed and dynamically negotiated [23]. Blockchain/Bitcoin is clearly a distributed technology as the main purpose of its design has been to avoid central control, e.g. by trusted third parties. It was developed as a peer-to-peer technology from the beginning [8]. The recent debate over the block size [24] shows that no party is in control of the changes to be made and that these changes must be negotiated dynamically: miners have their say, full node clients have their say as well as core developers, but none of the groups can dictate the terms. This has been, and is currently, a subject of heated debate, and the community has not yet reached a conclusion [25].

3.2 The Installed Base of Blockchain Technology

Of particular importance in an information infrastructure is its *installed base,* including both technical and non-technical elements. The evolution of IIs are thus path-dependent due to this "living legacy" of existing technical solutions along with organizational, economic and legal elements, interconnected practices and regulations that are often institutionalized in the organization [22]. An adequate understanding of the installed bases is particular important in building IIs in governments (eGovIIs), as an increasing number of information systems are shared in order to provide online government services., and the dynamics related to these systems often require both forward flexibility and backward compatibility.

Hanseth and Lyytinen (op. cit.) emphasize that the understanding of the installed base of an information infrastructure is essential for its governance, not least in order to handle the existing collection of possible legacy systems, which may be barriers for innovations. Currently, the installed base of the blockchain technology is limited, as its applications have short history (less than 10 years). However, we see significant social and technical diversity where new applications and platforms are emerging, e.g. new altcoins, smart contracts [26], sidechains [27]. In comparison, it took more than 20 years for the Internet to gain acceptance.

The limited installed base may both stimulate and inhibit innovations. On the one hand, it may stimulate the development and diffusion of new applications as there are few "technical bindings" such as, for example, legacy systems, and new users will adopt innovative solutions if they are sufficiently attractive or meet specific needs. The growth of cryptocurrency and various electronic cash systems clearly illustrates this. On the other hand, the lack of bonds to an existing installed base – for example, users of existing applications in relevant areas (such as payment systems, secure document handling and asset management etc.) – may imply that there are few incentives for adoption of applications based on blockchain technology unless they are made more attractive.

However, as we illustrate below, the blockchain technology is evolving beyond its primary application area and already supports a range of secure document and asset management in other areas. We summarize our discussions in Fig. 2.

Internet		**Blockchain technology**
Applications		Applications
HTTP/HTML/...		Bitcoin/other currency
TCP/IP		Consensus rules,peer-to-peer, security
Physical and logical link		Distributed blockchain database

Fig. 2. The layered structure of Internet and the Blockchain

Hanseth and Lyytinen [28] distinguish between two types of horizontal IIs: *application and support infrastructure*. We may conceptualize the blockchain technology platform as an emerging support infrastructure, while the Bitcoin and other digital currencies are part of the application layer. By so doing, we do not impose any restriction on how these technologies may evolve, as we do not yet know how new applications, such as secure document handling, smart contracts, digital ID management etc. will be realized on a growing support infrastructure.

Table 1. The characteristics of different types of infrastructures

Property	Platform	Information infrastructure, e.g. Internet	Blockchain/Bitcoin
Shared	Yes, across involved user communities and across a set of IT capabilities	Universally and across multiple IT capabilities	Potentially shared among those who are involved in building and maintaining this platform
Open	Partially, depends on design choices and managerial policies	Yes, allowing unlimited connections to user communities and new capabilities	Partly yes. Bitcoin is (in principle) open to any users and offers a platform for payment system and secure document/asset handling
Installed base	Growing, but limited to its intended applications and users.	The current Internet applications integrated with its users and use practices, still growing exponentially	The present installed base is limited, which may stimulate innovations but lack the networks effects
Evolving	Yes, limited by architectural choices and functional closure. Linear growth. Path dependent	Yes, unlimited by time or user community. Both linear and nonlinear growth	Yes, although it may be too early to say how. Although it is a new technology, Bitcoin has demonstrated innovative potential.
Control	Centralized	Distributed and dynamically negotiated	Distributed control based on open source software. Changes are dynamically negotiated in user community

3.3 Blockchain Technology and the Internet – Similarities and Differences

The structure and development trajectory of the blockchain technology has been compared to that of the Internet [3]. Although such a comparison may result in misleading associations, we believe there are some lessons to be learned from the history of building the Internet.

The kernel of Internet architecture is essentially the TCP/IP protocol suite, built in a layered and modular way. TCP/IP offers a completely distributed, packet-switched network in that it requires no central control when in operation; new nodes may be added or removed in a dynamic way. Internet (IP) packets may be transmitted over any type of physical medium and TCP/IP supports all types of applications. Furthermore, the

Internet is transparent and neutral to any type of information being sent across the network (as unfiltered data). As important is its basic characteristic; being open, global and borderless with no censorship. Thus, based on the end-to-end-principle (see e.g. [29]), the Internet may be considered an "unintelligent" network, meaning that there is minimum functionality inside the network, making it efficient, flexible and dynamic.

Similarly, the blockchain platform, including Bitcoin is a dumb transaction-processing network because it pushes all of the intelligence to the edges, thus being able to support various smart devices. It does not offer a range of financial services and products, and it does not have automation and various features built in, thus making the interfaces much simpler, and thereby simpler to support innovations. analogous to Internet [30] The basic properties of the blockchain technology includes consensus rules, peer-to-peer mechanism, security functions such as cryptography and hash functions etc., which are not part of the blockchain database but have to implemented in the hardware/software controlling and verifying the blockchain.

We do not believe it is fruitful to (strictly) compare the architecture of the Internet with blockchain technology. However, in the figure below we illustrate the analogous structure of these two architectures.

3.4 Infrastructure Growth Through Bootstrapping

Hanseth and Lyytinen [21] have outlined a strategy for a set of design principles and rules to guide the design so that a set of system features is selected to meet chosen design goals. They exemplify the bootstrap problem (to come up with solutions early on that persuade users to adopt while the user community is non-existent or small): How can ICT solutions in an information infrastructure get a value? We clearly understand that IIs need to meet early users' needs directly in order to fulfill their mission. They thus outlined the following design strategy: (i) design initially for usefulness, (ii) draw upon existing installed base, (iii) expand installed base by persuasive tactics. IIs are often bootstrapped, by experimenting and thereby enrolling new communities, as e.g. Berners-Lee who designed the first WWW services to meet information-sharing needs among high energy physicists, however expanding to a growing, worldwide community [22].

Thus, we believe that the bootstrapping approach is useful to foster the growth of Bitcoin/Blockchain. Although this technology is not yet mature, the technology has shown a significant development from being used by a handful of persons the first year to today's millions of users (nodes) and links [31], significant investment rate indicating lots of start-ups, and expansion in terms of diversity of components and services added to the technology [32] (e.g. different wallets) and platforms (e.g. Ethereum and Lightning network) have found place [33, 34]. In particular, we believe that successful applications in public sector will stimulate such developments.

4 Blockchain Technology in e-Government

4.1 Blockchain and Innovations

Our research question is "To understand Bitcoin and the underlying blockchain network(s) as (1) an emerging platform and (2) potentially as a support infrastructure". One way to study this is to investigate its generative capacity.

According to Zittrain [35], generativity is a function of a technology's capacity for leverage across a range of tasks, adaptability to a range of different tasks, ease of mastery and accessibility. Generativity denotes a technology's overall capacity to produce unprompted change driven by large, varied and uncoordinated audiences.

Leverage. Describes the extent to which objects enable valuable accomplishments that otherwise would be either impossible or not worth the effort to achieve. The Bitcoin/ blockchain does offer a platform for secure and transparent payment and other financial operations in hostile environments, with no adequate technical or institutional infrastructure in place. For many countries where corruption often appears as a threat to ordinary ways of doing business, not least with the Government, tamper-evident and tamper-resistant ICT systems can provide significant benefits. For example, the Government of Honduras recently started collaborating with the blockchain company Factom (ibid.) aiming to use this technology for storing land title deeds and thereby rendering corruption much more difficult [36].

Adaptability. Refers to both the breadth of a technology's use without change and the readiness with which it might be modified to broaden its range of uses. As an illustration of blockchain potential, the UK's Government Office for Science [37] have proposed several use cases for blockchain technology that point to using the technology for (1) protecting critical infrastructure, (2) novel payment systems for work and pensions, (3) strengthening international aid systems, (4) document authentication and smart contracts, and (5) handling European VAT. Of these suggested application areas, we think authentication of documents (CVs and other certificates, licenses, intellectual properties and patents, wills etc.) is the most interesting in terms of short–term realization. Thus, using blockchain technology for land title registry is an interesting use case for the public sector, highlighting the use of blockchain technology for secure storage of authentic documents as part of the effort to innovate e-Government solutions. The Swedish Lantmäteriet, responsible for land title and estate registries, collaborates with business partners to investigate the possibilities of using blockchain technology to innovate their ICT solutions [38].

Ease of Mastery. A technology's ease of mastery reflects how easy it is for broad audiences both to adopt and to adapt it. Academic certificates have already been stored on the Bitcoin blockchain. The University of Nicosia was probably the first institution to do this with their course "Introduction to Digital Currencies" [4]. The individual certificates from this course were first hashed to produce a fingerprint of the document. The hashes of all certificates from the course were then gathered in one document, which was again hashed, and the resulting fingerprint was stored on the Bitcoin blockchain (ibid.). The MIT Media Lab took this proof of concept further and developed an open source solution called *Blockcert* [39]. The *Blockcert* system is a complete system for storing, verifying and also revoking academic certificates using the Bitcoin blockchain [40]. The overarching idea is that the students should own their own records; this can be achieved by using the technology of open blockchains

Accessibility. The more readily people are able to use and control a technology, along with the information that might be required to master it, the more accessible the technology is. The above examples also show that the blockchain technology is becoming more easy to use. The open and global nature of public blockchains means that the technology is available and accessible to all people, and the only requirement is an Internet or mobile network connection. However, usability has not been given high priority thus far, and the crucial management of keys shares much of the same challenges as similar management from other domains [41].

5 Conclusions and Further Research

This paper has argued that Bitcoin and the underlying blockchain technology is an emerging platform for further innovation not just in financial systems but also in the public sector. The technology seems to be evolving into a support infrastructure for secure document handling and is thus positioned to have a significant impact on future digital innovations, including in the public sector.

We therefore argue that ICT systems based on blockchain technology, implying decentralized management and control, offer more robust and flexible solutions that cannot be corrupted. However, lessons learned from earlier efforts to introduce new technology underscore the importance of following a realistic, systematic approach. As a first step, we have provided examples of applications areas where the solutions are technically rather uncomplicated, and where there are few organizational or institutional barriers. However, given the promising benefits that blockchain technology holds, it is also important that researchers in the field of e-Government begin discussing important questions: Are governmental agencies ready to investigate the potential of blockchain technology, and what are the main barriers? What are the important factors determining whether to adopt Bitcoin technology in the public sector?

References

1. Böhme, R., Christin, N., Edelman, B., Moore, T.: Bitcoin: economics, technology, and governance. J. Econ. Perspect. **29**(2), 213–238 (2015)
2. Crosby, M., Pattanayak, P., Verma, S., Kalyanaraman, V.: Blockchain technology: beyond bitcoin. Appl. Innov. **2**, 6–10 (2016)
3. van Valkenburgh, P.: Open Matters—Why Permissionless Blockchains are Essential to the Future of the Internet. Coin Center, December 2016
4. Ølnes, S.: Beyond bitcoin enabling smart government using blockchain technology. In: International Conference on Electronic Government and the Information Systems Perspective, pp. 253–264 (2016)

5. Briner, R.B., Denyer, D.: Systematic review and evidence synthesis as a practice and scholarship tool. In: Handbook of Evidence-Based Management: Companies, Classrooms and Research. pp. 112–129 (2012)
6. Manrique, C.G., Manrique, G.: The evolution of virtual currencies: analyzing the case of bitcoin. Inf. Commun. Technol. Public Adm. Innov. Dev. Ctries **195**, 213 (2015)
7. Karlstrøm, H.: Do libertarians dream of electric coins? The material embeddedness of Bitcoin. Distinktion Scand. J. Soc. Theory **15**(1), 23–36 (2014)
8. Nakamoto, S.: Bitcoin: a peer-to-peer electronic cash system. Consulted **1**(2012), 28 (2008)
9. Antonopoulos, A.M.: Mastering Bitcoin—Unlocking Digital Cryptocurrencies, 1st edn. O'Reilly Media Inc, San Francisco (2014)
10. Chaum, D.: Blind signatures for untraceable payments. In: Advances in Cryptology, pp. 199–203 (1983)
11. Back, A.: Hashcash—A Senial of Service Counter-Measure (2002). http://www.hashcash.org/papers/hashcash.pdf
12. Dai, W.: B-money (1998). Blog post. http://www.weidai.com/bmoney.txt
13. Szabo, N.: Bit gold. Website/Blog (2005). http://unenumerated.blogspot.com/2005/bit-gold.html
14. Finney, H.: RPOW: Reusable Proofs of Work. Cypherpunks (2004). http://nakamotoinstitute.org/finney/rpow/theory.html
15. Wikipedia: Hash Function. Wikipedia. 18 January 2017. http://en.wikipedia.org/wiki/Hash_function
16. Let's Talk Bitcoin: Proof of Work and the Monument of Immutability, vol. LTB, 310 vols (2016). Podcast. http://letstalkbitcoin.com/blog/post/lets-talk-bitcoin-310-proof-of-work-and-the-monument-of-immutability
17. Schneier, B.: Applied Cryptography, 3 edn. Wiley, New York (1996)
18. Buterin, V.: Ethereum white paper: a next-generation smart contract and decentralized application platform. Ethereum White Paper (2014). http://github.com/ethereum/wiki/wiki/White-Paper
19. Noether, S., Mackenzie, A.: Ring confidential transactions. Ledger **1**, 1–18 (2016)
20. De Filippi, P.: Blockchain-based Crowdfunding: what impact on artistic production and art consumption? Obs. Itaú Cult. **19** (2015)
21. Hanseth, O., Lyytinen, K.: Design theory for dynamic complexity in information infrastructures: the case of building internet. J. Inf. Technol. **25**(1), 1–19 (2010)
22. Star, S.L., Ruhleder, K.: Steps toward an ecology of infrastructure: design and access for large information spaces. Inf. Syst. Res. **7**(1), 111–134 (1996)
23. Weil, P., Broadbent, M.: Leveraging the New Infrastructure. Harvard Business School Press, Boston (1998)
24. Croman, K., et al.: On scaling decentralized blockchains. In: Proceedings of 3rd Workshop on Bitcoin and Blockchain Research (2016)
25. Pilkington, M.: Blockchain technology: principles and applications. In: Olleros, F.X., Zhegu, M. (ed.) Research Handbook on Digital Transformations. Edward Elgar, Northampton (2016)
26. Szabo, N.: Formalizing and securing relationships on public networks. First Monday **2**(9) (1997). http://firstmonday.org/ojs/index.php/fm/article/view/548/469-publisher=First
27. Back, A., et al.: Enabling blockchain innovations with pegged sidechains (2014). http://www.opensciencereview.com/papers/123/enablingblockchain-innovations-with-pegged-sidechains
28. Hanseth, O., Lyytinen, K.: Theorizing about the design of Information Infrastructures: design kernel theories and principles. Sprouts Work. Pap. Inf. Environ. Syst. Organ. **4**(4), 207–241 (2004)

29. Saltzer, J.H., Reed, D.P., Clark, D.D.: End-to-end arguments in system design. ACM Trans. Comput. Syst. TOCS **2**(4), 277–288 (1984)
30. Antonopoulos, A.: The Internet of Money. Merkle Bloom LLC (2016). ISBN: 1537000454
31. Kondor, D., Pósfai, M., Csabai, I., Vattay, G.: Do the rich get richer? An empirical analysis of the Bitcoin transaction network. PLoS ONE **9**(2), e86197 (2014)
32. Edwards, P.N., Jackson, S.J., Bowker, G.C., Knobel, C.P.: Report of a workshop on history & theory of infrastructure: lessons for new scientific cyberinfrastructures. Underst. Infrastruct. Dyn. Tens. Des. (2007)
33. Wood, D.G.: Ethereum: a secure decentralised generalised transaction ledger (2014). http://pdfs.semanticscholar.org/ac15/ea808ef3b17ad754f91d3a00fedc8f96b929.pdf
34. Poon, J., Dryja, T.: The bitcoin lightning network: Scalable off-chain instant payments. Technical Report (draft) (2015). https://lightning.network
35. Zittrain, J.L.: The generative internet. Harv. Law Rev. **119**, 1974–2040 (2006)
36. Lemieux, V.L., Lemieux, V.L.: Trusting records: is Blockchain technology the answer? Rec. Manag. J. **26**(2), 110–139 (2016)
37. UK Government Office for Science: Distributed Ledger Technology: beyond block chain. Government Office for Science, London (2016)
38. Lantmäteriet: 'Framtidens husköp i blockkedjan' ('Future real estate trade through the blockchain'). Lantmäteriet, June 2016. http://www.lantmateriet.se/contentassets/6874bc3048ab42d6955e0f5dd9a84dcf/blockkedjan-framtidens-huskop.pdf
39. M. L. MIT Media Lab: Blockcerts-An Open Infrastructure for Academic Credentials on the Blockchain. Medium, 24 October 2016
40. MIT Media Lab: What we learned from designing an academic certificates system on the blockchain. Medium, 02 June 2016
41. Eskandari, S., Clark, J., Barrera, D., Stobert, E.: A first look at the usability of bitcoin key management. In: Workshop on Usable Security (USEC) (2015)

Comparing a Shipping Information Pipeline with a Thick Flow and a Thin Flow

Sélinde van Engelenburg(✉), Marijn Janssen, Bram Klievink, and Yao-Hua Tan

Delft University of Technology, Delft, The Netherlands
{S.H.vanEngelenburg,M.F.W.H.A.Janssen,A.J.Klievink,
Y.Tan}@tudelft.nl

Abstract. Advanced architectures for business-to-government (B2G) information sharing can benefit both businesses and government. An essential choice in the design of such an architecture is whether information is shared using a thick or a thin information flow. In an architecture with a thick flow, all information is shared via a shared infrastructure, whereas only metadata and pointers referring to the information are shared via the shared infrastructure in a thin flow architecture. These pointers can then be used by parties to access the information directly. Yet, little is known about what their implications for design choices are. Design choices are influenced by the properties of the architecture as well as the situation in which B2G information sharing takes place. In this paper, we identify the properties of architectures with a thin and thick flow. Next, we determine what this implies for the suitability of the architectures in different situations. We will base our analysis on the case of the Shipping Information Pipeline (SIP) for container transport. While both architectures have their pros and cons, we found that architectures with a thin flow are more suitable when non-standardized, and flexible sharing of sensitive information is required. In contrast, we found that architectures with a thick flow are more suitable when in-depth integration is required.

Keywords: Business-to-government information sharing · Information sharing · Shipping information pipeline · Supply chain · Thick flow · Thin flow · Information architecture

1 Introduction

Governments require businesses and other actors to report information, for example for purposes of taxation or keeping statistics. Most Business-to-Government (B2G) reporting is highly regulated, with obligations pertaining to scope, scale, timing and format for sharing. However, more information can be shared than is formally required, which can result in advantages for companies and governments. For instance, some Customs organizations put businesses that share additional information in a trusted,

M. Janssen et al. (Eds.): EGOV 2017, LNCS 10428, pp. 228–239, 2017.
DOI: 10.1007/978-3-319-64677-0_19

green trade lane, in which there are less and more conveniently timed physical inspections of their goods [1]. Each inspection delaying the delivering of goods causes additional work. In a green late companies will have less inspections resulting in lower costs and faster delivery.

Anything beyond obligatory information sharing is more difficult to arrange and relies on collaboration between government and businesses [2]. Organizations seek control over what happens to their information and how information is being shared [3]. Any information sharing that is not required by law for B2G reporting encounters the challenge of balancing this desire for control with the autonomy of other actors in the network, i.e. those you use data of or share data with [4]. Hence, any information sharing architecture will have to accommodate this balance.

In the many possible B2G information sharing architectures all information can be shared indirectly via the architecture or some information can be shared directly between parties. The former is called a thick information flow architecture, whereas the latter is called a thin information flow architecture. In a *thick* flow, the actual information itself is shared via the architecture [4]. In a *thin* flow, information shared via the architecture is limited to metadata and pointers to the information businesses intend to share [4]. The pointers can be used to directly access the shipping information in the systems of the businesses.

Which architecture is best for which circumstances is not known. There are only limited insights in the implications for design choices of these two types of architectures. The objective of this paper is twofold: we inventory the essential properties of these two types of architecture, and based on them, we analyse their implications. To this end, we focus on the case of container supplying in which the Shipping Information Pipeline (SIP) is used to share information with Customs.

In the next section, we will describe the SIP with a thick and a thin flow. Subsequently, we present a list of properties relevant to making a choice in design for the architectures. Section 4 contains the actual comparison of the thin flow and the thick flow using this list. In Sect. 5 we discuss what this implies for design choices for the SIP in different situations.

2 A Shipping Information Pipeline

The sharing of shipping information in supply chains can benefit businesses as well as Customs [5–7]. Reliable shipping information allows businesses to work together more effectively and efficiently and for synchro-modality to optimize the goods flow [7, 8]. Customs is tasked with monitoring the flow of goods and interfering with it if necessary for security, safety or public policy [5]. It is not feasible to physically inspect all goods they need to monitor and they thus have to rely on the shipping information of businesses in the supply chain to fulfil their responsibilities [9, 10].

In the current situation, the shipping information shared is often not timely, not originating from the source, filtered and altered, which might result into inaccurate information [6, 10, 11]. Yet, the information that businesses in the supply chain gather is of high quality, since their own commercial operations depend on it [5]. Customs often is expected to make it attractive for companies to trade in their country. For this reason, they reward businesses who do share information voluntarily (see e.g., [1]).

2.1 The Shipping Information Pipeline

The idea of a SIP was first proposed by UK and Dutch Customs [12, 13]. It was developed to allow original information to be captured in real-time at the source to increase reliability [6]. The data that are made available in the SIP are the raw and original data that companies have in their systems to base their own operations on [6]. When this data are made available in the SIP, they could be reused for other purposes than that they were gathered for, according to the piggy-backing principle [14, 15]. According to Hesketh [10], the information that is shared between the parties describes the transactional data that is captured by the parties in the supply chain, the physical data that is captured by tracing, tracking and monitoring devices and relevant commercial risk management data such as quality and technical compliancy tests. In the pipeline, data on goods and people are distinguished from data on different modes of transport (e.g. ship, rail, truck etc.) [8].

The SIP is based on a Service-Oriented Architecture (SOA), in which resources are made available as independent artefacts that can be accessed in a standardized way [6, 16]. SOAs are the de facto standard for data integration [8]. In the SIP, each subsequent party in the supply chain makes their source data accessible as soon as it becomes available [6]; for example a seller starts with a purchase order, then sends an invoice, and when his goods are received by the buyer a payment transfer is made. With each step, the data is enriched with new data [6]. By linking the data that becomes available in this manner, an integrated data view is created, providing a full view of the trade lane [6]. The SIP is therefore referred to as an integrated data pipeline or seamless integrated data pipeline as well [8, 10].

The main differences between the SIP and other kinds of data pipelines are that in the SIP data is shared between parties in a supply chain and with Customs and that it only supports the sharing of shipping information. Furthermore, it allows for a transition from the current data push approach in which businesses push documents to Customs, to a data pull approach in which Customs pulls the data they require [6]. Naturally, the access to data in the SIP is only allowed for parties that are authorized to do so by the owners of the data [6].

Whether the SIP supports thick or thin information flows highly influences the properties of the architecture. In the literature on its more practical design, usually the SIP involves a single or limited number of central components that the information goes through [11, 17]. Such a central component can be a port community system or business community system acting as a central hub, or an event repository [11, 17]. Considering the emphasis on more centralized versions of the SIP, it makes sense to compare a centralized SIP with a thick flow with a centralized SIP with a thin flow in this paper. It is important to note that technical centralization not necessarily means centralized control [18].

2.2 A Thick and a Thin Flow

In a B2G information sharing architecture with a thick flow, the messages sent between services contains the actual information that a party wants to share [4]. The information flowing in our case of the SIP thus includes the shipping information (hence, the name "thick flow"). In the case of a SIP with a thick flow, the systems of the businesses containing the shipping information are linked to the SIP using a standardized interface. When new shipping information becomes available, it is pushed or pulled from them to the central component (step 1 thick flow, Fig. 1) where it is linked to the data already available. Other parties can then pull the information from the SIP (step 2 thick flow, Fig. 1).

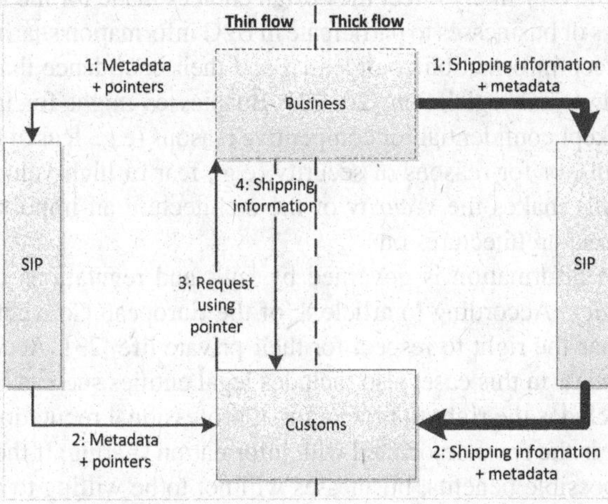

Fig. 1. A SIP with a thin flow and a SIP with a thick flow

In an architecture with a *thin* flow, the messages that parties send via the architecture only contain metadata and pointers to the actual information. The pointers that are sent via the architecture can be used to access the information in the systems of the businesses directly via another data exchange platform (e.g. Internet, VPN etc.). In the case of the SIP, the information flowing through the architecture, thus does not include the shipping information itself (hence, the name "thin flow"). In a SIP with a thin flow, only the systems containing the metadata need to be connected to the SIP via a standardized interface.

For the thin flow, when new data becomes available, its metadata and a pointer is added to a reference index (step 1 thin flow, Fig. 1), where the new data is linked to the data already available. This reference index is the central component of the SIP. Parties that are in need of information consult the reference index (step 2 thin flow, Fig. 1) and use the pointers to pull data directly from the system where it is stored (step 3 and 4, Fig. 1), without intermediation of the SIP. They could even be kept up-to-date using a publish/subscribe mechanism [19]. The sharing of the actual information in the thin flow is thus distributed and arranged between two parties.

3 Properties to Compare the Architectures

In this section, to select the relevant properties of thin and thick flow architectures, we first discuss some factors impacting the choice for a design of a B2G information sharing architecture. Then, we will discuss the properties of the architecture these factors are influenced by. In the next section, we will use these properties to compare the architectures with a thick and a thin flow. Based on this comparison, we will describe what they imply for design choices in different situations.

The voluntary sharing of information in addition to the information that businesses are obligated to share can be valuable to businesses as well as governments. However, this voluntariness makes the willingness of businesses to participate vital. Therefore, this willingness will very likely affect the design choices made for the architecture.

The willingness of businesses to participate in B2G information sharing is influenced by their need to keep information confidential and their confidence that the sharing is compliant with laws and legislation [20, 21]. Businesses might for instance require information to be kept confidential for competitive reasons (e.g., fear of being bypassed in the supply chain), or for reasons of security (e.g., fear of high-value goods getting stolen) [7, 22]. This makes the *security* of the architecture an important property to compare the different architectures on.

The sharing of information is governed by laws and regulations that require the *protection of privacy*. According to article 8, of the European Convention on Human Rights everyone has the right to respect for their private life [23]. According to jurisprudence, "everyone", in this case, also includes legal entities such as businesses [24]. Furthermore, it includes the right to protection of professional reputation [24].

Another factor is the *costs* associated with information sharing. If these are too high compared to the possible benefits, businesses will not to be willing to participate. We expect the initial investment and the resources required over time to play a role.

For businesses to be willing to share their information, they might want to have some form of control and influence on the way in which decisions about the architecture are made. The *governance* of the architecture might be as important as its infrastructure [22]. Therefore, businesses could require that the architecture is governed in a certain way. Whether a SIP with a thin or a thick flow allows for such governance thus might be an important property for making a decision as well.

The degree to which the architecture can adequately support the sharing of reliable information, is also important for the decision-making process. In fact, it is vital for the usefulness of the architecture. There are two important properties of the architecture that affect the reliability of information sharing.

When information is transferred it might be corrupted or lost. When this happens, the architecture cannot deliver its intended functionality, namely providing access to reliable information. The chances for and possible extent of issues with *data integrity* can therefore be important for design choices in architecture.

In a similar fashion, the way in which the architecture deals with faults and errors is vital for the reliability of information sharing. The *fault tolerance* of the architecture determines its coping with errors [25]. It determines to what extent data can still be shared in the architecture when something goes wrong and components fail.

The design of the architecture influences for how long it will be able to support information sharing in the future. Therefore, anticipation of future changes in the situation in which B2G information sharing needs to be supported will be an important factor influencing design choices.

Not all businesses that are a source of information might immediately be willing or able to connect to the architecture. This might change in time and the load on the architecture might grow. The architecture should then accommodate a growing number of connections and a larger volume of data. This makes its *scalability* an important property. Furthermore, in time more and unforeseen types of data might become available for sharing. For the architecture to accommodate this, it should be scalable on this dimension as well.

Other kinds of foreseen and unforeseen future changes might occur, changing the way in which the SIP should support information sharing. Examples are changes in the laws on data protection or the evolvement of new types of security attacks. Its *flexibility* is therefore another important property.

Table 1 shows the factors impacting design choices we focus on and the properties of the architecture that they in turn are affected by, based on our discussion. We will use this list of properties for comparing a SIP with a thick flow and a SIP with a thin flow. The number of each property corresponds with a subsection of Sect. 4.

Table 1. List of properties for comparing the architectures

Main factors	Properties
Willingness of businesses to participate	1. Security and privacy protection
	2. Costs
	3. Possibilities for governance
Reliability of the information sharing process	4. Data integrity and fault tolerance
Flexibility for anticipating future changes	5. Scalability
	6. Flexibility

4 Comparing the Thin and Thick Flow Architectures

In this section, we will describe the properties of a SIP with a thin flow and with a thick flow. In the next section, we will discuss how these influence the suitability of the thin and thick flow in different situations.

4.1 Security and Privacy Protection

In a technically centralized SIP with a thick flow, the shipping information and metadata goes through some kind of central component in the SIP. A security failure in this component would mean that the security and privacy of all shipping information and metadata is compromised. Encryption of the messages and sending and storing metadata and shipping information separately are possible solutions [26].

Since metadata is already shared via the reference index in the thin flow, there is no need to send it again with the follow-up message containing the shipping information; a reference number should be sufficient. As a result metadata and shipping information cannot be accessed at the same time.

In the thick flow, there is central accessibility to detailed shipping information. When the information is stored in the central component it could be immediately accessed. If it is not stored, or only temporarily stored in the central component, then the information sharing through this component might still be monitored. This is a concern for some stakeholders in the SIP [13]. In the thin flow, there is also central access to metadata. It depends on the content of the metadata in the thin flow whether similar big brother issues or global security and privacy issues could occur there. Security problems with shipping information will only be local.

In the thick flow, access will have to be controlled centrally. The more information and parties are involved, the more complex the rules for controlling access may become. In the thin flow, the reference index is a central component and will also require some central access control. However, for the shipping information itself, businesses can locally define roles and access rules. This might lead to less complex rules and provides businesses with more direct control.

In the thick flow security measures and access control can be developed and maintained centrally. In the thin flow there are a lot more connections between parties that need protection using local security measures. In a thin flow, security measures thus are as strong as the weakest link.

4.2 Costs

The SIP with a thick flow allows parties to combine forces and share part of the maintenance and keeping up to date of the central component of the SIP and its connections. This might lead to lower costs for individual parties. For the thin flow such possibilities are more limited. Additionally, sharing costs for e.g., developing security measures could lead to problems on a global scale that are avoided otherwise.

The interface of the systems of the businesses in a thick flow needs to contain many data elements, in other words, it is a 'thick' interface [4]. This requires initial investments to make it conform with an extensive standard. In the thin flow, the interface with the central component can be thin. Such a thin interface seems less costly to implement at first sight. However, the metadata still requires standardization.

In the thin flow, the shipping information itself needs to be shared as well. Since this is arranged between two parties, it might be the case that parties need to share or receive information according to different standards. Investments are needed by companies to work with these different standards.

Costs for implementation might be affected by how easy it is to use existing connections between parties for information sharing. For the thick flow, this might be easier with existing "thick" connections, such as those using a port community system. In the thin flow existing peer-to-peer connections for the sharing of the shipping information might be used as a basis.

4.3 Possibilities for Governance

In the thick flow, a lot of agreements are required initially, since once the system is setup everything has to work. Realizing such agreements is extremely difficult, especially in international settings such as that of the SIP. In the case of a thick flow, a large group with a great variety in parties, have to give up some of their autonomy to a system they do not have control over.

The governance in the case of the thin flow has to focus on agreements on the sharing of metadata, but not on the sharing of the shipping information, as that remains under control of the parties. As a result, without a clear incentive, the sharing of the shipping information might be perceived as contributing to a vulnerability or might result in opportunistic behaviour of other parties (e.g., inappropriately using the information) [27]. The thin data flow is therefore likely to start with low depth of integration ([28] in [27]). Only gaining a sufficient level of trust between parties will lead to higher levels of integration and more benefits of the information sharing. The paradox is that it also requires governance to create a situation that warrants against opportunism or at least bilateral agreements. This results in a fragmented system, where parties cannot rely on (all) shipping information actually being shared via the SIP.

4.4 Data Integrity and Fault Tolerance

In the thick flow, if shipping information is corrupted during sharing from the source to the central element, then all other parties with which the data is shared, receive the corrupt data. In the thin flow, issues with corrupt shipping information are only local. However, for the metadata central problems with data integrity might occur.

The centralized sharing of shipping information in the SIP with a thick flow, introduces a single point of failure. The reference index is a central element of the SIP with a thin flow and also constitutes a single point of failure. If the reference index cannot be used, parties might not know where to find shipping information and this will make sharing harder.

4.5 Scalability

For both architectures, scaling up the number of users would in general mean a higher volume of information that is shared via the SIP. The increase of volume of information per user is higher in the thick flow, since the shipping information itself is shared via the SIP. Therefore, it will require better scalability than a thin flow SIP.

In the thick flow, parties can use a standardized interface to link to the SIP and then they can exchange information with all other parties. For the thin flow, there is a possibility that all parties agree on such an interface as well. If not, adding a new party means that new arrangements about interfaces need to be made. This might involve a lot of work if it is a regular occurrence. At the local level there might be more heterogeneity and even manual work required without agreements on standards.

An effect of sharing new types of data is that new elements need to be added to the interfaces involved in the sharing of the shipping information. For the thick flow, depending on the design of the interface, this might be difficult to arrange since it involves adding an element to the interfaces of all parties in the SIP. The thin flow might have the same problem, depending on whether changes to the interfaces for metadata need to be made as well. However, for making additions or changes to the interfaces required to share the shipping information, less parties are involved.

4.6 Flexibility

A thick flow entails that the shipping information is shared via the architecture. This means that no large changes can be made to the route of information while still being a SIP with a thick centralized flow. Such a change might also be difficult to realize due to the changes in agreements and adaptations required by a lot of parties involved. For the thin flow, the route the information takes could be changed simply by changing the pointer so that the information is pulled from a different system.

In the thick flow, a component (e.g., for anonymization) can be added centrally, affecting the sharing of all shipping information such that it e.g., conforms with new legislation. In the thin flow, when a lot of parties are sharing their shipping information using the same newly added component, it is questionable whether we can still talk about a thin flow. It might be useful to switch to a different kind of architecture when adaptations are needed that require highly complex components that are hard to implement and develop for individual parties. However, in that case there are similar problems as in the thick flow, since a lot of parties need to agree.

5 Impact on the Design of B2G Information Sharing Architectures

The properties of the thick and the thin flow are important for several factors that impact the design choices for a B2G information sharing architecture. The way in which they impact the design choices depend on the situation in which B2G information sharing takes place. It is very hard, if not impossible, to say something in general about which choice for a design is more suitable, without taking the situation into account. Therefore, to say something about the impact on design choices, we have to say something about the situations in which a thick or thin flow is suitable.

In the previous section we discussed different properties of the architectures with a thick and a thin flow. Based on these, we present an overview in the tables below of the suitability of the architectures in different situations, with respect to these properties. Based on the factors, a thick or thin flow is considered suitable in a situation if in that situation the architecture: improves or not decreases willingness of businesses to participate, supports a sufficient level of reliability of information sharing, or is flexible enough to adequately adapt to anticipated future changes (Tables 2, 3, and 4).

Table 2. Thick and thin flow suitability: willingness of businesses to participate

Property	Thick flow suitable when:	Thin flow suitable when:
1. Security and privacy protection	No serious consequences of (global) security issues	Serious consequence of (global) security issues
	No concerns for big brother issues	Concerns for big brother issues with information, but not metadata
	Simple access rules sufficient	Complex rules required
	Parties do not need to control access directly	Parties need to control access directly
	Parties do not trust others to take sufficient security measures	Parties trust others to take sufficient security measures
2. Costs	Low costs required for development, maintenance etc.	Higher costs for development, maintenance etc. permitted
	High short-term costs for implementing thick interface permitted	Low short-term costs for implementing thin interface required
	Low long-term costs for connecting to new parties required	High long-term costs for many different connections permitted
	Existing connections are "thick"	Existing connections are "thin"
3. Possibilities for governance	Easy to get agreements between parties	Hard to get agreements between parties
	Actually sharing is important	Commitment to share not required

Table 3. Thick and thin flow suitability: reliability of information sharing

Property	Thick flow suitable when:	Thin flow suitable when:
4. Data integrity and fault tolerance	Incorrect data has no serious consequences	Incorrect data can have serious consequences
	Not being able to share has no serious consequences	Not being able to share has serious consequences

Table 4. Thick and thin flow suitability: flexibility for anticipating future changes

Property	Thick flow suitable when:	Thin flow suitable when:
5. Scalability	Not expecting to add a high number of parties in the future	Expecting to add a high number of parties in the future
	Not expecting to share many new data elements in the future	Expecting to share many new data elements in the future
6. Flexibility	Low need for a flexible route of information	High need for a flexible route of information
	Expecting to make changes that affect all information sharing	Not expecting to make changes that affect all information sharing

6 Conclusions and Suggestions for Further Research

In this paper we compared a B2G information sharing architecture with a thick flow and with a thin flow. We found that the choice for a thick flow or a thin flow causes properties of architectures to be quite different. The main cause for this is that in a thick flow more information is shared over an central infrastructure. Design choices for an architecture are not only influenced by the properties of the architecture, but also the situation in which B2G information sharing takes place. In every specific case in which a design choice is made, advantages and disadvantages of design choices need to be weighted carefully. However, in our case we found that an architecture with a thin flow would be more suitable when sensitive information is shared, it is hard to get parties to agree or commit, there is a need for high scalability and reliability and sharing between individual parties should be flexible. In contrast, we found an architecture with a thick flow to be more suitable when information is not sensitive, it is easy to get parties to agree, commitment to actually share information is important, the architecture does not need to be scalable or very reliable and future changes affecting all information sharing are expected.

There are some limitations to this research. We only compared a centralized SIP with a thick flow with a centralized SIP with a thin flow in a case of information sharing for container supply chain. Distributed variants of thick and thin flow architectures should be subject to further research. Furthermore, the comparison in this research is purely analytical. Evaluating thick and thin flow architectures in practice might provide further insight. Additionally, there might be other properties and factors that are important herein other cases. This can be investigated in future research as well.

References

1. Customs Administration of the Netherlands: Pushing boundaries: The Customs Administration of The Netherlands' Point on the Horizon for the Enforcement on Continuously Increasing Flows of Goods (2014)
2. Klievink, B., Bharosa, N., Tan, Y.H.: The collaborative realization of public values and business goals: governance and infrastructure of public-private information platforms. Gov. Inf. Q. **33**, 67–79 (2016)
3. Homburg, V.M.F.: The political economy of information exchange politics and property rights in the development and use of interorganizational information systems. Knowl. Technol. Policy **13**, 49–66 (2000)
4. Klievink, B.: Unravelling Interdependence: Coordinating Public-Private Service Networks. Delft University of Technology, Delft (2011)
5. Bharosa, N., Janssen, M., van Wijk, R., de Winne, N., van der Voort, H., Hulstijn, J., Tan, Y.-H.: Tapping into existing information flows: the transformation to compliance by design in business-to-government information exchange. Gov. Inf. Q. **30**, S9–S18 (2013)
6. Klievink, B., van Stijn, E., Hesketh, D., Aldewereld, H., Overbeek, S., Heijmann, F., Tan, Y.-H.: Enhancing visibility in international supply chains: the data pipeline concept. Int. J. Electron. Gov. Res. **8**, 14–33 (2012)
7. Fawcett, S.E., Osterhaus, P., Magnan, G.M., Brau, J.C., McCarter, M.W.: Information sharing and supply chain performance: the role of connectivity and willingness. Supply Chain Manag. Int. J. **12**, 358–368 (2007)
8. Overbeek, S., Klievink, B., Hesketh, D., Heijmann, F., Tan, Y.-H.: A web-based data pipeline for compliance in international trade. Witness **2011**, 32–48 (2011)
9. Levinson, M.: The world the box made. In: The Box: How the Shipping Container Made the World Smaller and the World Economy Bigger, pp. 1–15. Princeton University Press, Princeton (2010)

10. Hesketh, D.: Weaknesses in the supply chain: who packed the box. World Cust. J. **4**, 3–20 (2010)
11. Klievink, B., Aldewereld, H., Tan, Y.-H.: Establishing information infrastructures for international trade: discussing the role and governance of port-community systems. In: 5th International Conference on Information Systems, Logistics and Supply Chain (ILS2014), pp. 1–10. Dinalog (2014)
12. Pruksasri, P., van den Berg, J., Hofman, W.: Global monitoring of dynamic information systems a case study in the international supply chain. In: Computer Science and Engineering Conference (ICSEC) (2014)
13. Thomas, J., Tan, Y.-H.: Key design properties for shipping information pipeline. In: Janssen, M., Mäntymäki, M., Hidders, J., Klievink, B., Lamersdorf, W., Loenen, B., Zuiderwijk, A. (eds.) I3E 2015. LNCS, vol. 9373, pp. 491–502. Springer, Cham (2015). doi: 10.1007/978-3-319-25013-7_40
14. Tan, Y.-H., Bjørn-Andersen, N., Klein, S., Rukanova, B.: Accelerating Global Supply Chains with IT-Innovation. Springer, Berlin (2011). doi:10.1007/978-3-642-15669-4
15. Hofman, W.: Supply chain visibility with linked open data for supply chain risk analysis. Witness **2011**, 20–31 (2011)
16. Graham, I.: Business Rules Management & Service Oriented Architecture. Wiley, New York (2006)
17. Lucassen, I., Klievink, B., Griffioen, H., Commission, E.: Cassandra—WP400—Asia-NL/UK trade lane Living Lab Report (2010)
18. Janssen, M.: Insights from the introduction of a supply chain co-ordinator. Bus. Process Manag. J. **10**, 300–310 (2004)
19. Papazoglou, M.P., Van Den Heuvel, W.J.: Service oriented architectures: approaches, technologies and research issues. VLDB J. **16**, 389–415 (2007)
20. Urciuoli, L., Hintsa, J., Ahokas, J.: Drivers and barriers affecting usage of e-Customs—a global survey with customs administrations using multivariate analysis techniques. Gov. Inf. Q. **30**, 473–485 (2013)
21. van Engelenburg, S., Janssen, M., Klievink, B.: Design of a business-to-government information sharing architecture using business rules. In: Bianculli, D., Calinescu, R., Rumpe, B. (eds.) Software Engineering and Formal Methods. LNCS, vol. 9509, pp. 124–138. Springer, Heidelberg (2015). doi:10.1007/978-3-662-49224-6_11
22. Klievink, B., Janssen, M., Tan, Y.-H.: A stakeholder analysis of business-to-government information sharing. Int. J. Electron. Gov. Res. **8**, 54–64 (2012)
23. European Court of Human Rights: European Convention on Human Rights (2010)
24. Karampetsou, A.: Container information & privacy concerns: opening the ``Pandora's" box? In: Legal challenges of a Business-to-Customs Information Sharing with Regard to Containerized Cargo. Current Issues in Maritime & Transport Law, pp. 1–17. Bonomo Editore, Bologna (2016)
25. Lee, P.A., Anderson, T.: Fault Tolerance: Principles and Practice. Springer, New York (2012). doi:10.1007/978-3-7091-8990-0
26. O'Brien, L., Merson, P., Bass, L.: Quality attributes for service-oriented architectures. In: Proceedings of the International Workshop on Systems Development in SOA Environments. IEEE Computer Society (2007)
27. Hart, P., Saunders, C.: Power and trust: critical factors in the adoption and use of electronic data interchange. Organ. Sci. **8**, 23–42 (1997)
28. Massetti, B.L.: The Effects of Electronic Data Interchange on Corporate Organization. Florida State University in Tallahassee, Florida (1991)

Coordinated Border Management Through Digital Trade Infrastructures and Trans-National Government Cooperation: The FloraHolland Case

Boriana Rukanova[1(✉)], Roel Huiden[2], and Yao-Hua Tan[1]

[1] TUDelft, Jaffalaan 5, 2628 BX Delft, The Netherlands
{b.d.rukanova,y.tan}@tudelft.nl

[2] Royal FloraHolland, Middel Broekweg 29, 2675 KB Honselersdijk, The Netherlands
roelhuiden@royalfloraholland.com

Abstract. Digital infrastructures (DI) that support information exchange related to international trade processes (here referred to as Digital Trade Infrastructures (DTI)) have been seen as an instrument to help address the trade facilitation and security challenges. Data pipelines can be seen as an example of a DTI. Data pipelines are IT innovations that enable the timely provision of data captured at the source from different information systems available in the supply chain. Using the pipeline companies can share information with authorities and enjoy trade facilitation in return. The benefits of such data pipelines have been showcased in demonstrator settings. However, outside the controlled environment of demonstrator installations, the adoption and growth of these DTIs has been limited. The benefits based on purely implementing the data pipeline are limited. Combining data pipeline capability with Coordinated Border Management (CBM) has potential to articulate more clear benefits for stakeholders and push further investments and wider adoption. In this paper based on the FloraHolland trade lane related to exporting flowers from Kenya to the Netherlands we discuss a data pipeline/CBM innovation. Through the conceptual lens of DI (examining architectural, process and governance dimensions) we demonstrate the potential benefits of data pipeline/CBM innovation and the complex alignment processes between business and government actors needed for the further adoption. From a theoretical point of view we enhance the understanding regarding the governance dimension of such data pipeline/CBM innovations by identifying four type of alignments processes involving businesses and government actors nationally and internationally. As such the paper contributes to the body of research on DI and more specifically DTI. Form a point of view of practice, the insights from our analysis can be used to better understand other data pipeline/CBM innovation alignment processes in other domains as well.

Keywords: Digital trade infrastructures · Data pipelines · Coordinated border management · Cost-benefit · International government collaboration · Governance

M. Janssen et al. (Eds.): EGOV 2017, LNCS 10428, pp. 240–252, 2017.
DOI: 10.1007/978-3-319-64677-0_20

1 Introduction

In the international trade domain digital infrastructures, here referred to as Digital Trade Infrastructures (DTI), have been seen as an instrument to help address the trade facilitation and security challenges. It has been argued that DTI can transcends the current information silos and can enable more efficient risk assessment, supply chain optimization and cost savings [1, 14, 20]. Data pipelines can be seen as an example of DTI, where a data pipeline can be defined as "an IT innovation to enable capturing data at the source" [11, p. 14]. A data pipeline can enable the timely provision of data captured at the source from different information systems available in the supply chain [8, 11]. Solutions like the data pipeline rely on re-use of business data by multiple government authorities involved in cross-border inspections of goods for government control purposes. The benefits of DTI such as the data pipeline have been showcased in demonstrator settings in various EU projects including ITAIDE, CASSANDRA and now in CORE. However, beyond the pilots in these projects, the adoption and growth of these DTIs have been limited. One factor that makes DTI initiatives come to a halt relates to lack of financing and fair cost-benefit distribution among the DTI partners [12]. Significant investments need to be made for scaling up from a demonstrator to a real-life setting and that requires much sharper articulation of the benefits and the value propositions. In order to secure commitment from parties to invest and further adopt these DTI a better articulation of the value proposition for the parties involved in necessary.

As there are substantial risks involved in international trade activities, border management and safety inspections by the authorities have increased in complexity and can cause delays, extra cost, and negatively impact the competitiveness of supply chains [9]. An aggravating factor is the lack of coordination among the different inspection agencies at the border such as Customs, and National Plant Protection Organizations. Coordinated Border Management (CBM) aims to improve this inter-government agency collaboration and thus to achieve greater efficiency. According to the World Customs Organization, the term Coordinated Border Management (CBM) refers to a coordinated approach by border control agencies, both domestic and international, in the context of seeking greater efficiencies over managing trade and travel flows, while maintaining a balance with compliance requirements [21]. CBM according to the EU (Integrated Border Management) is referred to as national and international coordination and cooperation among all the relevant authorities and agencies involved in border security and trade facilitation to establish effective, efficient and integrated border management systems, in order to reach the objective of open, but well controlled and secure borders [5]. Both these definitions distinguish between national collaboration (collaboration among number of authorities in the same country) and international collaborations (i.e. collaborations between authorities of different countries) transcending national borders. Developing Coordinated Border Management solutions holds potential to reduce delays and reduce costs. Developing data pipeline innovation to achieve Coordinated Border Management solutions will potentially reduce inspection delays and costs at the border even further. This would it its turn enable a sharper articulation of the value of proposition for the data pipeline solutions.

In this paper, we conduct an in-depth interpretative case study of the trade lane for flower import from Kenya to Royal FloraHolland in the Netherlands. Building on the Digital Infrastructure literature we examine the FloraHolland innovation efforts related to data pipeline/CBM innovation. By doing so, we demonstrate the potential gains, as well as the complex governance and alignment processes between business and government actors (nationally and internationally) needed to develop such innovations. The remaining part of this paper is structured as follows: In Section Two we introduce the problem context and the theoretical background. In Section Three we discuss our interpretative case methodology. The case analysis of the FloraHolland case is presented in Section Four. We end the paper with conclusions and recommendations.

2 Theoretical Framework: Digital Infrastructures and Digital Trade Infrastructures

In order to provide a better understanding of the context complexity, we start with a brief explanation of the import procedure of flowers From Kenya to the Netherlands (see Fig. 1 below).

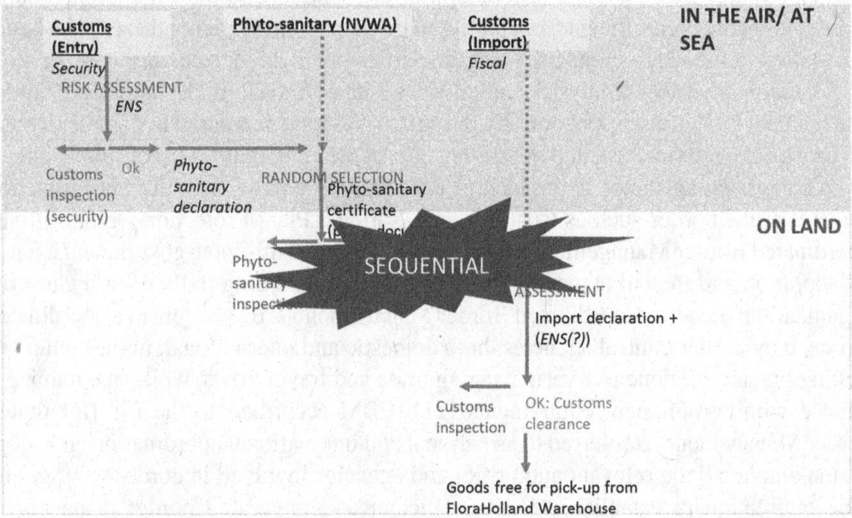

Fig. 1. Sequential procedure, most of the risk analysis done on land

The essential part of an inspection procedure is to conduct a risk assessment of goods to identify whether or not there is a potential risk. When flowers are imported from Kenya to the Netherlands there are three risk assessment processes (see Fig. 1), namely: *(1) safety and security risk assessment by Customs at entry in the EU*, *(2) phytosanitary product safety risk assessment by the National Plant Protection Organization (NVWA)*, and *(3) a Customs import risk analysis* related to the fiscal aspect and related import duties. While we will not go in detail in the documents exchanged, there are a number of issues with the current procedure. First, this is a sequential process, where one assessment cannot start before the other is finished. This sequential dependency of various border inspections is a typical example of lack of CBM. Second, most of the procedures take place once the goods are on the ground. Authorities can also ask for additional information to perform their risk analysis which adds extra delays and for businesses that translates in extra costs. In the FloraHolland pilot as part of the CORE project, FloraHolland together with the Dutch authorities designed a new procedure called *Clearance in the Sky/at Sea*. This new procedure shows how to develop a data pipeline that contributes to achieve CBM and is considered very beneficial for both the authorities and for the horticultural supply chain. For this procedure to be implemented however, complex alignment processes need to take place between business, the customs and phytosanitary authorities both nationally and internationally. While the further details of these alignment processes will be discussed in the Case analysis section, this brief example already gives an idea of the context and complexities involved.

Conceptually the data pipeline/CBM innovation can be seen in the context of Digital Infrastructures (DI) and more specifically Digital Trade Infrastructures (DTI). DI can be seen as a System-of-Systems [6, 7] that transcends organizational and systems domains, reducing information fragmentation. DI that support information exchange related to international trade processes are referred here as Digital Trade Infrastructures. The DI literature identifies a variety of challenges faced by the DI development. As digital infrastructures span among diverse set of stakeholders and develop over time, challenges include the inertia of the installed base [19], coordination challenges among the stakeholders [3], conflicts and struggles for influence and control [17]. DI literature also include critique of existing traditional systems development methods to deal with the complexity of digital infrastructures [4, 13, 18] and it has been suggested that different approaches are needed for DI development [6].

When thinking of development approaches there are two specific aspects that set DTI apart from other Dis such as e.g. infrastructures for the healthcare domain that are solely on a national level. The first aspect refers to the international dimension of international trade, where goods transcend national borders and regulatory regimes [14, 20]. The importance of the international dimension has been also highlighted in a stream of research focusing on Transnational Information Systems [2] and can be traced to other domains such as banking as well. The second aspect that is very specific for DTI is the high level of involvement of authorities both on the import and the export side in the business-to-business supply chain processes [8], which also leads to high influence on the system development efforts [15]. It is these two aspects in combination that distinguish DTI from other DI and that needs to be reflected in development approaches targeted at DTI. Identifying these specifics and based on the DI literature Rukanova et al. [16] propose a DTI framework to study DTI by looking at three dimensions, *(1) architecture*, *(2) process*, and *(3) governance*. For simplicity we will not discuss the full DTI framework but what is important to mention is that the concepts of *levels,* and *actor* as part of the architectural dimension of the DTI framework can be used to capture the distinguishing characteristics of DTI. More specifically the *levels* can be used to capture the increasing complexity related to legislation and alignment needed when dealing with trade relationships that transcend the national context towards the international and global level. The *actors* will capture the interrelationships between the business and government actors. To sum up, in this paper we will use the high-level dimensions of the DTI framework [16], namely *(1) architecture*, *(2) process* and *(3) governance* to steer our analysis of the data pipeline/CBM innovations of the FloraHolland pilot.

3 Method

In this study, we build on the interpretative and contextualist tradition that is well-established in Information Systems (IS) research [10]. The focus of this study is the trade lane for importing flowers from Kenya to FloraHolland in the Netherlands via Sea and Air by the support of data pipeline, which is part of the EU-funded research project CORE. FloraHolland, as a growers' cooperative, represents the growers and facilitates them in their trade. This trade lane further zooms in on how data pipeline can enable CBM. The data was collected as part of the FloraHolland pilot of the CORE project. The authors have been actively involved in the project in different roles. The data has been collected from the start of the project in May 2014 till January 2017. Data collection included participating in meetings, workshops including FloraHolland, Dutch Customs and the Dutch Plant Protection Organization, and document analysis. Two visits to Kenya took place, the second one in December 2016. In the second visit a delegation from the FloraHolland pilot including also the Dutch Customs and The Dutch Plant Protection Organization (NVWA) visited among others the Kenyan counterpart authorities to gain understanding about export procedures in Kenya. Next to that, via the participation in another pilot also including Kenyan authorities the authors were following closely the developments related to further alignment of the authorities on the Kenyan side driven by TRADEMARK, an international development organization that supports the development of the East Africa Customs Union. Regarding the data analysis, as discussed earlier we used the three high-level dimensions from the DTI framework [16], i.e. *(1) architectural* (including levels and actors), *(2) process*, and *(3) governance* as a conceptual lens. We further detailed and elaborate these dimensions based on the case findings to capture the specifics related to data pipeline/CBM innovations.

4 Case Analysis

4.1 Architecture

The first dimension of the DTI framework [16] is the *architectural dimension*, which includes analysis of *actors*, and *levels*. The FloraHolland initiative focusses on the import of Flowers from Kenya to The Netherlands. In terms of *actors* both business and government actors are involved on both sides.

Key business actors on the Kenyan side are the Growers, the Freight Forwarder responsible for arranging transport and necessary paper documents needed for export. On the Dutch side the key business actors are the Freight Forwarder, and FloraHolland. FloraHolland either prepares the flowers for auctioning or delivers them to the Importer. The (sea/air) carrier is responsible for transporting the flowers between Kenya and The

Netherlands and for preparing Entry Summary Declarations (ENS) required before entering the EU. The process steps are visualized below. The key government actors are as follows: Kenyan Customs Administration (KRA), Kenyan Plant Protection Organization (KEPHIS), Dutch Customs Administration (DCA) and the Dutch Plant Protection Organization (NVWA). In the development of the DTI for the FloraHolland pilot, two intermediary actors are of key importance. The first one is the data pipeline provider (DESCARTES) for sharing supply chain information such as invoices and packing lists between the business parties. The second one is the IT provider Intrasoft which develops a customs dashboard, which is an interface linked to the business data pipelines that can be used by the Dutch Authorities. Through this interface Dutch Customs can access additional business information (such as pro-forma invoice) and reuse it for risk assessment purposes such as cross-validation of information that appears in customs declarations.

The *levels* (national, international, and global) are used to define the scope of the initiative, as well as to trace legal and regularly developments (see Fig. 2).

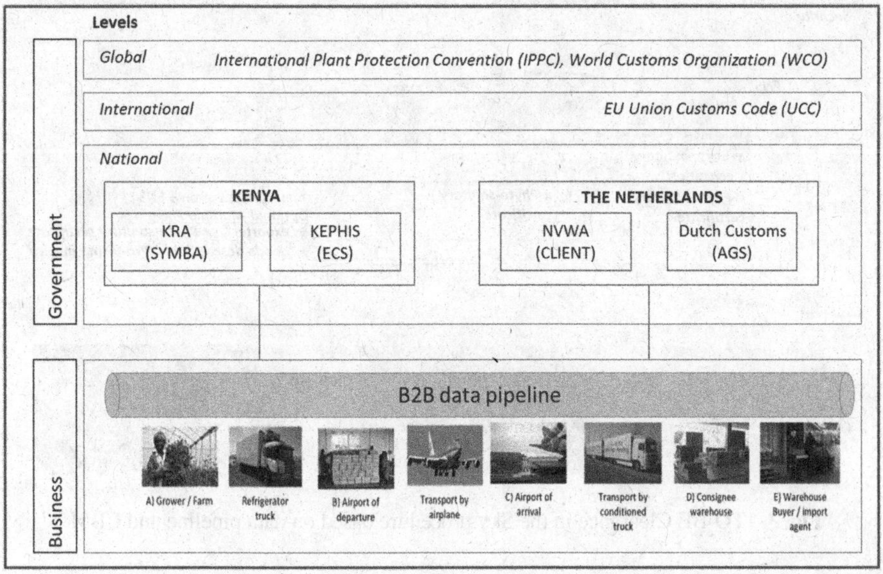

Fig. 2. FloraHolland data pipeline/CBM: Architectural dimension

The scope of the FloraHolland initiative is international, as it focusses on DTI in combination with CBM that can support trade processes between two countries, namely Kenya and the Netherlands. Due to the involvement of the Customs and The Plant Protection Organizations, there are two important legislative and regulatory developments which have an influence on the DTI development. The first one is the International Plant Protection Convention (IPPC), which sets the international rules for national Plant Protection authorities. One important development related to that is the legal requirement set for the EU for having a paper Phytosanitary certificate present during the physical inspection, which is a major barrier to achieving CBM solution that utilize the possibilities of digital documents to a full potential. The discussions around the possible use of electronic Phytosanitary certificates is very important for data pipeline/CBM innovation to achieve further simplifications. On the Customs side, the new Union Customs Code (UCC) that came in force in 2016 for the European Union is a very important legal framework, as it enables CBM solutions such as clearance at sky (see also the process section) to become possible.

4.2 Process

The second element of the DTI Framework [16] focusses on the process dimension. In Sect. 2 we discussed the inefficiency of the sequential AS-IS procedure. Below we present the new procedure *Clearance in the Sky* that was developed in the FloraHolland pilot (see Fig. 3 below).

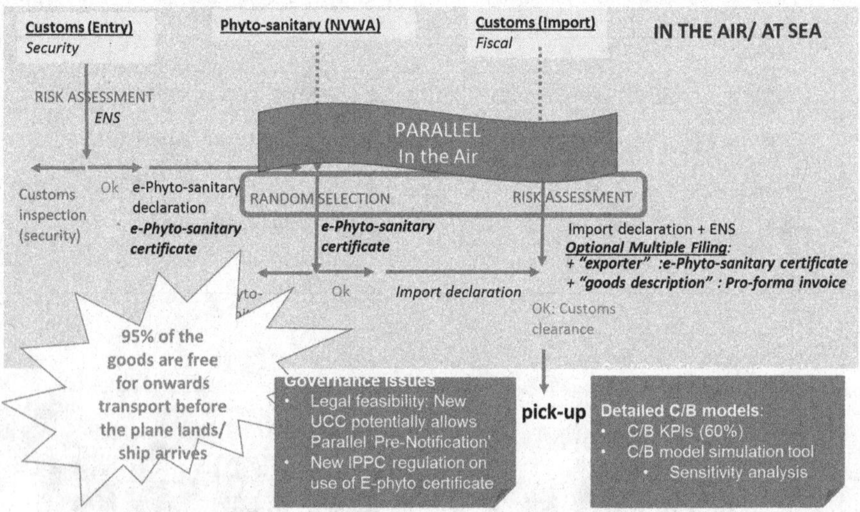

Fig. 3. TO-BE Clearance in the Sky procedure based on data pipeline and CBM

This procedure builds on the data pipeline which enables sharing information in advance with the authorities (also known as Optional Multiple Filing). Importers are obliged to send two mandatory documents to Customs, namely Import Declaration, and Entry Summary Declaration (ENS). To cross-validate the data accuracy of these mandatory documents, Customs would like to collect two additional documents from other parties in the supply chain; namely the pro-forma invoice from the grower of the flowers, which contains the most accurate goods description and the Phytosanitary certificate from KEPHIS which contains information about the real exporter. In such a way, by getting these documents via the pipeline, Customs does not need to ask and wait for additional information but can have access to additional cross-validation information earlier through the data pipeline (in Fig. 3 above the documents highlighted in bold/italic are shared via the data pipeline). The import process could be also further optimized by moving from a sequential procedure, most of which takes place on land to a parallel procedure, where all the risk assessments related to the three procedures described above are done in parallel in the air/at sea. This redesign also becomes possible due to the new EU Customs legislation set in the new Union Customs Code[1]. This means that the importer can be notified in advance whether the goods will be selected for inspection for one of the three procedures ((1) Customs security, (2) Phytosanitary, or (3) Customs import) already before the plane lands. As in the current situation only about 5% of all the FloraHolland flowers undergo any kind of inspection but all the goods need to go through the current risk assessment process, the new procedure allows for 95% of the flowers to proceed further immediately after the plain arrives. For the other 5% the new procedure allows for better planning of inspections and related efficiency gains and cost savings.

4.3 Governance

Implementing the new procedure requires complex alignment processes, which are examined through the Governance dimension [16]. Figure 4 outlines four types of key alignment processes needed for the data pipeline/CBM innovation that we identify and describe based on the case.

Alignment type 1: Business-to-Business (B2B) alignment of data sharing between all parties in the supply chain to enable the data pipeline (arrow 1).

Alignment type 2: Government-to-Government (G2G) alignment between different authorities on a national level (at import (2A) and export (2B)).

Alignment type 3: Government-to-Government (G2G) alignment between the same type of authorities on international level (Customs (3A) and Plant Protection (3B)).

Alignment type 4: Business-to-Government alignment (B2G) (Import side (4A) and export side (4B)).

Below we provide further details about how each of these alignment processes took place in the context of the FloraHolland pilot. The first alignment that was essential in the FloraHoland pilot was the B2B alignment (Alignment type 1, Arrow 1). In the FloraHoland sea trade lane, where FloraHolland is in control of large parts of the chain, aligning the parties was relatively easy. In the air trade lane it took more efforts to achieve

[1] While the full vision of Clearance in the Sky is to have full pre-clearance, for the full scenario legal changes are needed. However, the new UCC allows for prior declaration (i.e. import declaration to be submitted earlier), prior notification (in case of inspection decision), and prior verification (i.e. that the customs officer can ask for additional information (and this can be made available via the pipeline)). As such, the businesses can be notified about the outcome of the assessment (for logistics planning), while the administrative procedure would still need to be finalized independently from the logistics flows.

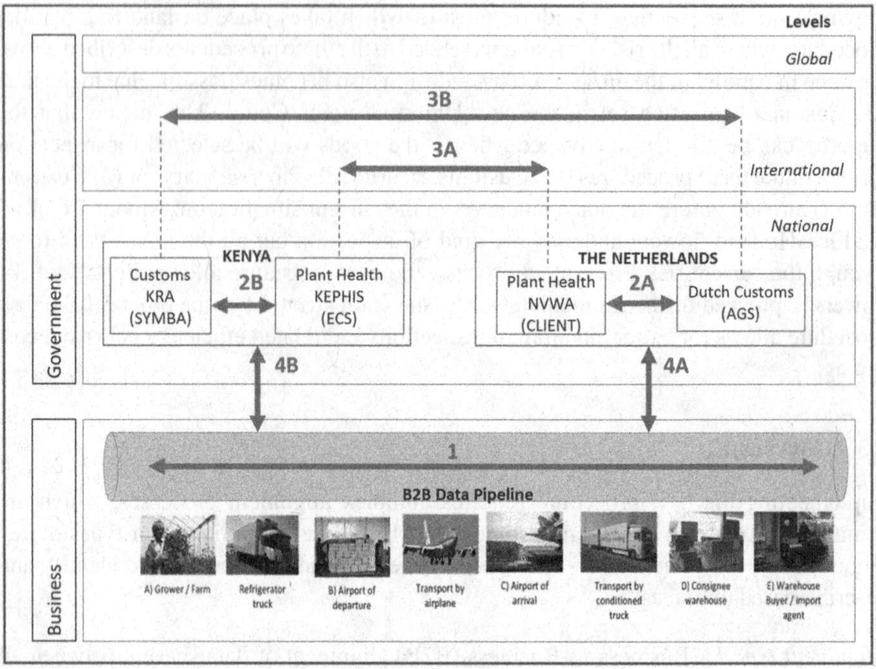

Fig. 4. Alignment processes related data pipeline and CBM

such an alignment and commit parties to join. However, due to the long business relationship this alignment was successful. A data pipeline was built and piloted in both trade lanes.

Once the data pipeline was available, the key question was whether data from this pipeline could be reused for government control purposes. Therefore, the second key alignment process started, namely B2G alignment (Alignment type 4, Arrow 4A). As part of the pilot FloraHolland initiated a number of workshops to discuss with the Dutch Authorities (NVWA and Customs) which data they would need in advance. Two elements. i.e. information about the goods description and information about the real seller are crucial for risk assessment. Having that in mind during the FloraHolland pilot an inventory was made of what information do businesses have in the data pipeline and what information they need to provide to other agencies.

By following that process the pro-forma invoice (a business document containing detailed goods description of what was actually shipped that can be made available to Customs via the data pipeline) and the Phytosanitary certificate (a document that provides information about the real seller and the real buyer of the goods) were identified as two documents which could be reused for improving Customs risk assessment processes. There were benefits through this solution especially for speeding up the last step for the import process (i.e. the import clearance), because the more accurate the data about imported goods is, the more Customs at import could de-risk the goods and then they do not need to inspect the goods. Implementation of this concept was also legally possible under the new Union Customs Code (UCC) of the EU. The FloraHolland pilot participants however wanted to look further than that. In a series of workshop, the concept of Clearance in the Sky/at Sea was developed. But the implementation of this concept required further alignment between the two Dutch authorities, namely Customs and NVWA (Alignment type 2, Arrow 2A). The participants of Dutch Customs and NVWA also collaborated in developing the Clearance in the Air scenario, which would allow for the two agencies to perform the risk analysis in parallel and in the air rather than after the goods have arrived at the airport. As part of the further alignment Dutch Customs and NVWA needed to check the legal feasibility and this seemed possible in the new UCC. Dutch Customs was very interested to pilot in the CORE project the new "pre-declaration, pre-notification, and pre-verification" clauses of the UCC; i.e. that the risk assessment can be done by Customs before goods arrive at the border, and businesses could also be notified of the results of the risk analysis whether their goods are selected for physical inspection before their goods have arrived. While the goods still needed to go through administrative customs procedures, the simplification for the physical flow of the goods was significant. This efficiency gain implies lower operational costs for the logistics service provider (LSP), and hence lower costs for the seller and/or buyer that pays the LSP for its transport services. The realization of the full benefits of the clearance in the sky scenario also depended on further collaboration with the Kenyan side, as ideally Dutch Customs wants to reuse the electronic phytosanitary certificate issued by Kephis. As a result, alignment Type 3 started to take place between NVWA and KEPHIS (Arrow 3A) to discuss the possibility to exchanging ePhyto certificates.

Historically there has been collaborations between NVWA and KEPHIS when developing their electronic declaration systems. There were even pilot projects parallel to the FloraHolland pilot for exchanging ePhyto certificates between the systems of KEPHIS and NVWA. For the FloraHolland pilot it was very interesting to link the ePhyto certificate exchange to the data pipeline. The direct link between the systems of KEPHIS and NVWA would allow for the ePhyto certificate to be exchanged directly via the G2G channels, assuring even higher data quality, compared to the alternative version when a pdf document issued by KEPHIS is shared via the commercial parties in the data pipeline with Dutch authorities. In December 2016 a delegation of the FloraHolland pilot including representatives of FloraHolland, Dutch Customs, NVWA visited Kenyan Customs (KRA) and KEPHIS to discuss the clearance in the sky scenario and align further collaboration related to the data pipeline/CBM innovation and more specifically the possibility for including ePhyto in the pilot. Next to that, in the context of the FloraHolland pilot discussions were started about further collaboration also between Dutch and Kenyan Customs (Alignment type 3, Arrow 3B). While historically there has been less collaborations between the two Customs administrations, there is an interest for closer collaboration between the two Customs administrations due to the data pipeline developments. By collaborating closely Dutch Customs can better understand how the Kenyan Customs is performing the controls during export of the flowers, and if the control measures are strict on the export side, Dutch customs may be able to rely on these controls and simplify the checks on the import side.

The alignments discuss above are essential for proceeding further with piloting with the Clearance in the Air scenario. This scenario concerns combining data pipeline capabilities with CBM to realize benefits on the Import side. Further potential for exploring the possibilities of additional procedure simplification lies on the Export side. This relies on further alignment between the Kenyan Customs and KEPHIS (Alignment type 2, arrow 2B), as well as B2G collaboration building on the data pipeline capabilities on the Kenyan side (Alignment type 4, Arrow 4B). These latter two alignments are the least developed in the FloraHolland pilot but there are intentions to develop these further. There is willingness for further collaboration between KRA and KEPHIS. In the context of the FloraHolland pilot, further contacts and alignments will be maintained and regular visits are envisaged to explore further possibilities for collaboration between the Kenyan and the Dutch authorities and possibilities offered by the data pipeline. In addition, the Kenyan authorities are also part of another alignment and mobilization effort driven by TRADEMARK. Also in these other mobilization efforts, the data pipeline in combination with CBM is the focus but more from the point of view of the exporting country. This link (4B) will be developed in the future, these efforts are likely to elicit additional benefits form combining the data pipeline and CBM.

5 Discussion and Conclusions

How to ensure safety and security while at the same time reducing the administrative burden has been a challenge for businesses and government for almost two decades. By looking at the FloraHolland pilot and through the conceptual lens of DI (looking at (1) architectural, (2) process, and (3) governance dimensions) we examine the potential benefits of data pipeline/CBM innovation. From a theoretical point of view we also enhance our understanding regarding the governance dimension of such data pipeline/CBM innovations by identifying and illustrating four type of alignments processes needed for supporting data pipeline/CBM innovation involving businesses and governments nationally and internationally. As such we contribute to the body of research on DI and more specifically DTI. This study is limited to a trade lane involving The Netherlands and Kenya representing EU and East Africa respectively. Further research can explore the applicability of our findings to trade lanes involving other countries or regions. Regarding the practical contribution: In many cases for various reasons such as supply chain efficiency, response to market demands for visibility regarding fair trade or environmental concerns businesses are investing heavily in IT systems to achieve end-to-end visibility. On the government side, different authorities have already been investing or are in the process of developing IT systems to control businesses. For realizing further value of these systems the art is to identify the important information exchanges and identify the alignment processes that need to be put in place to realize the potential gains. Due to the high level of complexity, identifying the links and the alignment processes needed may be a very lengthy process. The four alignment types that we identify allows us to understand that complexity. They can be used as an analytical lens to identify what parts of the data pipeline and government systems are already available, identify existing alignments and collaborative relationships among agencies on which the data pipeline/CBM solution can rely on. This would allow to a more efficient process of identifying and realizing the benefits of data pipeline/CBM solutions.

Acknowledgements. This research was partially funded by the CORE Project (nr. 603993), which is funded by the FP7 Framework Program of the European Commission. Ideas and opinions expressed by the authors do not necessarily represent those of all partners.

References

1. Baida, Z., Rukanova, B., Liu, J., Tan, Y.H.: Rethinking EU trade procedures—the beer living lab. Electron. Mark. **18**(1), 53–64 (2008)
2. Cavaye, A.L.M.: An exploratory study in investigating transnational information systems. J. Strateg. Inf. Syst. **7**(1), 17–35 (1998)
3. Ciborra, C., Hanseth, O.: Introduction: from control to drift. In: Ciborra, C. (ed.) From Control to Drift, pp. 1–12. Oxford University Press, Oxford (2000)
4. Damsgaard, J., Lyytinen, K.: The role of intermediating institutions in the diffusion of electronic data interchange (EDI): how industry associations intervened in Denmark, Finland, and Hong Kong. Inf. Soc. **17**(3), 195–210 (2001)
5. EU: Guidelines for Integrated Border Management on the EU Accession Program (2007)
6. Hanseth, O., Lyytinen, K.: Design theory for dynamic complexity in information infrastructures: the case of building internet. J. Inf. Technol. **25**(1), 1–19 (2010)
7. Hanseth, O., Monteiro, E., Hatling, M.: Developing information infrastructure: the tension between standardization and flexibility. Sci. Technol. Hum. Values **21**(4), 407–426 (1996)
8. Hesketh, D.: Weaknesses in the supply chain: who packed the box. World Cust. J. **4**(2), 3–20 (2010)
9. Holloway, S.: Measuring the effectiveness of border management: designing KPIs for outcomes. World Cust. J. **4**(2), 37–54 (2010)
10. Klein, H.K., Myers, M.D.: A set of principles for conducting and evaluating interpretive field studies in information systems. Manag. Inf. Syst. Q. **23**(1), 67–93 (1999)
11. Klievink, A.J., Van Stijn, E., Hesketh, D., Aldewereld, H., Overbeek, S., Heijmann, F., Tan, Y.H.: Enhancing visibility in international supply chains: The data pipeline concept. Int. J. Electron. Gov. Res. **8**(4), 14–33 (2012)
12. Klievink, B., Janssen, M., Tan, Y.H.: A stakeholder analysis of business-to-government information sharing: the governance of a public–private platform. Int. J. Electron. Gov. Res. **8**(4), 54–64 (2012)
13. Rodon, J., Silva, L.: Exploring the formation of a healthcare information infrastructure: hierarchy or meshwork? J. Assoc. Inf. Syst. **16**(5), 1 (2015)
14. Rukanova, B., Henningsson, S., Henriksen, H.Z., Tan, Y.H.: The Anatomy of Digital Trade Infrastructures. Working paper, January, 2017. doi:10.13140/RG.2.2.23382.04167 (2017)
15. Rukanova, B., Van Stijn, E., Henriksen, H.Z., Baida, Z., Tan, Y.H.: Understanding the influence of multiple levels of governments on the development of inter-organizational systems. Eur. J. Inf. Syst. **18**(5), 387–408 (2009)
16. Rukanova, B., Wigand, R.W., van Stijn, E., Tan, Y.H.: Transnational information systems: a multi-level, conflict management perspective. Gov. Inf. Q. **32**, 182–197 (2015)
17. Sanner, T.A., Manda, T.D., Nielsen, P.: Grafting: balancing control and cultivation in information infrastructure innovation. J. Assoc. Inf. Syst. **15**(4), 220–243 (2014)
18. Sauer, C., Willcocks, L.: Unreasonable expectations—NHS IT, Greek choruses and the games institutions play around mega-programmes. J. Inf. Technol. **22**(3), 195–201 (2007)

19. Star, S.L.: The ethnography of infrastructure. Am. Behav. Sci. **43**(3), 377–391 (1999)
20. Tan, Y.H., Bjorn-Andersen, N., Klein, S., Rukanova, B.: Accelerating global supply chains with IT-innovation. Springer, Berlin (2011)
21. WCO: Research Paper No. 2: Coordinated Border Management—A Concept Paper (2009)

Big and Open Linked Data

An Evaluation Framework for Linked Open Statistical Data in Government

Ricardo Matheus(✉) and Marijn Janssen(✉)

Faculty of Technology, Policy and Management,
Delft University of Technology, Jaffalaan 5, 2628 BX Delft, The Netherlands
{r.matheus,m.f.w.h.a.janssen}@tudelft.nl

Abstract. Demographic, economic, social and other datasets are often used in policy-making processes. These types of statistical data are opened more and more by governments, which enables the use of these datasets by the public. However, statistical data needs often to combine different datasets. Data cubes can be used to combine datasets and are a multi-dimensional array of values typically used to describe time series of geographical areas. While Linked Open Statistical Data (LOSD) cube software is still in an initial stage of maturity, there is a need for evaluation the software platforms used to process this open data. Yet there is a lack of evaluation methods. The objective of this ongoing research paper is to identify functional requirements for open data cubes infrastructures. Eight main processes are identified and a list of 23 functional requirements are used to evaluate the OpenCube platform. The evaluation results of a LOSD platform show that many functions are not automated and need to be manually executed. We recommend the further integration of the building blocks in the platform to reduce the barriers for the use of datasets by the public.

Keywords: Linked open statistical data · LOSD · Open data · Big data · Open government · Data cube · Evaluation · Parameters · Requirements · Agile development

1 Introduction

A large number of datasets, such as demography, economic indexes, or public policies results, are statistical types of data [1]. Often these data need to be combined to create value. Data cubes are useful for combining data [2]. Data cubes are the array of 2 or more datasets based on the Structured Query Language (SQL) join functionality [3]. Data cubes enable data analysis of for example time-series to detect trends, abnormalities, unusual patterns or can be used to compare geographic regions with each other. The authors of [4] show that data cubes can be used to aggregate unemployment and election datasets to explore the relationship between them.

Organising and reusing datasets is often found to be hard due to challenges like access to data [5], manipulation of data [6], accuracy of data [7], and a long list of other data quality issues [8–12]. Linking those datasets using the Linked Open Statistical Data (LOSD) approach enables the creation of data cubes. Statistical datasets have their peculiarities and due this reason, the W3C adopted the Resource Description Framework

M. Janssen et al. (Eds.): EGOV 2017, LNCS 10428, pp. 255–263, 2017.
DOI: 10.1007/978-3-319-64677-0_21

Data Cube (QB) vocabulary to standardise the modelling of cubes as RDF graphs [13]. While statistical data cubes platforms are still on an initial mature stage [6], there is a need to evaluate OpenCube platforms. Yet no models exist to evaluate open cubes platforms.

2 Research Approach

The objective of this project paper is to develop an evaluation framework to evaluate an open data cubes platform (ODCP). Eight main processes are identified and a list of 23 requirements are derived which can be used to evaluate OpenCube platforms and applications. Using the evaluation model six cases were evaluated. The first three cases were developed by students at Delft University of Technology (https://goo.gl/y5HgJq), whereas the other three cases have been developed within the OpenGovIntelligence project (www.opengovintelligence.eu).

Table 1. Open statistical data cube parameters, requirements and questions

Parameters	#	Requirements	Questions
Functionality	1	Functional Completeness	The set of functions on the platform covers all the needs of pilots and users to perform their specific tasks?
	2	Functional appropriateness	The set of functions on the platform covers all the needs since the beginning to the end to accomplish theirs initial objectives?
Performance	3	Resource utilization	The ODCP is able to deal with amounts (quantity) and types of resources (data)?
	4	Capacity	There is a known limit capacity of any dimension (storage, processing, etc.) that platform will face during any pilot phase?
Compatibility	5	Coexistence	The ODCP is able to perform required functions efficiently while shares a common environment with other products?
	6	Interoperability	The platform is able to create an interoperable environment for exchange and use of information?
Usability	7	Learnability	The ODCP has appropriate documentation for beginners use?
	8	Operability	The ODCP has attributes that makes easy to operate and control?
	9	User error protection	The ODCP protects users to make errors? What are the functions or attributes that helps users and/or avoid errors?
	10	Accessibility	The ODCP is prepared for the widest range of characteristic and capabilities of users?
Reliability	11	Maturity	The ODCP has reliability under normal operation.
	12	Availability	The ODCP will be available to all users at same time without losing any other requirement performance?
	13	Fault Tolerance	The ODCP has fault tolerance?
	14	Recoverability	The ODCP has data recovery function?
Security	15	Confidentiality	The ODCP has any confidentiality issues concernment?
	16	Integrity	The ODCP has any function that prevents unauthorized access, modification of system and data?
Maintainability	17	Modularity	The ODCP has the modular characteristic?
	18	Reusability	The ODCP has reusable characteristic?
	19	Analysability	The ODCP has documentation for failures and errors?
	20	Modifiability	The ODCP has characteristics of improvements without degrading existing efficient and effective characteristics?
Portability	21	Adaptability	The platform is prepared to have a adaptable language or building blocks?
	22	Installability	The ODCP can be easy installed and uninstalled?
	23	Replaceability	The ODCP has flexibility on changing to other software parts?

In the literature there is no overview of functions needed by data cubes. Nevertheless ISO/IEC 25010:2010, the standard for Systems and Software Quality Requirements and Evaluation [14] can be of help, as these present a structured list of requirements. This list of requirements will be used for evaluating statistical cubes platforms. Further, based on the description of ISO 25010:2010, we created questions to evaluate each of the requirements, as presented in Table 1.

The questionnaire was used to evaluate 6 case studies in which open data cubes were designed using the OpenGovIntelligence platform. The survey was conducted on a qualitative way to identify if the platform could be used to design statistical data cubes. The answers allowed us to evaluate the data cubes by looking at which requirements were fulfilled by the open data cube platform. Also this allowed us to identify the main issues that open statistical data cubes designers face during the design and implementation of open data cues. The requirements covered were used as an indication for the maturity of development.

3 Background

Statistical data is often organised in a multidimensional manner where a measured fact is described based on a number of dimensions. As an example, Olympics statistics can bring three different dimensions: countries (USA, GB, China), medal (gold, silver, Bronze) and year (2004, 2008, 2012) and summarised on the Fig. 1 [15]. In the example, each of the cells contains a measure referring to Olympian statistical data, but together, they form a data cube.

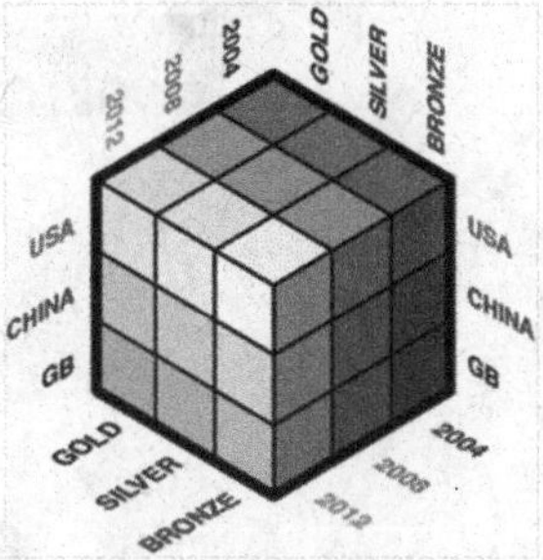

Fig. 1. Olympics Medals distributed by countries within the years.

The functionality we derived is created by adapting the Linked Open Statistical Data Cubes (LOSDC) cycle consisting of eight steps [1] modified by [16]. The steps are divided into (1) Data Cubes Creation and (2) Data cubes Analysis processes. Figure 2 shows the main steps which are described hereafter. Also the typical software tools used for supporting each step are presented.

A-Data Cubes Creation Processes

Step 1-Discover and Pre-process Raw Data

This first step is aimed at handling and preparing the file formats to be ready for the next steps. As an example XLS (spreadsheets file format), Comma-Separated Values (CSV) and JavaScript Object Notation (JSON) is used as an input. One of the most used tool for this step is the OpenRefine (http://openrefine.org/). This steps is needed for increasing the capacity and resilience for managing, updating and extending data because they are on an greater interoperable format (CSV, JSON) than XLS as an example.

Step 2-Define Structure and Create Cubes

The objective of the second step is to define the structure of the data cube using the Resource Description Framework (RDF) data cube vocabulary. For this own code lists or standard taxonomies created by external, supranational or international organisations like the W3C data cubes (https://www.w3.org/TR/vocab-data-cube/) can be used [13]. After this, the data in RDF format is validated. The tool used for this step is Cube Builder (https://github.com/OpenGovIntelligence/data-cube-builder) and Grafter (http://grafter.org/). This step is necessary for enabling ontology and concept scheme management.

Step 3-Annotate Cubes

The third step creates metadata about the datasets. Metadata explains the meaning of the datasets. Metadata enabled data provenance, understanding data production processes and cube structures. In this way data can be reused by others and the effort and cost for publishers to integrate with other data sources are reduces. Annotation can based on standard thesaurus of statistical concepts, validate the metadata and can

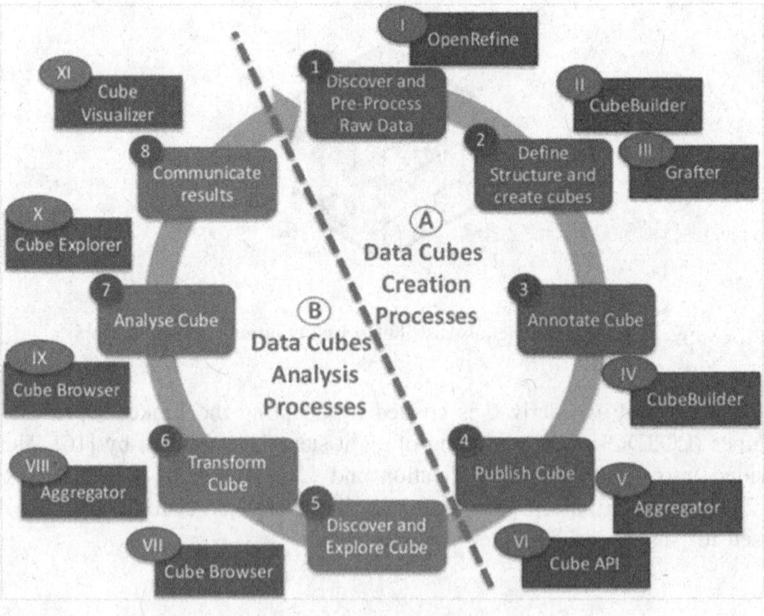

Fig. 2. Data cubes steps.

include the creation of links with compatible (external and internal) data cubes. As an example, the W3C also created the Vocabulary of Interlinked Datasets (VoID), aiming to be the connection between publishers and users of RDF datasets [17]. On the practice, OntoGov (Ontology-Enabled Electronic Government service configuration) defined a vocabulary with well-defined term that enabled automated discovery, composition, negotiation and reconfiguration of services between departments and governments [18]. The latter facilitates the analyses and even automatic combining with other datasets.

Step 4-Publish Cube

The fourth step finishes the Data Cubes Creation Process by publishing data cubes in data catalogues. This step also can use a Linked Data API (Application Programming Interface) or a SPARQL endpoint, the query language of RDFs. For this step, example of tool is the Cube API (https://github.com/OpenGovIntelligence/json-qb-api-implementation) or the aggregator (http://opencube-toolkit.eu/opencube-aggregator/).

B-Data Cube Analysis Processes

Step 5-Discover and Explore Cube

Based on the metadata, analysts can start to discover the cubes browsing the datasets and pivot them. This step enables the expansion of cubes, what means combining other data resources. Standardised semantic annotation helps users to find data of interest faster and easier.

Step 6-Transform Cube

The sixth step expands cubes and also allow analysts to create slices or dices, using pre-compute summarisations and other statistical functionalities. This can also help users to understand the content and structure of datasets faster and easier. The tool used on this step is the aggregator.

Step 7-Analyse Cube

This step enables statistical analysis on the cubes created using comprehensive Online Analytical Processing (OLAP) operations. The tools Cube Browser (https://github.com/OpenGovIntelligence/qb-olap-browser) and Cube Explorer (https://github.com/OpenGovIntelligence/data-cube-explorer) allow analysts to create and evaluate learning and predictive models or estimate dependencies between measures. Further, it is possible to publish the descriptions of resulting models into the Web of Linked Data. This enables the connection of data cubes with each other.

Step 8-Communicate results

This final step concludes the data cubes analysis processes and the cycle can start over again. The main objective of this step is to create visualisations and reports which can be used in policy-making efforts. As an example, analysts can create charts (bar chart, pie chart, sorted pie chart, area chart) and maps (heat maps) based on the LOSD and data cubes. The tool used for this step is the Cube Visualizer (https://github.com/OpenGovIntelligence/CubeVisualizer). The Cube visualizer is a web application that creates and presents to the user graphical representations of an RDF data cube's one-dimensional slices. It also enables non-technical users to re-use data more efficiently, in new and innovative ways without high level of technical skills.

4 Open Cubes in Practice: Case Studies

This paper selected six cases to evaluate its implementation of statistical data cubes. The first three cases were developed by students at Delft University of Technology (https://goo.gl/y5HgJq). The other three cases have been developed as part of the OpenGovIntelligence project (www.opengovintelligence.eu). The six applications are:

1. The "world most suitable country to live" (http://kossa.superhost.pl/sen1611/app/);
2. The "Gender Inequality in Europe" (http://raditya.me/genderinequality/paymentgap/mapview/);

Table 2. Open statistical data cube platform benefits and challenges

Requirements	Benefits	Challenges of development
Functional Completeness	The purposed platform has tools to open and link datasets. Also has functionalities to browse, expand, analysis and visualisation	The platform is hard to use for beginners and management level
Functional appropriateness	All the steps on the Fig. 1 (data cube cycle) can be realised if tools used properly	The platform has no manual or documentation for proper use. Examples of usage could be created to encourage and inspire usage
Resource utilization	The platform is able to deal with the amount and quantity of datasets. They are yet on the scale of Megabytes (MBs)	Quantitative analysis will be conducted on the next round of evaluation to identify if Gigabytes (GBs) scale can be processed
Capacity	This limit was not yet reached. Capacity is not an issue because datasets are on the scale of MBs	No challenges of development identified on this requirement
Coexistence	The platform has no limitations of Coexistence with other products/tools functioning in the same environment	No challenges of development identified on this requirement
Interoperability	The platform was created interoperable by default. Considering data source on an interoperable format such as tabular CSV, and output data (Data Cubes format, RDF and Turtle (TTL))	JSON API could be enhanced to increase interoperability level of platform
Learnability	If proper documentation and manual be created, the usage of platform can be done easier than learning from the scratch	Proper documentation and manual should be created to increase the capacity building (skills), for beginners and management level
Operability	Data cubes were created based on easy of usage attributes	If proper documentation, manual and also examples of usage be created, the operation of platform can be easier than current status
User error protection	Currently the platform has some functions that verifies user actions and disable options that would lead the user to commit errors. As example, some users cannot insert another CSV file after first upload	Any challenges of development for user error protection was mentioned
Accessibility	Not all the accessibility attributes had been developed on the platforms	Platform still has no accessible functions that should be adjusted according to user profile. An example, Linked data conversion will be allowed for service creators not consumers
Maturity	The initial version of platform is offering demo services on a testing server. For normal	There were no maturity issues described by any student or technical expert partners

(*continued*)

Table 2. (*continued*)

Requirements	Benefits	Challenges of development
	conversion, loading and visualisation operation the % of Uptime is around 98%	
Availability	The probability of the "Linked Data" service to be available shall be *at least* 99% of the time. In essence, the system *shall* be available "24 × 7" except for scheduled downtime related to configuration or system upgrades	There were no availability issues described. Except when system was down due human error (power off server)
Fault Tolerance	The known degree to which a system, product or component operates as intended despite the presence of hardware or software faults	There were no fault tolerance issues identified by any student or technical partner
Recoverability	The known degree to which, in the event of an interruption or a failure, a product or system can recover the data directly affected and re-establish the desired state of the system	Platform has no data recoverability functionality
Confidentiality	Statistical datasets has no issues about confidentiality, security, privacy, etc.	This requirement had no issues identified
Integrity	There is a function defining the level of user and what actions they can perform on the platform. Open access to system only provided to users of the pilot data dashboards	No complains observed about this requirement
Modularity	Platform is a loosely coupled application	No complain about this requirement
Reusability	Platform components can be reconfigured to work with other data sources/applications. As an example, the R libraries can be used	No issues identified for this requirement
Analysability	A list of errors code and documentation can enhance and encourage the use by external people to OGI Project	Students complained about no error code list or documentation
Modifiability	Platform is able to keep running the current version and suffer improvements on the background, being easily replaced by new version	No issues identified on this requirement
Adaptability	Platform components were written in different languages, but all components are communicating via APIs	No complain about this requirement
Installability	Platform components are web services and can be easily installed/uninstalled and run at any environment	Users had issues while performed local installation due Java, mainly Macintosh OS X users. Suggestion to create web version based in only one server for a group of users
Replaceability	Platform components can be reconfigured to work with other data sources/applications. As an example, visualisation service can be run using any Fuseki instance containing data cubes	No issues identified on this requirement

3. The "Best places for automotive industry install your plants in Europe";
4. The "Environmental monitoring centre" of The Flemish Government (Belgium);
5. The "Irish System of Maritime tourism, search and rescue" from Galway (Ireland);
6. The "Real Estate Market Analysis Dashboard" from Estonian Ministry of Economy (Estonia).

All cases took similar approaches of development, but have different objectives and audiences. Using the 22 requirements a questionnaire was designed to evaluate the benefits and identify the challenges of the data cube. The questionnaire was filled in by 40 students and 6 technical experts of the OGI Project. The benefits and challenges of the platforms are summarized in Table 2.

5 Discussions and Conclusions

More and more statistical data have been disclosed by organizations, which enables people from around the world to use these data. Yet data cube platforms are not a mature technology yet. This paper purposed a model for evaluation open statistical data cubes using a list of 23 requirements derived from the ISO 25010:2010 standard for Systems and Software Quality Requirements and Evaluation. Based on this list of 23 requirements, a questionnaire was developed which was used to evaluate six cases which makes use of the same platform for processing LOSD using open data cubes. The questionnaire was filled in by 40 persons and using this benefits and challenges of using open statistical data cubes were determined. The identified benefits include ease of use, the easy creation of open cubes when available in linked data format, and the flexibility of open cube platform to integrate with other software for enable the use of functionalities provided by other software. Challenges of development identified include no single platform for covering all steps, a lack of proper documentation, no guidelines for open data cube creation (which blocks capacity building and learning skills), fragmentation of tools, need for much manual work, and, installing and running issues with software which is needed to run OpenCube. The results show that Open Cubes can be used, but that there is still a lot of manual effort necessary and a variety of tools are needed that are not build to interoperate with each other. We recommend the further integration of the building blocks in the platforms to reduce the barriers for use of LOSD by the public.

Acknowledgement. Part of this work is funded by the European Commission within the H2020 Programme in the context of the project OpenGovIntelligence (www.opengovintelligence.eu) under Grant Agreement No. 693849.

References

1. Kalampokis, E., et al.: Creating and utilizing linked open statistical data for the development of advanced analytics services. In: Second International Workshop for Semantic Statistics, SemStats2014. CEUR-WS.org. (2014)
2. Sterling, T.D., Pollack, S.V.: Introduction to Statistical Data Processing. Prentice Hall, Englewood Cliffs (1968)
3. Gray, J., et al.: Data cube: a relational aggregation operator generalizing group-by, cross-tab, and sub-totals. Data Min. Knowl. Discov. **1**(1), 29–53 (1997)
4. Kalampokis, E., Tambouris, E., Tarabanis, K.: Linked open cube analytics systems: potential and challenges. IEEE Intell. Syst. **31**(5), 89–92 (2016)

5. Janssen, M., Charalabidis, Y., Zuiderwijk, A.: Benefits, adoption barriers and myths of open data and open government. Inf. Syst. Manag. **29**(4), 258–268 (2012)
6. Kalampokis, E., et al.: Exploiting linked data cubes with opencube toolkit. In: Proceedings of the 2014 International Conference on Posters and Demonstrations Track, vol. 1272. CEUR-WS.org (2014)
7. Wang, R.Y., Strong, D.M.: Beyond accuracy: what data quality means to data consumers. J. Manag. Inf. Syst. **12**(4), 5–33 (1996)
8. Wang, R.Y., Ziad, M., Lee, Y.W.: Data Quality, vol. 23. Springer, Cham (2006)
9. Pipino, L.L., Lee, Y.W., Wang, R.Y.: Data quality assessment. Commun. ACM **45**(4), 211–218 (2002)
10. Strong, D.M., Lee, Y.W., Wang, R.Y.: Data quality in context. Commun. ACM **40**(5), 103–110 (1997)
11. Matheus, R., Janssen, M.: Transparency of civil society websites: towards a model for evaluation websites transparency. In: Proceedings of the 7th International Conference on Theory and Practice of Electronic Governance. ACM, New York (2013)
12. Matheus, R., Janssen, M.: Transparency dimensions of big and open linked data. In: Janssen, M., Mäntymäki, M., Hidders, J., Klievink, B., Lamersdorf, W., Loenen, B., Zuiderwijk, A. (eds.) I3E 2015. LNCS, vol. 9373, pp. 236–246. Springer, Cham (2015). doi:10.1007/978-3-319-25013-7_19
13. Cyganiak, R., Reynolds, D., Tennison, J.: The RDF data cube vocabulary. W3C Recommendation (January 2014) (2013)
14. ISO/IEC: ISO/IEC 20510:2010 Systems and Software Engineering-Systems and Software Product Quality Requirements and Evaluation (SQuaRE)-System and Software Quality Models. International Organization for Standardization, Geneva (2010)
15. SWIRRL: How the Olympics Explains Multidimensional Data (2016). https://medium.swirrl.com/how-the-olympics-explains-multidimensional-data-8e58b127edb2-.glchsby71
16. Matheus, R., Janssen, M., Praditya, D.: Project Deliverable: D4. 1-Pilots and Evaluation Plan-v1, p. 100 (2016)
17. Alexander, K., et al.: Describing linked datasets with the void vocabulary (2011)
18. Tambouris, E., Gorilas, S., Kavadias, G., Apostolou, D., Abecker, A., Stojanovic, L., Mentzas, G.: Ontology-enabled E-gov service configuration: an overview of the OntoGov project. In: Wimmer, M.A. (ed.) KMGov 2004. LNCS, vol. 3035, pp. 122–127. Springer, Heidelberg (2004). doi:10.1007/978-3-540-24683-1_13

A Framework for Data-Driven Public Service Co-production

Maarja Toots^{1(⊠)}, Keegan McBride¹, Tarmo Kalvet¹, Robert Krimmer¹, Efthimios Tambouris², Eleni Panopoulou², Evangelos Kalampokis², and Konstantinos Tarabanis²

¹ Tallinn University of Technology, Tallinn, Estonia {maarja.toots,keegan.mcbride,tarmo.kalvet,robert.krimmer}@ttu.ee

² University of Macedonia, Thessaloniki, Greece
tambouris@uom.gr

Abstract. Governments are creating and maintaining increasing amounts of data, and, recently, releasing data as open government data. As the amount of data available increases, so too should the exploitation of this data. However, this potential currently seems to be unexploited. Since exploiting open government data has the potential to create new public value, the absence of this exploitation is something that should be explored. It is therefore timely to investigate how the potential of existing datasets could be unleashed to provide services that create public value. For this purpose, we conducted a literature study and an empirical survey of the relevant drivers, barriers and gaps. Based on the results, we propose a framework that addresses some of the key challenges and puts forward an agile co-production process to support effective data-driven service creation. The proposed framework incorporates elements from agile development, lean startups, co-creation, and open government data literature and aims to increase our understanding on how open government data may be able to drive public service co-creation.

Keywords: Open data · Public services · Co-production · Co-creation · Agile development

1 Introduction

Currently, there is a trend among governments to try to become more 'open'. One aspect of an open government is opening up government data [1–3]. However, it is known that simply providing open government data (OGD) does not automatically result in significant value for society [1]. The literature often cites the many potential benefits of OGD [1, 4–6], however, the point still holds that these benefits will not be realized unless data is actually used. Thus, a concrete understanding of barriers that prevent OGD from being utilized to produce public value is essential. As a continuance to this, a framework is needed to guide the use of OGD in an effective and efficient manner producing as much public value as possible.

© IFIP International Federation for Information Processing 2017 Published by Springer International Publishing AG 2017. All Rights Reserved M. Janssen et al. (Eds.): EGOV 2017, LNCS 10428, pp. 264–275, 2017. DOI: 10.1007/978-3-319-64677-0_22

This paper aims to address the current gap in literature related to the usage of OGD for the co-production of new public services. To this end, the paper proposes a conceptual framework based on current knowledge from literature, as well as an empirical survey conducted within six EU countries, and aims to help make sense of the ways that OGD may be turned into services that create public value. The survey was carried out with the aim of eliciting responses on the core needs and expectations for service co-production; the survey also sought understanding of how the co-production of public services may be applied to the production of data-driven public services. Once the survey results had been received, analyzed and interpreted, work on the proposed framework began.

The proposed framework takes a unique approach in three main areas: Firstly, we suggest a change in understanding from the traditional definition of a public service as something produced and provided by the government to society. Secondly, we argue that OGD-driven service creation is, by its nature, a process of co-production, conducive to collaboration between different kinds of stakeholders such as public administrations, citizens and businesses. Thirdly, the framework proposes to consider the use of agile development practices in the creation of data-driven services.

The paper is structured as follows. Section 2 presents background information on key elements of OGD-driven public service delivery based on a review of relevant literature; this is then followed by a brief overview of the empirical results. Section 3 outlines the proposed framework for data-driven public service co-production. This is followed by Sect. 4, which provides some reflections on the framework. Lastly, Sect. 5 gives conclusions and suggestions for further research.

2 Background

The initial starting point and goal for this research was to define and understand OGD. To this end, a literature search was conducted for articles that contained the phrases "open data" or "open government data" in the e-government reference library as well as Google Scholar. Though there are many different ways to interpret OGD, for this paper the definition proposed by [1] is used: "non-privacy restricted and non-confidential data which is produced with public money and is made available without any restrictions on its usage or distribution". To further expand on this, OGD should also be machine readable, discoverable, and usable by end users (see, for example, [7, 8]).

There is rich evidence stating that OGD has the potential to drive innovation [1, 9, 10, 36], it allows for increased levels of transparency [1], helps drive the creation or implementation of new public services [1, 4, 9, 36] and helps empower citizens and communities [1]. However, there are also barriers that seem to inhibit these benefits from manifesting. Some of the main barriers in the literature include issues with data quality [1–3, 36], lack of government willpower [1–3, 11, 26], confidentiality issues [5, 10, 12], and absence of understanding of OGD [1, 3, 11, 13, 36]. It is clear that OGD may be used to drive innovation and change how public services are created. This in turn could, potentially, empower citizens by providing easier ways to interact with government data and play a role in the public service creation process.

An important use of OGD is in its potential contribution to public services, though this is another area where future research is needed. As Janssen et al. (2012) suggest "little is known about the conversion of public data into services of public value. Hence, we strongly suggest further research in this area" [1]. A recent paper by Foulonneau et al. (2014) finds that there are three main roles which data plays in a new service: "the service is based on data, the service uses data as a resource, and the service is validated or enriched with data but the data is not directly used or is not directly visible in the service." [4]. They also find that OGD is currently underutilized, and applications that create public value only utilize a small number of datasets. Charalabidis et al. (2016) find that OGD can allow services to be co-created by non-typical service producers which results in the building of new and innovative applications [12]. Thus, OGD may be used for the co-creation of public services. The process of using OGD in public service co-production may be summarized as follows: governments make open data available, potentially anyone can use this data to create a new service, and it is this interaction that allows a service to be 'co-produced'.

Co-production was initially defined by Elinor Ostrom in 1972, and it can be understood as "the process through which inputs used to provide a good or service are contributed by individuals who are not 'in' the same organization" [14]. Since this initial definition, co-production has gained increasing attention in the academic literature. What is, generally, agreed upon is that the value of a public service is very much determined by not just the provider of the service but also by the interaction between the consumer of the service and the provider [14–16]. Since OGD allows many new interactions to take place between government and society, it follows that these interactions have the potential to lead to 'co-produced data-driven public service'.

When looking at the current literature on co-production, two different categorization schemes can be extracted. The first categorization takes a more hierarchical approach where co-production is categorized based on different levels of co-production within a service (for examples, see: [2, 16–18]). In contrast to the first categorization, the second defines co-production differently depending on what stage it occurs in during the creation or implementation of a new public service (for examples, see: [15, 19, 20]). What can be seen from this is that the idea of 'co-production' is still heavily debated, but it does provide an important way to look at and understand how public services are designed, created, implemented, maintained, and used.

As the literature study was ongoing, the survey was also started. The goal of this survey was to collect empirical data on the practical challenges that have been met by different actors in using OGD for the co-creation of new services. The survey elicited responses from experts and practitioners and was conducted in 6 EU countries (Belgium, Estonia, Greece, Ireland, Lithuania and the UK)[1]. In addition to their differences in terms of the political system and public administration tradition, these countries also differ for their government data exchange systems and level of open data maturity, involving early adopters, such as the UK, as well as laggards, such as Estonia or Lithuania. The survey yielded 63 responses from public administration, business, civil society and research

[1] The study was conducted as part of the OpenGovIntelligence project, a research and innovation action funded from the EU's Horizon 2020 program under grant agreement no 693849.

actors and revealed a number of barriers and drivers that are seen to affect OGD-driven service co-production (a more detailed overview of the study has been published in [36]). Some of the key barriers that came out of the survey include lack of availability of open data, little awareness of the benefits and uses of OGD, lack of feedback loops between public service providers and users, missing data-related skills in the public sector, lack of collaboration between stakeholders, low political priority and organizational resistance in the public sector, etc. The drivers seem to be polar opposites of the barriers, for example, lack of funding is a barrier whereas access to funding or external funding acts as a driver. Other examples are seen as well, for example, low political priority or lack of awareness of OGD benefits may be a barrier, but a clear demand from citizens and demonstrating tangible benefits can be used to counteract this.

From the literature it does appear that OGD may be used to help drive public service co-creation, but from the survey it is also clear that there are many barriers that stand in the way. It seems that a new approach is needed in order to help overcome these barriers so that OGD-driven public service co-creation may begin to thrive. This new approach should allow other stakeholders to take the driver's seat in exploiting OGD to create services and generate public value. In Sect. 3, one possible solution – a co-production framework for OGD-driven public service co-creation – is presented.

3 Proposal for a Co-production Framework for Data-Driven Public Services

3.1 The Concept of Open Government Data-Driven Public Service Co-production

In order to understand the building blocks of OGD-enabled public service creation, it is useful to look at services as open systems that are inseparable of the environment in which they operate. According to an emerging view in service management research, the production of a service is a "product of a complex series of, often iterative interactions, between the service user, the service organization and its managers and staff, the physical environment of the service, other organizations and staff supporting the service process, and the broader societal locus of the service" [21]. This view is supported by the current trends in public sector innovation and e-government literature, where the importance of context is increasingly emphasized (see, for example, [22, 23]). This framework for data-driven public services, therefore, looks at OGD as part of a broader service ecosystem that consists of the technological infrastructures needed for the publication and exploitation of OGD, interactions between stakeholders, and the social, organizational, cultural, legal and political environment where services are created.

Traditionally, public services have been understood as something designed and delivered by public administrators to the public. In this traditional system, public administrators act as "brokers" between society and the political system, attempting to feed society's needs to the relevant political bodies who, in turn, produce public services to meet these needs [24]. This understanding is beginning to erode both in the political realm (e.g. [25]) and research (e.g. [26, 27]), being supplemented or even replaced by a co-production-oriented approach where governments are encouraged to open their data and service creation process to non-governmental stakeholders. However, there are also more radical visions; the European Commission [28] proposes an approach according to which public services are any services which are offered to the general public with the purpose of developing public value, regardless of the role that the public sector plays in the process. In this view, the creation and provision of public services is no longer a monopoly of the public sector. Instead, any public or private actor may take the lead in developing a new service that creates public value, and any actor can participate in the co-production of this service. This is believed to lead to more user-friendly, proactive and personalized services, increased trust in administrations, and empowerment of citizens [28].

The concept of OGD naturally fits this scenario. When government data is made accessible and reusable by the public, it is possible for any interested party to use this data to offer new data-driven public services. If a problem or need is perceived, citizens and businesses are able to easily take the initiative and build their own services based on OGD, engaging other stakeholders in the process of co-production as needed. In the context of such services, data may have different roles, as explained by Foulonneau et al. [4]. Data may also come from various sources and in various volumes – from large open government datasets to data provided by individual users. In short, it may be said that any service that provides public value by using or exploiting data may be considered a data-driven public service.

The adoption of a collaborative model of data-driven service creation entails the need to redefine the traditional roles of public and private actors in the process. The concept of New Public Service [29] provides useful guidance in this respect. This approach places citizens at the center, emphasizing serving over steering, the importance of public interest, a view of service users as citizens not customers, and the value of people and partnerships. As suggested by Hartley et al. [22], collaborative innovation requires a thorough rethinking of the roles of all stakeholders: politicians need to redefine their role from "political sovereigns who have all the power and responsibility" to ones setting the agenda through dialogue with relevant actors; public managers should redefine their role from experts-technocrats to "meta-governors" who orchestrate collaborative arenas; private companies and voluntary organizations need to become "responsible partners in the production of innovative solutions for public value" rather than promoters of their own interests; and citizens should assume the role of "co-creators and co-producers" rather than "clients, customers, or regulatees". Therefore, a co-produced data-driven public service not only needs data to be provided and used, but also stakeholders need to assume new roles in the creation of public value.

3.2 The Process of Open Data-Driven Public Service Co-production

Co-production of Data-Driven Services. Pollitt and colleagues 2006 divide the service co-production process into four phases: co-planning, co-design, co-delivery, and co-evaluation [20]. It has been found vital to sustain close collaboration with users and stakeholders throughout this cycle to ensure the quality of services [30]. In the context of data-driven services, this collaboration involves the provision and use of data in these different phases. While public organizations have the key role in publishing government datasets as open data, citizens can also contribute their data in different ways, depending on their level of interest and skills. For instance, any citizen may notify the government about problems such as potholes or graffiti using smartphones or web apps. Such crowd-sourcing models are used in the well-known services of FixMyStreet and StreetBump[2]. At the same time, citizens with more advanced skills can engage in mining and analyzing OGD to explore patterns or discover problems [31]. As an example, residents of an area could scan data provided in waste collection plans and report problems to improve the collection schedule or locations [32]. Citizens may contribute to service design and partake in the development of data mashups and apps to address needs that have been discovered [31]. Similarly, citizens may be co-implementers of services by contributing user data (e.g. through sensors) or giving feedback for monitoring and evaluation [32]. Although citizens and other stakeholders may be valuable data providers, the provision of OGD remains a key driver in this process due to the volume and value of government datasets.

Agile Development and Continuous Improvement. In order for OGD-driven co-production to be effective, we suggest to move away from the traditional waterfall-like service development model (see: Fig. 1) and learn from the agile approach. The agile approach has become the norm in private sector ICT projects, but is still relatively new to the public sector. In the traditional waterfall model there is a linear approach to development where the project requirements are all outlined at the beginning and the development happens late into the project design cycle. In this traditional model, the public administrators are steering and controlling the whole process with citizen input being occasionally, but not necessarily, sought. In the traditional model, a service is slow to create, not easily adaptable, and may not have many adequate ways to receive feedback from the service user.

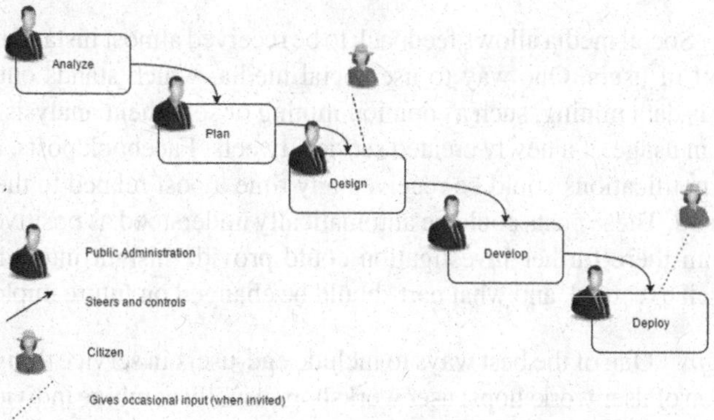

Fig. 1. Traditional model of public service creation

[2] See www.fixmystreet.com; www.streetbump.org.

Agile development focuses on being able to adapt quickly to changes by following an 'agile' approach that is based on multiple sprints made up of four main stages: plan, build, test, release [33, 34]. One concept within agile development is the idea of the Minimum Viable Product (MVP). The goal of an MVP is to develop a product or service, at its most basic and functional form, and release it as quickly as possible. Once the MVP has been released, it allows for fast feedback from service users. Ultimately, this allows for rapidly generated understanding of service use, which may then be used to adapt and change the service; this also leads to a cheaper service that is more in tune with the users' wants and needs.

Society's Feedback. Feedback from users and stakeholders is a core aspect of the data-driven public service. This feedback comes in many forms, but ultimately has one goal: improving the offered service. Feedback may be received in relation to the data that is being offered, the exploitation methods, and the new services themselves. Many different methods could be utilized for obtaining feedback. Some of the most likely feedback forms are (1) feedback mechanisms for user-provided data built directly into the public service, (2) social media, and (3) user workshops. A successful process for feeding feedback into the new public service will likely utilize some combination of these proposed feedback mechanisms.

User-Provided Data. When creating a new public service, it is important to make sure that the proper feedback mechanisms are in place. For a data-driven public service, users should be able to either upload their own data, suggest changes to datasets, or be able to participate directly in data creation for a service (this could be done via a phone app, sensors, etc.). The goal is to make sure that service users have some direct role in the creation/design of a service, and that they are able to provide continuous feedback into the service that is listened to and utilized.

Social Media. Social media allows feedback to be received almost instantaneously from a large amount of users. One way to use social media, which stands out in terms of effectiveness, is data mining, such as opinion mining or sentiment analysis. When there is an increase in usage of a newly created service, tweets, Facebook posts, etc. could be followed and notifications could be received any time a post related to the new public service is created. These posts could be automatically understood as positive or negative or neutral, from there further investigation could provide insight into what part of a service was well executed, and what part should be changed on future implementations.

User Workshops. One of the best ways to include end-users in service design is through the organization of user workshops; user workshops usually combine individual ideation with group discussion. These workshops should be repeated throughout the lifecycle of the new data-driven service. In terms of outcomes, user workshops should be able to produce a list of issues with the new service, a list of potential solutions, basic thoughts on the usability and functionality of the service, user stories, a list of user personas of individuals who could use the service, and any other information that may come out of the workshop organically. This information will allow government and citizens to work together and get a better understanding of the content, functions and goals of the service.

Towards Agile Co-production of Open Data-Driven Services. When examining the aforementioned definitions, it is important to pick up the commonalities between these different ideas: focus on the service user, be agile, develop quickly, listen to the service user, and be able to adapt quickly to changing needs. The service innovation process can be summarized with the following points:

- The government and citizens should be partners at all stages from ideation to creation to implementation of the new data-driven public service.
- There should be an initial release of the public service at an early stage, or an 'MVP' of the public service, which allows the cycle to be started as quickly as possible.
- The public service should be able to respond to user feedback from the initial launch.
- User input should be sought and utilized at all stages of the public service creation.

4 Discussion

In public service provision, a shift from a public administrator-centric view towards wider collaboration and interaction made possible by technological advances is observed [35]. We present a framework (Fig. 2), for data-driven public services that includes a wider view of stakeholders and is built around two key elements – co-production and agile development.

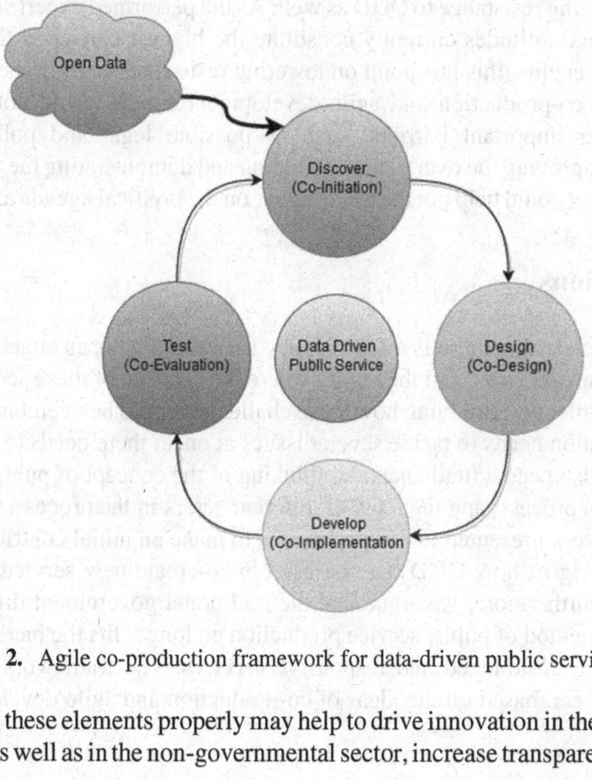

Fig. 2. Agile co-production framework for data-driven public services

Addressing these elements properly may help to drive innovation in the public sector, private sector as well as in the non-governmental sector, increase transparency, empower citizens and other stakeholder groups as well as achieve more effective and efficient public service delivery, and thus enhance public value.

The framework places a large focus on agile development and co-production/co-creation. It is believed that the focus on these attributes may allow for barriers that emerged from the literature and the survey to be overcome. The co-production element may help to overcome several data and technology related key barriers, such as limited supply and fragmentation of OGD (as other stakeholders could complement public OGD with their own data) and the overall development of data infrastructures, standards as well as specific tools, applications and demos that facilitate service creation. The agile development focus would help to keep the cost down for developing OGD driven applications while also allowing for more opportunities for co-creation of the service to emerge. This would, potentially, initiate a virtuous circle – if better data infrastructures and services are made available, new services could be built on the basis of those. Also, they potentially fuel the demand for additional services.

Agile development and continuous improvement are principles widely used in private sector ICT projects; it seems that they may also be incorporated in public service creation to help realize the future of public service delivery. The implementation of this framework would enable a new understanding of the costs and benefits of OGD services more promptly, open opportunities for further synergies (as contributions from other stakeholders can be incorporated immediately into public service), and make the delivery more effective and efficient, potentially increasing the legitimacy of public sector and lowering resistance to OGD as well. As the performed expert survey revealed that stakeholders' attitudes currently constitute the biggest barrier as OGD generally lacks tangible benefits, this last point on lowering resistance seems to be important.

The use of co-production and agile development surely would not help directly overcome other important barriers, such as possible legal and political barriers. However, by improving the overall understanding and demonstrating the value of OGD-driven services, it could help put the topic higher on the political agenda and lower fears.

5 Conclusions

It has become clear that there is a discrepancy between the hopes attached to OGD as an enabler of new services, and the reality where the creation of these services is facing a number of challenges. Studying how these challenges could be overcome, we find that any viable solution needs to tackle several issues at once: there needs to be a supply of OGD, but we also need a fundamental rethinking of the concept of public services, the service creation process, and the roles of different actors in the process.

The framework presented in this paper aims to make an initial contribution towards the understanding of how OGD may be used to co-create new services that produce public value. Furthermore, we argue that the traditional government-driven top-down waterfall-like method of public service production no longer fits the increasing demand for needs-based, customized and responsive services. The framework puts forth an innovative process, based on the ideas of co-production and agile development, in the hope that it may lead to the creation of new services in a more efficient and collaborative way.

The framework views service development as part of an ecosystem that consists of different actors, processes, and drivers and barriers related to the broader environment. While we strongly believe in the value of a systemic approach, we also acknowledge the limitations of our current understanding of the obstacles that may affect the implementation of this framework in practice. As the next step, it is therefore vital to test this on real-life cases in different contexts, so that further development and refinement of the framework may take place as new lessons are learned.

Acknowledgements. This work was supported by the European Commission (OpenGovIntelligence H2020 grant 693849), Estonian Research Council (PUT773, PUT1361) and Tallinn University of Technology Project B42.

References

1. Janssen, M., Charalabidis, Y., Zuiderwijk, A.: Benefits, adoption barriers and myths of open data and open government. Inf. Syst. Manag. (ISM) **29**(4), 258–268 (2012)
2. Martin, S., Foulonneau, M., Turki, S., Ihadjadene, M.: Open data: barriers, risks and opportunities. In: 13th European Conference on eGovernment (ECEG 2013), Como, Italy, pp. 301–309 (2013)
3. Zuiderwijk, A., Janssen, M., Choenni, S., Meijer, R., Alibaks, R.S.: Socio-technical impediments of open data. Electron. J. Electron. Gov. **10**(2), 156–172 (2012)
4. Foulonneau, M., Turki, S., Vidou, G., Martin, S.: Open data in service design. Electron. J. e-Gov. **12**(2), 99–107 (2014)
5. Janssen, K.: The influence of the PSI directive on open government data: an overview of recent developments. Gov. Inf. Q. **28**(4), 446–456 (2011)
6. Rebooting Public Service Delivery—How Can Open Government Data Help Drive Innovation? OECD (2016). http://www.oecd.org/gov/digital-government/rebooting-public-service-delivery.htm
7. OMB, Memorandum M-13-13: Open Data Policy—Managing Information as an Asset (2013). https://project-open-data.cio.gov/policy-memo/
8. Open Definition 2.1. http://opendefinition.org/od/2.1/en/
9. Chan, C.M.L.: From open data to open innovation strategies: creating e-services using open government data. In: Proceedings of the 46th Hawaii International Conference on System Sciences (HICSS-46), Wailea, HI, USA, pp. 1890–1899. IEEE Computer Society (2013)
10. Juell-Skielse, G., Hjalmarsson, A., Johannesson, P., Rudmark, D.: Is the public motivated to engage in open data innovation? In: Electronic Government: Proceedings of the 13th IFIP WG 8.5 International Conference, EGOV 2014, Dublin, Ireland, vol. 8653, pp. 277–288 (2014)
11. Gonzalez-Zapata, F., Heeks, R.: The multiple meanings of open government data: understanding different stakeholders and their perspectives. Gov. Inf. Q. **32**(4), 441–452 (2015)
12. Charalabidis, Y., Alexopoulos, C., Diamantopoulou, V., Androutsopoulou, A.: An open data and open services repository for supporting citizen-driven application development for governance. In: 49th Hawaii International Conference on System Sciences (HICSS 2016), Kauai, HI, USA, pp. 2596–2604. IEEE, Kauai, HI, USA (2016)

13. Misuraca, G., Viscusi, G.: Is open data enough? E-governance challenges for open government. Int. J. Electron. Gov. Res. **10**(1), 18–34 (2014)
14. Ostrom, E.: Crossing the great divide: synergy, and development. World Dev. **24**(6), 1073–1087 (1996)
15. Osborne, S.P., Radnor, Z., Strokosch, K.: Co-production and the co-creation of value in public services: a suitable case for treatment? Public Manag. Rev. **18**(5), 639–653 (2016)
16. Osborne, S.P., Strokosch, K.: It takes two to tango? Understanding the co-production of public services by integrating the services management and public administration perspectives. Br. J. Manag. **24**, S31–S47 (2013)
17. Bracci, E., Fugini, M., Sicilia, M.: Co-production of public services: meaning and motivations. In: Fugini, M., Bracci, E., Sicilia, M. (eds.) Co-production in the Public Sector. SAST, pp. 1–11. Springer, Cham (2016). doi:10.1007/978-3-319-30558-5_1
18. Pestoff, V.: Co-production and third sector social services in Europe. In: Verschuere, B., Brandsen, T., Pestoff, V. (eds.) New Public Governance, the Third Sector and Co-production. Routledge, New York (2012)
19. Pestoff, V.: Co-production as social and governance innovation in public services. Polittyka Spoleczna **11**(1), 2–8 (2015)
20. Pollitt, C., Bouckaert, G., Loeffler, E.: Making quality sustainable: co-design, co-decide, co-produce, co-evaluate. In: Presented at the 4QC Conference (2006)
21. Radnor, Z., Osborne, S.P., Kinder, T., Mutton, J.: Operationalizing co-production in public services delivery: the contribution of service blueprinting. Public Manag. Rev. **16**(3), 402–423 (2014)
22. Hartley, J., Sørensen, E., Torfing, J.: Collaborative innovation: a viable alternative to market competition and organizational entrepreneurship. Public Adm. Rev. **73**(6), 821–830 (2013)
23. Dwivedi, Y.K., et al.: Research on information systems failures and successes: status update and future directions. Inf. Syst. Front. **17**(1), 143–157 (2015)
24. Peristeras, V., Tarabanis, K.: The governance architecture framework and models. In: Saha, P. (ed.) Advances in Government Enterprise Architecture. IGI Global Information Science Reference, Hershey, PA (2008)
25. European Commission: EU eGovernment Action Plan 2016–2020: Accelerating the Digital Transformation of Government (2016). http://ec.europa.eu/newsroom/dae/document.cfm?doc_id=15268
26. Bovaird, T., Loeffler, E.: From engagement to co-production: the contribution of users and communities to outcomes and public value. Int. J. Volunt. Nonprofit Org. **23**(4), 1119–1138 (2012)
27. Galasso, G., Farina, G., Osimo, D., Mureddu, F., Kalvet, T., Waller, P.: Analysis of the value of new generation of eGovernment services and how can the public sector become an agent of innovation through ICT (2016)
28. A vision for public services. In: European Commission. Directorate-General for Communications Networks, Content and Technology (2013)
29. Denhardt, R.B., Denhardt, J.V.: The new public service: serving rather than steering. Public Adm. Rev. **60**(6), 549–559 (2000)
30. Together for better public services: partnering with citizens and civil society. In: OECD Public Governance Reviews. OECD (2011)
31. Nambisan, S., Nambisan, P.: Engaging citizens in co-creation in public services: lessons learned and best practices. In: Collaboration. IBM Center for The Business of Government (2013)

32. Scherer, S., Wimmer, M., Strykowski, S.: Social government: a concept supporting communities in co-creation and co-production of public services. In: dg.o 2015, New York, USA, pp. 204–209. ACM (2015)
33. Beck, K., et al.: Manifesto for Agile Software Development (2001). http://agilemanifesto.org/
34. Highsmith, J., Cockburn, A.: Agile software development: the business of innovation. Computer **34**(9), 120–127 (2001)
35. Kalvet, T.: Innovation: a factor explaining e-government success in Estonia. Electron. Gov. Int. J. **9**(2), 142–157 (2012)
36. Toots, M., McBride, K., Kalvet, T., Krimmer, R.: Open data as enabler of public service co-creation: exploring the drivers and barriers. In: Parycek, P., Edelma, N. (eds.) Proceedings of the 7th International Conference for E-Democracy and Open Government, pp. 102–112. Danube University Krems, Krems an der Donau (2017)

Big Data in the Public Sector. Linking Cities to Sensors

Marianne Fraefel(✉), Stephan Haller, and Adrian Gschwend

Bern University of Applied Sciences, Bern, Switzerland
{marianne.fraefel,stephan.haller,adrian.gschwend}@bfh.ch

Abstract. In the public sector, big data holds many promises for improving policy outcomes in terms of service delivery and decision-making and is starting to gain increased attention by governments. Cities are collecting large amounts of data from traditional sources such as registries and surveys and from non-traditional sources such as the Internet of Things, and are considered an important field of experimentation to generate public value with big data. The establishment of a city data infrastructure can drive such a development. This paper describes two key challenges for such an infrastructure: platform federation and data quality, and how these challenges are addressed in the ongoing research project CPaaS.io.

Keywords: Big data · Internet of things · Open government data · Linked data · Public sector · Smart city · Data quality · Platform federation

1 Introduction

The digitization of the economy and society becomes apparent in the many applications and devices that use and produce data. As businesses and individuals use available technological innovations to improve business and facilitate the demands of everyday life, governments around the world are struggling with how to best put these advancements to use in the public sector and create public value. The European Commission for example has acknowledged that "data has become an essential resource for economic growth, job creation and societal progress" [1] and is working on a policy and a framework for the free flow of data to reap the potential benefits and address challenges both in the technical as well as in the societal and legal fields. One of the primary difficulties lies in the diversity and the speed of the technological developments: The deployment of sensors delivers a multitude of new data sets, but with sometimes unreliable data, big data and machine learning is deployed for data analysis, and linked data and open government data approaches are used to make data more accessible to a wider clientele. The societal challenges that digitization will bring about manifest themselves first in the metropolitan, urban environment; hence the so-called "smart city" is an ideal field for experimentation to better understand and learn about the opportunities and potential pitfalls. While the term "smart city" is certainly hyped and many different activities are carried out under this label, two points are interesting when looking at cities that are generally regarded as pioneers in the field, e.g., Amsterdam, Barcelona, or Vienna.

M. Janssen et al. (Eds.): EGOV 2017, LNCS 10428, pp. 276–286, 2017.
DOI: 10.1007/978-3-319-64677-0_23

They all use a private-public-partnership (PPP) model in order to bring together actors from different sectors and with different expertise and interests [2, 3], and the establishment of a platform for information exchange and data access is seen as a key enabler for an effective implementation of a smart city programme [4].

With the main goal of developing such a platform for smart city innovation, we launched in 2016 the CPaaS.io project.[1] In this 30-month research and innovation action between Europe and Japan, data from various sources are made accessible via a cloud-based platform to application developers and service providers. Data sets from open government data portals and other administrative or publicly available data can be linked with Internet of Things (IoT) data, e.g., data from sensors deployed in the communal infrastructure or from sensors worn by participants in a city event. The project is also developing several application use cases in the domains of event management, water management, and public transportation and pilots these in partnering cities like Amsterdam, Sapporo and Tokyo. The aim of this paper is to discuss the particular challenges of implementing a smart city platform related to data management and in particular data quality management of various data sources, including IoT data in particular. The use of this type of data is relatively new to governments and irrespective of the usage context, the question of how to validate IoT data is still quite open. In order to be adopted, a city data infrastructure needs to provide information on data quality in form of metadata and, as will be shown, linked data provides several advantages in that respect. At the current stage of the project, we provide generic considerations on the named challenges, based on selected research in the field. Thus, we do not account for potentially differing requirements depending on e.g. the size or smart city maturity (cf. [2]) of a city.

The remainder of this paper is structured as follows: in the following section we summarize the state of adoption of big data in the public sector, with a special focus on the context of smart cities and the usage of the Internet of Things. Section 3 provides an overview of two challenges that need to be addressed for the successful deployment of such a platform: improving data quality and facilitating platform federation. Section 4 then describes linked data as a solution approach to tackle these issues and describes the state of the art in the field, while Sect. 5 goes into more detail how the solution is implemented in the context of the CPaaS.io project. Section 6 finally contains the conclusions and outlines future work.

2 Big Data in the Public Sector

2.1 Big Data Opportunities for the Public Sector and State of Adoption

Big data is about generating value through collecting and analysing information to extract knowledge and insight (cf. [5, 6]). Governments are increasingly aware that big data offers value potentials for the public sector [7]. As scholars point out however, implementation by now tends to be limited [7, 8] or as Desouza and Jacob put it, there

[1] The abbreviation stands for "City Platform as a Service – Integrated and Open". See http://www.cpaas.io for further details about this Horizon 2020 project.

is "some tension between the promise of big data and reality" [9]. Accordingly, big data in the public sector has only recently started to raise academic interest (cf. [10]), but is expected to gain more attention within big data research [11]. A first set of studies and reports rather looks at the public sector as a *data producer* for big data applications in other sectors (e.g. [12, 13]). Governments generate and collect large amounts of data through their everyday operations and the public sector is thus one of the most data-intensive sectors. Since public sector sources comply with high quality standards, they are considered an essential resource for the data-driven economy, which is reflected in the many open government data (OGD) initiatives that seek to make this data available for re-use [14]. A second stream of research focuses explicitly on governments as *big data user*. This work includes cross-case studies on existing cases of big data implementation [15, 16], general considerations on the opportunities and challenges of big data adoption by the public sector (e.g. [7, 9, 17, 18]), considerations on the preconditions for using big data [8] and/or specific fields of application, such as policy-making (e.g. [19] also [15, 16]).

Based on available research, *potential benefits* of big data adoption in the public sector can be categorized as follows [7]: A first set of opportunities relates to *improving the knowledge base*. As in other sectors, data analysis is used for generating new insights. Big data analytics can be applied to various domains of public administration (cf. [15–18]) and holds promises to improve all stages of policy-making [16]: Better and faster insights derived from big data analysis (e.g. through machine learning) may help to better react to unintended effects of a policy decision [19]. It may help to earlier detect mistakes, frauds or security threats [20]. Policy-makers can also use big data technologies to conduct policy impact assessments or gain a better understanding of citizen interests and opinions through the analysis of new data sources, e.g. social media, helping them to prioritize policy issues [7, 15].

A second set of opportunities relates to *improvements in effectiveness*. Data analysis may be used to tailor service provisioning towards the needs of different citizen groups, increasing their satisfaction [18]. Better insights can also contribute to solving social problems related to public transportation, healthcare provision or energy production [8]. Provided as open data, the public sector may facilitate the innovation of products and services by third parties.

A third set of opportunities relates to *improvements in efficiency*. Big data can be used to achieve greater internal transparency and to improve data sharing across administrative organizations. Available estimates suggest that the public sector could generate considerable revenues through better exploitation of data [12, 13]. Leveraging new data sources may also positively impact data generation by public administrations, e.g., when producing official statistics [15].

2.2 Smart Cities as Big Data Application Domain in the Public Sector

Depending on the application domain and the type of data generated, big data analysis in the public sector is closely related to the concept of smart cities [18] (for a definition see [21]). Cities are considered as distinct domain, in which the use of ICT in general [22] and big data in particular are expected to generate impact [7, 17, 23–25]. Thought leaders in the field expect that innovative examples of big data usage are more likely to be found at the city or regional level, since it is easier to get policy makers involved in small-scale initiatives, in new forms of collaboration and data usage [16]. Also, a mapping of smart cities in Europe reveals that there are more smaller than large smart cities, while larger cities have more resources and tend to be more ambitious in scope and more mature regarding implementation [2]. As several authors stress, the Internet of Things is an important data source in the smart city context: "The public sector is increasingly characterized by applications that rely on sensor measurements of physical phenomena such as traffic volumes, environmental pollution, usage levels of waste containers, location of municipal vehicles, or detection of abnormal behaviour" [7]. The analysis of such IoT data sources in combination with other data has the potential to improve urban management and the quality of life of city inhabitants: "Data from different sources need to be integrated and analyzed for smart urban planning, smart transportation, smart sanitation, smart crime prevention, etc." [17]. As Scuotto et al. point out however, "the relationship between IoT and smart cities is still largely unexplored" [26], which requires more research, e.g. on typical technological challenges to be tackled (cf. [23]).

3 Technological Challenges of Implementing a Smart City Platform

While governments are considered as catalysts for boosting a data-driven economy and growth through opening up their data, big data adoption in the public sector is also confronted with a range of constraints and challenges [7]. These are related to *governance* (e.g. agreements for integrating data sources across organizations, data-driven culture), *implementation* (e.g. organizational maturity in terms of IT facilities and data systems, required skills) and *risk management* (privacy, security) (cf. [7, 8, 17–19]).

As Munné points out [7], it is important that the public sector gains "adoption momentum", moving from marketing around big data to real experience, to derive lessons learned on which applications are valuable and how to deploy them: "This requires the development of a standard set of big data solutions for the sector." The CPaaS.io project provides such a solution for the smart city context and supports experimentation and capability building. One of several challenges to be addressed relates to the federation of existing platforms. Another typical challenge relates to data management. A linked data approach is suited to address both the challenge of ensuring system interoperability as well as data interoperability (cf. [27]).

3.1 Federation of Smart City Platforms

To exploit the full potential of a big data strategy, it is not enough that cities just implement a big data platform on their own. Unfortunately, this approach is still common today, leading to data silo solutions lacking interoperability (cf. [17]). Cities though are not standalone entities, they are embedded in a region, in a country, and they often cooperate with other cities – today also on a global scale. Cities thus need to strive for interoperability of their platforms and the possibility to federate instances: This will enable data analysis across regions from which all participating cities can profit, for example by better understanding traffic patterns or in order to provide better services to an increasingly mobile population. Standards can help to achieve this, but often are not enough, as the adoption especially of data standards on a global scale is slow due to historic, legal and cultural differences.

3.2 Governance and Management of Data

In the age of big data, datasets become increasingly "complex", which requires adequate capabilities for managing the data [9]. With the growing need to integrate data from multiple sources, data quality management becomes both more important but also challenging [28]. In the context of developing city data infrastructures, data management and in particular the management of data quality, i.e., ensuring that data is fit for use and free of defects [29] are important aspects (cf. [28, 30]) and part of an organization's overall data governance [31] (see Fig. 1).

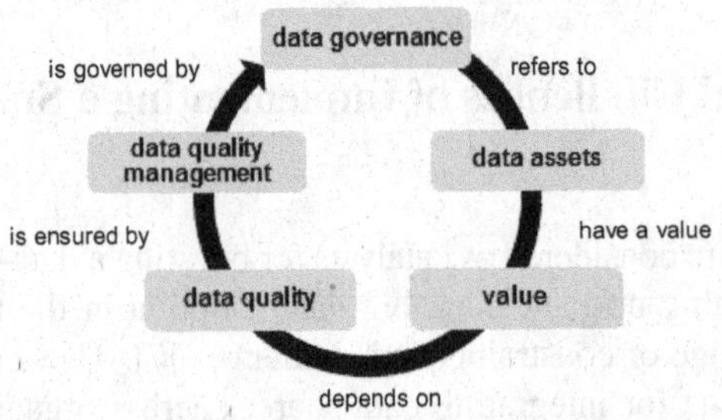

Fig. 1. Data governance and related concepts (adapted from [31])

Smart city platforms are used for making decisions and providing services based on the results of querying various datasets, which entails that applications need to be trusted and accepted and data quality plays a major role in that respect (cf. [32–34]). For a city data infrastructure aimed at integrating IoT data, managing data quality is particularly crucial, as sensors are an inherently unreliable data source. Sensors can become decalibrated, delivering inaccurate data readings, or they can fail or lose connectivity completely. Resolution, sensitivity, timeliness and provenance are other factors affecting the validity of IoT data.

As a requirement, data quality is well understood [35] and there are many methodologies to conduct data quality management (cf. [36]) as well as models and frameworks for assessing the quality of specific types of data, such as linked data [32], IoT data [33], open government data [37] or more generic big data [28]. What constitutes "good data quality" is however depending on the context of its use and thus very much application-dependent. A city data infrastructure aiming to support a multitude of possible applications must provide sufficient metadata about the data quality, while it is left to the application to decide if the data is good enough to be used. This requirement is also grasped by the emerging "Smart Data" paradigm, according to which successful big data implementation has "a clear meaning (semantics), measurable data quality, and security (including data privacy standards)" [35]. This entails making data more accessible through adding metadata for structuring and integration across separate data silos and for storing information on data quality as well as benefitting from already available open and linked data.

4 Linked Data as Solution Mechanism

In the context of big data, *linked data* is both a specific type of *data source* and an *approach* for facilitating data integration and re-usage through providing clear meaning. This is essential, since only through understanding the context sensitive meaning of data can one assess whether data can be combined to generate value [27]. As Shiri points out: "the formalized, structured and organized nature of linked data and its specific applications, such as linked controlled vocabularies and knowledge organization systems, have the potential to provide a solid semantic foundation for the classification, representation, visualization and the organized presentation of big data" [38].

As the cross-case study on big data adoption in policy-making shows [16], public administrations use a variety of data sources from administrative data, official statistics, surveys, sensors and social media. The data used may be either open or restricted. These siloed data sources are typically accessed over platform-proprietary APIs. To gain new insight about the data it is vital to fuse it from these different sources. This can be done by transforming the data into a more generic form, which is more accessible and provides standardized APIs on top of it. Such a generic API needs to provide a common way to exchange information between these sources and help the API consumer to understand the semantics and the meaning of the information. The W3C *semantic web and linked data technology stack* [24] aims at solving these problems. The *RDF data model* provides well-known schemas and ontologies as lingua franca, HTTP as transport layer, URIs as decentralized identifiers and multilingualism in its core. This makes it the data model of choice for bridging between data silos (cf. [27]).

In the past few years a lot of effort went into publishing best practices. In 2016, W3C released the "*Data on the Web Best Practices*" recommendation [38]: After roughly 10 years of open data movement [39], the document summarizes best practices and recommendations about how to publish open data, especially in the context of what needs to be taken into consideration to ensure that the published data is of maximum value for the public. Most of the recommendations are related to machine readability and discoverability of open data.

In the domain of *schema* and *ontologies*, several search engine giants launched schema.org [39], an initiative to "create and support a common set of schemas for structured data markup on web pages" Meanwhile schema.org seems to use "a simple RDF-like graph data model" and exposes its schema as embedded RDF. Over the past years schema.org had a huge impact; many sites started to include structured information within their websites and the support of first RDFa[2] and later JSON-LD[3] made people use semantic web technologies without being really aware of it. This increases visibility and perception of the semantic web as a whole.

Developments that are still work in progress revolve around *constraint languages*; examples of that are Shapes Constraint Language (SHACL) and Shape Expressions (ShEx). RDF is a graph data model and by design it is possible to express any relationship between a subject and an object. In real world applications, it is often necessary to define structural constraints and validate RDF instance data against those. This can be done with both of the languages.

In the domain of *IoT related ontologies* there are even more options available and under discussion. Several groups are pushing their own concepts and ontologies, among others: Spatial Data on the Web Working Group's SSN Ontology, IoT + schema.org, Web of Things (WoT) Interest Group and the EU H2020's FIESTA-IoT project. It is too early to tell yet which of the proposed constraint languages and IoT ontologies will see wider adoption in the next years.

5 Implementation in the CPaaS.io Project

The smart city platform as developed by the CPaaS.io project is based on a common reference architecture, but is for pragmatic reasons – mainly in order to have instances up and running quickly in the two main regions of the project – implemented on top of existing frameworks (see Fig. 2).

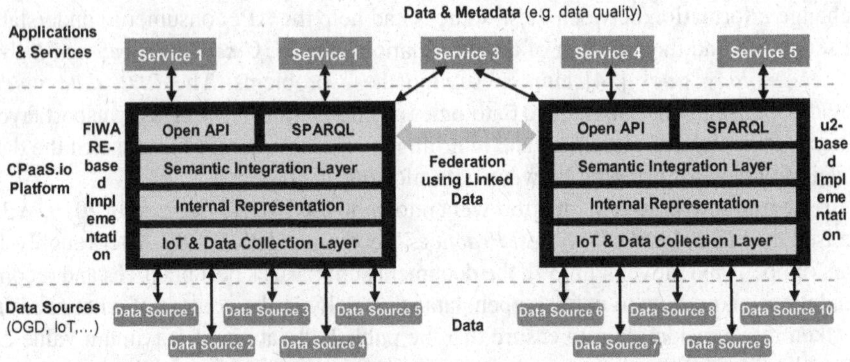

Fig. 2. Simplified CPaaS.io implementation architecture

The implementation in Europe is based on FIWARE [41], and the one in Japan on the u2 architecture [42]. The disadvantage of having two different platform implementations within the project is that data federation across instances becomes more challenging. However, in real life it cannot be expected that all cities will use the same

---

[2] RDF in Attributes, see RDFa Primer: http://www.w3.org/TR/xhtml-rdfa-primer.

[3] JSON for Linking Data (JSON-LD) is a JSON based RDF serialization. See json-ld.org.

platform implementation anyway, so the two implementations within the project serve as a test regarding the real-world viability of the platform. For example in the domain of public transportation, it is important that innovations developed in one city can easily be transferred to another city.

The CPaaS.io Platform aims at fusing data from different sources, in particular the FIWARE platform in Europe and the u2 platform in Japan. From a data consumer perspective, it should not matter where the data is stored, CPaaS.io will facilitate discovery and access to information in these data storages via generic APIs.

For that reason, CPaaS.io will use linked data and RDF to facilitate integration of data from platforms like FIWARE and u2. Neither of the two platforms is currently supporting RDF and linked data out of the box. CPaaS.io will integrate a semantic layer that enables mapping existing data to RDF. This semantic integration layer can be implemented in different phases and levels.

Initially the semantic layer will simply expose metadata as linked data, using common vocabularies and best practices as described in [38]. This enables users to query information about available data within the FIWARE and u2 platform as linked data. Access to this metadata layer will be done by providing a SPARQL endpoint that can be queried.

In a second step, data residing in FIWARE or u2 is mapped to RDF by extending the respective data model of each platform. In the case of FIWARE, this can be done by using the new NGSIv2 data model that supports JSON-LD representations. By providing appropriate tools and user interfaces, FIWARE users can thus map existing data to RDF representations. The ucode data model of u2 is close to RDF as it stores information in a triple-like data model. The semantic integration layer only needs to map internal ucode IDs to publicly used and dereferencable URIs, preferably as HTTP URIs to allow linked data usage like it has already been done for the Tokyo Metro real time data system.

To be able to query this kind of data, a SPARQL endpoint will proxy requests to the platform. CPaaS.io will provide a virtual-graph feature similar to what RDF graph databases provide to access relational data, using W3C standards like R2RML. Users will thus be able to run SPARQL queries on data residing in FIWARE or u2. In a final step FIWARE and u2 will implement its own SPARQL endpoint.

6 Conclusions and Outlook

While the public sector can be considered one of the most data-intensive sectors, actual use of big data in this sector is still rather limited. With the increased deployment of Internet of Things technologies and the international competition for cities to become smart, however, this is likely going to change. A lot of experimentation is still going on in this area to understand both the technologies as well as the applications that create real public value. To reap the potential benefits, cities will need an open city data infrastructure, where third parties can access the relevant city data, including data coming from the Internet of Things, and provide additional services on top. The platform that the CPaaS.io project is developing could serve as the basis for such an infrastructure if the two crucial issues that we highlighted in this paper are addressed: the ability to federate platform instances, and data quality. Linked data can serve as a possible mechanism to address both. The semantics behind linked data allow combining differently structured data from technically different platforms. And linked data can be used to annotate data sets with quality parameters so that an application using that data can decide if the data quality is good enough for the intended purpose. It is thus a fruitful approach for reaching the "smart data" paradigm.

Using linked data requires adequate vocabularies both for data integration into CPaaS.io and for re-usage by use case applications as well as for data dimensions and measures, accounting for the different types of data used in the project. Standards for such vocabularies and for validating data are still emerging; at this point in time none of these is well accepted yet. In the further course of the project, we will have to define which of the emerging vocabulary standards are suitable for the project and its use cases, and where we need to define our own. Furthermore, we plan to validate the applicability and the value of linked data, as well as the platform as a whole, in real-world use case implementations in European and Japanese cities. Both, the relationship between IoT and smart cities and the adoption of big data in the public sector in general require more research based on real applications. The CPaaS.io project will contribute to gaining new insights in these emerging research fields.

Acknowledgements. This work is supported by the Horizon 2020 EUJ-02-2016 Research and Innovation Action CPaaS.io; EU Grant number 723076, NICT management number 18302.

References

1. European Commission: Building a European Data Economy (2017). http://ec.europa.eu/newsroom/dae/document.cfm?doc_id=41205
2. Manville, C., et al.: Mapping Smart Cities in the EU (2014). http://www.europarl.europa.eu/RegData/etudes/etudes/join/2014/507480/IPOL-ITRE_ET(2014)507480_EN.pdf
3. Walser, K., Haller, S.: Smart governance in smart cities. In: Meier, A., Portmann, E. (eds.) Smart City. EH, pp. 19–46. Springer, Wiesbaden (2016). doi:10.1007/978-3-658-15617-6_2
4. Vega-Gorgojo, et al.: Case Study Reports on Positive and Negative Externalities (2015). http://byte-project.eu/wp-content/uploads/2015/06/FINAL_BYTE-D3-2-Case-studies-report-1-1.pdf
5. NIST Big Data Public Working Group: NIST Big Data Interoperability Framework: Volume 1, Definitions (2015). http://dx.doi.org/10.6028/NIST.SP.1500-1
6. Curry, E.: The big data value chain: definitions, concepts, and theoretical approaches. In: Cavanillas, J.M., Curry, E., Wahlster, W. (eds.) New Horizons for a Data-Driven Economy, pp. 29–37. Springer, Cham (2016). doi:10.1007/978-3-319-21569-3_3
7. Munné, R.: Big data in the public sector. In: Cavanillas, J.M., Curry, E., Wahlster, W. (eds.) New Horizons for a Data-Driven Economy, pp. 195–208. Springer, Cham (2016). doi:10.1007/978-3-319-21569-3_11
8. Klievink, B., Romijn, B.-J., Cunningham, S., de Bruijn, H.: Big data in the public sector. Uncertainties and readiness. Inf. Syst. Front. 1–17 (2016)
9. Desouza, K.C., Jacob, B.: Big data in the public sector: lessons for practitioners and scholars. Adm. Soc. 1–22 (2014)

10. Gaardboe, R., Svarre, T., Kanstrup, A.M.: Characteristics of business intelligence and big data in e-government: preliminary findings. In: Tambouris, E., et al. (eds.) Electronic Government and Electronic Participation, pp. 109–115. IOS Press, Amsterdam (2015)
11. Akoka, J., Comyn-Wattiau, I., Laoufi, N.: Research on big data—a systematic mapping study. Comput. Stand. Interfaces (2017). doi:10.1016/j.csi.2017.01.004
12. OECD: Exploring Data-Driven Innovation as a New Source of Growth: Mapping the Policy Issues Raised by "Big Data". OECD, Paris (2013). doi:10.1787/5k47zw3fcp43-en
13. Manyika, J., et al.: Big Data: The Next Frontier for Innovation, Competition, and Productivity. McKinsey Global Institute, New York City (2011)
14. Carrara, W., et al.: Analytical Report 1: Digital Transformation and Open Data (2015). https://www.europeandataportal.eu/sites/default/files/edp_analytical_report_n1_-_digital_transformation.pdf
15. Barbero, M., et al.: Big Data Analytics for Policy Making (2016). https://joinup.ec.europa.eu/sites/default/files/dg_digit_study_big_data_analytics_for_policy_making.pdf
16. Poel, M., Schroeder, et al.: Data for policy: a study of big data and other innovative data-driven approaches for evidence-informed policymaking. Report about the State-of-the-Art (2015). http://media.wix.com/ugd/c04ef4_cee7fd39eed342beb059526226e6a86e.pdf
17. Aggarwal, A.: Opportunities and challenges of big data in public sector. In: Aggarwal, A. (ed.) Managing Big Data Integration in the Public Sector, pp. 289–301. IGI Global, Hershey (2016)
18. Chen, Y.-C., Hsieh, T.-C.: Big data for digital government: opportunities, challenges, and strategies. Int. J. Public Adm. Digit. Age **1**, 1–14 (2014)
19. Höchtl, J., Parycek, P., Schöllhammer, R.: Big data in the policy cycle. Policy decision making in the digital era. J. Organ. Comput. Electron. Commer. **26**(1–2), 147–169 (2015)
20. Eckert, K.-P., Henckel, L., Hoepner, P.: Big data—Ungehobene Schätze oder digitaler Alptraum (2014). https://www.oeffentliche-it.de/documents/10181/14412/Big+Data+ungehobene+Schätze+oder+digitaler+Albtraum
21. ITU-T: Shaping Smarter and More Sustainable Cities (2016). http://wftp3.itu.int/pub/epub_shared/TSB/ITUT-Tech-Report-Specs/2016/en/flipviewerxpress.html
22. Castelnovo, W., Misuraca, G., Savoldelli, A.: Smart cities governance. The need for a holistic approach to assessing urban participatory policy making. Soc. Sci. Comput. Rev. **34**(6), 724–739 (2016)
23. Hashem, I.A.T., et al.: The role of big data in smart city. Int. J. Inf. Manag. **36**(5), 748–758 (2016)
24. Domingue, J., Lasierra, N., Fensel, A., Kasteren, T., Strohbach, M., Thalhammer, A.: Big data analysis. In: Cavanillas, J.M., Curry, E., Wahlster, W. (eds.) New Horizons for a Data-Driven Economy, pp. 63–86. Springer, Cham (2016). doi:10.1007/978-3-319-21569-3_5
25. OECD: Data-Driven Innovation: Big Data for Growth and Well-Being. OECD Publishing, Paris (2015)
26. Scuotto, V., Ferraris, A., Bresciani, S.: Internet of Things: Applications and challenges in smart cities. Bus. Process Manag. J. **22**(2), 357–367 (2016)
27. Janssen, M., Estevez, E., Janowski, T.: Interoperability in big, open, and linked data—organizational maturity, capabilities, and data portfolios. Computer **47**(10), 44–49 (2014)
28. Merino, J., et al.: A data quality in use model for big data. Future Gener. Comput. Syst. **63**, 123–130 (2016)
29. Fürber, C.: Data Quality Management with Semantic Technologies. Springer, Wiesbaden (2016)

30. Bertot, J.C., Choi, H.: Big data and e-Government: issues, policies, and recommendations. In: Proceedings of the 14th Annual International Conference on Digital Government Research (dg.o 2013), pp. 1–10. ACM, New York (2013)
31. Otto, B.: Organizing data governance: findings from the telecommunications industry and consequences for large service providers. Commun. Assoc. Inf. Syst. **29**(1), 3 (2011)
32. Zaveri, A., et al.: Quality assessment for linked data: a survey. Semant. Web J (2015). http://www.semantic-web-journal.net/content/quality-assessment-linked-data-survey
33. Karkouch, A., et al.: Data quality in Internet of Things. A state-of-the-art survey. J. Netw. Comput. Appl. **73**, 57–81 (2016)
34. European Commission: Commission Staff Working Document. Advancing the Internet of Things in Europe (2016). http://ec.europa.eu/newsroom/dae/document.cfm?doc_id=15276
35. Becker, T.: Big data usage. In: Cavanillas, J.M., Curry, E., Wahlster, W. (eds.) New Horizons for a Data-Driven Economy, pp. 143–165. Springer, Cham (2016). doi:10.1007/978-3-319-21569-3_8
36. Batini, C., Scannapieco, M.: Methodologies for information quality assessment and improvement. In: Batini, C., Scannapieco, M. (eds.) Data and Information Quality. DSA, pp. 353–402. Springer, Cham (2016). doi:10.1007/978-3-319-24106-7_12
37. Vetrò, A., et al.: Open data quality measurement framework: definition and application to Open Government Data. Gov. Inf. Q. **33**(2), 325–337 (2016)
38. W3C: Data on the Web Best Practices. W3C Recommendation 31 January 2017 (2017). http://www.w3.org/TR/dwbp/
39. Shiri, A.: Linked data meets big data: a knowledge organization systems perspective. Adv. Classif. Res. Online **24**(1), 16–20 (2014)
40. Guha, R.V., Brickley, D., Macbeth, S.: Schema.org: evolution of structured data on the web. Databases **13**(9), 1–28 (2015)
41. Hierro, J.: FIWARE: An Open Standard Platform for Smart Cities (2014). http://www.slideshare.net/JuanjoHierro/fiware-a-standard-platform-for-smart-cities
42. Sakamura, K.: Open IoT Platform & IoT-Engine (2016). https://www.tron.org/wp-content/uploads

Tracking the Evolution of OGD Portals: A Maturity Model

Charalampos Alexopoulos[1(✉)], Vasiliki Diamantopoulou[1,2], and Yannis Charalabidis[1]

[1] University of the Aegean, Samos, Greece
alexop@aegean.gr
[2] University of Brighton, Brighton, UK

Abstract. Since its inception, open government data (OGD) as a free re-useable object has attracted the interest of researchers and practitioners, civil servants, citizens and businesses for different reasons in each target group. This study was designed to aggregate the research outcomes and developments through the recent years towards illustrating the evolutionary path of OGD portals, by presenting an analysis of their characteristics in terms of a maturity model. A four-step methodology has been followed in order to analyse the literature and construct the maturity model. The results point out the two greater dimensions of OGD portals, naming traditional and advanced evolving within three generations. The developed maturity model will guide policy makers by firstly identify the current level of their organisation and secondly design an efficient implementation to the required state.

Keywords: Open government data · Maturity model · Semantic Web

1 Introduction

Since its formal inception in 2003, when European Union (EU) adopted the 'Directive on the Re-use of Public Sector Information'[1] [1], open government data (OGD) as a free re-useable object has attracted the interest of researchers and practitioners under the notion of research efficiency and effectiveness. Governments and high level policy makers have realised the potential of publishing public sector information as the last stand of earning back citizens' trust, as well as the importance of the national context on government information and knowledge sharing [2, 3]. Lower level civil servants, as always reluctant to the change this new entry, will enforce in terms of new systems, new procedures and effort. Citizens are becoming more aware of the benefits that OGD may offer, by using secondary services towards accountability and transparency. Businesses develop and/or redesign their business models to be in alignment with this great development of our century, exploiting the numerous benefits and turn it into profit. For these reasons, OGD initiatives have burgeoned over the last years worldwide, both in developed and in developing countries [4–6].

---

[1] http://ec.europa.eu/information_society/policy/psi/rules/eu/index_en.htm.

M. Janssen et al. (Eds.): EGOV 2017, LNCS 10428, pp. 287–300, 2017.
DOI: 10.1007/978-3-319-64677-0_24

Quite a lot of studies position OGD and its exploitation as the 'new gold' [7, 8], resulting in the establishment of opening government datasets as a 'political orthodoxy' in numerous countries worldwide (e.g., in the USA [9], in the UK [10], in Australia [11] and across Europe [6, 12]).

Big investments that have been made for the development of 'OGD sources', defined as various types of portals enabling access to government datasets by the public through the Internet. These OGD portals provide various capabilities/functionalities in this direction by a variety of government organisations with different strategies and technical capacities, and under different social, political and legal conditions worldwide [13]. Immense research has been conducted on these OGD sources to better understand their main characteristics from various perspectives, and identify their strengths and weaknesses over the recent years [4, 14–17]. The authors at [8] conclude that the success of the developed OGD infrastructures requires more than the simple provision of access to data; it is necessary to make progress towards (i) the improvement of the quality of government information, (ii) the creation and institutionalisation of a culture of open government, and (iii) the provision of tools and instruments for the most beneficial data utilisation. The realisation of the 'Open Government' paradigm, in general, seems to be a demanding and complex task, requiring combined efforts of multiple actors, from both the public and the private sector, and gradual development of 'open government ecosystems' [18].

The contribution of this paper is the aggregation of this research effort towards illustrating the evolutionary path of OGD portals, by presenting an analysis of their characteristics in terms of a maturity model. Our study provides an aggregation of the abovementioned characteristics, examining the development of OGD portals including the factor of time, by proposing an OGD maturity model.

This paper structures as follows; Sect. 2 describes the followed methodology. Section 3 presents the identified and integrated analysis framework of our study in order to categorise the different maturity stages. Section 4 enlists the maturity model for Open Government Data Platforms which is validated by the research literature concerning Greece and the EU in general in Sect. 5. Finally, Sect. 6 concludes the paper by raising issues for further research.

2 Methodology

The paper makes use of a methodology consisting of 4 stages. Firstly, a literature review was conducted in order to identify the documents containing the required information. Secondly, an integrated analysis framework was developed to identify the common elements of analysis in order to maintain coherence. The third step presents the facts that have been identified in the literature and lastly, the fourth step concludes to the construction of the OGD maturity model. More specifically:

Stage 1: *Identification of basic literature*

The first stage of our research method refers to the identification of the basic literature underlying the characteristics of OGD portals through time [19–25]. Since there is a great diversity of analytical methods as well as types of portals (European, national, regional, local and thematic) we proceeded to the next step of our methodology.

Stage 2: Formulation of an Integrated Analysis Framework

After the necessary adaptations, we concluded the integrated analysis framework for the construction of the OGD portals maturity model, which consists of elements categorised in 4 dimensions: general; information quality; system quality and service quality.

Stage 3: Analysis and presentation of facts and results

This stage, which is thoroughly analysed in Sect. 4, presents the aggregated results of the studies in terms of the IS Success model of analysis, which we consider it as the most efficient approach for the presentation. The case studies that could provide results in chronological order are those concerning Greece [20, 21] and EU as a whole [19, 22]. A few more studies indicate the development of marketplaces [24] and services repositories [25].

Stage 4:Maturity model construction

At the final stage of the methodology, which is presented in detail in Sect. 5, the maturity model in terms of the analysis framework is presented.

3 Integrated Analysis Framework

After the thorough examination of the literature on OGD evaluation metrics, stage models and portals functionality, we concluded the following dimensions for the development of a maturity model on OGD portals. The identified OGD sources constitute a new type of Information Systems (IS), so in accordance to previous relevant research on IS Success [26–29], their success relies critically on three main characteristics of them; their 'information quality', i.e. the quality of the information they provide, their 'system quality', i.e. their quality viewed as technological systems, and their 'service quality', i.e. the support provided to its users, such as training, helpdesk, etc. The "general" category introduces characteristics from the recent literature on OGD metrics that could not be categorised in the previous ones.

General

- *Internet presence*: This chronically placed element identifies the web presence of datasets. First was the closed silos and then the open data portals which all are characterised by internet presence. This factor was mostly included to point out time zero.
- *Users*: It specifies the different type of users according to their capabilities [29–31]. Collaboration spaces provide a wider range of functionalities, influenced by the principles of the new Web 2.0 paradigm [32, 33]. They support the main feature of this new paradigm: the elimination of the clear distinction between the 'passive' content of users/consumers and the 'active' content of producers (which characterises Web 1.0), and the shift towards highly active users (who assess the quality of the data they consume and intervene in order to enhance them) who are potentially data 'prosumers' (both consumers and providers of data). In particular, collaboration spaces increasingly offer to data users capabilities for comments provision and rating upon

the datasets; for processing them in order to improve them, adapt them to specialised needs; link them to other datasets (public or private); and then for uploading-publishing new versions of them, or even their own datasets. In general, collaboration spaces aim at fulfilling the needs of the emerging OGD 'pro-sumers' [33].

- *Open Government level*: Assessing the open government level of each type of OGD portal, regarding its functionality and scope, according to the study in [34]. The highest the maturity level, the highest the public engagement and thus greater public value of open government is realised.
- *Value:* The authors in [35–37] argue that there can be four types of values that generated from the OGD, which differ based on the sector generating the value (public or private), and the kind of generated value (social or economic): (i) transparency related value (public sector organisations generate social value by offering increased transparency into government actions, which reduces misuse of public power for private benefits and corruption), (ii) efficiency related value (public sector organisations generate economic value through OGD by increasing internal efficiency and effectiveness), (iii) participation related value (individuals and private sector generate social value through participating and collaborating with government), (iv) innovation related value (private sector firms generate economic value through the creation of new products/services).

Information Quality

- *Thematic perspective*: It includes analysis of the thematic categories of the datasets provided by the OGD sources. It has been conducted using the nine main thematic categories of OGD, identified by the [1, 38].
- *Format*: It defines the portals' available data representation formats of the published information and their categorisation, according to the 5-stars Berners Lee's Rating Scheme for Open Data.[2] The authors in [41] define LOGD as "all stored data of the public sector connected by the World Wide Web which could be made accessible in a public interest without any restrictions for usage and distribution", and argue that "the cross linking of Open Data via the Internet and the World Wide Web as "Linked Open Data" (LOD) offers the possibility of using data across domains or organisational borders for statistics, analysis, maps and publications", which can lead to the generation of more insight, knowledge and innovation from OGD, implementing generic applications that can operate over the complete data space.
- *Metadata*: It concerns (a) the metadata openness: Portals' provided metadata schemas and their categorisation, according to the 5-stars Maturity Scheme of Metadata Management [42–44] and (b) their capabilities of flat metadata descriptions (based on a specific metadata models) and/or contextual metadata descriptions and/or detailed metadata of any metadata/vocabulary model [51].
- *RDF-compliance*: It concerns the use or not of relevant technologies that support RDF (binary indicator), including technical products of open data initiatives publishing structured data in a way that it can be interlinked. It is quite important, both for enabling more effective browsing and discovery of datasets, and for linking

[2] http://lab.linkeddata.deri.ie/2010/star-scheme-by-example/.

and combining OGD from multiple sources [39, 41]. The use of Semantic Web technologies (such as "Uniform Resource Identifiers" (URI) for the identification of certain resources, the "Resource Description Framework" (RDF) for relating elements, and also vocabularies and ontologies that give meaning to the datasets) in OGD provides a common framework that allows various datasets to be shared and reused. Semantic Web technologies enable a more effective browsing and discovery of datasets through distributed SPARQL queries, and also linking and combining OGD from multiple sources across the Web, which can increase significantly the usefulness of the OGD and the value generated from them (e.g., it allows discovering new correlations and gaining deeper insights, or developing new advanced value-added e-services by combining different datasets from multiple OGD sources). Also, the value of any kind of data (including OGD) increases each time it is being re-used and linked to another resource, and this can be facilitated and triggered by providing informative and explanatory data about each available dataset, i.e. metadata, which can be used as a systematic way to describe datasets, based on pre-agreed meanings, thus facilitating the usefulness of the data.

System Quality

- *Functionality*: It includes analysis of the functionalities provided by the OGD portals [45], in terms of datasets discovery (simple document list, free text search, browsing through categories, browsing through filters, browsing through interactive map and SPARQL search), data provision (download file, online view of dataset, API), data visualisation (charts and maps) techniques, multi-linguality and data and metadata processing (e.g. enrichment, data cleansing and data format conversions).
- *Type*: It contains the types of OGD portals, as they have been identified in [19]. It has been revealed that two distinct types of OGD sources/portals have been developed with respect to the capabilities/functionalities provided to the user: (i) *OGD direct provision portals*: constitutes the main category of OGD portals, which are 'primary sources' of OGD, publishing original government datasets provided by either one government agency, or a small number of similar government agencies (who are the legal owners/licensers of the data). These portals usually offer a wide range of functionalities supporting the whole lifecycle of OGD, from the creation of datasets to the update and finally to the archiving of them. (ii) *OGD aggregators*: this category includes OGD aggregator portals, which are 'secondary sources' of OGD, coming from a big number of government agencies, publishing and maintaining lists of other 'primary' OGD catalogues and links to them. They constitute single access points to multiple OGD direct provision portals, and make it easier for a user to locate the OGD they are interested in. Usually they include descriptive information about datasets and sources, which is quite useful for the users to get a first impression of what is available. Many of them act as highly structured registries of OGD primary sources and datasets, storing structured and machine processable information, and provide 'index'-like features, such as automated registration and discovery of OGD.
- *Technology*: It includes analysis of the technologies and products that have been used for the development of the OGD sources at the main technological layers: (i) web

server, (ii) Content Management System (CMS) or platform and (iii) user interface, which is categorised either as open or not open source software.

Service Quality

- *License*: It concerns license information related to the use of the published datasets. This is one of the most important characteristic of OGD sources, since it defines the allowed ways of OGD utilisation and exploitation for generating various types of social and economic value, and reduces all relevant legal uncertainties and risks (e.g., see [39, 41]).
- *Rating and Feedback mechanisms:* It concerns capabilities to communicate to the other users and the providers the level of quality of the datasets that I perceive and get informed on the level of quality of the datasets perceived by other users through their ratings (e.g. five stars rating system). Another feedback and discussion mechanism that was investigated was the discussion of what can be learned from data use by looking at previous uses of the data; expressing your own needs for additional datasets; getting informed about the needs of other users and getting informed about datasets extensions and revisions [51].

4 The Maturity Model for OGD Portals

Based on the essential elements that have been identified and presented in Sect. 3, we are creating the maturity model presented in Table 1, categorising the capabilities of OGD infrastructures through time. Following the observations of the analysed literature, we concluded the following abstract maturity model:

Table 1. The Maturity Model for OGD Portals

	Time	Traditional OGD Infrastructures		Advanced OGD Infrastructures	
		Point Zero	1st Generation	2nd Generation	3rd Generation
General	Internet presence	OGD existence in silos accessed by application	OGD web presence	OGD web presence	OGD web presence
	Users	Distinction between Data Providers and Data Users	Distinction between Data Providers and Data Users	Data Procumers	Data Procumers
	Open Government level	Initial: Information broadcasting	Data Transparency: processes and performance	Open participation: Data quality, Public feedback, conversation, voting, Interactive communications, Crowd-sourcing	Open Collaboration: Interagency and with the public, Co-creating value-added services
	Value	N/A	Transparency & Accountability	Participation	Efficiency & Innovation
Information Quality	Thematic perspective	N/A	Statistical, economical, census	Law, Transportation, GIS	All categories with proper data modelling
	Format	.xls,.pdf	html,.xls,.pdf	+.csv + URLs	+ Linked data
	Metadata	Metadata Ignorance or Closed flat Metadata	Metadata Ignorance or Closed flat Metadata	Open Metadata for Humans or Open Reusable Metadata + contextual or detailed metadata models	Linked Open Metadata 3-layer metadata model (flat, contextual, detailed)
	RDF-compliance	No	No	Partially yes	Yes
System Quality	Functionality	N/A	Basic Web 1.0	Advanced Web 2.0	Supporting value creation
	Type	N/A	OGD direct provision portals	OGD direct provision & OGD aggregators	Collaboration Spaces
	Technology	N/A	Custom technologies	Open source	Open Source
Service Quality	License	N/A	Custom or N/A	CC share-alike	CC share-alike
	Quality Rating and Feedback Mechanisms	N/A	Web forms	+ Rating and feedback mechanism	+ Collaboration Environments

5 Validation of the Maturity Model

5.1 Information Quality

Analysing the *thematic perspective*, we remark that the thematic category with the highest publication rate in Greece (having a significant difference from the second one) is the economic and financial one, concerning mainly public spending data for various government agencies and also data about economic activity and firms [21]. This is strongly associated with two important facts: the growing citizens' distrust in government (so many government agencies respond by publishing data on their spending), and the existing severe economic crisis (which necessitates an increase in economic activity, so it is useful to provide data on existing economic activity/firms, which allow a better understanding of it, and support a better design and planning of its increase). Therefore, it is concluded that the first attempt of opening data was restricted in a narrow thematic range, focused mainly on the provision of economic/financial data. Next to that, statistical offices open their census and unemployment data. It should be noted that the European Union member states' OGD portals, has the highest publication rate in the thematic category of 'Law Enforcement, Courts and Prisons' (probably reflecting the increasing criminality and security concerns in many EU countries) [22] and then in economic and statistical data. We also remark that there are also four thematic categories (social, natural resources, legal and geographic information) with much lower publication rate, while the remaining four thematic categories (traffic/transport, meteorological/environmental, agricultural/farming/forestry/fisheries, tourism/leisure and geospatial data) have quite low frequencies, despite their importance (e.g., the importance of agriculture and tourism). In the next developments we observe the increase of publication rate in the categories of GIS and transport data, since they are characterised of great innovation value.

For the *semantic perspective*, the analysis shows that currently the majority of open data providers aim to adopt an already available metadata standard that fits within their context. Data providers that are based on the CKAN engine also adopt the CKAN metadata schema for the data catalogue and data discovery. Other governmental sites adopt a custom metadata schema for the data discovery and preserve the datasets in vertical-domain metadata standards. Noteworthy cases include open data initiatives that have developed detailed metadata standards to become EU recommendations (e.g., INSPIRE[3] directive for geospatial information and SDMX for statistical information), which tend to be included in the current phases of development. Furthermore, the majority of longstanding OGD sites indicate their intention not to follow the Linked Data paradigm, as opposed to more recent "data gov" efforts. There is a growing rate of RDF-compliance of OGD portals towards the connection to linked open data cloud and much more standardised ontologies have been used for data modelling. Additionally, the analysis indicates that almost all initiatives (with the exception of EUR-Lex) limit their internationalization efforts (if any) to the user interface level not respecting multilinguality in their published datasets.

[3] http://inspire.ec.europa.eu/.

For the *data perspective,* the data formats provided are more or less common between all initiatives, while the vast majority of OGD sites tend to provide data only in the format of the original source. Greece seems to be far behind since the studies indicate a stable position in publishing data in not machine-processable formats (.pdf, .rar and .html instead of .csv, .json and .xls). The current developments and after the launch of Greek open data portal is characterised by a small increase towards machine-processable formats. EU-wide the same course have been followed only quicker.

5.2 System Quality

Our analysis indicates that in Greece only a few OGD aggregators exist; all the others are OGD direct provision portals. EU-wide and as we moving to the next generation of developments, we observe an increase of OGD aggregators at the national level, since the majority of countries (with only a few exceptions) maintain an OGD national portal. In addition EU has launched two versions of its own OGD aggregator. Next to that, we remark some new attempts of collaboration spaces and marketplaces development characterised by higher level of open government and value but not yet with great success and recognition [24, 25].

The analysis of the system quality from the *functional perspective* identifies that only a few OGD providers offer advanced data acquisition capabilities. The majority of data providers are internally linked to the relevant data repositories and provide only interfaces for data provision. It is especially common for organizations and agencies that are responsible for the complete life cycle of data (from creation to update/archiving), such as statistical offices. Furthermore, the majority of OGD providers offer simple free-text search and theme-browsing functions for the discovery and cataloguing of datasets, whereas only recent open data initiatives start to appreciate the advances of Semantic Web by providing semantically enriched discovery services such as performing SPARQL queries. Additionally, most local public agencies limit their data provision services to a simple download functionality whereas agencies addressed to a wider network (country-level or European level) typically include the capability to view datasets on a map or various types of charts. Nevertheless, the range of visualization facilities offered by each provider varies significantly. This is mainly due to the fact that during the last years visualisation engines have become more comprehensive, flexible and light-weighted. The next generations of OGD platforms are characterised by the provision of more collaborative capabilities such as: Grouping and Interaction, Data Processing, Data Enhanced Modelling, Feedback and Collaboration, Data Quality Rating, Data Linking, Data Versioning, Advanced Data Visualisation and Advanced Data Search.

The analysis from technological perspective shows that there is a strong preference for open-source and free underlying platforms and content management systems in OGD sites with the exception of the Data.gov initiative which is based on the proprietary platform Socrata[4] that receives widespread adoption in the US (State of Oregon, State of Oklahoma, City of Chicago, City of Seattle, etc.). For data visualization, OGD sites are turning from heavy and proprietary engines to free and light-weighted javascript

[4] Socrata, the Open Data platform, http://www.socrata.com/.

frameworks (Google charts, JQuery, JavaExts). Lastly, relatively few data providers offer APIs for data and metadata interactions, whereas the paradigm of restful web services that output JSON objects is becoming the common approach in the new generations.

5.3 Service Quality

The first generations of OGD portals are characterised by the absence of service quality mechanisms. Neither guidance in how publicised data could be used nor communication channels supporting feedback and needs input were provided.

The analysis indicates that there is no common policy for *license* issues as the license for use and reuse of data vary significantly. Most of the OGD portal do not specify their licencing mode but there is a clear move towards open licences and more specifically, Creative Commons Attributes.

One essential element of OGD portals concerns their service quality development *"through user adaptation, feedback loops and dynamic supplier and user interactions and other interacting factors"* [46]. However, discussion and feedback loops appear barely to be part of existing open data practices and infrastructures. The authors at [33] argue that after open data have been used, the provision of feedback to data providers or a discussion with them is quite important by not facilitated by existing open data infrastructures, though such mechanisms might be useful for improving open data service quality, data release processes and policies. The authors at [47] found that such mechanisms can help users to obtain insight in how they can use and interpret open government data and generate value from them.

Only a few efforts concentrate on receiving the needs of users in a formal and systematic manner. In the majority of service providers comments and suggestions from users is limited to general-purpose feedback web forms that typically address comments on technical aspects of the site rather the actual datasets. On the other side, moving to the next generations of OGD portals there is a clear move towards the inclusion of dataset rating and commenting, as well as viewing and voting users' demands for specific datasets, that are not yet public or that follow strict data license [48].

6 Conclusions

This paper aggregates the research outcomes and developments, including the factor of time, towards illustrating the evolutionary path of open government data. It presents an analysis that has been conducted based on the basic identified characteristics of them, proposing a maturity model, in terms of traditional and advanced OGD infrastructures. As a next step in our study we have identified the assignment of relevant best practices to each layer, thus assisting policy makers to better design the implementation of each state. The identification of the proposed OGD portals maturity model is based on the distinction of the OGD sources with respect to the capabilities/functionalities they offer, namely to the 'traditional' Web 1.0 paradigm and to Web 2.0 paradigm [49, 50].

The 'traditional' first generation OGD portals have been influenced by the Web 1.0 paradigm, in which there is a clear distinction between content producers and content users. They are characterized by datasets publishing in non-machine-processable formats (i.e. PDF), without providing any contextual information or linkage capabilities to other datasets. Also, they are limited to offering basic functionalities to data users (consumers) for datasets downloading, and to data providers for uploading datasets. They do not support improvements of their published datasets by their users (e.g., through cleaning and further processing), or feedback provision by datasets users to their providers so that the latter can understand better the needs of the former.

The advanced second generation Web 2.0 OGD portals follows the advent of the Web 2.0 paradigm, which facilitates the generation of content of various types by simple and non-expert users, the development of relationships and online communities among them, and the extensive interaction, collaboration and sharing of content and information. These attributes have led to the emergence of a second generation of OGD portals, which have been influenced by the Web 2.0 principles. They provide, in addition to the basic functionalities of the traditional first generation OGD portals mentioned in the previous paragraph, functionalities for commenting and rating datasets, forming groups around common interests, visualising and processing datasets, improving or adapting them to specialised needs, and then publishing them again, uploading new datasets, enabling OGD users to become data 'pro-sumers' (both consuming and producing datasets). Their main objective is to support and facilitate extensive communication between OGD users (citizens, journalists, businesses, scientists, etc.) and providers (government agencies), and also collaborative value generation from OGD.

References

1. European Commission.: Directive 2003/98/EC of the European Parliament and of the Council of 17 November 2003 on the Re-use of Public Sector Information (2003). http://eur-lex.europa.eu/LexUriServ/LexUriServ.do?uri=OJ:L:2003:345:0090:0096:EN:PDF
2. Gharawi, M., Dawes, S.: Conceptualizing knowledge and information sharing in transnational knowledge networks. In: Proceedings of the 4th International Conference on Theory and Practice of Electronic Governance (ICEGOV 2010)
3. Dawes, S., Gharawi, M., Burke, B.: Knowledge and information sharing in transnational knowledge networks: a contextual perspective. In: Proceedings of the 44th Hawaii International Conference on System Sciences (2011)
4. Huijboom, N., Van Den Broek, T.: Open data: an international comparison of strategies. Eur. J. Epractice **12**, 1–13 (2011)
5. Harrison, T.M., Guerrero, S., Burke, G.B., Cook, M., Cresswell, A., Helbig, N., Hrdinova, J., Pardo, T.: Open government and e-government: Democratic challenges from a public value perspective. Inf. Polity **17**(2), 83–97 (2012)
6. European Commission.: Directive 2013/37/EU of the European Parliament and of the Council of 26 June 2013 amending Directive 2003/98/EC on the re-use of public sector information (2013). http://eur-lex.europa.eu/LexUriServ/LexUriServ.do?

7. Manyika, J., Chui, M., Groves, P., Farrell, D., Van Kuiken, S., Almasi Doshi, E.: Open data: unlocking innovation and performance with liquid information. McKinsey Global Institute, McKinsey Center for Government and McKinsey Business Technology Office (2013). http://www.mckinsey.com/insights/business_technology/open_data_unlocking_innovation_and_performance_with_liquid_information
8. Digital Agenda Assembly: Report from the workshop "Open Data and re-use of public sector information", Brussels 16–17 June 2011. (2011) http://ec.europa.eu/information_society/events/cf/daa11/item-display.cfm?id=5963
9. Lathrop, D., Ruma, L.: Open government: Collaboration, transparency, and participation in practice. O'Reilly Media, Inc. (2010)
10. Cameron, D.: Letter to Government departments on opening up data (2010). https://www.gov.uk/government/news/letter-to-government-departments-on-opening-up-data
11. AGIMO: Declaration of Open Government (2010). http://www.finance.gov.au/e-government/strategy-and-governance/gov2/declaration-of-open-government.html. Accessed 25 Feb 2011
12. European Commission: Decision C (2014) 4995 of 22 July 2014. "HORIZON 2020 LEIT ICT Work Programme" (2014). http://ec.europa.eu/research/participants/data/ref/h2020/wp/2014_2015/main/h2020-wp1415-leit-ict_en.pdf
13. Zuiderwijk, A., Janssen, M., Jeffery, K.: Towards an e-infrastructure to support the provision and use of open data. In: Conference for E-Democracy and Open Governement, p. 259 (2013)
14. Zhang, J., Dawes, S.S., Sarkis, J.: Exploring stakeholders' expectations of the benefits and barriers of e-government knowledge sharing. J. Enterp. Inf. Manag. **18**(5), 548–567 (2005)
15. Conradie, P., Choenni, S.: Exploring process barriers to release public sector information in local government. Paper presented at the 6th International Conference on Theory and Practice of Electronic Governance (ICEGOV), Albany, New York, United States of America (2012)
16. Meijer, A., Thaens, M.: Public information strategies: making government information available to citizens. Inf. Polity **14**(1–2), 31–45 (2009)
17. Janssen, M., Charalabidis, Y., Zuiderwijk, A.: Benefits, adoption barriers, and myths of open data and open government. Inf. Syst. Manag. **29**, 258–268 (2012)
18. Harrison, T.M., Pardo, T.A., Cook, M.: Creating open government ecosystems: a research and development agenda. Future Internet **4**, 900–928 (2012)
19. ENGAGE: Analysis Report of Public Sector Data and Knowledge Sources (D7.7.1) (2011). http://www.engage-project.eu/engage/wp/wp-content/plugins/download-monitor/download.php?id=4. Accessed 12 Dec 2012
20. Alexopoulos, C., Spiliotopoulou, L., Charalabidis, Y.: Open data movement in Greece: a case study on open government data sources. In: Proceedings of the 17th Panhellenic Conference on Informatics, pp. 279–286. ACM (2013)
21. Alexopoulos, C., Loukis, E., Mouzakitis, S., Petychakis, M., Charalabidis, Y.: Analysing the characteristics of open government data sources in Greece. J. Knowl. Econ. **6**, 1–33 (2015)
22. Petychakis, M., Vasileiou, O., Georgis, C., Mouzakitis, S., Psarras, J.: A state-of-the-art analysis of the current public data landscape from a functional, semantic and technical perspective. J. Theor. Appl. Electron. Commer. Res. **9**(2), 34–47 (2014)
23. Alexopoulos, C., Zuiderwijk, A., Charapabidis, Y., Loukis, E., Janssen, M.: Designing a second generation of open data platforms: integrating open data and social media. In: Janssen, M., Scholl, H.J., Wimmer, M.A., Bannister, F. (eds.) EGOV 2014. LNCS, vol. 8653, pp. 230–241. Springer, Heidelberg (2014). doi:10.1007/978-3-662-44426-9_19
24. Zuiderwijk, A., Loukis, E., Alexopoulos, C., Janssen, M., Jeffery, K.: Elements for the development of an open data marketplace. In Conference for E-Democracy and Open Governement, pp. 309–322 (2014)

25. Charalabidis, Y., Alexopoulos, C., Diamantopoulou, V., Androutsopoulou, A.: An open data and open services repository for supporting citizen-driven application development for governance. In: 2016 49th Hawaii International Conference on System Sciences (HICSS), pp. 2596–2604. IEEE (2016)
26. DeLone, D.H., McLean, E.R.: Information systems success: the quest for the dependent variable. Inf. Syst. Res. **3**(1), 60–95 (1992)
27. DeLone, D.H., McLean, E.R.: The DeLone and McLean model of information systems success: a ten-year update. J. Manag. Inf. Syst. **19**(4), 9–30 (2003)
28. Urbach, N., Mueller, B.: The updated DeLone and McLean model of information systems success. In: Dwivedi, Y., Wade, M., Schneberger, S. (eds.) Information Systems Theory-Explaining and Predicting Our Digital Society. Springer, New York (2012)
29. Bovaird, T.: Beyond engagement and participation: user and community coproduction of public services. Public Adm. Rev. **67**(5), 846–860 (2007)
30. Jaeger, P.T., Bertot, J.C.: Designing, implementing, and evaluating user-centered and citizen-centered e-government. Int. J. Electron. Gov. Res. **6**(2), 1–17 (2010)
31. Pieterson, W., Ebbers, W., Dijk, J.: The opportunities and barriers of user profiling in the public sector. In: Wimmer, M.A., Traunmüller, R., Grönlund, Å., Andersen, K.V. (eds.) EGOV 2005. LNCS, vol. 3591, pp. 269–280. Springer, Heidelberg (2005). doi: 10.1007/11545156_26
32. Charalabidis, Y., Ntanos, E., Lampathaki, F.: An architectural framework for open governmental data for researchers and citizens. In: Janssen, M., Macintosh, A., Scholl, J., Tambouris, E., Wimmer, M., Bruijn, H. D., Tan, Y. H. (eds.) Electronic Government and Electronic Participation Joint Proceedings of Ongoing Research and Projects of IFIP EGOV and ePart 2011, pp. 77–85 (2011)
33. Zuiderwick, A., Janssen, M., Jeffery, K.: An e-infrastructure to support the provision and use of open data. In: International Conference for eDemocracy and Open Government 2013 (CEDEM 13), 22–24 May 2013, Krems, Austria (2013)
34. Lee, G., Kwak, Y.H.: An open government maturity model for social media-based public engagement. Gov. Inf. Q. **29**(4), 492–503 (2012)
35. Jetzek, T., Avital, M., Bjorn-Andersen, N.: The generative mechanisms of open government data. In: Proceedings of the 21st European Conference on Information Systems (ECIS), Utrecht, The Netherlands (2013a)
36. Jetzek, T., Avital, M., Bjorn-Andersen, N.: Generating value from open government data. In: Proceedings of the 34th International Conference on Information Systems (ICIS), Milan, Italy (2013b)
37. Dawes, S.S., Helbig, N.: Information strategies for open government: challenges and prospects for deriving public value from government transparency. In: Wimmer, M.A., Chappelet, J.-L., Janssen, M., Scholl, H.J. (eds.) EGOV 2010. LNCS, vol. 6228, pp. 50–60. Springer, Heidelberg (2010). doi:10.1007/978-3-642-14799-9_5
38. OECD Working Party on the Information Economy: Participative Web: user-created content. In: DSTI/ICCP/IE(2006)7/FINAL (2006)
39. Wood, D. (ed.): Linking Government Data. Springer, New York (2011)
40. Geiger, C.P., Luecke, J.V.: Open government and (linked) (open) (government) (data). J. e-Democr. Open Gov. **4**(2), 265–278 (2012)
41. Bauer, F., Kaltenböck, M.: Linked Open Data: The Essentials—A Quick Start Guide for Decision Makers. Monochrom Editions, Vienna (2012)
42. ISA Programme, Interoperability Solutions for European Public Administrations, "Towards Open Government Metadata" (2011). https://joinup.ec.europa.eu/sites/default/files/towards_open_government_metadata_0.pdf

43. Shukair, G., Loutas, N., Peristeras, V., Sklarß, S.: Towards semantically interoperable metadata repositories: The asset description metadata schema. Comput. Ind. **64**(1), 10–18 (2013)
44. Zuiderwijk, A., Jeffery, K., Janssen, M.: The potential of metadata for linked open data and its value for users and publishers. JeDEM-eJ. eDemocr. Open Gov. **4**(2), 222–244 (2012)
45. Zuiderwijk, A., Janssen, M., Parnia, A.: The complementarity of open data infrastructures: an analysis of functionalities. In: Proceedings of the 14th Annual International Conference on Digital Government Research, pp. 166–171. ACM (2013)
46. Zuiderwijk, A., Helbig, N., Gil-García, R., Janssen, M.: Special issue on innovation through open data—a review of the state-of-the-art and an emerging research agenda: Guest Editors' Introduction. J. Theor. Appl. Electron. Commer. Res. **9**(2), I–XIII (2014)
47. Dawes, S., Helbig, N.: Information strategies for open government: challenges and prospects for deriving public value from government transparency. Paper presented at the 9th International Conference on e-government (EGOV), Lausanne, Switzerland (2010)
48. Alexopoulos, C., Loukis, E., Charalabidis, Y.: A platform for closing the open data feedback loop based. JeDEM-eJ. eDemocr. Open Gov. **6**(1), 62–68 (2014)
49. Alexopoulos, C., Loukis, E., Charalabidis, Y., Zuiderwijk, A.: An evaluation framework for traditional and advanced open public data e-infrastructures. In: Castelnovo, W., Ferrari, E. (eds.) Proceedings of the 13th European Conference on Egovernment, pp. 102–111 (2013)
50. Charalabidis, Y., Loukis, E., Alexopoulos, C.: Evaluating second generation open government data infrastructures using value models. In: 2014 47th Hawaii International Conference on System Sciences (HICSS), pp. 2114–2126. IEEE (2014)
51. Zuiderwijk, A., Janssen, M., Davis, C.: Innovation with open data: essential elements of open data ecosystems. Inf. Polity **19**(1, 2), 17–33 (2014)

Open Government

Exploring on the Role of Open Government Data in Emergency Management

Yumei Chen[1], Theresa A. Pardo[2(✉)], and Shanshan Chen[1]

[1] School of Public Administration and Emergency Management, Jinan University, Guangzhou, China
tchenym@jnu.edu.cn, xchenshanshan@foxmail.com

[2] Center for Technology in Government, University at Albany, SUNY, Albany, NY, USA
tpardo@ctg.albany.edu

Abstract. Analysis of the U.S. government response to Hurricane Katrina in 2005 and Hurricane Sandy in 2012 remind us that inter-governmental and intra-governmental communication plays an important role in effective response to disaster. Hurricane Katrina highlighted the lack of information sharing across levels of government and sectors and showed that such gaps in sharing contribute to slower and uncoordinated response and insufficient deployment of resources. The response to Hurricane Sandy was much more effective because of the lessons learned from Katrina about cross-boundary information sharing but problems still existed. The conclusion that more complex and severe incidents require more coordination and information sharing across levels of government and functional agencies makes it increasingly important to increase information sharing capability as part of EM. This paper presents the argument that the unique and important opportunity of leveraging OGD in this regard requires continued attention and investment in ways that maximize value in the form of more effective and efficient emergency response efforts.

Keywords: Open Government Data · Emergency management · LEHD program

1 Introduction

Emergency Management (EM) typically involves multiple jurisdictions as well as a number of governmental ministries, departments and agencies, non-governmental organizations (NGOs), private sector entities, and citizens. In addition, the number and type of actors involved emergency response varies depending on the context and severity of the event [1]. Information flow and interaction among the many actors are important factors in making decisions about response activities, as well as preparedness and recovery plans. Governments are among the largest creators and collectors of data. The data held by governments provides insight into the critical infrastructure of countries

Submitted Track: Open Government & Open and Big Data.

M. Janssen et al. (Eds.): EGOV 2017, LNCS 10428, pp. 303–313, 2017.
DOI: 10.1007/978-3-319-64677-0_25

includes transportation, health care, financial services, weather and agricultural conditions, population and housing trends and any number of characteristics of the society from a geographical perspective. Increasingly, governments and other emergency management professionals are looking to both governmental and non-governmental actors to provide access to the vast store of government information to guide emergency response decision making. In particular pressure to provide open government data as input to emergency management and in particular emergency response efforts, is increasing.

This in progress research paper presents the first phase of a study designed to provide new understanding about global practices in the use of Open Government Data (OGD) in emergency response. The complete study will focus on the US, the EU and China. This first paper will start with a focus on the United States. Once complete, the collected set of papers will propose a model of the use of OGD in emergency response, identify a common set of global practices and present a set of guidelines for the use of OGD in the various stages of EM. Questions being examined in this study include where and how is OGD playing a role in EM, how do OGD initiatives facilitate EM in terms of increasing efficiency and effectiveness, how does the use of OGD impact EM procedures and organizing frameworks, do current OGD efforts provide data to support the full life cycle of EM, and are there requirements for government data that the OGD efforts are not providing. This paper begins to develop a mapping between the EM lifecycle and OGD and highlights where and in what way OGD efforts are creating public value in EM efforts.

This paper is organized in five sections including this introduction. Section 2 briefly introduces the edge research on OGD and EM interaction, and the trends of OGD applied in EM area. Section 3 provides a brief introduction to Emergency Management and Open Government Data practices in the U.S.A, and tries to analyze the interaction between EM and OGD via a typical application such as LEHD project. Followed by Sect. 4 the paper introduces a discussion of EM and OGD as a foundation for the analysis and conclusion which provides a model of the use of OGD across the lifecycle of EM.

2 Literature Review

In recent years, OGD have been accepted and used in more and more countries. OGD is commonly seen as a strong driver in society, and many OGD strategies have also been taken, such as website, platform, policy and Hackathons. Although open data exploiting potential value have become a popular trend globally, different countries open data policies and application are different, such as the degree of open data and application of it are higher in the US, UK and UN.

2.1 The Relationship Between Open Government Data (OGD) and Emergency Management (EM)

OGD is one of the important initiatives to support decision-making in emergency management protocol. A disaster happened, social data and information will increase rapidly, so the need for various information outlets need to be linked from an open data cloud is critical [2]. Janssen et al. shows that data analytics plays a role by providing deep insight and influences the decision making processes of public organizations [3]. In order to identify vulnerable places, assets, population and infrastructure facilities, it necessary to balance resource requirements. And Olyazadeh et al. believed that open-source data, techniques and solutions will decrease the time and efforts needed for rapid disaster and catastrophe management [4]. It means that open data can support government or citizens making decisions in a shorter amount of time, in order to better prepare for and respond to disasters.

OGD is seen as a tool to strengthen the collaboration in emergency management. Harrison et al. pointed out that openness changed the nature of relationships between stakeholders and governments, and enables them to link across organizational boundaries and functions [5]. In addition, Meijer and Bolívar highlighted that open data can strengthen the collective intelligence of cities by enabling companies, innovators, NGOs and citizens to extract value from this data [6]. In this sense, openness can increase stakeholders' collaboration, because open data supplied a data-sharing platform. Not only does it provide information quickly, but it can also promote and support team-work.

2.2 The Attempts of Open Government Data Applied to Emergency Management

The web of OpenDRI [7] introduced a lot of examples for analyzing open data which can be used for government to reduce vulnerability and build resilience to natural hazards. Open government data, such as GIS, can be used for forest conservation planning [8], health care [9], detect malaria incidence in Vietnam [10], build disaster management system [2], set the course of emergency vehicle route [11] and disaster risk management [10]. These scholars introduced typical cases to analysis that OGD is on the need of emergency management. For example, Balbo et al. introduced the Malawi government setting up MASDAP (a public platform) based on GeoNode (a platform for the management and publication of geospatial data) as a case, to prove geospatial data sharing can be help for disaster risk management [12]. This means that OGD is an important resource for emergency management, and to identify the relationship between them will help stakeholders to build correct corporation.

3 Open Government Data Attempted to Apply in Emergency Management

In fact with the transformation of Emergency Management coordination among government agencies and NOGOs, private companies and individuals becomes more and more important. OGD is commonly used to create new economic and social values via the government information efficiently disseminated and reused. As the basis of coordination of information could be disseminated to the public and be used by more and more involved parties will impact the response to the accidents.

3.1 Emergency Management Transformation in U.S.A

EM in the United States (U.S.) was fragmented and managed by several federal agencies until Federal Emergency Management Agency (FEMA) was authorized as an independent federal agency to coordinate emergency management functions in 1979. At the beginning the Federal Response Plan (FRP) was released to coordinate multi-level and multi-sector efforts respond to and prepare for incidents. In the aftermath of the 9/11 attack, the FRP was released to a new National Response Plan (NRP) in 2003. The new NRP came with a new perspective on homeland security, included a stronger focus on intergovernmental networks among state, local and federal levels, as well as the vital role of private and nonprofit sectors been increasing recognition.

In the aftermath of Hurricane Katina, NRP was replaced by National Response Framework (NRF) in 2008. NRF is built upon scalable, flexible, and adaptable coordinating structures to align key roles and responsibilities across the Nation, linking all levels of government, nongovernmental organizations, and the private sector [13].

EM functions in the U.S. are generally grouped into four phases: Mitigation, Preparedness, Response, and Recovery. In the U.S. EM is managed according to the principles of the National Incident Management System (NIMS), which is a preparedness and response management model based on the Incident Command System (ICS) [14]. Each of these four phases is introduced below.

- Mitigation activities often have a long-term or sustained goal to improve resilience to reduce or eliminate the impact of an incident in the future;
- Preparedness is the process of enhancing capacity to respond to an incident by taking steps to ensure personnel and entities are capable of responding to incidents, such as training, planning, exercising, procuring resources and intelligence and surveillance to incidents;
- Response activities are immediate actions to save lives, protect property and the environment, such as evacuation, deployment of resources and establishment of incident command operations;
- Recovery activities are intended to restore essential services and repair damages.

3.2 Open Government Data Practices in U.S.A

President Barack Obama signed the Open Government Directive on December 8, 2009. This Directive set forth three principles of transparency, participation, and collaboration as the cornerstone of an open government. Over the past few years, the Obama Administration has launched a number of Open Data Initiatives aimed at scaling up open data efforts across the Health, Energy, Climate, Education, Finance, Public Safety, and Global Development sectors [15].

The White House launched the Open Government Directive with one of the most important practice changes in terms of government data: the creation and release of Data.gov. Data.gov, a government web portal, comprises hundreds of thousands of raw data streams from different agencies available to citizens, private companies and NGOs. With this paradigm shift in the accessibility of government data the concept of Open Government Data (OGD) emerged. OGD, as a unique concept from Open Government gained attention, particularly in the U.S., as a strategy for creating greater government transparency, participation and collaboration.

More and more countries now have data platforms created for selected purposes such as economic analysis and development, environment protection, transportation schedule, emergency management, and so on. One such platform is the Longitudinal Employer-Household Dynamics (LEHD) program, which is part of the Center for Economic Studies at the U.S. Census Bureau and focuses on data gathered from economic-related agencies and all 50 states of the U.S. The mission of the LEHD is to provide new dynamic information on workers, employers, and jobs with state-of-the-art confidentiality protections and no additional data collection burden. New data is uploaded on a regular basis and some services are provided such as partially synthetic data and statistics for detailed levels of geography and industry and for selected demographic groups.

The Toxics Release Inventory (TRI) provided by the U.S. Environmental Protection Agency (EPA) provides another example. TRI is a starting point for communities to learn about toxic chemicals that industrial facilities are using and releasing into the environment, and whether those facilities are doing anything to prevent pollution. Its mission is to protect human health and the environment [16]. TRI data supports informed decision-making by communities, government agencies, companies, and others. It releases Pollution Prevention (P2) Data and Tools for TRI Data Analysis as well.

In accordance with the OG Directive and the foundational principles, Data.gov and other such open data programs provide some new understanding of the characteristics of OGD initiatives, including:

- They contain large amounts of data and comprise various themes;
- Raw data streams from different agencies as well as partially synthetic data and statistic data are uploaded to an integrated portal;
- Data products are released to the public via a wide variety of dissemination and analysis tools. The data sets are provided in different formats, and analysis tools are provided to support users in data analysis and reuse;
- For special purposes or different domains, data are sorted into different data communities (data.gov/health for example), or integrated to a special portal.

3.3 Open Government Data Practice in Emergency Management: Case OnTheMap

The LEHD program provides new dynamic information on workers, employers, and jobs with state-of-the-art confidentiality protections and no additional data collection burden. LEHD Origin-Destination Employment Statistics (LODES) are used by OnTheMap, Data files are state-based and organized into three types: Origin-Destination (OD), Residence Area Characteristics (RAC), and Workplace Area Characteristics (WAC), all at census block geographic detail. Data is available for most states for the years 2002–2014.

Under the LEHD Partnership, states agree to share Unemployment Insurance earnings data and the Quarterly Census of Employment and Wages (QCEW) data with the

Census Bureau. The LEHD program combines these administrative data, additional administrative data and data from censuses and surveys. From this data, the program creates statistics on employment, earnings, and job flows at detailed levels of geography and industry and for different demographic groups. In addition, the LEHD program uses this data to create partially synthetic data on workers' residential patterns.

The LODES dataset is highlighted in OnTheMap, a mapping and reporting tool showing employment and home locations of workers with companion reports for user-defined areas. OnTheMap has been selected as a representative U.S. statistical innovation for the United Nations in 2009, and received the U.S. Department of Commerce Gold Medal, its highest recognition for scientific achievement, in 2010 [17].

OnTheMap for Emergency Management is a public data tool that provides an intuitive web-based interface for accessing U.S. population and workforce statistics, in real time, for areas being affected by natural disasters. The tool provides users this information for rapidly changing hazard event areas. OnTheMap for Emergency Management automatically incorporates real time data updates from the National Weather Service's (NWS) National Hurricane Center, Department of Interior (DOI), Department of Agriculture (DOA), and FEMA. Recent improvements have been made that advance the utility of the tool and its data offerings for users including newly added social, economic, and housing data from the American Community Survey (ACS), greater reporting flexibility to better analyze communities affected by disaster events, and a variety of user interface enhancements. The highlights are as follows:

- Addition of detailed social, economic, and housing data from the ACS;
- Generate reports for specific communities for regional, local, and comparative analyses;
- Linkable maps and reports for easier sharing (Fig. 1).

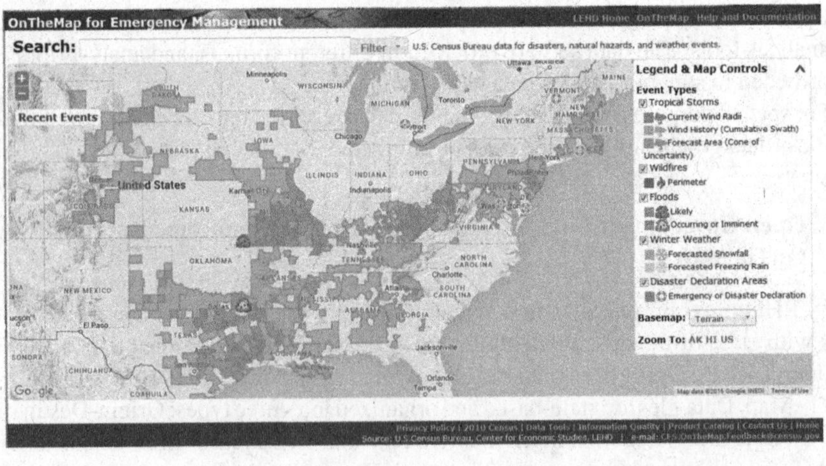

Fig. 1. LEHD Application OnTheMap for Emergency Management (http://onthemap.ces.census.gov/em/)

4 Analysis

As contemporary incidents become more and more complex, responses to these incidents have begun to exceed the capacity of any one agency and require coordination with other agencies to interact together [18]. A lack of coordination across the numerous U.S. federal agencies charged with some aspect of EM led to the formation, in 1978, of the Federal Emergency Management Agency (FEMA). The 9/11 attack caused significant changes to the federal and national emergency response coordination with the new released NRP (National Response Plan). Then in the aftermath of Hurricane Sandy, NRP was replaced by NRF, which not only was the public sector saying governments need to interact but all across the society including NGOs, private sectors and citizens need to be involved in emergency preparedness and response. Now, the most important consideration when accidents happen is how to make all the stakeholders respond quickly and collaboratively on accurate, timely and distributed information.

4.1 Open Government Data Needs in Emergency Management

During emergencies stakeholders respond according to the information and directives they receive. The painfully slow response to Hurricane Katrina was a national embarrassment. The response state governments were waiting for were the federal directives to act and to provide funding and support to the area. However the federal agencies involved didn't grasp the severity of situation immediately, which made the decision making slow, command vague and local governments response time insufficient. Further, government agencies, private sector companies and NGOs who might have been more responsive, knew little about the NRP. The public didn't know the government's rescue plan or evacuation schedule, nor the recovery plan for after the hurricane. There wasn't a uniform platform for disseminating the information and directives so the multiple layers of government nor the public knew what happened and how to address and solve the problems from the disaster.

Hurricane Sandy in 2012 was another test for the new NRF. The results were considered much more effective than the Katrina response. All the agencies prepared for the hurricane landfall and communicated with each other, deployment of resources and logistics were found to be more efficient and effective. Communication among responding governments was improved though communication between government and the public such as citizens, private companies and NGOs remained problematic. However, the assessment also found that few people used shelters, the evacuation was inefficient, situational awareness was limited, and the recovery plan lacked public support.

The newly released NRF improved the sharing of information and directives among governments, though interaction between government and other stakeholders did not improve. The NRF was not open to other stakeholders to help inform their decision making and communication strategies, and as a consequence, little improvement was evident.

4.2 Open Government Data Leveraging in Emergency Management

When emergencies happen governments making decisions quickly and correctly and both the government and the public acting according to unified directives and collaborating immediately are the determinants of the emergency response. And all the systems should be prepared as emergency management's main functions.

In the case of OnTheMap, firstly there is an unified platform based on the spatial geographic map which in the data publishing and data use phase it is published to the public via a wide variety of dissemination and analysis tools, and in the data collection phase it automatically incorporates real time data updates from the National Weather Service's (NWS) National Hurricane Center, Department of Interior (DOI), Department of Agriculture (DOA), and FEMA. And all 50 states, the District of Columbia, Puerto Rico, and the U.S. Virgin Islands have joined the LEHD Partnership, although the LEHD program is not yet producing public-use statistics for Massachusetts, Puerto Rico, or the U.S. Virgin Islands.

For the widely use of data the LEHD program staff includes geographers, programmers, and economists. With the integrity of information about people, weather, hurricane landfall changes, transportation etc. are all available on this unified spatial geographic map, firstly both governments and the public become very aware to the accidents and its changes in time, then without panic the response could be better-organized; Secondly governments can make decisions very quickly according to the real time situation, such as response plan, evacuation plan, deployment plan and even the recovery plan with appropriate schedule; Thirdly the public can get the directive at the first time, and get to know the relief goods and rescue facilities immediately such as shelters locations, safe or dangerous buildings, which can help people from the second disaster; Finally if there are some applications developed using the open data on mobile phones which can actively push the updated emergency information to the citizens to let everybody get the information as soon as possible, and on the contrary the citizens can access some special information by themselves for example to find the nearest shelter location, or to find safety and a shortcut route to evacuate. Not only in the phase of response but in other phases open data can help emergency management become more efficient and accurate. In the above case of TRI, the company and its facilities using or releasing toxic chemicals are strictly monitored. The industrial standards could be set according to historic data to avoid toxic chemical accidents, governments' supervision and administration can be based on data collected automatically instead of the data provided by the companies, which will be more reliable and respond quickly and accurately once accidents happen. To the public the data can be accessed easily which means they will know clearly where the dangerous locations are to be able to avoid themOpen data can be used to develop a "Toxic Chemical Maps" to help people far from the dangerous and also it will be very helpful for anybody to "monitor" the potential toxic chemical accidents happened.

5 Conclusion and Recommendation for Further Research

As incidents become more complex and severe, many more organizations are needed to as part of response efforts. Organizations tasked with addressing large scale events which affect many people and require significant resources are increasingly crossing traditional hierarchical boundaries to collaborate with other public, private, nonprofit organizations, and the media [19]. Multi-level, multi-sector, and cross-boundary information sharing is recognized as necessary for EM decision making.

The emergence of a new governance approach that combines the practices of traditional government with market driven approaches of the private sector and the resourcefulness of non-profit organizations is required. Coordination across the boundaries of government and non-governmental organizations, companies and citizens becomes a very important factor in the effectiveness of incident response.

As one important step toward more effective use of OGD in emergency management, Data.gov disseminates emergency preparedness information with the goal of helping the public prepare for many different kinds of incidents. Data such as that provided by LEHD, TRI and FGDC, are also resources for the public, in particular other governments, the private sector and NGOs, to produce applications that provide tools to visualize the data and visualizations themselves, for example, to support more rapid response by all stakeholders and improve the accuracy of decisions in routine emergency preparedness and response. Drawing on the experiences in the U.S. we propose a set of scenarios where the use of OGD in EM could be highlighted and cultivated to increase EM response capability.

- During mitigation stage, the analysis of the routine data from production and business can help government locate the city's vulnerability, and the usage of data will reflect the real production and business situation. Then governments can modified the industry standard or regulations to improve the city's resilience;
- During preparedness stage, preparedness will be more sufficient and well planned if government collects the updated data through a geographic platform like GeoPlatform.gov sharing geographic data, maps, and online services, the resources can be more efficiently reserved and shelters location can be more optimized according to the LEHD;
- During response stage, rapid action and accurate decision-making are the most important things. Evacuation will be more efficient and well planned if government combine the dynamic Employer-Household data from LEHD and geographical data from federal or state's geographic information center. And obviously it will be easier for the public to find the shelters if there is an application positioning nearest shelters via mobile phone;
- During the recovery stage, quick and easy access to the recovery plan and accessibility to the emergency government agencies will improve the plans.

Hurricanes Katrina and Sandy were typical of recent city-based responses to disasters. Hurricane Katrina highlighted the lack of information sharing across levels of government and sectors and showed that such gaps in sharing contribute to slower and uncoordinated response and insufficient deployment of resources. The response to Hurricane Sandy was much more effective because of the lessons learned from Katrina about cross-boundary information sharing but problems still existed.

The conclusion that more complex and severe incidents require more coordination and information sharing across levels of government and functional agencies, as well as across sectors and with the public is well accepted. This conclusion makes it increasingly important to increase information sharing capability as part of EM. The unique and important opportunity of leveraging OGD in this regard requires continued attention and investment in ways that maximize value in the form of more effective and efficient emergency response efforts.

Acknowledgements. The work is supported by Natural Science Foundation of Guangdong Province China (Grant No. 2015A030313315), the Fundamental Research Funds for the Central Universities (Grant No. 15JNKY002), Social Science Foundation of China Major Project (Grant No. 14ZDB166), and the Guangzhou City Construction of State-level Scientific Research Think Tank (Grant No. 2016SX013).

References

1. Lindsay, B.R.: Federal Emergency Management: A Brief Introduction. Congressional Research Service, 30 November 2012
2. Silva, T., Wuwongse, V., Sharma, H.N.: Disaster mitigation and preparedness using linked open data. J. Ambient Intell. Humaniz. Comput. **4**, 591–602 (2013)
3. Janssen, M., Matheus, R., Zuiderwijk, A.: Big and open linked data (BOLD) to create smart cities and citizens: insights from smart energy and mobility cases. In: Tambouris, E., Janssen, M., Scholl, H.J., Wimmer, Maria A., Tarabanis, K., Gascó, M., Klievink, B., Lindgren, I., Parycek, P. (eds.) EGOV 2015. LNCS, vol. 9248, pp. 79–90. Springer, Cham (2015). doi: 10.1007/978-3-319-22479-4_6
4. Olyazadeh, R., Aye, Z.C., Jaboyedoff, M., Derron, M.H.: Prototype of an open-source web-gis platform for rapid disaster impact assessment. Spat. Inf. Res. **24**, 203–210 (2016)
5. Harrison, T.M., Guerrero, S., Burke, G.B., Cook, M., Cresswell, A., Helbig, N., Hrdinová, J., Pardo, T.: Open government and E-government: Democratic challenges from a public value perspective. In: Proceedings of the 12th Annual International Conferènce on Digital Government Research, New York, pp. 245–253 (2011)
6. Meijer, A., Bolívar, M.P.R.: Governing the smart city: a review of the literature on smart urban governance. Int. Rev. Adm. Sci. **82**, 392–408 (2016)
7. The Global Facility for Disaster Recovery and Reduction (GFDRR). Open Data for Resilience Initiative. https://opendri.org/
8. Lehtomäki, J., Tuominen, S., Toivonen, T., Leinonen, A.: What data to use for forest conservation planning? A comparison of coarse open and detailed proprietary forest inventory data in Finland (2015)
9. Badawi, O., Brennan, T., Zimolzak, A., et al.: Making big data useful for health care: a summary of the inaugural MIT critical data conference. J. Med. Internet Res. (2014)
10. Bui, T., Pham, H.: Web-Based GIS for Spatial Pattern Detection: Application to Malaria Incidence in Vietnam. Springer, Cham (2016). doi:10.1186/s40064-016-2518-5
11. Consoli, S., Gangemi, A., Nuzzolese, A.G., Peroni, S., Reforgiato Recupero, D., Spampinato, D.: Setting the course of emergency vehicle routing using geolinked open data for the municipality of Catania. In: Presutti, V., Blomqvist, E., Troncy, R., Sack, H., Papadakis, I., Tordai, A. (eds.) ESWC 2014. LNCS, vol. 8798, pp. 42–53. Springer, Cham (2014). doi: 10.1007/978-3-319-11955-7_4
12. Balbo, S., Boccardo, P., Dalmasso, S., et al.: A public platform for geospatial data sharing for disaster. Risk Manag. **1**(5), 189–195 (2013)
13. U.S. Department of HomeLand Security, National Response Framework (2008)

14. Homeland Security Presidential Directive-5: Management of Domestic Incidents (2003)
15. Web. https://www.whitehouse.gov/open
16. Web. https://www.epa.gov/toxics-release-inventory-tri-program
17. Web. http://onthemap.ces.census.gov/em/
18. Wise, C.R., Nader, R.: Organizing the federal system for homeland security: problems, issues, and dilemmas. Public Adm. Rev. **62**, 44–57 (2002)
19. Kapucu, N.: Examining the National Response Plan in response to a catastrophic disaster: Hurricane Katrina in 2005. Public Adm. Rev.

Proactive Transparency and Open Data: A Tentative Analysis

Olivier Glassey(✉)

University of Lausanne, 1015 Lausanne, Switzerland
oglassey@unil.ch

Abstract. In this paper, we discuss the topic of governmental transparency, and more specifically in relation to Open Data. We look at governmental transparency in terms of channels, benefits, context, directions, etc., and we argue that there is an emergence of new intermediaries in the domain of governmental transparency, made possible mainly through information and communication technology. We then use the concept of public utility to integrate transparency and open data in a larger governmental perspective and we give a few examples of the use of open data to that effect. We propose an approach to support proactive transparency based on Open Data, based on a "lens" to be used to analyse transparency and open data in given contexts.

Keywords: Transparency · Open data · Intermediaries

1 Transparency and Information Technology

Transparency is a broad concept in social sciences. Derived from its literal definition, i.e. the physical capacity of an object to let light pass through, it means that a system or an organization lets third parties consider their internal knowledge, processes and decisions. According to [1] transparency can be applied to many areas: organizational transparency, accounting and budgetary transparency, transparency of government action and responsibilities, as well as documentary transparency. In this paper, we will discuss the topic of governmental transparency, and more specifically in relation to Open Data. Indeed, many argue that access to government information is essential for a working democracy, along with [2], who called upon Thomas Jefferson and his "information as currency of democracy" to declare that "the public must know what information is available from which government body, and how and where this can be located…". These ideas have found their way in many national regulations around the world. In 2010, more than 80 countries had passed Freedom of Information Acts or access to information laws and 50 additional countries were in the process of doing so [3].

[4] identifies 4 primary channels supporting government transparency:

- Proactive provision of information;
- Answers to precise requests;
- Public meetings;
- Leaks or disclosures (whistleblowing).

M. Janssen et al. (Eds.): EGOV 2017, LNCS 10428, pp. 314–323, 2017.
DOI: 10.1007/978-3-319-64677-0_26

Here it will be only a question of the proactive provision of information, an approach greatly facilitated by information and communication technology and particularly by the Internet. [5] make a brief review of the literature on the subject and conclude that the overall trend is the use of eGovernment to reduce costs and facilitate access to information, thereby supporting transparency and accountability, or even reducing corruption. The cases of "whistleblowing" or of denunciation on the Internet, of which the best-known example is probably WikiLeaks, will not be discussed in this contribution.

To show the benefit of the use of ICT in a democratic perspective, [6] proposes three analysis scenarios:

- Minimal use of ICT: this would only enforce existing laws more efficiently, to collect, process, store and make available information.
- A revolutionary approach: ICT would allow a move towards an ideal type of deliberative democracy, where citizens can participate directly and transparently in decision making, based on objective and easily accessible data.
- A gradual transformation, where elected officials and public sector managers are "reactive" in relation to feedback and knowledge sharing enabled by ICT. A politician who relies on reading blogs to get an idea of public opinion and decides accordingly constitutes a simple example.

Regardless of the scenario that is played out in the coming years, the fact of using ICT as a support for transparency will have an impact. Before proposing a detailed analysis of what he calls "computer-mediated transparency," [7] traces the positions of two opposing camps. Proponents of computer-mediated transparency believe that it will provide better access to information for citizens, and thereby contribute to a more rational and democratic society. Critics of this form of transparency argue that the provision of a mass of unsorted or incorrect information will simply increase uncertainty and reduce public trust in institutions. Nonetheless, [7] argues that currently transparency is in any event mediated, in general by the press, radio or television and increasingly by the Internet. In contrast, face-to-face transparency, where citizens attend political meetings, is tending to disappear. The author gives an overview of the main differences between these two modes of transparency, including:

- The direction: mediated transparency is unidirectional, face-to-face transparency is bidirectional. Indeed, if the citizen knows who said what during a council meeting he attends, the counsellor can also know who was in the seating area to listen. During the broadcast of these same sessions on television or on the Internet, elected officials do not have any means of knowing who is listening to them.
- The context: data are sometimes available "in bulk" on the Internet, without any information about their meaning or the purpose for which they were collected. Conversely, a public administration employee who presents the same data should be able to explain the context of their use.
- The structured and quantitative nature of data that computers are capable of processing: a computer has tremendous capacities for the treatment of statistical data but is not necessarily able to interpret certain non-formalized elements. [7] gives the example of OPEN, a Korean system for monitoring administrative procedures, which

shows very effectively how many files were processed in a given time, but cannot explain why a decision was taken.

Without entering an academic discussion on the impact of ICT on transparency, it should nevertheless be noted that the relationship between transparency, technologies and trust are ambivalent. Optimists will see almost unlimited possibilities to improve democracy, pessimists will hold up the threat of a "Big Brother" type of society or of information overload, and pragmatists one tool among others to improve transparency. To borrow a comment from [8], "Information and communication technologies have been touted as the cure for all ills, from the rigid and silo architecture of public administration to the fall in participation rates in our democracies." [8] do not however criticize the technology, but they believe that eGovernment should not focus only on technology but rather explore in depth the flow of information within the public sector. In addition, they find that eGovernment has developed according to a transactional perspective, namely the simple and structured automation of routine services. They thus propose to widen this perspective and to integrate an informational vision of the State.

Regardless of the approach adopted in relation to ICT, it is clear that it has an impact on the functioning of the State in general, and in particular on transparency. To investigate this latter dimension, [6] uses a continuum, which goes from the simple use of ICT to make information available to passive citizens to tools to enable active citizens to participate fully in decision-making. Without providing definitive answers about the impact of ICT on transparency, let us mention some key points to conclude this section. The first one is the emergence of new intermediaries. [9] discuss the importance of NGOs and private companies that have access to government data and develop new or improved services. [6] talks about the arrival of "ersatz-Intermediaries", i.e. engaged citizens who are evaluating available information and issue reports, for example on their blogs. The wiki GuttenPlag counts thus more than 1'200 extracts plagiarized in the thesis of doctorate of the baron Karl Theodor Zu Guttenberg, who resigned of his post of German Minister for Defence after these charges of plagiarism [10].

Traditionally the appearance of new technologies (telegraph, telephone, television) has benefited the powers that be: the latter have used them as tools for control or propaganda [11]. There is no consensus however at the present time about the use of blogs, citizen journalism or social media such as Twitter: does it neutralize or counterbalance the media industry [12], allowing it to circumvent censorship, as seems to have been the case during the Arab Spring [13], or on the contrary does it allow governments to monitor or imprison dissidents? Cases are not lacking, we can mention for example that of a Chinese blogger arrested and placed under house arrest in August 2011 [14]. Are governments overwhelmed when it comes to filtering content from social media [15] or is it enough to unplug the Internet in the case of a serious crisis, as was the case in Egypt [16]? What is certain however is that the traditional barriers to ICT use also exist in the context of transparency [5]: usability of tools, computer skills, infrastructure problems, availability of Internet access, etc.

Finally, ICTs have the same general impacts on transparency as they have had on trade or administrative services: distance in time and space [7], to the effect that exchanges do not occur in a unit of time and place; availability 24 h a day, 7 days a week

[17]; potential cost reductions and economies of scale [18]. The topic of ICTs in government is discussed in more detail in the next section.

2 Government and ICT

Different "labels" apply to the use of information and communication technology in the public sector: electronic or online administration, eGovernment, Government 2.0 or even "Open Government". Without entering a thorough discussion of what these concepts cover, it is all the same necessary to position them before going further. Online administration, or eGovernement, relates to the development and the provision of electronic administrative services, mainly in a managerial approach [19]. Government 2.0 or Gov 2.0, is a term that was coined by symmetry with Web 2.0 [20]: it thus refers to the application of key concepts of Web 2.0 to the functioning of a State, namely co-creation, sharing, user experience, etc. The founding text of [21] provides a good introduction to Web 2.0. Quite quickly, some have questioned whether it was a fad, destined for oblivion, or if Web 2.0 contributions were positive and concrete, such as [22]. The Open Government approach was launched by President Obama, who on in his first day in office signed a Memorandum on Transparency and Open Government [23]. This gave 120 days to the Department of Management and Budget to pass a directive emphasizing transparency, participation and collaboration in government, which was done on December 8 with the Open Government Directive [24]. The term "Open Government" then spread like wildfire across the world and is used generically for all projects within the public sector which include the three dimensions: transparency, participation and collaboration.

[20] made a brief review of the literature on expectations of Government 2.0: these range from improved efficiency and effectiveness to public awareness in public policy, from the possibility for citizens to give their opinion, or to participate in solving collective problems. The author paints a mixed picture for real improvements in transparency and openness by asking whether it relates to a glass that is half full or half empty. Moreover, [5] believe that excessive enthusiasm for technologies known as 2.0 can only lead to failure in a government which still functions in mode 1.0. [25] have meanwhile not wished to dwell on the term "Open Government" which they consider ambiguous, they offer however a typology of the stakeholders involved:

- Proponents of transparency consist of researchers, associations, or activists, who believe that to "shed light" is the best way to control government action and inspire public confidence.
- Futurists have a technological vision of Open Government and are inspired by the philosophy of free and open software (Open Source).
- Democrats see in Open Government a means of making society more democratic, allowing a more direct involvement of citizens.
- Bureaucrats focus on ICT and openness in order to evaluate the performance of the public sector.

This typology is obviously based on "ideal types", but it provides an interesting and accessible perspective on the potential contributions of Open Government. Whatever the term used to describe the use of ICT in administration and government, it is certain that the spread of the Internet, "smart" phones, as well as tools such as Facebook, Twitter, YouTube, Wikipedia, has an impact on the industrialized society. It is not appropriate to make a sociological analysis here, some authors such as [5] note the gap between the technology used day to day by citizens and public policy.

Before moving on to more concrete examples and in an attempt to reconcile the perspectives presented above, let us consider the work of [19] who argue that the government 2.0, transparency, collaboration and participation are only means to serve a larger purpose, public utility. These authors consider in fact these means as "utility generators", just like efficiency or effectiveness. They also offer six measures of public utility, in terms of financial, political, social, strategic, and ideological impact, on public opinion in matters of trust and legitimacy.

This discussion of the relationship between information technology and communication, transparency and the state, was to enable the reader to understand the issues and challenges faced by a proactive approach to the provision of information, in particular as regards the contribution to the public good and the gap between technology and public policy. The following section illustrates them in a more concrete way.

3 Open Data

According to [26], the "Open Data" movement was born in the mid-1990s in the North American academic world. The basic idea was that researchers share their experimental data. It was taken up again in 2003 by the creators of the Open Knowledge Foundation and in 2006 by those of the Open Data Foundation. These associations promote the use of standardized metadata and interchange formats, to maximize the potential of reuse of these open data.

Both the Open Knowledge Foundation and the Open Data Foundation have defined criteria, respectively eleven [27] and eight [28] to check whether data are considered open and free for use. These criteria are well documented on the websites listed above and it does not seem appropriate to list and describe them here, but it is particularly necessary that the data are complete, raw, recent, accessible, usable, and available in non-proprietary formats. Producers of open data are mainly public administrations, companies with a public-service mission and researchers, while "reusers" can equally be citizens or associations, other public services or supervisory authorities, press or economic actors [26]. These authors also cite a figure of 3.7 billion euros for the information market in France, a market of which 60% would consist of public data. Their report also describes several examples of reuse of data at national and regional levels.

Beyond difficulties to measure economic aspects, [29] believes that "these data are a tremendous resource that could be of much wider benefit to the citizens who financed their production." However, he notes that "most of the time they are at best offered for sale or made available to some actors under less than transparent conditions, and most often they are not shared at all." With this in mind, he proposes the "release of data", which "constitute a common good". By the release of data, [29] means "to give them, in the hands of private parties, a purpose other than the public service mission for which they were originally produced." In his report, he lists data that can be released by an administration, of which here is a brief selection given as an illustration: measurements of pollution or traffic; land register and water networks, energy, transport; statistics; archival data and documentary holdings; bills; investigations; deliberations; subsidies.

Several major competitions were organized to promote the emergence of new uses, in particular The Open Data Challenge [30]. This European competition, with a prize of 20,000 euros and open to participants for 60 days between April and June 2011, attracted 430 contributions from 24 Member States Among the winners are notably:

- "Nomen est Nomen" from Finland, which gives access to all the entries of the public information databases concerning a surname.
- "European Union Dashboard" which shows how the Member States contribute to, and profit from, the common public policies.
- "ZNasichDani" which lists the people who hide behind the companies that obtain public contracts in Slovakia (including the politicians).
- "Mapping Europe's Carbon Dioxide Emissions": all is in the name.
- "Bike Share Map" which posts the state of the systems of bicycles in self-service in 30 towns of Europe and of the world.
- "Evolution of European Union Legislation" which makes it possible to visualize the activity about public policies through time, by field and topic.

Examples of use of open data abound and evolve too quickly for it to be relevant to list more in this section. The Apps for Democracy site gives an order of magnitude of the potential of these ideas and these new uses, certainly to be considered prudently: [31] said it had received 47 Web, iPhone and Facebook applications in 30 days, for an estimated value of $ 2.3 million in exchange for $ 50,000 distributed in prizes

At first sight the use of the open data thus appears very promising, but there remain many prerequisites to be set up before being able to exploit this potential fully. [32] point out that these data were defined and collected in very different contexts, for specific operational objectives. They thus do not have the same characteristics, in particular with regard to the temporal framework. As they were not created in anticipation of purposes other than those originally intended, it is common that they do not contain contextual information, i.e. metadata. Another important criticism raised by [32] is that no mechanism for feedback or improvement is envisaged. Thus a "reuser" of data who finds errors or has updated data generally has no automated way to return this information to the producer of the original data. [32] even mention the case where end users have corrected the data and where errors would be reintroduced during updates "at source". They conclude their case study on data from the land records of the State of New York with an emphasis on the need to implement data management processes, in particular metadata creation and updating, in order to fully benefit from these open data. [9] accentuate this point when they write that the new relations between data producers and intermediaries "cannot be built solely on the basis of data exchange between the stakeholders."

A quick review of a classification system of open data based on assigning one to five stars, like hotels, allows us to conclude this section on a note of pragmatism. For each level, the page Linked Open Data Star Scheme by Example [33] shows the minimum requirements, examples, as well as the costs and benefits for users and producers. Thus, the award of two stars requires the provision of data in a structured but proprietary form (e.g. Excel) and without metadata, allowing users to process this data and export it to other formats, while the effort is minimal for the producer because he just released an existing file. To get the maximum score of five stars, the data should be structured, under a free license and in a non-proprietary format, with a unique identifier that allows easy retrieval and metadata describing the context of use. For users, the main benefit is the ability to create a data network, and thus discover relevant new data, whereas producers must invest resources to identify and contextualize data to facilitate discovery. In return for this effort, they increase the intrinsic value of their own data.

4 Proactive Transparency

This article is devoted mainly to the study of the proactive provision of information, with a focus on the transformations that this approach might induce in the public sector. The main findings about the impact of information technology and communication on transparency focus on the "direction" of transparency, the context and nature of the data, as well as the emergence of new intermediaries. Moreover, the expectations for ICTs and transparency are very varied: some want to draw inspiration from the world of open source, others believe in their potential to strengthen democracy, still others see them as a tool for improving performance. The fact of considering both transparency and ICT as a means among others, to use in order to achieve a higher goal (the public interest), can reconcile these expectations. Thus, the most enthusiastic, such as [29], see clearly an objective of public interest in data openness. However, the potential of ICT is partially limited by barriers, including traditional problems of access and skills, as well as the gap between technology on the one hand, and public policy and administrative practices on the other. Furthermore, [32] emphasize the need to establish mechanisms for feedback, and thus reintroduce bidirectional transparency, and the importance of contextual data or metadata. Finally, examples of the use of open data clearly show the emergence of new intermediaries, with public authorities willing to organize competitions with cash prizes to support innovative ideas. Some results of the Open Data Challenge competition [30] further illustrate how certain expectations can be met: "ZNasichDani" brings into the open the links between politicians and public procurement; "European Union Dashboard" is a typical example of an approach oriented towards performance management; "Evolution of European Union Legislation" aims to provide better information to citizens; and "Bike Share Map" is a composite application, or "mash-up", which is based on values from the open-source world (collaboration, sharing, reuse). The conclusion to draw is certainly that more information from the public sector is available via the Internet, thus contributing to proactive transparency, but that a number of prerequisites are to be put in place before being able to profit from it fully. The solutions necessary to the implementation of these prerequisites exist, both at technical and managerial levels. However, they require additional resources on the part of public administrations, and these requirements are potentially conflicting in relation to those of the core business of a department or office. Note that these requirements are not necessarily just financial, they can also include skills, such as information management [32].

Figure 1 shows the different dimensions discussed in this article in the form of an overview diagram. To measure the impacts of transparency, and more particularly of the proactive provision of information, it is necessary:

- to take a position in relation to the perspective adopted, for example using the typology of [25] discussed in Sect. 2;
- to decide on objectives to be achieved or expectations: the concept of generator of public interest of [19] may be used;
- to think in terms of prerequisites to implement or barriers to remove: the work of [7] provides very interesting theoretical avenues in terms of mediated transparency, while [32] have a more practical approach to information management; the Open Data Foundation provides in addition very specific recommendations about data openness.

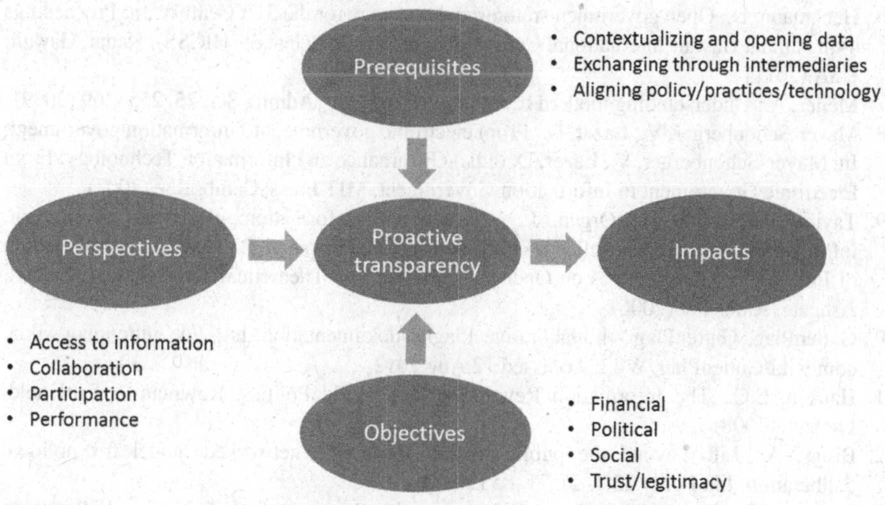

Fig. 1. An integrated vision of proactive transparency

The above works are given as reference or source of inspiration; anyone is free to adjust the dimensions of the model depending on context or needs.

5 Conclusion

In this paper we discussed transparency and various underlying concepts, particularly the idea of proactive transparency. We used these concepts to analyse the potential contributions of Open Data to proactive transparency. Finally we proposed an integrated vision of this proactive transparency that we believe could be used in different context to analyse the potential contributions of Open Data to transparency for public administrations.

References

1. Pasquier, M., Villeneuve, J.: Organizational barriers to transparency: a typology and analysis of organizational behaviour tending to prevent or restrict access to information. Int. Rev. Adm. Sci. **73**, 147–162 (2007)
2. Kierkegaard, S.: Open access to public documents—more secrecy, less transparency! Comput. Law Secur. Rev. **25**(1), 3–27 (2009)
3. Holsen, S., Pasquier, M.: What's wrong with this picture? The case of access to information requests in two continental federal states—Germany and Switzerland. Public Policy Adm. **27**(4), 283–302 (2012)
4. Piotrowski, S.J.: Governmental Transparency in the Path of Administrative Reform. SUNY Press, New York (2007)
5. Bertot, J.C., Jaeger, P.T., Grimes, J.: Using ICTs to create a culture of transparency: E-government and social media as openness and anti-corruption tools for societies. Gov. Inf. Q. **27**(3), 264–271 (2010)
6. Heckmann, D.: Open government-retooling democracy for the 21st Century. In: Proceedings 44th Annual Hawaii International Conference on System Sciences (HICSS), Kauai, Hawaii, USA (2011)
7. Meijer, A.: Understanding modern transparency. Int. Rev. Admin. Sci. **75**, 255–269 (2009)
8. Mayer-Schönberger, V., Lazer, D.: From electronic government to information government. In: Mayer-Schönberger, V., Lazer, D. (eds.) Governance and Information Technology: From Electronic Government to Information Government. MIT Press, Cambridge (2007)
9. Taylor, J.A., Lips, M., Organ, J.: Freedom with information: electronic government, information intensity and challenges to citizenship. In: Chapman, R., Hun, M. (eds.) Freedom of Information: Perspectives on Open Government in a Theoretical and Practical Context. Ashgate, Aldershot (2006)
10. GuttenPlag, GuttenPlag - kollaborative Plagiatsdokumentation. http://de.guttenplag.wikia.com/wiki/GuttenPlag_Wiki. Accessed 12 Aug 2012
11. Hanson, E.C.: The Information Revolution and World Politics. Rowman & Littlefield, Lanham (2008)
12. Bruns, A.: Life beyond the public sphere: towards a networked model for political deliberation. Inf. Polity **13**(1–2), 71–85 (2008)
13. Huyges, F.B.: Facebook, Twitter, Al-Jazeera et le "Printemps arabe", Institut de Relations Internationales et Stratégiques. http://www.iris-france.org/docs/kfm_docs/docs/2011-04-04-facebook-twitter-al-jazeera-et-le-printemps-arabe.pdf (2011). Accessed 12 Aug 2012
14. Reporters Without Borders, Blogger Released from Prison but Placed under Residential Surveillance. http://en.rsf.org/chine-jailed-human-rights-lawyer-allowed-29-03-2012,39918.html (2011). Accessed 12 Aug 2012
15. Faris, R., Wang, S., Palfrey, J.: Censorship 2.0. Innov. Technol. Gov. Glob. **3**, 165–167 (2008)
16. Williams, C.: How Egypt Shut Down the Internet, The Telegraph, 1 Jan 2011
17. Wimmer, M., Tambouris, E.: Online one-stop government. In: Traunmüller, R. (ed.) Information Systems: A Working Framework and Requirement. IJIP, vol. 95, pp. 117–130. Springer, Boston (2002). doi:10.1007/978-0-387-35604-4_9

18. Bertot, J.C., Jaeger, P.T., McClure, C.R.: Citizen-centered E-government services: benefits, costs, and research needs. In: Proceedings 9th Annual International Digital Government Research Conference (dg.o), Montreal (2008)
19. Harrison, T.M., Burke, G.B., Cook, M., Cresswell, A., Helbig, N., Hrdinová, J., Pardo, T.: Open government and E-government: democratic challenges from a public value perspective. In: Proceedings 12th Annual International Digital Government Research Conference (dg.o), College Park (2011)
20. Nam, T.: New ends, new means, but old attitudes: citizens' views on open government and government 2.0. In: Proceedings 44th Annual Hawaii International Conference on System Sciences (HICSS), Kauai, Hawaii (2011)
21. O'Reilly, T.: What Is Web 2.0—Design Patterns and Business Models for the Next Generation of Software. http://oreilly.com/web2/archive/what-is-web-20.html (2005). Accessed 12 Aug 2012
22. Zajicek, M.: Web 2.0: Hype or happiness?. In: Proceedings International Cross-Disciplinary Conference on Web Accessibility (W4A) (2007)
23. Obama, B.: Transparency and Open Government. http://www.whitehouse.gov/the_press_office/TransparencyandOpenGovernment/ (2009). Accessed 12 Aug 2012
24. Office of Management and Budget, Open Government Directive, Executive Office of the President. http://www.whitehouse.gov/sites/default/files/omb/assets/memoranda_2010/m10-06.pdf (2009). Accessed 12 August 2012
25. Linders, D., Copeland Wilson, S.: What is open government ? One year after the directive. In: Proceedings 12th Annual International Digital Government Research Conference (dg.o), College Park (2011)
26. Lacombe, R., Bertin, P.-H., Vauglin, F., Vieillefosse, A.: Pour une politique ambitieuse des données publiques (2011). http://www.scribd.com/doc/59939293/Pour-une-politique-ambitieuse-des-donnees-publiques-Ecole-des-Ponts-ParisTech-Rapport-Donnees-Publiques-2011. Accessed 12 Aug 2012
27. Open Knowledge Foundation, Defining the Open in Open Data, Open Content and Open Services (2011). http://opendefinition.org/okd/. Accessed 12 Aug 2012
28. Open Government Data Foundation, 8 Principles of Open Government Data (2007). http://www.opendatafoundation.org/. Accessed 12 Aug 2012
29. Genoud, P.: Opening of the public data: an opportunity for Geneva. http://www.slideshare.net/patgen/ouverture-des-donnes-publiques-une-opportunit-pour-genve (2011). Accessed 12 August 2012
30. Gray, J., Meller, P.: The Open Data Challenge. http://opendatachallenge.org/ (2011). Accessed 12 August 2012
31. Kundra, V.: Apps for Democracy. http://www.appsfordemocracy.org/ (2009). Accessed 12 August 2012
32. Dawes, S.S., Helbig, N.: Information strategies for open government: challenges and prospects for deriving public value from government transparency. In: Wimmer, M.A., Chappelet, J.-L., Janssen, M., Scholl, H.J. (eds.) EGOV 2010. LNCS, vol. 6228, pp. 50–60. Springer, Heidelberg (2010). doi:10.1007/978-3-642-14799-9_5
33. Linked Data Research Center Laboratory, Linked Open Data Star Scheme by Example. http://lab.linkeddata.deri.ie/2010/star-scheme-by-example/ (2010)

Trusting and Adopting E-Government Services in Developing Countries? Privacy Concerns and Practices in Rwanda

Chantal Mutimukwe(✉), Ella Kolkowska, and Åke Grönlund

School of Business, Örebro University, Fakultetsgatan 1, 701 82 Örebro, Sweden
Chantal.Mutimukwe@oru.se

Abstract. E-government is a strong focus in many developing countries. While services can technically benefit from solutions developed elsewhere, organizational development and user trust and acceptance are always local. In Least Developed Countries (LDCs) such issues become more dramatic as services are transformed quickly from traditional manual procedures to digitized ones copying models from developed countries. One of the most critical trust issues is privacy protection; e-government services must be developed in balance with citizens' privacy views.

To understand how to design trusted services in an LDC this study investigates information privacy concerns, perceptions of privacy practices, trust beliefs and behavior intentions towards using e-government services in Rwanda. The study was conducted by means of a survey (n = 540).

A majority of the respondents had a considerable level of trust, and a positive view of the effectiveness of service providers' privacy practices. Most respondents expressed positive intentions towards using e-government services. Still, a majority of the respondents expressed considerable privacy concerns. Men were more concerned than women and reported a higher reluctance to use e-government service. As this study is one of the few studies of privacy, trust and adoption of e-government in LDC, it contributes to broadening the context in which such issues have been researched.

Keywords: E-government · Privacy · Trust · Behavior intentions · Rwanda

1 Introduction

As many developing countries, including LDCs (Least Developed Countries), now move ambitiously towards developing e-government they can technically build on more than two decades of developments in the industrialized world. The required technology is readily available, affordable, and to a large extent standardized, and can hence quickly be installed. Users in developing countries, including LDCs, are rapidly becoming comfortable with the digital world, perhaps most immediately through the rapid uptake of smart phones and social media.

While technology is universal, the organizational development and user acceptance necessary to achieve the benefits of e-government are always local [1]. They both rest on local practices, customs, and views developed over long time, and are hence difficult to change quickly; "all business is local" – even the global ones, as for

M. Janssen et al. (Eds.): EGOV 2017, LNCS 10428, pp. 324–335, 2017.
DOI: 10.1007/978-3-319-64677-0_27

example Google has learned from the discussions about use of user data which have occurred in many countries.

Information privacy, typically defined as the individuals' ability to control information about themselves [2], is one of the major factors affecting the development of e-government services [3, 4]. Government organizations' practices in collecting, handling, and disseminating citizens/users personal information are important for preserving privacy, and these procedures need to be known and trusted by citizens [5]. People need assurance from service providers that their personal information is not changed, disclosed, deleted or misused in any way. Therefore, government organizations require to adopt adequate privacy practices in order to assure users' privacy protection.

But even if privacy practices are adopted, there is no way citizens can themselves inspect how data is handled in any depth, so they must trust the organization and the procedures involved. Trust is therefore a critical issue for sharing personal information in the context of online services [6] and is considered as one of the major factors influencing users' adoption of e-services [4]. Trust is defined as "the willingness of a party to be vulnerable to the actions of another party based on the expectation that the other will perform a particular action important to the trustor, irrespective of the ability to monitor or control that other party" [7]. Earlier studies show that trust affects users' adoption of e-government services [8]. Adoption of e-services is usually studied by assessing the users' behavior intentions into using these services [9].

Impact of privacy issues on trust and adoption of e-government have been considered in a substantial amount of the research literature, but even though e-government is now rapidly growing in developing countries and LDCs, these countries are yet under-researched [10, 11]. There are many reasons to try to bridge that research gap. Previous studies show that privacy issues vary from country to country due to many factors such as differences in culture, regulation, laws and technical arrangements [12]. A literature review by Nkohkwo and Islam suggests that for successful implementation of e-government in LDCs it is very important to understand privacy issues in these countries as privacy is among the major challenges to e-government implementation in Sub-Saharan countries [13].

This paper takes one step in that direction by presenting a study from Rwanda, an LDC in Eastern Africa with high ambitions for not just e-government but generally for IT and moving into the information society, and with a good development record for the past two decades [14]. The study asks (1) *what are Rwanda citizens' concerns about information privacy*? (2) *What are their perceptions of effectiveness of privacy practices?* (3) *to what extent do they trust the ways in which government organizations handle their personal information*, and (4) *What are their behavior intentions towards using e-government services*?

2 Privacy Concerns, Privacy Practices, Trust and Acceptance in E-Government

In the literature, the concept of privacy concerns is conceptualized in various forms and assigned different meanings. A commonly used definition is "beliefs about who has access to information disclosed when using internet and how it is used" [15].

Many studies have investigated the impact of privacy concerns on trust and adoption of e-government services. For example, Cullen and Reilly [16] investigated New Zealanders' concerns in relation to information privacy and the impact of these concerns on the trust they place in government. The study found that most respondents had low levels of confidence in the privacy of online communication but still used it for convenience. They also had greater confidence in government than in commercial organizations. In another study Cullen investigated Japanese's information privacy concerns found considerable differences compared to the earlier New Zealand study. The Japanese had major concerns about information privacy and had considerably less trust in government than the New Zealanders [17].

Choudrie, Raza, and Olla investigated the relationships between privacy, trust and adoption of e-government in the UK and found that respondents who were concerned about their information privacy reported significantly less intention to use e-government services than those who were less concerned [18]. Sarabdeen, Rodrigues, & Balasubramanian investigated the impact of privacy and security concerns on e-government adoption in Dubai and found that security and privacy concerns were important factors influencing e-government adoption [19]. Similarly, Abri, Mcgill, and Dixon investigated the impact of privacy concerns on Omani citizens' intentions to use e-government services [8]. Their findings indicate that people with high privacy concerns have low perceptions of trust in e-government services and low intention to use them. Another empirical study conducted in Jordan investigates the antecedents of trust in the context of e-government [20]. The study shows that numerous factors such as privacy concerns, information quality, trust in technology and trust in government affect trust in e-government. All in all, the literature strongly indicates that privacy concerns are antecedents for trust and as well as adoption of e-government services.

In the information system literature indicated that possible consequences of privacy concerns mentioned include for instance lack of trust and/or weak intentions to use online service [21].

To reduce privacy concerns, organizations need to provide privacy assurances, which can also increase trust and intentions to use e-services. Organizational privacy assurance are the practices that an organization applies to ensure service users that enough effort has been devoted to protect personal information [22]. Studies of e-government privacy practices focus on checking the availability of privacy policies on e-government websites, assessing the comprehensibility and clarity of the available privacy policies and investigating users' level of awareness of privacy policies [23, 24]. Most studies conclude that an effective privacy policy reduces users' lack of trust in e-government and unwillingness to use e-government services. The present study investigates service users' perceptions of the effectiveness of privacy policies and organization's privacy self-regulation. According to Culnan & Bies, privacy policy and self-regulation are two common types of practices that an organization can apply [25].

It is generally agreed in the literature that privacy concerns and privacy protection practices within e-services are both important for citizen/user trust and their intentions to adopt and use those e-services. However, research is inconclusive about the influence of various personal factors such as age, gender, personal experience, and level of technical skills. Some studies have suggested that younger people are less concerned with information privacy issues than older [26]. Other studies have shown that young people's privacy concerns in online environments do not differ from those of older people [27]. Some studies have found that women are more concerned about privacy of their personal information than men [28] but there are also other studies indicate that men expressed a higher level of concerns regarding privacy than women [29]. There are also studies that show that people who are employed in government trust government more than people who work in the private sector, and vice versa [30].

One reason that research is inconclusive on factors like age and gender might be that they come out differently in different countries or cultures. For example, gender issues and age are very differently viewed in Asian and European cultures. While such factors are likely situated it still makes sense to include them in studies as they potentially have great influence over local development.

3 E-Government and Information Privacy in Rwanda

Rwanda is a small (26,388 km2) and landlocked country located in East Africa, with an estimated population of 11,609,666 and GDP per capita of 697.3 USD (World Bank, 2015). The Rwandan economy is based largely on agricultural production with 80% of the population engaged in (mainly subsistence) agriculture [31]. Striving for poverty reduction, the government of Rwanda formulated the Vision 2020 policy, whose over-arching aim is to transform the country into a knowledge based, middle income society and modernize agriculture [32]. Rwanda identified advancing science, technology and ICT as an approach to achieve this vision. It therefore facilitates the creation of technology enterprises and develop access to ICT within government, in accordance with the national ICT plan, called NICI, National Information and Communication Infrastructure. The first NICI plan was launched in 2000, and so far there have been four phases of the NICI plan, each covering 5 years.

The Government of Rwanda have initiated e-government projects since 2005. The main goal is to facilitate government service delivery to citizens and businesses and bring people close to Government through the use of ICT [33]. So far, notable progress has been achieved and e-government is changing the service delivery schemes. Many initiatives including the launch of the "Irembo" portal to e-government services are deployed. Irembo is a big e-government portal currently providing access to 40 e-services from 6 different government agencies [34]. Rwandans can access Irembo services online or via smartphone.

As in other LDCs, infrastructure challenges including insufficient network access and power supply hamper use of e-government services. Rwanda puts a lot of effort in overcoming that, and significant developments have taken place. For example, national fiber optic backbone network has been completed and is available in all 30 districts [35]. As of December 2015, Rwanda had 33.5% internet penetration rate, and 77.8% mobile phone penetration rate [36].

Interaction between citizens and e-government services also requires a legal infrastructure to cater for, among other things, information security and privacy. The government has enacted laws to govern electronic messages, electronic signatures, transactions, data protection, cyber-security and ICT usage.

A Rwanda cyber security policy has been established, a security infrastructure is established and security applications are deployed in government offices. A cyber security capacity building project is initiated so as to keep on pace with the ongoing development in the field [35].

Concerning privacy, the Rwanda Constitution Article 22 ensures the protection and respect of the rights to privacy [37]. Besides that, other laws have been established to protect individuals' right to privacy in the context of digital information, for example; law no 02/2013 regulating media (article 9); law no 03/2013 regulating access to information (article 4); law no 60/2013 regulating the interception of communication [37]. This regulation has been established during the time of e-government and is hence generally designed to cover also the digitized world.

The existing e-government services and the supporting privacy laws and policies are newly established and represent a new phenomenon to Rwandans. It is of great importance to learn how Rwandans are adopting them.

4 Method

The aim of this study is to investigate to Rwandans' privacy concerns, their perceptions of the effectiveness of privacy practices, their trust in the way the e-government services use personal information, and their intentions to use e-government services.

The study is conducted by means of a questionnaire based on five constructs adapted from the previous literature: privacy concerns [22], perceived effectiveness of privacy policy [22], perceived effectiveness of organizations self-regulations [22], trust beliefs [38] and behavior intentions [9]. Statements for each of the constructs are shown in the Results section. All items are measured on seven-point, Likert-type scale where 1 = strongly disagree, 2 = mostly disagree, 3 = slightly disagree, 4 = neutral, 5 = slightly agree, 6 = mostly agree, and 7 = strongly agree.

The questionnaires were distributed to 700 individuals. 604 were returned and 540 could eventually be used, which yields a response rate of 77%. For data collection, an intercept approach was adopted by visiting shops, public servants organizations, private companies, churches, banks and universities from selected interview sites to achieve a high response rate. Five sites were chosen; City of Kigali, the capital; the Huye district of the Southern Province; the Musanze district of the Northern Province; the Rubavu district of the Western province, and Nyagatare City of the Eastern Province. These sites were chosen so as to provide geographic diversity and generalizability of the sample to the entire country. The survey was conducted during three months from June to September 2016.

In terms of demographic characteristics, the sample is fairly representative for Rwanda as concerns age and geographic distribution (Table 1). However, there is a considerable bias towards well educated people. One reason for these biases is that it is well-educated people in the cities people who mainly use electronic services, and views on services have to be collected among people who actually use them. Men are also overrepresented.

Data was analyzed using descriptive statistics. By displaying mean and standard deviation of the statements, the respondents' level of concerns, perceptions of

Table 1. Respondents demographic

Demographic variables	Category	Frequency(Percentage)
Gender	Men	330 (60.3%)
	Women	217 (39.7%)
Age	18–30	248 (45.3%)
	31–45	215 (39.3%)
	46–55	71 (13%)
	>55	13 (2.4%)
Occupation	Government staff	92 (16.8%)
	Private organization staff	167 (30.5%)
	Students	127 (23.2%)
	Businessman	138 (25.2%)
	Unemployed/retired	23 (4.2%)
Education level	Training/instructions	8 (1.5%)
	Primary school	35 (6.4%)
	Secondary school	79 (14.4%)
	University degree	425 (77.7%)

effectiveness of privacy practices, trust beliefs and behavior intentions were recognized. Furthermore pairwise correlation tests were done in order to see the effect of demographic factors (gender, age, occupation). The software used for data analysis was STATA.

5 Results

This section presents the results from the study organized by the four research questions.

5.1 What are Rwanda Citizens' Concerns About Information Privacy?

The privacy concerns construct is composed of four statements (Table 2). Respondents are concerned about their information privacy. The majority of the respondents answered "slightly agree" for PCON2, PCON3 and PCON4 and by "mostly agree" for PCON1. Means for all statements are above 4.50 and their standards deviations are between 1.59 and 1.80. The correlation test between privacy concerns and different respondents' demographic factors (gender, occupation and age) indicated that there is a significant correlation between gender and privacy concerns. Men's level of concern is higher than that of women; the mean for men are between 4.67 and 4.80 for the four items, and between 4.40 and 4.51 for women.

5.2 What are Rwanda Citizens' Perceptions of Effectiveness of Privacy Practices?

The perceived effectiveness of privacy practices is examined through two constructs; perceived effectiveness of privacy policies (POLICY) and perceived effectiveness of organizational self-regulation (SREG). As Table 3 shows, respondents' perception of effectiveness of privacy practices is generally high with a mean of 4.99 for POLICY and 4.95 for SREG. A majority of the respondents answered "strongly agree" for POLICY1, POLICY3 and SREG1. Similarly, a majority answered "mostly agree" for POLICY 2 and SREG 2. Means for all statements are between 4.92 and 5.18, with a standard deviation between 1.67 and 1.71. The correlation test indicate that there is no correlation between perceptions of effectiveness of privacy practices constructs and respondents demographics factors (gender, age, occupation).

Table 2. Privacy concerns.

Privacy Concerns (PCON): Mean = 4.60, Std. Deviation = 1.21
PCON1: I am concerned that the information I submit could be misused
PCON2: I am concerned that others can find private information about me
PCON3: I am concerned about providing personal information because of what others might do with it
PCON4: I am concerned about providing personal information because it could be used in a way I did not foresee

Table 3. Perceived effectiveness of privacy practices.

Perceived effectiveness of privacy policy (POLICY): Mean = 4.99, Std. Deviation = 1.33
POLICY1: I feel confident that privacy statements from service providers reflect their commitments to protect my personal information
POLICY2: With their privacy statements, I believe that my personal information will be kept private and confidential
POLICY3: I believe that privacy statements are an effective way to demonstrate their commitments to privacy
Perceived effectiveness of privacy self-regulation (SREG): Mean = 4.95, Std. Deviation = 1.39
SREG1: I believe that privacy related regulations will impose sanctions for service providers' noncompliance with privacy policy
SREG2: Privacy related regulation will stand by me if my personal information is misused during and after transactions

5.3 To What Extent Do Rwanda Citizens Trust the Way Government Organizations Handle Their Personal Information in E-services?

The citizens' trust in the way government organizations handle their personal information is examined though the trust belief construct which is composed of 5 statements. Table 4 shows that respondents to some extent trust the way the e-government service

Table 4. Trust beliefs.

Trust Beliefs (TRUST): Mean: 4.56, Std. Deviation = 1.28
TRUST1: E-service providers are trustworthy in handling personal information
TRUST2: I trust that e-service providers tell the truth and fulfill promises related to my personal information
TRUST3: I trust that e-service providers keep my best interests in mind when dealing with personal information
TRUST4: I trust that e-service providers are in general predictable and consistent regarding the usage of personal information
TRUST5: I trust that e-service providers are always honest with customers when it comes to using (the information) that I would provide

providers treat their personal information. The majority of the respondents answered "slightly agree" on four of the statements and were neutral to TRUST4. The means for the statements vary from 4.35 to 4.71, with a standard deviation between 1.52 and 1.80. Correlation test indicates that respondents trust beliefs do not correlate with any of their gender, age or occupation.

5.4 What Are Rwanda Citizens' Behavior Intentions Towards Using E-government Service?

The construct 'behavior intention' is composed of four statements. As Table 5 shows, a minority of respondents had refused to give their personal information or to use e-service due to the concerns of their personal information. The majority answered "strongly disagree" for all statements. The means for all the four statements are below 3.50 and the standards deviations are between 1.65 and 1.87, which is rather high. The correlation test indicates a significant correlation between respondents' behavior intentions and their gender – men are more prone to refuse to provide information than women.

Table 5. Behavior intentions

Behavior intentions (BEHAV): Mean = 2.77, Std. Deviation = 1.27
BEHAV1: I decide not to use e-service because I don't want to provide certain kind of my personal information
BEHAV2: I refuse to give personal information
BEHAV3: I refuse to use e-service because I disagree with the way e-service providers use personal information
BEHAV4: I take action to have my name removed from direct mail list

6 Discussion and Conclusion

This paper set out to investigate Rwandans' concerns about information privacy, their perceptions of effectiveness of privacy practices, the extent to which they trust the way government organizations handle their personal information, and their intentions to use e-government services.

Overall, Rwandans mainly perceive e-government privacy practices as effective, and they trust the way governmental organizations handle their personal information. They are not inclined to refuse using e-government services although their privacy concerns are rather high.

Regarding trust, the majority answered "slightly agree" for four out of five statements. This indicates that Rwanda citizens have a certain level of trust. However, they were "neutral" to the statement "I trust that e-service providers in general are predictable and consistent regarding the usage of personal information". This may indicate that trust varies across different organization so each service provider needs to show users that they have trustworthy procedures. This appears as a critical factor in previous studies where citizens trust in e-government is found to be a primary input of transactional usage [4].

Regarding behavior intentions, only a minority of respondents were negative towards using e-government services and report they may refuse to provide personal information. Even though only a minority holds these views they must be taken into consideration as provision of personal information to government organizations is sometimes compulsory [16]. Even though such requests for personal information are supported by governmental mandates [39], it is important to take measures to assure service users that personal information is in fact handled correctly from the point of view of privacy.

Rwandans are concerned about their information privacy – the respondents answered "slightly agree" or "mostly agree" for all of the privacy concerns statements. This is a critical issue as the privacy literature recognizes privacy issues as one of the biggest barriers to a successful e-government development [3, 4]. Even though the results suggest that users trust that privacy practices are effective, measures need to be taken in order to overcome their concerns. This study found that privacy concerns correlate significantly with gender and that men are more concerned than women.

In Rwanda, there is a quite comprehensive e-government initiative aimed at improving the integration of government information and services to business and citizens [24]. In order to sustain this initiative, government organizations must find ways to build relationships with people within the new environment of e-government and work to increase citizens' trust.

In sum, this study results suggest that e-government in Rwanda has a good potential. Citizens trust e-government services and have positive intentions towards using them. However, they also have considerable concerns about information privacy, and overcoming these is one important issue. Some measures toward that end have already been practiced successfully elsewhere; it is, for example, common practice in both e-government and e-commerce to provide adequate privacy practices and explain how personal information that is requested is processed and stored. Obviously it is not enough to provide good practices, these also has to be effectively communicated to service users.

Governments in developing countries, including Rwanda, are increasingly adopting e-government and this study contributes to this work by assisting e-government project leaders, policy makers, and private sector organizations involved in developing e-government services in obtaining a better understanding of citizens privacy concerns, trust and adoption. For academics, this research provides an extended empirical base concerning privacy issues by investigating the situation in a least developed country. The limitations of this research includes a considerable bias towards well educated people in the sample. While this is unavoidable in a country where use of electronic services is yet limited to such groups, future research should investigate the views of other groups as they start using such services. Another complementary study would be using focus groups or individual interviews to investigate more in depth the reasoning and perspectives of Rwandans toward e-government services.

References

1. Grönlund, Å., Horan, T.A.: Introducing e-gov: history, definitions, and issues. Commun. Assoc. Inf. Syst. **15**(39), 713–729 (2005)
2. Westin, F.: Privacy and freedom. Atheneum, New York (1967)
3. Fedorowicz, J., Gogan, J.L., Culnan, M.J.: Barriers to interorganizational information sharing in e-government: a Stakeholder analysis. Inf. Soc. **26**(5), 315–329 (2010)
4. Park, R.: Measuring factors that influence the success of e-government initiatives. In: Proceedings of the 41st Hawaii International Conference on System Sciences (HICSS-41). IEEE Computer Society Conference Publishing Services, Waikoloa, Big Island, Hawaii, p. 218 (1–10) (2008)
5. Carter, L., McBride, A.: Information privacy concerns and e-government: a research agenda. Transform. Gov. People Process Policy **4**(1), 10–13 (2010)
6. Liu, C., Marchewka, J., Lu, J., Yu, C.-S.: Beyond cocnern a privacy-trust-behavior intention model of electronic commerce. Inf. Manag. **24**(2), 289–304 (2005)
7. Mayer, R.C., Davis, J.H., Shoorman, F.D.: An integrative model of organizational trust. Acad. Manag. Rev. **20**(3), 709–734 (1995)
8. Abri, D., Mcgill, T., Dixon, M.: Examining the impact of E-privacy risk concerns on citizens' intentions to use E-government services: an oman perspective. J. Inf. Priv. Secur. **5**(2), 3–26 (2009)
9. Stewart, K.A., Segars, A.H., Albert, H.: Examination empirical for information privacy of the concern instrument. Inf. Syst. Res. **13**(1), 36–49 (2002)
10. Makulilo, A.B.: Privacy and data protection in Africa: a state of the art. Int. Data Priv. Law **2**(3), 163–178 (2012)
11. Bélanger, F., Crossler, R.E.: Privacy in the digital age: a review of information privacy research in information system. **35**(4), 1–36 (2011)
12. Almagwashi, H., Gray, A.: Citizens' perception towards preserving privacy in e-government services : a cross-sectional study (2014)
13. Nkohkwo, Q.N., Islam, M.S.: Challenges to the successful implementation of e-government initiatives in sub-Saharan Africa: a literature review. Electron. J. e-Gov. **11**(2), 253–267 (2013)

14. UNPAN: Rwanda: Citizens Commend E-Government Services. http://www.unpan.org/Library/MajorPublications/UNEGovernmentSurvey/PublicEGovernanceSurveyintheNews/tabid/651/mctl/ArticleView/ModuleId/1555/articleId/50072/Rwanda-Citizens-Commend-EGovernment-Services.aspx (2016)
15. Dinev, T., Hart, P.: An extended privacy calculus transactions model for e-commerce transactions. Inf. Syst. Res. **17**(1), 61–80 (2006)
16. Cullen, R.C.R., Reilly, P.R.P.: Information privacy and trust in government: a citizen-based perspective from New Zealand. In: 2007 40th Annual Hawaii International Conference System Science, no. January 2007
17. Cullen, R.: Citizens' concerns about the privacy of personal information held by government: a comparative study, Japan and New Zealand. In: Proceedings of the 40th Annual Hawaii International Conference on System Science, pp. 1–10 (2008)
18. Choudrie, J., Raza, S., Olla, P.: Exploring the issues of security, privacy and trust in eGovernment: UK Citizens' perspective. In: 15th Americas Conference on Information Systems (AMCIS 2009), vol. Paper 347. pp. 1–9, AIS, San Francisco, CA (2009)
19. Sarabdeen, J., Rodrigues, G., Balasubramanian, S.: E-Government users' privacy and security concerns and availability of laws in Dubai. Int. Rev. Law Comput. Technol. **28**(3), 261–276 (2014)
20. Abu-Shanab, E.: Antecedents of trust in e-government services: an empirical test in Jordan. Transform. Gov. People Process Policy **8**(2), 283–308 (2014)
21. Hong, W., Thong, J.Y.L.: Internet privacy concerns: an integrated conceptualization and four empirical studies. MIS Q. **37**(1), 275–298 (2013)
22. Xu, H., Dinev, T., Smith, J., Hart, P.: Information privacy concerns: linking individual perceptions with institutional privacy assurances information privacy concerns: linking individual perceptions with institutional privacy assurances. J. Assoc. Inf. Syst. **12**(12), 798–824 (2011)
23. Al-Jamal, M., Abu-Shanab, E.: Privacy policy of e-government websites: an itemized checklist proposed and tested. Management Research and Practice http://U6-ctx_ver=Z39.88-2004&ctx_enc=info%3Aofi%2Fenc%3AUTF-8&rfr_id=info:sid/summon.serialssolutionscom&rft_val_fmt=info:ofi/fmt:kev:mtx:journal&rft.genre=article&rft.atitle=PRIVACY+POLICY+OF+E-GOVERNMENT+WEBSITES%3A+AN+IT, vol. 7, no. 3. Academia de Studii Economice din Bucuresti, Research Center in Public Administration and Public Management, Bucharest, p. 80 (2015)
24. Kuzma, J.: An examination of privacy policies of US Government Senate websites. Electron. Gov. Int. J. **7**(3), 270–280 (2010)
25. Culnan, M., Bies, J.: Consumer privacy: balancing economic and justice considerations. J. Soc. Issues **59**(2), 323–342 (2003)
26. Steijn, W.M.P., Vedder, A.: Privacy under Construction: a developmental perspective on privacy perception. Sci. Technol. Hum. Values **1**, 23 (2015)
27. Hoofnagle, C., King, J., Li, S., Turow, J.: How young adults differ from older adults when it comes to informatin privacy attitudes and policies (2010)
28. Sheehan, K.B., Hoy, M.G.: Flaming, complaining, abstaining: how online users respond to privacy concerns. J. Advert. **28**(3), 37–51 (1999)
29. Alasem, N.: Privacy and eGovernment in Saudi Arabia. World Congr. Eng. Comput. Sci. **II**, 21–24 (2015)
30. Christensen, T., Lægreid, P.: Trust in government: the relative importance of service satisfaction, political factors, and demography. Public Perform. Manag. Rev. **28**(4), 487–511 (2005)
31. World Bank: Agricultural Development in Rwanda (2013). http://www.worldbank.org/en/results/2013/01/23

32. Rwanda: Rwanda vision 2020. Revised in 2012, pp. 1–40 (2012)
33. N. I. I. Socio-economic: Government of Rwanda the Nici-2010 Plan, Development (2010)
34. RwandaOnline, Irembo. http://www.rwandaonline.rw/in-the-works.php (2015)
35. G. of Rwanda, National ICT Strategy and Plan NICI 2011- 2015 (2011)
36. Rwanda Utility and Regulatory Authority: Statistics and tariff information in Telecom Sector as of December 2015 (2015)
37. R. N. C. for Human: The Rights to privacy in the digital age (2013)
38. Malhotra, N.K., Kim, S.S., Agarwal, J.: Internet users' information privacy concerns (IUIPC): the construct, the scale, and a causal model. Inf. Syst. Res. **15**(4), 336–355 (2004)
39. BeVier, L.R.: Information about individuals in the hands of government: some reflections on mechanisms for privacy protection. William Mary Bill Rights J **4**, 455 (1995)

All Citizens are the Same, Aren't They? – Developing an E-government User Typology

Bettina Distel(✉) and Jörg Becker

University of Münster, Leonardo-Campus 3, 48149 Münster, Germany
{bettina.distel,joerg.becker}@ercis.uni-muenster.de

Abstract. Taking a closer look at current research on e-government diffusion shows that most studies or conceptual works deal with citizens as one broad mass that is not further described or divided into smaller subgroups. Such efforts are mainly limited to the digital divide discourse and distinguish at most between haves and have-nots or younger and older parts of the population. Understanding why and how citizens use public online services also requires an understanding of how different segments of the population react to IT in general as well as to e-government in particular. To date, no meaningful attempts to develop such an e-government user typology have been undertaken. Therefore, the study at hand aims at developing a user typology for the e-government context. To this end, we chose an explorative design and conducted a qualitative interview study in Germany in 2016 with 18 respondents from all age groups. We qualitatively analyzed the sample regarding usage behavior, variety of use, and e-government specific uses and perceptions. Our research reveals six user types differing in quality and quantity of use with regard to internet-based technologies in general and e-government services in particular. Understanding how different populations perceive e-government and contextualizing their behavior can help explaining why some citizens are making advanced use of e-government while others widely ignore these services.

Keywords: E-government · Usage · User typology · Citizens

1 Introduction

Although a plethora of electronic government (e-government) services have been available for many years now, most western countries are still facing low adoption rates, despite the fact that citizens are repeatedly referred to as a main stakeholder of e-government. Most current research focuses on 'the' citizen, i.e. treating the customers as a broad and rather undefined mass. There are only few exceptions to this approach and these studies typically focus on broad populations like elderly citizens [e.g. 10, 17]. Moreover, research tends to neglect the majority of citizens who are not using e-government services by not distinguishing between users and non-users [e.g. 9]. A common assumption in this context is that citizens expect their governments and administrations to provide their services electronically [e.g. 12], which is striking for two reasons. First,

M. Janssen et al. (Eds.): EGOV 2017, LNCS 10428, pp. 336–347, 2017.
DOI: 10.1007/978-3-319-64677-0_28

this assumption is highly normative and treats e-government as an undoubted necessity. Second, it views the citizens as a uniform and unspecified mass. This perspective suppresses the fact that 'the' citizen does not exist and that the population consists of a multitude of different groups with different needs and expectations regarding new technologies. To our best knowledge, a systematic clustering of citizens regarding their e-government specific perceptions has not yet been applied. In the light of the diversity of modern societies, it seems rather short-sighted to not further differentiate populations beyond some socio-demographic factors (e.g. age, income, or education) – a perspective with a long tradition in sociology [e.g. 22], adopted in this paper.

We assume that 'the' citizen can be grouped into user types according to differing needs and requirements regarding the use of information technology (IT), both in general and with regard to public (online) services. Therefore, the present study sets out to answer the following research questions (RQ). *RQ1: What types of e-government users exist? RQ2: How do these types differ in terms of their perceptions off e-government?*

The RQ are answered based on an inductive interview study, conducted in Germany in 2016. We chose an inductive approach, because to date, there is only limited research on user types in the e-government context. The aim of this explorative study is to identify different patterns of e-government use and IT usage behavior and to shed light on the individuals' motivations.

2 Background and Literature Review

2.1 E-government Diffusion Research

Whenever new technologies enter the market, researchers want to understand how these new technologies diffuse, what influences usage, and also what hinders usage. E-government research is no exception here. Most works in this area are built on commonly used technology acceptance models [e.g. 3, 24]. Institutions like the United Nations conduct their own studies [e.g. 23] to measure the diffusion rates of e-government in general and of certain services. These studies in particular reveal that citizens in many countries are still reluctant to use e-government services [23]. This finding has induced research on non-adoption of e-government as a counterpart to the broad field of adoption and acceptance research [e.g. 2, 13]. Despite the undoubtedly important strides the field has made, there is still need for further research: Studies in current diffusion studies often focus on 'the' citizen without further distinguishing different segments of the population or use only socio-demographic and digital divide factors to describe the citizenry in more detail. One major problem inherent to this approach are the heterogeneous and sometimes contradicting empirical findings when it comes to digital divide factors [11]. E-government research has not yet considered segmenting citizens into more detailed groups to study perceptions about and consequently the diffusion of e-government. Instead, most studies do not distinguish between different user groups [e.g. 4, 5] or focus their attempts on single factors like users' internet competencies [e.g. 1]. This sheds light onto general patterns of adoption decisions but neglects differences in these patterns relating to general usage behavior and different segments in the population.

2.2 Media User Typologies

Presumably, the perceptions about IT and internet use can to a certain degree explain how people behave in technological contexts and in turn, why some citizens make use of services like e-government while others still prefer on-site services. We hypothesize that the way citizens perceive e-government is influenced primarily by their general technology behavior rather than by the service itself. Thus, understanding how citizens react to IT in general can add to the understanding of e-government specific behavior. User typologies have a long tradition, especially in communication and media research and exist for diverse media [e.g. 7], the internet in general [e.g. 16, 26], and different media like online news [e.g. 25]. Up until now, most works on in the IS discipline focus rather on e-democracy and e-participation than e-government [e.g. 18]. Others use the digital divide framework – a perspective focusing solely on demographic patterns [e.g. 19] or single user groups [e.g. 10, 20]. Therefore, the present study aims at creating a specific e-government typology but uses media user typologies as a starting point. For example, Brandtzæg [6] developed a unified media-user typology, which distinguishes *non-users* (no use at all), *sporadic users* (occasional and rare use, low interest), *debaters* (information search, information exchange with others), *entertainment users* (use for entertainment purposes), *socializers* (seeking social contacts, spontaneous and flexible usage), *lurkers* (use to while away the time), *instrumental users* (utility-oriented use and information search), and *advanced users* (all purposes). To build the different user types, frequency and variety of use, typical activities and used media platforms were considered.

Similarly, a German study reveals six different types of media users [14]. Socio-demographic factors, the access to the internet and e-services, digital competencies and knowledge, intensity of use and variety of use, and openness towards digital trends and innovation, were used as indicators for one's type of usage. As the study at hand also was conducted in Germany, we take this typology into account, with its types ranging from *outside skeptics,* described as having the lowest digital potential, *conservative occasional users, cautious pragmatists, reflecting professionals* and *progressive users* to *technique enthusiasts,* described as having the highest digital potential.

Although both these exemplarily cited and other typologies [e.g. 16, 26] use different labels, they are mainly based on similar concepts. The main category used to identify different user types can be labeled *resources,* encompassing financial resources [e.g. 21], the available infrastructure [e.g. 14], i.e. number of internet enabled devices but also more intangible resources like knowledge and experience [e.g. 6]. Besides the *perceived importance of the internet*, major influences seem to be the *media behavior* and the *variety of use*. The media behavior can best be described with the question: Why and for what purposes are certain technologies or e-services used? *Variety of use* [14] describes the number of different platforms or applications a person regularly uses. Additionally, the *frequency or intensity of use* [14] plays a major role in defining user types. Even though this is not a comprehensive summary, it still offers a reasonable starting point for the development of an e-government user typology.

3 Method

To answer the RQ, we conducted a *qualitative* and *exploratory* interview study with 18 German participants. Since we know little about different types of e-government users, such a research design seems appropriate. Qualitative interviews are used to uncover patterns or relations that have not yet been researched or are considered to be influential [e.g. 8]. The interview guideline was semi-structured, meaning that we predefined a set of important questions but kept the interview open for topics and aspects that were important to the interviewee. The guideline consisted of five major blocks: general use of IT and the internet (1), reasons for (non-)adoption of electronic services (2) and e-government (3), image of public administrations (4), and concluding remarks (5). The interviews, taking on average half an hour, were recorded, transcribed and analyzed using inductive qualitative content analysis [15].

As a sample, we chose eight men and ten women from different parts of Germany, aged between 23 and 63 years. Unfortunately, the sample was not as well distributed over other socio-demographic variables as we would have expected. Thus, the influence of socio-demographic variables should be interpreted carefully, if this is possible at all.

4 Analysis – Developing an E-government User Typology

4.1 Approach

For the development of the typology, we compared every respondent with each other. At first, we only considered the *variety of use*, i.e. the different online services that were actually used, and grouped respondents with similar service use together. Then we also considered the *time spent online*, *personal importance of the internet*, *frequency of use*, *number of internet enabled devices*, and the *perceived own competencies* in handling (new) IT. Respondents were regrouped if considerable differences occurred. Finally, we included all remaining variables (*age, gender, size of household, net income, education, profession,* and *employment status*) and formed the final types with these variables. While the assignment of each respondent to one type changed from the first to the second step, the consideration of socio-demographic variables did not change this mapping. This may be due to the fact that the sample was biased. In total, six different user types were defined, which overall fit the typologies discussed in the previous chapter. After we assigned every respondent to one type, we analyzed their general and e-government specific usage behavior using MAXQDA, a software for qualitative analyses.

4.2 User Types

The analysis of the citizens' perception of e-services in general and e-government in particular is based on visual tools. The distribution of the different factors across the user types is shown in Figs. 1 and 2. All descriptions are based on these displays.

Minimal Users (Type 1) are characterized by a limited time spent online (<7 h per week) and a very low variety of use, which is focused on functional services like online

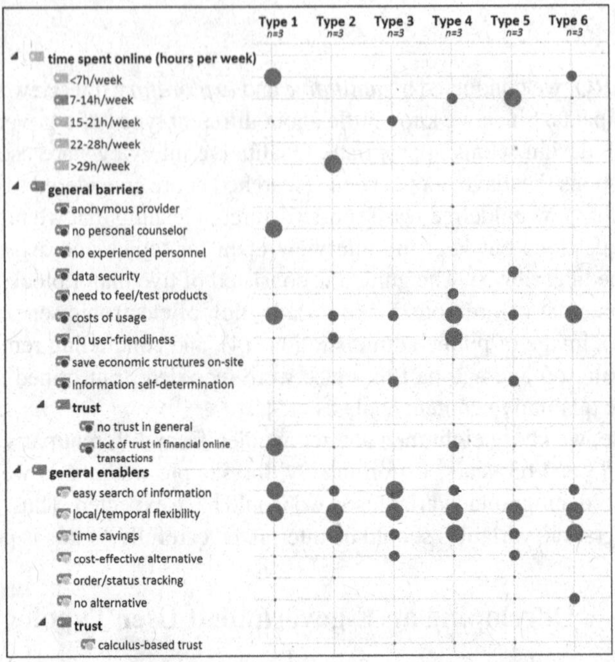

Fig. 1. Perceptions of enablers and barriers to technology adoption by user types

banking and e-mails. The internet is of small importance in their life and they describe themselves as having low technological competencies. Regarding their perceptions of e-services in general, not having *personal contact* and a *physical experience* are the main barriers to IT adoption. Additionally, they name *costs of usage* and a *lack of trust in financial online transactions* as inhibitors. Thus, the online environment is perceived as uncomfortable. Their aversion is also reflected in the main use they see in the internet which is the *ease of information search* and a *local/temporal flexibility*.

Regarding their e-government specific perceptions, their general behavior is partially reflected. The main barriers to e-government use are *convenience* and *no need to use*. For this type, the offline services work well and their sporadic contact with public administrations (no/one contact during the last year) does not make the use of e-services necessary, although two of the respondents work full-time and have already used an e-government service. As enablers to e-government use, the respondents stated a *reduced workload* and *time savings*. For this type, e-government services are not out of question in general but have to fulfill needs and are used only if it seems to be indispensable or in all respects beneficial. In addition, this type *prefers paper documents* over digital documents and also *prefers the personal contact* to administration employees, especially if problems or questions occur. Furthermore, this user type expresses a high degree of trust towards administrations concerning data security: All respondents think that public administrations handle their data carefully and can guarantee data security.

Type 2: **Power Users** can be described as the very opposite to minimal users. They use the internet and IT for all purposes, value the internet as a very important part of

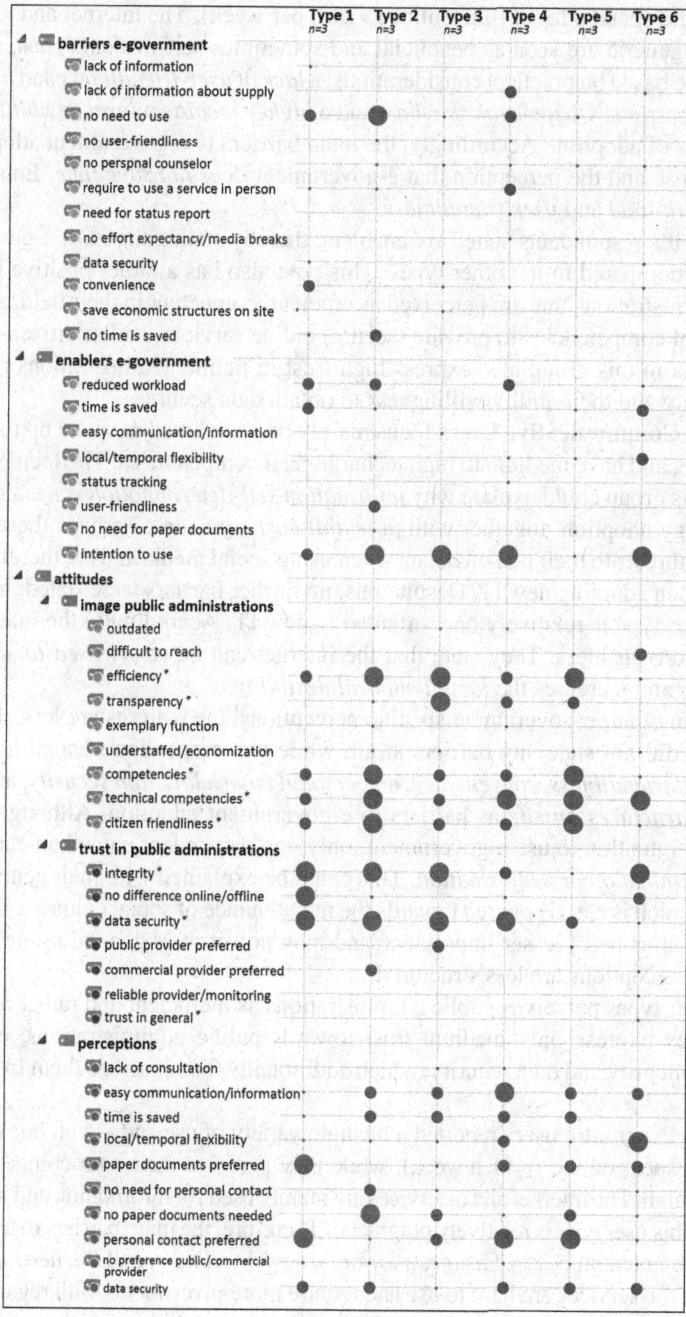

Fig. 2. Perceptions e-government by user types (*positive *or* negative evaluation)

their lives and spend a lot of time online (>29 h per week). The internet and new technologies in general are seen as beneficial and sometimes self-evident. Thus, adoption decisions are based on practical considerations: a *lack of user-friendliness* and *high costs* are seen as barriers, whereas *time savings* and a *higher local/temporal flexibility* are the main drivers of adoption. Accordingly, the main barriers to e-government adoption are *no need to use* and the perception that e-government *does not save time*. Enablers are *reduced work-load* and *user-friendliness*.

In total, the respondents stated six enablers, thereby stating the most e-government enablers as compared to the other types. This type also has a rather positive image of public administrations that are perceived as efficient, competent in their field, as having the technical competencies to provide (secure) online services, and as citizen-friendly. Respondents in this group also express high trust in public administrations regarding their integrity and their ability/willingness to obtain data security.

Type 3: **Communicative Users** focus mainly on social media, spend up to 21 h per week online, and have medium to high technological competencies. The focus on social media in this group could explain why *information self-determination* is a major barrier to technology adoption, together with *potential costs of usage*. Perhaps these persons experience threats to their personal data when using social media and are therefore more cautious when adopting new IT. Despite this, no further barriers were stated, indicating that this user type is relatively open-minded to new IT. Accordingly, the interviewees perceive more enablers. They state that the internet can be *easily used to search for information* and increases the *local/temporal flexibility*.

Regarding their e-government specific perceptions, the patterns are less clear: One respondent did not state any barriers at all, while two respondents stated *no need to use*, *no user-friendliness*, *convenience*, *no personal counselor*, *data security*, and *saving economic structures on site* as barriers to e-government adoption. Although they all express the intention to use e-government, only one respondent named an enabler, i.e. *easy communication and information*. This could be explained with their general usage behavior, which is clearly geared towards the maintenance of social contacts. E-government could thus be of lesser importance and may not fit their general usage behavior wherefore perceptions are less structured.

This user types perceives public administrations as inefficient and rather non-transparent. They express only medium trust towards public administrations, especially regarding integrity and data security, which additionally distinguishes them from power users.

Type 4: **Pragmatic users** reported a medium variety of use and – with one exception – low time spent online (≤14 h/week), while they perceive their own competencies as medium to high. The internet and e-services are mainly used for information and job related purposes. This user type is relatively pragmatic. Therefore, the main barriers to technology adoption are potential *costs of usage*, a *lack of user-friendliness*, and the *need to feel/test products*. If the services are hard to use and require more investments with regard to costs and efforts, this type tends to not adopt e-services. In contrast, if the services promises *time savings* or greater *local/temporal flexibility* (enablers), the interviewees are more willing to use them. This user type expresses a *lack of trust in financial online transactions*, which also fits the image of a pragmatic use of IT.

The pragmatism characterizing this type also becomes obvious with regard to the perceptions of e-government. The major barriers for this group are a *lack of information about supply*, *no need to use*, and the impression that one is *required to use a service in person*, whereas the major enabler is *reduced workload*. Hence, the adoption decision mainly relies on the degree to which an e-government service fulfills the personal needs and fits established usage behavior and routines. This also means that *personal contact* is preferred whenever problems occur. At the same time, respondents think that the use of e-government services can make *communication with and information about public administrations easier*, can *save time*, and can *increase the local/temporal flexibility*.

Type 5: **Goal-oriented occasional user.** Goal-oriented occasional users show a small to medium variety of use and time spent online ($\leq$14 h/week) but think that the internet is important. They use the internet and e-services purposefully and mainly for job-related issues. In contrast, entertainment or the maintenance of social contacts takes place offline. Since this type is very goal oriented, one barrier seems to play a major role in the adoption decision: *costs of usage*. The potential use of new IT or e-services has to clearly outweigh its costs. For two respondents, perceptions about *data security* and *information self-determination* are important as well. On the other side, *local/temporal flexibility* is the main driver of adoption decisions for this user type.

Prima facie, this type seems to be a mismatch regarding the e-government perceptions: One interviewee stated only barriers (*no effort expectancy* and *no time savings*), whereas another interviewee stated only enablers (*time is saved, local/temporal flexibility, no need for paper documents, intention to use*). The third respondent named both barriers and enablers (*no need to use, required to use a service in person* and *easy communication/information*). Still, their goal-orientation is the unifying characteristic: For all respondents, reaching a certain goal is of top priority. In the case of one interview, this leads to the perception of barriers, whereas in the case of the other interview, this leads to the perception of enablers. In addition, the respondents reported several contacts with public administrations in private and in job-related contexts. Thus, their image of public administrations is rather balanced: all interviewees tie their perceptions to individual employees and their local administrations instead of rendering a general judgement. In general, they have a positive image of administrations and, accordingly, express high trust in public authorities, especially regarding data security.

Type 6: **Versatile occasional user.** The occasional users spend limited time online (<7 and $\leq$14 h/week), attribute less importance to the internet and describe their technological competencies as low to medium. Although this type of user seems more heterogeneous regarding the variety of use, perceptions of barriers and enablers regarding general as well as e-government specific use are quite similar. The *costs of usage* are the major adoption barrier, whereas *time-savings* and the perception of online services as a *cost-effective alternative* are major enablers. Two respondents also stated as an enabler that, oftentimes, *e-services are without alternative*.

In contrast, the evaluation of the e-government specific perceptions is rather difficult: Two out of three respondents named barriers, however not the same and one interviewee named only one barrier. Since all three respondents have already used e-government, this could explain the differing perceptions of barriers, according to the type of service that has been used and problems that may have been encountered with the respective services. More of a consensus was reached with regard to the enablers: The most important drivers of e-government adoption for this group are *potential time-savings* and a *higher local/temporal flexibility*. Accordingly, all respondents in this group are *willing to use e-government* and perceive public administrations as having the needed competencies to provide secure e-services and as having integrity.

5 Discussion

Regarding RQ1, we built six user types (*minimal users, power user, communicative user, pragmatic user, goal-oriented occasional user, versatile occasional user*) using an iterative analysis process. The comparison showed that these types not only behave differently in online or electronic environments but also perceive IT in general differently, primarily according to personal technological needs and established usage routines – a result that is in accordance with prior research on different user types [e.g. 26].

Concerning the second RQ, it becomes clear that the user types also differ with regard to their perceptions of e-government. The first user type, **minimal users**, has a low usage profile and is oriented towards functional services. As described, the use of e-government is not out of question in general but has to fulfill needs. Consequently, this type presumably uses informational services, while more complex transactional services are of less interest due to the respondents' need for personal contact. This type could be also less inclined to e-government use due to the infrequent contacts to administrations and, thus, a lack of necessity. The **power users**, in contrast, have the highest potential to use e-government services, as the internet is an environment in which these persons feel comfortable and which is used, together with IT in general, for multiple purposes and seen as beneficial. Once this user type has the need to use governmental services, it is very likely for him to use them online as long as they are user-friendly and cost-effective, both with regard to material and immaterial resources.

The remaining types lie in between these two poles: The **pragmatic user** also has more potential to use e-government as the services promise time savings and higher flexibility. At present, they lack information about which services are supplied and how they function as they spend less time online and have medium competencies and thus, less experience. But in general, they are open minded towards e-government use.

The **pragmatic** and **goal-oriented users** may be slightly harder to reach with e-government services since the internet and electronic services are used mainly for job-related purposes and, additionally, both types spend limited time online. If administrations' on-site services have the same service level as e-government, both types presumably tend to use the former instead of e-services, especially regarding the pragmatic users' need for personal consultation in case of problems or questions.

The **versatile occasional users** attach great importance to time and cost savings and higher flexibility. For them, e-government usage is tied to benefits, especially time-savings, since this type spends less time with the internet or IT in general. Finally, the **communicative users** are less inclined to use e-government, as they use e-services and the internet mostly for communication and the maintenance of social contacts.

Moreover, they perceive administrations as inefficient and non-transparent, which could affect their perceptions about e-government and make them the least accessible group.

The comparison of the user types highlights two important aspects. First, it becomes obvious that citizens perceive e-government in accordance with their general usage behavior, needs, and attitudes. These perceptions may differ from individual to individual and thus also the importance of e-government for each citizen. Second, this result leads to the conclusion that low adoption rates cannot solely be explained by a lack of usability or usefulness. Research should also re-estimate the population that can actually be reached with e-government services and start evaluating adoption rates not for the complete citizenry but with regard to different segments of the public since, presumably, adoption rates differ from user type to user type.

6 Conclusion and Outlook

This study's aim was to uncover what types of e-government users exist (RQ1) and to reveal how these types differ in terms of their perceptions of e-government (RQ2). Our analysis led to the development of six user types: minimal users, power users, pragmatic and goal oriented users, versatile occasional users, and communicative users. These types can be distinguished according to their variety and frequency of use, the importance assigned to the internet, technological competencies, their perceptions about IT/e-services and about e-government and public administrations.

We are aware that our study has some limitations, which are mainly due to its explorative design. Since we have a very small number of respondents and focused solely on Germany, our results are not generalizable, especially since our sample was biased and the influence of socio-demographic variables thus remains unclear. Due to the small sample, it was sometimes difficult to clearly differentiate the user types and to assign each respondent to only one type. Thus, we are aware that the presented typology is by no means comprehensive and should be carefully validated with a larger sample and a quantitative research design. Furthermore, we focused on perceptions of e-government, which omits the effect of these perceptions and other influences on the actual behavior – a research question that should also be investigated with quantitative data.

Nonetheless, our study still contributes to current e-government research by revealing that citizens perceive e-government in accordance with their general IT behavior. From a scientific position, understanding how user groups differ in terms of needs and requirements, helps explaining why e-government adoption rates are stagnating and what impacts citizens' usage behavior. This research can also add to a better understanding of how e-government diffusion research differs from general technology research. From a practical viewpoint, understanding how user groups differ can help creating tailored e-government services that are actually used by a broad mass.

References

1. Araujo, M.H., Reinhard, N.: Categorization of Brazilian Internet users and its impacts on the use of electronic government services. In: Janssen, M., Scholl, H.J., Wimmer, M.A., Bannister, F. (eds.) EGOV 2014. LNCS, vol. 8653, pp. 242–252. Springer, Heidelberg (2014). doi: 10.1007/978-3-662-44426-9_20
2. Barth, M., Veit, D.: Electronic service delivery in the public sector: understanding the variance of citizens' resistance. In: Proceedings of the 44th Hawaii International Conference on System Sciences (HICSS 2011), pp. 1–11 (2011)
3. Belanche, D., Casaló, L.V., Flavián, C.: Integrating trust and personal values into the Technology Acceptance Model: the case of e-government services adoption. Cuadernos de Economía y Dirección de la Empresa **15**(4), 192–204 (2012)
4. Bélanger, F., Carter, L.: Trust and risk in e-government adoption. J. Strateg. Inf. Syst. **17**(2), 165–176 (2008)
5. Beldad, A., van der Geest, T., de Jong, M., Steehouder, M.: Shall I tell you where I live and who I am? Factors influencing the behavioral intention to disclose personal data for online government transactions. Int. J. Hum. Comput. Interact. **28**(3), 163–177 (2012)
6. Brandtzæg, P.B.: Towards a unified media-user typology (MUT). A meta-analysis and review of the research literature on Media-User Typologies. Comput. Hum. Behav. **26**(5), 940–956 (2010)
7. Brandtzaeg, P.B., Heim, J.: A typology of social networking sites users. IJWBC **7**(1), 28–51 (2011)
8. Brinkmann, S.: Qualitative Interviewing. Understanding Qualitative Research. Oxford University Press, New York (2013)
9. Carter, L., Bélanger, F.: The utilization of e-government services: citizen trust, innovation and acceptance factors. Inf. Syst. J. **15**(1), 5–25 (2005)
10. Choudrie, J., Ghinea, G., Songonuga, V.N.: Silver surfers, e-government and the digital divide: an exploratory study of UK local authority websites and older citizens. Interact. Comput. **25**(6), 417–442 (2013)
11. Distel, B., Ogonek, N.: To adopt or not to adopt: a literature review on barriers to citizens' adoption of e-government services. In: Proceedings of the 24th European Conference on Information Systems (ECIS 2016), pp. 1–17 (2016)
12. Evans, D., Yen, D.C.: E-government. An analysis for implementation: Framework for understanding cultural and social impact. Gov. Inf. Q. **22**(3), 354–373 (2005)
13. Gilbert, D., Balestrini, P., Littleboy, D.: Barriers and benefits in the adoption of e-government. Int. J. Public Sect. Manag. **17**(4), 286–301 (2004)
14. Initiative D21 e.V.: D21-Digital-Index. Jährliches Lagebild zur Digitalen Gesellschaft, Berlin, pp. 1–64. (2016). http://initiatived21.de/publikationen/d21-digital-index-2016/. Last accessed 3 May 2017
15. Mayring, P.: Qualitative Inhaltyanalyse. Grundlagen und Techniken, 12th edn. Beltz, Weinheim, Basel (2015)
16. Meyen, M., Pfaff-Rüdiger, S., Dudenhöffer, K., Huss, J.: The internet in everyday life: a typology of internet users. Media Cult. Soc. **32**(5), 873–882 (2010)
17. Molnar, T.: Improving usability of e-government for the elderly. Electron. J. e-Gov. **13**(2), 122–135 (2015)
18. Nam, T.: Determining the type of e-government use. Government Information Quarterly **31**(2), 211–220 (2014)

19. Niehaves, B., Gorbacheva, E., Plattfaut, R.: The digital divide vs. the e-government divide: do socio-demographic variables (still) impact e-government use among onliners? In: Gil-Garcia, J.R. (ed.) E-Government Success Factors and Measures. Theories, Concepts, and Methodologies, pp. 52–65. IGI Global, Hershey (2013)
20. Pethig, F., Krönung, J.: Social inclusion through e-government? Developing an inclusionary framework of e-government adoption. In: 36th International Conference on Information Systems (ICIS 2015), pp. 1–13 (2015)
21. Rogers, E.M.: Diffusion of Innovations, 5th edn. Free Press, New York (2003)
22. Ueltzhöffer, J.: Europa auf dem Weg in die Postmoderne. Transnationale Soziale Milieus und gesellschaftliche Spannungslinien in der Europäischen Union. In: Merkel, W., Busch, A. (eds.) Demokratie in Ost und West. Für Klaus von Beyme. Suhrkamp Taschenbuch Wissenschaft, vol. 1425, 1st edn, pp. 624–652. Suhrkamp, Frankfurt am Main (1999)
23. United Nations Department of Economic and Social Affairs: United Nations E-Government Survey 2014. E-Government for the Future We Want. https://publicadministration.un.org/egovkb/Portals/egovkb/Documents/un/2014-Survey/E-Gov_Complete_Survey-2014.pdf. (2014). Last accessed 28 Nov 2016
24. Wang, Y.-S., Liao, Y.-W.: Assessing eGovernment systems success: a validation of the DeLone and McLean model of information systems success. Gov. Inf. Q. **25**(4), 717–733 (2008)
25. Zeller, F., O'Kane, J., Godo, E., Goodrum, A.: A subjective user-typology of online news consumption. Digit Journal. **2**(2), 214–231 (2014)
26. Zillien, N., Hargittai, E.: Digital distinction: status-specific types of internet usage. Soc. Sci. Q. **90**(2), 274–291 (2009)

Evaluation

Value-Based Decision Making: Decision Theory Meets e-Government

Leif Sundberg(✉) and Katarina L. Gidlund

Mid Sweden University, Holmgatan 10, 851 70 Sundsvall, Sweden
{leif.sundberg,katarina.l.gidlund}@miun.se

Abstract. Electronic government, or e-Government, is the use of information and communication technology in the public sector. As a research field, it is characterized as multi-disciplinary with heritage from both the information systems and public administration fields. This diverse background may be beneficial, but it may also result in a fragmented theoretical base and conceptual vagueness. This paper applies decision theory to e-Government to tie a number of theoretical and practical concepts together. In particular, five concepts from decision theory (i.e. objectives, stakeholder inclusion, weighting and resource allocation, risk analysis, and outcomes assessment) are compared with counterparts in e-Government. The findings have both theoretical and practical implications. First, they add to and unite e-Government theory. Second, practical methods for operationalizing the theoretical concepts are proposed. This operationalization includes using a holistic approach to e-participation throughout decision processes.

Keywords: Public values · Decision theory · Decision making · e-Government

1 Introduction

Electronic government, or e-Government, is the use of information and communication technology (ICT) in the public sector to create better government [1]. As a research field, e-Government is studied by multiple disciplines utilizing a variety of theories and methods. Some scholars define the field as theoretically weak and assert that much of the research lacks practical implications. They also express concerns about conceptual and definitional vagueness [2, 3]. However, others have a more optimistic view; for instance, Bannister and Connolly [4] argue that a great deal of valuable theory exists in the e-Government field.

e-Government is often mentioned in relation to a paradigm shift in which a full range of democratic and institutional values are relevant. To realize these values, government agencies are supposed to collaborate and include citizens in their processes. The citizen becomes a problem solver who is actively engaged in producing values [5]. Dunleavy et al. [6] use the term "digital era governance" to describe these changes in government. They identify three characteristic themes: reintegration (as opposed to fragmentation), needs-based holism (i.e. reorganization

M. Janssen et al. (Eds.): EGOV 2017, LNCS 10428, pp. 351–358, 2017.
DOI: 10.1007/978-3-319-64677-0_29

to create seamless, non-stop solutions) and digitization processes (electronic service delivery).

Nonetheless, the outcomes of the above-described change have many uncertainties and alternate possibilities. For instance, Budzier and Flyvbjerg [7] have examined high-risk e-Government projects, which they refer to as "black swans." As a counter-measure against black swans, they suggest establishing efficient decision making to enable the early detection of anomalies. Pardo and Burke [8] argue that unstructured and non-transparent decision processes hinder the realization of public values and citizen trust. A longitudinal field study of the private sector reveals that managers who apply a high degree of procedural rationality in strategic decision making generally take better decisions [9]; unfortunately, few such studies have been conducted in relation to the public sector. Andersson et al. [10] investigate the challenges of implementing decision support systems (DSS) in a political context and conclude that a number of issues affect the outcomes, including a lack of impact on final decisions: the attitude among some of the decision makers in the study was that the political decision process could not be reduced to science, which meant they did not consider the DSS results when taking their final decisions.

Against this backdrop, the purpose of this paper is to apply decision theory to e-Government. The aim of doing so is to contribute to the theoretical base of the e-Government field and to tie several research issues within this field together by merging them with concepts from decision theory. The results should also offer practical benefits, by inspiring public managers to adapt more holistic and structured decision making.

This paper proceeds as follow. The method used is described in Sect. 2. Section 3 then presents a literature study, which is the main part of this paper. The results are then summarized in Sect. 4, which also contains suggestions for further research.

2 Method

The underlying method used in this paper is concept analysis, as visualized in Fig. 1. Concept analysis can be described as clarifying and describing the characteristics and relations that concepts have within a system.

Concept analysis is applied as follows in the current study. The goal (1.1 in the figure) is stated in the above introduction and the domains (1.2 in the figure) are the research fields of decision theory and e-Government. The premise is that the domains have concepts (1.3 in the figure) that overlap or are close. Decision theory can be used to gather the fragmented concepts from e-Government into one system.

Concept analysis has been operationalized by identifying five concepts that represent a structured decision-making procedure, namely:

- Objectives
- Stakeholder inclusion
- Weighting and resource allocation
- Risk analysis
- Outcomes assessment

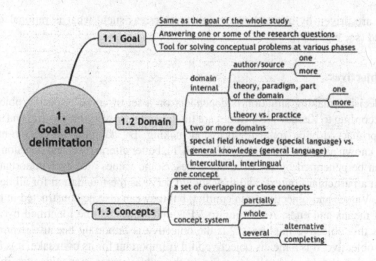

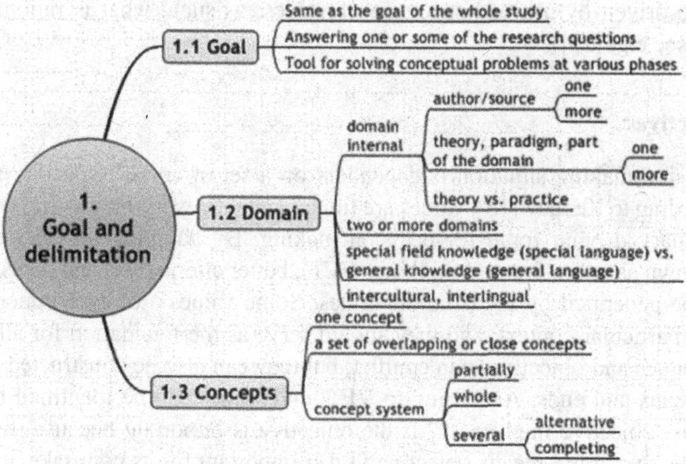

Fig. 1. Concept analysis [11]

These concepts are described using decision theory literature and then compared with their counterparts from the e-Government literature.

3 Applying Decision Theory to e-Government

This section starts with a general description of decision theory, which is followed by an introduction to the concepts explored in the study (namely objectives, stakeholder inclusion, weighting and resource allocation, risk analysis, and outcomes assessment). In addition, each concept is matched to an e-Government counterpart. Where applicable, a practical method for operationalizing it is also suggested.

3.1 Overview of Decision Theory

Humans make a number of decisions every day. The science of decision theory aims to understand the reasoning behind an agent's choices as well as to improve decision making. Descriptive decision theory is concerned with how people actually make decisions, whereas prescriptive decision theory is devoted to providing assistance that improves decision making [12]. The underlying goal of the decision analysis field is to contribute to rational decision making, and thus to increase the likelihood of fulfilling the decision maker's objectives and acting in accordance with his or her desires and values. However, no clear definition of rationality exists and a successful decision might not always be based on rational grounds.

In situations with high uncertainty, it might be nearly impossible for a decision maker to know which path to choose [13]. To reduce uncertainty in decision making and thereby improve outcomes, decision theory provides several structured proceedings to aid decision makers. However, decision problems are often complex and not ideally framed and humans are driven by a broad spectrum of values; as such, what is rational is also contested (see e.g. [14]).

3.2 Objectives

Every decision-making situation is dependent on a set of context-specific objectives [13]. According to Keeney [15], values are fundamental to everything we do and should be the primary driving force for decision making. By adopting a decision-making method known as value-focused thinking (VFT), better alternatives and decision situations can be generated by focusing on values: Some values are more important than others in a particular context, and they should serve as the foundation for all decision making. Values and objectives can conflict, but they can also be constructed in hierarchies of means and ends. According to VFT, end values can be identified by asking "Why is this objective important?" If the objective is important because if promotes another objective, it is a means objective; if it is important for its own sake, it is an end objective that should guide all decisions. In the public sector, a specific classification range of public values is frequently mentioned [16]. Bannister and Connolly [17] define public values as a mode of behavior that is held to be right. According to Bozeman [18], public values can be described as a normative consensus about rights, obligations and principles between citizens and the government. Values in e-Government can be classified in different ways depending on their properties in relation both to each other and to governmental paradigms [19, 20].

3.3 Stakeholder Inclusion

Values are subjective by nature, which means they can be ascribed to individuals or groups. To incorporate public value thinking into decision-making practices, public managers need to rigorously identify stakeholders [21]. Involving important stakeholders throughout a decision process enables both a better decision-making situation and the construction of additional alternatives [15]. Zhu and Kindarto [22] observe that participative decision structures are associated with IT project success in developing countries while more hierarchical structures hurt performance. The link between stakeholders and success is especially important in the public sector, since a system's user group may be both extensive and varying. A large stream in the e-Government literature is devoted to issues concerning e-participation and citizen empowerment. While participative governance is often treated as a success factor, concerns about how to extract a representative number of values from a limited pool of stakeholders also exist [23].

3.4 Weighting and Resource Allocation

Strategic decision making includes allocating limited resources in a way that achieves objectives [24, 25]. Fiscal funds are a democratic government's basic resource. As Moore [16] points out, public managers cannot produce desirable results without utilizing limited resources that have value for multiple uses. When conflicting objectives exist, they must be properly weighted as part of resource allocation and activity planning.

Tools such as multi-criteria decision analysis (MCDA) can be used to quantify independent criteria in order to associate them with different weights. Riabacke et al. [26] suggest utilizing MCDA to improve decision quality in large-scale participatory processes.

In the e-Government context, the difficulty becomes prioritizing a broad range of public values; some services might target most of a country's population. As Bannister and Connolly [17] point out, implementing ICT:s is not value free but requires decisions about – and sometimes trade-offs between – values. Rose et al. [19] describe how public managers in a case study tended to prioritize administrative efficiency values while neglecting citizen engagement values. The findings of these studies illustrate that rationality is thus both contested and context-dependent. However, some researchers are attempting to identifying ways to make value prioritization more inclusive; for instance Robbins et al. [27] introduce resource allocation to eParticipation by using a web-based survey tool that enables respondents to take the fiscal impacts of their choices into consideration.

3.5 Risk Analysis

The definition of risk varies to some extent [28], with the common denominators being (a) uncertainty concerning future events and (b) the potential loss of something of value to humans. Epistemologically, risk is often divided into two categories: objective and subjective. Objective risk is based on statistics and earlier experiences, from which the probability that events will occur in the future can be extracted. Aven and Renn [29] argue that uncertainties are not objective parts of the world, but rather human constructs that an individual needs to assess. Subjective risk is dependent on personal beliefs. In the heart of subjectivist theory lies Bayes' theorem, which tells us that we can largely create any probability statement based on current information. New information makes it possible to revise earlier statements. Bayesian risk analysis has been adapted to e-Government in a handful of cases [30, 31].

The word "risk" came to the English language in the 1660s through a French adoption of the Italian word *"riscare,"* which means to navigate among dangerous rocks (as mentioned by Rosa [32]). An early paper on risk in relation to e-Government (with the suitable title of "Walking atop the cliffs") states that the causes of failures in this context are intertwined with technical, social and behavioral factors [33]. Røberg et al. [34] mention that research on risk and risk management in relation to e-Government is sparse. However, "challenges," "barriers" and similar terms are used as opposites to success factors in both information systems and e-Government literature. Sundberg [35] suggests defining risk in e-Government as potential threats to public values.

3.6 Outcomes Assessment

The final concept is a highly debated topic in the information systems literature: How do we assess the outcomes of implementing technology in a specific context? The main challenge is putting hard numbers on soft values. Traditional assessment methods such as cost-benefit analysis might fail to reflect the true costs and benefits of e-Government

[36]. As such, frameworks that consider dimensions beyond monetary/efficiency values are needed [37, 38]. Scott et al. [39] suggest applying public value theory in order to evaluate e-Government success. Their approach consists of considering three categories of net benefits that comprise several public values, namely efficiency (cost, time, communication), effectiveness (avoid personal interaction, control, convenience, personalization, ease of information retrieval) and improved democracy (trust, well-informedness and participation in decision making).

4 Conclusions and Future Research

This paper has compared five concepts of decision theory to their theoretical counterparts in e-Government. The results reveal that a number of theoretical concepts of e-Government fit well within decision theory, as shown in Table 1 where each concept is also accompanied by an example of a practical method.

Table 1. Concept system: Decision theory meets e-Government

	Decision theory concept	e-Government concept	Examples of methods	
Stakeholder inclusion	Objectives	Public values	Value-focused thinking	eParticipation
	Weighting and resource allocation	Prioritizing between values and allocating public funds	Multi-criteria decision analysis; web-based surveys (with fiscal implications)	
	Risk	Barriers and challenges that prevent value realization	Bayesian risk analysis	
	Quantitative outcomes assessment	Multi-dimensional evaluation	Public value net benefits	

Stakeholder inclusion and eParticipation are placed on the sides of the table since they are frequently mentioned as success factors in the concepts, with the exception of risk analysis. Risk in e-Government still lacks clear conceptualization, even though implementing ICTs in the public sector is often seen as high-risk initiatives. This paper suggests using a risk analysis method that is based on subjective Bayesian probabilities which could enable future research to base risk assessment on participatory processes (through stakeholder-based probabilities).

The practical output of this paper is a holistic approach to (e-)participation in which different methods are used to include stakeholders throughout the decision process and participation is actually assessed as an outcome. The authors believe that this approach would benefit public managers by helping them to navigate an uncertain reality. Decision theory is not suggested as a universal solution to complex problems such as participative government and outcomes assessment; however, it does both improve structuring and help to fit these problems into a holistic theoretical and practical context. At the same time, decision theory could benefit from the e-Government field by addressing the challenges of a complex socio-technical field in which rationality is contested through paradigms, politics and organizational and stakeholder diversity.

This paper is based on a small sample of studies from two diverse research fields. Future research could add more to the topic by taking a more systematic approach to the literature, as well as by considering cases in which practical methods have been successfully applied.

References

1. OECD: The e-Government Imperative. OECD Publications, Paris (2003)
2. Heeks, R., Bailur, S.: Analyzing e-government research: perspectives, philosophies, theories, methods and practice. Gov. Inf. Q. **24**, 243–265 (2007)
3. Yildiz, M.: e-Government research: reviewing the literature, limitations and ways forward. Gov. Inf. Q. **24**, 646–665 (2007)
4. Bannister, F., Connolly, R.: The great theory hunt: does e-Government really have a problem? Gov. Inf. Q. **32**, 1–11 (2014)
5. Bryson, J.M., Crosby, B.C., Bloomberg, L.: Public value governance: moving beyond traditional public administration and the new public management. Public Adm. Rev. **74**, 445–456 (2014)
6. Dunleavy, P., Margetts, H., Bastow, S., Tinkler, J.: New public management is dead—long live digital-era governance. J. Public Adm. Res. Theory **16**, 467–494 (2005)
7. Budzier, A., Flyvbjerg, B.: Overspend? Late? Failure? What the data say about IT project risk in the public sector. In: Commonwealth Governance Handbook (2012/2013)
8. Pardo, T., Burke, B.: Government Worth Having: A Briefing on Interoperability for Government Leaders. Center for Technology in Government, University of Albany, Albany, NY (2008)
9. Dean Jr., W.D., Sharfman, M.P.: Does decision process matter? A study of strategic decision-making effectiveness. Acad. Manag. J. **39**, 368–396 (1996)
10. Andersson, A., Grönlund, Å., Åström, J.: You can't make this a science! Analyzing decision support systems in political contexts. Gov. Inf. Q. **29**, 543–552 (2012)
11. Nuopponen, A.: Methods of concept analysis—towards systematic concept analysis. LSP J. **1**, 5–14 (2010)
12. Keeney, R.L.: On the foundations of prescriptive decision analysis. In: Edwards, W. (ed.) Utility Theories: Measurement and Applications. Kluwer Academic, Boston (1992)
13. Eisenführ, F., Weber, M., Langer, T.: Rational Decision Making. Springer, Heidenberg (2010)
14. Webler, T., Renn, O., Jaeger, C., Rosa, E.: The rational actor paradigm in risk theories: analysis and critique. In: Risk in the Modern Age: Social Theory, Science, and Environmental Decision Making, New York, pp. 35–61 (2001)
15. Keeney, R.L.: Value Focused Thinking: A Path to Creative Decisionmaking. Harvard University Press, Cambridge (1992)
16. Moore, M.H.: Creating Public Value: Strategic Management in Government. Harvard University Press, London (1995)
17. Bannister, F., Connolly, R.: ICT, public values and transformative government: a framework and programme for research. Gov. Inf. Q. **31**, 119–128 (2014)
18. Bozeman, B.: Public values theory: three big questions. Int. J. Public Policy **4**, 369–375 (2009)

19. Rose, J., Persson, J.S., Heeager, L.T.: Competing value paradigms of e-Government managers: the efficiency imperative. Inform. Polity **20**, 35–59 (2015)
20. Jørgensen, T.B., Bozeman, B.: Public values: an inventory. Admin. Soc. **39**, 354–381 (2007)
21. Cook, M.E., Harrison, T.M.: Using public value thinking for government IT planning and decision making. In: Proceedings of the 15th Annual International Conference on Digital Government Research, pp. 54–60 (2014)
22. Zhu, Y.Q., Kindarto, A.: A garbage can model of government IT project failures in developing countries: the effects of leadership, decision structure and team competence. Gov. Inf. Q. **33**, 629–637 (2016)
23. Gidlund, K.L.: Designing for all and no one-practitioners understandings of citizen driven development of public e-services. In: Proceedings of the 12th Participatory Design Conference 1, pp. 11–19 (2012)
24. Kleinmuntz, D.: Resource allocation decisions. In: Edwards, M., von Winterfeldt, D. (eds.) Advances in Decision Sciences. Cambridge University Press, Cambridge (2007)
25. Phillips, L.D., Bana e Costa, C.A.: Transparent prioritisation, budgeting and resource allocation with multi-criteria decision analysis and decision conferencing. Ann. Oper. Res. **154**, 51–68 (2007)
26. Riabacke, M., Åström, J., Grönlund, Å.: Eparticipation galore? Extending multi-criteria decision analysis to the public. Int. J. Public Inf. Syst. **7**, 79–99 (2011)
27. Robbins, M.D., Simonsen, B., Feldman, B.: Citizens and resource allocation: improving decision making with interactive web-based citizen participation. Public Adm. Rev. **68**, 564–575 (2008)
28. Hansson, S.O.: The epistemology of technological risk. Tecné **9**, 68–80 (2007)
29. Aven, T., Renn, O.: On risk defined as an event where the outcome is uncertain. J. Risk Res. **12**, 1–11 (2009)
30. Vrček, N., Peharda, P., Munđar, D.: Methodology for risk assessment and costs associated with risk occurrence in e-Government projects. In: Transportation Systems and Engineering: Concepts, Methodologies, Tools and Applications. IGI Global (2013)
31. Xia, A.: Research of e-Government security risk assessment method using bayesian network. In: International Conference on Web Information Systems and Mining (2009)
32. Rosa, E.A.: Metatheoretical foundations for post-normal risk. J. Risk Res. **1**, 15–44 (1998)
33. Pardo, T.A., Scholl, H.J.: Walking atop the cliffs: avoiding failure and reducing risk in large scale e-Government projects. In: Proceedings of the 35th Annual Hawaii International Conference on System Sciences (2002)
34. Røberg, P.M., Flak, L.S., Myrseth, P.: Unveiling barriers and enablers of risk management in interoperability efforts. In: Proceedings of the 47th Hawaii International Conference on System Science (2014)
35. Sundberg, L.: Risk and decision in collaborative e-Government: an objectives-oriented approach. Electr. J. e-Gov. **14**, 36–47 (2016)
36. Heeks, R.: Implementing and Managing e-Government: An International Text. Sage, London (2006)
37. Chircu, A.M.: e-Government evaluation: towards a multidimensional framework. Electr. Gov. Int. J. **5**, 345–363 (2008)
38. Luna-Reyes, L.F., Gil-Garcia, J.R., Romero, G.: Towards a multidimensional model for evaluating electronic government: proposing a more comprehensive and integrative perspective. Gov. Inf. Q. **29**, 324–334 (2012)
39. Scott, M., DeLone, W., Golden, W.: Measuring eGovernment success: a public value approach. Eur. J. Inf. Syst. **25**, 187–208 (2016)

Information Artifact Evaluation with TEDSrate

Hans J. Scholl(✉), William Menten-Weil, and Tim S. Carlson

University of Washington, Seattle, WA, USA
{jscholl,wtmenten,timca}@uw.edu

Abstract. The evaluation of systems or artifacts as "outcomes" of software engineering (SE) projects has been a focus of study in SE-related research for quite some time. In recent years, evaluating artifacts, for example, mobile applications or websites has become more important, since such artifacts play increasingly critical roles in generating revenues for businesses, and the degree of artifact effectiveness is seen as a competitive factor. With the TEDS framework/procedure a novel and comprehensive approach to systematic artifact evaluation and comparison had been presented a few years ago, whose effectiveness and analytical power in comprehensive and highly detailed artifact evaluations and comparisons was empirically shown; however, despite its demonstrated capability TEDS still proved to be time and resource consuming like other evaluation approaches before. In order to overcome these constraints and provide evaluative feedback more quickly to developers and service providers, TEDSrate, a Web-based evaluation tool employing the TEDS framework/procedure, was developed. The tool was tested with two real-world organizations, the City of Seattle Emergency Operations Center (EOC) and the Seattle Sounders Football Club. The tests suggest that the highly configurable TEDSrate tool can fully implement and administer the TEDS framework/procedure and, at the same time, provide instantaneous, cost-effective, comprehensive, and highly detailed artifact evaluations to both developers and service providers.

Keywords: TEDS framework and procedure · TEDSrate · Information artifact evaluation · Information artifact comparison · Usability studies · Value added criteria · Government websites · Government apps

1 Introduction

Assessing the aptitude and appropriateness of software systems relative to both purpose and requirements along with evaluating their performance relative to user expectations has been a recurring theme in software engineering research for a long time. Investigations in these areas intend to contribute to improving overall system design and support the initial development and further evolution of an artifact in use so that systems better match purpose, requirements, and users' expectations. In a more general sense, such studies help to better understand the factors, which lead to software engineering success. However, for reasons of high cost, heavy time commitments on part of both developers and user-evaluators, and institutional barriers among other hindering factors, systematic

M. Janssen et al. (Eds.): EGOV 2017, LNCS 10428, pp. 359–377, 2017.
DOI: 10.1007/978-3-319-64677-0_30

software artifact assessments and evaluations have been found difficult to conduct persistently [4].

Furthermore, numerous aspects have to be considered when assessing and evaluating software systems ranging from internal architecture and code efficiency investigations, over studies on the effectiveness of human–computer interaction to user satisfaction and usability among others so that the purposes and foci of evaluative studies can vary widely. What constitutes ultimate software engineering success, hence, is still an open debate [15]. As shown in the next section, user satisfaction and effective use-related studies have been conducted in increasing numbers in recent years; however, criteria and frameworks used in such studies are also of a wide variety making it difficult to compare study results.

Interestingly, in times of burgeoning mobile and web-based applications (apps), which compete for market share, evaluative user satisfaction and effective-use studies have rarely been used to compare such artifacts, which could greatly help ongoing software engineering efforts in such markets. A few years ago, the TEDS framework and procedure was introduced [21] and successfully utilized in a number of empirical user satisfaction and effective-use studies, which also encompassed detailed artifact comparisons [10, 19, 20, 22].

While TEDS has demonstrated its effectiveness and analytical power in these studies leading to highly detailed and comprehensive results, it nevertheless also demonstrated its limitations with regard to the aforementioned constraints of high cost, heavy time commitment, and difficulties in user-rater/evaluator recruitment. In order to address and mitigate these three specific barriers, the researchers developed, introduced, and tested TEDSrate, a Web-based application (app), which allows recruiting and employing user-rater/evaluators anytime and everywhere. In this paper, TEDSrate, its uses, and the initial experiences with using it in evaluative studies, are presented and discussed.

The paper is organized as follows: In the next section, related work is reviewed leading towards the research question. Then, the design of TEDSrate is presented followed by the description of real-world pilot tests of the application. The results of the pilot tests are discussed, followed by the presentation of future work building on this discussion. The paper then concludes that frameworks/procedures like TEDS and supporting applications such as TEDSrate can effectively help conduct systematic user satisfaction and effective-use studies.

2 Literature Review

As mentioned before, determining and measuring the ultimate success of a software engineering project and its resulting artifacts has been a focus of debate for a long time. Already in the early 1980s fairly detailed categories had been specified for determining and assessing the relative value added by information systems regarding the specific contexts of their use and the respective information environment, in which they operate [25]. Later, the DeLone & McLean (D&M) model of information system success in its various evolutionary versions [7, 8] has served as a reference on a high level of abstraction in a number of SE-related fields and subfields [15, 23]. The D&M model basically relates three high-level variables of quality (information quality, system quality, and service quality) to equally high-level variables of system use (or, the intent of its use) and the user satisfaction, which in turn are said to lead to measurable or perceived net benefits, which feed back on system use and user satisfaction, the latter two of which are also connected via feedback [8]. Addressing these feedback relationships another recent study pointed at the importance of project efficiency, artifact quality, market performance, impact on stakeholders, and time as influential dimensions of software engineering success [11, 15]. Software engineering success along with overall information system or artifact success apparently depends on interacting and interdependent variables [9], which render the respective outcomes to factors not completely controllable by designers, developers, and project leaders.

As a result, multiple studies focused on better understanding these context-related factors and feedbacks. For example, recent workshops and studies emphasized user involvement in design and testing [3, 4, 14, 24]. Others highlighted the importance of continuous feedback on artifact (use) performance [1, 17]. Yet, others have relied on built-in monitoring and self-tuning functionalities as well as automatic user review scanning and salient-issue ranking methods [5, 6, 13]. Also, although not new, recent studies have reintroduced the utilization of personae and scenarios in both artifact design and artifact evaluation [2, 18].

However, the D&M model variables can hardly be studied in isolation, nor can they be effectively addressed when just employed on a high level of abstraction when it comes to design-relevant and artifact-specific recommendations (or comparisons). The TEDS framework and procedure [21], which represents a substantial extension to the aforementioned "Value-added Processes" work advanced in the 1980s [25], not only breaks down into detail the six high-level variables of the D&M model, but also accounts for the interaction between the variables within a given context by employing the concepts of personae and scenarios. The TEDS framework distinguishes six major categories of (a) ease of use/usability, (b) noise reduction, (c) quality, (d) adaptability, (e) performance, and (f) affection. These main categories are further broken down into 40 subcategories further specifying and detailing the main categories. The TEDS procedure, then, specifies thirteen steps of evaluating what is called an "information artifact," which, as a summary term, is used to represent any information technology or software artifact that a human actor may use for her or his purposes within a certain context. The term "information artifact" encompasses "both sources and pieces of information as well as information systems and other information technology artifacts" [20, p. 141]. The concept acknowledges that "information" is a context-dependent entity providing a certain meaning in the eyes of a beholder, and technology carrying and containing this very information can no longer sharply be distinguished from each other.

As mentioned, the TEDS framework and procedure has demonstrated its analytical power in various empirical studies [19, 20, 22], in which it was able to help derive detailed recommendations for developers and designers, and it also provided valuable competitive information to service providers who intended to improve their online offerings. However, while the results quite strongly proved the effectiveness and the overall concept of information artifact evaluation by means of the TEDS framework and procedure, it was still subject matter experts who had to carry out the detailed assessments and evaluations in a rather time-consuming and costly fashion [4] and also in geographically limited areas, all of which would present serious constraints for the future use of TEDS.

3 Research Question and Methodology

As a natural next step, the authors considered building a web-based tool for using the TEDS framework and procedure, which would reliably facilitate the issuance of artifact assessments and evaluations to both subject matter experts and laypersons alike on a broad and potentially global scale. With increasing sample sizes and controllably established demographics, it was reasoned that this would enable information artifact evaluations rather inexpensively while comprehensively at the same time. In the following, requirements, design criteria, and design options for a web-based tool enabling the use of the TEDS framework and procedure are discussed. This addresses the research question:

RQ: *What kind of Web-based tool can help subject matter experts and laymen alike perform TEDS-based evaluations capably and with global access?*

3.1 Design Considerations

Overall Requirements: When analyzing how TEDS was "manually" used in projects of empirical information artifact studies, that is, when the projects followed the 13-step procedure as described elsewhere [21] without the use of information system technology (ICT) support, the authors identified functional and non-functional requirements of a to-be ICT-supported TEDS tool.

3.1.1 Functional Requirements

Rating/Evaluation Component: The TEDS tool had to be able to input, record, and display scale ratings (for example, on a 1–5 Likert scale) from human raters for up to six main categories and up to forty sub-categories of TEDS in a pre-specified number of scenarios and for a pre-specified number of personae. As part of the evaluation component the TEDS tool had to further be able to calculate and present/print average scale ratings per category/sub-category for each persona and scenario along with the standard deviation. Beyond recording numerical scale values the TEDS tool had to be able to record free-format text comments along with screenshots of a rated artifact for each category and sub-category in any persona-scenario couplet. Recording the ratings needed to occur in an IRB acceptable and human subjects protecting space along with online raters' detailed demographic information. The TEDS tool report component had also to be able to pivot results along each dimension. It also had to be able to include raters' comments and screenshots in reports. Rater-provided screenshots and comments had to be searchable/findable per artifact, scenario, persona, and rater.

Administration/Configuration Component: In order to make the TEDS tool usable for multiple projects and studies, a configuration tool was required; also, for the analysis of results an administration tool for projects and configuration was needed. The TEDS tool admin/configuration had to be able to freely configure categories and sub-categories (all, sub-sets, or extensions). It also had to be able to cluster and re-cluster sub-categories. The TEDS tool admin/configuration further had to be able to add, modify, and remove artifacts, scenarios, and personae. It had to be able to modify the descriptions of categories, sub-categories, and topical clusters. It had to be able to add, modify, and delete collected rating data. For use with external tools rating data and reports had to be exportable into CSV format. The export or handover to other utilities such as the R project for statistical computing had to be provided for post-processing of results.

3.1.2 Non-functional Requirements

For reaching out to expert and layman raters without geographical and time constraints, the TEDS tool needed to be Web-based and work on any Web browser. The browser-based user interface had to be easy to navigate and operate. For easy and straightforward rating and recording, the TEDS tool had to be able to display the information artifact to be rated without interfering with the artifact's functionality alongside the rating tool in a browser window. Given the electronic mass recruitment of raters, for example, via Facebook advertisement, the rater population would be diverse, and so would be their devices and platforms. Consequently, TEDS tool had to be able to support a wide range of devices. The user interface of the TEDS tool had to be adaptable and adjustable depending on the artifact under evaluation, for example, for mobile applications versus web pages, or for full-blown TEDS evaluations versus subset evaluations. Demographic questions had to be configurable relative to the respective TEDS study design. Ratings were to be recorded instantaneously. Rating sessions were to be able to be temporarily suspended and resumed at a later point in time without the loss of data. Raters were to be informed about the progress of the rating exercise relative to completion. Rating results were to be searchable instantaneously. High standard deviations in ratings along with other outliers were to be made visible. Graphics and charts were to support the analysis of rating results. Finally, recruiting and signing up raters, conducting ratings, recording and storing large amounts of data were to be performed in a fashion allowing for comprehensive empirical studies with low or no budgets.

3.2 Design Criteria

When reviewing and considering the requirements, it quickly became clear that publicly available and generic tools such as Google Forms or SurveyMonkey were no suitable solutions for meeting IRB requirements and human subject protection needs and/or would carry prohibitively high price tags when signing up raters. Also, for the inaccessibility of respective data, statistical analyses on raters' demographics would have required significant overhead when using those generic tools. Furthermore, some essential functionality along with the need for flexible and robust configurability options would not have been attainable with such publicly available tools. Consequently, the researchers decided to build a homegrown tool, which would meet all requirements including the storage of collected data on secure institutional servers. Moreover, it was reasoned that a homegrown tool would far better fit the flexibility and configurability needs of future TEDS-based empirical projects.

3.3 Design Options

When analyzing various (also alternative) tool design options, we ultimately settled on utilizing the LAMP (Linux, Apache, MySQL, and PHP) stack. In our reasoning, while LAMP was popular, cost effective, and open source, it also provided the advantages of known runtime robustness along with generally high performance, global resource and support bases, excellent documentation, and sustainability for future development. Along these lines the high potential for continued future talent recruitment from a vast pool of knowledgeable developers for this platform was another important argument in favor of LAMP.

Among other options considered were Windows as server platform, noSQL as database, .Net as alternative to PHP, and native code development as opposed to Web-based application (app) development. In each single area as well as for the whole platform, we concluded that LAMP was favorable. Windows as proprietary server platform appeared more costly in terms of available development resources, installation cost, and upgradeability/version sustainability. The enterprise-grade .NET framework seemed to be overkill relative to the foreseeable present and future research needs of the envisioned relatively small system, which were seen as fully covered via PHP, the latter of which also provided rapid prototyping and app development along with boilerplate constructions of Web-based application program interfaces (APIs). Also, we did not expect much server-side logic to be needed. As a result, we saw PHP as a right-size/right-weight choice. On the client side, we could have opted for developing a native application instead of using a Web-based application. However, this would have led to a proprietary and high load of custom development and maintenance along with portability issues among others, whereas a Web-based client would be easier to develop, maintain, and distribute. Finally, relational characteristics are a mainstay of TEDS-based use and usability studies so that a relational database concept was the natural choice over non-relational concepts. Among relational databases, MySQL had advantages of cost effectiveness, slimness, platform independence, robustness, and non-proprietariness over other options such as Microsoft SQL Server, Oracle, or others. In summary, the LAMP stack appeared as a logical platform for the development and implementation of the Web-based TEDS rating tool, which was dubbed *TEDSrate*.

3.4 The TEDSrate Approach

According to the functional requirements, TEDSrate would need three main architectural components: (1) an administration and configuration component, (b) a rating or evaluation/assessment component, (c) a database component for storing study configurations as well as evaluation results and ratings along with qualitative data such as comments and screenshots, and (d) a result query and presentation component (see

Fig. 1). A fifth architectural component, that is, an automatic statistical post-processor was and still is under consideration for a future version of TEDSrate. In its current implementation, TEDSrate uses both plain php scripts and the object-oriented CodeIgniter (CI) PHP framework (Fig. 2).

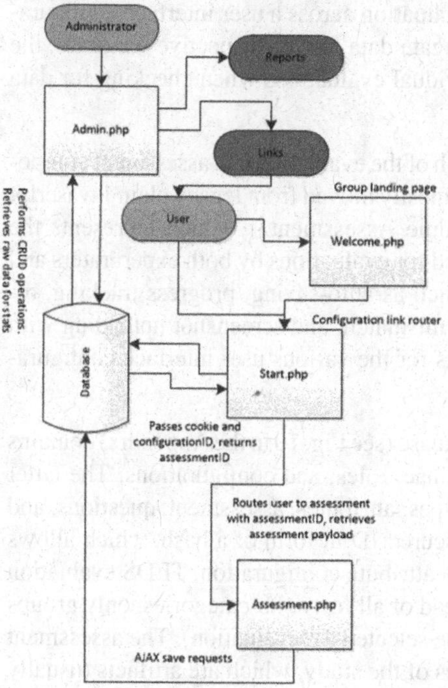

Fig. 1. TEDSrate overview

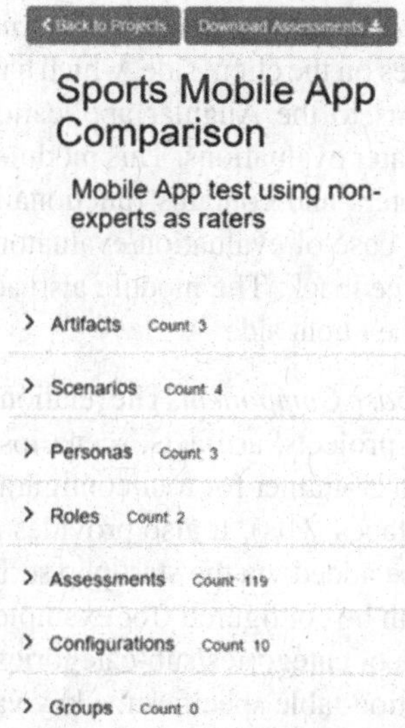

Fig. 2. TEDSrate admin/configuration tool (project: sports mobile app comparison)

The Admin/Configuration Component allows to create and manage TEDS research projects. On the server side, a new project is started in the admin function by defining and attaching the project's use facets such as artifacts, personae, scenarios, and roles. Several scripts handle project setup and management including adminproc.php (for admin login/logout), start.php (for handling the routing logic for new assessments and new users), assessment.php (a misnomer for legacy reasons, now containing an Angular template for issuing assessments), upload.php (for uploading rater screenshots and providing feedback to the raters), and welcome.php (for helping raters navigate configurations). In recent rewrites and updates to TEDSrate, CodeIgniter has been used as an efficient replacement method for previously used plain php models to interact with the data layer, since it also allows for the creation of a REST (representational state transfer) API, which is now the primary means of interacting with the database facilitating CRUD (create, read, update, and delete) operations on all entities of the data schema.

Furthermore, the Internal API handles specific processes such as receiving project overviews and generating report tables. On the client side, Admin.js is an Angular script, which supports the creation of project entities such as artifacts, scenarios, personae, roles, user interface configurations, and evaluations. Admin.js allows administrators to view rating results in the form of pivot tables presenting means and standard deviations. It further provides access to and graphically presents raters' demographic information. Moreover, Admin.js presents statistics along three dimensions: artifacts across a scenario, scenarios for one artifact, and an evaluation across a user interface configuration. The former two statistics provide aggregate data for the respective variables, the latter allows the granular inspection of individual evaluations when checking for data consistency and quality.

The Evaluation/Assessment Component. Much of the evaluation and assessment component resides on the client side, which has also mostly moved from legacy plain Javascript components to the Angular application module Assessment.js, which represents the logic for rater evaluations. This module is used for evaluations by both expert raters and layman raters and contains functionalities such as auto-saving, progress tracking, re-routing in case of evaluation/evaluator-rater mismatch, and screenshot uploading with progress feedback. The module also accounts for the various user interface configurations on the client side.

The Database Component. The relational database (see Fig. 10 in the Appendix) contains tables for projects, artifacts, scenarios, personae, roles, and configurations. The latter serves as a container for four configuration types: attributes, assessment, questions, and user interfaces (UIs). It also provides an obscured ID in form of a hash, which allows raters to be added via the start.php script. Via attribute configuration, TEDS evaluation subsets can be configured (for example, instead of all forty sub-categories, only groups or clusters of categories/sub-categories can be selected for evaluation). The assessment configuration table specifies the key variables of the study, which are artifacts (usually a website or mobile app) and the scenarios, personas, and roles. The question configuration table serves as a target to associate the project with a group of survey questions. The UI configuration table contains the specification of the rating style (for example, Likert scale). The assessment table is the reference point for ratings, comments, and screenshots. It also holds time stamp information. The attribute table specifies the TEDS category/sub-category or configured cluster. It further holds the attribute description or explanation in academic or layman language. The rating table stores the rating value for a single attribute. It also serves as the reference to attach attribute-related textual rater comments and screenshots. The question table holds the information on demographics questions (question title/name, description, and requirement status), whereas the response table stores the respective rater responses. Finally, the user table stores personal identifiers such as email address, first name, last name, and password along with the respective users' authorization level.

The schema also contains a number of associative entities such as project (parent), artifact, scenario, persona, role (children) or question (parent), project, artifact, scenario, persona, role, attribute (children).

Stored Procedures and Worked Scenarios. TEDSrate also contains about thirty stored procedures such as addPersona, addPersonaScenario, addProject, addProjectArtifact, addRating, addResponse, addScenario, addScreenshot, addUser, getAllArtifacts, getAllPersonae, getAllProjects, getCategories, getCriteria, getProject, getUser, updateCategory, and updateUser, among others.

Further, worked scenarios include starting a project, creating a configuration, and running a report.

4 Pilot Tests with Real-World Organizations

Concurrently, two TEDSrate-based evaluations of different artifacts were carried out, one of which in the environment of professional disaster response management at the City of Seattle's Emergency Operations Center (EOC), and the other with a major league soccer club (Seattle Sounders FC). In the case of the Seattle EOC a Web-based artifact was evaluated, which responders mainly work with on desktop computers during the response to an emergency or a disaster. In the other case, a mobile application was rated, which ticket holders, fans, and supporters of the Sounders FC franchise use to keep up to date about their team and to shop for franchise-related merchandise or tickets.

4.1 Government-Internal Website Evaluation (WebEOC)

Intermedix' WebEOC® is a Web-based application suite, which is tailored to help Emergency Operations Centers (EOCs) manage the response to and early recovery from disasters. The suite is configurable and expandable and enjoys a relatively large user base among EOCs in the United States. In recent years WebEOC has been criticized for its cumbersomeness, complexity, and old-fashioned user interface.

The City of Seattle's EOC had a vested interest in identifying the exact problem areas of WebEOC from a user's perspective, that is, from a disaster responder's view. TEDSrate was configured and used to receive ratings and feedback from responders who had recently used WebEOC during a disaster response or exercise.

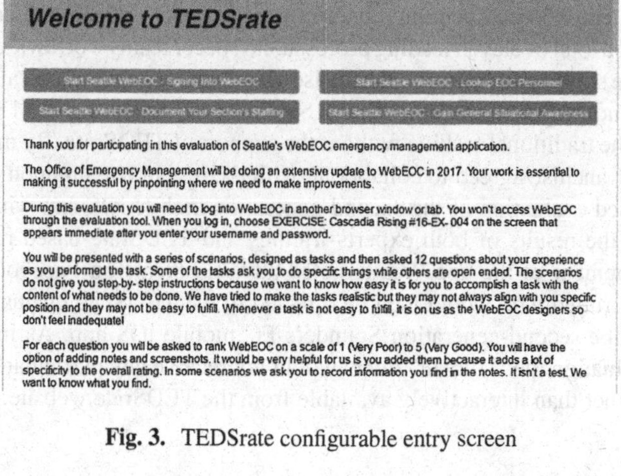

Fig. 3. TEDSrate configurable entry screen

In particular, four scenarios of utilization, each of which comprises one or more use cases, were seen as potentially in need of improvement along several lines (UI, performance, logic, etc.). The four utilization scenarios were (1) Signing into WebEOC, (2) Lookup EOC Personnel on duty, (3) Document Your Section's Staffing, and (4) Gain General Situational Awareness. The evaluation was carried out before and immediately after a major exercise was conducted involving over 200 responders in June 2016. The purpose of the evaluation was explained to responders on the entry screen (see Fig. 3).

It is noteworthy that except for the introductory information in the entry page no further training of tool or method was required for responders to perform the requested evaluations for the four scenarios. The evaluation would be taken on a split screen, that is, the WebEOC artifact alongside the TEDSrate window.

4.2 APP Evaluation (SoundersS FC's Mobile IOS APP)

Almost every franchise in the US Major Soccer League (MLS) has implemented a mobile application for smart phones or notepads. While the websites of all franchises are designed, operated, and maintained by the League, the franchises have greater leeway to develop and implement their own mobile apps. The various MLS team websites are distinct in appearance (logos, team colors, etc.) and content (team-related information); however, they are uniform in terms of functionality and style guidelines. When it comes to mobile apps, the League appears to mandate only the adherence to guidelines of presentation style and merchandising, whereas the functionality of apps may widely differ between franchises.

Since its introduction to the League in 2009, Seattle Sounders FC has developed into a commercially highly successful MLS franchise with the far highest average attendance in the League (44,247 in 2015), which is more than double the League's average (21,574 in 2015), and even exceeds the average attendance of the league with the highest attendance worldwide, that is, the German Bundesliga (43,177 in 2015) [12, 16].

A comprehensive TEDSrate-based evaluation of an early version of the second generation of the Sounders FC's mobile iOS app was conducted at a time, when the app development process had not concluded and was still open to extensions and modifications based on the evaluation results. The evaluation was performed in two rounds, first with expert raters who had been involved in a larger study, which had compared the mobile apps of a total of eleven leading professional soccer teams worldwide. The results of this separate study have been published elsewhere. These expert raters also evaluated the early second-generation mobile app of Sounders FC following the 13-step TEDS procedure in the traditional fashion without the support of TEDSrate. By mid-2015, the Sounders FC franchise agreed to collaborate with the research team upon organizing a TEDSrate-based evaluation of the second-generation mobile iOS app with the aim of incorporating the results of both experts' ratings and TEDSrate-based ratings in the further development of the app. Via targeted advertisements on Facebook "layman" raters were recruited who would then be directed to the TEDSrate evaluation site and asked to rate the second-generation Sounders FC mobile iOS app. As in the case of WebEOC evaluation the "layman" raters would not receive any particular introduction nor training other than interactively available from the TEDSrate website. As intended the Facebook recruitments of "laymen" raters provided a wide spread of geographical, age, gender, and other backgrounds in the sample.

4.3 Demographics Module

When moving from purposively selected expert raters to a wider population of non-expert ("layman") raters it was imperative to collect demographic data in order to better quantify and qualify the results. More detailed and more specific demographic data would be needed for larger populations (for example, "Asian soccer fans," "North American soccer fans," or "European soccer fans", see Fig. 5) than for smaller and more homogeneous populations such as "City of Seattle Emergency Responders" when making sense of and relating the rating results to demographic characteristics in the analysis phase.

As mentioned before, demographic questions are configurable accounting for larger and diverse populations.

4.4 The Rating Procedure

TEDSrate allows for configuring and adjusting the categories and sub-categories of the TEDS framework. As mentioned before, the framework consists of six main categories and forty sub-categories, which can be expanded or consolidated depending on the desired granularity of the specific evaluation project. In the case of "layman" evaluations fewer and consolidated categories/sub-categories serve the evaluation purpose more effectively than too specific and too detailed rating schemes, which typically only experts fully understand and then rate in an informed fashion. We are referring to "experts," in the context of TEDS, as individuals who have attended a TEDS framework and procedure training and, after completing an artifact rating, have also attended an inter-rater validity and consistency checking session (Fig. 4).

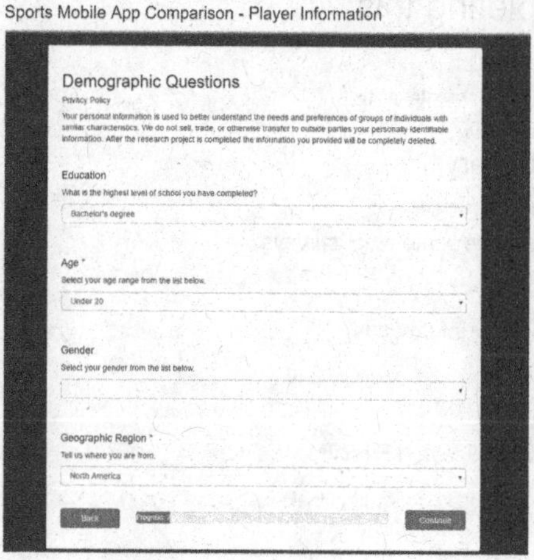

Fig. 4. Sample demographic questions (configurable)

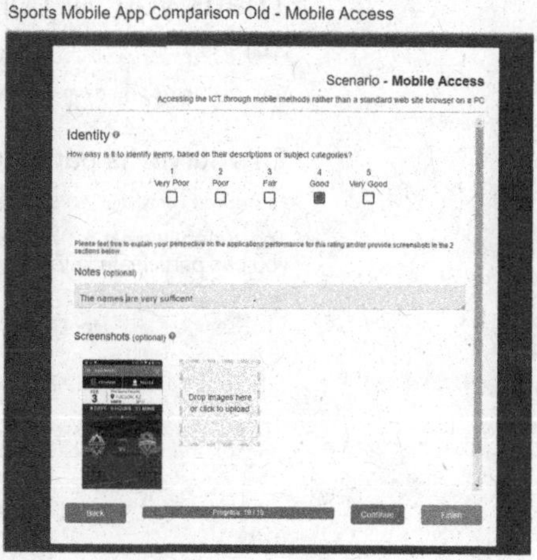

Fig. 5. Sample rating screen with Likert scale, free-format text comments, and screenshots (configurable)

In the case of the WebEOC website evaluation as well as in the case of the "layman" evaluation of the second-generation Sounders FC mobile app a consolidated framework was used, which was reduced to twelve sub-categories (two for each main category—see sample screen in Fig. 5), whereas the expert evaluation of the mobile app used the entire framework of forty sub-categories.

Transparent to the individual rater who uses the rating tool TEDSrate saves all data entries immediately via AJAX calls to the server. Each entry, whether it is a Likert scale radio button tick, a text comment, or an artifact screenshot is saved individually, so that client-to-server communications are relatively small and therefore fast.

Whatever configuration is used, the rater sees her advancement towards completion of the evaluation by means of a progress bar displayed at the bottom of the rating screen.

If raters have to postpone the completion of the evaluation for some reason, they find the latest data they had entered before pre-filled in the form, so that they can continue the rating exactly at the point, where they left it off.

Most artifacts are designed to serve multiple purposes and subsequently are used in practice in more than one scenario of utilization. However, the evaluation with TEDSrate has to distinguish between scenarios, since an artifact might be highly rated for some uses and certain scenarios, while it may fall short in others.

As an example, for the mobile apps of soccer clubs such as Sounders FC, Real Madrid, of FC Barcelona, the scenarios of "player information" and "schedule and results" might be evaluated among others. A rater, hence, has to go through the rating procedure as many times as separate scenarios were configured for evaluation. Once one scenario evaluation is completed, the rater needs to be reminded that other scenarios still need ratings. Once raters complete or leave a rating session unfinished, upon exiting the

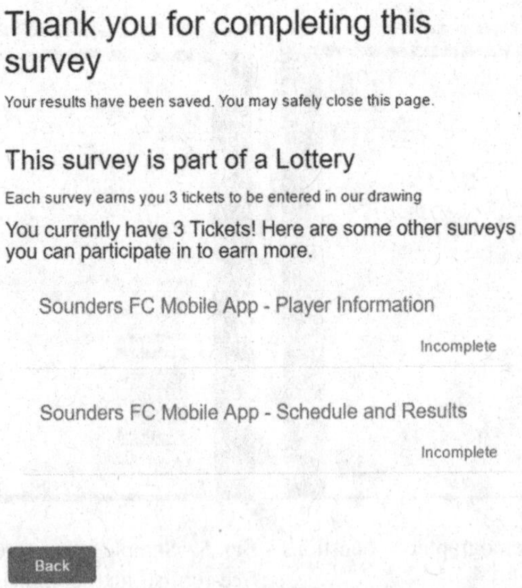

Thank you for completing this survey
Your results have been saved. You may safely close this page.
This survey is part of a Lottery
Each survey earns you 3 tickets to be entered in our drawing
You currently have 3 Tickets! Here are some other surveys you can participate in to earn more.
Sounders FC Mobile App - Player Information
Incomplete
Sounders FC Mobile App - Schedule and Results
Incomplete
Back

Fig. 6. Survey completion update

rating of a scenario, they are reminded of the overall completion status of their assignments (see Fig. 6).

In evaluation assignments with several pre-configured scenarios or attributes, TEDSrate also allows for the randomization of the order, in which the various scenarios or attributes are presented to the rater.

4.5 Mitigating Rater Fatigue

In the course of both artifact evaluations, the WebEOC website and the Sounders FC mobile app, rater fatigue was discovered. Some "layman" raters would leave the rating sessions behind incomplete even after repeated reminders. While the randomization of the order of assignments appeared to have already had some mitigating influence on rater fatigue, other means such as incentives were considered and became part of the TEDSrate tool during the practice test phase. In particular, when populations with potentially short attention spans are targeted, the incentive module can be configured. The implementation was performed in the format of a lottery, in which raters who completed the assignments would earn them "tickets" with certain material value, which could then be used for purchases or other benefits. In the case of the Sounders FC's

	Player Information			Schedule and Results		
	Average	Std. Dev.	Count	Average	Std. Dev.	Count
Navigation and Findability	3.43	0.97	55	3.67	0.92	33
Structure	3.55	1.02	60	3.45	0.96	31
Identity	3.96	0.91	57	3.68	0.94	[illegible]
Substantiality	3.67	1.09	57	3.68	0.91	31
Completeness	3.91	0.88	56	3.71	1.04	31
Trustworthiness	4.04	0.99	56	3.90	0.98	[illegible]
Interaction	3.33	1.03	54	3.17	1.21	30
Customization	3.49	0.97	53	3.39	[illegible]	31
Savings	3.62	1.16	53	3.48	1.20	31
Confidence	3.79	[illegible]	52	3.81	1.14	31
Attractiveness	3.60	1.16	52	3.48	1.18	31
Enjoyment	3.44	1.07	52	3.42	0.89	31

Fig. 7. Likert ratings for two scenarios along twelve sub-categories for the sounders FC mobile app

mobile app, the lottery-based mitigation strategy worked satisfactorily leading to much increased completion rates. The researchers also successfully experimented with giving out $5 gift certificates to the first 25 raters who completed the TEDS surveys for two scenarios by using timestamp and user ID information. Likewise this led to more and faster completion of surveys in this particular pilot.

4.6 Presentation and Analysis of Results

In both pilot tests, the feature of the TEDSrate Admin utility, which lets the researchers track evaluations and lets them see even preliminary results in real time while the evaluations are still underway, was found highly informative and beneficial. All analytical functions can be performed this way, for example, inspecting pivot tables of ratings along the lines of configurations, scenarios, or artifacts, or after the evaluation project has ended. The utility also allows for selection and instantaneous analyses of demographic sub-samples, comment presentations, screenshot inspection, and data export to external analysis tools (for an example, see Fig. 7).

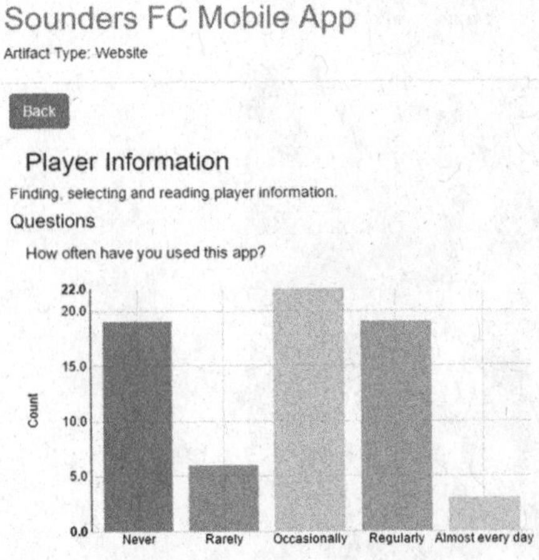

Fig. 8. Visualization of usage frequencies in support of interpreting the weight and validity of ratings

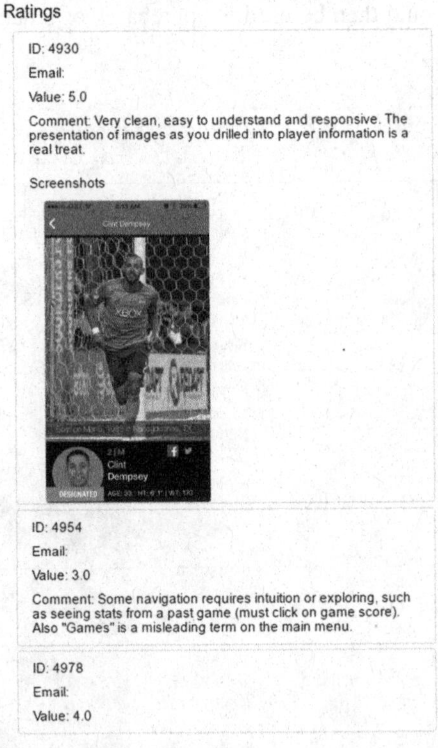

Fig. 9. Inspecting raters' comments and screenshots in a target area based on clean and formatted displays

The visualization and formatting of results was found essential for analytical interpretation, also due to the sheer amount of detailed data, which was produced. Not only numerical data were target of visualization and formatted display but also comments, screenshots, and demographic information helping focus the analytical treatments and speed up the overall analysis process (for example, see Fig. 8). In ongoing rating campaigns the immediacy of information availability, in particular, with regard to demographic information helped target the rater recruiting so that the various identified personae could exactly be represented and matched by the sample of raters. Formatted displays for comments and screenshots supported the straightforward inspection of data and their analytical interpretation. When numerical data showed both relative strengths and weaknesses in a particular area, for example, "navigation and findability" in the scenario of "player information," then the comments and screenshots, which raters had provided, could be inspected in that particular area (see Figs. 7 and 9).

5 Discussion

As shown in the section on related work above, software engineering success depends on a number of interacting and interdependent variables, some of which escape the developers' span of control, whereas others, which can be directly influenced, have so far gone unattended for the most part due to prohibitive cost and overwhelming commitment of resources and time needed to uncover deficiencies in, for example, artifact quality, attractiveness, user satisfaction, and system use among others.

Feedback, if any, which could practically and effectively influence how developers and designers tweak or reshape an artifact to better meet expectations and needs, would be slow in coming and probably incomplete. While the TEDS framework and procedure might be the most comprehensive and systematic analytical lens available for assessing, evaluating, and comparing artifacts, it also suffered from the high cost incurred, long time to conclude, and heavy resource commitment necessary in order to arrive at detailed, conclusive, and robust results. In many instances, however, even if such a level of effort had been expended, it would not have produced the needed feedback in due time, and, for example, market opportunity might have already vanished, or worse, damage had already been inflicted. The critical question then became how the prohibitive high cost, long turnarounds, and excessive resource commitments for systematic artifact evaluations could be cut down without compromising the validity and robustness of results. This led the research group to consider, specify, design, develop, and test TEDSrate in practice.

The tool underwent two real-world tests, one with the City of Seattle Emergency Operations Center (EOC) for a desktop-operated web-based application suite (WebEOC), which serves as the Center's linchpin in disaster response. The other real-world test was simultaneously conducted with Seattle Sounders FC for the soccer franchise's mobile application, which is the centerpiece of interaction between the club and its supporters and match attendees.

These two tests greatly demonstrated the effectiveness and utility of the tool, which produced robust and reliable results, which were used by both organizations to make targeted changes to the configuration of their respective artifacts. In the case of Sounders FC, the test identified in fine detail such areas that needed improvement. Moreover, informed by rater comments and screenshots and through pinpointed comparisons with other "best-in-class" implementations, detailed design recommendations were given to the mobile app developers, many of which have meanwhile been developed and implemented into version 2 of the Seattle Sounders FC mobile app.

The two tests were conducted over a period of six weeks. A total of 90 raters were involved, most of whom completed all Web-based TEDSrate surveys in all scenarios, to which they were assigned. The recruiting of "laymen" raters was found easier, when certain material incentives were offered, for example, gift cards. Recruiting raters for the Seattle Sounders FC app via the Sounders' Facebook site by means of targeted Facebook advertisement was straightforward. In the case of WebEOC, the raters were recruited via EOC-internal email invitation. However, in other artifact evaluation and comparison studies, different recruiting approaches may also be effective.

Since TEDSrate works web-based, the reach of this artifact evaluation and comparison tool is global, so that literally any target audience can directly be reached. Results of TEDSrate-based artifact evaluations and comparisons become available instantaneously, which provides a great benefit also to developers if TEDSrate is used in pilot testing and iterative development cycles. The tests proved that time was little, cost was low, and resources were few that were needed to produce detailed artifact evaluations and real-world feedback.

These results give us confidence for asserting that TEDSrate has successfully addressed a core issue when it comes to improving and enabling timely and effective artifact evaluation.

6 Conclusion and Future Work

Software engineering success hinges on a number of variables, not all of which developers and software engineers are able to directly influence. However, many of those that can be directly addressed have also gone unattended for reasons of high cost, long time to complete, and prohibitive resource commitments necessary for producing meaningful and detailed feedback on artifacts. With the introduction of TEDSrate a tool has been created and tested that overcomes the cost, time, and resource barrier. It helps collect, analyze, and present detailed feedback data, which can immediately be used to adjust and change designs and improve artifacts.

In the next version of TEDSrate we will implement a post-processor, which transfers the numerical data to statistics packages for appropriate automatic analyses. We also consider the transfer of comments to an automatic text-mining post-processor.

Acknowledgment. Our thanks go to then graduate assistant Gary Gao, the developer of the alpha version of TEDSrate in 2013, who was followed by graduate students Delong Gao and Donghe Xu who added the initial version of the Admin Utility in 2014. Since 2015 William Menten-Weil has performed the technical design and development. We would also like to thank Janet Boyd, head of the graduate assistants crew at the Information School in the University of Washington, who helped get this project off the ground.

Appendix

See Fig. 10.

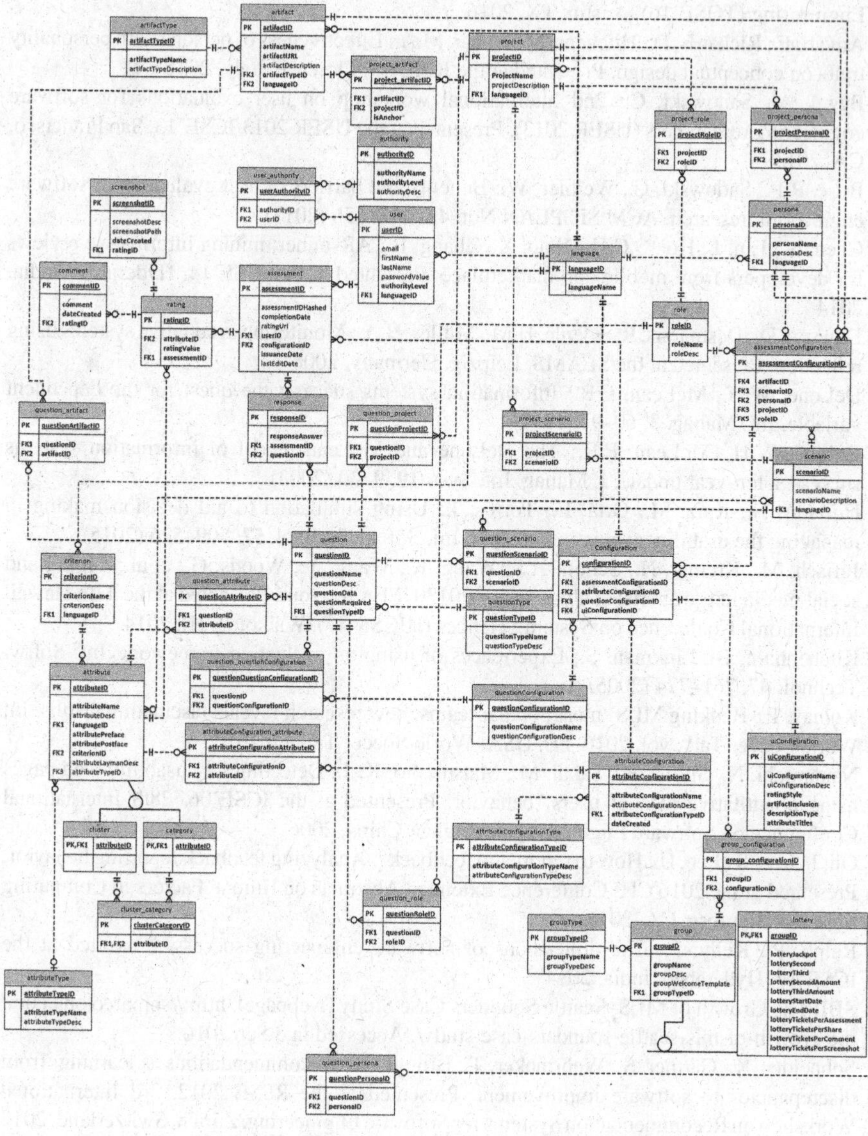

Fig. 10. TEDSrate Entity Relationship Diagram

References

1. Abdelzad, V., Lethbridge, T.C., Hosseini, M.: The role of semiotic engineering in software engineering. Presented at the 5th International Workshop on Theory-Oriented Software Engineering (TOSE'16), Austin, TX, 2016
2. Anvari, F., Richards, D., Hitchens, M., Babar, M.A.: Effectiveness of persona with personality traits on conceptual design. Presented at the ICSE'15, Florence, Italy, 2015
3. Begel, A., Sadowski, C.: 2nd International workshop on user evaluations for software engineering researchers (USER 2013). Presented at the USER 2013/ICSE'13, San Francisco, CA, 2013
4. Buse, R.P., Sadowski, C., Weimer, W.: Benefits and barriers of user evaluation in software engineering research. ACM SIGPLAN Not. **46**, 643–656 (2011)
5. Chen, N., Lin, J., Hoi, S.C.H., Xiao, X., Zhang, B.: AR-miner: mining informative reviews for developers from mobile app marketplace. Presented at the ICSE'14, Hyderabad, India, 2014
6. Dawson, D., Desmarais, R., Kienle, H.M., Müller, H.A.: Monitoring in adaptive systems using reflection. Presented at the SEAMS, Leipzig, Germany, 2008
7. DeLone, W.H., McLean, E.R.: Information systems success: the quest for the dependent variable. Inf. Manag. **3**, 60–95 (1992)
8. Delone, W.H., McLean, E.R.: The DeLone and McLean model of information systems success: a ten-year update. J. Manag. Inf. Syst. **19**, 9–30 (2003)
9. Hurtado, N., Ruiz, M., Orta, E., Torres, J.: Using simulation to aid decision making in managing the usability evaluation process. Inf. Softw. Technol. **57**, 509–526 (2015)
10. Jurisch, M., Krcmar, H., Scholl, H.J., Wang, K., Wang, Y., Woods, G., et al.: Digital and social media in pro sports: analysis of the 2013 UEFA top four. Presented at the 47th Hawaii International Conference on System Sciences (HICSS-47), Waikoloa, HI, 2014
11. Kitchenham, B., Linkman, S.: Experiences of using an evaluation framework. Inf. Softw. Technol. **47**, 761–774 (2005)
12. Kolnay, P.: Ranking MLS' most popular teams; new research reveals fascinating results. In: World Soccer Talk, vol. 2016. FL, USA: World Soccer Talk (2015)
13. Nakamichi, N., Shima, K., Sakai, M., Matsumoto, K.-I.: Detecting low usability web pages using quantitative data of users' behavior. Presented at the ICSE'06. 28th International Conference on Software Engineering, Shanghai, China, 2006
14. Oh, J., Lee, S., Lee, U.: How to report app feedback?: Analyzing feedback reporting behavior. Presented at the 2016 CHI Conference Extended Abstracts on Human Factors in Computing Systems, San Jose, CA, 2016
15. Ralph, P., Kelly, P.: The dimensions of software engineering success. Presented at the ICSE'14, Hyderabad, India, 2014
16. SBI: The Growth of MLS–Seattle Sounders Case Study [webpage]. http://sbibarcelona.com/the-growth-of-mls-seattle-sounders-case-study/. Accessed in 3 Sep 2016
17. Schneider, K., Gärtner, S., Wehrmaker, T., Brügge, B.: Recommendations as learning: from discrepancies to software improvement. Presented at the RSSE 2012. 3rd International Workshop on Recommendation Systems for Software Engineering, Zurich, Switzerland, 2012
18. Schneidewind, L., Hörold, S., Mayas, C., Krömker, H., Falke, S., Pucklitsch, T.: How personas support requirements engineering. Presented at the UsARE 2012. 1st International Workshop on Usability and Accessibility Focused Requirements Engineering, Zurich, Switzerland, 2012
19. Scholl, H.J.: Evaluating sports websites from an information management perspective. In: Pedersen, P.M. (ed.) Routledge Handbook of Sport Communication, pp. 289–299. Routledge, New York (2013)

20. Scholl, H.J., Carlson, T.S.: Professional sports teams on the web: a comparative study employing the information management perspective. Eur. Sport Manag. Q. **12**, 137–160 (2012)
21. Scholl, H.J., Eisenberg, M., Dirks, L., Carlson, T.S.: The TEDS framework for assessing information systems from a human actors' perspective: extending and repurposing Taylor's value-added model. J. Am. Soc. Inf. Sci. Technol. **62**, 789–804 (2011)
22. Scholl, H.J., Wang, K., Wang, Y., Woods, G., Xu, D., Yao, Y., et al.: Top soccer teams in cyberspace: online channels for services, communications, research, and sales. J. Market. Anal. **2**, 98–119 (2014)
23. Seddon, P.B.: A respecification and extension of the DeLone and McLean model of IS success. Inf. Syst. Res. **8**, 240–252 (1997)
24. Shekhovtsov, V.A., Mayr, H.C., Kop, C.: Stakeholder involvement into quality definition and evaluation for service-oriented systems. Presented at the USER 2012. 1st International Workshop on User Evaluation for Software Engineering Researchers, Zurich, Switzerland, 2012
25. Taylor, R.S.: Value-added processes in the information life cycle. J. Am. Soc. Inf. Sci. **33**, 341–346 (1982)

Understanding Public Value Creation in the Delivery of Electronic Services

Luis F. Luna-Reyes[1(✉)], Rodrigo Sandoval-Almazan[2], Gabriel Puron-Cid[3], Sergio Picazo-Vela[4], Dolores E. Luna[4], and J. Ramon Gil-Garcia[1]

[1] University at Albany, State University of New York, Albany, NY 12222, USA
lluna-reyes@albany.edu

[2] Universidad Autonoma Del Estado de Mexico, 50130 Toluca, EdoMex, Mexico

[3] Centro de Investigacion y Docencia Economicas, 20313 Aguascalientes, AGS, Mexico

[4] Universidad de las Americas Puebla, 72810 Cholula, PUE, Mexico

Abstract. Understanding public value creation through electronic services is a complex and important research problem. Recent attempts to understand electronic services value from the citizen perspective suggest that dividing service delivery in several stages could be a valuable approach to understand ways in which information technologies support value creation when providing electronic services. Therefore, we propose the use of this process model as a tool to analyze and define public value creation through electronic services. We show the potential value of the model using birth certificate requests as a hypothetical example. We conclude the paper by describing how we are applying the model to our current research.

Keywords: Public value · Electronic services · Digital government · Citizen behavior model · Electronic government

1 Introduction

The concept of public value has become increasingly important in the field of digital government, public administration, and a few other related disciplines. However, in spite of some efforts to clarify the concept and its implications for digital government research [1], public value is not yet clearly defined. In fact, there is not a clear agreement on the definition of Public Value even among Public Value scholars [2]. On the other hand, conducting some preliminary focus groups related to the use of digital government services, one of the main problems identified by the researchers was the difficulty of framing the creation of value in the conversation with focus groups participants [3].

In this way, we propose in this paper a process model that may serve as a framework to understand public value creation in the delivery of electronic services. The model is an adaptation from consumer behavior models developed in the field of marketing, and commonly used in electronic commerce applications [4–6]. We believe that this process model provides a framework to think about public value creation in a more operational

M. Janssen et al. (Eds.): EGOV 2017, LNCS 10428, pp. 378–385, 2017.
DOI: 10.1007/978-3-319-64677-0_31

way, making easier to connect specific technology-supported processes with the creation of values to the public.

The rest of the paper is organized in three sections. The second section includes preliminary conceptual ideas associated to public value and the process model. Section 3 introduces a conceptual analysis of the potential use of the model to understand public value creation. We finish the paper with a reflection on the potential use of the model, and the ways in which we are using it in our current research.

2 A Framework for Public Value Creation in Electronic Services

The present section is an introduction to the main concepts in public value creation and also includes a brief presentation of our preliminary process model. The model was developed by the authors as part of a project in which we are looking to better understand the creation of public value in electronic services from the citizen perspective. The model is a way of connecting the use of electronic services to the creation of public value.

2.1 Approaches to Public Value

Information technologies in government have played an important role in government modernization agendas [7, 8]. The use of technology has always been associated with value creation. In the early days of information technology use in government, efficiencies and cost savings were the most important sources of value [9]. The New Public Management and collaborative governance approaches have emphasized on applications looking beyond the organizational boundaries of government, adding focus on program effectiveness, citizen participation and improved democracy [9, 10].

Digital government creates value by applying information technologies in support of core government tasks and public service delivery. Public value management has been recently identified as an approach to public administration that is still in the process of being defined [2]. Although there are competing definitions, in this paper we are understanding public value creation as an strategic approach to public management [11]. This approach to public management was proposed by Moore [12], who introduced the concept as a way to understand the creation of value by public managers in contrast to the approach to value in the private sector, where the emphasis is in the creation of value for the stockholders. In the public sector, as a contrast, value is to be created for the public. According to him, value creation was the result of aligning three interrelated processes in a strategic triangle [11]: (1) defining public value, (2) building and sustaining a group of diverse stakeholders to create an authorizing environment, and (3) mobilizing the resources from inside and outside the organization to achieve the desired outcomes.

Parallel developments have been more focused on defining value to the public. In the area of digital government, for example, public value has been defined as the result of seven value generators [13, 14]. These seven generators include efficiency, efficacy, enablement, intrinsic enhancements in government actions, transparency, participation, and collaboration. This work emphasizes the multiple and diverse stakeholders that would be involved in any in-depth analysis of an initiative designed to create public value.

In the broader Public Administration literature, Jørgensen and Bozeman have defined seven constellations of values [15]. The constellations involve lists of values such as the ones mentioned above, but organized from the perspective of public administration and its relationships with inside and outside actors. For example, efficiency and effectiveness belong to the constellation of intraorganizational aspects of public administration. Transparency and collaboration, on the other hand, related to the constellation of relationships between public administration and its environment. Other constellations include relationships between public administration and the citizens, politicians and the society at large.

2.2 A Process Model for Government Electronic Services Delivery

In an effort to better understand consumers buying decision process, marketers have developed process models that start with identifying a need or problem, and continue with acquiring information about potential solutions, assessing the alternatives, buying, and finally, assessing the results of the product acquired [4–6]. This type of models have been evolving by recognizing that consumers use traditional and on-line channels in different steps of the buying decision process [16]. This models have been useful in the design of e-commerce websites and defining conversion goals, which involve developing strategies to promote consumers to move from one step to the next in the buying process, such as requesting for a quote, moving a product to a shopping cart or buying it.

We argue that the use of an adaptation of this type of process models can help to understand information technology value creation through electronic services in government. The idea was derived from our efforts on understanding electronic services public value creation from the citizen perspective. Focus groups with citizens revealed the difficulty on eliciting the public value creation from citizens' perspective. Our adaptation of consumer behavior models includes five stages: Information search, form preparation, submitting forms, payment, and getting results (see Fig. 1).

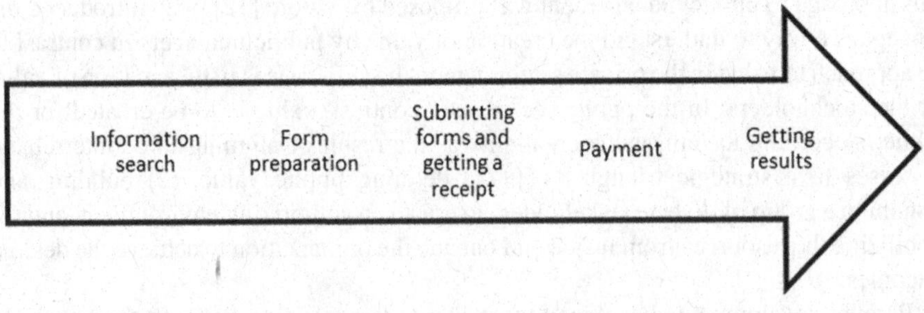

Fig. 1. Citizen behavior model. Source: Adapted from [4].

Information search involves citizen behavior oriented to find the requirements, costs and documentation of specific services provided by government. Important information for the citizens also includes addresses of public offices where they can apply for the services as well as their hours of operation. The second stage involves the preparation of the forms required to apply for the service. Form completion may require data that is not at the citizen's finger tips, and that is our main rationale on separating this stage from the submission of the forms. Submitting the forms constitutes the third step in our service delivery model, which includes processing of the form and usually issuing a receipt. Although not all public services involve a payment, there are some public services that involve a fee, such as applying for a passport, a driver's license or a birth certificate. Finally, many public services involve some result from the process, and this constitutes the last component of our model.

In the following section, we use the case of requesting a copy of a birth certificate as an example to illustrate the use of the model to understand public value creation through electronic service delivery in government.

3 Exploring the Potential Utility of the Framework: Obtaining Birth Certificates

In order to show the usefulness of the proposed process to understand public value creation in the delivery of electronic services, we decided to analyze one public service using the five-step process model. First, we described the five stages for the service including also mechanisms in which information technologies can be used to support each stage of the process. Then, we include examples of individual and public values that are created through the use of information technologies and electronic services. We chose obtaining a copy of a birth certificate as the example or case for this section of the paper. The process may differ from country to country. We are using Mexico as the context for this electronic service.

First of all, it is worth to notice that in the Mexican context, issuing copies of birth certificates is a State level service in charge of the State's Civil Registry. The Civil Registry in each state has offices in major cities, sometimes in each municipality, but sometimes only in major urban centers. Before the introduction of electronic records around 10 years ago [17], obtaining a copy of a birth certificate in Mexico and living in a rural area, implied traveling to the city where the citizen had been registered to search for the original book where the birth was registered and made a copy on this basis. The copy was usually hand-written or typed in a form. Finding the record use to take several days. Another important note is that the postal service in Mexico is not reliable enough to support this type of official requests. In this way, a citizen that needed a copy of his or her birth certificate needed to cover costs of travel and other incidentals to obtain it. It is also important to note that in the context of Mexico, a copy of a birth certificate is a common requirement to apply for school, a scholarship, government benefits, or a job. Currently, and after the introduction of electronic records, it is possible to obtain a birth certificate in any office of the Civil Registry using a shared database with a unique population registry.

When the state regulations include a standard for electronic signatures, it is also possible an electronic birth certificate. This is possible on very few states.

Table 1. Stages in applying for a copy of a birth certificate in Mexico. Source: Authors' own preparation.

Step in the behavior model	Activity in the context of obtaining a birth certificate	Potential support by information technologies
Information search	The citizen looks for information about the requirements, fees, forms, times and places to apply for and get a birth certificate	Information technology can be used to ask for or distribute the information via telephone, email, social media, or a web page. Citizens usually combine more than one of these technologies in their process of search
Form preparation	Birth certificates require filling a form with basic information of the person that is applying for a copy, including his/her name, place of birth and date of birth. Additionally, citizens can provide information to ease the search such as their Unique Registry Identifier (CURP) or currently, a code associated directly to the birth registry	Information technology can be used to distribute the form (such a pdf) through email or a web page. The form itself can be filled online by the citizen and submitted via the web page. In some places in Mexico, the Civil Registry Office has a self-service kiosk where the citizens input the required data to obtain the birth certificate
Submitting forms and getting a receipt	Submitting the form to apply for a copy of the birth certificate	The same electronic media used to distribute the form can be used to submit the form (email, web pages, kiosks, etc.)
Payment	There is a fee associated to the service	Again, credit cards, ATMs and Internet-based electronic payments are ways in which technology can be used to facilitate the transaction. Several Mexican States also use networks of convenience stores to collect payments for government fees
Getting results	Obtaining a copy of the birth certificate	In its most basic form, printers facilitate the copying process. Moreover, self-service kiosks have the potential of being also dispensers of documents. In the cases of states with a regulation for electronic signatures, the Internet can also be used to issue an electronic document

Table 1 describes the main tasks related to each of the five stages in our process model as they relate to the application for a copy of a birth certificate in Mexico. Recently, one of the authors of the paper had to obtain copies of his birth certificate. He started, as the model suggest, by searching for information about requirements and places to apply for a copy of his birth certificate. Given that he is not living in the place where he was registered, he started by looking in the website of the Civil Registry of the State where he was born. In that particular State, the website only provided limited information and a phone number to ask for the birth certificate. Using the phone, he provided some basic personal information, including name, city of birth, date of birth, date of registration, and he got in exchange a number associated with the registry in the national population registry. Using this number, he could go to the Civil Registry in the city where he lives now and obtain a copy of his birth certificate. He came in person to the office of the Civil Registry in his current home town, and got a copy of the birth certificate in the same day of the application. The payment of the fee was made on site, using his credit card.

The use of the model to understand specific uses of technology in the process of applying for and getting the service, provides a framework to better understand value creation at the individual and collective levels. Table 2 presents preliminary ideas of individual and public value produced by electronic services from the point of view of the citizen. These initial ideas were originated through preliminary focus groups made in the State of Puebla, Mexico. It is important to point out that it is not easy to elicit public values through open-ended interviews. During the focus groups sessions, we found that citizens can articulate easily the individual value produced by a service, but it is harder for them to articulate the value for the society as a collective. It was also challenging for them to identify the value generated in each of the stages as oppose to the electronic service as a whole. In this preliminary exercise, we are supporting our selection of public values on the inventory proposed by Jørgensen and Bozeman [15].

Table 2. Value creation through electronic services. Source: Authors' own preparation.

Step in the behavior model	Individual Value	Public Value
Information search	Time and cost savings	Timeliness
	Convenience	Accountability
		Equity
		User orientation
Form preparation	Convenience	Timeliness
		User orientation
		Equity
Submitting forms and get a receipt	Time and costs savings	Timeliness
		User orientation
		Equity
Payment	Security	Timeliness
	Convenience	User orientation
Getting the results	Time and cost savings	Timeliness
	Convenience	Equity
		Competitiveness

4 Final Comments

Our current research involves the use of the process model to understand value creation through electronic services in Mexico. Our final goal in this particular project is to gather data through a citizen survey to understand relationships between system quality, information quality, user satisfaction, system use, individual benefits, and public value (see Fig. 2). The research model in its current form is inspired by Delone and McLean's research [18]. Given initial difficulties in eliciting value from citizens, we are using the process model proposed in this paper as a way of unfolding the concept of use, and understand the mechanisms of public value creation.

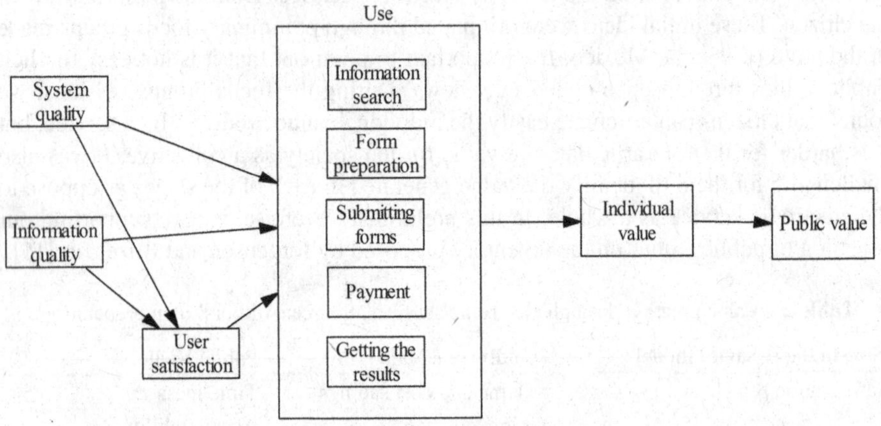

Fig. 2. Research model in current research. Source: Adapted from [4, 18]

Currently, we are using the model in a new series of focus groups to refine the concepts and develop the survey instrument. We are planning to conclude the focus groups in the first half of 2017, with the objective of developing the survey instrument during the Summer. We expect that the focus groups data will provide rich information and a better understanding of individual and public value from the citizen perspective.

References

1. Cordella, A., Bonina, C.M.: A public value perspective for ICT enabled public sector reforms: a theoretical reflection. Gov. Inf. Q. **29**, 512–520 (2012)
2. Bryson, J.M., Crosby, B.C., Bloomberg, L.: Public value governance: moving beyond traditional public administration and the new public management. Public Adm. Rev. **74**, 445–456 (2014)
3. Luna-Reyes, L.F., Gil-Garcia, J.R., Sandoval-Almazan, R.: Avances y Retos del Gobierno Digital en México. UAEM-IAPEM, Toluca (2015)

4. Comegys, C., Hannula, M., Väisänen, J.: Longitudinal comparison of Finnish and US online shopping behaviour among university students: the five-stage buying decision process. J. Target. Meas. Anal. Mark. **14**, 336–356 (2006)
5. Dewey, J.: How We Think. Cosimo, New York (2007)
6. Engel, J.F., Kollat, D.T.: Blackwell: Consumer Behavior. Holt, Rinehart and Winston Inc., New York (1968)
7. Gil-Garcia, J.R., Arellano-Gault, D., Luna-Reyes, L.F.: Even if we build it, they may not come: Reformas de e-Gobierno en México (2000–2009). In: Valverde Loya, M.A., Hilderbrand, M. (eds.) ¿Transformación, lo mismo de siempre, o progreso lento y con tropiezos? Reformas recientes al Sector Público en México, pp. 137–171. Graduate School of Public Administration, Instituto Tecnologico de Estudios Superiores de Monterrey-Harvard Kennedy School-Miguel Angel Porrua, Mexico (2012)
8. Morgeson, F.V., Mithas, S.: Does E-government measure up to E-business? Comparing end user perceptions of U.S. Federal Government and E-business web sites. Public Adm. Rev. **69**, 740–752 (2009)
9. Dawes, S.S.: The evolution and continuing challenges of egovernance. Public Adm. Rev. **68**, S86–S102 (2008)
10. Clark, B.Y., Brudney, J.L., Jang, S.-G.: Coproduction of government services and the new information technology: investigating the distributional biases. Publ. Adm. Rev. **73**, 687–701 (2013)
11. Benington, J., Moore, M.H. (eds.): Public Value: Theory and Practice. Palgrave Macmillan, New York (2010)
12. Moore, M.H.: Creating Public Value: Strategic Management in Government. Harvard University Press, Cambridge (1995)
13. Harrison, T.M., Guerrero, S., Burke, G.B., Cook, M., Cresswell, A., Helbig, N., Hrdinova, J., Pardo, T.: Open government and e-government: democratic challenges from a public value perspective. Inf. Polity **17**, 83–97 (2012)
14. Cresswell, A.M., Cook, M., Helbig, N.: Putting public value to work: a framework for public management decision making. In: Bryson, J., Crosby, B., Bloomberg, L. (eds.) Public Value and Public Administration, pp. 204–219. Georgetown University Press, Washington, DC (2015)
15. Beck Jørgensen, T., Bozeman, B.: Public values an inventory. Adm. Soc. **39**, 354–381 (2007)
16. Rippé, C.B., Weisfeld-Spolter, S., Yurova, Y., Sussan, F.: Is there a global multichannel consumer? Int. Mark. Rev. **32**, 329–349 (2015)
17. RENAPO: Modernizacion Integral del Registro Civil: Conceptos y Estructura (2005). https://www.renapo.gob.mx/swb/work/models/RENAPO/Resource/317/ConceptosMIRC.pdf
18. Delone, W.H., McLean, E.R.: The DeLone and McLean model of information systems success: a ten-year update. J. Manag. Inf. Syst. **19**, 9–30 (2003)

Electronic "Pockets of Effectiveness": E-governance and Institutional Change in St. Petersburg, Russia

Yury Kabanov[1(✉)] and Andrei V. Chugunov[2]

[1] National Research University Higher School of Economics, St. Petersburg, Russia
ykabanov@hse.ru

[2] ITMO University, St. Petersburg, Russia
chugunov@egov-center.ru

Abstract. The paper explores the patterns and factors of e-governance development in ineffective institutional settings. Although it is assumed that most of e-projects in such countries failed, we argue that in some contexts such initiatives can survive in the hostile environment and achieve relatively positive results, leading to limited institutional changes. We adapt the *pockets of effectiveness* framework in order to analyze the Our Petersburg portal (St. Petersburg, Russia). Our findings suggest that such electronic "pockets" may emerge as a deliberate policy of the political elite in an attempt to make institutions work properly. The key factors of such projects' success relate to agency, namely the political patronage and control, policy entrepreneurship, as well as organization autonomy and the power of the initiative.

Keywords: E-government · E-governance · Institutional change · Pockets of effectiveness

1 Introduction

A substantial part of e-governance research aims at revealing when, how and if ICTs lead to institutional changes in public administration or citizen-government relations [3, 15]. In fact, a plethora of works has found little impact of the e-mechanisms on democratization and the quality of governance, especially in ineffective institutional contexts, developing, neopatrimonial[1] or authoritarian countries [24, 27, 30], limiting the role of such instruments to legitimation and PR [2, 34]. But is this always the case? If incumbents may be interested in malfunctioning institutions to gain rents [19], can they eventually make use of e-government as a working tool? Although ICTs can consolidate the regime and empower autocrats [20], can they in fact strengthen the state capacity [23]? For instance, some empirical findings suggest that such relatively successful examples can be found on the subnational level [26].

The *research goal* is hence to reveal the factors such effective e-governance instruments emerge in the potentially hostile (authoritarian or neopatrimonial)

[1] For discussion on the concept of neopatrimonialism see [51].

M. Janssen et al. (Eds.): EGOV 2017, LNCS 10428, pp. 386–398, 2017.
DOI: 10.1007/978-3-319-64677-0_32

institutional environment. To do this, we apply the *pocket of effectiveness* (PoE) concept [42] to the case of the *Nash Peterburg* (Our Petersburg, OP) portal, St. Petersburg, Russia,[2] a government – initiated platform, launched in 2014, showing relative viability and effectiveness particularly against the overall ambiguous performance of the national initiatives [5, 9, 19], and in the context of the Russian political regime [17]. We investigate if the OP portal is an example of PoE, and why.

2 Factors of ICT-Enabled Institutional Change: "Pockets of Effectiveness Framework"

The concepts like e-government, e-participation, e-democracy etc. have always been surrounded by myths and normative implications on better government and democracy. But challenged by reality, they often fail [4]. Potentially, the directions of ICT-led institutional change are different and overwhelming [36]. For instance, e-mechanisms can affect bureaucracy by reducing administrative discretion via the automated information systems [7, 32: 223–224, 40, 41], eliminating corruption [11, 46], cutting the red tape [48], improving public services' delivery or enhancing participation [28, 31]. All improvements do not follow immediately and with necessity, though [8, 13: 88–89, 12].

The factors influencing the success of e-government are conceptualized differently. An important aspect is *agency*, or *entrepreneurship* [14], and its interaction with *structures*, i.e. institutions and organizational settings [3, 15, 35, 50]. Leadership and political power are crucial when bureaucracy is reluctant to changes and hinders the reform [1, 44]. Other possible factors include stakeholders' engagement, communication and feedback [33], public value and trust [6], institutional design [6, 49]. Plenty of research has been conducted so far to systemize all factors in one framework [38].

The problem is that ICT-enabled institutional change, as previous research shows, often emerges in polities with already sufficient institutional quality and democracy. Developing, neopatrimonial and authoritarian countries usually lag behind in terms of e-participation development [25]. Even when they have enough capacity to introduce technological advancements [47], new instruments serve other goals: to be a façade for legitimation, international socialization or investment [1, 34]. Even if a strong political will for reforms is observed, they usually fail due to the informal norms and rent-seeking behavior of public officials [19].

In such context, a full-scale reform cannot be accomplished successfully. However, in some cases scholars observe that new institutions and organizations can resist the hostile environment and show relatively effective performance, Such organizations are called *pockets of effectiveness*, or PoE - "public organizations that deliver public goods and services relatively effectively in contexts of largely ineffective governments" and "operate in politico-administrative systems that are primarily based on personal networks instead of … impartiality and formal, law – based rules" [42]. Roll distinguishes several characteristics of the PoE: "relative effectiveness", contribution to public good and "persistence as PoE for at least three years" [43]. There is a question why a PoE

[2] Our Petersburg Portal, http://gorod.gov.spb.ru [in Russian].

emerges, and several frameworks were proposed. The discussion is basically focused on what factors are necessary and sufficient. Based on Leonard and Roll [29, 42, 43], we may discern the following variables:

- *political factors*, including the strong leadership of the political elite, and its interest in effective institutions. As Leonard argues, the PoE is related to the "benefits and costs … for the politically powerful groups" [29: 97];
- *managerial factors,* ranging from proper training, commitment and "merit-based recruitment" and "inclusive leadership" and entrepreneurship to the ability of a public organization's leader to get political support and protection, remaining "autonomous of an operational political direction" [29: 95];
- *organizational and institutional factors,* such as the autonomy and powers of the organization to perform their tasks through legal and enforcement mechanisms;
- *other factors,* distinguished by Roll include, for instance, PR and external pressures.

Although the studies on PoE mostly relate to developing countries in Africa, we suppose that this concept is applicable to any context when institutions do not work properly, such as Post-Soviet countries, including Russia [18]. In some cases, the creation of PoE becomes the final resort to increase governmental performance in time when a more overall reform is hindered by the existing institutions. The key implication of this framework to the e-governance studies is that the ICT – enabled instruments or public organizations may perform the functions of a PoE. The research strategy is to distinguish such successful cases and explain the factors of their success. We can draw several *hypotheses* from the framework. First, we hypothesize that e-governance initiatives can survive in the hostile institutional environment as a PoE, leading to some limited positive changes (*H1*). Secondly, we hypothesize that the development of PoE will depend on: (1) *political control* (*H2*), meaning the leadership and attention of the chief executive to the development of the policy; (2) *institutional entrepreneurship* (*H3*); (3) *autonomy* (*H4*) of the key executives in charge of OP.

3 Case of PoE Emergence: *Our Petersburg* Portal

3.1 Research Design

To accomplish the research goal of discovering an electronic PoE and explaining its emergence, we do the case study. We take the *Our Petersburg* Portal (OP), created by the government of St. Petersburg. The case selection is justified by the fact that St. Petersburg shows relatively high level of the regional e-government development. On the one hand, it does not have as much resources as another federal city, Moscow.

The first task is to discern the characteristics that attribute OP to the PoE. Namely, we need to conceptualize *success*. As PoE framework suggest, success can be understood as a relatively better service provision, internal efficiency and persistence. To explore if the OP meets these criteria, we explore the development of its institutional design, popularity with citizens and effectiveness in citizens' complaints resolution. The more elaborate the OP becomes, the more complaints it processes and the more spheres it covers, the more successful the OP is supposed to be. The empirical data here is the descriptive statistics on the OP functioning, gathered by the automatic monitoring system developed at the ITMO University [52] or provided by the city government, as well as official documents that regulate the OP.

The second task of revealing success factors, we have conducted five in-depth semi-structured interviews with public officials, related in various capacities to the OP emergence and operation. We asked them to share their own vision on how the OP had been initiated, on the role of decision-makers and civil servants, on the problems, current state and perspectives of the OP. The thematic and discourse analysis was then used to combine these subjective stories into a general, collective experience on the OP. Along with documental and mass media data, these interviews (some quotes are given) used to explore the formation and success factors.

3.2 *Our Petersburg* Portal as an Emerging PoE

Although the situation in Russia cannot be compared to the situation in some developing countries, it sill faces difficulties in maintaining effective institutions of good governance, mainly due to ineffective bureaucracy and informal ties [18], as well as corruption [22]. In this respect, the real impact of the e-governance is doubted [5]. Against this picture, St. Petersburg presents a relatively better picture compared to other regions. It is considered to be relatively democratic [39], having a relatively effective bureaucracy and quality of life. In May 2014 the St. Petersburg Government adopted the ambitious Strategy 2030,[3] aiming at restructuring the city administration, strengthening control and eliminating information asymmetry for better urban planning. In accordance with this, in 2015 the regional administrative reform was launched, to deliver quality service and implement new ICTs into the urban planning.[4] The launch of the OP could serve this end.

The Portal was officially launched in early 2014 as a government – led portal, initiated by St. Petersburg Governor Georgy Poltavchenko. It serves to gather online complaints from citizens, devoted to the wide spectrum of urban problems, such as roads and housing etc., and process and solve them through the ICT with minimum delays.[5] In short, to solve a problem related to the urban environment, a citizen needs to register in the OP and submit an application. Each registered complaint is classified and processed through the moderator/coordinator to the executive in charge of its resolution. Then the executive agency should report on the results.

It was neither the first project of that kind in Russia, nor the only platform for urban problems solution in the city. In 2012, a group of civil activists launched the online platform "Beautiful Petersburg" (BP). As a legal basis, the BP uses the federal legislature on citizens' addresses (Law 59 "On Handling Citizens' Appeals"), allowing their

[3] St. Petersburg 2030 Strategy, http://spbstrategy2030.ru/?page_id=102 [in Russian].

[4] Administrative reform in St. Petersburg, http://gov.spb.ru/gov/otrasl/c_information/adm_ref/ [in Russian].

[5] Our Petersburg Portal, http://gorod.gov.spb.ru [in Russian].

transmission in electronic form.[6] Although it was novel for the e-governance practices then, it could have in fact not been called true institutional innovation, as the internal bureaucratic workflow remained pretty much the same [10]. On the contrary, the OP provided a brand new and ambitious regional legislation.

The key agencies involved in innovation are the Committee on Information and Communication (CIC), headed by Ivan Gromov, dealing with technological issues, the Gubernatorial Control Board (GCB) in charge of the administrative and legal aspects, and the City Monitoring Center (CMC), as a moderator and information processing unit. The first version of the portal (Fig. 1) was limited in scope, but required much effort in order to provide a technological and legal basis. As our interviewee notes, they needed to restructure all administrative workflow from "the Governor to housing offices and road services". Complaints were to reach the exact agency or municipality, and it was crucial to clarify the competence of all divisions and the ownership of each city object, from "roads to trash cans". The portal has been constantly modernizing. In 2015 the Interdepartmental Commission was established in order to resolve possible conflicts between the agencies. In 2016 the public control was introduced, when users could check the completion of a task.[7]

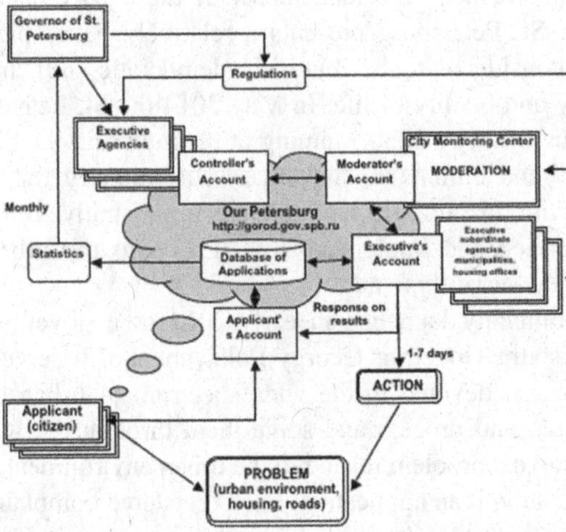

Fig. 1. The OP Portal's Technological and Institutional Ecosystem, Version of 2014. Source: Authors' picture based on open documents.

The recent scheme of the OP is presented in Fig. 2. In theory, the OP implies an unprecedented transformation of bureaucratic practices. In comparison to the ordinary procedure, enshrined in Federal Law 59 used by the BP portal, it shortens the time for complaints' processing, and clarifies agencies' responsibilities and control. If Law 59 gives agencies 30 days to respond, in the case of the OP they should do it in 7 days or

[6] Federal Law 59 On the Order of Consideration of Addresses from Citizens of the Russian Federation. Adopted on 02.05.2006, http://www.consultant.ru/document/cons_doc_LAW_59999/ [in Russian].
[7] Changes in the work of Our Petersburg Portal, http://gorod.gov.spb.ru/content/news/36/ [in Russian].

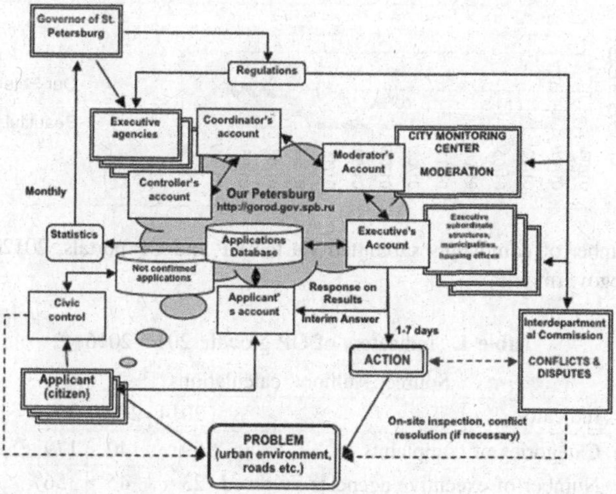

Fig. 2. The OP Portal's Technological and Institutional Ecosystem, Version of 2016. Source: Authors' picture based on open documents.

less. It cuts red tape and sets the interoperability of executive bodies based on ICT. So, the OP has been evolving as a PoE in legal and technological terms.

From the start, the new initiative had to compete with the abovementioned civic initiative, as well as to deal with the internal bureaucratic rigidity. The founder of the BP Krasimir Vransky accused the OP of being a stillborn PR project,[8] while shortened time limits and procedures negatively affected the ordinary bureaucratic workflow, making Ivan Gromov "the personal enemy of some districts' administrations".[9]

Our interviewees emphasize that the implementation was challenged by a "silent rebellion" against the OP and the CIC, especially from the housing services. The latter had to use the portal, but could discredit the portal, attempting to present reports with Photoshop-edited images, or even threaten the applicants. Some services adapted to new regulations by creating separate positions or units to handle complaints, which protect the rest of the structure from changes. Hence, the establishment of a dispute-resolving Interdepartmental Commission was a timely measure. The institutional resistance is constant, as new executive agencies are included into the system, being "not eager to help in developing technological routes of applications processing" and "trying to postpone it by any means".

Despite this, the OP seems to have won the competition for efficiency and popularity against the BP by the end of 2015 (Fig. 3). Official statistics claim that as of February 2016, about 169 thousand urban problems out of 1935 thousand reported via the portal were resolved.[10] Our interviewees suggest that the key achievement of the

[8] Portal for Self-Glorification, https://www.zaks.ru/new/archive/view/127361 [in Russian].

[9] Ivan Gromov's speech on the IT Forum, 2015. Authors' notes.

[10] Our Petersburg Portal, http://gorod.gov.spb.ru [in Russian].

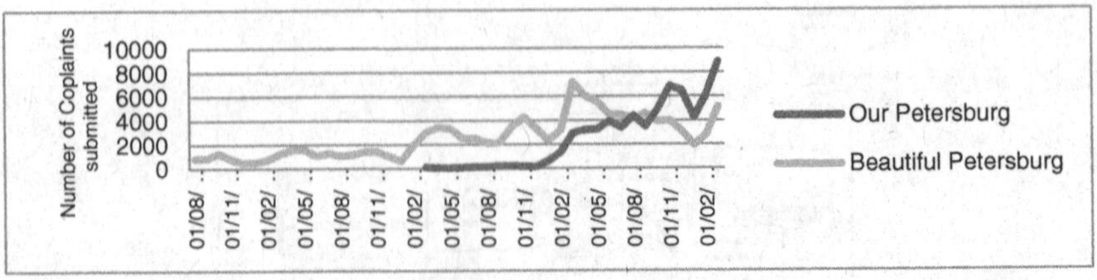

Fig. 3. The number of complaints submitted via the BP and OP portals, 2012–2016. Source: http://analytics.egov.ifmo.ru/

Table 1. Indicators of OP growth, 2014–2016

Source: Authors' calculations

Indicator	2014	2015	2016
Categories of complaints	59	140	179
Number of executive agencies involved	23	45	56

OP is the increase in efficiency and quality of governance. The portal is expanding in terms of problem categories and the agencies involved (Table 1).

While it positively affects the principal – agent problem, discretion and corruption by transparent rules and meaningful control mechanisms, it in unclear if the portal is viable in the long run. The goal of the OP was not to reform the entire system of governance from scratch. All previous legal regulations, such as Federal Law 59, remain in power, with persisting red tape and inefficiency problems. As North argues, formal institutions can be easily altered, but time is needed to change informal rules [37].

To summarize here, we suppose that OP represents a case of PoE in several respects. It was deliberately excluded from a different legislative basis, creating an alternative system of urban governance beyond the persistent informal norms. It meets the criteria of relative effectiveness, persistence and contribution to public goods, and manages to survive and develop in the potentially hostile institutional environment. It proves the thesis that sometimes the incumbents need working e-governance instruments that function well beyond legitimation, supporting our hypothesis (H1).

3.3 Factors of PoE Emergence

Political Control. It's quite clear from the interviews' analysis, that the role of the Governor in success of the OP is crucial. The positioning of the portal as a gubernatorial initiative gave necessary incentives to comply with new rules. The gubernatorial powers and executive domination in Russia have significantly increased since the 2000s [21]. Supplemented by the so-called *power vertical,* a hierarchal system of governance and informal rules [16], it made governors the key political actors able to concentrate resources in order to implement policies, provided there are incentives. Although the launch of the portal might have been linked to the election campaign, the main rationale, we argue, was to increase the gubernatorial control over bureaucracies at all levels, centralizing the system of governance and strengthening political power.

Such goal seems more plausible, as neither the OP was banned after the elections, nor the OP substantially increased the level of citizen engagement in decision-making [10]. The context is important as well: in 2012 e-government and e-participation became a national priority, and Moscow was the first to initiate an innovative portal for urban problems reports. Hence, the OP could help St. Petersburg show loyalty to the federal policy and be competitive against other regions.

Such personal political patronage was accompanied by effective control mechanisms. The GCB was empowered to formulate the reports on executive discipline. These documents contain the indicators of agencies' work with the OP. Each executive body should report on a monthly basis. The Governor may take disciplinary measures on the results. As formulated by Ivan Gromov, "… the Governor of St. Petersburg constantly pays attention to it [the OP]. If he didn't systematically check it, the portal wouldn't have raised so high".[11] The transparency of the portal, allowing mass media and citizens to control the work of the executive agencies, has contributed to the gubernatorial control. Falsified images in reports that were found by mass media were met with severe criticism from the Governor.[12] The existing "power vertical" rendered the transmission of gubernatorial incentives through all bureaucratic levels very fast, contributing to the success of the OP. Though it was necessary for the rapid implementation, it seems to be insufficient, as the operative control is needed. Otherwise, when the patronage is over, the initiative will fade with comparable velocity.

Institutional Entrepreneurship. The role of institutional entrepreneurs is crucial in policy changes [14]. Somebody had to persuade the Governor to implement the policy and level the interests of political actors. Here we can mention the role of Ivan Gromov, a former CIC head, who performed the classical role of an institutional entrepreneur. He was appointed in 2012 when, as he noted, the regional IT system needed more centralization and economic efficiency.[13] His motivation to launch the OP is not clear, but the easy answer obtained from an interview, "he just wanted something working properly to help people". Due to his previous work in Moscow, he might have learnt about the success of a similar project.

Despite his motivation, Gromov possessed sufficient political authority, being a trustee member of the Governor's team.[14] He managed to acquire political support of his initiative, and demonstrated "inclusive leadership" to motivate the employees. To leverage the system of administration, Gromov took the medium position between the Governor, the GCB and the rest of the executive bodies, as he had to sustain the political interest in the OP and ICTs in general, on the one hand, and amortize the

---

[11] Ivan Gromov: "Our Petersburg" Solves Problems Quickly, http://www.spbdnevnik.ru/news/2016-08-30/nash-sankt-peterburg–reshaeyt-problemy-bystro/ [in Russian].

[12] Governor: The official who repaired road with Photoshop is fired, http://www.fontanka.ru/2016/11/29/068/ [in Russian].

[13] St. Petersburg: Informatization, http://www.tadviser.ru/index.php/ [in Russian]; New St. Petersburg IT Director, http://www.cnews.ru/news/top/novyj_itdirektor_sanktpeterburga [in Russian].

[14] Persona: Ivan Gromov, http://www.tadviser.ru/index.php/Персона:Громов_Иван_Александрович [in Russian].

possible negative effects on the other. Until 2015, when he was appointed the head of one of St. Petersburg's districts, he had supported (and still does) the project.

Organizational Autonomy. In 2015 Gromov resigned from his position as CIC head, but it did not affect the efficiency of the OP. Is it inertia or regularity? From the framework, we know that the autonomy and sufficient powers are important for the PoE emergence and survival. Furthermore, as literature suggests, the ICT can lead to a reinforcement of the existing power relations [45], allowing those controlling the ICTs to concentrate more recourses and authority.

This hypothesis is partially confirmed in our case. During the OP establishment, the CIC, led by Gromov, has sufficiently raised its status, mostly informally through the association to the gubernatorial initiative. The importance of ICTs in public administration has also generally increased. In terms of finance allocation, the CIC is the key recipient of funds with an annual average budget of 6 billion rubles,[15] and the regional expenses on IT remain one of the highest in Russia.[16] Sufficient resources and patronage have provided the CIC with sufficient autonomy and status to implement the OP and other projects. However, the raise in status was implicit, as no changes in the administrative position of the committee occurred.

Crucial is that the successful implementation of the OP helped to achieve new powers in adjacent spheres, mainly in the administrative reform. First, in 2014 the division in charge for developing new administrative procedures was transferred from the Committee on Executive Agencies under the CIC. The Committee took responsibilities on the administrative reform in the area of electronic services and interdepartmental interaction. As the reform itself was connected to the development of the ICT infrastructure, the CIC acquired new opportunities to influence decision-making on the informatization of government. Second, the CIC became responsible for the Commission on administrative reform (Gromov was appointed its deputy head), raising its steering role.[17] Although the CIC has never been a sanctioning body, the CIC managed to raise its own status and autonomy and secure the development of the OP.

Hence, we can summarize that the case study confirms the hypotheses that the political control (H2), institutional entrepreneurship (H3) and organizational autonomy (H4) became the key factors of the PoE emergence.

4 Conclusion

Our findings from the case of the OP contribute to the knowledge on e-governance and institutional change in several respects. First, we suggest the PoE can be a valuable research framework to be used in e-governance studies. It helps to grasp an ambiguity

---

[15] Committee on Information and Communications of St. Petersburg, http://www.tadviser.ru/index.php/Компания:Комитет_по_информатизации_и_связи_Санкт-Петербурга [in Russian].

[16] Informatization of Regions: Russian Market, http://www.tadviser.ru/index.php/Статья:Информатизация_регионов_(рынок_России) [in Russian].

[17] Resolution of St. Petersburg Government N 548 dated 25.06.2014, http://gov.spb.ru/law?d&nd=822403644&prevDoc=537976863 [in Russian].

of e-governance projects in ineffective institutional settings, and its heuristic value is linked to the variety of hypotheses on why such electronic *pockets of effectiveness* emerge and persist.

Secondly, the research expands, and to a certain degree challenges the opinion that e-governance projects cannot function properly in ineffective institutional settings. Although most e-mechanisms are in fact legitimacy tools, in some cases they can serve incumbents better as working instruments, positively affecting the institutional development and public services provision. Here we can refer to one of our interviewees, who said that "no matter whether it were a PR-action, if it achieved real results and benefited the citizens".

The case of the "Our Petersburg" Portal provides an excellent example of such PoE, and proves that such electronic *pockets* can emerge and survive. Our study shows the crucial importance of agency in creating and maintaining successful e-mechanisms, namely the political control, institutional entrepreneurship and the organizational autonomy.

It is important to continue the analysis to and to compare the OP with other cases in Russia and abroad.

References

1. Ahn, M.J., Bretschneider, S.: Politics of e-government: e-government and the political control of bureaucracy. Public Adm. Rev. **71**(3), 414–424 (2011)
2. Åström, J., Karlsson, M., Linde, J., Pirannejad, A.: Understanding the rise of e-participation in non-democracies: domestic and international factors. Gov. Inf. Q. **29**(2), 142–150 (2012). doi:10.1016/j.giq.2011.09.008
3. Barrett, M., Grant, D., Wailes, N.: ICT and organizational change introduction to the special issue. J. Appl. Behav. Sci. **42**(1), 6–22 (2006). doi:10.1177/0021886305285299
4. Bekkers, V., Homburg, V.: The myths of e-government: looking beyond the assumptions of a new and better government. Inf. Soc. **23**(5), 373–382 (2007). doi:10.1080/01972240701572913
5. Bershadskaya, L., Chugunov, A., Trutnev, D.: e-Government in Russia: is or seems? In: Proceedings of the 6th International Conference on Theory and Practice of Electronic Governance, 22–25 October 2012, pp. 79–82. ACM, New York (2012). doi:10.1145/2463728.2463747
6. Bertot, J.C., Jaeger, P.T., Grimes, J.M.: Using ICTs to create a culture of transparency: E-government and social media as openness and anti-corruption tools for societies. Gov. Inf. Q. **27**(3), 264–271 (2010). doi:10.1016/j.giq.2010.03.001
7. Buffat, A.: Street-level bureaucracy and e-government. Publ. Manag. Rev. **17**(1), 149–161 (2015). doi:10.1080/14719037.2013.771699
8. Chadwick, A.: Web 2.0: new challenges for the study of E-democracy in an era of informational exuberance. I/S J. Law Policy Inf. Soc. **4**(3), 9–42 (2008)
9. Chugunov, A.V., Kabanov, Y., Zenchenkova, K.: Russian e-petitions portal: exploring regional variance in use. In: Tambouris, E., Panagiotopoulos, P., Sæbø, Ø., Wimmer, M.A., Pardo, T.A., Charalabidis, Y., Soares, D.S., Janowski, T. (eds.) ePart 2016. LNCS, vol. 9821, pp. 109–122. Springer, Cham (2016). doi:10.1007/978-3-319-45074-2_9

10. Chugunov, A.V., Kabanov, Y., Misnikov, Y.: Citizens versus the government or citizens with the government: a tale of two e-participation portals in one city-a case study of St. Petersburg, Russia. In: Proceedings of the 10th International Conference on Theory and Practice of Electronic Governance, pp. 70–77. ACM, March, 2017. doi:10.1145/3047273.3047276
11. Elbahnasawy, N.G.: E-government, internet adoption, and corruption: an empirical investigation. World Dev. **57**, 114–126 (2014). doi:10.1016/j.worlddev.2013.12.005
12. Fountain, J.E.: On the effects of e-government on political institutions. In: Kleinman, D.E., Moore, K. (eds.) Routledge Handbook of Science, Technology, and Society, pp. 462–478. Routledge, London (2014)
13. Fountain, J.E.: Building the Virtual State: Information Technology and Institutional Change. Brookings Institution Press, Washington (2004)
14. Garud, R., Hardy, C., Maguire, S.: Institutional entrepreneurship as embedded agency: an introduction to the special issue. Organ. Stud. **28**(7), 957–969 (2007). doi:10.1177/0170840607078958
15. Gascó, M.: New technologies and institutional change in public administration. Soc. Sci. Comput. Rev. **21**(1), 6–14 (2003). doi:10.1177/0894439302238967
16. Gel'man, V., Ryzhenkov, S.: Local regimes, sub-national governance and the 'power vertical' in contemporary Russia. Eur. Asia Stud. **63**(3), 449–465 (2011). doi:10.1080/09668136.2011.557538
17. Gel'man, V.: The rise and decline of electoral authoritarianism in Russia. Demokratizatsiya **22**(4), 503–522 (2014)
18. Gel'man, V., Starodubtsev, A.: Opportunities and constraints of authoritarian modernisation: Russian policy reforms in the 2000s. Eur. Asia Stud. **68**(1), 97–117 (2016). doi:10.1080/09668136.2015.1113232
19. Gel'man, V.: The vicious circle of post-soviet neopatrimonialism in Russia. Post Sov. Affairs **32**(5), 455–473 (2016). doi:10.1080/1060586X.2015.1071014
20. Göbel, C.: The information dilemma: how ICT strengthen or weaken authoritarian rule. Statsvetenskaplig tidskrifts arkiv **115**(4), 385–402 (2013)
21. Golosov, G.V., Konstantinova, M.: Gubernatorial powers in Russia: the transformation of regional institutions under the centralizing control of the Federal authorities. Probl. Post Communism **63**(4), 241–252 (2016). doi:10.1080/10758216.2016.1146906
22. Goncharov, D.V., Shirikov, A.: Public administration in Russia. In: Liebert, S., Condrey, S. E., Goncharov, D.V. (eds.) Public Administration in Post-communist Countries: Former Soviet Union, Central and Eastern Europe, and Mongolia, pp. 23–43. CRC Press, Boca Raton (2013)
23. He, B., Warren, M.E.: Authoritarian deliberation: the deliberative turn in Chinese political development. Perspect. Polit. **9**(02), 269–289 (2011). doi:10.1017/S1537592711000892
24. Heeks, R.: Most e-government-for-development projects fail: how can risks be reduced? iGovernment Working Paper Series, Vol. 14. Manchester: Institute for Development Policy and Management, University of Manchester (2003)
25. Jho, W., Song, K.J.: Institutional and technological determinants of civil e-participation: solo or duet? Gov. Inf. Q. **32**(4), 488–495 (2015). doi:10.1016/j.giq.2015.09.003
26. Johnson, E., Kolko, B.: e-Government and transparency in authoritarian regimes: comparison of national-and city-level e-government web sites in Central Asia. Digital Icons Stud. Russian Eurasian Central Eur. New Media **3**, 15–48 (2010)
27. Katchanovski, I., La Porte, T.: Cyberdemocracy or Potemkin e-villages? Electronic governments in OECD and post-communist countries. Int. J. Publ. Adm. **28**(7–8), 665–681 (2005). doi:10.1081/PAD-200064228

28. Kim, S., Lee, J.: E-participation, transparency, and trust in local government. Public Adm. Rev. **72**(6), 819–828 (2012)
29. Leonard, D.K.: 'Pockets' of effective agencies in weak governance states: where are they likely and why does it matter? Publ. Adm. Dev. **30**(2), 91–101 (2010)
30. Linde, J., Karlsson, M.: The Dictator's new clothes: the relationship between e-participation and quality of government in non-democratic regimes. Int. J. of Public Adm. **36**(4), 269–281 (2013). doi:10.1080/01900692.2012.757619
31. Linders, D.: From e-government to we-government: defining a typology for citizen coproduction in the age of social media. Gov. Inf. Q. **29**(4), 446–454 (2012). doi:10.1016/j.giq.2012.06.003
32. Lipsky, M.: Street-level bureaucracy. In: 30th ann (ed.) dilemmas of the individual in public service. Russell Sage Foundation, New York (2010)
33. Luna-Reyes, L.F., Gil-Garcia, J.R.: Digital government transformation and internet portals: the co-evolution of technology, organizations, and institutions. Gov. Inf. Q. **31**(4), 545–555 (2014). doi:10.1016/j.giq.2014.08.001
34. Maerz, S.F.: The electronic face of authoritarianism: e-government as a tool for gaining legitimacy in competitive and non-competitive regimes. Gov. Inf. Q. **33**(4), 727–735 (2016). doi:10.1016/j.giq.2016.08.008
35. Meijer, A.J., Zouridis, S.: E-government as institutional transformation. In: Khosrow-Pour, M. (ed.) Innovations Through Information Technology, pp. 565–568. Idea Group, Hershey (2004)
36. Nograšek, J., Vintar, M.: E-government and organisational transformation of government: black box revisited? Gov. Inf. Q. **31**(1), 108–118 (2014). doi:10.1016/j.giq.2013.07.006
37. North, D.C.: Institutions, institutional change and economic performance. Cambridge University Press, NY (1990)
38. Panopoulou, E., Tambouris, E., Tarabanis, K.: Success factors in designing eParticipation initiatives. Inf. Organ. **24**(4), 195–213 (2014). doi:10.1016/j.infoandorg.2014.08.001
39. Petrov, N., Titkov, A.: Rating of Democracy by Moscow Carnegie Center: 10 Years in Service. Moscow Carnegie Center, Moscow (2013)
40. Reddick, C.G., Abdelsalam, H.M., Elkadi, H.: The influence of e-government on administrative discretion: the case of local governments in Egypt. Public Adm. Dev. **31**(5), 390–407 (2011). doi:10.1002/pad.615
41. Reddick, C.G.: Citizen interaction with e-government: from the streets to servers? Gov. Inf. Q. **22**(1), 38–57 (2005). doi:10.1016/j.giq.2004.10.003
42. Roll, M. (ed.): The Politics of Public Sector Performance: Pockets of Effectiveness in Developing Countries. Routledge, London (2014)
43. Roll, M.: The state that works. Pockets of effectiveness as a perspective on stateness in developing countries. Institut für Ethnologie und Afrikastudien, Johannes Gutenberg-Universität. Working Paper No. 128 (2011)
44. Schlæger, J.: Digital governance and institutional change: examining the role of e-government in China's coal sector. Policy Internet **2**(1), 37–61 (2010). doi:10.2202/1944-2866.1014
45. Schlæger, J.: E-Government in China: Technology, Power and Local Government Reform. Routledge, London (2013)
46. Shim, D.C., Eom, T.H.: E-government and anti-corruption: empirical analysis of international data. Int. J. Public Adm. **31**(3), 298–316 (2008). doi:10.1080/01900690701590553
47. Stier, S.: Political determinants of e-government performance revisited: comparing democracies and autocracies. Gov. Inf. Q. **32**(3), 270–278 (2015). doi:10.1016/j.giq.2015.05.004

48. Welch, E.W., Pandey, S.K.: E-government and bureaucracy: toward a better understanding of intranet implementation and its effect on red tape. J. Public Adm. Res. Theor. **17**(3), 379–404 (2007). doi:10.1093/jopart/mul013
49. Wright, S., Street, J.: Democracy, deliberation and design: the case of online discussion forums. New Media Soc. **9**(5), 849–869 (2007). doi:10.1177/1461444807081230
50. Yang, K.: Neoinstitutionalism and e-government beyond jane fountain. Soc. Sci. Comput. Rev. **21**(4), 432–442 (2003). doi:10.1177/0894439303256508
51. Erdmann, G., Engel, U.: Neopatrimonialism reconsidered: critical review and elaboration of an elusive concept. Commonwealth Comp. Polit. **1**(45), 95–119 (2007). doi:10.1080/14662040601135813
52. Chugunov, A.V., Kabanov, Y., Zenchenkova, K.: E-participation portals automated monitoring system for political and social research. In: Chugunov, A.V., Bolgov, R., Kabanov, Y., Kampis, G., Wimmer, M. (eds.) DTGS 2016. CCIS, vol. 674, pp. 290–298. Springer, Cham (2016). doi:10.1007/978-3-319-49700-6_27

Outcome Evaluation of StartBiz

How a Governmental Online-Tool Can Quantitatively Assess Its Benefits for SME

Kristina Zumbusch[1(✉)], Philippe Zimmermann[2], and Emamdeen Fohim[1]

[1] University of St. Gallen, 9000 St. Gallen, Switzerland
{kristina.zumbusch,emamdeen.fohim}@unisg.ch

[2] State Secretariat for Economic Affairs SECO, 3003 Bern, Switzerland
philippe.zimmermann@seco.admin.ch

Abstract. The following paper presents the results of the outcome evaluation of StartBiz; an online tool for start-ups in Switzerland. StartBiz is provided by the State Secretariat for Economic Affairs (SECO) and allows start-ups to enroll with trade registers, VAT, social insurances and accident insurances without any additional fees directly via the internet. The outcome evaluation was required to learn about generated benefits for start-up companies that have used StartBiz so far. At the same time, the evaluation was aimed at providing decision-makers in the SECO with strategic information for their future e-governmental activities (esp. planned expansion of StartBiz to an electronic One-Stop-Shop for small and medium sized enterprises). The paper contributes to the debate of evaluating e-governmental activities by emphasizing an outcome orientation based on the assessment of quantitative benefits. It underlines the advantages but also the disadvantages of such a focus for future outcome evaluations in the field.

Keywords: E-government services · Outcome evaluation · Start-up companies

1 Introduction

The following paper presents the results of the outcome evaluation of StartBiz, an online tool for start-ups in Switzerland. StartBiz is provided by the State Secretariat for Economic Affairs (SECO) and allows start-ups to enroll with trade registers, VAT, social insurances and accident insurances without any additional fees directly via the internet. The intended benefit of StartBiz for its users was to offer them a single portal to complete various government transactions with different administrative offices. Using this portal, start-up companies need to undertake one login exclusively. In this way, they can use the same web-frontend and reuse their previously entered data. This procedure confirms with the "Once-Only" Principle Project (TOOP), which has been launched by the European Commission [1]. Besides start-up companies, other important stakeholders, which might benefit from StartBiz were assessed in a first phase: for instance, trustees or bankers. However, due to their low usage rate, their potential benefit was not explicitly considered within the presented analysis. Hence, the presented outcome evaluation was applied to

M. Janssen et al. (Eds.): EGOV 2017, LNCS 10428, pp. 399–410, 2017.
DOI: 10.1007/978-3-319-64677-0_33

learn about the benefits, generated for start-up companies that have used StartBiz so far. At the same time, the evaluation was aimed at providing decision-makers in the SECO with strategic information for their future e-governmental activities – that is an envisaged expansion of StartBiz to an electronic One-Stop-Shop (OSS) for small and medium sized enterprises (SME). The objective of the OSS is to offer companies, in particular to SMEs, the possibility to undertake any public services fully online and through a single portal. To advance with the OSS effectively and to set up an optimal solution for Swiss companies, it was essential to generate know-how on the created benefits of StartBiz so far and on the mechanism behind these benefits. Therefore, the outcome evaluation had to combine summative as well as formative evaluation-elements.

1.1 The Rise and the Challenges of Outcome Evaluations

Public managers are under increasing pressure in order to report the outcomes and results of their programs, their activities as well as their investments. With both internal and external demands for information, public managers not only need to provide an accounting for expended resources and for provided services, but also have to report on performances and outcomes [2]. The assessment of generated outcomes gains importance to justify public fund expenditure on the one hand, but also to optimize future projects on the other hand. Consequently, outcome evaluations show an inflationary implementation in many different policy fields and for many different policy tasks [3]. Outcome evaluations assess the effectiveness of a program in producing change. They focus on difficult questions such as: *"what happened to the target groups of a program?"* and *"how much of a difference the program made for them?"* [4]. Thus, in any program the crucial questions are *"what do you want to change?"* and *"how would you know if you have changed it?"*. These evaluation questions are not just bureaucratic requirements, but meanwhile the essence of a good project management [5]. Outcome evaluation mobilizes scientific and statistical tools to follow up on these questions.

The term *'outcome'* refers in this context to all induced changes that can be causally attributed to a particular activity, as not all observed changes are categorically an intended and direct consequence of the corresponding activity [6]. That is why outcomes are defined by their causality with the interventions carried out. So-called 'Outcome-models', or' 'impact-models', attempt to map these causalities on the basis of hypotheses in the form of outcome- or causal action chains, more complex circuits of activity, or also as partially highly complex networks of effects [7]. Thinking in outcome-models, such as in the mentioned outcome-chains, begins from the (policy) objectives over the taken (policy) measures to the generated (policy) outcomes or benefits.

In other words, the identified (policy) problems and their corresponding objectives determine the basis of the outcome-model. They build the reference framework for assessing the outcome in the sense of target achievements as outcome evaluations are undertaken when it is important to know whether and how well the objectives of a project or program were met [6]. On this basis, the model leads to the question whether the respective measures exist for the defined objectives as well as whether they are also used by the planned target groups accordingly. If measures are used by the target groups, intended benefits are generated [6]. Based on this framework, corresponding variables should be identified to measure – as far as possible – the *output* (i.e. the concrete measure as well as the usage of this measure) and the *outcome* (i.e. the causally justified effects) (see Fig. 1). Ideally, the long-term *impact* should be measured by adequate variables as well. However, the impact is often influenced by other factors, which is why its allocation to the initial objectives is often difficult to determine.

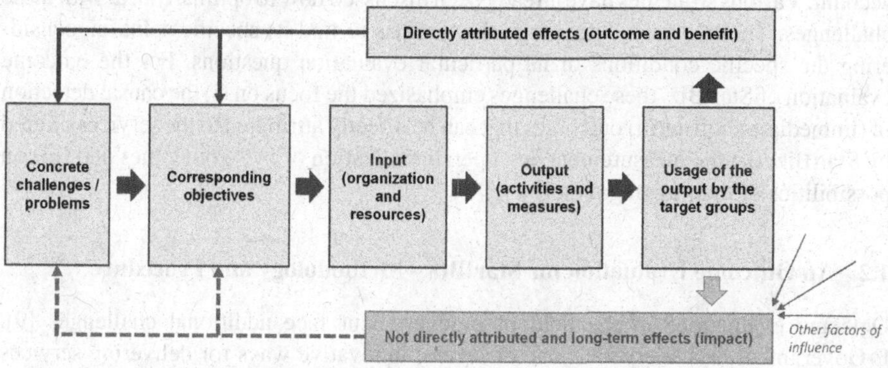

Fig. 1. Outcome chains as the basis of the outcome evaluation: own illustration, 2016.

Consequently, a strict focus on measuring the direct outcomes allows identifying causal outcomes, which can be directly related to the taken measures and their objectives. In this way, the target achievement of these identified outcomes can be assessed and the underlying mechanisms about success factors but also about inefficiencies or other shortcomings can be detected [7]. While outcome models also support the accuracy of outcome evaluations, some main challenges remain, that have to be met by all different outcome evaluations. These challenges had to be considered in the outcome evaluation of StartBiz as well [6]:

- The problem of causality: The central problem is the proof that certain changes (or conservative effects) are causally related to certain activities. For even if the desired condition, the intended effect occurs, other factors can be responsible for it.
- The problem of detectability: Since the comparison with a development without intervention (zero variant) is not possible in start-up promotion and in many other areas, the proof of the effects is a challenge. Counterfactual analyses may offer a resilient approach.
- The problem of time: Most effects occur in the medium to long term exclusively and can then no longer be attributed to a single, concrete activity. The long-term nature of the effects thus makes both the detectability and the causality more difficult.
- The problem of operationalization: Which indicators can be used to reliably quantify outcomes? Do we have the necessary data and information? Actuality, quality, spatial perimeter and comparability of the data are only some of the problems that can become critical here. At the same time, the generic requirements for any kind of quantitative analysis, such as objectivity, reliability and validity, have to be guaranteed.

- The problem of aggregation: The effects of individual activities/offers cannot be simply summed up due to their partly completely different characteristics. However, individual indicators cannot adequately reflect the overall target achievement of an offer such as StartBiz.

Each outcome evaluation is confronted with these problems and must take them into account. Various strategies have already been discussed how to optimally deal with these challenges. Though, each outcome evaluation has to find its specific solution, considering the specific conditions of its particular evaluation questions. For the outcome evaluation of StartBiz, these challenges emphasized the focus on (i) the causal detection of (immediate short-term) outcomes that can be directly attributed to the services offered by StartBiz, (ii) the measurement and operationalization of these outcomes and (iii) on possibilities of their aggregation [8].

1.2 An Outcome Evaluation for StartBiz – Methodology and Procedure

Outcome evaluations in the field of e-government face additional challenges [9]. E-Government has emerged as one of several innovative ways for delivering services to citizens and companies. It is providing governments with new opportunities for bringing services closer to (small and medium sized) companies in cost-effective, efficient, and transparent ways [10]. Also Switzerland intends to reduce, with electronic tools, the administrative burden for companies. Its e-government is based on the Federal Council's strategies "Information Society Switzerland" and "E-Government Switzerland" that are jointly pursued by the Confederation, the cantons, and the communes. The first e-government strategy was adopted in 2007. The second and current strategy was signed at the end of 2015 [11]. Simplified electronic licensing, application and registration processes are seen as important for reducing red tape. Electronic services of the authorities are increasingly popular with the economy, not only with regards to digitalizing the processes, but also simplifying them and gearing them towards the customers. That is why the Federal Council considers e-government to be an important pillar of growth policy [12].

For this purpose, various initiatives were undertaken, amongst others also for the small and mediums sized companies in Switzerland. In this context, also StartBiz was created to facilitate the process of setting up a new company (www.startbiz.ch). StartBiz offers both informational and transactional services. In the first part (without registration), companies can check their obligations depending on their individual characteristics such as their legal form, their number of employees, their planned turnover or their industry. In this way, StartBiz provides start-ups with relevant information before starting the official registration of the enterprise. This clarification of requirements also allows start-ups to test various scenarios for their enterprise and to find out, which requirements apply in each case.

Once this informational part is completed, StartBiz allows start-ups to create an account and to register their enterprises fully online with the major administrative offices in Switzerland, which are the trade registry, the VAT, the social insurances as well as the accident insurances. This service, free of charge for the start-ups, is available regardless of the country level and its specific requirements, which are given by the confederation and the cantons.

Unquestionably, an underlying assumption for offering administrative tasks as electronic services is, that these services create benefits for the users of the tool. General advantages and disadvantages of e-government services have already been subject to a wide range of scientific discussions. Usually, by analyzing the potential of e-government solutions, a distinction is made between general and specific benefit potentials. The general benefit potentials are independent of the specific stakeholders. They mainly consist of increased efficiency and effectiveness in the management of administrative procedures. This is reflected in time and financial savings, comfort gains, lower error rates, greater transparency of service provision and expansion of services [13]. The specific utility potentials, on the other hand, are exclusively accessible to the respective stakeholders. These specific benefit potentials were the focus of the present outcome evaluation of StartBiz.

The SECO has already analyzed the benefits of its e-governmental services some years ago. At this time, all e-governmental services were considered at once, so that specific information for certain services were difficult to segregate [14]. Therefore, the purpose of the present evaluation was to provide the SECO with specific insights concerning the generated benefit by each StartBiz service. What kind of benefit has StartBiz generated for its users so far? Is an e-government tool like StartBiz able to cause significant positive outcome for the start-ups? How can these outcomes be assessed quantitatively and qualitatively to legitimize the corresponding public investments? And by which means might the outcomes even be strengthened? What kind of lessons learned can be transferred to the planned OSS?

All in all, the two main objectives of the present study were (i) to develop a theoretical model for analyzing the benefits of the online tool StartBiz and of future e-government services within the planned OSS, and (ii) to summarize the benefits created by StartBiz so far based on this model [8]. To allow resilient answers to the research questions mentioned, the methodology of the present outcome evaluation combined the model of theoretical based outcome-chains on the one hand and a counterfactual analysis on the other hand.

- The outcome-model is essential to assure the causality, to understand the mechanisms of creating the benefits. It is crucial to identify bottlenecks, inefficiencies and to emphasize potential improvements.
- The counterfactual analysis shows simply what would have happened without the given intervention. A comparison group of start-ups, that have not used StartBiz so far, serves as an estimate for this counterfactual. The difference in outcomes between the StartBiz user group and the control group allows the quantification of outcome and impact. Hence, the strength of counterfactual approach lies in quantified estimates of impacts at the micro level: *"how much has changed because of the use of StartBiz?"*.

Hence, the two approaches were used complementary [8]: counterfactual methods to quantitatively assess the outcome, theory-based methods to understand the underlying mechanisms, thus helping to identify the need and possibilities for optimizations. The methodology was based on various approaches:

- a series of in-depth interviews with a broad range of experts of the entrepreneurship ecosystem,
- one online survey amongst all start-ups in Switzerland of the last 5 years (sufficient representative response of 500 start-ups) for information with regard to the comparison group and to the embeddedness of StartBiz in the ecosystem,
- data analysis of anonymized user data of the StartBiz tool from the last 5 years,
- another online survey amongst the StartBiz users of the last 5 years (sufficient representative response of 250 StartBiz users of the last 5 years).
- two reflection workshops with the responsible decision-makers of the SECO.

The evaluation was implemented between January 2016 and October 2016. After concerting the results in a workshop, the evaluation was finalized in autumn 2016. Additional measurements and quantifications of the benefits created by StartBiz as well as by the future OSS are planned to be undertaken every two years from now on.

1.3 The Developed Outcome-Model

The developed outcome-model allows the causal deduction of StartBiz-/OSS-benefits by considering specific groups of users, their use of the services offered and the outcome created. The outcome-model for StartBiz is based on the before outlined model of outcome-chains, although it emphasizes the link between the output (specific services of StartBiz and its different components) on the one hand, and the benefit generated by the use of the output on the part of the target groups on the other hand. The further elements of the outcome-chain (problem/need, objective, inputs etc.) are taken into account as well, but are primarily in the way of additional explanation factors. This means that the developed StartBiz outcome-model focused on the three parts (i) output (=specific services of StartBiz), (ii) their usage by the target groups and (iii) the directly attributed and short-term outcome for these target groups (Fig. 2).

The reason to focus the evaluation on short-term outcomes (in particular savings in time and costs by StartBiz-users) was the following: intended long-term impacts of StartBiz (such as the increase of location quality due to efficient administration processes) could have been influenced by other external factors and would not be meaningful enough in order to assess the online tool. The focus on short-term outcomes, on the other hand, allows the identification of the direct generated benefits for each target group as well as for each of the StartBiz-services separately. In this way, the benefits of StartBiz can be assessed ex-post for the last five years. Due to the counterfactual analysis, the intensity of the benefit and quantification at an individual level of a single company was possible. In order to reach an aggregated scale of outcome based on individual-level information, an aggregated monetarization of the achieved benefits was calculated. This in turn permitted the benefits of StartBiz to be put in relation to the invested costs in the sense of a cost-benefit assessment.

In order to best monetarize the benefits of StartBiz, a methodology was used, which is based on two complementary central pillars and a willingness-to-pay approach as a

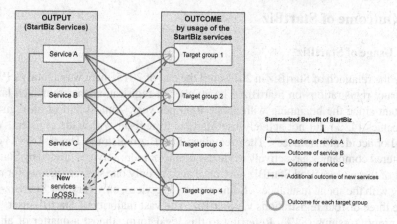

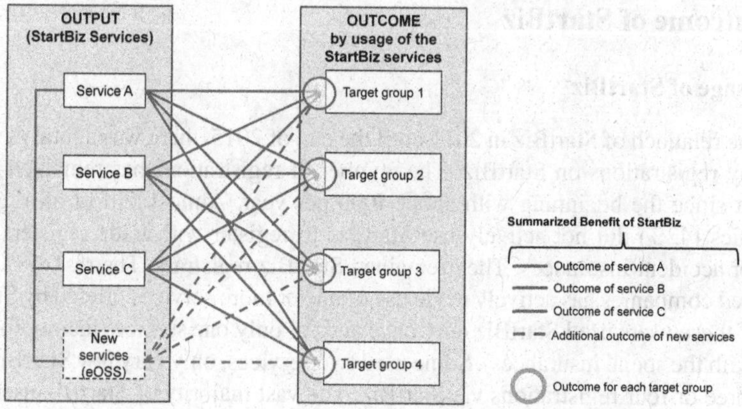

Fig. 2. The developed outcome-model for StartBiz [8].

relativizing third pillar. The following listing shows this threefold hedge of the utility montage of StartBiz.

- The first pillar is the personal assessment of time and cost savings thanks to StartBiz. For this purpose, StartBiz users of the last 5 years were asked in the second survey, how they estimate their time savings (working days) and their additional cost savings (in CHF) thanks to the use of StartBiz. By means of the conversion of the working days into CHF (1 working day = 425 CHF), the calculation of the respective mean values and their summation, a first monetary benefit per company founder could be determined.
- The second pillar of monetarization is based on the counterfactual analysis. It is a calculated difference between time and cost investments between the group of entrepreneurs who have used StartBiz and the group who make the administrative registrations without StartBiz independently or with other support services. By asking the two groups for their work (in working days) and the cost (in CHF) for the formal start-up process, the two groups were again able to calculate the mean values for the respective categories per founder group. The difference between the two aggregated mean values per group served as a second basis for the calculation of the monetary benefits per company founder.
- The calculated sum from these two pillars was compared to the amount resulting from the willingness-to-pay approach (Pillar 3). In this case, the determination of the benefit of the StartBiz services from the user's viewpoint is classified by the recording of a maximum payment for the benefit achieved [15]. For this purpose, the StartBiz users were asked about their potential willingness to pay, which is what they would have been willing to pay for the use of StartBiz and the resulting benefits [16, 17]. The mean value calculated for this category does not flow into the benefit calculation, but serves as a comparison value to the supplementary interpretation. It shows how much the benefit of the user side is appreciated and perceived.

2 Outcome of StartBiz

2.1 Usage of StartBiz

Since the relaunch of StartBiz in 2011 until the end of 2015, there was a total of 19'626 company registrations on StartBiz. The number of registrations has remained largely constant since the beginning with about 4000 per year. Almost half of all registered companies (42%) did not actively use StartBiz to register with trade registers, VAT, social or accident insurances. They remained StartBiz registrars. The rest (58%) of all registered companies has actively made use of one or more services offered by StartBiz. Most of these users used StartBiz only once and for only one service (mainly for registering with the social insurances). Some used two services, only very few StartBiz-users made three or four registrations via StartBiz. The vast majority of StartBiz-users were sole proprietorships (84%). Referring to this legal form, almost a quarter of all new companies in Switzerland over the last years has formally been established by using StartBiz [18] (Fig. 3).

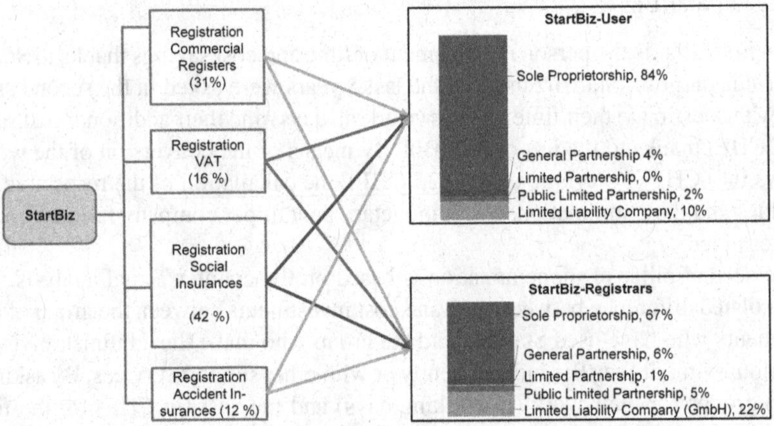

Fig. 3. Specified benefit model for StartBiz according to its user data 2011–2015 [8].

2.2 Identification and Quantification of Generated Benefits

What kind of benefits did StartBiz-users derive from using StartBiz services? In principle, companies which had used StartBiz, were highly satisfied with the StartBiz offer. They mainly expected savings of time and money. These expectations were largely met. To quantify these benefits, the three pillars explained in Sect. 1.3 were used, encompassing the following three approximations: (i) the personal assessments of time and cost savings by StartBiz-users; (ii) the calculated differences of time and cost requirements for the formal establishment of a new company, indicated by StartBiz-users on the one hand and those who did not use StartBiz on the other hand; and (iii) the willingness to pay, which expresses the value of benefits in terms of money as it is perceived by the StartBiz-users themselves. However, the quantification of the benefit generated over the last five years was only possible for sole proprietorships, since only for this user group a sample of sufficient size was available (Fig. 4).

Pillar 1	Pillar 2			Benefit of StartBiz for one SP	
Estimated difference			*Calculated difference*	*Averaged difference*	
SP by using StartBiz Survey 2 (n=130) *Arithmetic mean*	SP without StartBiz Survey 1 (n=111) *Arithmetic mean*	SP by using StartBiz Survey 2 (n=130) *Arithmetic mean*	SP with & without StartBiz Based on indicated expenses (Survey 1 & 2)	Pillar 1 & Pillar 2	Savings by using StartBiz
4.7 WD	4.3 WD	2.8 WD	1.5 WD	~ 3 WD	**2/3 of WD**
820.- CHF	2'125.- CHF	710.- CHF	1'415.- CHF	~ 1'100.- CHF	**1/2 of CHF**
				Total (monetized): **~ 2'200.- CHF**	

Fig. 4. Time and cost savings (in working days/WD or CHF) by formally establishing a sole proprietorship (SP) with StartBiz [8].

The calculations show that the use of StartBiz reduces the time required for formally establishing a sole proprietorship by approximately two-thirds. In addition, the costs for the formal establishment of a sole proprietorship is cut down by half in case of using StartBiz compared to the procedure without StartBiz. Hence, Swiss sole proprietorships can save time and money by using StartBiz, which they can invest otherwise. Especially during a company's founding phase when resources are usually scare, their saving is important, since investments have to be carefully taken in order to succeed.

To make these benefits comparable and summable, a monetarization was undertaken. It has to be considered that this monetarization represents only a partial benefit, since only the two parameters (time, costs) can be assessed in monetary terms. Consequently, the calculated benefit in terms of money indicates only the order of magnitude. An exact indication in Swiss francs would represent a spurious accuracy that is not reliable.

Based on the three abovementioned approximations, time and cost savings for formally establishing a sole proprietorship by using StartBiz can be assessed with approximately CHF 2200.-. With regard to 9'448 sole proprietorships in the years 2011 to 2015 using StartBiz, StartBiz has generated a total benefit of about CHF 21 million over these past five years. This results in an average benefit of CHF 4 million per year by sole proprietorships using StartBiz. Since 84% of the current StartBiz users are sole proprietorships, this amount already represents the largest share of the generated benefit [8]. Further calculations show that the benefit of StartBiz for companies with different legal forms seems to be at least as high as that for sole proprietorships – a distinction between different types of legal forms was undertaken, because the number of possible service uses depends on the legal form of a company due to legal conditions. However, for all legal forms of start-up companies other than sole proprietorships, the sample sizes were not large enough. Yet, assuming a similar benefit like that realized by sole proprietorships, one can estimate a total benefit of almost CHF 25 million generated by the total of 11'293 companies (irrespective of their legal form) using StartBiz for formally establishing their company in the years 2011–2015. This results in a total benefit of almost CHF 5 million per year generated by the use of StartBiz services.

Considering furthermore all StartBiz-registrars, who used the online tool for information reasons exclusively, additional generated benefits by StartBiz could be identified too. Pursuant to the above mentioned procedure among StartBiz-registrars from the years 2011–2015, a generated benefit by StartBiz of additional CHF 800,000 could be approximated (Fig. 5).

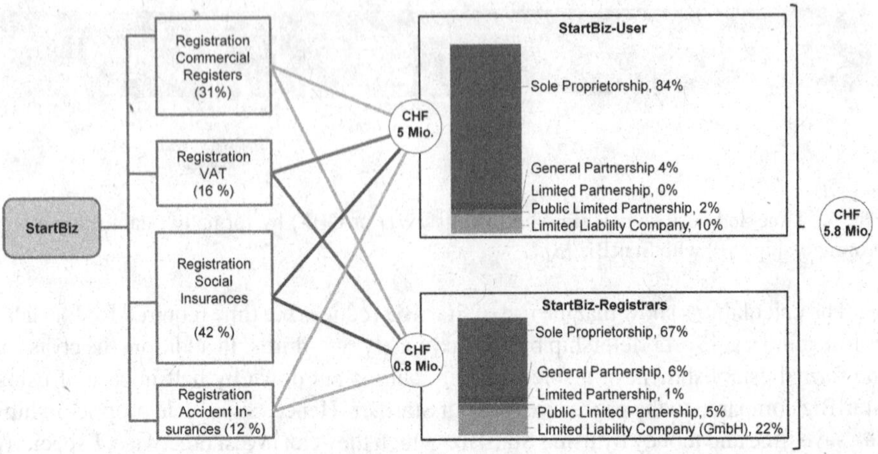

Fig. 5. Generated benefits by StartBiz per target group and year [8].

These benefits are offset by costs for the development of StartBiz and its operation as well as personnel costs for its maintenance and care. Between 2010 and 2015 SECO has invested around CHF 440,000 per year. Thus, the benefits for start-ups exceed the public investments by far. If these costs are taken into account in the benefit assessment, the total benefit of StartBiz amounts CHF 5.36 million per year [8].

3 Conclusions and Implications for the Planned OSS

In summary, StartBiz exhibits a constant number of users per year who are very satisfied with the StartBiz offer and have a proven benefit from the use of StartBiz. Nevertheless, it should also be pointed out that StartBiz addresses a comparatively small group of users. This is due to the limitation of its services only to the formal establishment of companies out of all the various phases that a start-up company has to go through. In addition, one has to note a limited degree of brand awareness for StartBiz. The great potential to increase the target group is not yet fully exploited. In particular, there is no possibility to use StartBiz under mandate (potential use by third parties such as trustees, lawyers or consulting companies on behalf of founders). This aspect restricts the positioning of StartBiz as a « tool » and fuels the reservation of other institutions in the start-up community, who perceive StartBiz as a competitive offer. In this regard, a clear and active communication of StartBiz (as well as of the future OSS) as an online tool seems advisable, which intends to facilitate administrative obligations of companies. Such a communication could sharpen the profile, reduce perceptions of StartBiz as a competitive offer, and could address additional user groups. In this sense, it should be a matter of course, that the future OSS also enables the use of its services under mandate.

In order to be able to identify the specific benefits generated by the use of StartBiz/OSS, more information on individual target groups would be necessary. For this purpose, a standardized, automated feedback loop could be established in order to measure customer satisfaction of all users promptly after they have used a certain service either of StartBiz or of the future OSS. This feedback may provide essential information specifically for each target-group as well as important strategic knowledge for required adjustments and optimizations of the services offered. At the same time, this may help to document reliable and sufficiently robust feedback information – so that in the future, amongst other things, one will be able to evaluate the benefits of each StartBiz-/OSS service and each user group separately.

In general, for outcome evaluations of e-governmental offers we see, that benefit models can significantly help to identify and quantify the benefits generated for the specific target groups. At the same time, it has to be taken into account that quantified benefits alone only show one puzzle piece in the vast fields of outcomes. So it is of great importance that all discussions emphasizing monetary effects of e-governmental services always underline their embeddedness in a broader field of qualitative outcomes and benefits. Public investments in e-government can no longer be legitimized only by cost-benefit ratios. In many areas, e-governmental services have become a matter of course as the low willingness to pay shows clearly. In this context, it is also clear that e-government solutions are increasingly of interest to companies. Simple and fast administrative processes, as promoted through e-government solutions [19], are gaining in importance as a location criterion. In a time of increasing location competition, in which many of the infrastructural location factors are now largely ubiquitous, such e-government approaches can certainly make a significant contribution to keeping companies at the location or gaining a location [20, 21]. Thus, the question, what kind of e-governmental services have already to be seen as a matter of course on the one hand, and what kind of respective services constitute an additional offer on the other hand, will gain importance during future outcome evaluations of e-governmental activities.

References

1. European Commission Homepage. https://ec.europa.eu/digital-single-market/en/news/once-only-principle-toop-project-launched-january-2017. Accessed 05 Oct 2017
2. Schedler, K., Proeller, I.: Outcome-Oriented Public Management: A Responsibility-Based Approach to the New Public Management. Information Age Publishing, Charlotte (2010)
3. Van Wouter, D., Bouckaert, G., Halligan, J.: Performance Management in the Public Sector. Routledge, London (2015)
4. Gertler, P.J., Martinez, S., Premand, P., Rawlings, L.B., Vermeersch, C.M.: Impact Evaluation in Practice. World Bank Publications, Washington DC (2016)
5. European Commission: Guidance Document on Monitoring and Evaluation: Concepts and Recommendations. Evaluation Unit of the Directorate-General for Regional and Urban Policy, Brussels (2014)
6. Scherer, R., Zumbusch, K.: Wirkungsmessung als Strategieinstrument. IMPacts **10**, 8–12 (2015)
7. Scherer, R.: Wirtschaftsförderung – Erfolg ist schwer zu messen. kommunal **32**(1), 22–23 (2015)

8. Zumbusch, K., Fohim, E., Scherer, R., Krüger, K., Vogel, P.: Nutzenbewertung des Online-Schalters StartBiz. State Secretariat for Economic Affairs (SECO), Bern (2016)
9. Ward, J., Daniel, E.: Benefits Management: How to Increase the Business Value of Your IT Proejcts, 2nd edn. Wiley, Chichester (2012)
10. European Commission: Future-proofing eGovernment for a Digital Single Market: Final Insight Report. Directorate General for Communications Networks, Content and Technology, Brussels (2015)
11. Schweizerische Eidgenossenschaft, Konferenz der Kantonsregierungen, Schweizerischer Städteverband, Schweizerischer Gemeindeverband: E-Government-Strategie Schweiz. egovernment schweiz, Bern (2014)
12. Institut für Wirtschaftsstudien Basel AG: eEconomy in der Schweiz – Monitoring und Report. State Secretariat for Economic Affairs (SECO), Bern (2014)
13. Scheer, A.W., Kruppke, H., Heib, R.: E-government – Prozessoptimierung in der öffentlichen Verwaltung. Springer, Berlin (2013)
14. Summermatter, L., Cristuzzi, A., Rohrer, D.: Evaluation von E-Government Angeboten. State Secretariat for Economic Affairs (SECO), Bern (2009)
15. Sattler, H., Nitschke, T.: Ein empirischer Vergleich von Instrumenten zur Erhebung von Zahlungsbereitschaften. Zbetriebswirt Forsch **55**(Juni), 364–381 (2003)
16. Völckner, F.: Methoden zur Messung individueller Zahlungsbereitschaften – Ein Überblick zum State of the Art. Journal für Betriebswirtschaft **56**, 33–61 (2006)
17. Bhatia, M.R., Fox-Rushby, J.A.: Validity of willingness to pay: hypothetical versus actual payment. Appl. Econ. Lett. **10**(12), 737–740 (2003)
18. Federal Statistical Office Start-Ups in Switzerland. Bern (2016)
19. Lenk, K.: Bürokratieabbau. In: Brüggemeier, M., Lenk, K. (eds.) Verwaltungsvollzug. Nomos, Baden-Baden (2011)
20. Göbel, A.: Kommunalverwaltung und Wirtschaftsförderung als Standortfaktor. Forschungsbeiträge zum Public Management. LIT Verlag, Berlin (2013)
21. Westerfeld, H.: IT - Entwicklung und Stand in der öffentlichen Verwaltung. In: Hill, H., Martini, M., Wagner, E. (eds.) Die digitale Lebenswelt gestalten, vol. 29, pp. 197–208. Nomos, Baden-Baden (2015)

Correlation Between ICT Investment and Technological Maturity in Public Agencies

Mauricio Solar(✉), Sergio Murua, Pedro Godoy, and Patricio Yañez

Department of Informatics, Universidad Técnica Federico Santa María, Santiago, Chile
mauricio.solar@usm.cl

Abstract. This article shows the results obtained with a model to assess the digital maturity of a government at country level. The model is based on maturity model concepts with focus on the digital strategy of the country. The application of the model to public agencies shows the weaknesses of the digital strategy that should be improved as country, but more interesting is the correlation that exists between the ICT investment in a public agency and its maturity.

Keywords: Maturity model · E-government · ICT investment

1 Introduction

The e-government survey of the United Nations [1], divides the evaluated countries in 4 categories: Low income countries; Lower Middle income countries; Upper Middle income countries; and High income countries, giving an idea that there is a correlation between level of development of the country and Information and Communication Technologies (ICT) investment at country level. Unfortunately, there is no information related to the ICT investment at country level.

As a fact, the UK Government based its ICT strategy [2] ensuring it is vital for the delivery of efficient, cost-effective public services which are responsive to the needs of citizens and businesses.

As example, in Kuppusamy, Raman and Lee [3], the empirical results suggest that ICT has had a significant impact on Malaysia's economic growth during the period 1992–2006, suggesting good payoffs from the investment.

The Australian Department of Finance released (in January 2015) a revised set of Whole-of-Government ICT Investment Principles. The Principles are high-level statements of best practice aimed to ensure that ICT investment aligns with whole-of-government vision, strategy and policy [4].

This article presents a study that was carried out between February and July 2015, with the main objective of measuring the degree of maturity of the capacities to manage the ICT of the central State agencies, with the purpose of guiding the development of digital government strategies. To this end, a maturity model was developed to diagnose the digital governance capacities in the main axes that drives the Digital Government development strategy [5].

M. Janssen et al. (Eds.): EGOV 2017, LNCS 10428, pp. 411–420, 2017.
DOI: 10.1007/978-3-319-64677-0_34

Section 2 presents the **Maturity Model of Digital Government** (MMGD) that was applied in a massive way to 121 agencies of the central government for which the information was collected through a web tool developed for these purposes. Section 3 shows the scheme used to classify agencies by segment according to reality in terms of ICT investment and their budget.

Section 4 presents the descriptive results of the evaluation process of the captured data. The analysis is presented from the point of view of the average maturity of the 121 state agencies that participated in this self-assessment. As a result, an **average maturity level of 2.3** was obtained, which on an organizational maturity scale corresponds to the level of maturity 2. This level is defined as a level of **incipient development**, which is the average level of the state agencies that participated in the study. The description of the results is carried out following the logic of the model, but is analyzed by segment to allow a comparison of critical success factors for agencies to implement their digital governance strategy.

Finally, Sect. 5 provides the general recommendations of the variables that were identified as those that can add value, and present opportunities for improvement, as well as institutional challenges.

2 Digital Government Maturity Model (MMGD)

The areas considered in the design of the MMGD model are aligned with the lines of action of Digital Government, being these: General Capacities, Citizen-centered Services, Enablers of Digital Government, and Open Government. In this way, four (4) domains were defined, 12 subdomains in total (3 for each domain) and 41 variables distributed in the 12 subdomains, based fundamentally on the objectives and goals of the digital government development strategy, such as interoperability, single key, electronic signature, and open data policy, among others (see Fig. 1).

The evaluation process corresponds to a self-assessment scheme carried out by each agency, and therefore does not require means of verification. Consequently, with the results obtained it is not possible to "determine" the specific level in which each variable is found, but is an approximation coming from the perception of what each agency responds. The results indicate an adequate level of validity, given the overall knowledge of the level of development of each variable in the central State at present.

For each variable of the model there is a scale of measurement of increasing levels of development from 1 to 4, ranging from a level 1 called "no development" to a maximum level 4 of "advanced development".

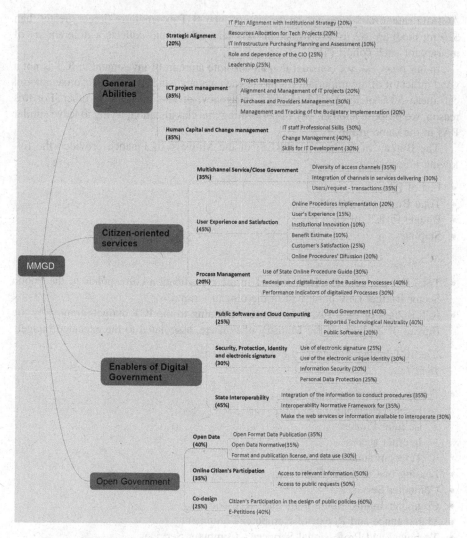

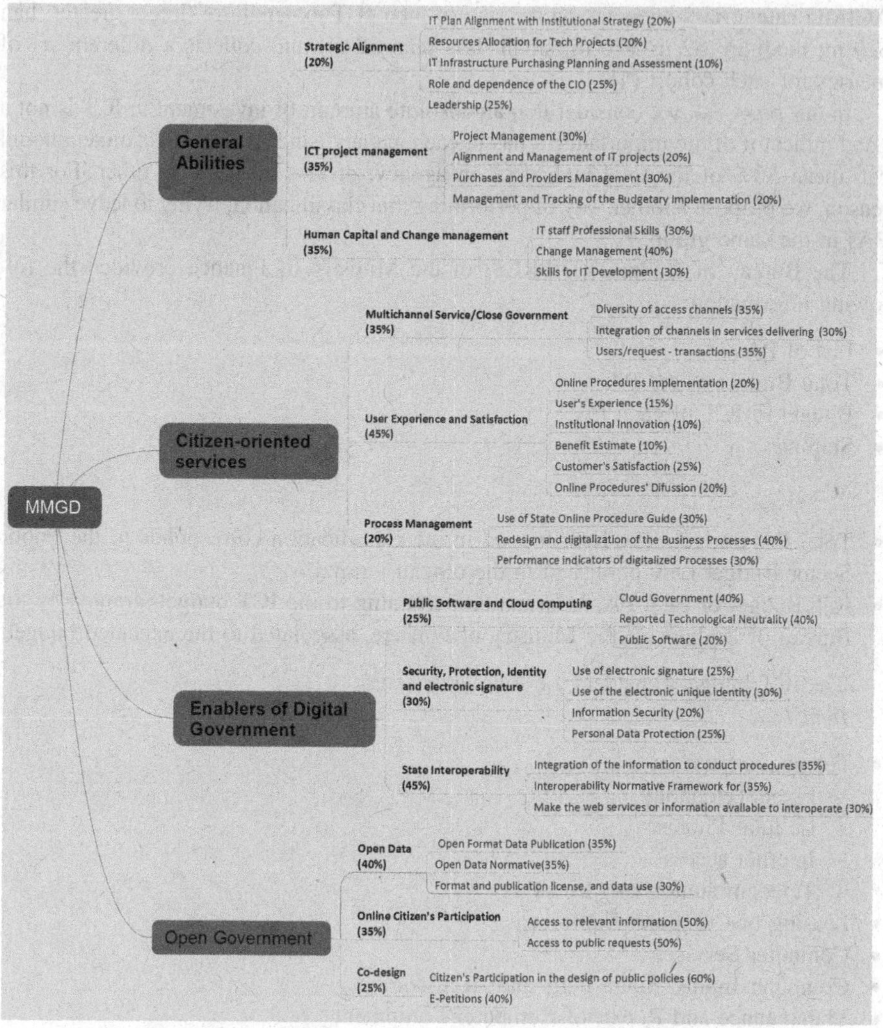

Fig. 1. Digital government maturity model: domains, subdomains and variables.

3 Classification

We first present the classification that was made to group the agencies of similar characteristics in order that the results of the evaluation are compared between pairs of similar level of development.

In this way, the Public Agencies (PAs) has been segmented so that when applying the maturity model, the results of the agencies can be compared between PAs that have similar characteristics between them.

The *Australian Government Information Management Office* (AGIMO) calculates a range of benchmarking metrics, which vary depending on the size of the agency.

AGIMO categorizes agencies by the size of their ICT expenditure (large: greater than $20 m; medium: $2 m–$20 m; small: less than $2 m) and collects a different set of metrics for each cohort [4].

In our proposal, we consider that an absolute amount of investment in ICT is not a good indicator of the importance it has in each agency, since a certain absolute amount can mean 50% of the total budget of an agency, or less than 1% in other. For this reason, we propose another way of performing this classification, trying to leave similar PAs in the same group.

The Bureau of Budgets (DIPRES) of the Ministry of Finance provided the following information:

- List of PAs
- Total Budget of the PA
- Budget in ICT of each PA
- Staffing

Where:

- Total PA Budget: The budget used in the classification corresponds to the Public Sector Budget Law published in the official journal.
- ICT Budget of each PA: Information pertaining to the ICT budget, granted by the Bureau of Budgets of the Ministry of Finance, associated to the executed budget.

The ICT budget considers the following items:

Item 1:

- Telephone Service:
  - Fixed Telephony
  - Cellular Phones
  - Internet access
  - Telecommunications Links
- Leasing of Computer Equipment
- Computer Services
- Computer Inputs, Spare Parts and Accessories
- Maintenance and Repair of Computer Equipment
- Technical and Professional Services - Computer Services

Item 2:

- Computer and peripheral equipment
- Communication Equipment for Computer Networks
- Information Systems
- Computer Programs

In order to formulate a classification of the PAs that participated in the application of the MMGD model it is suggested based on the information given to classify as follows:

(a) Classification Criteria

Each PA is classified relating the budget dedicated to ICT and total budget that has that agency. The results reflect the level of technological infrastructure that this PA has to develop its services offering with citizens and with the rest of the actors that interrelate with the public sector (Eq. 1).

$$\text{ICT percentage} = (\text{ICT budget}/\text{Total Budget}) * 100 \tag{1}$$

(b) Segments:

From the ICT percentage of each agency, four (4) segments were identified and distributed as shown in Table 1.

Table 1. Classification of agencies

Segment	Range percentage in ICT	Number of agencies
I	>5%	24
II	2–5%	34
III	0.5–2%	35
IV	<0.5%	28
		121

The results of this segmentation reveal that:

- 24 agencies have an ICT budget above 5%.
- Some highly specialized ones such as the Financial Analysis Unit, the Purchasing and Public Procurement Department and the Superintendence of Gambling Casinos.
- Segments II and III have a balanced number of agencies, 34 and 35 respectively.
- Segment IV corresponds to 28 agencies that have an investment of less than 0.5% in ICT.

4 Descriptive Data Analysis

This section presents a descriptive analysis of the results in the massive application of the MMGD model to 121 state agencies. Results are presented by segment according to the level of ICT investment and analysis of critical success factors for agencies to implement their digital development strategy.

4.1 Outcome of Maturity of State Agencies

Recalling that the objective of the study is to measure the capacity of public agencies to implement the digital development strategy, as a result of the self-assessment of the 121 state agencies that participated, an average level of maturity of 2.3 was obtained. On an organizational maturity scale, it corresponds to the level of maturity 2, which is defined as an incipient level of development, that is to say, that is the average level of the state agencies that participated in the study.

The average maturity of self-assessed public agencies is the average of the results obtained in the four domains of the model: General Capacities, Citizen-centered Services, Digital Government Enablers, and Open Government. All domains have the same importance in defining the maturity state.

As for the domains, the following was obtained: The Domain for Citizen-centered Services is the most developed domain of the State with an average maturity of 2.5. The domain Digital Government Enablers has an average maturity of 2.3, and Open Government with an average of 2.2. Finally, the General Capacities domain has the lowest level of development of all domains, with an average maturity of 2.1.

4.2 Relation of ICT Budget and Degree of Maturity

As part of the study, a classification of agencies was carried out to group similar characteristics so that the results of the evaluation are compared among agencies of similar size.

From the results obtained, it can be verified that segment I, where the agencies with the greatest investment in ICT in relation to their budget are the segment where the largest number of mature agencies are located, considering that there are 4 agencies with level of maturity above level 3.

Segment II has a single agency with an average of more than 3, which is actually the one with the highest maturity among all agencies surveyed, with an average level of 3.4. The other two segments, III and IV, do not have any agency with maturity level greater than 3.

It is possible to verify that 70.8%, corresponding to 17 agencies of the 24 that compound the segment I, have a maturity less than 2.5. This ratio increased to 79.4% (27 of 34 agencies), and in segments III and IV, the ratio increased to 94% (33 out of 35 agencies) and 93% (26 out of 28 agencies).

In fact, the average maturity by segment is 2.4 for segment I, 2.2 for segment II, and for segments III and IV, the maturity averages are 2.0 and 2.1, respectively, recalling that they are the segments with investment levels lower than 2% in ICT.

In segment I we have a single subdomain with an average less than 2, which increases to 3 subdomains in the case of segment II, and passes to 5 subdomains and 4 subdomains in the case of segments III and IV, respectively.

Percentage of Agencies per Segment that have a Level 4

Figure 2 shows the distribution by subdomain of the percentage of agencies per segment that have a level 4 evaluation in that subdomain. As an example, it is observed that:

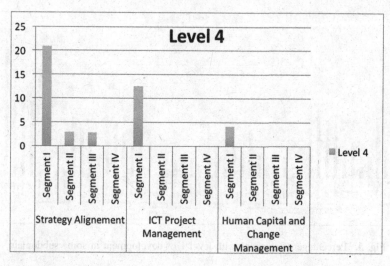

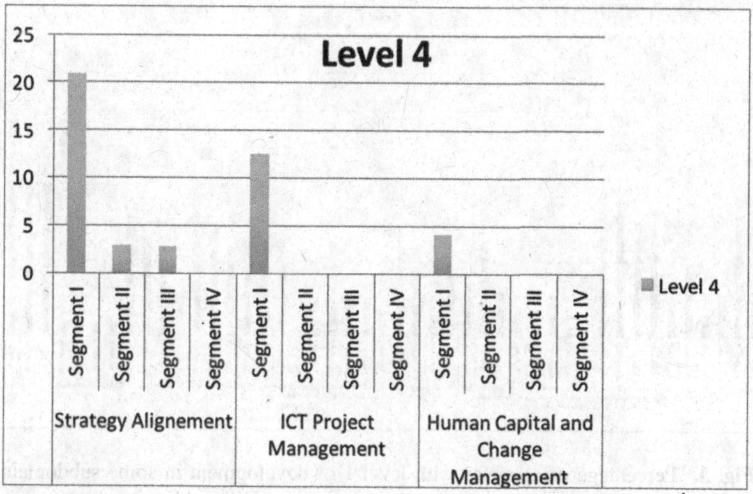

Fig. 2. Percentage of agencies in level 4 of development in domain general capacities.

- Segment I is the one with the highest percentage of agencies in level 4 in all subdomains that have reached this level.
- In the sub-domains "ICT Project Management" and "Human Capital and Change Management", segment I is the only one that has agencies with a level of development 4.
- In segment III, some agencies have a level 4 in the subdomains "Strategic Alignment" (3%).

Figure 2 shows that in all subdomains of the "General Capabilities" domain, i.e. "Strategic Alignment", "ICT Project Management" and "Human Capital and Change Management", some agencies in the segment of highest ICT budget are at the highest level of development. This would explain why it is necessary to have adequate resources.

Percentage of Agencies per Segment that have a Level 1

Figure 3 shows the subdomain distribution of the percentage of agencies per segment that have a level 1 evaluation in that subdomain. As an example, it is observed that:

- Segment IV has the highest percentage of agencies in level 1 in more subdomains (but only reaches 6 subdomains).
- In almost all subdomains there are agencies with level 1, except for the subdomain "Multichannel Service/Open Government", where in segment I there are no agencies with this level of development, and being the subdomain with fewer agencies at that level, and the subdomain "Security, Protection, Identity and Electronic Signature", where in segment II there are no agencies with this level of development.
- Within the Open Government domain there is a very dispersed behavior of its subdomains. On the one hand, two of the subdomains are evaluated as the worst-developed in all segments, in particular, the subdomain "Co-Design", which is the worst subdomain in all segments.

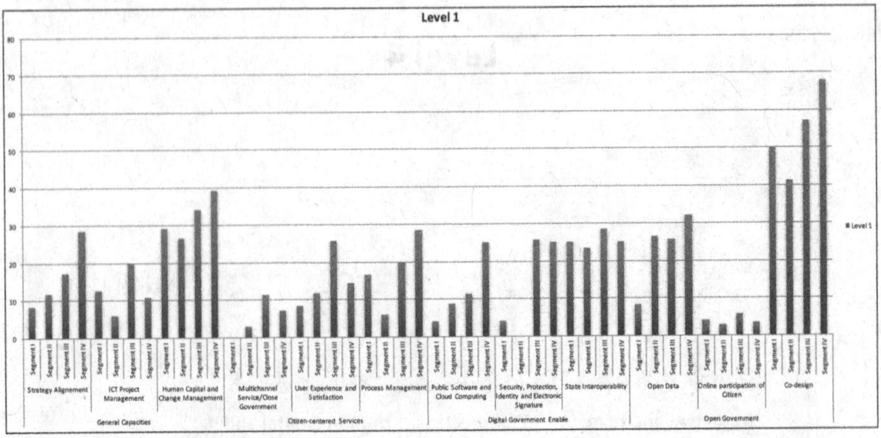

Fig. 3. Percentage of agencies with level 1 of development in some subdomain

- The other badly evaluated subdomain is "Open Data", which contrasts with the subdomain "Citizen Online Participation", which is among the well-evaluated subdomains in each segment.

In relation to Fig. 3, agencies with lower ICT budget are in a lower degree of development (level 1) in the subdomains of "Strategic Alignment", "Human Capital and Change Management", "Process Management", "Public Software and Cloud Computing", "Open Data" and "Co-Design", where government probably have to work on introducing these topics at a more basic level.

The results of this study show a direct relationship between the level of investment in ICT and institutional maturity, since agencies with higher levels of investment in ICT (by segment) have a higher average level of maturity.

Another aspect that reinforces the above is that the maturity average of the most developed subdomain belongs to segment I, with an average of 2.8 (Multi-channel Service/Close Government), and the less developed subdomain belongs to segments III and IV, being the lowest average of 1.5 for the "Co-Design" subdomain.

4.3 Analysis by Segment

Table 2 shows the distribution by segment for each level of the 121 agencies that were self-evaluated in this study. For example, for the first bar showing the Tier 1 distribution, it is indicated that one agency belongs to segment II, 4 agencies are from segment III and 2 agencies from segment IV. It is observed that if 57% of the 7 agencies that are in level 1 belong to segment III, with a low percentage of the ICT budget in relation to the total budget, this could be a factor that would affect the level of maturity in digital government.

In general, from the data collected it can be seen as described in Table 2.

The results of the study reveal that in those agencies where the level of investments in ICT is high, their level of maturity is also high. Therefore, it is highly recommended

Table 2. Interpretation by segment/levels

Level 1	• There are 7 agencies with this level of maturity and correspond to 6% of the total • At this level there are no agencies (0) belonging to segment I • At this level, 57% are segment III
Level 2	• At this level of maturity are the most agencies (98) account for 81% of the total • They are distributed evenly between segments II, III, and IV, with 28.6%, 29.6% and 24.5%, respectively
Level 3	• At this level of maturity, there are 16 agencies and correspond to 13% of the total • 75.1% is concentrated between segments I and II, with 43.8% and 31.3%, respectively
Level 4	• There are no agencies with this level of maturity

to suggest that in the budget discussion incorporate the concepts of digital government as an element that increases and contributes to the efficiency of public agencies and increases the public value of benefits to citizens.

As a result we recommend:

- To increase the efficiency of public investment in ICT.
- Implement measures to rationalize the ICT infrastructure through the sharing of resources between administrations that allow to reduce costs and im-pulsate strategies of collaboration between the different agencies.
- Align efforts of the administrations of all services, homogenizing objectives and coordinating measures to optimize the use of resources.
- Maximizing efficiency in the management and allocation of training and training funds for continuing training in ICT for public servants.

5 Conclusions

In this section we propose recommendations aimed at increasing the level of maturity of public agencies of the State. The recommendations were elaborated based on the results obtained from the application of the maturity model, the objectives and strategic axes of Digital Government.

The recommendations are organized according to the degree to which public agencies improve their General Capacities, develop Digital Government Enablers, increase Citizen–centered Services and extend the scope of Open Government in public agencies.

We recommend to create an institutional framework that takes charge of incorporating the aspects of the new technologies both at the level of the organization of the State to increase the level of efficiency and at the level of the citizens so that they participate in the discussions related to the changes in the life of the citizen. We recommend to create a Specialized Agency on Digital Government issues, to ensure the good use of State resources, to support the implementation of the digital strategy at the level of all public agencies, to advise on the design of technological projects of high impact and propose models of digital government governance.

This Agency should encourage the undertaking of open data initiatives and should monitor closely to encourage their use, as well as to improve internal processes. The Agency can also foster an environment of exchange and collaboration between public agencies, citizens, civil society organizations and other stakeholders.

An Agency can help build a key integrated infrastructure, deploy an unified knowledge base, establish common standards, and invest in training to facilitate multi-channel delivery of public services. This, in order to establish common service standards that help guide consistency in service and interoperability needs. Taking into account the concern about data security and privacy of users in cloud systems, it can take advantage of the dissemination, communicate the advantages of availability and the reduction of costs offered by integrated cloud technology.

Finally, another proposal for improvement at the institutional level is the creation of a portfolio of public projects that, to the extent that more agencies are supporting the execution of a project, is a sufficient reason to obtain resources and execute it, for the benefit of all agencies that supported it.

Acknowledgements. This work was partially supported by the grants DGIP-UTFSM.

References

1. UN: United Nations E-Government Survey 2016: E-Government in Support of Sustainable Development (2016). http://workspace.unpan.org/sites/Internet/Documents/UNPAN96407.pdf
2. Cabinet Office: Government ICT Strategy, March 2011. https://www.gov.uk/government/uploads/system/uploads/attachment_data/file/85968/uk-government-government-ict-strategy_0.pdf. Accessed Jan 2017
3. Kuppusamy, M., Raman, M., Lee, G.: Whose ICT investment matters to economic growth: private or public? The Malaysian perspective. Electron. J. Inf. Syst. Dev. Ctries. **37**(7), 1–19 (2009)
4. AGIMO (2015). http://www.finance.gov.au/policy-guides-procurement/ict-investment-framework/ict-investment-principles/
5. Solar, M., Murua, S., Godoy, P., Yañez, P., Monge, R., Vasquez, A., Schramm, K., Arismendi, T.: A tool to generate public policies. In: Scholl, H.J., et al. (eds.) Electronic Government and Electronic Participation, pp. 279–286. IOS Press, Amsterdam (2016). doi:10.3233/978-1-61499-670-5-279

Author Index

Printed in the United States
By Bookmasters